D1301103

Faithful Servants

Faithful Servants

The Story of
Florida Woman's Missionary Union
1894 - 1994

By Martha Pope Trotter

Florida Woman's Missionary Union
Jacksonville, Florida

© 1994
Florida Woman's Missionary Union
a department of the
Florida Baptist Convention
1230 Hendricks Avenue
Jacksonville, Florida 32207

Scripture taken from
the HOLY BIBLE, KING JAMES VERSION
and NEW INTERNATIONAL VERSION,
© Copyright 1973, 1978, 1984
by International Bible Society.
Used by permission.

Library of Congress Catalog Card Number 94-61132
ISBN 0-9643065-0-6
Manufactured in the United States of America
Printed by PEC Printing & Publishing
Pensacola, Florida

To
Robert W. Trotter, Ed.D.
1934 - 1993

As a pastor, Bob Trotter believed in Woman's Missionary Union and trusted the organization's commitment to making known the name of Jesus.

As my husband, Bob fully supported my commitment to writing the history of Florida WMU. He believed it to be a story whose telling could renew and energize women as they confront the missions challenge of the future.

Despite Bob's death in the midst of the writing process, if one detects among these pages a spirit of inquiry, a sense of humor, and a love for missions, the credit is due in great part to my husband.

For these reasons, I dedicate this book in love to the memory of Robert W. Trotter and to the glory of the God whom we served as partners for 33 years.

CONTENTS

FOREWORD

A wise WMU leader of the past said, "A heritage is a precious thing, not to be squandered, but to be treasured, added to, and transmitted." It is my prayer that through the publication of *FAITHFUL SERVANTS: The Story of Florida Woman's Missionary Union 1894-1994,* our rich heritage will be treasured, added to, and transmitted to future generations.

I have been intrigued, humbled, and inspired by those who have gone before us. Their singleness of purpose and gentle, Christ-like tenacity secured for us a strong missions foundation. Our history is filled with courageous and visionary women who faced challenging circumstances and yet remained undaunted, faithful to their Lord. How thankful I am for Faithful Servants who have taken great risks and made significant sacrifices for the expansion of God's Kingdom!

With love and gratitude we acknowledge our author Martha Pope Trotter, who poured her life into this two-year project. She spent untold hours doing extensive research to ensure accuracy and credibility. In the midst of writing the book, Martha's husband, Bob, was diagnosed with a fast-growing, malignant brain tumor. For six months, until Bob's death, Martha's role shifted from author to care-giver. As Bob's condition deteriorated, Martha wrote in a letter to the Centennial Committee, "God is good. He has supplied us bountifully with His sufficient grace. And I have great hopes for picking up the trails and moving forward once again with the book." Martha's personal journey and this book are testimonies of God's grace and sufficiency.

We are grateful to Toni Clevenger for her part, from the very beginning to the very end, in making the "book" a reality. Her vision and creative touches have helped to make this a book to treasure.

Annie Armstrong's words in 1890 bear repeating today: "Past successes should only be stepping stones to future endeavors. Rewards await us yonder, work awaits us here. And while so much work has been left undone, we have no time to stop even for congratulations or praise." As we in Florida Woman's Missionary Union look to our second century, may the Lord rekindle in us the spirit and the passion that burned within the hearts of our early leaders.

Happy birthday, Florida WMU. And many, many more.

Barbara Curnutt
Director, Florida Woman's Missionary Union

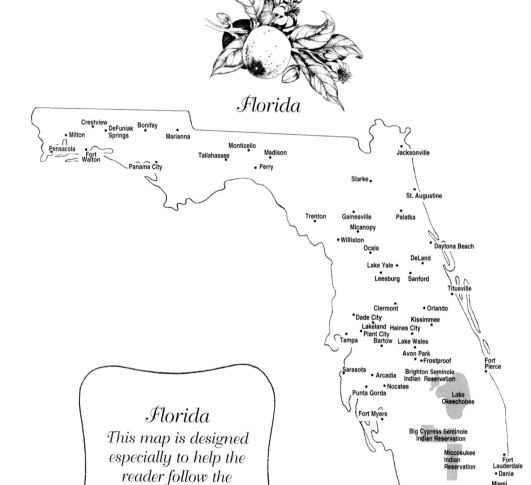

Florida

Florida
This map is designed especially to help the reader follow the paths of WMU's Faithful Servants

Crestview
Milton • DeFuniak Springs • Bonifay
Pensacola • Marianna
Fort Walton
Panama City • Monticello
Tallahassee • Madison
Perry

Jacksonville

Starke

St. Augustine

Trenton • Gainesville • Palatka
Micanopy
Williston
Ocala • Daytona Beach
Lake Yale • DeLand
Leesburg • Sanford
Titusville

Clermont • Orlando
Dade City • Kissimmee
Lakeland • Haines City
Plant City
Tampa • Bartow • Lake Wales
Avon Park
Frostproof
Fort Pierce
Sarasota • Brighton Seminole Indian Reservation
Arcadia
Nocatee
Punta Gorda • Lake Okeechobee
Fort Myers

Big Cypress Seminole Indian Reservation

Miccosukee Indian Reservation
Fort Lauderdale
Dania
Miami

Cutler Ridge

Florida City

Key West

Havana

Cuba

PREFACE

The story of Florida Woman's Missionary Union is the story of God's call to individual women and to the missions organizations which they formed. From the earliest years, Florida WMU has seen its work as a response to God's call to service.

The book *FAITHFUL SERVANTS* is also a response to God's call. When the invitation of the Centennial Committee to write a "new" history of Florida WMU came, I was stunned. I felt totally inadequate for such a monumental task. And yet I knew that only one question really mattered: Was the committee's invitation also God's call?

Through scripture, prayer, and conversations with my husband Bob, I explored that issue. God seemed to be saying, "Look at the path behind you." As I mentally retraced my steps over the past several years, I could see a pattern, with each decision of faith, each act of obedience, leading to the next, until my path intersected with the plans of the Centennial Committee. Then I understood that God had been preparing me all along, not by instructing me in history, but by teaching me dependence upon Him.

To read this book is to see God at work in similar fashion in the lives of Florida Baptist women. *FAITHFUL SERVANTS* is the story of women whose lives intersected with the great missions purpose of God. Individually and collectively their decisions and actions nurtured a fledgling organization into a strong corps of faithful servants. Looking back over the past 100 years, women of Florida WMU declare with gratitude, *Lord, you establish peace for us; all that we have accomplished you have done for us* (Isaiah 26:12).

My previous participation in the writing and editing of *On the Bay—On the Hill,* the history of First Baptist Church, Pensacola, authored by Toni Clevenger, gave invaluable guidance for this project. Principles I learned from that experience guided both my research and my writing. In order to re-create the aura of the past, I have told the story as often as possible in the words of the persons involved. Some readers may be disappointed not to find in these pages certain deserving individuals, memorable events, or worthy projects. As I accept responsibility for my choices, I also pray the readers' forbearance in understanding the restraints of both space and time. While of necessity I focused primarily on leaders, my prayer is that the reader will see those women as representative of all the thousands of faithful servants who created the complete story.

Having lived in Pensacola only since 1979, with virtually no background in Florida history and little in Florida WMU, everything was new to me. As I waded through reams of minutes, checked statistics, read newspaper accounts, and conversed with participants, the old truth emerged: rarely do two people have precisely the same recollections and understandings of an event or a process. The richness of varied perspectives is woven into the story wherever possible.

Letting go of some of my preconceived conclusions that research disproved was sometimes difficult. But more often, the in-depth view gave me much greater appreciation for the sensitivity, tact, ingenuity, and persistence of women who refused to surrender their vision for making known the name of Jesus.

Acknowledgements

Writing is often an isolating experience. Many days over the last two years I have spent alone, tethered to my computer. But this book is in no way the product of one person. Rather it represents the combined work of many persons. Because Toni Clevenger has helped with so many aspects of the process, we have laughed about what her title should be. Early on, she was dubbed "friend

Toni Moore Clevenger

and co-worker," but that does not begin to impart the extent of her involvement, which ranged from chauffeuring me to Richmond, Birmingham, and Jacksonville, where she joined in the research process, to guiding the production of the book itself. While designing the layout, choosing pictures and illustrations, and planning art work, she was also my guide in questions of content and helped me to eliminate thousands of useless words, for which the reader will be especially grateful. Our roles in this book were reversed from those in producing our church history. That we could make such a switch is a tribute to our unique partnership, which I consider one of God's richest blessings in my life.

Readers can also be grateful for Dr. Allison Chestnut, associate professor of English at William Carey College, who contributed her expertise to the writing process. Her sometimes not-so-gentle urging to shorten sentences, clarify ideas, and seek continuity challenged me to excellence. Allison also compiled the computer files for the index base.

For Diane Goeller, *FAITHFUL SERVANTS* artist, I am especially thankful. Both the text illustrations and the lovely "A New Dwelling Place" watercolor on the jacket are her creations. Hers is a newly discovered talent in our church, and now the secret is out for the longtime member of Pensacola First Baptist WMU.

Gary Garland, First Baptist Minister of Education, designed and produced the graphs. I am grateful for his skills, patience, and friendship. My thanks also go to Lanny Anderson of DeFuniak Springs, who helped with the original print design and produced the promotional brochure announcing the book's pre-publication availability. Barbara Denman, Florida Baptist Convention Public Relations Department, and Jack Brymer, *Florida Baptist Witness* editor, quickly responded to every request for photographs and information. My thanks to them for their cooperative spirit in the midst of busy schedules.

In approaching a history project, where does one begin? In the library, of course, and to the archives I went immediately. To express fully my appreciation to Dr. Earl Joiner, curator and secretary-treasurer of the Florida Baptist Historical Society, and his secretary Pat Nordman would be impossible. They provided every possible support, including the reading of old Florida Baptist Convention annuals and copies of the *Witness* in search of pertinent data, the photocopying of reams of pages, and the hospitality of Pat's home during research visits in DeLand. Pat and Dr. Joiner were always just a phone call away when any Florida history question arose. Equally as much I appreciate their encouragement during the difficult days of my husband's illness and death.

Ron Tonks and Cindy McMurtrey, WMU, SBC, archivists; Edie Jeter, Foreign Mission Board archivist; and Bill Sumner with the Southern Baptist Historical Commission gave valuable assistance, as did Fred Anderson, director of the Virginia Baptist Historical Society, and his research assistant, Darlene F. Slater.

My deep appreciation goes to Catherine Allen, who read the manuscript for historical accuracy in connection with WMU, SBC, and to Earl Joiner, who read for accuracy in regard to the Florida Baptist Convention. Each gave helpful counsel for improving the final product.

My readers—Jill Findley, Pat Nordman, Jackie Draughon, Debbie Bozeman, and Sue Holladay—managed quick turn-arounds as they received manuscript chapters, and always gave useful suggestions for corrections and clarifications. Sue Holladay went the second mile in working up the original list of events for inclusion in the Chronology. Vanita Baldwin scheduled interviews and assisted with the officers' list.

Numerous others joined the process support team. Among them were Beth Puckett, who provided both typing skills and moral support; Lucy Gray, who researched census records; WMU office secretaries, who answered dozens of questions and always stood ready to copy "just a few more pages" of needed records; and those who helped with transcribing manuscripts. For all of these, and many other unnamed helpers, I am grateful.

Perhaps the greatest blessing for me came in new relationships engendered through this writing project. Former members of the Florida WMU professional staff showed why they were so beloved in "their day." Graciously they wrote or taped answers to detailed questions, spoke with me for hours on the phone, and/or gave their time for personal interviews. The stories and insights which they shared provided useful background information and helped to make the history come alive. Their openness and honesty in reflecting on issues gave me courage to explore beneath the surface for cause and meaning. Current staff members were equally helpful.

State presidents added immeasurably to my storehouse of information and to an understanding of the "feel" of their eras. I am grateful for the supportive way in which each one responded.

Family and friends of WMU leadership also were essential in producing the book. With unusual generosity they shared their treasures: photographs, unpublished writings, mementos, and insights into family relationships.

A word of thanks must also go to the Florida missionaries who graciously responded to my questionnaire. Florida-born missionaries have been important to the story of Florida WMU; interaction with missionaries has enriched the journey we have traveled together.

Equally as important as those to whom I went for help and information were those who provided a base of support from which I could work. From the first day Barbara Curnutt shared an inner strength which God used to sustain me in the difficult times. Her unusual sensitivity discovered and ministered to my deepest needs. In my first meeting with the Centennial Committee, members offered to become a prayer support team, each taking one day of the week. What a good feeling to know that they were holding up to the Father my needs and the needs of the book!

My very special prayer support organizer in Pensacola was Pat Evans, who had to buy extra pages for her prayer journal in order to keep up with all my requests. Her home became a cloister for retreat when the turmoil of strenuous days brought exhaustion.

My church, Pensacola First Baptist, extended sustaining grace when I all but disappeared from my accustomed places of service. Most especially am I grateful to my WMU for providing the dust jacket for *FAITHFUL SERVANTS*. Such support brings both exhilaration and humility.

Throughout this project my family has stood by me with unusual strength and patience. Had God not given me such deep peace and assurance that, in spite of all obstacles, this "God-sized project" was in His eternal plan for me, I might have given it up. But never did my mother or children suggest that I should consider such a possibility. They rejoiced with me, as did Bob, that through the book the story of Florida WMU would reach beyond today into God's tomorrow.

"For I know the plans I have for you,"
declares the Lord,
"plans to prosper you and not to harm you,
plans to give you hope and a future."
Jeremiah 29:11

PART ONE

Preparing the Way
1881 – 1893

PROLOGUE

We've gathered here tonight in this light-filled place, His faithful servants celebrating what He has done for us.

We've gathered here tonight in this light-filled place, His faithful servants, responding to His call.

We've gathered here tonight in this light-filled place, while around our world millions who live in black flag countries grope in darkness—without hope, without peace, without ever having heard of Jesus.

The last rays of the late afternoon sun beamed through the stained glass windows of the Deermeadows Baptist Church sanctuary. The beautifully crafted windows portrayed essential points in the development of the Gospel: Nativity, Crucifixion, Resurrection, Pentecost, Ascension, and Mission. Silhouetted against the windows, black flags gave mute reminder of a world groping in darkness. The question for the evening: How will members of Florida Woman's Missionary Union, who live in a world of light, respond to those living in darkness?

More than a thousand people gathered for the closing segment of the Centennial Annual Session of Florida WMU. Awed by the impressive scene, they watched members of Girls in Action and Royal Ambassadors parade the flags of nations. The moving lyrics of "They've Never Heard of Jesus" stirred the hearts of women, women committed to making known the name of Jesus to *every nation, tribe, language, and people. . . .*

For 100 years, making known the name of Jesus had been the driving purpose of Florida Woman's Missionary Union. For 100 years, members of Florida WMU had faithfully served their Master, sharing the light of Jesus in dark corners of Florida, the United States, and around the world. Even before 1894, God began calling Florida women to serve His cause through missions.

Who were those women? What drew them together? What are the stories of those faithful servants? . . .

I

Are Ladies Entitled . . . ?

1881 – 1886

Serve the Lord with gladness.
Psalm 100:2

January 1882

Ann Bailey lay under her goose-down cover watching the early morning light consume the darkness. She couldn't sleep. Her thoughts darted between the December meeting in Ocala of the Florida Baptist Convention and the events in her life which had brought her to that place.

Before moving back to Florida in 1880, she had worked hard for the progress of woman's mission work in both Alabama and Georgia. Aware that such work was very limited in Florida, she had wondered what God had in mind for her in the move to Micanopy. . . .

As the rooster crowed in the chicken yard, Ann tiptoed across the cold plank floor to the bedroom fireplace. With the bellows she pumped up a spark from the banked ashes, and as it took flame, she tossed two pieces of kindling on the fire, just to get the chill off. "When people hear the word *Florida*," she mused, "they think of warm weather. They don't know that in the northern interior of this state, it gets pretty cold!"

She extended her hands toward the fire as if to grasp its warmth more quickly. As she stared into the flames, the state meeting again invaded her thoughts. She could see her husband Napoleon stand last month before the assembled delegates in Ocala and ask, "Are ladies entitled to seats as members of this body and upon what terms?"

The answer went beyond her hopes: "They are and upon the same terms as brethren." With that response, she and three other ladies she barely knew—Mrs. James Hobkirk, Mrs. J. H. Wentworth, and Mrs. J. M. Beggs — took their seats as members of the Convention. Even with the four of them,

3

there were only a few more persons in attendance than the thirteen who had been present in Madison just the year before, when the State Board of Missions was organized.

Then her thoughts focused on the moment later in the meeting when her husband rose to make his report on state missions. He had told her it would contain a surprise, but she still shivered when she recalled his words:

Mrs. N. A. Bailey
1881-1886

"We cannot too earnestly urge the importance of our sisters organizing societies in all our churches for systematically collecting funds for missions. Appreciating the efficiency of our sisters in working for the Master, we recommend that the Corresponding Secretary of the State Board of Missions be authorized to appoint a sister State Secretary and a sister in each association as associational secretary for more efficiently organizing the sisters in our churches into Ladies Mission Societies to work in connection with the State Board of Missions."

She and Brother Bailey had been happily surprised to find that many Florida Baptists possessed a more open spirit toward women than they had found in Georgia. She had known Brother Chaudoin, secretary of the new Florida State Board of Missions, since their days in Monticello, near Tallahassee. It was he who had pulled her aside after the afternoon session in Ocala and said, "Mrs. Bailey, if I asked you to become my 'sister Secretary,' would you consider the possibility?"

She had promised that she would consider his offer carefully and pray for the Lord's guidance. Before retiring in the home of friends, she and Napoleon discussed the invitation. Asking God to make His will clear, she spent most of that night "considering."

Again, in her memory she heard Brother Chaudoin call out, as they were climbing into their wagon after the final session of the three-day convention, "Mrs. Bailey!" Stepping closer he asked, "Have you reached a decision?"

Hardly realizing that she was ready for such a commitment, she burst out, "Yes! Oh, yes! I know this is the call of the Lord!"

Breaking the eggs she had gathered yesterday, Ann beat them into a frothy liquid and added them to the sausage frying on the wood stove. She could hear Napoleon pulling on his boots, whistling as if happy to be up so early. As she stirred his favorite breakfast dish, she whispered to herself, "Mrs. N. A. Bailey, secretary for Woman's Mission Work in Florida! I still can hardly believe it. I know I can go along in the wagon to visit with the women while Napoleon does his missionary-ing, but we just may have to get that old carriage in the barn fixed up if I'm going to meet with women in other parts of the state." She smiled as she placed hot biscuits, sausage, and eggs on her husband's plate.

Napoleon Bailey continually encouraged his wife to be all that God had created her to be. Perhaps it was those two years as president of the female college in Perry, Georgia—or maybe it was just his nature to believe that God created women to serve Him, just as He created men. Whatever the reason, Ann was very grateful that Napoleon had encouraged her to read, to study, to take leadership roles in every church they had served. As she sat across the table from her husband, Ann silently thanked God for this special man. She knew that Napoleon's support had given her the courage to accept Brother Chaudoin's offer in spite of her delicate health.

"Well, Madam Secretary," Napoleon broke into her reverie as he finished the last bite of warm biscuit, "what are your intentions for today? Now that you have this job, I'm going to have to consult with you, I'm sure, to know where I can fit into your plans." He tried to hold back a smile, but his eyes gave away his humor.

"Oh, Napoleon, now you know better than that! You'll always be first in my plans." Pausing to catch his eyes directly, she spoke with urgency, "But I do have to begin thinking about how I can influence the women of Florida to support missions. Brother Chaudoin said he'd heard of several mission societies around the state, but he didn't know much about any others except the one in our church and the one in Peniel. I must visit churches and encourage women to form societies. We must, we *must* be about the business of expanding the Master's kingdom."

"You're right, Annie," Napoleon responded to her serious turn. "I'll tell you what. When I go into town today, I'm going to buy you a supply of writing paper, and some pens, and some ink, and you can start writing to the women. And then you can write to the pastors. I have a list from the State Board of Missions. Or better yet, you could send a letter to the Florida department of the Georgia *Christian Index*. Address it to Florida pastors and ask them to get the women of their churches organized in support of missions."

"I wish I thought they'd do it," she said. "You know, some really oppose supporting missionaries. They say if God wants people to be Christian, He'll make them Christian. But we know that's not the answer." She paused, adding, "Do you suppose that next week you could take me over to Stafford's Pond? They don't have a mission society, and I think that's a good place to start."

"Sure thing, Annie, I'm glad to be part of the Woman's Work Department. The church of the living God needs women's vitality as much as it needs men's." Pulling on his coat, Napoleon headed out the back door.

Ann realized that sometimes the work would take her away from home and from her husband. Sharing in his ministry had always been important to her. But her soul warmed with the assurance that God had chosen her for that special work and had been preparing her for it throughout her marriage. As far as she knew, not a single other state convention had taken the bold step of officially authorizing woman's work by appointing a woman to lead it. She would be pioneering new paths for women in Florida, and maybe for the whole Southern Baptist Convention.

In several other states of the Southern Baptist Convention (SBC), Central Committees had been appointed to organize and channel the work of ladies' missionary societies. But for some reason Dr. Tupper, the Foreign Mission Board secretary, had not initiated a committee in Florida.

"I wonder why," she thought. "Does he suppose there are too few Baptist women in the state to make it worthwhile? Does he assume that women are too widely scattered across this vast state, more than a thousand miles from Pensacola down to the Keys, to work together effectively? Or has he just forgotten about Florida, here at the farthest corner of SBC territory?" She did not know the answer, but she did know that before her lay the greatest challenge of her life.[1]

When the Reverend and Mrs. N. A. Bailey moved to Micanopy, Florida, in early 1880, Baptists in the state gained a wealth of experience both in the pulpit and in woman's mission work. The couple joined the meager ranks of Baptists scattered up and down the state from Monticello in the north to Key West in the south, from St. Augustine on the east coast to Pensacola in the western panhandle. Each of the Baileys contributed to Southern Baptist work both in Florida and beyond its borders. From the day she was selected as the first "sister Secretary," Mrs. Bailey received recognition for her contributions to woman's mission work in Florida; little has been said, however, about her husband's significance to that same endeavor.

Napoleon Alexander Bailey was born September 5, 1833, in Lawrence County, Alabama. After a childhood baptism by Methodist sprinkling, Bailey, at age seventeen, was baptized by immersion into the Liberty Baptist Church. His home church licensed him to preach in 1853, the year before the organizing of the Florida Baptist Convention. Soon after his graduation from college in 1857, he was ordained to the ministry. On January 18, 1858, only two weeks after he began his first pastorate, the promising young pastor "secured a most intelligent and zealous helper in his work" when he married Miss A. B. Hester of Fayetteville, Tennessee.[2]

A Pilgrimage of Service

Within a few months, however, Brother Bailey's enthusiasm for the gospel led him into difficulty. Weeks of preaching revivals in bad weather in neighboring Tennessee caused chronic health problems. When a physician finally advised him to seek a milder climate, Bailey moved his young wife to Monticello, Florida, where he "took charge of" the Baptist church January 1, 1860.[3] That same year, Bailey, an innovator by nature, and W. N. Chaudoin [Shoh-doh'-in] of Thomasville, Georgia, "issued a prospectus of a Baptist paper for Florida."[4] Apparently that was the first effort to provide a state paper. The project did not materialize, perhaps done in by the Civil War.

In 1860, as war threatened the very structure of the nation, the population of Florida numbered about 144,000, with only 14,373 men of voting age. Only eight towns could boast more than 1,800 citizens in a state classified in 1850 as 100 percent rural. Baptists in Florida totaled only about 5,529 in 1859; probably more than half of those were slaves.[5]

The Civil War certainly interrupted any progress Baptists might have been making in Florida, but the effects of the war were felt unevenly throughout the state. In some localities, such as Tallahassee and Tampa, the conflict destroyed church buildings and largely disrupted Baptist work. In other instances life in the church continued almost as if no war were scourging the nation.[6] The Baileys' location apparently remained for a time a pocket of tranquility; they were reported to have spent the next several years "delightfully in Monticello." Nonetheless, "Federal incursions from the coast" prompted the couple to move to Georgia in 1863.[7]

While Brother Bailey served several country churches, he also led the Houston Female College in Perry, Georgia. After two years the Baileys moved on to pastorates in Milledgeville, then Albany, and later Dalton. As they served in Georgia, a missionary vision for planting the gospel on the other side of the nation entered their thinking.

To move more than 3,000 miles required a long-term commitment. Not shying away from God's assignment, they left for California in the spring of 1873. However, when the California climate caused health problems for Mrs. Bailey, they were forced to give up their mission and to repeat in the opposite direction the eternal train ride across the country. In 1875 they returned to Napoleon's home territory in north Alabama.[8]

From there God's guiding hand led the couple immediately to Talladega, when Brother Bailey was called as interim pastor of the notable First Baptist Church. Although that "bold and able preacher" served the Talledega church less than a year, there Mrs. Bailey apparently began her involvement in the growing movement of women's mission societies.[9]

Progress in Woman's Mission Work

During those years of the Baileys' marriage—difficult years of war and reconstruction for the nation—the involvement of Southern Baptist women in the support of missions gained strength and recognition. Despite indifference on the part of some Convention and local leaders, and outright opposition on the part of many others, women continued responding to their hearts' cry for ways to serve their Master. By the end of 1871, Woman's Mission to Woman, a strong and influential organization located in Baltimore, had articulated its purpose: "to give light to the women that sit in darkness because of Bible destitution, by taking the gospel of Christ in their homes, through the agency of native Bible women, aided and superintended by their Christian sisters from Bible lands."[10] Each member was to collect funds for carrying out that purpose by placing two cents in a "mite box" every Lord's Day.

Until Dr. Henry Allen Tupper became secretary of the Foreign Mission Board (FMB) in January 1872, FMB leadership had declined a working relationship with Woman's Mission to Woman. "Sensitive, charming, wealthy, aristocratic," Tupper acknowledged the significance of the women's endeavors and set about to develop a climate of cooperation. Working quickly, he returned the FMB to an earlier policy of appointing women missionaries. Among the first to receive appointment at that time and to sail for China was Edmonia Moon, who would soon be followed by her sister Lottie.[11]

Under Tupper's extraordinarily smooth guidance, the FMB in successive quarterly meetings made several other significant decisions regarding women. They "promised to keep separate accounts of the women's contributions." Thus ladies' mission societies could confidently send their money directly to the FMB. The Board also "agreed to help the Baltimore women foster women's societies elsewhere" by encouraging the formation of Central Committees. A Central, or Executive, Committee in each state would promote the organization of women and youth into societies and further the support of missions through their cooperative work. In a third move the Board agreed "to emphasize the evangelization of women."[12] This led to the appointment of more women missionaries and more support for "Bible women," native women who could have access to other women when the prevailing culture would forbid contact with a man.

Women were sacrificially filling their mite boxes, cent by cent. The money not only supported missions, but also accentuated the importance of the women's involvement: "In 1873 [FMB] contributions increased by 75 percent, the first fiscal sign of life since before the Civil War." The turnaround in financial support of the FMB was later attributed to Tupper's encouragement of the women during "the gloomiest period of [Convention] suffering and privation."[13]

Try it, Sisters!

By the time the Baileys arrived in Talladega in 1875, a number of ladies' mission societies had entered the records of the Alabama Baptist Convention.[14] Mrs. Bailey quickly began such a society in First Baptist Church and became its secretary. In that same year, South Carolina organized the first state Central Committee.[15] Soon South Carolina leaders asked the Alabama women to help with a project to build a home for missionaries in China. Mrs. Bailey's group must have responded immediately, for Alabama leaders reported, "Our sisters in Talladega have gone into it, and resolved for the present to cooperate with the Baptist ladies of South Carolina." Encouraging the formation of other similar groups, the Alabama women urged: "The mite box is the plan . . . and the inventive head and heart of woman will fall on other plans to get small sums of money. Try it sisters."[16]

Writing to Mrs. Bailey in the fall of 1875, Dr. Tupper expressed his confidence in her and her organization by requesting that the Talladega group

> "invite the co-operation of the ladies in the other churches of the State to form societies and report to the one in Talladega," thereby making it "a central society, through which the concentrated results of Alabama Baptist ladies . . . should be known." Responding favorably to this request, the local society sent out an "Appeal to the Baptist Ladies of Alabama."[17]

That appeal for the organizing of an Alabama Central Committee had hardly gone out when the Talladega ladies lost their "leading spirit."[18] In 1876, the Baileys accepted the call of the Baptist Church in Quitman, Georgia.

Kindred Spirits and a Beloved Cause

The women of Georgia had diligently supported missions for several years. In 1873, while principal of the Female Seminary in Cartersville, Lottie Moon reached a decision "to offer herself to the Foreign Mission Board as a missionary to China."[19] Developing support for Moon galvanized into action the Cartersville women, and soon women across the state. Their interest in China spilled over into increased offerings and support of other mission efforts.[20]

Georgia's Central Committee was organized in 1878, with Mrs. Stainback Wilson as president. As they came in contact through woman's work, Mrs. Wilson and Mrs. Bailey sensed their kindred spirit. Wilson credited Mrs. Bailey with the suggestion for organizing associational unions.[21]

Any woman who has ever had to move, leaving behind a wealth of friends and departing a beloved cause, would understand Mrs. Bailey's heart when the decision was made to move to Micanopy, Florida. While Baptists in neighboring Alabama and Georgia made hardy strides, Florida Baptists still struggled to emerge from the depressive conditions following the Civil War. Sister Bailey knew of no organized missionary societies. But surely the

Lord's purpose would become clear; surely God would continue to direct His committed servants along His chosen paths.

Reconstruction and Rededication

By 1880 white Baptists in Florida numbered 8,410; colored Baptists, 8,776.[22] Dr. S. B. Rogers, third corresponding secretary of the Florida Baptist Convention, evaluated the situation which faced the Baileys as they returned to the state in 1880. Through "personal, heroic, and sacrificial efforts in the field of evangelism," he said, the scattered churches were winning converts. However, the territory of the Florida Convention "was so extended, its churches so weak and scattered, mediums of communication so exceedingly poor and methods of travel so difficult, that any form of concrete organization was well nigh impossible."[23]

Associations tried to support mission efforts, but no statewide cooperative endeavors among the churches had developed. Baptists limped along under those circumstances, with few choosing, or perhaps able, to attend the annual state Convention sessions. During the 1870s, attendance ranged from nine to twenty-one and sometimes included women and children.[24] When no others offered to host the 1879 meeting, two men, the only male members of the Tallahassee Baptist Church, invited the Convention to meet in Tallahassee in May 1879. Only those two and six out-of-town delegates attended, and only six dollars was sent as offering. The group transacted no regular business other than to elect a president and a secretary.[25] The Tallahassee men invited the Convention to return in January 1880. Although nineteen delegates, plus several out-of-state visitors, accepted,[26] one of the two hosts reflected: "The Florida Baptist Convention had been about as badly wrecked as the church house at Tallahassee, which, having been used by both armies as a hospital during the War, was in an utterly dilapidated condition."[27] Another meeting was set for December 1880 in Madison.

A Spirit of Hope and Vision

Like a fresh wind blowing across the landscape, Rev. N. A. Bailey entered the meeting in Madison. Arriving a day late, he brought a daring idea: why not form a board of missions to organize and oversee mission work throughout the state? The 12 others present at the meeting, also knowing that drastic action was needed, responded enthusiastically to Bailey's idea. A spirit of hope and vision emerged.[28] The delegates pledged an astonishing $185 for state mission work, and a committee named the first members of the State Board of Missions. The selection of W. N. Chaudoin as corresponding secretary provided the key to the organization's success.

Chaudoin had been a friend of Florida Baptists for years. As an agent of the Home Mission Board (HMB), he was well known in the state. He also knew the Baileys and perhaps influenced the choice of N. A. Bailey as one of two missionaries appointed by the State Board of Missions (SBM) in its first quarterly meeting, March 1881. Each man was to be paid $25 per quarter for nine months. Promising such a salary demonstrated an act of faith, for the previously pledged $185 had not materialized.[29]

With those encouraging developments, the Baileys settled into life in Micanopy. Brother Bailey traveled many miles as a state missionary. Not one to waste time, Mrs. Bailey picked up in Micanopy where she had left off in Georgia—she organized a ladies' missionary society in the Micanopy church.[30] Her missions vision moved toward reality when the 1881 Florida Baptist Convention in Ocala voted to appoint a secretary for Woman's Mission Work and Brother Chaudoin chose Mrs. Bailey. Now she would have an avenue for leading Florida women to join women of other states as servants supporting the "fundamental" work of "the God of Missions."[31] Her husband's words recommending such an office[32] echoed supportively, as Florida women followed the way prepared originally by Mrs. Bailey.

Micanopy Baptist Church

During her first year in office, Sister Bailey worked in spite of "a long and severe illness." She organized 26 missionary societies (including one at Stafford's Pond) in 9 of the 13 Florida associations, and began "Little Helpers," a children's mission band in Micanopy. She also managed to organize 2 associational missionary unions, in Alachua and Santa Fe River Associations.

At the December 1882 Convention meeting in Lake City, the "special order of business" for an entire evening session was "ladies' mission work." Such exceptional attention by a state Convention demonstrated again the progressive attitudes of Florida Baptist leadership. While woman's mission work gathered support from "a growing fraternity of sympathetic pastors, usually the most eloquent and most progressive in each state,"[33] the Foreign Mission Board in 1882 rejected the SBC recommendation to "employ a woman to superintend and promote women's work." Even though women's contributions to foreign missions filled the Board's coffers, the FMB recoiled at such a thought, responding "a false step now might entail fatal embarrassments."[34]

Ability and a Mind to Work

Because women did not speak before such gatherings, a man read Sister

Bailey's first report. In it, she listed the new societies and gave details of the monies collected for missions. The total of $295.65 had been divided among Foreign, Home, and State Mission Boards. Acknowledging that "the number of societies is less than we had desired," she expressed gratitude nevertheless: "what has been accomplished is sufficient to cause us to thank God, take courage and persevere."[35] One way of taking courage was to call the women to meet separately on the Sunday afternoon of the convention. For the first time, women from societies scattered across the state gathered to praise God and seek support from each other.

George Allen, chairman of the all-male committee on Woman's Work, gave his committee's report. Before bringing recommendations, he proclaimed the rightful place of woman "in promoting the cause of truth and righteousness in the earth":

> A godly woman, intent on serving and honoring the Master, can do some things for him just as effectually as a godly man can do them; and there are some pious tasks that she is peculiarly fitted to perform and can perform even better than the man. . . .
>
> Although instances of woman's activity and services in furthering the great, beneficient [sic] undertakings of our denomination have hitherto been rare, still it has not been for the reason that her help was not needed, or that she had not the ability and a mind to work.[36]

After affirming woman's capabilities, he fervently declared the heights to which woman might rise:

> She is a living power in our churches and a significant figure in the enumeration of their forces, and she must be recognized and appreciated as such if we would see our denomination putting on its whole strength and increasing its capacity for evangelistic achievement to the full measure of its possibility.
>
> Woman has a head to think and plan, a heart to feel and desire, and a hand to execute and serve.

Allen then commended Florida women in particular:

> We, therefore, rejoice in the work that the Baptist women of Florida have done during the past year in the interest of missions, and commend heartily the earnestness, diligence, and faithfulness which . . . they have manifested in this broad field so new to them.

Adopting a Plan

One can hardly assume that Allen spoke for all Baptist men in Florida; certainly his endorsement of Adam's helpmeet would have irritated many Southern Baptist men. To the credit of the Florida Baptist Convention, early in its history it feared no "fatal embarrassments"; rather the State Board of Missions had both the wisdom to recognize the value of women to Kingdom's work and the openness to act on that recognition.

Allen also brought several recommendations, including the following: 1) that the title of the office held by Mrs. Bailey be changed from state secretary to corresponding secretary and that "Sister N. A. Bailey be reappointed to the position"; 2) that "there shall be, for obvious reasons, no Central Committee appointed to supervise woman's work in this State"; 3) that money be provided for missions education literature by taking an offering at the close of the session; 4) that "pastors and preachers of the different Associations of our State do all they can to multiply, encourage, and render effective Women's Missionary Societies and Children's Mission Bands."[37] Apparently the assumption was that the support of the State Board of Missions and the provision of state leadership for woman's work negated the need for a Central Committee.

A new title, affirmation of the effectiveness of her work, a few dollars to help provide literature (the offering taken had amounted to $12.50), and a call for support from "pastors and preachers" across the state—those were the currency, in lieu of a salary, with which Sister Bailey entered her second year at the head of Woman's Missionary Work in Florida.

For Jesus' Sake

In her second year Mrs. Bailey determined to make "For Jesus' sake" the "keynote" of her efforts. She entered the new year "confidently expecting that the embarrassments and peculiar difficulties surrounding the work would not be wholly insurmountable."[38] The second annual (1883) report of the "Corresponding Secretary" included this significant paragraph:

> It affords me much pleasure to state that valuable and efficient aid has been received from some of our pastors. . . . Much has been done in this way in removing the prejudices existing in the minds of some good brethren and sisters to this work. As these prejudices give way under the light of correct information, the natural sanctified impulses of women's hearts lead them at once into this new field of usefulness; they realize that *God has honored them with a place beside their brethren in the great work of evangelizing the world.*[39]

One of the churches in which Sister Bailey reported a new women's society was at Campbellton. The second oldest church in Florida, the Campbellton Church, in an informal history, noted records of a female missionary society as early as 1848. The 1852 minutes showed Bethlehem (the original name of the church) with "prayer meeting, S.S. & Female Miss. Soc."[40] What may have happened to that society is unknown, but Mrs. Bailey's diligence in promoting work in the far reaches of the West Florida Association demonstrated the perseverance which she modeled for the women of Florida.

Mutual Recognition and Honor

When the standing committees were appointed at the 1883 annual convention, the committee on Woman's Work for the first time included a woman, Mrs. Walter Gwynn. The State Board of Missions spoke with exuberance in its 1883 report on Woman's Mission Work:

> The Board feels some embarrassment in reporting on this department of our work, or rather on this *auxiliary* in our work, because we have such reasons for self-congratulation, that we might be thought to be *bragging* when simply stating facts. We . . . emphasize two facts. The *first* is, the almost, if not altogether *unparalleled progress* we have made in the organization of Ladies' Mission Societies in the State, considering the length of time we have been at work. . . . Secondly, your Board feel that in *organization*, for us in Florida at least, we have improved upon the older States. It is simple, not complicated, effective, and withal we think tends to educate our sisters in a proper, broad, high, unsectional missionary spirit.
>
> We take much pleasure in saying to the Convention, that in addition to infusing an increased mission spirit, these societies have rendered much material aid to us in carrying on the work with which we have been charged, having raised over one-third of what has been contributed for Foreign Missions, and about $300 for State Missions. To our Sister Bailey's consecrated energy and arduous work we are under many obligations, as a Board, and wish she could be compensated, and in some proportion to the value of her labors.[41]

Though certainly not in proportion to her value, the State Board voted Mrs. Bailey a yearly salary of $100, to be paid by the Home Mission Board. That the Florida Board could direct the HMB to pay a salary is unlikely. Perhaps the action was a designation of funds annually allotted to Florida by the Home Mission Board. Or perhaps because Dr. Chaudoin represented and was paid by the HMB, he had the prerogative of such a decision. Whatever the case, at that point both of the Baileys received wages, small though they were, from the Home Mission Board. It is quite likely that their arrangement was unique in their day.

Comparison of the reports from the women's leader and from the State Board of Missions shows that those two courses of Convention leadership flowed together in harmony and cooperation. Beginning in the earliest days of the forerunner to Woman's Missionary Union in Florida, the theme of mutual respect between Florida WMU and the Florida Baptist Convention has intertwined the history of both institutions.

The Totals Grow

One opportunity that fell to the Woman's Work secretary required that she communicate with the *Heathen Helper*, a monthly newspaper published by the women's missionary organization, or Central Committee, of Kentucky. Introduced in 1882, it communicated the SBCwide news and concerns of women endeavoring to support home and foreign missions. A woman leader in each state served as a contributing editor. Mrs. Bailey made the first reports from Florida. In the June 1884 issue she wrote:

> We can now report fifty-two Societies, and for the year ending April, 1884, have raised $645.85. As there are less than 10,000 Baptists in the State of Florida, and, with less than half-a-dozen exceptions, our Churches are not self-sustaining, and many of the Churches to which our Societies belong are either trying to build new Churches or repair old ones, we feel that no invidious comparisons will be made with the reports of other States.[42]

In the months between June and the December 1884 Florida Baptist Convention, the secretary organized a number of new women's societies and children's bands, bringing the total to 71 begun during her tenure. In addition, she launched the distribution of mite boxes. Among the contributions through mite boxes she recorded: "Dr. Harrison's three children, Manatee county, $5; Mildred Harrison (aged two years, now deceased), of Monticello, 25¢; Mrs. W. N. Chaudoin, $5.45, and Mrs. A. B. Bailey, $11." She reported a "grand total" of $833.22.[43] Delegates to the 1884 meeting reelected Sister Bailey to office, gave her a rising vote of confidence, and, because of her "feeble" health, granted her three months' vacation.[44]

This Side of Eternity

In the meantime, in May 1884 Mrs. Bailey had attended the women's meeting held alongside the annual Southern Baptist Convention. Gathering in Baltimore, the women assembled in organized fashion for the second year in a row. No record indicates her attendance at the 1883 meeting in Waco, Texas, but reverberations of Mrs. Bailey's presence in Baltimore have carried over the years.

With high hopes of formal organization,[45] or at least SBC sanction of their work, the women convened at the Westminster Presbyterian Church. Although bolstered by the stirring address of Adele Fielde, an American Baptist missionary to China, their spirits deflated when the SBC refused a proposal "to employ a woman to superintend and organize women's societies."[46] Mrs. Bailey could praise the Lord that Florida's vision exceeded that of the Southwide organization.

As the meeting concluded, "representative women from each State" were asked to "meet in an upper room in one of the hotels for prayer and consultation." Mrs. Stainback Wilson, friend of Mrs. Bailey and a forceful Georgia leader, described that prayer meeting:

> Only three responded, enough, however, to claim the promise—Mrs. F. B. Davis, of San Antonio, Texas; Mrs. N. A. Bailey, of Florida, and the writer. We had a precious hour, and after earnest prayer by each, we covenanted to pray on the morning of the first Sunday of each month for the success of Woman's Mission Work.[47]

Publicity through the Georgia *Index* and other state papers regarding that "concert of prayer" reached all the way to China, where Mrs. T. P. (Martha) Crawford, longtime SBC missionary, responded: "I think of your hour of special prayer, and join you in spirit, though so far away in my home among the heathen." Some years later, Mrs. Wilson concluded: "The full results of that little prayer service in that upper room will not be realized this side of eternity."[48]

On The Same Terms as Brethren

Southern Baptists assembled in Augusta, Georgia, for their May 1885 convention. Tension over the status of women, their missions work, and their standing (if any) in the SBC pervaded the atmosphere. When two women, authorized as delegates of the Arkansas Baptist Convention, presented themselves for seating, their appearance provoked consternation from many of the men. A divided committee reported that, on the one hand, the Convention constitution did not ban women as messengers; on the other hand, if the possibility of women messengers had entered their minds, the writers "would have written more carefully." Finally, the two women withdrew their names. To avoid future problems over the issue of women delegates, those present amended the SBC constitution to require that delegates be men.[49]

That action must have caused Mrs. Bailey to remember the moment in 1881 when her husband asked, "Are ladies entitled to seats as members of this body and upon what terms?" And she must have reflected with gratitude on the Florida Convention's amazing answer: "They are and upon the same terms as brethren."

Doing Nobly

Mrs. Bailey's fourth annual report, delivered in Jacksonville at the 1885 Florida session,[50] contained accounts of moderate progress, pleas for patience in seeing results of the work, and an ardent appeal for supportive pastors:

> I do believe if all our pastors were in active sympathy with the work, and appreciated its potency in the development of the benevolence of the churches in every way, there would scarcely be a church in the whole State that would not have the women thoroughly organized and actively working before the next Convention. Some of our pastors are doing nobly; would that I could say that for all.

She also introduced a dilemma characteristic of children's work through the ages. Children are ready for organization and eager to learn, she explained, but in many churches no woman has stepped forward to lead:

> If we only had one earnest, consecrated woman in each of our churches, who would gather the children and form them into bands and meet with them monthly, so as to train them in mission work, what a power for good would these children be.

Among the "past year's labors," she recorded the writing of 493 letters and (with the help of a state missionary) distribution of over 1,000 mite boxes, emphasis on the development of more children's mission bands, and organization of additional ladies' societies. Mission offerings for the year totaled $1,225.38.

In closing her report, Sister Bailey introduced a name which would soon rank with her own in woman's mission work: "I wish gratefully to acknowledge the assistance rendered me, this fall, by Sisters Telford and Guild." Because Mrs. Bailey had laryngitis, Mrs. S. K. Leavitt of Jacksonville presided at the ladies' meeting, held at the Congregational Church of Jacksonville, and read the secretary's report. Mrs. L. B. Telford of DeLand, former American Baptist missionary to Siam and China, also spoke. After her address, she presented "a beautiful bouquet of flowers" to Mrs. Bailey "in the name of the women of heathen lands, in whom she was so deeply interested."[51] That meeting has carried an extra measure of impact through the years because for the first time the women's minutes were printed in the Convention annual.

The Sweetest Sorrows of Life

Because of his wife's poor health, Brother Bailey went alone to the 1886 Southern Baptist Convention in Montgomery. He was one of five men who "tried to get the SBC to invite the women to attend the Convention 'as visitors.' The idea was rejected on the familiar basis, 'The women do not want it.' "[52] Certainly he knew better, for he had walked beside his wife along the rigorous paths of woman's mission work in Florida.

The paths, in fact, led through the valley of the shadow of death. In April 1886, Mrs. Bailey wrote her Georgia friend, Mrs. Wilson:

> "My health is too feeble to admit of my leaving home. I can not attend the S.B.C. in Montgomery. I presume the next meeting I shall enjoy with my friends of other States will be in heaven. If I can have God's sustaining grace in the future, as I have had for months past, death will have no terrors for me."[53]

On September 26, 1886, the grace of God at last carried Mrs. Bailey into the very presence of the One whom she had served so constantly.

During the 1886 Florida Baptist Convention in Ocala, delegates again devoted an evening session to woman's work. That time, however, the occasion was a memorial service for "our much lamented sister, A. B. Bailey." Tributes and musical presentations dedicated to Mrs. Bailey filled the evening. Brother J. J. W. Place of Palatka called her "a mother to her mission enterprise" and "a helpmeet to her husband in all his work in the ministry." Her co-worker, state missionary G. W. Hall, recalled how she had inspired him, citing his participation in her memorial service as "one of the sweetest sorrows of his life." Brother S. K. Leavitt of Jacksonville "spoke of faith as exercised by Sister Bailey." His "beautiful and pathetic words" defied reporting in "condensed form."[54]

A Solid Foundation

The women also held a memorial service which included the reading of a paper written by "Mrs. Dr. Mays" of Apopka on "The Life and Works of Mrs. A. B. Bailey," and a choir rendition, "Sister, thou was't mild and lovely." On behalf of the DeLand LMS, Mrs. Telford presented to Rev. Bailey "a beautiful memorial motto, artistically painted in two tints and handsomely framed, and decorated with white flowers."[55] The inscription read:

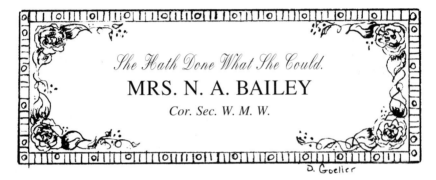

The 1886 report from the committee on Woman's Mission Work concluded:

> We acknowledge, with gratitude to God, the earnest, persevering labor of our late Sister Bailey, in awakening so largely the missionary spirit among the Baptist christian women throughout the State, and in establishing mission bands among the children; and while we would bow submissively to our all wise Providence in removing her by death from her work, and sometimes feel our loss irreparable, we pray that her mantle may fall on some one chosen of God who, under him, may carry forward to perfection what she had so well begun.[56]

Confidence in the Lord, unswerving devotion to the cause of missions, courage in facing opposition and optimism in confronting obstacles, a focus on the future—Florida WMU could find no stronger foundation upon which to build a second century than those stones laid by God's faithful servant, Mrs. N. A. Bailey.

A Place Beside Their Brethren

1887 – 1893

I know your deeds, your love and faith, your service and perseverance. . . .
Revelation 2:19

May 17, 1887

Lucina Beach Telford sat in her Windsor chair, her journal resting in her lap. The quill pen on the table beckoned her to one more entry in the diary that for thirteen years had lain unopened in a drawer of Mr. Telford's roll-top desk.

From time to time she glanced out her parlor window, watching for her beloved husband to return from his afternoon errands. His mysterious smile when he said goodbye told her he had remembered today was her birthday. Mr. Telford couldn't keep a secret! He didn't know that, however.

Mrs. L. B. Telford
1887-1893

Lucina had already spent two hours writing letters and postal cards to churches in nearby associations; she still had a long list of literature packages that needed to be gathered and prepared for mailing to the Ladies' Missionary Societies which had requested them. Yet, on that 61st anniversary of her birth, for some strange reason she felt drawn to her past, compelled to read through the entries of her journal.[1] She had started the journal so long ago—January 27, 1854—that the paper had yellowed, and an occasional fragment broke off as she gently turned the pages.

Lucina read aloud from the first entry:

> After we had met in our quiet little parlor, with our beloved mother, dear sister, and a few devoted friends, prayer was offered by our faithful pastor. In the midst of tears, the last kiss was impressed and farewells hastily repeated.
>
> I love mother, sister, brother, home and country, as much as anyone can; yet I love Jesus more. How thankful I feel that Mother endured the parting so well! . . . Truly her sacrifice has been a great one. Few mothers would have felt at the age of 74 that they could give up the youngest of their family, but she has done this for Jesus and great will be her reward.

"What a Godly woman!" she thought, remembering her mother's joy when as a 17-year-old Lucina had received Christ as her Savior in 1843. Lucina had never wavered from that commitment. Her mother had also rejoiced the day in 1853 when Miss Lucina Beach of Brockport, New York, became the bride of the Reverend Robert Telford of Hall, New York. She might not have been so happy, Lucina thought, had she realized then that the newlyweds would soon be sailing as American Baptist missionaries to Siam. Reading the February and March entries, Lucina felt again a surge of the terrible nausea which daily had gripped her as the boat tumbled in the high waves.

Mr. Telford had wanted to labor in China, but because the Chinese government would not open the country's borders to outsiders, they had decided to go to Bangkok, Siam, to work with Chinese immigrants. A collage of recollected sounds and odors assaulted her as she pictured the streets of Bangkok, crowded with lost souls who needed Jesus. She felt again the fear which struck her heart when she heard that the king had summoned several missionaries to the Palace of the Prime Ministers. Irate over an uncomplimentary article appearing in a local newspaper, and erroneously assuming that one of the missionaries had written it, he threatened to banish them from the country. A few days later, however, the king invited them all to dine at the palace on his birthday! Lucina recalled her frustration when she and two other missionary wives were no longer welcomed at the palace as teachers. The king believed that they were proselytizing as well as teaching.[2]

March 23, 1855—the day she received the dreadful missive from her sister Jenny informing her of their mother's death in October, only nine months after their farewell embrace. How could she envision life without the loving support of her mother's prayers? But how could she question the God who never errs? Blessed be the name of the Lord.

The difficulties of those days washed over her like the waves that had continually beset their vessel—the problem of getting flour, no matter the cost of a barrel; the dilemma of building and furnishing a house so far from home; the struggles to learn a language that twisted her tongue until she almost choked on it; the sad effects of the demon opium, invading even the lives of native Christians. How impatient she sometimes felt with a people whom she loved but never quite understood!

May 29, 1858—a day of pure joy, when their first son, Robie, was born. It had taken more than two years for her to overcome the effects of the long voyage to Siam and adjust to the local climate, but she felt strong as Mr. Telford placed little Robie in her arms for the first time. Her husband's good health never seemed to vary. She praised God for her helpmeet's unflagging patience and sympathy as she fought sieges of illness and despondency.

March 2, 1861—she had often longed to return to America for a visit. She wanted her sister Jenny and her brother Sammy to see Robie while he was still a baby. After the Chinese borders opened to foreigners, however, Mr. Telford began to talk of an eventual move to China. Problems in the mission further encouraged them to look at a move. By now, she was expecting their second child.

August 13, 1861—she had only recently received the horrifying news that war had split her country, but on that day when precious Willie arrived safely, peace flooded her heart. As the months passed, Willie's health never seemed quite as robust as his brother Robie's; she prayed that the planned move to China would bring him vitality and strength.

June 27, 1863—after years of preparation and weeks aboard a sea vessel, at last they arrived in Swatow, Double Island, China. Finally reaching their elusive destination should have heightened Lucina's sense of victory, but already an uneasy shadow clouded the future.

While her husband sought a permanent location for their mission, they lived in rented rooms that seemed to spawn pulmonary problems. Just after Christmas, she succumbed to an attack of pleurisy and was put to bed while Chinese women cared for the boys. She had scarcely recovered when little Willie contracted croup. For ten days high fever and wracking coughs attacked her baby. Then the unthinkable happened.

February 4, 1864—At age two years, five months, and twenty-two days, little Willie died. Hardly a day went by now that Lucina did not think of him. As she read that entry, the wrenching grief stabbed her heart just as it had 23 years ago, when Mr. Telford and a fellow missionary buried Willie's tiny hand-made casket in Swatow. There he was to remain separated from them until they would meet again in eternity. Sometimes she wished that the Lord would hasten the day.

Those memories, she supposed, had pushed the development of Children's Mission Bands in the churches of Florida to the top of her priorities as corresponding secretary for Woman's Mission Work.

March 27, 1864—Jenny's birthday anniversary. But that very day the mail boat delivered a packet from Sammy with word that their sister had joined their mother in the presence of the Lord. Could a heart so heavy bear yet another burden? Or, should she not rejoice that, unknown to them, Jenny had already gone before to welcome their precious Willie Boy? Lucina found God's grace sufficient.

March 30, 1864—The family visited Willie's grave before leaving for Hong Kong. Even now tears brimmed her eyes when she remembered Robie's solemn face as he covered the grave with roses. Only the Lord knew how she was able to hold mind and body together as they departed.

April 22, 1864—after seeking passage for weeks, they boarded a boat to return to the United States.

June 9, 1864—With six-year-old Robie, they set foot on American soil for the first time in more than ten long years.

In the years after their return, Robert Telford served churches in five midwestern states. Lucina saw that she had written only two journal entries during all those 23 years. Their mission call, however, had continued its claim, and in 1883 they made a bold move away from familiar territory. They chose DeLand, Florida, for their new home, first because they hoped the milder Florida climate would favor Lucina's health, and second, because they believed God would show them ways of serving Him in an area of the country known for its spiritual destitution.

As Lucina recalled the move, Mr. Telford's step interrupted her thoughts. His return temporarily diverted her from her journal, and she restored it carefully to its long accustomed place.

Her husband beamed with pleasure as he brought forth a small vial of perfume, reminiscent of bottles they had seen in the Orient. "I know it's not much, Lucina," he said hesitantly, "but it says I love you."

"Oh, dear Mr. Telford, thank you!" she exclaimed, the color rising in her cheeks.

After their supper of cold roast beef, sour dough bread, and rich buttermilk, they sat for a time in the rocking chairs on the front gallery. The natural perfume of nearby orange trees hung in the early evening air.

They talked of days in Siam and China and pondered the future of missions among the heathen. When their neighbor, Mr. Williams, stopped to speak during his evening stroll, they invited him in to share her modest birthday celebration.

Later that evening she took out the old journal[3] again and once more sat in her chair. That time the pen could not be ignored, and by lamp light she wrote one final entry:

> *May 17, 1887*—Many long years have passed since any record has been made upon these pages. But the record has been kept by Him who never errs or sins.
>
> Today I have recalled the past with pleasure and pain. Many, very many, recollections give me great joy, but the one great sorrow gives me pain, and I sometimes feel that the Lord will bring comfort out of it in the near future.
>
> I am in usual health on this my anniversary day. Have written letters and postals in regard to arranging for a tour among the Churches to organize Societies and Children's Mission Bands. Though the work is arduous, yet I love it for it is in line with the work I gave my life to. I do thank God that He gives me something to do for Him.
>
> Mr. E. P. Williams spent the evening with us.
>
> Had cake and orangeade.

The Reverend and Mrs. Robert Telford arrived in DeLand in 1883, as Florida Baptists were envisioning extraordinary progress in evangelism, missions, and education. "Spiritual destitution" among the state's small population troubled Baptist pastors and lay leaders alike, and they resolved to bring the gospel to bear on their entire state. Woman's Mission Work, one of the primary instruments for accomplishing their noble vision, progressed under the devout guidance of Mrs. N. A. Bailey.

Other areas of state life also quickened. Rail transportation was a major factor. In 1883, the year of the Telfords' move, Mr. Henry M. Flagler, vice-president of the Standard Oil Company, visited Florida. "Irked by the poor facilities of St. Augustine," where Baptists were struggling to gain a foothold, he, too, determined to bring about a change. There, at a cost of $2 million and five years of planning and work, he built the magnificent Ponce de Leon Hotel. To transport visitors to his grand palace on the Atlantic, he also developed a rail line, the Florida East Coast Railway, which by 1890 extended to Daytona Beach.[4]

In 1881 Mr. H. B. Plant, New York "railroad magnate," began developing a system of railroads, from Jacksonville to Palatka, on to Sanford, and from there to Tampa. In February 1884, soon after the Telfords' arrival in Florida, "the first train over the new road reached Tampa, then a town of about 700 inhabitants with a few small shops. There [Plant] erected the great Tampa Bay Hotel."[5]

Meanwhile Colonel W. D. Chipley of Pensacola ramrodded the completion of a railway across the northern borders of the state. The first through trip from Pensacola to Jacksonville ran April 26, 1883.[6] Those lines unlocked Florida's great undeveloped regions and carried a burgeoning population to the southern reaches of the state. They also opened the way for Baptists to spread the gospel at a more rapid pace. Brother N. A. Bailey recognized such implications early on; at the 1884 Florida Convention he offered an insightful resolution on appointing an agent to buy lots in all the "rising towns" along rail lines or lines under construction.[7]

As Robert and Lucina Beach Telford established their home in DeLand, the town's most well-known citizen, Mr. Henry A. DeLand, was establishing a school that trustees would later name DeLand Academy and that would ultimately evolve into Stetson University.[8]

Finding Places of Service

The Telfords found in their new hometown a strong Baptist church with a building, a pastor, and a Ladies' Missionary Society (LMS). Many of the 49 members had also migrated from the North. While awaiting God's direction for service, the Telfords invested themselves and gave leadership in the church.[9] The earliest printed reference to Brother Telford's work came in the October 1884 Minutes of the Wekiwa Baptist Association, where his name and post office (DeLand) appeared in a list of ministers living in the association. Although Florida Baptist Convention records do not indicate that he served any Florida church as pastor, he established himself as a man of ability, energy, and sensitivity to the spiritual needs of all men.

His wife, who routinely and affectionately called him "Mr. Telford" and referred to herself as "Mrs. L. B. Telford," quickly earned the respect of both men and women in Baptist work. Her past created an aura that fascinated her contemporaries. The 1885 minutes of the South Florida Association recorded that when "visiting brethren" were invited to seats, "Sister Telford was present from DeLand, having been a returned Missionary from China."[10]

Entering quickly and effectively into the work of the LMS of the DeLand church, Mrs. Telford also began to help Mrs. Bailey in expanding woman's mission work throughout the area. The former missionary was a delegate from her LMS to the state Convention and a featured speaker at the annual meeting in 1885. That year Convention delegates voted to publish for the first time the minutes of the concurrent ladies' meeting in the annual records of the Florida Baptist Convention.

The next year Sister Telford represented her church as a delegate to the

Convention, still a rather rare assignment for a woman; she was named to the often all-male committee on Woman's Work; and she presided over the annual ladies' meeting after the death of Mrs. Bailey. The 1886 Home Missions committee report spoke again to "the religious destitution of our own State" and asked, "Is it possible for the Baptists of Florida to supply this widespread destitution?"[11]

Replacing the Mantle

At its winter meeting in 1887, the State Board of Missions (SBM) chose Mrs. Telford as the new "Corresponding Secretary for Woman's Mission Work," with an annual salary of $200, provided by the Home Mission Board.[12] When she accepted the position, no one could doubt that Mrs. Bailey's mantle had fallen on a special lady chosen by God to lead Florida women in serving Him.

Throughout the year Mrs. Telford traveled, by the new rail lines, by wagon, and by river steamer. She and Brother Chaudoin, corresponding secretary of the SBM, often traveled together; he frequently visited in the Telfords' home. Many years after her death he recalled: "She at first shrank from addressing mixed audiences [men and women], but I insisted and she yielded, and oh, the impressions she made! They are alive yet."[13]

Lucina Telford found joy in visiting different churches. In that first year, she helped to establish 16 new ladies' mission societies and 25 children's mission bands. An outbreak of yellow fever thwarted her vision for establishing unions in every association.[14]

The corresponding secretary spent a great portion of her time in organizing literature packets; in her annual report she noted over 2,000 pieces distributed. Those included the *Foreign Mission Journal, Heathen Helper, Baptist Basket,* tracts, leaflets, prayer cards, Bibles, and mite boxes.[15]

Holding the Fort

The FBC did not meet in 1887, extending the time between annual sessions from November 1886 to January 1888. Brother Telford opened the first afternoon session of 1888 in prayer.[16] Under a section of the State Board of Missions report titled "Encouragements," Brother Chaudoin noted the starting of a church in St. Augustine, beginning with 19 members in 1887 and now having 63. Hearing that those members now "maintain a lively Sunday-school and Woman's Missionary Society" cheered the ladies present. He also identified as cause for rejoicing the "wonderful work in Cuba, started by you [Florida Convention]."

In 1885 Brother W. F. Wood, a home missionary who worked with the Cuban population in Key West, had urged the Florida Baptist Convention to inaugurate a mission on the island of Cuba. The FBC foreign missions committee sought the counsel of Dr. H. A. Tupper, secretary of the Southern Baptist Convention Foreign Mission Board, who was attending the 1885 Florida meeting. After consultation, the committee unanimously agreed: "This Macedonian cry from these islands of the sea *must* have our *prompt* attention." They concluded that "this convention is able to *undertake* this work at once—that is, the preliminary or provisional work . . . and to hold the fort till the Foreign Mission Board of the Southern Baptist Convention can

come to the rescue." They also proposed the appointment of Brother Wood "to guard the Cuban Mission, his home being in Key West, with authority to visit the Island of Cuba at least quarterly, to direct, encourage, and foster the various missions there." A "subscription" (solicitation of money or pledges) was taken at that convention to begin the Cuban mission, and the sale of "two collars, sent by a sister" elicited a collection of $15.75 for that purpose.   Miss Adela Fales, "our Cuban Missionary in Key West," received the collars.[18] The women of Florida would continue to play a significant role in the work in Cuba. They would also become closely involved in work with Cubans who, when the rail lines opened, moved in large numbers to Tampa.

True to her nature, in her first report (1888) Mrs. Telford mingled "sunlight and shadow," recording "advancement" in some parts of the state, "retrograde steps" in others. She found the missionary spirit deepening "in the hearts of our ladies throughout the State." Their leader desired above all else to "enlist *all* the *women* and girls in our churches to have a part in this work for their Saviour."[19]

Journey to Prominence

In the 1880s, churches in the far western panhandle of Florida, which had traditionally looked to the Alabama Baptist Convention for support, began turning toward the Florida Baptist Convention instead. While Colonel W. D. Chipley, the railroad baron, carved a place of prominence in the business and politics of the area, his wife, Ann Elizabeth Billups Chipley, entered wholeheartedly into the life of Pensacola First Baptist Church. In 1878, she had organized a Ladies' Aid Society to help raise money for the church's needs.

Her personal contributions often determined the church's ability to pay a pastor. Until her name was added to the "committee requesting the service," the local gas company refused to install gas lights in the church building for the promised $25. Under her tactful and intelligent influence, the struggling church began to show some signs of unity and progress. After her church officially became part of the Florida Convention in 1886, Mrs. Chipley regularly attended annual conventions and ladies' meetings. With her striking appearance, strong leadership qualities, and generous spirit, she commenced her own journey to prominence in an arena far different from her husband's.[20]

Mrs. Chipley and Mrs. Telford carefully planned their attendance in May 1888 at the Woman's Meeting in Richmond, Virginia. Since 1883, annual meetings of women from across the SBC territory had been held at the time of the Southern Baptist Convention sessions. The results of woman's work in support of the Southern Baptist Foreign and Home Mission Boards had garnered respect from some quarters of SBC leadership; others, threatened and even angry, supposed that the women sought independence or places of authority not considered scripturally appropriate. By 1887 missions contributions to the Boards were decreasing because of a stalemate over control of the Central Committees guiding woman's work in most states. That year some women called for quick action to establish their own national organization. Others, including Annie Armstrong of Maryland and Martha McIntosh of South Carolina, counseled patience and careful preparation. Rather than act precipitously, the women decided to invite each state's Central Committee to send three delegates to the 1888 meeting in Richmond. The 1888 group would consider organizing a general committee to oversee the dissemination of information and the collection of money for missions.[21]

Interest, Anxiety, and Prayer

Although Florida had no Central Committee, Mrs. Telford seemed the obvious person to represent the ladies' mission societies of the state. Mrs. Chipley had also proved her commitment to woman's work. While the men met in the Richmond First Baptist Church, the two Florida ladies met with the other women in the Broad Street Methodist Church, only a block away. When the presiding officer "called the roll of states to air their opinions on the subject of general organization,"[22] Mrs. Telford spoke firmly:

> Great interest, a little anxiety, and much prayer have preceded this meeting. It is a happy occasion. Ten years in a foreign land have made the need for missionary effort more apparent to my mind. If we follow the Bible teachings we are safe and success is sure. God gave women to men to be help-meets to them. Women can do work which men can not do. Florida has not sent instructions for action; but that method would meet with approbation by which the most good could be accomplished. Do not let us be swayed by prejudice. If God be for us, who can be against us?[23]

The Right for Service

Even though the year 1888 brought out the first woman candidate for the Presidency of the United States,[24] the issue at hand certainly was not women's rights. Fannie Breedlove Davis, responding for the Texas delegation, clearly rejected the notion that the women were agitating for power: "This movement is not for 'woman's rights,' though we have our rights, the highest of which is *the right for service*."[25]

Still sensitive to the concerns of the men, however, the women postponed final action until Monday. On May 14, 1888, after a time of prayer, representatives from ten states voted to establish the "Executive Committee of Woman's Mission Societies, Auxiliary to Southern Baptist Convention." As one of those ten states, Florida became a founding member of Woman's Missionary Union, Auxiliary to Southern Baptist Convention (WMU, SBC). A vice-president from each state would form an advisory board of the Executive Committee. Mrs. Chipley was named the vice-president from Florida.[26]

Serving the Needs of Cuba

One of the first issues dealt with by the ladies after they had concluded the business of organization was a request for support of the work in Cuba. The mission work there had developed quickly; a congregation of over 1,000 in Havana now stood in need of a church building. Rather than the Foreign Mission Board coming to the rescue as had been anticipated after Florida took the initial steps, the SBC had agreed that the Home Board would direct the work. In its first request of the new woman's organization, Dr. Isaac Taylor Tichenor, HMB secretary, asked the women to raise $5,000 to aid in the "work of building a church and enlarging the cemetery in Havana, Cuba." Annie Armstrong designed "a small card picturing twenty bricks for the proposed new building. Each member was to take a card and mark off a brick for each ten cents contributed." Along with representatives of the other states, Mrs. Telford accepted "brick cards" to distribute back home. As Florida women marked off their bricks, they joined women from other states in contributing several thousand dollars for that special project in Cuba.[27]

Prayer and praise, decision and action—Mrs. Telford and Mrs. Chipley left Richmond buoyed by the outcome of the meeting and the new Union forged with their Southern Baptist sisters.

*A*s the months passed, Mrs. Telford continued her efforts to involve in mission societies every female church member. Having spent the summer away from Florida,[28] she credited her husband and Brother W. H. Hall with "timely help in organizing societies" in her absence. She also maintained an ever increasing distribution of literature and encouraged support of the work in St. Augustine at every opportunity. While admitting in her next annual report that "we have been sorely afflicted," she nevertheless claimed that "we have no reason for discouragement." She recorded one special source of cheer: "A few societies whose light had grown dim, and they had changed their name, thus thinking they could work for other objects, have returned to their first love, and now are happy in sending their money through the right channel."[29]

The "other objects" to which Mrs. Telford referred may have been the causes espoused by the Ladies' Aid Societies, formed in many churches to develop financial aid for local purposes. They raised money literally to keep the home fires burning—to buy firewood for heat, and lamps and oil to light the often deficient buildings, and to pay the preacher. Sometimes a church would have either a Ladies' Mission Society or a Ladies' Aid Society. In some situations the groups worked side by side, with many of the same members and only a fine line separating them. In other instances, the mission society used some of its collections for local needs. Mrs. Bailey had refused to count those monies as missions contributions. Evidently Mrs. Telford thought some mission societies had drifted too far over the line into aid society work. Reports from several societies at the 1889 Ladies' Meeting, however, showed "an encouraging interest in the work throughout the State."[30]

Scriptural Salutations

When the ladies began their separate meetings during one day of the annual conventions, an interesting tradition started. Sending scriptural greetings between the groups became customary. The 1889 message from the women gathered in the Presbyterian Church read:

> *To the Florida Baptist Convention, Greeting:* First Cor., 15:58. "Therefore, my beloved brethren, be ye steadfast, unmovable, always abounding in the work of the Lord, forasmuch as ye know that your labor is not in vain in the Lord."

The Convention responded:

> *The Florida Baptist Convention in session, to the women's Missionary Meeting, sendeth Greetings:* "I entreat thee also, true yoke-fellow, help these women who labored with us in the Gospel."—Phil. 4:3.[31]

Mrs. Telford followed the pattern of using God's Word to communicate with the ladies gathered in Memphis for the 1889 meeting of the new general woman's organization. Each of the other eleven SBC states sent either three or four delegates, but Florida sent none. While other states recounted their work for the past year, Sister Telford's telegram reflected her discouragement in the rigorous days of a yellow fever epidemic and a freeze in the

DeLand area which severely damaged many of its fine citrus groves: "Greetings—Gal. 6:9 Mrs. L.B. Telford."[32]

For the group's reply to the message, *Let us not be weary in well doing . . .* , Martha McIntosh, the president, selected the encouraging words of Psalm 126:6, *He that goeth forth and weepeth, bearing precious seed, shall doubtless come again with rejoicing, bringing his sheaves with him.*[33] Such scriptural affirmation must have heartened the Florida secretary, despite the WMU treasurer's Annual Report showing that Florida societies had given only $1,110.91, the least of the twelve SBC states.[34]

The Right to Lay in Store

"How can the women find means to give to missions?" That question was central to teaching women about stewardship and sacrifice for the spread of the Gospel. The Report on the Plan of Work presented in Memphis suggested several options:

> As the best plan of raising money, we would recommend the setting apart and laying by in store, a certain proportion of earnings or spendings, or the doing without some object of convenience or self-indulgence. In the country, so many rows of potatoes, etc., such a proportion of eggs, butter, lard, or other farm products; in the towns, the denial of self, in attending entertainments, etc. We would earnestly deprecate the employment of any method that would put the cause of Christ before the world as a beggar, or one needing to seek aid from it in any way, by catering to the lower elements of human nature.[35]

Countering later arguments against the involvement of women in handling the Lord's money, Mary Gambrell, wife of Southern Baptist leader J. B. Gambrell, contended:

> "Is it not commanded, 'Let everyone of you on the first day of the week lay by in store as the Lord has prospered so that there be no gathering when I come'? Does that not include women, are they not a part of the Lord's church, and if He prospers them, have they not *a right to lay in store*? Are women transgressing any command of the Scriptures when they send their contributions for missions to the Boards? Look into the Scriptures and see."[36]

The right for service, the right to lay in store, such were the "rights" the women of WMU claimed under the banner of their Lord.

In the absence of both Mrs. Chipley and Mrs. Telford, the Executive Board named Mrs. Telford the new vice-president from Florida.

Laboring in the Gospel

Those attending Florida Baptist Convention meetings in that era might sometimes have thought they had stumbled into a quilt sale. Several times during the sessions in Monticello in January 1890, business ceased while a quilt "was spread." A handsome creation by Mrs. H. M. King of St. Augustine brought pledges and cash totaling $50.48. The money was contributed toward the $2,000 needed to build St. Augustine's Ancient City church, and the quilt was presented to J. F. Forbes, president of Stetson University.[37] Florida Baptists could take pride when the Ancient City building would finally rise from soil contributed by Mr. Flagler, not far from his renowned two-million-dollar Ponce de Leon Hotel.

In the January 1890 report from the committee on Woman's Work, the men again resounded their unequivocal endorsement:

> "Help those women who labored with me in the gospel," is at once divine authority, and example sufficient to allay all doubts and stimulate our sisters to become co laborers in extending the gospel and sharing its rewards.[38]

Recognizing the growing effectiveness of the ladies' work, they supported Mrs. Telford's desire to see all women church members taking part in those efforts. Their strategy differed, however. They recommended: "That a Woman's Mission society be organized in every church under the auspices of the church, including, *as a matter of course*, all female members of the church."[39] The women did not choose that path to success.

The year 1890 was a busy one for the Telfords. Florida Baptists for some time had attempted to assist their "colored brethren" in developing trained pastors and church leaders.[40] Brother Guild, who had come to Florida from "the extreme North," was hired as a state missionary to head that work. He gave himself so whole-heartedly to his task that his health broke.[41] The person chosen to carry on the assignment was Brother Telford, a fellow Northerner.[42] Brother Chaudoin said of his work during 1890:

> Dr. Telford has faithfully worked on, holding Institutes, and lecturing, and in whatever way he could, tried to build up and improve our colored brethern, and especially by seeking to help their ministers. He realizes more and more the need and importance of the work.

At the same time, Chaudoin praised Sister Telford as "faithful in her work, a valuable helper," and a co-worker who had aided and encouraged him.[43] Now both of the former foreign missionaries had found their special calling to work among the people of Florida.

When Mrs. Telford reported the contributions for 1890, she commended Indian River as the banner association, "the only one that gave over a dollar per member." The mission organizations of the DeLand church had made the largest contribution, $426.89, including, for the first time, "two barrels valued at $62.07."[44] Since women often had little money to contribute to mission causes, the resourceful Annie Armstrong had conceived the idea of sending boxes, or barrels, filled with goods the women could share, to missionary families on the frontier. Women of a mission society or an association might plan

and prepare their items, such as handwork, clothes, food, cloth, sewing supplies, and books, over several weeks, then gather for a festive afternoon to pack their goods. The value of a barrel could equal as much as one fourth of the recipient's income.[45] Mite boxes for their coins or mite barrels for their wares, the women would find a way to support missionaries.

God Gives the Harvest

In January 1891, delegates gathered in Pensacola for the annual state convention. While the men assembled in the meager accommodations of First Baptist Church, the women met on Saturday in a splinter church called Palafox Street Church. For the occasion, "First Baptist bought an organ and additional hymnals, while Palafox Street members made arrangements for some of their families to host the visiting Baptists."[46] Mrs. W. D. Chipley and Mrs. S. M. Loften, presidents of their respective societies, welcomed the participants.[47]

The program included the reading of a leaflet, "The Christian Education of Girls in Cuba," by Mrs. J. B. Stetson of DeLand. Mrs. Telford's heart was so touched by the project that she requested the group to consider pledges for the education of two girls in Cuba. The women pledged $75, with Mrs. Chipley and Mrs. Stetson personally promising the sizable amount of $10 each. Thus Florida women followed the example of the general Union in making Cuban missions an early object of their efforts.

Mrs. Telford's report, "a most interesting and ably prepared paper," was the next item on the agenda. Longer than customary, it included zealous rhetoric on the "world's evangelization" and urged involvement in "this wonderful story of missionary advance." The responsibility for results lies not with the workers, she said. Rather, "it is ours to work and pray, and pray and work and die. . . . God gives the harvest." Those words, from one experienced in the prayer and work of foreign missions, seriously challenged the women.

Coming Full Circle

A seemingly insignificant word slipped into the 1891 report when Mrs. Telford referred to "circles," a term which had not yet come into use by the general organization of WMU. She rejoiced that as she visited "with the circles" or in "the meetings of the Associations," some women responded, more quickly than she had anticipated, to her challenge to become assertive about mission support. Years later, in the *Encyclopedia of Southern Baptists,* Mrs. John Maguire would write that the "circle plan," adopted by WMU, SBC, in 1918, was "believed to have originated in Florida."[48]

Neither insignificant nor inadvertent, however, was the title which Mrs. Telford signed to her 1891 report: "Corresponding Secretary and Organizer." For the uninformed or skeptical, she left no doubt about her priorities! Mrs. Telford seemed unusually optimistic in that report. Perhaps the friendship of Jennie Lucena Spalding, a young lady who had recently moved from New Jersey to DeLand, fueled her enthusiasm. Only recently, the *Florida Baptist Witness,* a weekly news journal, had begun carrying a column on Woman's Work, often written by Miss Spalding. It provided information useful to women "desirous of being helped" in carrying on the work of their mission societies.

From Scraps to Schools

What happened when a small group of women, usually called a "Ladies' Mission Society," gathered once or twice a month? Many early churches in Florida had no building. In rural areas, attending home meetings often required lengthy travel. Members might bring with them items for sewing. Others might gather around quilting frames, working on patterns like Sunburst, Wedding Ring, or Snail Trail, made with batting of homegrown cotton. On occasion a society or an individual would send the quilt to an annual state convention to be sold for a designated mission cause. The focus of the meeting, of course, was praying for and learning about missions.

From time to time they brought their mite boxes and counted out the coins so lovingly saved. Sometimes they shared ideas on how to earn money for current projects like the missionary home in China, the Cuban Girls' School, the work in Key West, or a church building in Brazil. Or they could plan for the filling of a missionary barrel as they sewed baby clothes for the family to receive it. Sharing a letter from a missionary always brought excitement and frequently tears. Perhaps they talked of ways to relate to husbands who resisted their involvement outside the home.

Women generally lacked opportunities for public speaking. Limited education hampered some. Learning to pray in a group or to present information—received through the *Baptist Basket,* literature sent by the Secretary, or columns in the *Witness*—presented a challenge. Convinced of their cause, they persisted against obstacles. In their timidity and lack of experience, they simply followed the Psalmist's counsel: *Serve the Lord with fear, and rejoice with trembling* (Psalm 2:11 KJV).

Let the Little Children Come

With the passing of time, women from local societies began to emerge as leaders in the associations and at the annual state meeting. As other women learned the art of leadership from Mrs. Bailey and Mrs. Telford, names of individuals began to appear more frequently in minutes and reports, for example, Mrs. A. L. Jones of Fernandina, Miss Lily Clubbs of Pensacola, and Mrs. J. F. Forbes of DeLand.

Mrs. Forbes, the secretary at the Pensacola meeting, closed the record with a brief account of an activity first organized by Mrs. Telford in 1886. Each year, at the end of the ladies' session, she held a special meeting for children. There she would draw the imagination of the children into the mysterious country of China and win their hearts for missions. At the Pensacola meeting, as a girl modeled a Chinese costume, Mrs. Telford told them about the life of Chinese boys and girls. "She had the most perfect attention of her audience and especially pleased them by reciting the Lord's prayer in Chinese, and showing idols and the little shoes worn by Chinese women." Perhaps as she looked into the eyes of the eager children, she saw the face of her own little Willie Boy and felt again the pain of the "one great sorrow" that still lingered in her heart.

The ladies' and children's meetings dismissed in time for them to join the men "for a delightful excursion on Pensacola Bay," hosted by Colonel W. D. Chipley and Mr. W. K. Hyer.

In Perfect Sympathy

A new name appeared in the committee appointments at the 1891 meeting of WMU, SBC. "Mrs. N. A. Bailey" was named to the Committee on Nominations.[49] After his first wife's death, Brother Bailey evidently had "secured" another "intelligent and zealous helper in his work."

Mrs. Telford was appointed to the pivotal Committee on Plan of Work; she also led devotional services at one session and was one of four women who spoke at a children's missionary service. Mrs. Chipley was selected for the committees on resolutions and obituaries. Two other women from Florida, Mrs. Ferrias and Miss M. Curry, also attended the national meeting in Birmingham.

Women of the state were recognized and respected on the national level, even though Florida was now the only SBC state without a Central Committee. Mrs. Telford acknowledged that unique position in her report to WMU, SBC:

> Woman's work in our State is steadily taking hold of the hearts of our people. Our plan of work is unlike that of any other State and yet, when we come up to our meeting, we are astonished at the amount of work done and money raised for the various benevolent objects. We are in perfect sympathy with our Missionary Union in all its plans of work.[50]

"And yet"—even though the leadership of the state Convention praised and supported the work of the women, the reports of Mrs. Bailey[51] and Mrs.

Telford occasionally hinted of some inadequacy in the organizational structure. Intimations of a growing desire for change began to surface.

Drawing the Line for Missions

In the year 1892 Baptists in Florida joined others throughout the SBC and around the world in celebration of the centennial anniversary of William Carey's historic mission to India. On October 2, 1792, the day when Carey, an English cobbler, made his commitment to a new vision for reaching the heathen in foreign lands, Christianity "came to a new life and usefulness," declared Brother Chaudoin. "That day," he said, "began to draw the line of demarkation between a religion which was formal, selfish, worldly, dead, and one which was spiritual, self-sacrificing, heavenly, vital."[52]

To celebrate the centennial of modern missions, the Southern Baptist Convention set expansive goals, calling first for 100 new missionaries in the field. Reaching that goal would more than double the current mission force. Beyond support for newly appointed missionaries as well as their regular offerings, Southern Baptists were asked to raise yet another $250,000. The money would go equally to the Home and Foreign Boards for increased support of their work. Those objectives would challenge the commitment of state organizations and local churches.

The Seven-Step Plan

Perhaps the stress of work at the pace she normally set for herself caused problems for Mrs. Telford. Or she may have undertaken an undue burden as she faced the challenges of the centennial goals. Whatever the underlying cause, she explained that "on account of illness and nervous prostration" she could prepare only the statistical report for the January 1892 Florida convention. A notable achievement was the fulfillment of the $240 goal for the Cuban Girls' School "and $20 more."[53]

Although the committee included no women, the seven men who presented the report on Woman's Mission Work did a masterful job. They commended "our efficient secretary" for so ably carrying out the four features of the work: organizing new societies, distributing missionary literature, encouraging the weak and timid leaders, and visiting the societies and mission bands. Their report closed by naming seven steps for doubling the "power and efficiency" of the work in the coming year:

> 1. Let every pastor increase his interest in this work, and determine that his church or churches shall at once organize a Woman's Mission Society. 2. Let every S. S. Superintendent see to it that the children of his school are organized into a Mission Band. 3. Let every Woman's Mission Society increase its contributions. 4. Make good use of the literature sent you by Sister Telford. 5. Let the societies occasionally send for her to address

them, seeing to it that they pay her expenses. 6. Let this part of the work be constantly remembered in prayer by pastors and congregations. 7. Let our ladies, interested in this grand work, encourage each other and their Secretary by communicating with each other through the Florida Baptist Witness.[54]

After 100 years those principles still provide worthy guidance.

Trust Them, Brethren

The *Baptist Basket*, joining its cousin, the *Heathen Helper*, in January 1888 began providing missions news and emphases on stewardship and tithing. Edited by two sisters-in-law from Kentucky, the monthly publications supplied a unifying force as women worked through the issues of birthing and developing the national Union. By 1895 both had ceased publication.[55]

In 1892 other women from Florida besides the state secretary, who was called an "editor," wrote to the *Baptist Basket*. The letters of two ladies told some of the story of what was happening in Florida Woman's Work. Mrs. Eva A. MacMahon wrote optimistically:

> I have just moved to Lakeland from Pensacola, where I was a member of the First Baptist Church Society, Mrs. W. D. Chipley President. There is no Ladies' Missionary Society here, but I will do my best to organize one. Send me the BASKET.

Mrs. E. F. Booth of Anthony painted a more disheartening picture:

> Our society is still in existence, feebly striving to aid in spreading the Gospel in heathen lands and in our own loved country. We are a small band of twelve members, and appoint regular monthly meetings, but from sickness and other unavoidable causes, we have had but few to attend.[56]

On the same page as those letters appeared the picture of Dr. J. B. Gambrell "Who will Preach the Convention Sermon" in Atlanta. A handsome man with piercing eyes and full beard, Dr. Gambrell had been editor of the *Mississippi Baptist Record* for a number of years and was a well-known and respected leader. The July 14, 1892, edition of the *Alabama Baptist* published an extract of Dr. Gambrell's speech under the title "Results of Woman's Work." Woman's Work, he said, will "emphasize the Baptist doctrine of individuality in religion" and help men to realize that a "woman is a person" in her own right. "It is enlarging the character of our women," he declared, "and will greatly strengthen our churches." Perhaps most engaging of his arguments was Gambrell's word on the family:

> It will, as another result, give us better homes. If you don't understand this, it is because you are not married—that's all. When the mother becomes interested and absorbed in religion and missions she will talk it in the home, and as a result, a great uplift of morals will be seen. It breaks up

her monotony. Seventy per cent of insane women in the United States are wives of farmers. The ceaseless doing of one thing, a never-ending routine, no relief, no diversion. . . . mission work will enlarge her heart, her mind, her sphere, and it will be for the glory of God.

Gambrell concluded, "Women have sense. Trust them, brethren."

In Memory of "The Gift"

Dr. Gambrell's message encouraged the women at the 1892 SBC meeting in Atlanta, but the presence of Miss Lottie Moon at the Atlanta WMU sessions electrified them. The Foreign Mission Board had appointed her in 1873 to mission service in China. When she returned to the United States in 1891, she had not stood on American soil for fourteen years.

By the time of the founding of WMU in 1888, Moon's strenuous work and sacrificial spirit had become widely known. In urgent correspondence she proposed that the new organization undertake a Christmas offering to provide for two new women missionaries who could continue the work while she took a much-needed furlough.

"Need it be said why the week before Christmas is chosen? Is not the festive season, when families and friends exchange gifts in memory of The Gift laid on the altar of the world for the redemption of the human race, the most appropriate time to consecrate a portion from abounding riches and scant poverty to send forth the good tidings of great joy into all the earth?"[57]

At the encouragement of the Foreign Mission Board, the national WMU Executive Committee in its first meeting decided to promote the offering. They set a goal of $2,000, enough to send two women as Moon had requested. When the contributions finally were tallied and entered into FMB ledgers, over $3,000—enough to support three new women missionaries—had been laid on the Lord's altar by the women, and the men with whom they had shared their special envelopes.[58]

Both Mrs. Telford and Mrs. Chipley shared the excitement caused by Miss Moon's presence as they listened to her descriptions of the political situation in China, her work among the Chinese women, and "the crying need for more workers."[59] From its beginning, the Christmas Offering was a cause of great importance to Mrs. Telford. Her heart could resonate with the missionary needs described by Lottie Moon; she, too, had observed the heartbreak of Chinese women with bound feet and with hearts desperate to receive the gospel.

In a later business session, Mrs. Chipley moved the adoption of the FMB recommendation: " 'That the object of the next Christmas Offering be the increase of the missionary force in Japan.' " Even though Lottie Moon's heart beat with the mission force in China, it was large enough to approve that objective as well.[60]

Vigorous Efforts, Fervent Prayers

Although Mrs. Telford's health was growing more precarious, curtailing her travel, she continued her work as best she could. She maintained a steady correspondence with societies around the state and continued the distribution of literature. With enlarged vision, she began to supply literature for missions education to "not only the societies and bands, but [also] Sunday-schools and some of the churches."[61]

Mrs. Telford sent out 1,084 envelopes for 1889 and proclaimed, "The Christmas envelopes for Pingtu, China have been a perfect success." The Leesburg LMS claimed the banner for the largest contribution, giving $22 of Florida's $136.12 offering. In 1890, she reported "a vigorous effort," sending out 2,265 envelopes "accompanied with fervent prayer that they might return with an offering." They returned with $174.86. In 1891 and 1892 fewer than half as many Christmas envelopes went out. On the other hand, the money for missions raised by the societies and bands nearly doubled during 1892, reaching a total of $2,295.[62]

The State Board of Missions also aspired to "have the honor of supporting" a citizen of Florida in some mission field. Brother Chaudoin noted, "A worthy young woman has offered herself and awaits appointment."[63] What greater harvest could woman's mission work bring than to inspire one of Florida's own to enter the Master's service?

When Chaudoin gave the 1893 SBM report, he included statistics on missions organizations: "20 churches, 52 Sunday-schools (or one for every Sunday in the year), and 22 missionary societies and bands were organized; 374 people were baptized, 282 were received by letter, and 52 restored to fellowship."[64] Commending Sister Telford for the advancement of woman's work, he turned to the future:

> Nor can we believe that our women in Florida, seeing what progress the women in other States are making year by year, will fall out of line. . . . Let us encourage our women in Florida, and help them as they help us, and so be co-workers, in spreading the gospel that does so much for woman.[65]

Far from falling out of line, Mrs. Telford also looked to the future in her report: "The children who are at work in our Union Bands are delighted in doing their little deeds of kindness and acts of love. Soon they will be our standard bearers."[66]

Sentiments for Change

At the 1893 FBC meeting in Lake City, a recommendation with interesting overtones came from the committee on Woman's Mission Work. Besides the usual urging of cooperation from the pastors and the systematic distribution of "the best literature on the cause of missions," they further recommended "the intimate co-operation of Societies with their State Secretary, and through her with the Woman's Missionary Union, Auxiliary to the Southern Baptist Convention."[67] Perhaps Mrs. Chipley, the only woman on the committee, had shared with the men the growing sentiment of the women for a change in organizational structure.

At the 1893 women's meeting in the Methodist church, Mrs. Telford presided for what turned out to be the last time. The women pleased her greatly when they voted to continue the support of three Cuban girls in Havana Girls' School. In her last speech she urged the women to "constant, efficient work, the coming year."[68]

Receiving the Reward

During the years of her leadership of Florida Woman's Mission Work, Mrs. Telford's fellow workers had observed her obedience to Paul's teaching: *And whatsoever ye do, do it heartily, as to the Lord, and not unto men; knowing that of the Lord ye shall receive the reward of the inheritance: for ye serve the Lord Christ* (Colossians 3:23-24 KJV). She continued to work "even when prostrated by her last sickness." But on July 17, 1893, "she quietly passed to her rest 'in the sweet fields of Eden.' "[69]

When the Florida Convention met again, many accolades filled the sessions, as various reports referred to the death of the much beloved "Secretary for Woman's Mission Work." Her young friend, Jennie Spalding, spoke for the women:

> [Mrs. Telford's] devotion to her work was unfeigned and unceasing. She was equally loyal to Foreign, Home and State Missions.
>
> The words of love and praise in our denominational papers, both South and North, as well as many personal letters received by myself and others, bear strong testimony to her recognized worth.[70]

Rev. H. C. Speller, Mrs. Telford's pastor from DeLand, spoke for the Woman's Mission Work committee:

> Her qualities of head and heart, together with ten years of practical work in China, eminently fitted her to carry on the work among our women from the stage of healthful progress to which it had been brought, to its present splendid proportions.

He spoke of the committee's "entire satisfaction with her work" and "their sorrow at losing her." Speller also extended "tenderest sympathy with her bereaved husband, our Bro. Telford."[71]

After those two reports, Dr. Chaudoin exhibited Mrs. Telford's gold watch, which had timed so many women's meetings. She had donated it "on her death bed" to a cause most dear to her, the Girls' School in Havana. A collection of $100 "released" the watch to be sent to her husband, who, like his predecessor Brother Guild, had moved to the George Nugent Home, a Baptist institution in Germantown, Pennsylvania.[72] Later Brother Telford, conscious of his wife's devotion to the work in Cuba, sent the watch back to the Convention, "to be sold and the proceeds to be used for furnishing a room in the [Havana] hospital, to be known as the Telford Room." At the 1895 annual session the watch "sold" for $28.10; the money and the watch went to the hospital in Havana.[73]

Having faithfully served her Lord, Lucina Beach Telford joined little Willie Boy in the presence of her Master.

PART TWO

Making Known the Name of Jesus
1894 – 1994

III

An Uncharted Path

1894 – 1911

> *. . . sacrifice and service coming from your faith.*
> Philippians 2:17

July 1893

A tear spattered on her stationery, blurring the fresh ink. Jennie Lucena Spalding wept as she worked on the correspondence of her dear friend, Lucina Telford. Almost two weeks before, Mrs. Telford had asked Jennie to take over communications with the women who requested literature or sought help with the work of their societies.[1] Watching her mentor grow weaker each day, Spalding knew that death would soon take the corresponding secretary for Woman's Mission Work. Oh, woeful day for those left behind!

Young Jennie Spalding had come to Florida "to escape the rigors of the Northern climate." When she moved from Elizabeth, New Jersey, to DeLand in 1890, she found a community and a Baptist church largely filled with other settlers from the North. Finding a strong church with an active Ladies' Mission Society excited her, because she had grown up under the influence of "a godly mother and father, and a pastor who believed, and taught others to believe, in missions." Converted as a child, Jennie participated in the mission band of her church. As she learned about the "lost heathens" and the missionaries who helped them, she developed "a strong desire to become a foreign missionary, but God ordered otherwise." Spalding often pondered why God had not allowed her to pursue mission service. In truth, as she adjusted to her new situation in DeLand, she sometimes "felt rebellious at the apparent uselessness of her life." All the while, God was preparing a place of usefulness for her through her friendship and work with Mrs. Telford.[2]

More Than a Heritage

After Mrs. Telford's death, Dr. W. N. Chaudoin, corresponding secretary of the State Board of Missions (SBM), requested that Miss Spalding temporarily take over the leadership of the Woman's Work Department. With no hesitation, she "assumed full charge."[3] After all, she had worked with Mrs. Telford for almost three years, writing columns in the *Florida Baptist Witness* and assisting in other ways when illness more and more frequently beset her friend. She had learned much from her mentor about both Woman's Missionary Union, Auxiliary to Southern Baptist Convention (WMU, SBC), and the plan of work for the mission societies and bands in Florida. Despite their age difference, she and Mrs. Telford had shared more than a northern heritage and a name (Lucina/ Lucena). They had also shared a deep commitment to missions. Now Spalding, too, could serve God through Florida Woman's Mission Work, knowing that she could depend on His promise: *Commit thy way unto the Lord; trust also in him; and he shall bring it to pass* (Psalm 37:5 KJV).

Some Are Sound Asleep

Spalding immediately set a goal to communicate with every society and band in the state in the next six months, before the January 1894 state Convention meeting. She was not totally successful in rousing them to response, she said, "because some of those whose names appeared on the books were dead, and some were sound asleep."[4]

Rather than the regular monthly article, she developed in the *Florida Baptist Witness* a weekly column for the Woman's Work Department. In it she promoted the first observance of Sunday School Missionary Day. The Sunday School Board had joined the SBC family in 1891. WMU, SBC, had supported the new board just as it had the Foreign and Home Mission Boards.[5] In 1893 the mission boards recommended that Sunday Schools throughout the SBC observe "Missionary Day," with promotion and literature to be provided by WMU.[6] Although in Florida "only a few Sunday Schools engaged in the service," Spalding hoped that in the future "its observance will be more general and it will become a permanent institution."[7]

While the young acting-secretary carried on the work from her home in DeLand, women long active in Florida mission societies discussed a need for change. Many of the mission society members had learned to speak before a group, to write and present papers on pertinent mission topics, to preside at meetings, and to participate in business sessions, even at the national level. WMU work had earned the respect of Florida Baptist Convention leadership and many of the local pastors. Yet a restlessness had surfaced from time to time that took definite shape at Mrs. Telford's death. The time had come, according to the women, for a change that would put Florida in line with women's organizations in other states. That meant having a Central Committee of women to guide a statewide organization.

A Season for Change

Few delegates traveling to the state Convention meeting in Plant City in January 1894 knew that a historic moment was about to occur. But the long-skirted women gathering in the Presbyterian Church on the afternoon of

Mrs. T. D. Crawford
1894-1896

January 12 sensed both strong grief and an air of anticipation. After a touching memorial service for Mrs. Telford, the minutes said simply: "It was decided to change the plan of Woman's Work to the Central Committee plan, consisting of a President, Secretary, Advisory Committee, and a Vice-President from each Association." The ladies elected Mrs. T. D. Crawford, Ocala, as their first president under the new system; Miss Spalding, corresponding secretary; Mrs. E. D. Beggs, Kissimmee, recording secretary; and five members for an advisory committee: Mrs. N. A. Bailey, Leesburg; Mrs. E. W. Agnew, Ocala; Mrs. M. F. Hood, Lake Weir; Mrs. J. C. Newman, Gainesville; and "Mrs. Dr. Bruce," Tampa. They also chose the associational vice-presidents.

To the delegates meeting in the Baptist Church, the women sent a petition:

> We, the women of the Florida Baptist State Convention, believing that a distribution of labor would be conducive to the success and progress of the missionary work; and believing that a central committee, with vice-presidents in each Association, would awaken greater interest and enlist a larger number of workers, petition the convention to change the present system of woman's missionary work to the central committee.[8]

If anyone spoke to the issue, Convention minutes did not record it. The response of Florida Baptist Convention delegates was reported as simply as was the action of the women:

> The Constitution was changed by striking out [in the list of convention officers] the words, "also a Corresponding Secretary of Woman's Mission Work," and the matter of a central committee was committed to the Woman's Meeting.

Commenting on Woman's Work in his State Board of Missions report, Chaudoin, as always, commended the women: "Their system, liberality and self-denial is an inspiration, and is frequently heart-opening to our men and sometimes to pastors." He acknowledged Spalding's excellent help in keeping the work going after the death of Sister Telford. In closing his report, the great friend of Florida women emphasized, "Help these women (and children, too) who labor with us in mission work, and encourage them, and do not be jealous of them, or afraid of them—much."[9]

Instilling Confidence

Spalding's report to the 1894 Convention exhibited a style quite different from that of her predecessors.[10] Opening with the salutation, "Dear Brethren," she presented no introductory treatise on the scriptural basis for missions or appeal to reach the benighted heathen population of the world. Rather, she gave clear descriptions of Mrs. Telford's accomplishments and of her own subsequent work. She reported a marked increase in total giving for the second year in a row. The number of societies "on record" was 55; the number of bands "on record," 31.

The State Board of Missions, as well as the women, could relax as they listened to Spalding's report. The young lady instilled confidence with her direct approach and her optimistic assessment:

> Taking the reports as a whole and looking at the tangible evidence furnished by the money sent to Bro. Chaudoin for the various Missionary projects, it may be truly said that the Mission Work of the women of the Baptist churches of Florida is on a good foundation and promises most encouragingly for the future.

For the missionary societies throughout the state, January 12, 1894, marked the dividing line between that good foundation and that promising future. Conceived in the hearts of women devoted to the cause of Christ, from the womb of sacrifice and service was born the Woman's Baptist Missionary Union of Florida.

Jennie Lucena Spalding
1894-1911

*O*fficial FBC action and election of leadership were only the first steps in putting the new organization into operation. The women requested the newly-elected corresponding secretary to draft a constitution and bylaws for the Central Committee to consider in its first meeting in April 1894. The committee met in Ocala, home town of the president, Mrs. T. D. Crawford. Like most presidents who would be elected in the next half century, Leonora Grandy Crawford was a pastor's wife who had been active in her local organization. Like most inhabitants of Florida, she had come from another state. Born in 1846 in Camden County, North Carolina, she received an excellent education, "absorbing the best in literature, music, and the art of gracious gentle living." As a young woman she focused her primary attention on church activities, leading the choir and beginning a missionary society. When she moved to Ocala in 1889, "she entered heartily into the work of the church."[11]

The Central Committee adopted a constitution for the Woman's Baptist Missionary Union, which would be voted on formally at the next annual meeting.[12] They patterned the preamble after those in the constitutions of WMU, SBC, and other state WMU organizations:

> We, the women of the churches connected with the Florida Baptist Convention, desirous of developing and stimulating the missionary spirit and grace of giving among the women and children of the churches, do organize ourselves into a society. . . .

The bylaws gave the Central Committee "entire control of the mission work of the Union," from arranging programs for the annual meetings to planning for the extension of the work.

Delegating Authority

If the Central Committee formed the cornerstone of the new system, the associational vice-presidents were the load bearers. Each association was to elect two women—first called associational vice-presidents and later associational superintendents—for an advisory board to the Central Committee. Since Florida Baptists were divided into 19 associations,[13] a complete team of associational vice-presidents would spread leadership of WMU work among 38 women throughout the state. All were entitled to vote at Central Committee meetings. The bylaws gave them "general supervision of missionary work among the women and children" and instructed them to organize new societies and bands, visit organizations already in place, hold associational meetings, order and distribute literature, and make "a full report" each quarter.

The duties of the corresponding secretary, as described in the bylaws, included "general supervision of the work of the entire State," distribution of literature, editing of the Woman's Work column in the *Witness*, and monthly communication with the *Baptist Basket.* Quarterly and annual reports would communicate the progress of the work. A significant change occurred as the designation "treasurer" was added to the secretary's job. In addition to her other responsibilities, she would now keep records both of monies she received and sent on to the state Convention treasurer, and of monies he received directly from the women and reported to her. She should also "encourage the sending of all monies through the church Treasurer directly to the Treasurer of the State Convention." Meticulous record keeping on the part of Jennie Spalding assured accurate accounting from her direction.

However, inconsistencies in records furnished to her by the state treasurer or the State Board of Missions were an ongoing frustration and accounted in part for friction that eventually arose in regard to expenditures.

Miss Spalding's employment differed considerably from that of Mrs. Telford, who had worked full time and traveled extensively and who at the time of her death was receiving an annual salary of at least $200. Spalding only worked part time when she was elected. The women neither asked nor expected her to travel; they may have assumed that the work of the vice-presidents would now make travel and full-time work unnecessary. If Spalding received pay, it was minimal. She taught music lessons to supplement her income.[14]

Fiscal Disasters

Meanwhile, the women were giving generously to reduce the life-draining debt of the Foreign Mission Board (FMB). WMU, SBC, promised to raise $5,000 for the FMB; Florida's portion of that amount was $150. Enthusiasm for new leaders and new methods may have inspired Florida women and children to give more than double their apportionment. By the August 1 deadline, $386.14 had gone from Florida to the FMB in Richmond. Dr. Chaudoin attributed the good response to the efforts of Spalding, "aided by the wise counsel and help of the Central Committee."[15]

Because many of the states met their goals, WMU, SBC, eliminated over $5,000 of the FMB debt. Other financial climates, however, were not as healthy. Several reports at the 1894 annual meeting of WMU, SBC, revealed pervasive financial problems: Georgia, "unprecedented financial stringency"; Louisiana, "depressed financial condition of the State"; Mississippi, "small contributions . . . owing to the monetary depression"; Tennessee, "great financial depression of the past year"; Texas, "more hindrances during the past year than ever before . . . 'hard times' . . . drought-stricken counties."[16] In contrast, Florida's report spoke to the loss of Mrs. Telford and the change to the Central Committee form of organization.

In late 1894, however, Florida began experiencing the depths to which the economy can plummet when natural disasters occur. A freeze, hitting while the orange trees hung heavy with fruit, killed the oranges and any hopes for a profitable crop. Hardly had Floridians adjusted when a more devastating freeze occurred in February 1895. That time the trees themselves, as well as extensive vegetable crops, felt the death blow. Estimates of losses rose to $75 million. Many owners simply abandoned their groves. The citrus industry of necessity migrated farther south.[17]

In a largely agricultural economy, the effects of those disasters spilled into church life: smaller contributions to churches and to mission offerings made paying pastors and missionaries difficult and forced cutbacks in assistance for ministerial education and for building church houses. The work of Florida WMU, therefore, became all the more important.

Committed Hearts and Hands

Between the freezes of late 1894 and February 1895, the Florida Baptist Convention met in Leesburg in January. While delegates acknowledged "the great disaster that has befallen us," they expressed no spirit of despair. Always an encourager, Dr. Chaudoin blessed Miss Spalding in her new position:

> We feel that the same loving Father who brought to us our first leader, and then her successor, has been as good in giving us our present Secretary of Woman's Work. Seldom has one not known or never seen by but a few, been so generally loved, as our Miss Spalding.[18]

In turn, on behalf of the Central Committee, Spalding commended the pastors for not only aiding the women in their work but also helping to organize new societies: "In two Associations the pastors recommended the sisters of the churches to engage in organized mission work. It is just such an attitude by the pastors, that will be efficient in bringing into service the ladies of all the churches."[19]

The associational vice-presidents had directed the forming of 30 new women's societies and 11 new children's bands. Societies now totaled 73; bands, 25. Spalding reported that she had written 1,119 letters and 12 postal cards. She had distributed 300 copies of the *Foreign Mission Journal,* 240 copies of *Our Home Field,* 120 copies of *Young People's Leader,* 1,040 copies of *Kind Words* (Sunday School literature), and 120 copies of *Baptist Basket.* She had also sent out 3,075 Christmas Offering envelopes, 300 programs for Christmas meetings, 400 programs for Week of Prayer, 300 programs for Sunday School Missions Day, and 500 copies of the Sunday School Board's circular letter—and she worked only part-time! "Our only desire," she said, "is that we may be faithful to the trust committed to our hearts and hands, and to the God who has committed it."[20]

Give, Sisters, Give

In its early days the Christmas Offering was gathered primarily in January. Collected before the February 1895 freeze, gifts for the work in China more than doubled those given the year before. The Central Committee, worried that additional disasters would dishearten the women, encouraged them "to maintain their organizations and continue their meetings."[21]

In March 1895, the Home Mission Board (HMB) and Annie Armstrong appealed to Florida women to "join the Baptist women of the South in observing a Week of Self-Denial for the purpose of aiding in paying off the debt of the Home Board." The Central Committee debated asking the women to sacrifice any further but concluded that all should have the opportunity to participate. Of the $155 given to that first Self-Denial Offering, the Ocala ladies gave $45.90, "the most from any society in the state."[22] The committee felt that, though limited, the responses "represented such denial as people have seldom ever been called upon to make."[23]

Florida Baptists knew the importance of supporting the HMB, Florida's partner in conducting state missions since the formation of the State Board of Missions in 1880. "Our work is the Home Mission Board's work, and that Board's work is our work," explained Dr. Chaudoin. "All labor of missionaries is reported strictly to both Boards."[24] Annually the number of missionaries working in the state varied, usually between 30 and 50. Some were missionary pastors; some were associational missionaries; some worked only part-time. Salaries were marginal for all. Even as the women themselves experienced unusual deprivation, their sympathies for the struggling state missionaries led them to fill more mite barrels than ever before for missionaries in Florida. Over the year they supplied goods valued at $652.17, bringing "joy and comfort to our worthy workers and their families."[25]

Light in Dark Days

While helping construct new church houses as well as rebuild some destroyed by storms, the Florida Baptist Convention pushed to complete the building of the Ancient City church in St. Augustine. It was Baptists' only church house between Jacksonville and Key West.[26] At the same time, Henry Flagler was extending his rail lines to West Palm Beach and Miami. When the first train arrived in Miami in 1896, passengers saw "only a few wooden stores and not many houses. The streets were ruts through the sand."[27] Later as citrus growers moved south, and the trains carried both settlers and tourists to the area, Baptists would talk of evangelizing the growing population.

Meanwhile, dark days followed one after another. Bank failures were doubly painful, costing the Florida Convention its own, as well as borrowed money. Missionaries went without pay, and debts mounted. Yet God was faithful. John B. Stetson twice sent an extra $500 offering, and the HMB added another $1,000 to its regular Florida appropriation of $3,000. Dr. Chaudoin praised God for light in the midst of darkness. One ray of light, cast through the influence of WMU, spotlighted "four young [Florida] women, intelligent and consecrated," who were "desirous of devoting their lives to the work in foreign fields." Consecrated Florida Baptists prayed that God would call out Floridians as foreign missionaries.[28] At the same time, they renewed their resolve to shed the light of the Savior throughout their needy state.

Strength in Times of Stress

At the January 1896 meeting the women elected Mrs. J. E. Oates, also from Ocala, as president. They renamed the Central Committee as the Executive Committee and elected fellow workers with strong missions track records: Mrs. T. D. Crawford (outgoing president), Ocala; Mrs. N. L. Anthony, St. Augustine; Mrs. W. D. Chipley, Pensacola; Miss Mary A. Taylor, Tampa; and Mrs. M. B. Harrison, Palmetto.

Spalding gave consultation as needed and continued to promote the work from her home in DeLand. Her mother, Mrs. S. J. Spalding, shared her home and her interest in WMU. The two became familiar figures wherever the women gathered for annual meetings or other special occasions. Spalding often remarked, "I don't know what I would do without Mother. She's such a help and an inspiration to me."[29]

Although Spalding had not yet attended an annual session of WMU, SBC, frequent correspondence kept her in touch with the headquarters in Baltimore. She studied the published materials and kept the Florida work carefully in line with the goals and recommendations of national Union leadership. At the same time both she and the Executive Committee worked toward keeping the warmest relations with the State Board of Missions. On more than one occasion she reiterated: "We desire to strengthen and enlarge, more than ever before, by our prayers, gifts and labor, every work to which the [Florida Baptist] Convention and union are pledged, and this all the more because of the stress of the times."[30]

As the economic situation worsened, the women no longer could fill enough boxes to meet the needs of the state missionaries. WMU, SBC, came to the rescue by suggesting that several of the "abler states" to the north might help the Florida women. Spalding coordinated the combined efforts, seeing that every missionary working in Florida received the aid requested.[31]

Jesus Wants Me for a Sunbeam

Mission bands for children had been part of the Florida Woman's Work Department ever since the 1881 convention record mentioned the Peniel Band. Mrs. Bailey and Mrs. Telford had worked hard to involve children in missions education and giving. Jennie Spalding also felt great concern for the children. During 1896 WMU, SBC, gave that concern an "official" outlet when the national Union, in consultation with the Foreign Mission Board, took charge of the Sunbeam program. Sunbeams began in 1886 as the inspiration of George Braxton Taylor, a Virginia pastor, who provided missionary information for a Sunday School class called the Sunbeams. As the response of the children grew, Taylor broadened his outreach through state papers, inviting children "to form Sunbeam Bands and to correspond with Cousin George. The main work of the Sunbeams was to raise money" for missions.[32]

The organization's quick growth—284 bands with over 8,000 children within three years—outstripped Taylor's ability to foster it. The Union became the sponsor. In turn, the leaders recommended that every state organization appoint someone to lead the children's work.[33] With that recommendation from WMU, SBC, Spalding gave "special attention to organizing the children of our Sunday schools into mission bands or 'Sunbeam' societies." She wanted to instruct the children "in the great commission, in missionary history past and present, and in the grace of giving." She firmly believed that "the importance of this early seed-sowing in its relation to future missionary work can not be over-estimated."[34] Future generations of missionaries have proved her right. Despite her extra efforts, however, at the end of the year only 24 bands were recorded, down one from the year before.

Measuring Success

The 1897 state Convention, held in the fine new Ancient City church house in St. Augustine, represented a triumph for the patience and determination of church members and the Florida Baptist Convention alike. For the first time both the state Convention and the women could meet in the same building: the women convened in Sunday School space, while Convention sessions proceeded in the auditorium.

For the second consecutive year, illness prevented the WMU president's attendance. Mrs. Oates sent her husband, Rev. J. E. Oates, to read her address. The women thought it "deeply spiritual, and replete with helpful suggestions for the work." Miss Carolyn Palmer of Lake Helen reluctantly accepted election as the new president. Mrs. J. C. Porter, Lake Weir, became the new recording secretary. For the first time, the minutes included the names and home towns of the delegates. Thirty-four names were recorded.[35]

With finances dominating the thinking and the conversations of most Floridians, Dr. Chaudoin treated the subject in a special section of the State Board report. His words, like his praise, spilled almost uncontrollably across the page; much of the good news he attributed to WMU organizations:

> More churches have overpaid than have fallen behind. Some churches and women's mission societies have contributed more than they ever did any year before, as Whitney church and society, Bartow church, the Telford society at Palmetto. Apopka society gave $6.68 as a Christmas offering and three or four months later raised $12 by self-denial. Chipley societies increased in their contributions. Kissimmee church overpaid her pledge, and the Woman's Missionary Society paid $10 for Foreign Board debt, and a sister in heaven sent $5 for the [Cuban] girls' school (or it came to us in her name), and the Sanford Woman's Missionary Society sent $10 for the debt, and the Orlando Woman's Missionary Society overpaid, and DeLand overpaid her pledge; while some women sewed to make money, some washed clothes, some used no sugar for a week—all to increase the funds of self-denial week; so that, while we anticipated that 1896 would be a trying year, the faithfulness and self-denial of some of our people . . . have enabled us to keep up our work, in some parts of it to even advance.[36]

Unfortunately, Dr. Chaudoin's cause for optimism was short-lived. For the FBC, 1897 proved to be "the hardest of the three years" since the disastrous freezes. Yet the women persisted. The associational vice-presidents continued to organize new societies, strengthen old ones, and nurture the mission sympathies of the women. They counted success not only in increased numbers, but also in the report of "a society at work with only one member."

Charmed Circles

Four delegates from Florida—Miss Spalding, Mrs. J. C. Porter, Mrs. Murray of Citra, and Miss Carolyn Palmer, the new state president—made the trip to Wilmington, Delaware, for the 1897 meeting of WMU, SBC. Palmer had given her heart to Christ as a youth. She taught "a Sabbath School class" in Lake Helen and later in DeLand, where she worked as librarian for Stetson University. An admitted novice in the WMU arena, she wrote extensive reports of the Wilmington meeting for the *Witness*. Her insights are novel and refreshing:

—on the seating arrangement:

> Delegates [43 in number] were distinguished from visitors by small bows of lavender ribbon, and sat in a charmed circle, divided from their less favored but no less esteemed sisters by broad bands of the same.

—on Miss Fannie Heck's presidential address:

> She refrained from the too common mistake of placing undue importance upon the indispensableness of women in the plans of creation and salvation, and urged them to greater spirituality.

—on a Sunday School Board request for WMU to pledge $1,000 for the coming year:

> Dr. Frost, secretary of the Sunday School Board, made a patronizing but ineffectual plea of fifteen minutes duration, after which the Union amended the recommendation to read: "We pledge to the Sunday School Board our hearty cooperation," which seemed on the whole to be wiser than to promise a definite amount.[37]

Advancing the Gospel Wagon

The circumstances of the past several years might have dampened enthusiasm for the 1898 women's meeting, yet on Thursday before the first Sunday in January 106 delegates and visitors met in the Sunday School rooms of the Tampa First Baptist Church. That number far exceeded any past attendance and would stand as a record for several years to come.[38] An unexpectedly positive report from Miss Spalding elicited a strong response from Mrs. J. C. Porter, the recording secretary:

> We give thanks for the gift of our wise, consecrated leader, Miss Spalding, who is devoting time, talents, even her very life itself, to the upbuilding of the mission cause in our State. Her report showed an increase in the contributions of more than $200 over last year, and every department of the work is making steady advance.

At the same hour, in the church auditorium, Convention delegates heard Dr. Chaudoin address the issue of "some falling off in our work." Speaking of the "present embarrassment," he revealed that the Convention's debt exceeded $1,500; yet he believed that the coming year would bring improvement. Though other aspects of Convention work had declined, he rejoiced over "the work of our ladies and children, led by Sister Spalding."[39]

The women's program included speeches by the three SBC board secretaries. Several women also addressed the group, including Mrs. B. M Bean of Live Oak, who spoke on "Systematic Giving." Mrs. M. A. McIntosh of Pasco Association "gave a resume of her work, and showed the great good being accomplished by the 'gospel wagon' which she and her husband use as a means of locomotion into the far interior [of the state], off the lines of travel." As the January 1898 WMU meeting drew to an end, delegates voted to send their beloved Mrs. Chipley both a telegram and a letter expressing their love and sympathy at the recent death of her husband, Colonel W. D. Chipley. Mrs. Porter concluded the record: "Thus closed the best meeting ever held by the Woman's Missionary Union of Florida."

Before the Florida Baptist Convention meeting ended, however, a mystifying action occurred. FBC delegates "re-elected" Miss Spalding as corresponding secretary of Woman's Work, even though that office had been deleted from the FBC constitution when the Central Committee plan was adopted in 1894.[40] Until 1906, in fact, the WMU of Florida remained in many ways an integral part of Convention structure. Delegates to FBC annual meetings continued to vote on the election of the WMU corresponding secretary as well as her pay. They considered her report as part of Convention business and discussed it from the floor. Minutes of the WMU annual meeting were automatically included each year in the Florida Baptist Convention Annual. Yet, through the WMU Executive Committee the women planned and carried out their work.

The Cuban Connection

Florida women had begun their support of the Girls' School in Havana under Mrs. Telford's guidance. After her death, they added the hospital in Havana to their mission causes. Miss Spalding boosted the Cuban work, with its close connections to Florida, while WMU, SBC, also took up the promotion of Cuba as a Home Mission Board field. A Cuban rebellion, which broke out against the oppressive Spanish government in 1895, eventually forced the missionaries temporarily to evacuate to the United States. Some of the displaced national pastors migrated to Tampa, where a large number of Cubans had settled to work in cigar factories. Florida Baptists soon began work in Tampa.

In 1897 women attending the WMU meeting in St. Augustine had taken a special collection of $10 "for furnishing the Cuban chapel at Tampa." Later the Union added $70 more, "and it was the beginning of active interest on the part of Baptists in the work of Rev. J. V. Cova among his people." Soon the State Board of Missions saw the need for another Cuban missionary but had no funds for a salary. To the women they went, suggesting that the WMU take over the weekly rent ($3) for the chapel. Relieved of that obligation, the Board could employ a helper for Brother Cova. The Union received the suggestion "most cordially" and over the last six months of 1897 paid $71.43 in rent.[41] The work progressed rapidly. A second missionary was hired, and larger quarters were rented.

Cuba was on the minds of the women for more reasons than one. In 1898 the United States actually went to war with Spain over the liberation of Cuba. Hundreds of fresh-faced young men in new khaki uniforms arrived in Tampa to prepare for embarkation and battle. Rev. J. C. Porter, owner and editor of the *Florida Baptist Witness* and husband of the WMU state recording secretary, visited the "Ocala boys" in their tents and reported them "all well and happy." Distinguished Southern Baptist preachers conducted revival meetings "in the great army tabernacle morning and night," with "scores of conversions" recorded. Dr. H. M. Wharton of Baltimore "preached to Roosevelt's Rough Riders last Sunday afternoon," Porter wrote, "and some fifty or more stood up and asked Christians to pray for them."[42]

Investing and Harvesting

During 1899, Spalding began "earning" $25 a month to provide leadership for the 1,800 women enrolled in 139 societies and the 850 children in 43 bands.[43] At that time she may have been the only state WMU executive who received pay. Spalding's wages, plus "a small sum for stationery and postage" constituted "the entire expense connected with woman's work."[44]

After nearly six years of constant work, Spalding needed a rest and a change. In 1899 she attended a three-month "study course of missions" in the Chicago University divinity school. While there, she probably visited with Tampa native Mary Taylor. Taylor had surrendered publicly to mission work long before she ventured to Chicago to attend the Baptist Missionary Training School. She had actively served WMU in many ways, as recording secretary, as guest speaker, and as advocate for the Cuban work. At the 1899 annual meeting, Spalding asked the women of Florida to assume "the privilege of paying" $135 for Taylor's expenses during the last six months of her training. Although the women responded with gifts or pledges amounting to only $29, the Union paid the full amount.[45]

For the women, two developments during 1900 embodied the seed and the "fruitage" of missions. They planted seeds by establishing a new "branch" of WMU work, the "Babies' Branch." Spalding explained that the new organization carried two purposes:

> to enroll the little ones as contributing members of our Union, but equally, and far more important, to interest the mothers whose home cares make it impossible for them to attend the society meetings, and so secure for their children missionary training in the home.[46]

Fruitage occurred when years of missions education, prayer, and experience resulted in the Home Mission Board appointment of Mary Taylor as a missionary to Cuba. The HMB wanted Florida WMU to contribute $500 for her financial support. Raising $500 beyond their last year's contributions would not be easy. In Arcadia at the annual meeting, they discussed the matter "fully" and voted unanimously to undertake that responsibility. Pledges of $170 came from individual members, societies, bands, pastors, and others, including "Modest Brother," who promised $1.[47]

"Baptist Baby"

Men, except as guest speakers, generally did not attend the women's meeting. Before Mary Taylor was to deliver her talk, "Appropriating Christ," the women made an exception. "On motion of Mrs. Chipley, the gentlemen in the lobby were invited to hear Miss Mary Taylor." As she thought of the departure of Taylor for Cuba, Spalding exclaimed: "What an inspiration to more liberal giving of ourselves and of our means! What a call to prayer!"[48]

Into the Twentieth Century

The last years of the nineteenth century had brought both disasters and triumphs to the Florida Baptist Convention. The twentieth century would bring changes and challenges, including the resignation of Dr. Chaudoin, who had nurtured Woman's Work as the first department of the Convention. The loss of Chaudoin created a vacuum in the heart of Florida WMU, but it did nothing to diminish the cordial relationship between WMU and the State Board. The election of L. D. Geiger, a native of Old Town in Marion County, Florida, brought to the post of SBM corresponding secretary another advocate of woman's mission work.

Baptists in Florida were growing at a faster rate than the general population, which now numbered more than half a million.[49] In 1901, the state had 468 churches; few had buildings. Primarily because of the foresight and efforts of the State Board of Missions, however, almost every county seat had at least one Baptist church house. Churches in Daytona Beach, West Palm Beach, and Miami represented Baptist growth along the east coast. Unfortunately, the number of pastors lagged far behind,[50] and the number of Woman's Missionary Societies trailed a distant third. Yet Florida Baptists, including WMU, could see substantial progress. Ever dependent on God's guidance they looked forward with hope. They would not be disappointed.

Hopes for Youth Work

Jennie Spalding had high hopes for the development of work with young people. As early as 1897, she devised a reading club and solicited involvement through articles in the *Witness:* "Wanted—Fifty young ladies to join our 'Missionary Reading Circle.'"[51] In 1901 Spalding reported "two new societies distinctly known as Young Ladies' Mission Clubs."[52] "Our Girls" claimed Spalding's "special attention" in 1904.[53] Realizing that young ladies and girls desired "a place in the Union and a definite object to work for," the secretary in 1905 began the "What I Can" Societies. In May 1905 the Home Mission Board gave the children and young ladies of Florida "the privilege and honor of opening the first mission to the Pawnee Indians, near Pawhuska, Okla." By year's end, they had already given $200 for the Indian mission.[54]

Other states also organized groups for girls considered too old for Sunbeams. By 1906 over 600 such groups existed throughout the SBC; Fannie Heck, in her third term as president of WMU, SBC, set in motion the process of developing an organization to embrace them. The young ladies chose a name already in use in Alabama, Young Woman's Auxiliary. They also designed a pin and chose a watchword, Daniel 12:3, *They that be wise shall shine like the brightness of the firmament; and they that turn many to righteousness, as the stars forever and ever.* Thus, when Young Woman's Auxiliary was officially added to the WMU family in 1907, Spalding's "What I Can" Societies became YWA groups.[55]

Despite hesitancy on the part of many in WMU, Fannie Heck also pursued her vision for a boys' missions education organization. In 1908 Royal Ambassadors (RA) became the fourth WMU family member. Florida, however, had no special work among the boys, as Mrs. S. B. Rogers, the recording secretary, noted at the 1909 annual meeting:

> We have no Royal Ambassadors in Florida, so Miss Spalding had to tell us all about them. Her talk was so full of enthusiasm for this great work among our boys, that most of the ladies became enthused also, and we feel sure there will be a number of organizations for our boys before the next Convention.

Two Jacksonville churches, Riverside and Grace, soon organized the first and second RA chapters in the state.[56]

Hopes for Missionary Service

In the spring of 1902, hopes for the continued missionary service of Mary Taylor appeared doomed. Ill health forced her resignation from HMB service in Cuba. Rather than succumb to pessimism, the women clung to "the hope that very soon some field of labor within our own State will be opened to her." By the time of the January 1903 annual meeting, Taylor was ready to work again, "wherever the Lord would have her labor." During the meeting,

"Mrs. J. H. Tharp, Lakeland, presented the needs of the Cubans in Tampa and suggested the peculiar fitness of Miss Mary Taylor for that field." The women voted to provide a salary of $25 a month for three months if the SBM would open a mission among the Cubans in Ybor City, Tampa, and "engage Miss Taylor to labor there." If local pastors and the SBM decided to continue the work, WMU pledged their continued support of Taylor.[57]

Hopes for the State Work

In several visits to the state Miss Annie Armstrong, corresponding secretary of WMU, SBC, spurred the hopes of Florida women. "Sharp, forceful, tall, attractive,"[58] Armstrong had earned the admiration of Southern Baptists, from the most timid of WMU members to the heads of the Foreign, Home, and Sunday School Boards.

Armstrong began her 1902 train journey at Pensacola, home of her close friend, Bettie Chipley. Traveling 800 miles in 9 days, she stopped at 11 places and held 18 meetings, "five of them being given partly to the children and four of them held among the colored women." Florida women flocked to see "this noble woman." Some women traveled "sixty to ninety miles at night to spend an hour or two in the morning with Miss Armstrong." Men, however, were excluded from the meetings.[59] Armstrong might summon the heads of SBC boards to her Baltimore office, but lest she tarnish the reputation of WMU, she refused to speak before men in public meetings.[60]

In the spring of 1903, Armstrong again toured Florida, "visiting some new and untried fields" as well as meeting with "workers long in service."[61] When she returned to Florida for the 1905 annual meeting and a third state tour, the state president introduced Armstrong as "our very own," and the women greeted her "with the Chautauqua salute, a silent, yet speaking token of love."[62] The high point of the meeting came when Armstrong spoke on "Opportunities" of Home Missions:

> "A narrow life circumscribed by one's self, one's family, one's own neighborhood, is so poor a life. . . . God is working in two ways: Sending missionaries to the heathen and sending the heathen to this Christian land. Last year there came to the shores of America representatives from 97 other nations. These foreigners are coming with all their loose morals, their false religions, their dangerous tendencies and what shall we do for them. The question is confronting us.
> "Foreign Missions have been brought to our very door. . . . The heathen are here; what shall we do with them? Make answer to God; not to me."

Armstrong also promoted the Tichenor Memorial Church Building Fund, established "in honor of the magnificent work" of Dr. I. T. Tichenor, longtime head of the HMB. Weak churches could borrow money from the fund and repay it as they gained strength.[63] In 1906 Bettie Chipley gave $1,000 to the fund. In that same year, Armstrong, after 18 years of service, left her post as WMU, SBC, corresponding secretary.

Hopes for a Florida-born Missionary

For years Florida Baptists had hoped and prayed that a native Floridian would serve as a foreign missionary. God responded to their prayers through Frank J. Fowler. Born in 1870, Fowler grew up among his parents' orange groves near Melrose. He attended the Eliam Church, where he was baptized and later ordained to preach. While on summer vacation, he worked as a student missionary for the Santa Fe River Association, "to be paid what the Association thought his work was worth." He was worth the handsome sum of $85.[64]

After three years at Mercer University, Fowler went on to Southern Baptist Theological Seminary in Louisville, Kentucky. During one of the severe freezes of the 1890s, "his parents telegraphed him: 'Please come home. We need you.' He had to make a decision: 'Do I leave the ministry and go to farming or do I stay?' "[65] He stayed. While a pastor in Harriman, Tennessee, Fowler married Miss Daisy Cate. Active in WMU, she, like Fowler, had felt God's call to foreign missions. "One of the memorable and significant mileposts in the history of Florida Baptists" occurred July 18, 1904, when the Foreign Mission Board appointed the Fowlers "to serve in the unevangelized pioneer country of Argentina."[66]

To hail the importance of that event, the *Witness* editor traveled to Richmond to cover the story for Florida Baptists. Florida WMU members proudly read *Witness* accounts of the appointment process. At the 1905 annual meeting, the women volunteered "to assume the care of Brother and Sister Fowler" in Argentina. Their pledging the sizable amount of $1422.75 to the Fowlers' support underscored their love.

Supplying the hopes of many a young woman in Florida and across the SBC, the WMU Training School opened in 1907 in Louisville, Kentucky. Long in coming, the decision to undertake such an institution involved controversy and debate among WMU, SBC, leaders. Florida women by resolution had already endorsed a proposed home for females attending the seminary in Louisville and had promised to "assist in its support." Mrs. Chipley was named to the school's original board of trustees.

A Heritage of Service

A decade of service claimed the focus of Florida WMU members who gathered in Kissimmee for the tenth anniversary meeting. Miss Spalding detailed the progress of their work. Before the organization of the state Union, offerings had totalled $8,571.58. Since 1894 the women had given over $22,000. In 10 years the number of societies had increased from 55 to 144. Spalding noted that the Florida Union had "long since been generally recognized as an indispensable *auxiliary* to the State Board of Missions, with which body it has ever been in closest sympathy."[67]

Spalding expressed appreciation annually to the *Florida Baptist Witness.* That year she acknowledged ten years of cooperation: "The *Witness* has ever been a staunch friend and supporter of woman's work and without this medium of communication with the societies and churches our work could never have been as efficient as it has been."[68]

Bettie Chipley's paper, "Baptist Women's Missionary Work in Florida for the Past Twenty Years," emphasized the era of Mrs. Bailey and Mrs. Telford. "The fine, clear, annual reports of our present most efficient corresponding secretary," she modestly asserted, provide "the history of our last ten years much more fully, and a thousand times better than I can."[69] Only a few of the 49 delegates had known either of the previous secretaries, but all present praised the Lord for the heritage of those faithful servants.

After seven years in the presidency, Carolyn Palmer stated her belief in the rotation system for officers and firmly declined reelection at the anniversary meeting. With candor, humor, and dedication, she had led the women through difficult years, toward the promises of the twentieth century. Palmer died three years later in Denver, Colorado, where she had gone for treatment of a malignancy. Stetson president Lincoln Hulley spoke at her memorial service in the university auditorium. Jennie Spalding remembered that in spite of "peculiar discouragements, repeated and sore disappointments and the constant bearing of heavy burdens," her good friend had consistently displayed a "strong, generous heart and cheerful spirit."[70] Steadfast in her private struggles, unfailing in her public duties, Carolyn Palmer served God faithfully throughout her life.

Mrs. B. M. Bean
1904-1905

Ready to enter the second decade of Florida WMU, the women chose as their new president Mrs. B. M. Bean. She and her husband, as matron and manager, were readying the property for the orphanage which Florida Baptists would open later that year. After hearing Mrs. Bean excitedly recount the plans for the new home, delegates voted to support it. When much-loved causes such as the orphanage, aid to aged ministers, or help for Dr. Chaudoin's widow, "Aunt Carrie," claimed their attention, and particularly their money, the women conscientiously designated those causes as "benevolences," not missions.

Mapping the Future

From 1904 until Jennie Spalding's resignation in 1911, Florida WMU traveled an especially challenging trail. For the most part, the trail moved upward, guided by the aspirations of the women for an effective organization committed to the support of state, home, and foreign missions through offerings, mission study, and missions education for youth. The WMU Executive Committee and the corresponding secretary continued to work in close harmony with the State Board of Missions. Occasional internal WMU disagreements did not affect the mutually supportive relationship between Florida WMU and the Florida Baptist Convention.

The women, however, found much of the trail unmapped. No manual prescribed how to relate to a state convention, how to fund the organization, what officers to elect or appoint, and which to pay, what methods to use in forming new units in the churches. Each state organization found its own way, aided no doubt by correspondence and conversation with leaders of other states. WMU, SBC's first periodical, the quarterly publication, *Our Mission Fields,* began in 1906 to offer help with coordinated monthly program material. Despite their inexperience, the women achieved a pattern of organizational advancement because they recognized Christ above self and the cause of missions above their own desires.

The year 1904 brought a significant change in the Executive Committee's arrangement with Miss Spalding. Because she had worked only part time, the results of her ten years' work had been erratic. In April the Executive Committee asked the SBM to place "an organizer in the field" by the time of the 1905 annual meeting and to raise their secretary's salary from $300 to $500 a year, with travel and office expenses provided. The raise took place July 1. In the meantime, Spalding offered to visit fifth Sunday Union meetings and annual association meetings, "expenses guaranteed."[71]

Unleashed from the office in her home, Spalding set out with a will. By the end of the year she had traveled nearly 4,000 miles and had spent more than three months away from DeLand. The more than $1,000 increase in gifts to missions reported at year's end clearly demonstrated the value of her personal visits. More members and gifts meant more office work. To help her keep up, the Union bought a fine $80 typewriter. Later, the women provided funds for a mimeograph machine.

At the 1905 meeting, Dr. Geiger reported on the earlier proposal:

> It is the desire of the Executive Committee and State Board that the suggestion for a State organizer be reconsidered and that the work of the W.M.U. be carried on, as it was during the last six months, viz: That the Corresponding Secretary travel when and where she deems best for the good of the work, and that she be instructed to employ such clerical help as is necessary.

After adoption of the report, the ladies voted Spalding another raise, to $600 a year.[72]

The women had hardly adjusted to the new circumstances when all the rules changed. In 1906 the Florida Baptist Convention adopted a new constitution. Henceforth WMU annual meeting delegates would not be considered Convention delegates as well. Instead of the WMU corresponding secretary reporting to the "Brethren," Spalding now addressed her reports: "Dear Sisters." The women paid to have the minutes of their annual meetings published in the annual records of the FBC. As Spalding explained:

> The Union elects its own officers, decides upon its own policy, designates its own gifts and expenses, etc. The Union is not under the direction or control of either the State Board or the State Convention, though it has always worked in harmony with these bodies.[73]

The heart of the auxiliary status, as Spalding defined it, rested in the women's contributions to FBC causes and their hearty cooperation "in the evangelization of Florida through the State Board of Missions." For practical purposes, the Union continued to make the State Board the custodian of its funds, with WMU retaining "the right to direct the expenditures for expenses" out of its state missions contributions. Dr. Geiger agreed to make up, from SBM funds, any shortfall that might occur in the women's contributions, considering the money "a worthy investment in missions."[74]

Willingness, Diligence, and Ambition

Miss Spalding was growing weary. After the 1906 annual meeting, she took the month of February off. She reported, however, that the work went on, "under her direction and at her expense."[75]

Although the 1906 report showed some increase in gifts, contributions did not cover pledges. Spalding blamed the SBM; delayed money for clerical help resulted in less letter writing and less travel. To forestall a recurrence of the problem, at the 1907 meeting in Live Oak, "Miss Spalding *stipulated* that an allowance be granted for office help." The women reelected her at the same $600 salary and "added enough to defray her traveling expenses and necessary clerical work and office expenses."[76]

At the 1907 Live Oak meeting, the Executive Committee for the first time presented a list of recommendations. The ladies eagerly adopted the eight proposals having to do with their work. Only the proposal to hold the annual meeting at a time and place different from the state Convention meeting failed. That issue would arise again and again before a change finally occurred. In general, a spirit of enthusiasm prevailed in Live Oak. Spalding paid tribute to the "willingness, diligence and increased ambition" which had marked the service of the women over the past year.[77]

A Week for State Missions

In 1908 the State Board of Missions recommended:

> that there be a week of special prayer and study, and giving by the sisters and their friends for state missions; that our pastors and members be invited to assist in this good work in every way they can. We suggest that this week of prayer embrace the second week in November.[78]

The women responded cordially: "Resolved, That one week during the year shall be devoted to a week of prayer and effort for State Missions and that in cooperation with the State Board of Missions, suitable literature be prepared and distributed free."[79] WMU prepared the program for the first observance, scheduled for November 1908. Mrs. Annie O'Neal, secretary of the College Street Woman's Missionary Society, Dade City, wrote to Spalding about her society's experience with the first State Missions Offering:

> Each member of the Society had been requested to earn a dollar for this especial purpose.
> One lady sold vinegar, cleaned silver, and tacked a comfort. Another made hers by cleaning her husband's guns. Some made theirs by selling milk, butter and eggs. Another made a kimono for her neighbor.
> One lady . . . caught an o'possum that was disturbing her poultry during the wee small hours of the night, sold it for fifty cents, then sold the hen which the o'possum did not catch for another fifty cents.[80]

The College Street women collected $30.50, "only regretting while the needs are so great that we cannot do more." Dr. Geiger assessed the results of the first offering as "highly gratifying."[81]

The year 1908 also brought the first "field worker" to WMU in Florida. Mary Taylor was employed for one month to travel as an organizer, not for the state Union but for the South Florida Association. In order to "encourage others," she wrote for the *Witness* an account of her travels. Her first day could have discouraged the most seasoned missionary. "On April Fools' Day I started out on the campaign. . . . But I was April Fooled myself," Taylor recounted. "When the morning train refused to carry me to Seffner," she found herself

> stuck in the deep sand on the shore of Lake Thonotosassa in an automobile at the hour announced for the meeting. The mishaps of that eventful day were crowned at nightfall by my dress skirt being torn off by a big, ferocious dog. . . . I took courage in prayer and went forward.[82]

Since Florida probably had fewer than 500 automobiles in the entire state at that time, the story becomes even more memorable![83]

Knowing, Doing, Giving, Going

Mrs. M. B. Harrison
1905-1906, 1907-1911

"After 14 years of unremitting toil," Jennie Spalding requested a three-month leave of absence in 1908, "the alternative being, the acceptance of her resignation." The secretary and her mother headed to a favorite spot, the mountains of North Carolina, "to store up energy for another year's work in Florida." Meanwhile, the president, Mrs. M. B. Harrison of Palmetto, took charge of the *Witness* column, and Mrs. Frances Wooten did the routine office work.

After several relatively stable financial years, the state Convention suffered as a lengthy drought destroyed orange groves, pine forests, cattle, and truck crops. In addition, the whole nation experienced another economic decline. In January 1909 the Florida Baptist Convention and WMU annual meetings convened in DeFuniak Springs. The State Board report saw the FBC in debt for the second consecutive year. The women had also faced "the [financial] panic, the draught and untold difficulties," but Spalding's report trumpeted victory. The "faithfulness of the women" had won over the "financial stringency of the times." She praised God: "We rejoice that He enabled us to lay upon the alter [sic] of service not only as much as we gave last year [$6563.80] but $164.91 more."[84]

An Executive Committee recommendation in DeFuniak Springs helped establish definite training opportunities. From the early days of her tenure, Spalding had emphasized the importance of becoming informed. She believed that "to know is to do; to know is to give; to know is to go."[85] When in 1907 WMU, SBC, had recommended systematic mission study, Spalding feverishly pushed study, emphasizing not only knowing, but also knowing how. For several years, annual meetings devoted one session to discussions of the work, sometimes with papers read, sometimes with question and answer sessions. The women gradually developed a concept of method study that led to the state's first Missionary Institute. Held on January 2, 1908, in Tampa, it resulted in "a clearer understanding of W.B.M.U. methods."[86] The Executive Committee recommended that Missionary Institutes for training workers become a regular feature of the work.

Although Spalding's personal attentions helped lead the organization to greater growth, some members began to resent the use of state missions contributions for her salary and expenses. Perhaps they thought that their secretary should follow the example of Annie Armstrong, who adamantly refused any salary throughout her 18-year tenure as WMU, SBC, corresponding secretary. When concern for expenditures surfaced again during the 1909 meeting, Mrs. Harrison tried to quiet fears of extravagance. She explained "why the expenses of our Secretary appear in the record to be more than Dr. Geiger's," saying that hers were all under one head of "Expenses" and his were divided under several different "Heads."[87]

Oases for Our Journeys

The disputed expense report was Dr. Geiger's last. He died of a heart attack on April 20, 1909. Miss Spalding sang at his funeral, as she had sung at services for both "Uncle Chad" and "Aunt Carrie" Chaudoin. Upon the death of Dr. Geiger, the State Board of Missions chose Dr. S. B. Rogers, pastor of Gainesville First Baptist Church, as corresponding secretary. Rogers' wife had already served as a Florida WMU state officer; as SBM secretary he, too, would work closely with WMU leadership. Later as he wrote the report of the work for 1909, Rogers described the state Union as "the oases of our journey."[88]

In the hot summer months of 1909 Spalding took another extended leave:

> I was obliged to be out of the State four months to save my mother's life and to give my overworked body a chance to get stronger in a cooler climate—that was all. And some of you have thought I was "enjoying" myself all that time and forgetting you and my duty to you. You never were more mistaken.

Spalding contended that she had done the summer's work—mainly correspondence—"just the same as I would had I been in Florida."[89]

Stung by the criticism arising here and there, Spalding surveyed other state WMU organizations and published the responses in her column. The results clearly showed that Florida WMU was in line with a majority of other states, both in paying the secretary and in the amount of her salary.[90] By the end of 1909, however, relations between Miss Spalding and some of the women were strained. For the most part, they handled their difficulties privately, but a negative report on Spalding's work, given at a fall association meeting, appeared in the *Witness* in late October. It elicited strong letters of support for the secretary.

Including her "fall tourage," in 1909 Spalding traveled 6,396 miles—224 by boat, 23 by carriage, and the remainder by rail. In her report to the 1910 annual meeting in Gainesville, she acknowledged the help of many during her travels. After the ladies in Gainesville adopted her report, Spalding trembled as she listened to a beautiful duet, "Let Not Your Heart Be Troubled." Her heart was greatly troubled. At that point she "demanded that her books be examined by a committee appointed from the body. The President appointed Mrs. J. A. Lamb, Mrs. W. D. Chipley and Mrs. Standley."[91]

The Positive Prevails

In spite of the tension, the 1910 delegates dealt positively with several significant items: 1) they established requirements for receiving scholarships to the WMU Training School; 2) they adopted their first Standard of Excellence; 3) they created the office of state vice-president and elected Mrs. N. C. Wamboldt, Jacksonville; and 4) they appointed their first temperance committee. The fourth action reflected the growing concern among Florida Baptists over the moral condition of the state. The FBC had earlier initiated a statewide prohibition movement. The women had requested that the State Fair Association remove the "indecent exhibitions and demoralizing shows" from the midway of the annual state fair in Tampa.[92] Now the new WMU committee officially urged women to become involved in the temperance movement.[93]

The women also responded generously to the needs of the orphanage. When Mrs. Baker of Arcadia requested that 12 societies volunteer to provide sacks of groceries, one per month for the year, "the responses were so eager that the secretary could hardly write fast enough."[94]

Dealing with the conditions of Miss Spalding's employment was more difficult. The Executive Committee recommended that her expense money be cut and that she no longer be asked to travel. Instead, they proposed the hiring of a field secretary who, under the direction of the Executive Committee, would "travel not more than three months or less than two at salary of $40 per month while in actual service, and expenses."[95] After serious discussion and considerable disagreement, the recommendations passed. Mrs. H. C. Peelman was elected to the new position.[96] If some ladies saw that move as a reprimand of Spalding, others saw it as a means to relieve Spalding from the laborious travel which drained more of her strength with each passing year.

Working as Never Before

Mrs. E. Van Hood, widow of *Witness* editor Rev. J. C. Porter, was elected to replace Mrs. Peelman as recording secretary. Her account of the meeting, published in the *Witness,* gives insight into the proceedings. On the recommendations for two paid positions, she said:

> Many women throughout the State feel that the woman's work is costing too much for the returns. A divided vote however, gave a majority of those present as approving said recommendation. The delegates from Ocala, Gainesville, Arcadia, Kissimmee and Lady Lake opposed—not to the officers, but to the expense. Dr. Rogers was called in and stated that his Board did business on a 2 1/2 per cent basis.
>
> The women are spending 18 per cent for salaries and expenses. This, some did not consider the "best thing," but as loyal Baptists should do, all agreed to abide by the majority vote for the next twelve months and to work as never before for the success of our work.

Before the meeting concluded, the committee examining Spalding's books reported that they had found "not one item therein to which any reasonable woman could object." Spalding "thanked the body for the vindication and urged careful consideration of the feasibility of placing someone else in the office of Corresponding Secretary."[97]

Despite any rejection she may have felt, throughout 1910 Jennie Spalding persevered in the work to which she had dedicated herself. Encouraging, teaching, promoting, admonishing, informing—through correspondence, her *Witness* columns, attendance at meetings, and occasional visits, she stayed in close contact with local societies. She also traveled out of state, attending a BYPU encampment in Mississippi, the World's Sunday School Convention in Washington, D.C., and the annual meeting of WMU, SBC, in Baltimore.

Eleven delegates—including Spalding, her mother, and Mrs. Chipley—represented Florida WMU at the Baltimore meeting. As they listened to Miss Heck's presidential address on "Vision," perhaps no woman there could identify more than Spalding with Heck's closing words:

> We are discouraged with ourselves, O Lord, we are encouraged in Thee; we have no power for the task Thou hast set us; Thou hast that power. Undertake for us; work through us for the love of Thy great heart for all mankind.[98]

At the close of the first session, the Florida delegates met "under leadership of Mrs. Chipley" to discuss matters coming up for debate.[99] Because Bettie Chipley had participated in the early business sessions, those present on Saturday morning were surprised to hear the call for "special prayer for Mrs. Chipley in her sudden and serious illness." During that session, Spalding extended the greetings of the Florida women and invited delegates and visitors to attend the next annual meeting in Jacksonville, in May 1911.[100]

She Lived and Wrought Among Us

The editor's page of the May 26, 1910, *Witness* carried the sad news: "Mrs. W. D. Chipley Passes Away." While in Baltimore, she had been "taken suddenly and violently ill with peritonitis" and "died from the effects of an operation." The unexpected loss stunned Baptists throughout the state. The editor paid tribute to her as "a woman of the highest order of intelligence and refinement" and "one of the best friends the Witness had in the State." None was "more beloved and more thoroughly trusted" than Mrs. Chipley. "Every thought of her," he concluded, "will rekindle a gratitude to God that she lived and wrought among us."

After Mrs. Chipley's death, the Pensacola First Baptist Woman's Society immediately began planning

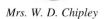

Mrs. W. D. Chipley

an appropriate memorial. Spalding encouraged women across the state to consider the matter and come to the annual meeting prepared to decide on a way "to honor her by extending the kingdom of Christ." Mrs. Peelman, the new field secretary, had spent a week in Bettie Chipley's home, just before the Baltimore meeting. Even though not feeling well, Mrs. Chipley traveled with her as she visited churches in the area. Their "heart to heart talks and seasons of prayer together" left a special impression on Mrs. Peelman, which she recalled time and again as years passed.[101]

Detailed travel reports from Mrs. Peelman began to appear in the *Witness* alongside Miss Spalding's column. Mrs. Peelman's encouraging words added a new strength to the "W.B.M.U. Department" page. As she completed her trip through the Florida panhandle, she reported: "The pastors showed me much courtesy and consideration in arranging for meetings. May the Lord abundantly bless all our dear sisters in their labor of love, and we trust many societies will become 'A1.' "[102]

Soft Answers and Wise Plans

Plans and work moved steadily toward the annual meeting to be held in DeLand in January 1911. The money issue, laid aside at the end of the 1910 meeting, would apparently lie dormant until the DeLand session. But, no! On December 8, "An Open Letter to the Woman's Missionary Union of Florida" appeared in the *Witness*. Mrs. Hood reopened the questions of the past, repeating the criticisms and adding suggestions for changes in almost every facet of the way the Florida Union did business. Insisting that her only concern was "how best to advance the Kingdom of our Lord," she proposed cutting back expenses and at the same time cutting back the work, passing the office work and bookkeeping altogether to the State Board of Missions.

Spalding did not respond for a time. In her January 12 column, two weeks before the annual meeting, she gave details of the planned program and commended the Executive Committee as a group "whom you can trust to plan wisely for the best interests of the Lord's work."[103] The *Witness* of January 19, however, gave two full pages to three WMU articles. In the first, Spalding announced her resignation. In the second, an open letter to the WMU, she responded to Mrs. Hood's previous article, refuting each charge as well as the value of each suggested change. The third article, "A Final Word with the Sisters of the W.M.U.," came from Mrs. Hood. Reiterating her previous comments, she expressed her opposition to the proposal—favored by Spalding and the president, Mrs. Harrison—that the Union have its own treasurer to receive and dispense funds. No matter what one's position on the question, no one could argue with Hood's final plea: "Sisters, go to DeLand from your knees. We need wisdom from on high to carry on this great work."

Looking Back, Looking Forward

The January 1911 meeting in DeLand was remarkably optimistic. While a memorial service for Mrs. Chipley and 11 other members brought sadness, delegates focused more on the Chipley Memorial Fund. After much discussion, they agreed on a recommendation:

> That the W.B.M.U. of Florida raise Chipley Memorial Fund of $15,000, payable in five years, to be equally divided between Home, Foreign and State Boards, to be used at their discretion, but if agreeable to the Boards, the W.M.U. prefers that it be used for church building.[104]

To start the fund, the women pledged $3,345.

Both Spalding and Peelman gave reports. The tithing system and the department of personal service had been introduced during the year 1910, but they remained undeveloped. "The Standard of Excellence," said Spalding, "has proven a power dynamic." About 20 societies had almost reached the "A1" mark. New units in every age level raised the totals for the year, even though other units had also dropped out. The "greatest hindrance" to growth remained lack of youth leaders "who know *how* and who will '*stick.*'" Contributions to missions had declined slightly, Spalding indicated, because of support for efforts to pass statewide prohibition legislation. "Our opportunities for service in Florida are great," said Peelman. "Our greatest need is not new methods or more methods, but more prayer and consecration."

Frank and Daisy Fowler, home on their first furlough from Argentina, spoke briefly to the women, as did Lulu Sparkman, recently graduated from the Training School and awaiting appointment to Brazil. To hear from those whom they supported encouraged the women as they looked to the future.

When the business session arrived, peace prevailed. Each Executive Committee recommendation was read, discussed, and approved. Changes in personnel policies carried long-range impact. The Union voted to elect its own treasurer, (the office to be combined with that of the corresponding secretary) who would have total responsibility for handling Florida WMU money. The secretary-treasurer would also do the necessary traveling. Sufficient clerical help would be provided. Delegates also voted to elect superintendents of YWA, Sunbeam, and Royal Ambassador departments, "who shall give gratuitous service." They then revised the constitution to reflect the changes they had made.

Before the election of new officers, Spalding spoke briefly, "emphasizing her decision not to accept the work" another year. The women gave her a unanimous vote of thanks "for her efficient work in the past." Separate ballots for each office resulted in the election of Mrs. N. C. Wamboldt, Jacksonville, president; Mrs. J. A. Mellon, Tampa, vice-president; Mrs. H. C. Peelman, Jacksonville, corresponding secretary and treasurer; Mrs. Van Hood, Ocala, recording secretary; Mrs. Lee MacDonell, Tampa, YWA

superintendent; Mrs. S. B. Rogers, Gainesville, Sunbeam and RA superintendent.

As the end of the session approached, the women felt "greatly cheered and
encouraged by the fine reports, plans for the future work, and the inspiration
and spirituality of this meeting."

Miss Spalding closed the meeting, and her WMU career, with prayer.

*Jennie Spalding's sharp mind did not lie idle long. She and her mother
moved to Missouri, where Jennie, at somewhere near forty years of age,
entered medical school. Her years of study required sacrifice and hardship.
Mrs. Spalding watched proudly as her daughter graduated with a Doctor of
Osteopathy degree. Jennie had established a successful medical practice in
Kirksville, Missouri, by the time of her mother's death, January 1, 1915.[105]*

*For the first time in her life, Spalding was now completely free to go where
she wished. By 1918, she had returned to the mountains she loved, establishing her medical office in Asheville, North Carolina. The Asheville City
Directories, 1918 through 1930, include her home and office listings and
occasional commercial announcements for Dr. J. Lucena Spalding. She died
suddenly in Asheville on October 17, 1931.[106]*

*As the first corresponding secretary of Florida Woman's Baptist
Missionary Union, Spalding holds a unique place in Florida WMU history.
Young and inexperienced when she began, she matured along with the organization. Time and again she ran ahead of WMU, SBC, in initiating components of the work, for example, the regular publication of a prayer calendar,
the launching of mission societies for young women, and the introduction of
a WMS Standard of Excellence. Perhaps she somewhat limited her influence
by focusing more on the work than on relationships. Nevertheless, Jennie
Lucena Spalding followed in the tradition of Mrs. Bailey and Mrs. Telford,
bequeathing a legacy of faithful service for Florida WMU.*

IV

Advancing the Cause

1911-1936

Serve him faithfully with all your heart.
1 Samuel 12:24

May 1897

Charlotte Peelman and eight-year-old Marion watched the landscape rush past their train window. "How much longer?" asked Marion, again.

"No wonder the child is restless," thought Charlotte. "We left Chicago three days ago. Even I'm beginning to doubt we'll ever get to south Florida." Aloud she said, "Only a few more hours to Jacksonville. We need a diversion. Can you still name the books of the Bible?" Reaching over to pat her daughter's hand, Charlotte resisted saying, "Sit still, Marion. Ladies don't wiggle in their seats." Instead she prompted, "Genesis, Exodus, Leviticus, . . ."

Well past dark, the train at last pulled into the little brick station in Jacksonville. Mother and daughter took a horse-drawn cab to a nearby rooming house. Only Marion slept. After spying a monstrous spider crawling into a crack, Charlotte sat up the rest of the night with shoe in hand, determined not to let the creature attack. The next morning they continued their journey south and west to Punta Gorda, where Mr. Peelman was waiting.[1]

Mrs. H. C. Peelman
1911-1936

Henry C. Peelman and Charlotte Rinkenberger had married in 1885. Older by 13 years than his 19-year-old bride, Henry had already unsuccessfully sought his fortune in New Mexico and returned to Chicago to make his living as a carpenter. The harsh Chicago winters aggravated Henry's asthma, until finally the doctor told him to move south or find his life cut short. His family spent the winter of 1895 in Chicago without him, while he went to Florida to find a healthful climate and make preparations for them to join him.

Henry found a log cabin in a little community about 25 miles into the Everglades from Punta Gorda. "You could raise oranges there, and cabbages as big as washtubs," Marion remembered.

"You won't mind it, Lottie," Henry persuaded his wife, using his pet name for her. "Before you know it, I'll have our new house built, with a bathroom in it, too!" The family settled temporarily into the cabin, while Henry set about to build a permanent house with lumber he carried by the wagonload from a nearby sawmill.

To help provide for the family, Charlotte taught in the one-room school-house where her daughter was one of the students. She and Marion learned from experience about overaged and unruly pupils who year after year managed to run the teacher off before the end of the school term. One little girl envied Marion's pretty clothes. "I had on my new plaid gingham dress one day, and she spit tobacco all over the back of it," recalled Marion. Charlotte proved her mettle, refusing to let difficult students get the best of either her or her daughter.

During the year as Henry worked on their house, he followed a sense of calling that had begun in Illinois. He visited in the country churches, sometimes preaching at their once-a-month services and starting Sunday Schools when he could. Eventually he was ordained to the ministry. Three years after their move to Florida, the Peelmans left the house Henry had built single-handedly, to answer the call of First Baptist Church, Nocatee. Although Charlotte had not married a pastor, she attended her first annual WMU meeting as a pastor's wife: she was listed as a visitor at the December 1900 meeting in Arcadia.[2]

After three years in Nocatee, Brother Peelman accepted the call of First Baptist Church, Fort Myers. To make the 45-mile move, the Peelmans rode in a buggy, slept outside in the Everglades, and crossed the Caloosahatchee River by ferryboat. Brother Peelman's new pastoral duties included ringing the bell and sweeping the floor of the one-room church house. Marion, an accomplished musician, played the organ for worship services. In 1905 Mrs. Peelman attended the WMU annual meeting as a delegate from Fort Myers.[3] Her interest in missions and her organizational skills gained the respect of the women. The next year they elected her state recording secretary, a position she held until she resigned in 1910.[4]

Although the Peelmans moved to Providence in Beulah Association in 1906, they remained tied to Fort Myers. Marion eventually married Dr. Dempsey Dubois Crews III, a dentist who had courted her while she was a high school student. After their marriage in Providence, they returned to Fort Myers, where he had set up his dental practice.

In each of his pastorates, Brother Peelman was employed as a missionary by the State Board of Missions (SBM). By 1907 Mrs. Peelman's work with her husband had caught the attention of Dr. L. D. Geiger, corresponding secretary of the SBM, who commented in the *Witness:* "In [Brother Peelman's] missionary evangelistic work, Mrs. Peelman travels with and assists her husband. She is one of the most intelligent and consecrated women we know."[5] While working beside her husband, her concern for lost souls spread beyond Florida to the far reaches of the world; she found an outlet for her expanding interest through WMU.

In 1909 the Grace Baptist Church called Brother Peelman to service in Jacksonville, and though he would serve another church, Brentwood Baptist, before his retirement, Jacksonville became the Peelmans' permanent home.

As the WMU Executive Committee planned recommendations for the annual meeting in January 1910, committee members struggled with the work and travel schedule of corresponding secretary Jennie Spalding. After much prayer, they recommended Mrs. Peelman's employment as a field worker for three months during 1910. Through her energetic work, Mrs. Peelman proved both her leadership aptitude and her capacity for a vigorous schedule. By the time Miss Spalding announced her resignation in January 1911, Mrs. Peelman had become the obvious choice as successor.

The new corresponding secretary met financial problems head on. During the first four months, WMU organizations did not send in enough state missions contributions to cover WMU expenses, including her salary. "Preferring not to be in debt to the bank," she herself "carried the work" until May, when contributions caught up with needs.[6]

For several years, Florida Baptists had anticipated the 1911 Southern Baptist Convention (SBC) and Woman's Missionary Union, Auxiliary to Southern Baptist Convention (WMU, SBC) meetings in Jacksonville. Mrs. Peelman worked with WMU leaders in the Jacksonville churches to prepare for the May gathering. SBC sessions met in the large Shriners' Temple. The women held their meetings at the First Baptist Church. Only 10 years earlier a tremendous fire had burned a large section of Jacksonville, including the First Baptist building. Now with gratitude, Mrs. W. A. Hobson, the First Baptist pastor's wife, welcomed nearly 300 WMU delegates and visitors.

One visitor noted, "Jacksonville people are glad to see us, for they even have the mules decorated with feathers and flowers."[7]

Doing "Whatsoever"

Mrs. Peelman's report to WMU, SBC, on the work in Florida highlighted the decisions and changes made at the time of her election in January:

> The new secretary was also elected to the office of treasurer, the W.M.U. voting to receive and disburse funds and not make the State Board of Missions custodian of their funds as heretofore. Headquarters were transferred from Deland to Jacksonville.

New officers included Mrs. Lee MacDonell, of Tampa, Superintendent of the Young Woman's Auxiliaries, and Mrs. S. B. Rogers, Superintendent of the Sunbeams and Royal Ambassadors.[8]

Mrs. Peelman also explained the $15,000 Chipley Memorial Fund, to be "equally divided among Foreign, Home and State Boards, for Church Building." Additionally, the state societies, she said, "are contributing regularly and cheerfully." Furthermore, adopting "a Standard of Excellence for the WMS and Honor Roll for Sunbeams and Royal Ambassadors" had promoted growth. "We study and pray for an increase of knowledge," she concluded, "that we may have a larger vision of the world's needs and do the 'whatsoever' the Lord may require."[9]

Mrs. Peelman saw positive results from the national meeting: "An impetus was received at the annual meeting of [WMU, SBC,] that has greatly stimulated missionary endeavor."[10]

Marking a History of "Firsts"

The year 1912 was notable for the election of Miss Kathleen Mallory of Alabama as executive secretary of WMU, SBC, as well as for two annual meetings of the Florida Baptist Convention. In Ocala in January, the presence of Rev. and Mrs. A. J. Terry, missionary appointees to Brazil, delighted the women. For several years they had followed the preparation of Lulu Sparkman (now Mrs. Terry), Florida's first female foreign missionary. "She will bear with her to her far away home our prayers and our dearest love," noted Mrs. Louise Porter Hood, recording secretary.[11]

The president, Mrs. N. C. Wamboldt, read a letter from the Micanopy missionary society asking that the women contribute money for a marker for the grave of Mrs. N. A. Bailey, "who began Woman's

BAILEY MARKER

Work in Florida." Mrs. Wamboldt expressed the hope that "sisters all over the State would respond."[12]

Another significant item of business was the appointment of Mrs. Hood "to complete the History of the W.M.U. of Florida, begun by the loved and lamented, Mrs. W. D. Chipley."[13] Mrs. Hood herself had also engendered the love and respect of Florida women. Her first husband, Rev. J. C. Porter, was a pastor, state missionary, and owner/editor of the *Florida Baptist Witness*. After his death, in 1905 she married Dr. E. Van Hood of Ocala. When she expressed public criticism of WMU work under Jennie Spalding's leadership, the women rejected Mrs. Hood's recommendations for change. However, to their credit, they continued to elect her to positions of leadership and honor. As a teacher, they considered her "preeminent," and she often "lectured extensively on cultural and ethical subjects" to men's as well as women's groups.[14] In the December 1912 meeting, the Executive Committee further recommended that the Florida WMU history to be compiled by Mrs. Hood "be published in book form and bound attractively" and sold, with the proceeds going "to the Chipley Memorial Fund."[15]

WMU, SBC, in 1909 had introduced "personal service" and in 1910 made it a regular department of WMU work.[16] At that December 1912 meeting, held in Lakeland, delegates for the first time elected a state Personal Service committee to lead the emphasis and guide them in meeting the Standard of Excellence requirements. They also unanimously chose Miss Maude Montague as their first college correspondent, a volunteer position.

Progressive Attitudes, Progressive Offerings

Women now served on major committees of the Florida Baptist Convention (FBC); the state missions committee, for example, included eight women and six men. The report on Woman's Work, however, came from a committee of 13 men, who hailed the progress of attitudes toward women:

> We earnestly assure these tireless workers that their efforts are no longer merely *tolerated* among us, but they are thoroughly *appreciated* and given *honored* recognition; fast becoming *indispensable* to the most successful church organizations everywhere.[17]

The years 1912 and 1913 brought together three significant emphases, two SBC and one WMU. The SBC promoted the Judson Centennial, which marked the hundredth anniversary of "systematic and organized" foreign mission work, stemming from Ann (Hasseltine) and Adoniram Judson's journey to Burma.[18] To celebrate the pivotal occasion, Southern Baptists established a $1,250,000 fund, above regular offerings, for equipment and capital improvements on foreign fields. Simultaneously, the Home Mission Board established a special $1,000,000 church building fund to help the 3,000 SBC churches without houses of worship.

From long experience, Florida Baptists understood the importance of

HMB assistance, both for buildings and for pastoral support. Dr. S. B. Rogers, who followed Dr. Geiger as corresponding secretary of the State Board of Missions, reminded Convention delegates: "Of the 639 organized Baptist churches in the state, 542 have only once a month preaching, if any at all, 224 have no house of worship." He called special attention to the plight of the Rocky Creek Association, with 800 members and no church houses, and the Miami Association, 262 miles long, with only 14 organized churches (13 of which were dependent missions) and 3 houses of worship.[19]

Although state Baptist work functioned in pioneer-like conditions, the women's years of dedicated service had resulted in more than 300 societies and bands (WMS, YWA, RA, Sunbeam) in Florida WMU. WMU members felt the excitement of the third conventionwide emphasis, the celebration in 1913 of the 25th anniversary of WMU, SBC. Entitled the "Jubilate," meaning "Rejoice Ye," the celebration took Psalm 100 as the Jubilate Psalm and "Joy to the World" as the first "official hymn of the year."[20] Mrs. P. P. Arnold, state YWA and GA leader, wrote Florida's Jubilate Hymn.[21] Special meetings in each state, often featuring national WMU leadership, and other promotional activities evoked a great surge of renewed enthusiasm and generous giving from the women. Special offerings supported both the Judson Centennial and the Million Dollar Church Building Funds. Over $81,000 from WMU, SBC, helped to fulfill the goals of each fund. Florida women met their offering objective, giving total Jubilate gifts of $1,716.61 in the anniversary year.

WMU Begins in Cuba

In early 1913, at the invitation of Home Mission Board secretary, Dr. B.D. Gray, Mrs. Peelman traveled to Cuba. During the three-week trip, she sent reports of her travels to the *Witness*. With Dr. M. N. McCall, leader of the Southern Baptist mission in Cuba, the Florida WMU secretary and others in their party visited many of the 24 mission stations, in the rural areas as well as the cities.[22] Of their journey, she wrote:

> To save expense, Dr. McCall travels third class (our day coaches in America are better than first class in Cuba) so we all did likewise. The seats were wooden benches with low backs, all of the men were smoking; pigs and chickens shared the car with us.[23]

The climax of their tour came at the West Cuba Baptist Convention. Dr. McCall invited Mrs. Peelman to speak at one of the sessions:

> We tried to [speak] through an interpreter and realized for the first time the difficulty of that method of addressing an audience. We told them something of our own W.M.U. and the helpfulness of woman's work to our women and to the churches. Both pastors and people became enthused and urgently requested that a W.M.U. be organized in Cuba. They also decided to send a banner and an exhibit to the Annual Meeting at St. Louis in May.[24]

The Cuban women agreed to organize groups in their local churches. Those societies would use a constitution similar to that of the WMU. Dr. McCall would devote to woman's work one page of the mission's semi-monthly paper.

Though she had helped establish a Cuban WMU, Mrs. Peelman still felt a burden for the people of Cuba: "There is still a very great work to be done and no funds to do it with. The results of the gift of life to Cuba are so apparent. Shall we not rally as never before to the cause of Home Missions?"[25]

At first, growth lagged for the Cuban WMU, Auxiliary to the West Cuba Baptist Convention. No Cuban woman felt capable of presiding over the meetings. For several years, the president of the convention conducted the women's annual meeting. Yet by 1942, as Dr. McCall looked back over his 37 years in Cuba, he concluded, "The Cuban W.M.U. is a real force in all phases of Cuban mission work."[26]

Come Women Wide Proclaim!

Seven Florida delegates joined more than 1,100 others[27] attending the Jubilate Annual Meeting of WMU, SBC, held in St. Louis in May 1913: Mrs. N. C. Wamboldt and Mrs. H. C. Peelman, Jacksonville; Mrs. E. R. Pendleton, Pensacola; Mrs. Jennie Bean, Arcadia; Mrs. E. Ray, Tampa; Mrs. A. A. Harris and Mrs. N. E. Norwood, Owens. Colorful pageantry characterized the sessions. Hundreds of women and children paraded, carrying state and organization banners and singing the hymn, "Come Women Wide Proclaim," written by Fannie Heck for the Jubilate. Mrs. Peelman described the Florida banner: " . . . white satin, with gold fringe, cord and tassels, green lettering. The words "Florida W.B.M.U." and the State seal are painted on the banner. Beneath the seal a red scroll with the motto, 'In God We Trust.' " The honor of carrying the banner went to Mrs. Pendleton, a member of the Pensacola First Baptist Woman's Missionary Society (WMS). One of three state honor societies, the Pensacola WMS had given the largest contributions for the year. The Florida exhibit for the meeting included photographs of the other two honor societies, Lakeland and Phoenix, as well as the Ocala YWA scrapbook, a "beautiful quilt" from the Phoenix Sunbeams, yearbooks from the First Baptist Churches of Jacksonville and Tampa, and "excellent exhibits from the Cuban and Italian missions of Tampa." Mrs. Peelman's seed planting in Cuba bore fruit with the attendance in St. Louis of Cuban WMU representatives. "We were especially proud of the Cuban banner," said the Florida secretary.[28]

From the Jubilate celebration came several significant contributions to WMU work. In addition to the hymn, Heck wrote the first book-length history of WMU, entitled *In Royal Service*. The WMU pin also was adopted. Kathleen Mallory described the pin's shape as representing "a double fish head" commemorating the sign early Christians used. She explained, "The letters which make up the Greek word for fish are the first letters in each word of the expression, 'Jesus Christ, God's Son.' "[29] Good will centers, as recommended in the celebration plans, became an important channel of ministry, or personal service. Girls' Auxiliary (GA), for preteen and young teenage girls, officially became a member of and completed the WMU family of organizations.[30] In line with the contemporary SBC fascination with "efficiency," WMU, SBC, also appointed commissions on Organized Efficiency (of which Mrs. Peelman was named vice-chairman), Rural Efficiency, and Urban Efficiency. The next year, *Our Mission Fields* took a new name, based on Heck's history, becoming *Royal Service.* "In every way," said Ethlene Boone Cox, "the Jubilate celebration was one of the high points, spiritually and financially, in the Union history."[31]

Florida WMU held several Jubilate meetings around the state, closed the year with a dramatic Jubilate service at the 1913 annual meeting, and continued to celebrate well into 1914. Mrs. Peelman could also celebrate her raise in pay to $75 per month!

A Permanent Home

The organizational framework for Florida Baptists had developed gradually, beginning with the founding of the State Board of Missions in 1880. In January 1914 the SBM established the first "permanent" Florida Baptist Convention state offices at 602-605 Heard Building, Jacksonville. Previously, the location had depended upon either the residence of the Board's corresponding secretary or the pleasure of Board members. With the move to Jacksonville, the FBC gained an identity and stability that often accompany a place of belonging. Graciously they shared that identity and location with WMU; at the invitation of the Board, the WMU office moved to room 603 Heard Building. "We appreciated the courtesy of the State Board in making this provision," said Mrs. Peelman. "The central location, better facilities, being in closer touch with the other State workers have made possible more efficient service."[32]

Ever optimistic, always urging the women of Florida to exceed past accomplishments, Mrs. Peelman also challenged their inner commitments: "Let us emphasize the spiritual life and aim to be better, kindlier, nobler women in all walks of life; to so live to show forth daily the Christ-life within."[33]

Florida WMU followed the national Union in completing the family of organizations, with the first GA group reported in 1914. With attention focused on other state and national emphases, however, the publishing of Mrs. Hood's history was the only other significant action marking the 20th anniversary of the founding of Florida WMU. Produced at a cost of $240.50, the book sold for 35 cents per copy.[34] In an "After-word" to the history, Dr. S. B. Rogers conveyed another "right" to the women:

> Our good women all over Florida have a right to thank God and take
> courage, and our good men throughout the State should not only lend them
> a helping hand and sympathetic encouragement, but might well learn from
> them the lessons of sacrifice, service, organization, progress, and devotion.
> . . . May heaven's richest benedictions abide upon this organization of
> splendid, faithful women, for their service, and sacrifice.[35]

The right to serve, the right to give, the right to thank God and take
courage—armed with those rights, the women of Florida WMU marched into
their third decade of missions advance.

From Campus to Encampments

As Floridians listened nervously to the echoes of war in Europe, Florida
Baptists faced difficult circumstances at home. While a poor economy and
inflated prices led to decreased giving, Dr. Rogers labored diligently to maintain the progress of state work within the limits of income. Perhaps the most
embarrassing and disappointing circumstances revolved around Columbia
College in Lake City. A dispute over control of the Board of Trustees had
caused a break in the Convention's relationship with Stetson University. In
July 1907, 1,500 messengers attending a special Florida Baptist Convention
session pledged almost $50,000 toward an endowment for the new college.
The institution opened its doors to students in fall 1907.

For several years, Florida Baptists proudly sent their sons and daughters
to Lake City for a Christian education. However, they did not send their
money through the FBC at a level necessary to sustain Columbia College.
By 1917, college debts had reached nearly $50,000. Considering both the
debt and the decline in enrollment, caused in part by the outbreak of World
War I, trustees decided to close the college, rather than open for the 1918
fall session.[36]

While Columbia College was in existence, however, Florida WMU gave
generously to various campus needs such as books for the library, upkeep of
buildings, and furnishings for guest rooms. A newly organized college YWA
quickly enlisted every young woman on campus and for several years earned
the only honor YWA award in the state.[37] Final WMU efforts sought $1,000
to help pay off the college indebtedness.

Beginning in 1912, the Columbia College facilities provided the site for
the first statewide summer "encampments." There Baptists of all ages gathered for a week of courses in spiritual development, methods, and missions,
interspersed with invigorating recreation, inspiring music, and rousing ser-
mons. State Sunday School, BYPU, and WMU leadership planned cooperatively to produce memorable experiences for all who attended. Mrs. Peelman
usually taught a class or two and often invited outstanding WMU leaders
from across the South to conduct others. On one occasion, Miss Marie
Buhlmaier, home missionary to the immigrants in Baltimore, spoke before

the entire assembly. According to Mrs. Peelman,

> her vivid portrayal of the immigrant problems . . . made us see, not the
> abstract problem, but the living, loving, feeling immigrant, homesick and
> alone in a strange land. Our viewpoint was changed and sympathies enlist-
> ed. We thank God for this vision.[38]

Even the small children had such special events as an afternoon story hour,
led one year by Mrs. C. D. Creasman, a popular WMU writer and speaker
from Tennessee, who frequently came to Florida to lead conferences.[39]

The name "Florida Baptist Assembly" was soon applied to the summer
gathering. With the closing of Columbia College and reestablishment of relationship with Stetson University, the Assembly moved to the Stetson facilities in DeLand.

The Women Speak for Themselves

A significant change in the reporting of Woman's Work to the FBC annual meeting occurred in January 1917. Since Brother N. A. Bailey's presentation in 1881, the report had come from a committee (usually all male) and
frequently had centered on scriptural support and the committee's enthusiasm for woman's place in kingdom work.
Beginning in 1917, when Mrs. Hood, WMU historian,
gave the report, it came from the women themselves.
For several subsequent years, the WMU secretary presented to the Convention a limited version of her
annual report to the Union.

Mrs. Hood called attention to WMU's "systematic
and thorough" graded system of missionary education and to the efforts at enlisting "every woman in
every church" as an active member of a Woman's
Missionary Society. The monthly magazine *Royal
Service* had already reached an SBC circulation of 27,000.
Hood commended its "superb programs arranged   *Mrs. Porter Van Hood*
to meet the needs of every society from the
Sunbeams to the grown-ups." She also took pride in reporting that the offerings for the past year had reached over $14,000, going beyond the aim for the
year and exceeding the previous year's gifts by some $3,000. Her concern
regarding expenditures under Jennie Spalding echoed in assessments of current activity:

> All this has been accomplished with practically no increase of expense, the
> added office work having been done without assistance by our incompara-
> ble Secretary. . . . We count ourselves blest to have as officers women of
> consecration, culture and business efficiency, and we believe we are doing
> the biggest work on the smallest capital of any business in the state.[40]

To conclude her report, Hood recalled for Convention messengers the matchless closing words of Fannie Heck's last message to WMU, SBC:

> See to it only, that you listen to His voice and follow only where Christ leads:
> Be gentle in your personal lives, faithful and shining.
> Be joyful, knowing His purposes are good, not evil, to His children.
> Be prayerful in your planning.
> Be patient and persistent in your fulfillment.
> Endeavor to see the needs of the world from God's standpoint.
> Plan not for the year but for the years.
> Think long thoughts.
> Strive for the conversion of those around you as faithfully as for the heathen.
> Train the children for world-wide service.
> Lead the young women gently in places of joyous responsibility.
> Bring all your powers into the best service of the best King.[41]

Since the days of that incomparable president of WMU, SBC, faithful servants have modeled their lives and work after her example. Mrs. Peelman, in a rare personal revelation, wrote to Heck just before Heck's death: "I have been striving to be more 'gentle' and 'faithful' in my personal life. . . . I had a great desire to tell you . . . how much you were to me and how much your messages have meant to the work."[42]

Later, in the new *Home and Foreign Fields* magazine, Kathleen Mallory, who had been present at the 1917 Florida annual meeting, gave her impression of the event:

> At the Florida W.M.U. seventeen states were represented. This will give some idea of the tourist problems there. Eighteen of the twenty-nine associations of the state were represented, showing how state-wide was the attendance in beautiful, orange-fragrant Orlando.[43]

As the Times Shall Demand

Within three months of the annual meeting, on April 6, 1917, the United States declared war on Germany. With fewer than one million citizens, Florida lent 42,030 of her sons to the armed forces.[44] Training camps, or "cantonments," and aviation schools in Florida instructed men in the arts of war. Patriotism ran strong among Florida Baptists.

Mrs. Peelman responded quickly to the situation. In her first *Witness* column after the United States took action, she wrote at length about "Our Task," saying: "Our nation is at war. We prayed for peace, but not peace at the cost of national honor. We bow to the inevitable and pray for courage, strength and fortitude." After encouraging women to take stock of their resources and to "renounce luxury and extravagance," she instructed them:

> It behooves every Christian woman especially, to serve plain food, dress her-
> self and her family simply, give time to meditation and prayer, that she may
> be able to minister to material and spiritual needs as the times shall demand.
>   Missionary societies should be ever ready to respond to calls involving
> labor and sacrifice. . . . Pray as never before. Come together for united,
> earnest prayer for victory that shall bring the war to a speedy close.[45]

Through her weekly "W.M.U. Department" columns, Mrs. Peelman
called members to consistent, faithful service despite trying circumstances.
The security and stability of their world might be sliding away like ocean
sand beneath bare feet, but Mrs. Peelman tried to keep them focused on
prayer, personal service, mission study, and giving. With promotion of special projects and ongoing activities, along with news about her field travels,
she continued to foster through the *Witness* a sense of unity among women
in societies scattered around the state.

The Gospel for Soldiers

Near the end of 1917, the WMU secretary pled with her readers to contribute to "an every member canvass for state missions." They not only
shared responsibility for the 950,000 lost persons in Florida, but also they
had the opportunity, she said, to minister to 40,000 soldiers encamped in
Jacksonville:

> These men are doing their "bit" toward causing Democratic principles to
> prevail in the world. Jesus was the first Democrat. A Baptist church repre-
> sents the purest Democracy. What an opportunity God is granting us to give
> the gospel in its simplicity to these 40,000 men who have left home and
> loved ones to give their lives, if need be for the cause of freedom.[46]

Despite the war—or perhaps *because* war conditions reflected the world's
desperate need of the gospel—Florida women gave more money to missions
causes and pushed the development of WMU organizations at an unprece-
dented pace. "The war has given impetus to our missionary endeavors," Mrs.
Peelman reported. One example was the distributing of soldiers' New
Testaments. Since the beginning of Florida WMU, small contributions had
gone yearly to the Sunday School Board for Bible distribution. Seeing the
Bibles go to their soldiers brought a clearer sense of the blessing of that annual contribution. A record 507 local organizations worked toward the
Psalmist's goal: *That thy way may be known upon earth, thy saving health
among all nations* (Psalm 67:2 KJV).[47]

Circles and Societies, Perfect Wholes

When the first *Manual of WMU Methods* came off the Sunday School
Board press in 1917, Mrs. Peelman urged its immediate study. A Florida
committee evaluated the new publication:

It gives minute details (yet it is not tiresome, but exceedingly charming) on how to carry on every department of woman's graded work. The last chapter is especially helpful, as most societies have very little, if any, knowledge of parliamentary usage.

In the manual, "WMU suggested that all women's organizations of the church be centralized under one Woman's Missionary Society." Within that society, circles could be organized according to the interests of the women, thus drawing the aid societies and other women's groups into the WMU framework. At least once a month the whole society would meet together to promote missions and take care of business.[48]

A few Florida societies had used a circle plan for some time before the manual's publication. In the beginning, the idea met with varying degrees of enthusiasm; some members resisted altogether such radical change. However, with women emerging from the shadows of the men who had gone to war, a plan allowing for a variety of interests found favor among many. "To make the Circle Plan a success," said Mrs. M. M. Taylor, chairman of a committee to promote the change, "the right leaders must be chosen. . . . The leader should constantly remind the Circles that they are part of the society, all working to make a perfect whole."[49]

Mrs. Peelman's report for the year 1917, presented in Tallahassee in January 1918, revealed that she had again worked the full year without vacation or office help. She had mailed 88,941 items, traveled 8,895 miles, attended 125 meetings, made 187 addresses, and received a salary of $100 a month. Florida women could also look to other longtime servants—for example, Mrs. E. C. Angell, Personal Service chairman; Mrs. B. W. Blount, WMU Training School trustee; and Mrs. N. C. Wamboldt, president—as models of devotion to the missions cause.

A decision concerning the WMU Training School (WMUTS) in Louisville, Kentucky, faced those attending the Tallahassee meeting. When a growing enrollment required larger facilities, WMU, SBC, built a handsome structure, costing $150,000. Quickly dubbed "House Beautiful," the building, which included the Heck Memorial Chapel, had opened virtually debt free for the fall 1917 session.[50] Florida WMU had already paid almost all its apportionment of $1,400 in only half the specified time. Each state was allotted several rooms as memorials; Florida had a music room and two bedrooms. The Executive Committee chose to name the music room for Mrs. Bailey. Delegates deliberated over the two bedrooms. They decided to follow a recommendation naming one for Miss Spalding, "the second [sic] Corresponding Secretary who served lovingly and faithfully for eighteen years," and one for Mrs. Blount, "who is ever ready to advance the interests of our splendid institution."[51] Somehow, the ladies seemed to have lost track of Mrs. Telford! Mrs. Peelman later attended the dedication of the new building and spoke to the student body in "beautiful Heck Memorial Chapel."[52]

The Executive Committee also suggested changes in the state organizational structure. "For greater efficiency," they recommended dividing the state into six districts, with a vice-president elected from each. Delegates ratified the new districts, and chose their vice-presidents: West Florida District, Mrs. Porter E. Webb; Tallahassee District, Mrs. W. A. Burns; Jacksonville District, Mrs. S. R. Skinner; Ocala District, Mrs. E. Van Hood; Tampa District, Mrs. O. K. Reaves; and Miami District, Mrs. L. H. Calkins. Another recommendation from the Executive Committee was the annual election of a press committee, with a chairman from Jacksonville who would serve on the Executive Committee.

A revision of the constitution renamed officers of the Union to include president, vice-president at large, six district vice-presidents, corresponding secretary and treasurer, recording secretary, superintendent of YWA and GA, and superintendent of Sunbeams and RA. Another change described an "Executive Board" composed of the officers of the Union plus the state vice-president of WMU, SBC, Training School trustee, Margaret Fund chairman, chairman of the press committee, and two others from Jacksonville. The bylaws gave no indication of the duties of the Executive Board. The Executive Committee would be allowed to function with a quorum of three members. Those various changes set into motion the trend toward concentration of leadership in Jacksonville. By 1924, five Jacksonville residents served on the Executive Board in addition to all other members.[53]

In the midst of serious circumstances and serious business, the ladies took time out to attend a reception held in their honor in the Governor's Mansion.[54] No doubt many of the guests had voted for Governor Sidney J. Catts, since he was an ordained Baptist minister and the nominee of the Prohibition party.[55]

Meeting Emergencies

As the months of war dragged on, conditions at home increasingly demanded the time, energy, money, and spiritual maturity of Southern Baptist women. Dr. Gray, Home Mission Board secretary, sounded the trumpet call:

> The day for woman has come. She is taking the place of man in multitudinous ways.
> Southern Baptist women have the supreme opportunity of all their history. . . . They must make good in a great fashion for the loss of their sons and brothers whose places are made vacant in the work of the churches at home.[56]

As they temporarily filled vacancies in routine church work, Florida women could still respond quickly to a calamity in Tampa. Mission work among Cubans in Ybor City and Italians in West Tampa had

*Italian child
at Tampa mission*

developed into strong ministries. Both day and night schools operated for each group. Miss Anna Merryman, a Training School graduate from Florida, worked as a teacher in the Cuban school.[57] In April 1918, a disastrous fire in West Tampa completely devastated the Italian mission property. Dr. Claude W. Duke, pastor of Tampa First Baptist Church, wrote to the *Witness* about the situation:

> This afternoon when the local committee met with the missionaries, every eye was suffused with tears, for their sorrow was keen. But there was no repining, no complaining. . . . Let our women over the state take special offerings for them. Remember that they have even lost their clothing.[58]

In the next week's *Witness*, Mrs. Peelman urged every WMS, auxiliary, and Sunbeam Band to help replace lost Bibles, sewing equipment, piano, Sunday school books, and furniture, plus personal items of the missionaries.

When WMU members gathered in Tampa for the next annual meeting, they visited the Italian and the Cuban missions. Women were urged to leave love offerings for the missionaries at each stop. "A most delightful visit was made to the House of Happiness,"[59] new home of the missionaries to the Italians, which, with the help of WMU, had risen like the phoenix from the ashes of the great Tampa fire.

The ladies met another emergency when Mrs. Peelman's Ford car was stolen. WMU members throughout Florida contributed to a replacement. The overwhelmed secretary expressed her deep appreciation: "I feel so unworthy of the sacrifice this represents. Pray for me that this noble gift may be used to advance the Master's service."[60] Although Mrs. Peelman herself did not drive and did much of her field travel by train, Brother Peelman often drove her to meetings. In later years, her daughter, Marion, took over chauffeur duties.

On the road – again

Something for Margaret

Needs of missionaries could have been overlooked in those stressful times, but the women managed to keep mission support, through prayer and gifts, at the core of their work. Ceasing its separate publication, the missionary prayer calendar became a regular feature in *Royal Service,* giving more than 43,000 subscribers access to the list and encouraging regular and concerted praying for home and foreign missionaries.[61] The WMU, SBC, treasurer reported that, for the first time, the Union had given over half a million dollars in one year.[62]

A favorite avenue of mission support was the Margaret Fund. A scholarship fund for missionary children, it had grown out of an original ministry known as the "Margaret Home." In 1904 Mrs. Frank Chambers had given WMU, SBC, $10,000 in honor of her grandmother, mother, and daughter, each named Margaret. The money provided a home for missionary children who remained in the United States for education while their parents served in foreign countries. Mrs. W. D. Chipley was Florida's first trustee of the Margaret Home, which was located in Greenville, South Carolina. Elvie Fowler, oldest child of Florida's first foreign missionary, Frank Fowler, lived briefly in the home.

As time passed and circumstances changed on the mission fields, the need for such a ministry diminished. In 1914, the Margaret Home was sold and the proceeds invested to produce scholarship money for missionary children. Florida women were gratified when Elvie Fowler became a recipient of a Margaret Fund scholarship.[63]

From Military to Spiritual War

ARMISTICE! proclaimed the newspaper headlines on November 11, 1918. A spirit of optimism, generated by the great military victory, pervaded the nation's thinking: Americans had indeed made the world "safe for democracy." As soldiers returned home, they found that the homefront had changed. The nation had prospered economically as a result of the war, and women had begun to recognize more of their potential in a man's world. Florida WMU members confidently joined their Southern sisters to declare their

> sympathy with the forces which make for righteousness, patriotism, peace, prohibition, Sabbath observance, sacredness of the home, establishment of the family altar and the crusade against poverty, disease, illiteracy and crime.[64]

On the other hand, Florida, like the rest of the nation, felt the mortal sting of a worldwide influenza epidemic. Dr. Rogers lamented: "Not since the great freeze of '95 have Florida Baptist churches and denominational activities been so completely undone."[65]

Still, Southern Baptists, buoyed by national successes in military combat, made preparations to expand their battle for men's souls. To do that required money, more money than the SBC had dared envision heretofore. Thus emerged the $75 Million Campaign. In May 1919, SBC messengers pledged to raise $75 million by 1925. Working as partners with SBC leadership, WMU joined in the strategies to meet the enormous goal. Plans involved seeking pledges for all denominational enterprises, beyond contributions for local church work, to be paid over a five-year period. All contributions given by women were to count toward the WMU apportionment of $15 million.

To raise pledges, "organizers" worked at every level of denominational life. WMU structures already in place provided a ready means for helping to reach every corner of the SBC. First, Kathleen Mallory, and then Janie Cree

Bose, appointed by WMU as national organizer, toured Florida with Mrs. Peelman. In her column Mrs. Peelman wrote of visits to dozens of Florida towns, including Live Oak, DeFuniak Springs, Chipley, Apalachicola, Lakeland, Orlando, and Tampa, where she, Miss Mallory, and Mrs. Bose spoke before numerous congregations. Before Victory Week, November 20-27, both Mrs. Bose and Mrs. Peelman spoke from Florida pulpits in morning and evening worship services.[66] Such presentations may have broken with tradition, but they also promoted a successful campaign. With help from the women, Florida pledges exceeded the state's $1 million apportionment. Nationally, Southern Baptists over-subscribed the goal by promising $92 million. Mrs. Peelman relished the apparent victory: "The Campaign has revealed to Baptists their strength and real unity. Old and young, rich and poor are interested in advancing the Kingdom of God."[67] Such overwhelming success caused SBC and state leadership to make commitments even more expansive than their original visions.

But promises do not equal cash. Despite desperate pleas from boards and institutions, contributions lagged farther and farther behind. At the end of five years, church members had given only $58 million, leaving Convention agencies floundering in an ocean of debt. WMU, SBC, however, met its $15 million goal. Both the Florida Baptist Convention and Florida WMU surpassed their quotas: Florida churches gave over $1 million, with nearly $300,000 coming from WMU. For the SBC, failure to bring in the original $75 million brought temporary pessimism, but Catherine Allen, WMU historian, described positive campaign results:

> For Woman's Missionary Union, a new day of influence and recognition had dawned. The campaign was a prototype for the Cooperative Program, the unified church budget, and the Every Member Canvass for contributions, a trio that revolutionized Southern Baptist life.[68]

Assemblies, Institutes, and the White Cross

Meanwhile, Florida WMU continued regular activities and even began new ministries. Added to the summer agenda, the West Florida Assembly in DeFuniak Springs brought to the Florida panhandle the wonderful opportunities of DeLand. Soon a third encampment, known as the East Coast Assembly, began meeting in Delray Beach. Several WMU classes at each assembly educated large numbers of adults and youth in missions.

WMU also agreed to cooperative efforts with the Home Mission Board for the Seaman's Institute in Jacksonville. "Thousands of sailor boys and men from all parts of the world enter Jacksonville harbor," said Mrs. Peelman, "and a Christian home is often their salvation. Women alone can make this Institute a real home."[69]

A third new enterprise picked up the work of the Red Cross during the war. Florida WMU accepted the assignment of furnishing supplies for the

Baptist Hospital in Yang Chow, China. Miss Eliza Powell, Jacksonville, first chaired the project, which became known as White Cross work and lasted through World War II.

A Witness to Stress

The strain of several years of uninterrupted and often stressful work began to affect Mrs. Peelman. Her occasional irritation with the *Witness* gave evidence. In one edition, an article on her WMU page urged Florida Baptist students to attend state colleges. In loyalty to the failing Columbia College, she publicly disclaimed, "I do not know who wrote or authorized the publication of this article." In another column she noted "several typographical errors and an omission of one line in our department last week, owing probably to the proof reader having the 'flu.'"[70]

After the January 1920 annual meeting, Editor J. W. Mitchell wrote:

> Mrs. Peelman, well known in Florida, lambastes us, personally, directly, and otherwise, for not reporting the Woman's work in our last issue. When Sister Peelman gets older she will learn that a man cannot be in two or three places at the same time.

He explained that "the dear sisters" had not "condescended" to send in any information on the "procedures." Noting that Mrs. Peelman had written a good account of the meeting for the current issue, he offered an olive branch: "Now we will all think as well of each other as we can under the circumstances."[71]

In addition to job stresses, Mrs. Peelman also had been adjusting to an additional family in her home. For two years, Marion and Dempsey Crews and their children lived with the Peelmans. Frances, the oldest grandchild, often visited her grandmother's office in the Professional Building.[72] One day Frances, who liked to look out the high windows, observed some men working on the ground below. She exclaimed, "I bet those men down there are hot!"

Mrs. Peelman, always proper, responded in typical fashion, "Ladies don't bet!"

When granddaughter Dorothy was old enough to visit the WMU office, she would walk beside her grandmother along the sidewalk, swinging her arms in exuberance. She received a similar admonition: "Calm down, Dorothy. Ladies don't swing their arms when they walk." In 1920 Dr. Crews moved his family and his dental practice to Avon Park.[73]

Making Life Easier

Because WMU leaders loved Mrs. Peelman and were sensitive to her needs, they did several things in 1920 to make life easier for her. They raised

Correspondence was a vital part of Mrs. Peelman's WMU work.

her salary to $150 a month. Then they hired Cecilia Nolan, a WMU Training School student from Florida, as office secretary; other WMUTS students assisted with field work for WMU, BYPU, and Sunday School. When Nolan returned to school, another office helper was provided.[74]

The women also insisted that their leader take three weeks of vacation. During a week at Ridgecrest, Mrs. Peelman "had the pleasure of seeing Dr. J. L. Spalding, our former Secretary who is a popular physician both in Asheville and Ridgecrest." After the trip to North Carolina, Mrs. Peelman returned to the office "refreshed in body and mind."[75]

Finally, the Executive Committee promoted the hiring of a "trained woman field worker" who would "help Mrs. Peelman in organizing and strengthening Women's Work."[76] Carrie Hobson Baer traveled the field during the last six months of 1921. Despite "many things to hinder," including lack of trained and willing leaders, she began 25 new WMU organizations.[77] Baer and Cecilia Nolan, who had returned to Florida WMU to work with young people, were both recent Training School graduates. During their senior year, nine Florida girls attended the school on scholarship. Such a strong group reflected the emphasis accompanying the $75 Million Campaign on giving oneself as well as one's resources to the Lord.

Official Recognition

Acting on a WMU recommendation, the Florida Baptist Convention in 1921 officially recognized WMU as the "Woman's Department" of Florida churches. The recommendation picked up an old theme, the enlistment of every woman in the church, and urged weekly meetings, "preferably Monday."[78] Mrs. Peelman believed that action accounted for a surge in the growth of societies, "both numerically and in efficiency." Women's Societies now totaled 457.[79]

Development of age-level groups also began to move at a faster pace. A 25 percent increase in 1921 brought the total number of bands and auxiliaries to 369. Delegates to the annual meeting voted—perhaps in an effort to elevate the status of the work—"that the name of the Y.W.A., G.A. and R.A. State leader be changed to State Young People's Secretary and Sunbeam leader to Sunbeam Secretary." Several years passed before the title "secretary" was actually applied to state youth leaders.[80]

Stockholm Sans Seasickness

The Peelmans could have used a youth leader when the Crews family returned to live with them in 1922. Four active children and their parents more than filled the three-bedroom, one-bath house on Herschel Street. The grandchildren felt the excitement as their "Granny" made plans for attending the Baptist World Alliance (BWA) in Stockholm, Sweden, in the summer of 1923. Christmas came in the summer when a group of ladies arrived at the house to bring gifts for her trip. Fearing that the long ocean voyage might cause seasickness, her son-in-law made her an extra set of false teeth. If she lost her original set overboard while seasick, she would be prepared!

The WMU Executive Committee was eager for Florida "to keep abreast of her sister states in religious activities." That reason had led them to decide, "after prayer and earnest consideration," to "send" Mrs. Peelman to the BWA. They firmly believed that "it was the best thing to do, not only for our W.M.U. but for our Baptist work generally." Florida women paid two-thirds of the $1,000 cost of the trip.[81]

Leaving Jacksonville on July 3, Mrs. Peelman traveled by train to New York City, where she took a Swedish liner bound for Stockholm. "Mal de mer seized many," she wrote in her three-by-five-inch journal, but she herself escaped seasickness, so she returned home with two sets of teeth. Perhaps her thoughts had returned to Cuba when she observed about Stockholm: "No shabby homes. No poorly clad children line roads." In preparation for the reports she would make back home, she took meticulous notes about the speakers and activities of the BWA meeting, as well as her tours through Sweden, Germany, and France.

President Emerita

The end of an era for Florida WMU came at DeLand in December 1923. Mrs. N. C. Wamboldt, who had taken office as president in 1911, bid her followers "adieu" with her thirteenth presidential address. Elected in the same year as Mrs. Peelman, Wamboldt had come to Florida from New York state. She had helped organize the first woman's mission society in Jacksonville's Tabernacle Baptist Church, which later became First Baptist. After her husband became pastor of Main Street Church, she also served there as WMU president.[82] As a presiding officer she was capable, courteous, just, and "strictly parliamentary in her rulings."[83] With themes such as "Efficiency," "Loyalty," "Progress," and "Light," her annual addresses pointed to the issues of the day. Following the American victory in 1918, in a speech entitled "Forward March," she used military images to encourage the women to reaffirm missions as their priority. In the $75 Million Campaign she focused on "Enlargement."[84]

The vote of the Florida Union in 1922 to limit the presidency to a two-year term set the stage for Wamboldt to step down. In her final address, she reminded the women of principles which they had already seen in her: "Cooperation is the key word, combined with willing service. The highest grace of living is not in getting but in giving; giving of ourselves and our all—to our Master's cause." The ladies responded with 13 rosebuds, "an expression of their love for her and their appreciation of her . . . faithful service." The recording secretary reported that "the [WMU] Convention honored itself" by electing Wamboldt president emerita. Delegates chose Mrs. J. A. Mellon, Tampa, as the new president.[85] Until Wamboldt's death in 1933, she remained actively involved in WMU.

Layers of Leadership

Over the next several years, the organizational structure of Florida WMU expanded, multiplying in levels and numbers of officers and adding staff

<table>
<tr><td>*Mrs. N. C. Wamboldt*
1911-1923</td><td>*Mrs. J. A. Mellon*
1923-1925</td><td>*Mrs. E. C. Bostick*
1925-1929</td></tr>
</table>

workers. In 1924 a move to the new building on Church Street, later named the Rogers Building, allowed more secretarial space and help. The number of districts increased from six to seven; the designation changed to "divisions." State leaders for stewardship and mission study were added to the officers. The Executive Committee in 1925 recommended that the state president and the state vice-president of WMU, SBC, "be recognized" as members of the State Board of Missions,[86] but no woman was named to the Board for two more decades. In 1926, through a constitutional change, the president automatically became the state vice-president of WMU, SBC. The two-year term limit was removed.

Districts, associations, and local organizations developed slates of officers to mirror those on the state level. Young people's counselors for each district and a roster of youth officers comparable to the women's roster added to the complexity of the organization. Standards of Excellence set excruciatingly meticulous goals for every unit, ranging from the state level to the individual circle, band, and auxiliary.

As more and more women took leadership responsibilities, the role of the corresponding secretary began to shift away from directing the work toward more emphasis on teaching, encouraging, and supporting. An Executive Committee report reflected the new direction as it acknowledged "the untiring and sacrificial co-operation" of Mrs. Peelman: "Her knowledge of the field and friendly counsel have greatly aided us in arriving at conclusions and formulating plans for the welfare of our State Work."[87] No change seemed to diminish Mrs. Peelman's enthusiasm for, or commitment to, her work.

From Theory to Practice

The Florida Union continued to reap a harvest from its scholarship investments as WMUTS students gave summer assistance in the office and on the field. Mrs. Willie Lee Harrell, a recent graduate, in 1924 began her work as full-time young people's leader and later added the college correspondent's duties. She spent much of her time visiting churches to encourage development of youth organizations, also including Sunday School and BYPU in her efforts. The state Sunday School department shared in support of field workers with assignments like Harrell's.

Work in rural areas of the state grew along with the rural population. Differing from the rapidly expanding urban areas, the needs and opportunities of rural churches called for special attention. Details from one of Harrell's trips through the Florida panhandle highlighted the commitment of rural members:

> How my heart was made to rejoice at Bethel. Hosts of young people are interested in Kingdom affairs. Although everyone was busy picking cotton I had crowds at night. At least five of the W.M.S. have promised a bale of cotton each, for missions and current expense. Think what this will mean when cotton is selling for over $100 a bale.[88]

Unfortunately, enrollment in the Training School took a downturn. Two circumstances gave even the most committed young ladies reason to consider their options carefully. The heavy debts of the SBC mission boards forced the boards to delay appointing any new missionaries, and deteriorating economic conditions in general led to fewer church job possibilities because salaries awaited contributions. Meanwhile, the Southwestern Training School in Fort Worth was in process of development, and from time to time claimed Florida students. Mrs. Peelman was named to its Board of Advisors.

Entering the Cooperative Program

As Florida Baptists struggled with their financial problems, they moved from the $75 Million Campaign to a new unified program of giving promoted by the SBC and eventually labeled the Cooperative Program (CP). "Not clearly defined" in people's minds, according to Dr. Rogers, the CP did little in its first years to relieve the financial burdens of either Florida or Southern Baptists.[89] But WMU, SBC, took up its promotion, as did the state unions, and helped over the years to move it from a meager stream to a mighty tide of support for state and SBC causes.[90]

Both the genius and the liability of the Cooperative Program lay in its elimination of special appeals for individual causes and of designated giving. WMU leaders fought successfully to protect the annual missions offerings from inclusion in the Program. To substitute those offerings for the mission boards' rightful CP allocations, they declared, would defeat a major purpose of the plan. Because Florida women had felt much unrest over the issue, they were greatly relieved by the decision to maintain the customary status of the mission offerings and continued to give faithfully to foreign and home missions.[91]

A Mantle of Sadness

Florida WMU met in 1925 under a "mantle of sadness." Two pillars of the organization, Mrs. M. B. Harrison and Mrs. S. B. Rogers, had died during the year. Mrs. Harrison was state president, 1905-06 and 1907-1911. Mrs. Rogers, wife of the SBM corresponding secretary, was the first state Sunbeam and RA leader and Florida's vice-president for WMU, SBC, 1916-1925. In her report Mrs. Peelman recognized Dr. Rogers' grief and expressed gratitude "for his ever ready sympathy and advice." She also thanked the Sunday School and BYPU secretary, W. W. Willian, and Rogers' assistant, C. M. Brittain, for "kindly cooperation."[92]

Mrs. Peelman worked well with all those gentlemen. Dr. Willian occasionally visited in the Peelman home, sometimes bringing his marble slab and making peanut brittle. That adventure was a favorite with Mrs. Peelman's grandchildren.[93] Her relationship with Dr. Brittain soon assumed more significance. After Dr. Rogers' resignation and death in 1926, the State Board of Missions elected Brittain executive secretary and treasurer. As he served during the next 14 years, Brittain proved to be "a mature, stabilizing force in a time of great crisis and difficulty."[94] In the tradition of previous secretaries, Brittain's wife took an active role in WMU, and he was "a loyal friend" of the Union, often praising the women for their faithful support of missions.[95]

Florida WMU members mourned not only the death of Dr. Rogers, but also the severe loss of lives and property in a deadly hurricane which struck the Miami area in fall 1926. Among those memorialized at the annual meeting were four WMS members and seven GAs who had "perished in the storm" in Moore Haven.[96]

The WMU Boom

The word that Florida WMU had won the 1926 national Union Banner for achieving the largest proportionate increase in all WMU organizations momentarily brightened the gloomy Florida circumstances. Unlike the land boom, which had "gone bust" and taken much of the state's wealth with it, the "WMU boom," according to Mrs. Peelman, "had just begun."[97] It may have been Florida WMU's substantial progress which opened the door to rumors and criticism.

Mrs. Peelman met the situation head on with a lengthy defense in the *Witness* entitled "A Frank Statement of W.M.U. Aims and Methods."[98] She dealt first with complaints about the quality of WMU mission study courses, carefully explaining how their requirements compared favorably with courses in any other department of Baptist work. A current rumor "that the W.M.U. department is not in harmony with the other departments of our Baptist work" especially grieved her: "It has been a matter of pride on the part of the Florida W.M.U. that no friction exists among the departments of our work and we are very sure that our W.M.U. organizations do not harbor other than a cooperative spirit."

Peelman also reminded readers that WMU field workers had always helped promote the work of other departments. WMU members in local churches regularly taught Sunday School, led BYPU organizations, and participated in training schools. "We do not know how the impression of lack of unity has gained ground and been fostered," she said, "but it is regrettable." Finally she declared definitively:

> None of our W.M.U. representatives aspire to preach. It is true that when invited to do so they have talked on missions at the Sunday services. Often this is the only time when the majority could be reached, but pastors, who are strict adherents of Paul's teachings with reference to women, have invited W.C.T.U. and Women's Club representatives to present causes in which Christian people should be interested and co-operate.
>
> We love W.M.U.; believe in her purpose and ideals; are jealous for her reputation and believe our people have a real appreciation for the organization.

We Can and We Will

In 1927 the national Union called all members to focus on an occasion which would lift their spirits in those troubled times, the 1928 Ruby Anniversary of WMU, SBC. To celebrate 40 years of service, goals called for 40 percent increase in number of organizations, 40,000 new members, and contributions of $4 million, "the value of four thousand one carat rubies."[99] For Florida that meant "organizing 320 new Woman's Missionary Societies, 240 young people's organizations, enlisting 4,500 new members and making an increase of $50,000 in gifts before January 1, 1929."[100] Such an undertaking would require tremendous dedication, but the magnitude of the project captured the burdened hearts of the women.

From mid-year on, Mrs. Brinson McGowan, state anniversary chairman, and the division presidents, who made up her committee, organized and encouraged, perhaps even prodded local and associational WMUs to meet the goals. Field worker Lucile Brown and young people's secretary Willie Lee

Harrell gave excellent assistance. Florida's slogan, "We Can and We Will," assumed success, while the young people's slogan instructed, "Say it with Service." A new arm of intercessory prayer supported the Ruby anniversary celebration: homebound women were organized as the Intercessory League of Shut-ins.[101]

The natural enthusiasm for missions of Florida WMU members, coupled with their pain over cutbacks by the mission boards, drove the women to establish new organizations and involve more women and youth.[102] The *Witness* gave a major push to those efforts by devoting the entire May 3, 1928, issue to WMU and the Ruby anniversary activities. In addition to inspiring messages from state and national WMU leaders, the issue carried strong words of gratitude from Dr. Brittain, a tribute "To Our Women" from editor P. L. Johnston, articles affirming WMU by several other Convention leaders, and special greetings from Dr. Jennie Spalding.

Saying It with Service

In the midst of the uplifting Ruby Anniversary emphasis, tragedy struck again. A fierce hurricane invaded the West Palm Beach area, killing more than 2,000 persons and causing damage of more than $75 million. Florida Baptists surely noted the irony of that figure. Many church buildings were completely destroyed; others, severely damaged. In large measure those losses accounted for the failure of Florida WMU to reach the Ruby goal for contributions. However, Dr. Brittain acknowledged the sacrificial quality of their gifts:

> [Our women] have kept a steady stream of money flowing into the mission treasury and have made it possible . . . to meet our obligations through the year. They . . . have always been the first to respond to calls for help when calamities and disasters have overtaken us. We thank God for them and their manifold organizations which have covered the State for Christ and His Kingdom.[103]

The good news was that they achieved victory in the other goals. Their unprecedented efforts brought the total number of Florida WMU organizations to 1,462 with 24,578 members.[104]

A special Florida project connected with the Ruby Anniversary celebration involved the preparation of a Book of Remembrance. Mrs. B. A. Inglis, WMU historian; Mrs. N. C. Wamboldt, president emerita; and Mrs. S. E. Driskell solicited pictures and information about outstanding WMU members and staff, from past and present. Names of associational and state officers and foreign missionaries (called "Torchbearers") were included. The section called "Memorials" contained information about those who had been honored by contributions of at least $40. Mrs. Driskell was the "amanuensis" for the beautifully bound, hand-written book, which in 1994 remained a treasure in the state WMU office.[105]

Prayers and Answers

Florida WMU also declared an additional prayer emphasis during 1928. The Executive Committee called for special times of prayer to intercede for faithfulness in paying off SBC mission board debts.[106] For several years the Foreign and Home Mission Boards had been unable to appoint new missionaries. In 1926, the HMB temporarily cut off its funding of work in Florida and other states. Then came the word that furloughing foreign missionaries would remain home unless the FMB had the assurance that their transportation costs and salaries for one year would be paid by churches or individuals "over and above regular program gifts."

As God often does, He began to use the pray-ers to effect the answers. Dr. and Mrs. D. F. Stamps had endeared themselves to Florida Baptists, and particularly to the Ocala Division, during their extended furlough. Still, they were anxious to return to their work in China. Because churches elsewhere in Florida as well as in Atlanta agreed to his support, Dr. Stamps made plans to sail for China in August. However, no provision was made for his wife and two children. That they would have to remain behind was too much for the Wekiwa Association ladies. They determined that something must be done.

They consulted with their pastors and with various missionary groups, wrote letters, and prayed. The Wekiwa Association history tells the story:

> Then it was all clear. Wekiwa would take the lead, and the other associations in Ocala Division would help. By faith these women would undertake to raise the $1,400 necessary to return Mrs. Stamps to China with her husband. This included $800 for her salary for one year, $200 allotment for the two children and $400 for the passage for the family. . . . Much prayer was made for the passage money which had to be forthcoming at once. God graciously heard and answered by giving more than was asked.[107]

Florida Baptists also supported other missionaries caught in similar circumstances, including the Frank Fowlers and Lulu Sparkman Terry.[108]

Born to the Field

Field work had been an essential component of woman's mission work in Florida from the time of Mrs. Bailey through the Centennial anniversary. As early as 1891, traveling often with Mrs. Telford, Dr. Chaudoin pointed to the value of field work:

> We are assured that nothing is [as] effectual in any kind of religious work, and particularly in work like [Mrs. Telford's], as *personal contact*. We all need to be visited, talked to, and with, and to have the work explained, demonstrated before us, by those fresh from it, and posted in it.[109]

A "born teacher" from a devout Baptist family of very meager circumstances in Middlesex County, Virginia,[110] arrived in Florida in time to put her hand to the plow of Ruby Anniversary goals. Of all the women who have led any phase of Florida WMU field work, none seems to have carved so distinctive a niche in such a short time as did Louise Fletcher. In early 1928, Mrs. Peelman invited the WMU Training School graduate and former mission school teacher to become a "rural field worker of the Florida Baptist Woman's Missionary Union." Through Mrs. Peelman, the WMU Executive Committee offered Fletcher "$100 per month and expenses while in service. The expenses include all those for traveling. Your board will be provided by the churches."[111] How could she turn down such a generous contract! Fletcher, however, considered only two concerns: her health, which had been unstable, and the Lord's will. She obeyed God's call to Florida.

The final words of Mrs. Peelman's letter implied the uncertainties inherent in field work: "You would begin Mar. 1 or sooner if we could arrange an itinerary." In fact, when plans did not materialize quickly, Fletcher's work began several days beyond March 1. During her early days in Florida, correspondence from Dr. J. W. Storey, pastor of the noted Grove Avenue Baptist Church in Richmond, offered her the position of director of young people's work at $125 a month. Surely that was a tempting offer. Nevertheless, as a woman of "intense loyalties, the most intense of which was her loyalty to God,"[112] she remained firm in her commitment to God's work in Florida.[113]

Fletcher had virtually no home of her own. Sometimes staying one night, sometimes as long as two weeks, she traveled from one rural church to another, often not knowing how she would be received. Undaunted, however, by erratic train and bus schedules and the uncertainty of her reception, she crisscrossed the Florida peninsula and panhandle, dispensing love and methods, encouragement and organization to Florida Baptists.

Detailed records of her travels and work filled several notebooks.[114] On April 2, as she recorded, she "left [Dunellon] on the 4:15 train for Lakeland," although she had not received confirmation of her schedule. When she arrived at 6:55 p.m., no one met her; she had to get a "hired car" to take her to the home of Mrs. McGinnis, the South Florida Association WMU president. Mrs. McGinnis was not "looking for me, but she was so nice—seemed as if they couldn't find work for me to do & had written Mrs. Peelman, but I didn't know."

The days were full of WMU and BYPU activities with all age groups. One journal entry listed the day's activities as personal washing, correspondence including letters about a girdle she had ordered, two walking trips to the post office, afternoon meetings with youth and an evening meeting with adults. One Saturday evening at 6:35 she took the bus to Homeland. "It only went as far as Bartow," she wrote, "but fortunately I had time to catch train which put me in H[omeland] about 8 o'clock. . . . No one to meet me. I didn't know whether they'd want me at Homeland or not."

Want her they did, and she spent a strenuous week in the small community, staying in one home, but eating supper with a different family each night. Fletcher closed her April notebook by listing the places visited, miles traveled, WMU expenses, including $.02 postage, and personal expenses, including a $3.00 dentist bill and $2.00 for a new hat.

Always Welcome

Almost the entire month of October 1928 saw Fletcher in Graves Association.[115] After she had stayed several days with a Mr. and Mrs. Cook, Mr. Cook took her on to Sandy Creek. Her notebook revealed details:

> At 3 o'clock Mr. C. & I left for Sandy Creek, it is a rough road there. One *bad* hill. Finally got up it. I stayed on the hill with Mr. & Mrs. Pope. The Argo's [sic] lived right in hollering distance. Each night we went to church on Mr. Argo's truck, feet hanging down at back, good jolly crowd. Got up every morning *early*. They get up about day break or before. Mr. & Mrs. Pope good souls. Didn't have the work at the church that I had hoped.

Still she organized a YWA and taught the girls the manual and yearbook and also taught the WMS manual to two women. When she left on Saturday, she promised the Sandy Creek folks she would try to meet with them again on the fourth Sunday.

From Sandy Creek she transferred to the Leonia Church: "Mrs. Essie Carter & Reece Pagett from Leonia Church at Dady came for me in a new Chevrolet sedan. (Quite a contrast to truck.) At Mrs. Pagett's I found a room all to myself and more conveniences; they have a bathroom."

Fletcher's job was almost cut off at the end of 1928. Letters from Mrs. Peelman on November 29 and 30 explained that the HMB and Dr. Brittain had said there would be no more money for rural field work in the coming year. "I cannot express to you my gratitude for the service you have rendered," Peelman emphasized. "You have certainly done your part to make Florida a victory state and I wish we might continue your services. The women love you and you will always receive a royal welcome in Florida."

By December 5, Mrs. Peelman had wired Fletcher a reversal of the bad news. She had decided to "make one more effort" and had asked Dr. Brittain to allow Fletcher to work for six more months. "He is so favorably impressed with your work and so reluctant to give you up he assented," she explained, adding that he hoped to have money for the second half of 1929 as well.

Actually, a serious illness, as well as the funding problem, prevented Fletcher from continuing her work in Florida beyond May 1929. In June she was scheduled to speak at the annual session of the West Florida Association in Lynn Haven, but according to her hand-written note on the printed program for the association meeting, she was "sick in Pensacola Hospital and couldn't attend."[116] An appendicitis attack led to surgery. Before she had fully recovered from the operation, she returned to the hospital with phlebitis. There she suffered yet another indignity. A loyal member of First Baptist WMS, performing her personal service ministry, had taken Fletcher's gowns home to wash. The local newspaper carried the story:

POLICE ARE HUNTING FOR PINK NIGHTIES

Five night gowns were stolen from the rear yard of the home of Mrs. B. I. Able, at 1301 East Lee street, about 8:30 p.m. yesterday, she reported to police. "Three were pink and two were white," she said.[117]

After several weeks of hospital convalescence but still not able to walk, Fletcher returned to Virginia. Depicted by others as a "beloved and faithful servant of the Master," she left a permanent record of her work engraved on the hearts of Floridians of all ages.[118]

To Miss Fletcher

Some people live in our midst for years, And when they leave we shed no tears.
For though their talents may be many We never feel they help us any.
While others come and quietly aid In any plans the church has made,
Or enter in with suggestions new Of things we never had thought to do,
And the seeds of love they so quickly sow That we never want to have them go.

Your life, Miss Fletcher, is like the latter. And though my poetical ability is small, no matter,
I want to express as best I can The appreciation of every woman and man
Who've been lifted and helped by your efforts here To get us running in higher gear.
And we know our children have been greatly blest
By the improvements they've made in the efficiency test.

To give our thanks we are ever slow, But I want to tell you before you go
Of the warm place we have in our hearts for you, And how we shall miss you from our view.
And we ask God to bless you through each day And give you health and happiness along your way.
—-Mrs. Dora Libby

Pressing On

With summer came the assemblies, bright splashes of color on a bleak landscape. The West Florida Assembly, which had moved to the Bob Jones College campus near Panama City, and the East Coast Assembly in Delray Beach ran smoothly. To all outward appearances, the Florida Assembly in DeLand also carried on its work with rousing fervor and few problems. What some on the Stetson campus knew, however, was that over $1,000 in registration receipts had been deposited in a bank just ten minutes before the bank closed its doors for good. Resolutely, assembly leadership "secured a loan" and took pledges for funds to continue the ten-day session. "There is a fine optimistic spirit," Mrs. Peelman emphasized, while admitting, in a letter to Louise Fletcher in Pensacola Hospital, that "the bank failures here added to our worries."[119]

October 29, 1929, Black Thursday. Was the great stock market crash the climax of burgeoning financial problems, or was it an early stage of a lengthy depression? No one knew the answer, but WMU activities and published materials, either national or state, paid little homage to the tyranny of the Great Depression. "Kathleen Mallory noted that if the letters *d, e, i* were removed from *depression,* the words *press on* would remain."[120] Mrs. Peelman refused to let a declining budget, a cut in salary, or added youth responsibilities inhibit her enthusiasm, or her encouragement of Florida women to give utmost support to missions. Even as Dr. Brittain commended Florida Baptists generally for "a rising tide of spirituality" and a "beautiful spirit of unity and harmony," he recognized that the women "have kept alive the spirit of missions in many churches." Women of WMU "have always been loyal to our denominational program, and organizations," he said, "and they have continued to function without let-up" in spite of a hostile economic climate.[121]

Matters of Heart and Pocketbook

When Baptist women looked for sources of joy, they could count on the Margaret Fund. The increasing numbers of college-aged missionary children strained the fund's resources and required additional investments to support it. The Margaret Fund Book of Remembrance, introduced in 1930, provided one means for raising additional endowment. A minimum $2 contribution would enroll any Baptist woman named Margaret, or a mother or daughter with that name. By the end of 1931, the book included over 50 Florida "Margarets."[122]

Supporting the Margaret Fund was a matter of the heart as well as the pocketbook of Florida WMS members. Nurturing Margaret Fund sons and daughters called forth their best motherly instincts. Methods of assignment by WMU, SBC, varied, but Florida sometimes had as many as nine students (1932). In 1927 Florida WMU was assigned Baylor freshmen Lois and Eloise Glass, whose parents were missionaries to China. Looking back from a perspective of more than 60 years, Eloise Glass Cauthen, widow of China missionary and former Foreign Mission Board executive secretary Baker James Cauthen, reflected on her student days and her relationship with her "Florida mothers":

> Florida women have always been special to me because they took in this little innocent, China-raised girl who was so unacquainted with American life and ways in those days of jelly beans and flappers—they were just shocking to us! Lois and I were just as unadjusted as could be. Really, the missionary kids have a lot to catch on to. They have to learn that there are some Christians among these wild boys and girls on campus.
>
> I never got to meet my wonderful ladies that corresponded with me and sent me things. But just when my hose began to have a runner all the way down and I didn't have another pair, I would miraculously get a gift from the Florida women, and I'd buy a pair of hose.
>
> I felt so grateful because the women took such an interest without ever seeing us. We'd get so busy trying to write our papers for courses and that sort of thing, but they always seemed to come up with something thoughtful just at the time of desperation. We called them Margaret Fund mothers. When I graduated in 1931, they all sent me graduation gifts. [123]

Somewhat to her surprise, Eloise's Florida mothers continued their ministry through her years in Southwestern Seminary. In a letter to the Pensacola

Foreign Mission Board, SBC

Because Eloise Glass had been Florida WMU's Margaret Fund student, when she married a young minister named Baker James Cauthen, Florida's ladies provided her wedding gown and accessories. Some even attended the wedding in Texas. Left to right: Sybil Leonard, W. A. Criswell, Lois Glass, W. L. Howse, Jr., bride, Eloise Glass, groom, Baker J. Cauthen, W. T. Conner, Ardell Watkins, Nane Starnes, Mrs. Edwin McNeely.

First WMS, dated April 29, 1933, Eloise thanked the ladies "each and every one" for a box of homemade candy. She had passed the candy around "just before class, the day that it arrived," and reported that "the teacher liked it so well I think he will give me a good grade!?" Then she added two lengthy pages about the work in China, information which she had just received in a missionary letter. The blessing of the relationship worked both ways.

When Eloise Glass and Baker James Cauthen planned to marry in 1934, again Eloise thought that would end the relationship, but not so. "I thought they'd just drop me right away when I decided to get married and go to the mission field," Mrs. Cauthen recollected, "but they celebrated me instead! They said they weren't going to cast me off—they were going to continue to pray for me." In fact, the women of the Pensacola Division gave a "shower of wedding dress and accessories" for Eloise. Two ladies from Pensacola attended the wedding.[124]

A very special wedding present, a beautiful quilt made by Florida ladies, went with the Cauthens to China. "We had cold winters in north China, and we needed it," she said. A move to the interior allowed the Cauthens to remain in China for a time after the Japanese invasion. Eventually, however, when they were forced to evacuate through Burma and India, they had to leave all their possessions behind, including the treasured quilt. "We never saw it again," Mrs. Cauthen said, smiling wistfully before turning her thoughts to God's blessings in their long and frightening journey back to the States.

On Loan to the Convention

Because of the financial crunch, Florida WMU, in early 1930, had "cheerfully loaned" Willie Lee Harrell, state young people's secretary, to the State Board of Missions for student work at Florida State College for Women (FSCW) in Tallahassee. "They did this without complaining, though their field work suffered as a consequence," said Dr. Brittain in expressing his gratitude. At the end of the spring semester, Harrell decided to return to her WMU work. In August she again reconsidered and decided to return to the FSCW campus, but "meager" state mission receipts necessitated cutting salaries and discontinuing student work. In a sacrificial move at a called meeting, the WMU Executive Committee voted to "release" $100 a month through December for continuation of Harrell's excellent work with the "364 Baptist girls" at FSCW.[125]

While Mrs. Peelman shouldered the young people's work in Harrell's place, she began "The Pepograph," a mimeographed missions newsletter.[126] Young ladies also read a new national monthly, *The Window of Y.W.A.* Uncertainty about budget money for someone to replace Harrell on the WMU staff could have stymied the Executive Board, but they had learned how to cope with a diet of financial uncertainties. In the hope of adequate budget, the president appointed a committee to "secure" a young people's secretary.[127]

Covenants and Rainbows

To remind women of the certainty of God's faithfulness and of the hope that lies at the heart of the gospel, the program committee wove a theme of covenants and rainbows into WMU's 1930 annual meeting in Tampa. Apparently that was the first time a theme was incorporated into every facet of the program from the reports to the decorations. At each division report, a map of the division, in a spectrum color, was pinned onto a large state map, with the completed picture showing the entire state covered in a rainbow.[128] Mrs. Peelman could point to the map when she spoke of the year's work as "colors radiant with beauty."

Mrs. G. J. Rousseau
1929-1936

Mrs. G. J. Rousseau organized her first presidential address around the seven colors and characteristics of the spectrum. Wife of Ocala First Baptist Church pastor Gideon Jacques Rousseau, Christine McConnell Rousseau had grown up under the strong influence of her father, Dr. F. C. McConnell. An outstanding Baptist pastor, McConnell served as Home Mission Board secretary, 1901-03, and as SBC vice-president, 1928. Because her mother was often ill, Christine as a young lady had frequently stood beside her father as hostess to Baptist leaders, and she moved easily in the highest circles of denominational aristocracy.[129]

While returning from studying voice in Europe, a "story book romance" developed after she met her future husband, a native of South Africa, aboard ship. Gideon Rousseau became a Christian and answered God's call to ministry only after he married Christine.[130]

During her husband's pastorate in Norman, Oklahoma, Mrs. Rousseau was state YWA president and member of the state Executive Board. For the $75 Million Campaign she wrote a pageant used throughout the SBC. Soon after her husband became pastor of Pensacola First Baptist Church, she was elected president of the Pensacola Division. By the time she became Florida WMU president, she had been a YWA counselor "almost continuously for fifteen years."[131] Like other effective leaders in whose steps she walked, Mrs. Rousseau gave herself as wholeheartedly to the ongoing work in the local church as she did to the places of honor which came so frequently to her. Her many talents attracted the attention of Florida women; her refined and gentle spirit drew their love.

The Executive Board report avoided any reference to the Depression. It included the recommendation of Miss Louise Smith, a native of Kentucky and WMU Training School graduate, as the new young people's leader. Smith would begin her work July 1, 1931.[132]

Dark Clouds, Brilliant Rainbows

In giving her report, Mrs. Peelman acknowledged "trials and hard won battles," but also reminded delegates that "the darker the clouds the more brilliant the rainbow of hope and love." She used the milestone of her 20th annual report to thank the women for their "loyalty and faithful service," which had "sustained and strengthened her" in spite of her "weakness and unworthiness." In a roll call of faithful servants, she named many whose commitments to the work had enabled not only survival but growth in hard times since 1894.[133]

Recognizing the 20th anniversary of Peelman's "faithful and steadfast devotion to Florida W.M.U.," Mrs. E. A. McDowell of Lake Butler presented her with a "pot of gold," a love gift from the societies of the state.[134] The 65-year-old secretary, who was "visibly affected by the demonstration," later expressed her gratitude through the *Witness:* "The thought and love that prompted [your golden gift] are more precious even than the gift itself. Pray that I may in a measure be a worthy servant."[135]

The remaining five years of Mrs. Peelman's tenure saw Florida WMU struggling under financial constraints, but growing in numbers. Mrs. Peelman kept up her rigorous schedule of travel and office work. The term "Executive Secretary" came into general use in reference to Peelman's office; however, the WMU constitution was not changed to reflect that usage until 1938.

A Fashion Challenge

Although Florida Baptist women conscientiously followed the guidelines of WMU, SBC, St. Petersburg leaders introduced an innovation for the national WMU meeting in their city. Speaking to a Mississippi WMU gathering in Columbus in April 1932, Mrs. W. J. Cox, national president, announced that the annual meeting in May would be "hatless"! No doubt an audible gasp went up from the ladies. "If you haven't a new bonnet, don't get one, for the St. Petersburg women have decreed none will be worn," she said. An ideal climate, she added, would make hats "useless and taboo."[136] The hatless women in St. Petersburg heard Cox launch a major emphasis on "enlistment and extension." She challenged them "to reach out and arouse other individuals and groups to their opportunities and responsibilities." Mrs. Rousseau, who also held the office of state extension and enlistment chairman, led in the establishment of 173 new organizations by year's end.[137]

The Hundred Thousand Club

While the WMU concentrated on enlisting more women and youth in the missions cause, the SBC focused upon ways to eliminate the debts which were strangling the mission boards and damaging the credibility of the entire denomination. After grappling with various strategies to accomplish their goal, in May 1933 SBC leaders announced a plan to enlist 100,000 Baptists who would pledge $1 a month, above their regular offerings, to debt retirement. The October *Royal Service* carried an article by Frank Tripp, originator of the plan, urging the importance of WMU to the outcome:

> The W.M.U. of the south can save the situation. I believe with all my heart that if the good women in our churches will get enthusiastically behind the Baptist Hundred Thousand Club, it will succeed as no debt-paying movement has ever succeeded.[138]

Florida women took up the challenge rather slowly, but persisted diligently in their support until all debts were paid.

Mrs. B. I. Able, the same faithful servant who washed Miss Fletcher's nighties only to have them stolen from the backyard clothes line, prepared this hand-painted poster of missions literature in 1933.

WMU Shows Her Age

Forty years old—what woman wants to admit to that milestone? Florida WMU proudly celebrated in 1933 the 40th year of faithful service for the Master. Program planners presented a "Living Album of History" at the state meeting in Pensacola. As persons important to the work stepped out of the album, the story of Florida WMU unfolded. "It was a most attractive and informing program," said a report in the *Witness*.[139] The WMU report to the Florida general Convention took the form of an acrostic spelling FORTY YEARS.[140] The women also sent a "memorial" to the general Convention "requesting that the date of the annual meeting be changed to January."[141] Whether leaders yielded to the desires of the women or had some other reason for the change, the FBC held its next annual meeting in January 1935. Annual conventions continued to meet in January through 1946.

For the Good of the Whole

Mr. H. C. Peelman poses with his WMU-leader wife as they prepare to embark on yet another "little trip." Mr. Peelman often drove her to speaking engagements. Mrs. Peelman never learned to drive.

As the heavy clouds of the Depression began to thin, Florida WMU leaders faced a different dilemma. Mr. Peelman's health problems and her own age had taken their toll on Mrs. Peelman. She had shared her husband's condition in a letter to Louise Fletcher: "Mr. Peelman has been ill since Sept., has arthritis & neuritis. Part of the time he has been almost helpless. He is now taking fume baths & massages."[142] During her 25-year tenure, Mrs. Peelman had become known for using the expression, "While I'm on my feet . . . ," as she added one item or another of importance to her presentations. In the latter years she had growing difficulty in finding a stopping place, while she was "on her feet."[143] Her increasing hearing loss also caused awkward moments as she participated in meetings. What should be done? Not everyone agreed on the problem, much less the solution, but the consensus was that any action taken must be for her good, as well as the good of the organization.

Arcadia, where Mrs. Peelman had attended her first WMU annual meeting 31 years before, hosted the January 1936 convention. Several concerns troubled Mrs. Rousseau, and her anguish was apparent in her president's address. She expressed regret that the mid-year Executive Board meeting had been "abandoned": now, unless a president lived in Jacksonville she had no opportunity over the course of the whole year for personal involvement in the decision-making process. Without a mid-year meeting, "there is no time nor place where we can discuss the ideas of our workers on improvements in our plans," said the president. She also cautioned the women against forsaking the divisional structure, a matter that had been considered several times. "I believe we would make a mistake in doing so," she said. "It has always been my hope that the Divisions would be made to function more effectively."[144]

Her concern for Mrs. Peelman, however, was the major issue:

> Sometimes we women of the W.M.U., upholding the best in life, find our-selves in a mess of misunderstanding and fault-finding, due to looking too closely at the shortcomings of a personality rather than at the result of the efforts of that person. . . . Wherever the work itself is not concerned, we should forget the mistakes of others, and correct as many of our own as we can.

Because she believed, as had Carolyn Palmer, that seven years at the WMU helm was enough for one person, Rousseau extended her resignation as president.

The End of an Era

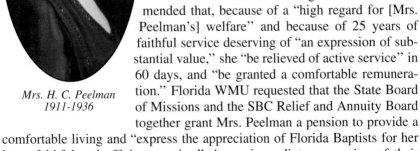

When the program turned to divisional reports, the atmosphere of the sessions brightened. Each report gave evidence of hard work by dedicated women and progress to show for it. Personal Service chairman Mrs. W. F. Brown reported: "All over the State our women are waking up to their duty in serving their Master." Support of mission work with the Seminole Indians, establishment of "open doors to teach the mothers of the colored race," and the opening of "several Good Will Centers throughout the State" pointed to a growing social consciousness among Florida WMU members.[145]

As the meeting drew to a close, the anticipated moment came. The nominating committee recommended that, because of a "high regard for [Mrs. Peelman's] welfare" and because of 25 years of faithful service deserving of "an expression of substantial value," she "be relieved of active service" in 60 days, and "be granted a comfortable remuneration." Florida WMU requested that the State Board of Missions and the SBC Relief and Annuity Board together grant Mrs. Peelman a pension to provide a

Mrs. H. C. Peelman
1911-1936

comfortable living and "express the appreciation of Florida Baptists for her long, faithful and efficient service." As an immediate expression of their love, members presented her with 34 silver dollars.[146]

When Mrs. Peelman took office in 1911, Florida WMU included 275 organizations: 188 WMSs and 87 auxiliaries. Total gifts were $5,588.51. At the end of her 25 years, the number of organizations had grown to 1,574: 470 WMSs and 1,104 auxiliaries with total gifts of $89,018.80.[147] At their height in 1926, before the Depression began its sinister intrusion, Florida WMU gifts had reached a total of $151,000.

Many expressions of love and appreciation came to Mrs. Peelman. The office force of the Rogers Building gave a "delightful" party for her in the home of *Witness* editor and Mrs. E. D. Solomon. There her co-workers presented her a chest containing 25 silver dollars.[148] Solomon dedicated the April 9 *Witness* issue to her. Glowing words of appreciation from WMU leadership, pastors, and state convention staff filled several pages. The sentiments of Dr. Brittain not only represented those many other accolades, but also spoke of the continuing bond of trust and respect between the Florida Baptist Convention and Florida WMU:

> We have labored at the side of Sister Peelman [since coming to work] for the denomination, and we have never known her to falter or lose courage. We have seen her at the battle front, but she never lost her poise or surrendered for one moment her womanly virtues and graces. She knew how to spend and be spent in the service of her Master without complaining of hardships or sacrifices. She stood foursquare for the doctrines and work of the denomination, and knew how to present the cause with convincing power.

Mrs. Peelman apparently never shared whatever pain she may have felt in leaving the work to which she had devoted her life. Perhaps she reminded herself, "Ladies don't cry in public."

Mrs. Peelman continued to serve as an honorary member of the local Executive Committee and took occasional other assignments. She was invited to write "a history of her twenty-five years of service, including intimate details of persons and performances, that would not ordinarily be contained in minutes."[149] Her own deteriorating health prevented her undertaking the strenuous project.

When Mr. Peelman died in 1940, she moved into the home of her daughter Marion. Although hardening of the arteries began to affect Mrs Peelman, God graciously called her home in 1943, before she became completely incapacitated. She had, indeed, served the Lord faithfully with all her heart.

They Are Precious in His Sight

1931 – 1936
1936 – 1943
1944

"Speak, Lord, for thy servant heareth."
1 Samuel 3:10

May 1926

*O*nly two more weeks of classes! Senior Louise Smith could scarcely picture herself as a graduate of the Woman's Missionary Union Training School. "How did a little country girl from Fordsville, Kentucky, get to this place?" Louise marvelled as she traced her steps to the Louisville campus. . . . [1]

The youngest of 11 brothers and sisters, Louise remembered her father, the town banker, as somewhat gruff, but her mother's gentle spirit prevailed more often, and their home exuded love, laughter, and constant activity. Theirs was a church-going family; in fact, her mother was "the most wonderful Christian" Louise had ever known. "Mama, did you hear the pastor stop his sermon and ask those two little girls on the front seat to be quiet?" Louise asked, as she set the table for Sunday dinner. "I promise I'm not going to whisper during the service any more!" Not long after that pledge, Louise made another, more important commitment. At 13, she invited Jesus into her life as Lord and Savior.

As a high school graduate, Louise felt God leading her to further education at Georgetown College, a Kentucky Baptist school. However, a cashier in her father's bank embezzled major funds, leaving her father with no money to send her back to college after her first year. After waiting for God to reveal the next step in his plan for her life, she again followed His leading, that time entering the WMU Training School.

Combined classes with the young men at Southern Baptist Theological Seminary may have thrilled many of the Training School students, but they had their liabilities, too. Large class enrollments often meant that each student recited for the professor only once during the quarter. Louise would never forget Dr. A. T. Robertson's class. When her time came, she stood, waiting anxiously for Dr. Robertson's question. He lectured on and on, seemingly unaware of the young lady awaiting her turn. When he finally paused long enough to ask her a question, she had lost track of her thoughts and was unable to respond. "I wouldn't answer that either," the famed New Testament professor declared with a smile. "You may be seated." And he gave her a good grade! . . .

The time for her last exams had come. Some of her friends already knew that they would be working in state WMU offices, as Girls' Auxiliary or Young Woman's Auxiliary leaders, or in associational good will centers. Some even had plans to go as foreign missionaries. When Miss Carrie Littlejohn, associate principal, sent for her, Louise hastily put aside her review notes, freshened her make-up, and hurried to the administrative office. Her heart raced as she tapped on the door. With no preliminaries, Miss Littlejohn pronounced Louise's future: "Miss Smith, I want you to go to Wallings Creek, Kentucky, where you will do mission work."

Louise's face flushed with disappointment. "Yes, Ma'am," she replied, backing out of the office as quickly as possible before her tears embarrassed her. "My own state—a coal-mining town in Kentucky—living in a pastor's home—somehow that's just not what I thought I'd be doing." Louise talked to herself as she walked slowly back to her room; and over the next few days, she talked again and again with the Lord, about her feelings and about His will for her. Finally, diploma in hand, the new Training School graduate moved directly to Wallings Creek, confident that God wanted her in the little mining town.

Louise lived with the pastor, his wife, and their little girl. On her first Sunday morning, when she walked into the church house and saw the children sitting on the front seats with their "funny papers" and their ice cream cones, she knew that the Lord had work for her to do. She remembered how the pastor in Fordsville had corrected the whispering girls in her own church, but she could see that it would be her job to teach these little ones how to behave.

With proper behavior in worship services as her first goal, Louise then developed one missions education organization after another. At first only one or two might attend the weekly meetings. Gradually, however, her genuine concern drew them in large numbers, many whose folks did not attend the Wallings Creek church; she and the youth developed a binding affection.

After working in a camp the next summer, Louise moved to New Orleans, where she took classes at Tulane University, and did work through Baptist Bible Institute (later renamed New Orleans Baptist Theological Seminary). Still lacking her college degree, she enrolled in Woman's College, a Baptist school in Hattiesburg, Mississippi (later renamed William Carey College).

Twenty-eight years old, she entered whole-heartedly into college life, joining campus clubs, serving as Student Government Association president, and winning the "Best Trooper" theater award. She graduated in 1930.[2]

While Smith was teaching in the public schools of Ashland, Kentucky,[3] Florida WMU hired her as young people's secretary. Her pay would be small. Economic conditions had required budget cutbacks for both the Florida Baptist Convention and Florida WMU. A strong commitment to continue missions education for youth, however, spurred state WMU leadership to "secure" the Kentucky school teacher.

Louise Smith completed her teaching contract and began her new work on July 1, 1931. The journey from Fordsville, Kentucky, to Jacksonville, Florida, had been a circuitous one, but she had faithfully traveled the road under the guidance of her mother's prayers and the hand of her heavenly Father.

*M*iss Louise Smith, young people's secretary—that had a nice ring to it, Smith thought, as she planned how she would arrange an office and begin her work in Florida. Her first day, however, brought a surprise. Mrs. H. C. Peelman, now 65 years old and a 20-year veteran as the

Louise Smith
Young People's Secretary
1931-1936

Florida executive secretary, had her own ideas about Smith's work. When Smith inquired about office space, Peelman replied, "Well, you can just work right here at the corner of my desk. Mrs. Wilson, the secretary, will take your dictation. You won't be in the office long enough to need a desk. You're going to be traveling."

Travel, she did. When anyone asked where she lived, she answered, "In my suitcase." She spent so few days in Jacksonville that she just rented a hotel room on the occasions when she was in town. By the end of her first six months in her new job, Smith had traveled 3,657 miles, mostly by bus, learning the state organization and earning the love and respect of young people and their leaders. Peelman praised her new staff member: "Louise Smith is winning a huge place in the hearts of our people. I like her very much. She is practical & self forgetting." The executive secretary confirmed what Smith had felt all along: "We believe God sent her to Florida."[4]

Influencing the Future

The story of Florida WMU during the years of Louise Smith's involve-ment is as much an account of individual lives influenced and changed as it is the record of organizational development. Smith brought to her work a genuine interest in other people and an ability to establish warm personal relationships. As a result of the 1931 YWA Conference at Ridgecrest Baptist Assembly, those qualities also significantly influenced the future of Woman's Missionary Union, Auxiliary to Southern Baptist Convention (WMU, SBC).

Beginning in 1923, a YWA Conference had been held each summer at Ridgecrest Baptist Assembly in North Carolina. Florida WMU arranged a "Florida Hut," just off the Ridgecrest grounds, where the girls and their chap-erons could stay with little cost. Afternoon recreation during the conference offered elaborate programs of sports, games, swimming, hikes, exercise, whatever creative leaders could design. In 1931 Louise Smith and a friend led the recreation program.[5] The two became very much impressed with a young YWA member from Virginia, who entered into the planned activities with skill and enthusiasm. Her name was Alma Hunt. Later Smith wrote to Juliette Mather, national WMU young people's secretary, recommending Alma Hunt as the recreation leader for the next year's YWA Conference.

When Hunt accepted Mather's invitation and took the job in 1932, a long relationship began. As Hunt continued through the years to lead the YWA recreation program at Ridgecrest, she became widely known among WMU leadership. According to Alma Hunt, that recognition, which had its roots in Louise Smith's personal interest in her, led to her election in 1948 as execu-tive secretary of WMU, SBC, a position she held for 26 years.[6]

An expedition into central Florida in late summer 1931 took Louise Smith to Williston for Girls' Auxiliary (GA) and Young Woman's Auxiliary (YWA) mission study classes. It also opened the door for a lifelong friendship. Etter Turner, an incoming freshman at Stetson University, attended a YWA class. A college freshman with a car was a rarity, but "because of a long history of broken legs," Etter had to have transportation to and from school. She offered to show Smith the city of Williston. A lengthy discussion during the drive convinced Etter to think more seriously about her relationship with the Lord and what He might have in mind for her future.[7]

Proclaiming Stewardship

"Jesus shall reign wher'er the sun does his successive journeys run." The words of the 1932 WMU hymn motivated Florida Baptist women "to go for-ward in their God-given task" of making the hymn's prophecy a reality.[8] Even in the declining economy, the women emphasized teaching youth the value of tithing. In early 1932, Smith and state Stewardship chairman, Mrs. Allen S. Cutts of Pensacola, introduced Stewardship Declamation contests for each auxiliary. GA and RA winners received scholarships to a summer assembly; Sunbeams received $2.50. With an award of $25 for a trip to Ridgecrest, the state YWA winner competed in the conventionwide contest during YWA Conference at Ridgecrest Baptist Assembly.

Two hundred young people entered Florida's various contests in 1932. Winners of the first state competition were, from the Sunbeams, Minnie Louise Kelley, New Port Richey; Junior GA, Eleanor Fokes, Ocala; Junior RA, Kenneth Crawford, Fort Pierce; Intermediate GA, Ellene Thompson, Mt. Dora; and Intermediate RA, William Stalvey, Jacksonville.[9]

Smith encouraged several Stetson girls, including Etter Turner, to take part in the local YWA competition. Turner recounted:

> As it turned out, I won that contest and then was fortunate enough to win the state competition in Ocala and the $25 stipend. About 20 of my friends had already talked about going to Ridgecrest, and that award spurred us on. We found a chaperon who was a great cook, and a cottage we could rent for a ridiculous price, and my dad helped us to arrange for a lady to drive us to North Carolina in a school bus. I decided that was a good place to put my winnings. My $25 helped to get us all to Ridgecrest.
>
> I didn't win the southwide contest. The judges picked the girl from Kentucky. That night Louise said to me, "You know, you really should have won, but to tell you the truth, I'm glad you didn't. This is my first year here, but the young people's leader from Kentucky, my good friend Jo Jones, has worked long and hard, so I'm glad for her YWA to win this time." Those words made me feel very comfortable about the experience.

Smith visited often in the Williston home of the Turners. Even after she left Florida in 1943, her friendship continued to influence Etter's life. Etter Turner stayed on at Stetson, eventually becoming dean of students and extending Louise Smith's influence to many generations of Stetson students.[10]

Of Such Is the Kingdom

WMU young people's organizations thrived with Louise Smith's leadership. Under her guidance, Baptists stretched their limited dollars to provide good missions training for their young people. A state-level young people's committee helped to develop plans. Smith's addition to the WMU *Witness* page, entitled "Our Young People," supplied weekly portions of news about activities, instructions on up-coming ventures, and encouragement for growth. In 1932 Smith directed 10 RA and GA camps for associations or local churches and helped YWAs to celebrate their organization's 25th anniversary. She encouraged mission study and the use of missions literature. Subscriptions to WMU youth magazines reached 206 for *The Window of YWA* and 437 for *World Comrades* (GA and Sunbeams). The women's magazine, *Royal Service,* also in its 25th year, elicited 2,733 subscribers.[11]

The women also reached out to youth having other kinds of needs. In 1932 Florida WMU mothered nine Margaret Fund students, sending them 88 boxes valued at $419.90, as well as $229.72 in cash. Residents of the Children's Home at Arcadia received 622 boxes valued at $6,648.27.[12]

From the birth of the children's home, Florida women had offered support and fulfilled requests from administrators, beginning with Brother and Mrs. B. M. Bean. However, enough money to meet all the needs of the institution or the children never seemed available. During the Depression, boxes and monetary gifts from WMU organizations became a necessary life-line. In 1934 the WMU Executive Committee appointed Mrs. C. M. Brittain, Mrs. R. C. White, and Mrs. J. E. Empie as a committee to explore a statewide auxiliary to the children's home. The committee proposed that the auxiliary be formed from the Tampa Division because of the home's location in Arcadia.[13]

Mrs. L. E. Womack, president of the Tampa Division, appointed the presidents of her seven associations, as well as the seven division presidents as members of the auxiliary, with Mrs. J. A. Lamb, state vice-president, as chairman. The auxiliary met with trustees of the home and "mapped out the repairs and necessities into seven projects, apportioning each Division a project according to its size and strength."[14] Such organized support began to effect substantial improvements for the children's home.

Rich Blessings Through Achievement

In 1933 Royal Ambassadors celebrated its 25th anniversary. The RA allegiance set strong guidelines of commitment:

> I pledge myself to try to live worthily of the name of our order; to guard my lips against profanity and untruth; to keep my body clean and useful; to study the lives of noble ambassadors set forth in God's Word and in world history; to give what I can to support missions, and in every possible deed of service to help bring in Christ's kingdom. I assert my allegiance to Jesus Christ, my desire to live for Him and serve Him always. I will "live pure, speak truth, right wrong, follow the Christ, the King. Else wherefore born?"[15]

Moving through six ranks from Page to Ambassador Plenipotentiary, Junior and Intermediate RAs studied and memorized scripture, learned denominational information, and developed handicraft skills. The year 1934 produced Florida's first Ambassadors Plenipotentiary: Joe McCullough and Earl McCullar, both from Mt. Olive Church, Hastings.[16]

Junior and Intermediate GA had similar rungs of achievement, known as Forward Steps. In 1933, Anna Marie Crane, First Baptist Church, Miami, became the first Florida girl to achieve the Intermediate GA rank, Queen with Scepter. She followed that with the first Florida Queen Regent recognition in 1934.[17] Reflecting on the "rich blessings" of Forward Steps, Anna Marie said: "In the study of the work of Southern Baptists the influence of

Girls' Auxiliary Coronation

Christianity was pictured to me clearly. It was through these steps that I came to see a life of Christian service as the goal of my life."[18]

YWA house parties and camps, as well as GA and RA camps, flourished wherever adult leadership gave the slightest encouragement. In both 1933 and 1934, Mrs. J. H. Matthews, Ocala Division young people's leader, held a YWA house party at her home near Leesburg. The second year, with 82 girls and counselors present, leaders may have felt that God had outstripped their prayers, but the impact of the occasion made the effort doubly worthwhile. "Only eternity can tell the results of the house party," said Division president Mrs. J. Ray Arnold, "as there were seven girls who gave their hearts to the Saviour, the others rededicating their lives to the Master's service."[19]

As Louise Smith guided YWA work, she began using the WMU, SBC, designations of "Ann Hasseltine YWA" for organizations on college campuses and "Grace McBride YWA" for those in hospitals or nursing schools. Named for the first American woman foreign missionary, Florida's two Ann Hasseltine groups, at Florida State College for Women and Stetson University, worked to develop leadership skills as well as personal service commitments among members. Named for a Southern Baptist nurse who died while serving in China, Grace McBride groups functioned in three Florida hospitals: Jackson Memorial in Miami, Orange General in Orlando, and Mound Park in St. Petersburg.[20] Both college and hospital YWA organizations received guidance and support from local WMUs.

The Florida Stewardship Declamation contest enrolled more than 250 participants in 1934. State winner Berta Fisher of Daytona Beach led a Florida delegation of 65 YWAs to Ridgecrest that summer. Competing with entrants from 11 other states, Fisher won first place. *Royal Service* magazine rewarded her with $50 in gold and a trip to nearby Mount Mitchell. That time, apparently satisfied that she had "paid her dues," Smith praised Berta Fisher, proclaiming, "Florida is truly proud of her contestant and of the honor she brought our state."[21]

To Every Land and Nation

With so many activities going on among Florida Baptist young people, Louise Smith was not sure she should accept an invitation to attend the 1934

"Miss Smith on a camel" is the simple caption under this photograph in an old WMU scrapbook from First Baptist Church, Pensacola.

meeting in Germany of the Baptist World Alliance (BWA). Three WMU leaders—national president Mrs. F. W. Armstrong, Oklahoma corresponding secretary Mrs. Berta K. Spooner, and Missouri WMU president Mrs. George McWilliams—had planned an extensive tour of Southern Baptist mission work, which also included the BWA meeting. They invited Juliette Mather, national young people's secretary, to go with them. Because Smith and Mather had developed a close friendship, they also invited Smith. Smith's meager salary barely covered her normal living costs, but as she prayed she felt God leading her to make the trip. The Executive Committee gave her a two-months' leave of absence; she went "without salary and at my own expense."[22]

In Berlin for the BWA, the five American ladies saw the shadow of Adolph Hitler's mad ambition, which would soon turn the continent into a battlefield. When German soldiers demanded that Mrs. Armstrong salute and say, "Heil Hitler!" she angrily refused. Perhaps the small contingent of soldiers did not want to take on five stalwart WMU leaders; the soldiers marched away.

The group, which included Foreign Mission Board executive secretary Dr. C. E. Maddry and his wife, traveled through Italy, Hungary, Rumania, Czecho-slavakia, Bessarabia, Yugoslavia, Egypt, Palestine, and England, often guided by missionaries in a particular area.[23] Although the pilgrimage through Europe made wonderful deposits in Smith's missions resource bank, the Florida lady wrestled with the proverbial "fifth wheel" syndrome. When room assignments were made, she usually ended up alone. For most of the trip, she refused to give in to her anxiety over being alone at night in alien surroundings. However, when the accommodations turned out to be tents raised in front of the Egyptian pyramids near Cairo, her self-control gave way. Hearing strange noises in the night, she screamed, waking the entire party of travelers. A gentleman in a long robe, who had entertained the group with magic tricks that evening, ran quickly to her tent, shouting, "What is it, Madam? What is it?"

"I want my cot put in there!" she cried, pointing to the tent of Mather and her roommate. "I'm not going to stay by myself! Move my cot!" And he did. Having cleared that agenda, Smith could enjoy the camel ride, sight-seeing, and souvenir shopping that filled the next several days.

When the Florida Baptist Convention met in DeLand in January 1935, Smith shared details of her trip in her annual report to WMU. Using young people to present various facets of her report, Smith had Stetson YWAs to wear national costumes from several countries she had visited and bring a special message from each. In conclusion, Smith wrote:

> My visit made me realize more than ever that . . . the cross of Christ alone has healing for the nations. Let us give Christ to the millions at our door, and send messengers to carry the banner of the Cross into every land and to every nation on earth.[24]

One aim of each WMU organization is to develop messengers who will reach unsaved persons. Beginning in 1935, Focus Weeks gave impetus to that goal and other work of each youth organization—Sunbeams, YWA, GA, and RA—one during each quarter of the year. Smith guided leaders in special planning and encouraged local church recognition. The *Witness* honored each of the four organizations in separate editions which carried a front page emphasis and gave several inside pages for special messages, histories, and program information.[25]

Unknown to Louise Smith, God was working his plans for her from more than one direction. As she occasionally checked into the hotel in Jacksonville, she began to notice a man who appeared to be a regular hotel guest. Eventually she met David Fair Boyd, a civilian contractor with the Navy. They first became casual friends, and then on the rare occasions when their schedules allowed, they began dating.

With her extensive travel schedule and her interest in David Boyd, Smith heard little of the discussions of WMU leadership concerning Mrs. Peelman's status. When the young people's secretary went to the 1936 annual meeting in Arcadia, according to her recollection, she knew nothing of the plans to "relieve Mrs. Peelman of her duties." Nor had the nominating committee consulted with Smith about her selection as the new executive secretary. She knew only that Mrs. Peelman's future was at issue, and, without knowing why, Smith feared that she was the cause of the problem. Certainly her fear was unfounded, for Mrs. Peelman had concurred with the Executive Committee that "the mantle of [Peelman's] years of fine service could fittingly rest on the young shoulders and splendid Christian spirit of Louise Smith."[26]

Smith was astonished when she heard the committee chairman name her as Mrs. Peelman's replacement. Unless she was certain that it was God's will for her, she could not embrace such a position. "I said I'd have to think it over, which I did, a great deal, before I accepted the job," she recalled.

The next two months created a buffer for both Mrs. Peelman and Louise Smith. Each had adjustments to make, and each graciously did so. Her regular travels, plus a case of the flu, kept Smith away from the office most of that time. After Mrs. Peelman's departure at the end of March 1936, Smith continued to demonstrate her respect and affection for the great lady. When Smith took over responsibility for the entire WMU page in the *Witness,* she included numerous tributes to the former leader, "who so greatly deserves all that we can say."[27]

Louise Smith was now ready to see what God had in store for her as the executive secretary of Florida WMU.

Louise Smith
1936-1943

The transition from young people's secretary to executive secretary and treasurer of Florida Baptist Woman's Missionary Union brought two other signficant moves for Louise Smith: her home and her office. Though she would spend more time in Jacksonville, she could not bring herself to rent a house, or even an apartment. She settled on a room in the home of a widow, "a beautiful place out on the river." Fortunately, her landlady also liked David Boyd and was "delighted" when he stopped by as often as possible to see the WMU leader. Besides moving into a home, Smith also moved to a desk of her own in the Rogers Building. There she planned her work, handled administrative details, and did writing assignments, shaping the personality of Florida WMU as it emerged from the Depression.

The Traumas of Travel

A heavy travel schedule still dominated Smith's calendar. She often traveled to schools of missions held throughout the state. Furloughing and retired foreign missionaries, home missionaries, Florida Baptist Convention employees, WMU leadership—there was a place for almost anyone willing to participate. The intensive missions emphasis, lasting from three days to a week, gained in popularity under Smith's planning. In 1936, her first year as executive secretary, 11 schools were held. By 1943, Smith's last year, the number had mushroomed to 61.[28]

On one of Smith's mission school trips, a young missionary to Europe asked if he might drive her car. As the young man slid into the driver's seat, he asked, "Where do you start it? What is this switch?" Within a second they hit a ditch.

"Why didn't you tell me you didn't know how to drive?" she gasped.

"Well, I thought you would teach me," he responded as they sat in the wrecked car![29]

Dr. J. F. Plainfield, missionary pastor to the Italians in Tampa, was another of Smith's fellow travelers. With good humor, she recalled:

> We were always entertained in a home, and one time this preacher's wife gave us two bedrooms with an adjoining bath. You can imagine my embarrassment the next morning when Dr. Plainfield met me in the kitchen saying, "If you lock that door again tonight, I'm going to fire you!" In the middle of the night I had locked his door to the bathroom and forgotten to unlock it![30]

Lay Leadership Shines

Having observed the growing capabilities of WMU members, Smith began delegating responsibilities and imparting leadership roles. To promote the seven state areas of emphasis—Mission Study, Personal Service, Stewardship, Margaret Fund, WMU Training School, White Cross work, and Publicity—she invited each state chairman to prepare material for one issue of the *Witness*. Mrs. C. H. Bolton, state vice-president at large as well as Miami Division president, prepared the program for the annual associational meetings. Mrs. G. A. Fellows, West Florida Division president, wrote the devotionals for the State Mission Season of Prayer. GA, RA, and Sunbeam materials on the State Missions emphasis came from Miss Dorothy Sparks, Miami, and Mrs. J. J. Cater, West Palm Beach.[31]

Smith herself was a favorite writer for WMU publications, and as she nurtured the skills of Florida WMU, members also shared their talents with a wider audience. Mrs. Allen S. Cutts contributed a stewardship article to the 1937 WMU, SBC, Yearbook; Mrs. C. R. Pittard, state Golden Jubilee chairman, wrote an "excellent article" for the next year's edition. Miss Addie Palmer, Jacksonville, designed the cover of the 1939 national Yearbook as well as the cover of the Foreign Mission Week of Prayer program booklet for that year. *Royal Service, World Comrades,* and *The Window of YWA* also published contributions from Florida WMU. Members of the Grace McBride YWA at Orange General Hospital, Orlando, supplied six articles for the 1939 *Window.* Passing assignments to different persons each year enlarged the base of capable members who could shoulder the ever-expanding work.

The work of lay leadership, including Mrs. Robert Walden, who was elected president at Mrs. Rousseau's resignation, helped to fill the gap when problems in securing a new young people's secretary arose. The executive committee had named Marguerite Lumpkin, a WMU Training School graduate who had done part-time and volunteer assignments, to fill Smith's vacancy. Fulfilling her teaching contract in Lakeland, Lumpkin did not actually begin her work until July 15; after only a few weeks she resigned and returned to her Lakeland classroom. Smith began the fall with no staff, but, according to Dr. C. M. Brittain, executive secretary of the state Convention, "the Lord directed" the Executive Committee to "a fine young Christian woman" who came highly recommended for "her spirituality and ability." Susan Adams, a Training School graduate from Lebanon, Missouri, began her work in November 1936.[32] In the meantime, Smith directed the 50th anniversary recognition for Sunbeams and the Stewardship Declamation contests. For the second time, Florida produced a national YWA winner from the Ocala Division, Frances Douglas of St. Augustine.[33] The contests ceased after one more year.

Hail the Women

At the 1938 Golden Jubilee celebration, WMU, SBC, observed 50 years of missions work in partnership with SBC boards. Recognition of WMU's value came from many sources, including Dr. W. O. Carver, renowned professor of missions at Southern Seminary in Louisville. Having taught every WMUTS student, Dr. Carver claimed 2,000 WMU "daughters" serving Christ around the world. As the women prepared for the Jubilee meeting in Richmond, he wrote:

> Every pastor of our twenty-four thousand churches ought to provide for a special, joyous recognition of this jubilee of W.M.U. Every church that has not done so already ought to make this year the occasion for seeing that the W.M.U. organization is formed in that church, along with all the subsidiary organizations for young people.
>
> The present income of our Convention boards for missions is due very largely to the missionary education which W.M.U. has carried on through these 50 years. Let everybody hail the women, and give special thanks to the Lord of the churches.[34]

Eighty-five Floridians traveled to Richmond for the Jubilee Celebration. As the trumpets sounded to open the first session, "delegates from the ten original states forming the union, marched in, followed by the nine other states in order of their joining the union." Florida's 50 delegates, second in line behind Arkansas, followed a new banner because "the Ruby Anniversary banner had burned." Personal items that had belonged to Mrs. L. B. Telford and Mrs. W. D. Chipley, Florida's delegates to the founding convention, formed part of the state's contributions to the Jubilee display.[35] *Following in His Train,* the 50-year history of WMU, SBC, written by former national president Ethlene Boone Cox, was introduced at the meeting. The book sold for 60 cents a copy.

Another processional took place in the session focusing on the WMU Training School. Miss Carrie Littlejohn led a group of WMUTS graduates down one aisle, while alumnae president Louise Smith, whom Miss Littlejohn had once sent off to the Kentucky coal mines, led a second group down another. With the alumnae seated on the stage, Mrs. George McWilliams announced that a "proposed new Training School building would be erected on seven and a half acres of suburban property near the new [campus of] Southern Baptist Theological Seminary."[36] Florida's young people's secretary, Susan Adams, sang in an ensemble which closed each session with a musical benediction.[37] WMU, SBC, published Adams' pageant, "The Candle of the Lord," which presented the story of WMU's 50-year history so effectively that orders required a reprint.[38]

More notable than the actual celebrations, however, was the stimulus for growth provided by the Golden Jubilee. Under the leadership of Mrs. Pittard, Florida WMU answered Annie Armstrong's challenge "to follow the original watchword," going forward in prayer life, enlistment, mission study, personal service, stewardship, and missionary education of young people. At the end of the year Smith reported several significant achievements including 1) 926 Sunbeam Babies enrolled; 2) 219 new organizations, surpassing the goal of 200; 3) 5,248 tithers, topping the goal of 5,000; and 4) 538 organizations reporting directed personal service. The financial goal for the year was $75,000, including $1,500 for the Jubilee offering. Contributions reached $82,062.80. The Jubilee offering surpassed its goal by almost $3,000, with the overage going to the Cooperative Program. During the year, Florida WMU also published a guidebook. Free copies of the 32-page booklet were given to divisional and associational officers. "Sold at 5 cents per copy to others, it practically paid for itself."[39]

Two innovations in youth work, state YWA house parties and state RA camps, marked the Jubilee year. Under Adams' direction, the five house parties held at scattered sites around the state attracted over 500 girls. Adams also planned two RA camps, one at Holland Springs near Monticello and one at Camp Foster near Jacksonville. Missionary W. W. Enete, on furlough from Brazil, and several local pastors led 84 boys in mission study, devotionals, and recreation. The year was also special for GAs, who celebrated the silver anniversary of their organization. Adams reported the coronation of 20 Queens and two Queens with Scepter.[40]

Living Among the People

The Jubilee year was almost over when, nearly 10 years after Louise Fletcher's departure, Florida WMU again appointed a field worker. "Realizing the needs of our state and prompted by the compelling motive of love for their Master," the Executive Committee on October 11, 1938, called Miss Theo Thomas, a recent WMUTS graduate from St. Augustine.[41] Theo was born in Fernandino Beach, where she received her introduction to missions through her Sunbeam leader. "I'll never forget Mrs. Boring," she said in 1992. "She really did do something to motivate me for missions." As Theo moved into adolescence, her family moved to St. Augustine, where they all joined Ancient City Baptist Church. Her pastor, Dr. A. E. Calkins, gave his young people frequent opportunities to develop their talents. As an 18-year-old, she won the Ocala Division YWA award in the 1933 Stewardship Declamation contest.[42] "My best school was my church," she recalled.

Migrating from church to church in her new job, Thomas carried a suitcase, a poster bag, memories of her youthful experiences, and a sense of humor. "Living among the people," she rarely knew where bedtime would find her. At the end of a daylong workshop or an evening speaking engagement, the host pastor would often ask, "Now who'll sleep and feed Miss Thomas?" The word *entertain* was "bad," she explained, and never used in making those last-minute arrangements.[43]

After a year of energetic and effective field work, Thomas resigned to marry Dr. Robert E. Lee, a Mississippian whom she had met at Southern Seminary in Louisville. An unforeseen situation, however, had her working through the Friday before her wedding on Monday, November 6. The ladies of the Ancient City Woman's Missionary Society rallied to Thomas' aid, and the wedding took place as if she had prepared for months.

After a brief time in Owensboro, Kentucky, Dr. Lee accepted the call of First Baptist Church, Fort Lauderdale; Theo Thomas Lee was back in Florida by January 1940. Her commitment to WMU was as strong as a pastor's wife, as it had been as a field worker. In only her second year in Fort Lauderdale, she accepted nomination as state president. A delicate situation had arisen when a lady from Jacksonville campaigned for the position. The women wanted another choice. "I was floored when they came to me," said Lee. At 27 years of age, she felt ill equipped to take the job, but her friend and mentor, Louise Smith, encouraged her to do so.

Sincerely Yours for a Debtless Denomination

As Smith moved through her years of Florida WMU leadership, four aspects rose like fresh cream to the top of her work. One was the campaign to pay off all SBC debts, which in 1933 had amounted to approximately $6 million, including state causes. Each year Smith encouraged more women to join the Hundred Thousand Club. She declared, "Our women hate debt and

Mrs. R. E. Lee
1941-1943

Mrs. Robert Walden
1936 – 1941

will do their part to erase it."[44] The women, in fact, preferred to avoid incurring debt in the first place. Florida WMU led all SBC states in paying its apportionment of $1,830 for the new WMUTS building. Mrs. B. W. Blount, who had been Florida's Training School chairman since 1911, made her first visit to the school for the ground-breaking in March 1940. The new building, which some called "House Magnificent," was dedicated "free of debt" in February 1942.[45]

Crippling debt continued plaguing most SBC interests into the 1940s. After WMU, SBC, re-emphasized the Hundred Thousand Club in its 1938 Golden Jubilee celebration, the Union in 1940 accepted responsibility for raising $1 million of the remaining $3 million debt. Florida WMU accepted a $35,000 apportionment. The theme "For a Debtless Denomination by 1945" energized stewardship promotion throughout the SBC, even as Japanese bombs finally forced the United States into war.[46] Smith's preoccupation with the debt burden lurked in the background, no matter what the context; in a letter to Foreign Mission Board secretary C. E. Maddry about missions needs in South America, it appeared in her complimentary close: "Sincerely yours for a debtless denomination."[47]

When Mrs. J. L. Rosser became state Stewardship chairman in 1940, she pushed to increase by 100 percent the number of women in the Hundred Thousand Club. The next year Rosser led an additional campaign to raise contributions for a Centennial Fund. Rosser's "ceaseless efforts and enthusiasm inspired the belief" that the denomination could indeed become debt-free by 1945, the centennial anniversary of the SBC.[48] In fact, offerings increased at such a rate that a new slogan appeared: "Debt-free in '43, Count on Me."[49]

As faithful servants, Florida women took the new motto seriously. With gratitude to the Father, Louise Smith announced, at the January 1943 annual meeting in Jacksonville, that Florida WMU had surpassed its $35,000 quota. Smith radiated her joy. Not only had WMU members fulfilled their secretary's dream of being the first state to reach its apportionment, but they also had surpassed last year's Cooperative Program gifts by almost $13,000. At the same time they had lived through more than a year of war-time conditions, a fact that somewhat tempered their exhilaration.[50]

As a pastor's wife, Theo Lee knew that the circumstances of war consumed the energies of many Christian women. In her second and final presidential speech, she addressed that issue:

> In these stressful and uncertain days when we are doing our best to aid in
> the war effort, we shall find it very easy to substitute other worthy work for
> our main business. Our name tells to the world what we are and what con-
> stitutes our supreme objective. We **must** make ourselves **primarily** and
> **fundamentally** missionary societies: we must **not substitute** canteen work
> for community missions; we must not substitute nurse's aid classes for mis-
> sion study classes; we must not substitute the study of the road maps and
> war maps of this world for the blood stained trail of human redemption
> taught us in the Bible; we must **not substitute** the giving of 10% in the pur-
> chase of War Bonds and Stamps for the bringing of the tenth to the store-
> house of God. Moreover, we must not lose ourselves in the doing of only
> humanitarian deeds. Our task is far more comprehensive than that. Our task
> is ever to hold before the world the Kingdom of God.[51]

Opportunity and Challenge

The second of Smith's emphases focused on work with Negroes. After the
Civil War, Negro Baptists in Florida had increased in number more rapidly than
had white Baptists. For a time, the Florida Baptist Convention (FBC) hired men
like Rev. Robert Telford as part-time missionaries to the Negro population.
Negro Baptists established successful schools before the FBC managed to do
so. Relationships between the two groups deteriorated in the 1890s, before
becoming "less strained" after the turn of the century. By 1912 the Home
Mission Boards of the Southern Baptist Convention and the Negro National
Baptist Convention were cooperating in sending out Negro missionaries in
Florida. Sometimes feeling a "bad conscience on the subject of race," the FBC
in the 1930s began to provide small amounts of financial help on a more regular basis and to assist with educational opportunities for Negro pastors.[52]

By 1926 the Florida WMU Executive Committee, in its recommendations
for personal service, was including annually the proposal that "wherever we
can be of service and opportunity offers, we help [Negro women and chil-
dren] plan and carry on their work in their missionary societies and auxiliaries."[53] Random reports sent to the Personal Service chairman indicated that
women and youth visited Negroes and held worship services for them. While
still young people's secretary, Louise Smith began to express her interest in
people of other races and nationalities. After trips to two Negro college campuses in 1935, she reported:

> Bethune-Cookman College at Daytona Beach, with an enrollment of 400,
> and Florida A. and M. College, Tallahassee, with 575 students, challenge
> us. We hope to formulate some plans for Y.W.A. work for these Negro
> students.

Within a year, Bethune-Cookman had an active YWA sponsored by the
Calvary Baptist YWA of Daytona Beach.[54]

In September 1936 the National Baptist Convention (NBC) met in Jacksonville. Guided by W. C. Sale, part-time employee of the State Board of Missions, white Baptists, primarily from Jacksonville, went all out to assist in preparations. After securing "the cooperation and financial aid of the entire City Administration and of the Duval County Board of Education," they built a lighted tabernacle large enough to seat 10,000 people and "organized a feeding force" capable of meeting "every demand" of those attending. "The delegation was housed in the homes of the colored people."[55]

The National Baptist WMU met concurrently with the NBC. Louise Smith, now Florida WMU's executive secretary, promoted the meeting through the *Witness.* Jacksonville Association WMU members decorated, made poster displays, and led conferences at the meeting.[56] "Over 500 official delegates and scores of visitors from 30 different States" as well as the Bahamas gathered for the women's meeting. Smith welcomed the guests on behalf of Florida WMU.[57] Kathleen Mallory, who spoke as WMU, SBC, representative, had felt some anxiety about attending the meeting. "Trembling all the way, Mallory prayed and read the latest books on the racial issue. Later she spoke of feeling God's presence throughout, and she greatly enjoyed herself."[58]

Both Shirley Willie Layten of Philadelphia, president of the National Baptist WMU, and Nannie Helen Burroughs of Washington, D.C., corresponding secretary, spoke. President Layten "paid tribute to Florida, to Viola T. Hill, president of the Florida Negro Baptist women, and expressed appreciation for the cooperation of the white Baptists." Burroughs, echoing her friend Annie Armstrong, said:

> The biggest word of any day is FORWARD. Our business is to push the program of Jesus Christ a little farther on than when we started the job. . . . This is a time of opportunity and challenge for both races. God grant that the cause of understanding, cooperation and good will shall be greatly advanced.[59]

Both the general convention and the women's meeting were successes by every standard. Hill expressed her appreciation to the Jacksonville WMU: "[Your contributions] brought success and honor to the Baptist womanhood of Florida. It is the talk of the country how beautifully we work together here in the south."[60] At the next WMU, SBC, Executive Board meeting, Una Roberts Lawrence, presenting the report for the Committee on Cooperation with the Woman's National Baptist Convention, noted: "The unselfish and generous example set by Florida Baptist women is worth years of theorizing and discussion of racial relations, in finding a common ground of Christian trust and understanding."[61]

While no large interracial projects developed over the next five years, individual members, societies, and auxiliaries made their own small advances in race relations. Theo Lee recalled a bitter winter morning in 1939 in the Florida panhandle:

It was raining—felt like ice. I had bought my ticket for the 6:30 train and was sitting alone in the waiting room. The wood stove was putting out good heat. Then I noticed several black people, even little children, standing outside in all that weather. They weren't allowed in the white waiting room. I just couldn't stand it. I gathered up all my posters and things I had to carry with me, and I went and stood outside with them.

Smith continued to visit Negro schools and became a familiar figure on the campus of Florida Normal and Industrial Institute in St. Augustine. Annual meetings under her leadership frequently spotlighted Negro work. In 1940, after attending the National Baptist Convention and NBC-WMU meetings, Smith came away feeling "a sense of shame."[62] In response, she organized Florida WMU's first statewide interracial institute. Funded partly by WMU, SBC, the institute was one of three held in Southern states in 1941.[63] Smith reported:

> The [meeting] held at Bethel Baptist Church (Negro), Jacksonville, July 17th, was a forward step in racial cooperation. In spite of [difficulties in advertising the meeting], four hundred registered. Many others failed to register because they anticipated a registration fee.

Those present represented 115 churches, 47 cities, and "five foreign countries (China, Nigeria, Liberia, Roumania and Central America)." Nannie Burroughs, Kathleen Mallory, Joy Chow from Shanghai, and M'bola Ayorinde, WMU leader from Nigeria, made inspiring presentations on the theme, "The Furtherance of the Gospel."[64] In 1942 and 1943 Smith scheduled the interracial conferences on the Florida Normal campus in St. Augustine. In late 1943, amid tributes and expressions of gratitude, the Florida WMU secretary was named a trustee of Florida Normal.[65] Having expended substantial energy in developing interracial cooperation, as she left the state she pondered Florida's future commitment:

> Most of us felt that during the past three years we have advanced in racial understanding and the ability to work together harmoniously. Florida Normal has many needs. Will Florida Baptists sit blindly unobservant of these needs? Florida W.M.U. has in a very small way helped, providing last year for furnishings for the chapel, and this year giving $500.00 through the State Mission Offering for scholarships and equipment. Can't we wake up and do something worthy of our missionary name?[66]

Reaching the Seminoles

The third of Smith's four emphases involved her concern for the Indians of Florida. Only after the turn of the century had Florida Baptists expressed interest in the "spiritual welfare" of the Seminole Indians. A 1913 Florida Baptist Convention committee recommended the securing of a Christian Seminole from Oklahoma to work among the Seminoles in Florida. Twenty years would pass before the recommendation came to fruition.[67] Meanwhile, in 1914 the FBC passed a resolution "protesting the expropriation of Indian lands by the State of Florida and asking that the land be given back to the Seminoles for a home." Two years later the state government heeded that appeal, and "the Federal government gave additional land."[68]

Early in 1934, Rev. Willie King, an Oklahoma Seminole, began his efforts to reach the 600-700 Seminoles living in south Florida. Through "slow and tedious" work, King built trust among the Indians and "made a place for himself in the hearts of his people." King quickly won the respect and love

Seminole Baptist Woman

of white Christians who rallied to the Indian mission. The Miami Association in 1935 secured a five-acre grant from the state and placed on it a "modest residence" for King's family. Miami Association WMUs furnished the home. The Miami women also voted to support another missionary to the Seminoles. "We are praying," said state chairman, Mrs. W. F. Brown, that "this personal service will be the means of more Indians being saved."[69] Rev. Amos Marks answered the call "as a missionary to the Seminoles in the Okeechobee section."[70]

The March 5, 1936, edition of the *Witness* carried a plea from the Miami Association:

> A crisis in the Baptist Seminole Mission on the reservation in Broward County west of Dania has arisen in which the help of all Florida Baptists is urged. It has become necessary to erect a meeting house for the Indians. . . . The churches of this association are contributing to the cost of the meeting house, but they need help.
>
> An Indian Baptist Church will be organized upon completion of the building with fifteen charter members, the fruit of Willie King's ministry.

Help came. When the church house stood completed, Willie King's converts constituted the first Indian Baptist church in Florida. Many Oklahoma Indians attended the dedication, and Miami WMU members "took food for a big spread." The next year, Miami Division women gave $529.93 to Indian work, while paying Amos Marks' salary.[71]

Appearances by King on the programs of the summer assemblies, as well as Florida Baptist Convention and WMU annual meetings, became the norm. In 1940 the Convention and WMU met jointly in the Lakeland city auditorium for a missions night directed by WMU. Rev. H. S. Inabnit, Indian River Association missionary at large, introduced King and a group of Seminoles from the Brighton Reservation. King read scripture and prayed "in his native tongue." After Richard Osceola, "a third generation descendant of the famous chieftain," spoke briefly, four Indian boys sang "America."[72] The spring of 1940 had brought another call for help. "Wanted—$1.00," a poem appearing on the WMU page of the May 23 *Witness,* requested one dollar from "each W.M.U. all over the state" to repair the roof and put screens on Willie King's house. Also in 1940, Louise Smith visited the Brighton Reservation to assess the needs which WMU could address. One of the projects she encouraged annually was the sending of gifts for the Seminole Christmas tree.[73]

In April 1942, as the Coast Guard patrolled against German U-boats, the government ordered "blackouts" and "dimouts" along Florida's east coast. Night rides along Highway 1 in public buses with lights dimmed became fearful adventures for WMU staff. Gasoline rationing interrupted travel routines, but the government granted exceptions for religious work, allowing Convention employees, including WMU, to continue some automobile travel.[74] Few Baptist women could obtain an exemption; yet attendance at meetings held up fairly well, and the women grew adept at "making do." Mrs. Ira D. S. Knight, Miami Division president, whose territory felt keenly the brunt of the restrictions but continued the ministry to Seminole Indians, commented: "We are grateful that there has been no 'blackout' or 'dimout' of God's love and care and that there has been some evidence on our part of love and loyalty to the Master's Cause."

In 1942 Smith again recorded a visit with the Seminoles. By that time she was acquainted with Billie Bowlegs, Susie Tiger, and other Indians who worked with Willie King. "After salutations," Smith wrote, "Susie Tiger, the oldest woman in the camp, stepped forward with a package neatly tied in a newspaper. Mr. King interpreted her words of love and appreciation as she presented the gift," a lovely multicolored Indian dress. Smith suggested that WMU members could furnish gas for King's car and write him encouraging letters, as well as send boxes of gifts for Christmas distribution.[75]

The opening session of the 1943 annual meeting in Jacksonville focused on the American Indian. "Behind the rostrum in the First Baptist Church was a colorful portrait of an American Indian, so realistic in appearance that some of those in the well-filled auditorium later declared they had seen the Indian move!" Mr. Aaron Hancock, a Choctaw Indian serving in Oklahoma, spoke. Several ushers wore bright Seminole dresses.[76] Later that year, Florida Baptists brought a new Indian couple, Rev. and Mrs. Stanley Smith from Oklahoma, to work with Rev. and Mrs. King. With the Kings and Rev. Smith, the WMU secretary in October visited Brighton Reservation to express her love and care for the last time before leaving Florida.[77]

A South American Tour

The fourth of Smith's major emphases actually occurred in 1943, but was rooted in a 1939 trip to South America. "Believing it God's will" for her life, Smith had asked for a leave of absence to make an extended tour of Southern Baptist mission stations in several Latin American countries. Her traveling companion was Mrs. George McWilliams, president of Missouri WMU, with whom she had also made her European pilgrimage five years earlier. After attending the Baptist World Alliance Congress in Atlanta, they traveled to New York, sailing on August 4 and expecting to return by the end of October.[78] Unforeseen circumstances—or the hand of God—took them to Mendoza, Argentina, a stop they had not planned. Delayed four days in Mendoza, the ladies visited the Godoy Cruz area where Florida's first foreign missionary, Frank Fowler, and his wife Daisy had served from 1918 until his death in 1933.

Dr. and Mrs. Frank Fowler in the courtyard of their residence in Mendoza, Argentina.

When the cable announcing Dr. Fowler's sudden death "flashed across the Caribbean," the news had shocked and saddened Florida Baptists. The circumstances made his loss seem even more poignant. While Mrs. Fowler was hospitalized in Buenos Aires with "severe crippling rheumatoid arthritis," Dr. Fowler became ill and required surgery. He entered the same hospital. Although he made excellent progress initially, a blood clot took his life. The Fowlers' older son and daughter were in the States, leaving only Franklin, a teenager, to assist his mother through that traumatic situation. Dr. Fowler was buried in the British Cemetery in Buenos Aires.[79] Heavy expenses prevented Mrs. Fowler from immediately purchasing a gravestone, but a 1933 Florida WMU Christmas gift of $6.35 helped her appropriately mark her "dear husband's" grave.[80]

When Smith left Mendoza, she carried both a fragment of adobe brick, made of mud and straw, and a burden for the completely inadequate adobe building of the Godoy Cruz church, which was closely identified with the Fowlers' mission service.[81] Over the next three years as she shared her overseas experiences in Florida meetings, at Ridgecrest Foreign Missions week, in *Commission* magazine, and in WMU publications, Smith experienced a growing vision for a bold project. But the time was not yet right.

During Smith's four-month absence for the South American tour, Theo Thomas, Susan Adams, and office secretary Helen Wilson, along with state president Mrs. Robert Walden, had handled the work admirably. The ensuing days brought a complete turnover in that group. By the time of Smith's delayed return, Thomas had married and gone to Kentucky. After managing the office work for fifteen years, Wilson resigned in July 1940.[82] In September Adams accepted the position of Oklahoma WMU young people's secretary and two months later married William Carden of Oklahoma City.[83] Mrs. Walden completed her presidential term in January 1941.

Replacing those valued leaders while maintaining effective work required the cooperation of all the state officers and especially the Executive Committee. Louise Smith emphasized the importance of every faithful servant: "Woman's Missionary Union is totally dependent on the faithfulness of its membership. . . . We are grateful for the host of women who have unfailingly kept at this task of missionary endeavor."[84] Mary Wilson, from Bagdad, Florida, started the replacement process. After volunteering for the month of August, in September 1940 she officially undertook the field work. Like Theo Thomas, she quickly won the women's loyalty as she traveled in the rural areas, sparking new commitments to the cause of missions. After a year with no permanent replacement for Helen Wilson, in 1941 Jo Withauer took up Wilson's tradition as faithful, efficient office worker. On November 1, 1940, Elsie Renfroe began her tour as young people's secretary.

That Thy Way May Be Known

The Executive Committee had moved quickly to employ Renfroe, a WMUTS graduate. Renfroe had been active in Florida WMU since she moved to the state as a nine-year-old GA and joined First Baptist Church, Tallahassee. An early encounter with Louise Smith foreshadowed the new job. Elsie recalled:

> In January 1933, when I was a high school sophomore, Louise Smith filled in for a few weeks as BSU secretary at FSCW.[85] Somehow my mother got the idea that Miss Smith was apprehensive about staying alone in the student house, so Mother sent me out to spend a few nights with her. Her beautiful Christian spirit and her enthusiasm for missions shaped my life from then on.[86]

As a young college freshman in 1935, Renfroe represented the state at the YWA Stewardship Declamation contest at Ridgecrest. As an older FSCW student, she appealed for the cooperation of WMU in establishing a student building at the college.[87] When the invitation to join the WMU staff came, "it seemed to me that it was the work God had been preparing me to do," she said.

Even before she moved from Tallahassee to Jacksonville, Renfroe traveled with other WMU leaders to numerous associational meetings, where she met many "wonderful WMU ladies and young people throughout the state." Psalm 67:2, *that thy way may be known upon the earth, thy saving health among all nations,* provided the devotional text for each meeting. "That Psalm," she reflected, "repeated over and over from Pensacola to Key West, set the tone and the purpose for my service in Florida."

Knowing the value of well-trained youth organization counselors, Renfroe provided leadership courses in 13 of the 35 associations and offered a parallel correspondence course. She continued YWA house parties in several different locations and each year took a large contingent of Florida girls to YWA Conference at Ridgecrest. In 1941, 48 girls each paid $26.60 to cover all their conference expenses including the chartered Greyhound bus. During that summer, 25 association and local camps provided missions education and recreation for 1,165 young people, with the heartening result of 95 professions of faith.[88]

When Renfroe had been on staff only six months, a major change in Florida Baptist leadership occurred. Declining health forced Dr. C. M. Brittain to resign in May 1941. His leadership as executive secretary and treasurer of the State Board of Missions had spanned the pre-depression boom, the struggle to survive the Depression, and the movement of the nation toward another world war. Throughout his tenure, he had befriended and encouraged WMU. His successor, Dr. C. H. Bolton, also walked that path. Florida women delighted in welcoming the Boltons back after his two years with the Relief and Annuity Board in Dallas, Texas. During her husband's previous 12-year pastorate of First Baptist Church, West Palm Beach, Mrs. Bolton had held several state WMU offices. By the end of the year, she was sharing her expertise as a member of the WMU Executive Committee.[89]

Mary Wilson's resignation in April 1942 to marry Rev. Willard Brown was the last staff change to occur during Smith's leadership. In her annual report, Smith commented about losing two field workers, Wilson and Theo Thomas, so quickly to marriage and asked: "Do you suppose they conclude that being a pastor's assistant is more important than a traveling job?" Smith herself also dealt with such questions. Whenever she and David Boyd were both in town, they managed to find moments to spend together. In those special encounters Boyd began talking of marriage. In Smith's mind, only God knew the answer.

Decisions, Decisions

Seeking a replacement for Mary Wilson, Smith visited Miami to interview Elizabeth Provence, director of the Miami Good Will Center. After talking with Provence about the job, Smith suggested they see a movie, a romance. In the dark theater, Provence contemplated becoming the next WMU field worker. The executive secretary contemplated her own pressing romance. As the movie ended Smith still had not decided to accept the engagement ring. At the train station, however, Provence told Smith that she had decided to accept the job.[90] On January 1, 1943, the newest staff member began her work.

On Track for Missions

When Elizabeth Provence moved from Miami to Jacksonville, she had hardly had time to catch her breath before Louise Smith sent her to the other

Elizabeth Provence
1943-1960

side of the state to teach mission study classes. Not being a "hat person" but now living in the hat world of WMU, Provence initiated a "serious conversation" with Smith on the subject. "Do I have to wear a hat all the way across north Florida?" she asked.

"Yes, you'd better wear one," Smith advised.

After a train ride to Pensacola, Provence started back east, visiting churches in every county seat town along the railway and teaching the 1943 Home Mission study book. She managed the hat in Pensacola, but when she left Milton, she forgot it. At her next stop, she just said, "I left my hat in Milton so I don't have one with me." The women readily accepted that circumstance, and she repeated the story all the way back to Jacksonville. "Nobody seemed upset by the fact that I didn't have a hat," Provence recalled, "so I never again wore a hat in Florida."[91]

After a session in Crestview she exited the train at Defuniak Springs, because she thought each day she was to move to the next county. When no one met her, she called the person who was to be her hostess. "Oh, you're supposed to be here tomorrow," she said. Sure enough, the schedule Smith had worked out said Bonifay before Defuniak Springs. After a call to explain the situation to her Bonifay hostess, she waited for a night train traveling east. In Provence's words,

> It was cold as Christmas, and there was a roaring fire going in a big pot-bellied stove. They had just painted the interior of the Defuniak station. I'd stay inside until the heat and the paint fumes drove me out, then I'd go outside and walk up and down until I was frozen, go inside to get thawed out, go outside so I could breathe. The result was that I caught a really bad cold.
>
> By the time I had taught the Bonifay class, returned to Defuniak, and taught there, I was really sick. Mercy, I did long to be at home in my own bed, but I was to spend the weekend there. My hostess put me to bed, fed me soup, and took care of me. By Monday I was able to function again, and I worked my way back to Jacksonville.

From the Soles of Their Feet . . .

Elizabeth "Lib" Provence learned to survive almost every imaginable crisis during her 18 years with Florida WMU. And well she should, for she was born with a WMU pedigree that should have prepared her for any situation. Her mother, she said,

> was WMU from the soles of her feet to the top of her head. Before her marriage she worked as a missionary to the Bohemians living in and around her

home town of Taylor, Texas. She was president of WMU in her church, her county, and her district, and on the state council. She was a volunteer state young people's leader in Texas before they had [paid] state young people's leaders. When my father was president of a small Baptist college in New Mexico, she was elected New Mexico state WMU president and also served on the Board of WMU, SBC.

Lib's grandfather, Dr. S. M. Provence, was pastor in Madison, Florida, before the Civil War. After the war, the State Board of Missions "asked him to go to Tallahassee, find the Baptists that were there, and reorganize the church." He walked his family, including Lib's father, from Madison to Tallahassee, stopping for the night in a farm home. Her father, who before his marriage had a brief mission tour in China, eventually became the first business manager of Baylor University, Waco, Texas.

After receiving a degree in journalism from the Texas State College for Women, Provence attended the WMUTS, graduating in 1939 at the age of 22. Her ambition had been to go to China as a missionary, but Foreign Mission Board policy would not allow appointment of an unmarried woman until she reached the age of 25. "I thought I'd be just as good a missionary as my classmates who were marrying and receiving appointment," she said in retrospect, "but I lived to be grateful they wouldn't send me. Several of those girls ended up in a Japanese concentration camp in the Philippines. In fact, the husband of one of them, Rufus Gray from Florida, died there."

Provence turned instead to a job in Kansas City, but a destiny in Florida awaited her. On the recommendation of her WMUTS prayer partner, Provence, "sight unseen," was hired as director of the Miami Good Will Center. And there Louise Smith found her.

The Mendoza Love Project

As Louise Smith coped with the numerous staff changes, the plight of the Godoy Cruz church remained in her thoughts. Could the women, who were already committed to eradicating the denomination's debts, support another major project. As the "Debt-free in '43" campaign concluded, Smith knew that the right time had come. Through correspondence, she had already laid an appropriate foundation with the FMB.[92] She discussed her proposal with Mrs. J. L. Rosser, state Stewardship chairman, and with the Executive Board.

PROPOSED BUILDING

With much prayer, but little fanfare, Smith presented her recommendation as part of the "Plan of Work for 1943." Number 10 under "Tithes and Offerings" stated:

> That we raise a minimum of $15,000 for the erection of a church in Mendoza, Argentina, in memory of Florida's first foreign missionary, Dr. Frank Fowler. This amount to be apportioned to the societies.

Explaining the proposal, Smith described the poorly located adobe structure, which also housed a good will center and quarters for the caretaker. She perceived the building as a tragic hindrance to God's work in Mendoza, where elaborate and beautiful Catholic churches beckoned the people in every section of the city.[93] Riding the wave of their previous financial successes, Florida WMU responded positively to the new venture. Limited opposition arose, but not from the women. "One or two brethren are afraid that it will interfere with the Co-operative Program," Smith wrote Dr. Maddry, "but they should realize from the past few years that we have not only increased our special offerings but the Co-operative Program gifts as well."[94]

God's timing brought two experienced state leaders to significant roles for the campaign. When Mrs. Lee could not accept renomination, 1943 annual meeting delegates elected as the new president Evelyn Rosser, whose husband, Dr. J. L. Rosser, was pastor of Ancient City Church in St. Augustine. He had been pastor of her home church, First Baptist of Selma, Alabama, when they married in 1909. After a 20-year pastorate in Bristol, Virginia, in 1932 the Rossers moved to Jacksonville at the call of Riverside Baptist

Mrs. J. L. Rosser
1943-1948

Church. Mrs. Rosser immediately became active in Florida WMU and over the intervening years held several different offices. Though they remained in Florida only 16 years, both Dr. and Mrs. Rosser made significant contributions on the state level, she as WMU president and he as Florida Baptist Convention historian. After her presidency ended in 1948, the Rossers retired and returned to Bristol.[95]

In Mrs. Rosser's place as state Stewardship chairman, the women elected Mrs. R. L. Lassiter, who was just completing a year as state White Cross chairman. She had led Florida WMU to send over $3,800 to purchase bandages and supplies for medical ministry in Kweilen, China. Although Japanese bombs had destroyed the Kweilen hospital and forced the departure of SBC missionaries, the Florida funds enabled native workers to continue limited treatment in four medical clinics.[96] Lassiter, Rosser, and Smith formed a powerful triumvirate for prayer and action, with Lassiter taking the lead.

Announcements and persuasive articles from Lassiter appeared almost weekly in the *Witness*. She requested that WMU members "pray daily for the success of our project and that God's Name be glorified in it all." She wrote suggestions for observing a "special day of prayer" on May 10 and "a splendid program" for presentation on June 16, designated as the day to receive the special love offering. Lassiter included young people's auxiliaries in all the planning. A $3,000 youth goal was added to the $15,000 women's goal.[97]

The Mendoza project took the spotlight at the DeLand Assembly in early June. While food and gas rationing and military use of Stetson space had required that registrations stop at 600, the attendance included a large, "most responsive" group of intermediates and young people. They were deeply touched by "an air mail special delivery letter" from Dr. and Mrs. G. Q. Holland of Miami. The letter brought a check for $100, "the savings of their 12-year-old son Freddie, who died just a week before the assembly." Freddie, whose mother was the WMU state Mission Study chairman, had recently acknowledged a sense of calling to medical missions in South America. Assembly participants gave $300 for the Mendoza project.[98]

The first "Mendoza Honor Roll" appeared on the *Witness* WMU page on July 8. Two associations, Lake County and Northeast Florida, had already reached their goals. Lake County youth had also met their goal. Week after week the list of contributing organizations appeared and the offering amounts climbed. By December 31, 1943, Florida WMU members had more than justified Smith's faith in them. Not only had they given $18,483.03 for the Godoy Cruz church, but also they had increased CP giving by almost $20,000 and surpassed each mission offering goal by several thousand dollars.

Gathering the funds only began the lengthy journey toward a new building for the Godoy Cruz church. Over the next five years, heavy correspondence between Florida WMU leaders and the Foreign Mission Board dealt with the progress of the project and the logistics of handling the money. The FMB experienced a great deal of confusion over the actual amount of money given because some money went directly to Argentina, some went to the FMB, some was designated as part of Lottie Moon Offering "over-and-above" gifts, and some was mistakenly counted as both Lottie Moon offering and a special love gift. Despite conflicting records and confusing letters, the correspondence was always cordial, respectfully seeking clarifications and demonstrating a meticulous concern for accountability to the last penny.[99]

Nine years had passed before Louise Smith's 1939 vision became reality in 1948. A beautiful stone edifice stood on the main avenue in Mendoza's Godoy Cruz section. Missionaries and church members planned an elaborate dedication ceremony, inviting government officials, local dignitaries, and leaders of the Argentine Baptist Convention. Having recently settled in Paraguay as a missionary doctor, Franklin Fowler, with his wife Dorcas and young baby, traveled to Mendoza to represent all his father's family at the "inauguration." The family had given $175 "for pulpit furnishings." The completion of the building represented a tremendous victory for Florida WMU and for the Baptists of Mendoza. For Franklin Fowler, the victory

came in the words of an elderly Argentine woman: "Franklin, there have been other missionaries that have come. They've started churches and built buildings; they've come and gone. But your father loved us." Throughout the whole Mendoza area, Frank J. Fowler was remembered as "the missionary that loved."[100]

An additional result of the Mendoza project carried Florida WMU's influence beyond expectations. With $2,000 left over from the new Godoy Cruz building, plus some Lottie Moon funds and the members' savings, the FMB provided a modest building for a small struggling congregation in Villa Atuel, a little town about fifty miles from Mendoza.[101] With the Godoy Cruz church still a strong Christian force in 1994, the influence of faithful service by Florida women continued to multiply.

Godoy Cruz Baptist Church in Mendoza, Argentina, built with Florida WMU contributions in honor of missionary Frank J. Fowler.

Throughout 1943, as she promoted the "love project" for Mendoza, brought membership lists up to date, and instituted improved methods for WMU work, Louise Smith wrestled with the question of marriage. Feeling that she "had to know that it was not my own selfish desire but God's will for my life," she prayed much over the matter.[102] She also made clear to Boyd that they would marry only if she could continue tithing, writing for WMU, SBC, and participating in WMU work whenever possible. He readily agreed to all stipulations. Finally she said yes. When the two decided to drive to Covington, Kentucky, to wed, she told no one except Elsie Renfroe. Smith left notes to all the associational WMU presidents telling them of her marriage, but she instructed Renfroe not to mail the notes until she received a call confirming that the wedding had taken place. Elizabeth Provence learned of the elopement only when an associational president told her. The whole state got the message when the October 7 WMU *Witness* page carried the wedding announcement.

In the remaining five weeks before she left Florida, Mrs. Boyd brought her work to conclusion. She visited the Seminoles at Brighton Reservation and accepted a trusteeship at Florida Normal and Industrial Memorial College. A check of the books showed that Florida WMU had given over $40,000 to achieve SBC freedom from debt and was approaching the $18,000 goal for the Mendoza project. She would carry lifelong joy in her four special areas of achievement.

Her last activity in office was a first for Florida WMU. The long-awaited state Leaders Conference, held in Jacksonville November 9-11, created an appropriate farewell occasion. At a special luncheon during the conference, Mrs. J. E. Empie, chairman of the Executive Committee, represented many who paid tribute to the departing secretary:

> With courage, tolerance, and cooperation, faithfully, prayerfully, humbly, with no count of personal cost, has this fine young woman led us in building a state Woman's Missionary Union of broad scope. . . . Lavishly the seed was sown in all seasons, in all weathers, and rich is the harvest.[103]

Louise and David Boyd moved to Mansfield, Ohio, then to Charlotte, North Carolina, and finally to Atlanta. As she had planned, she continued to write for WMU publications. So frequently did Juliette Mather use her friend's articles that she assigned different bylines to them—"Sally O'Neal" (the name of Louise's grandmother), "Mrs. David Boyd," and "Louise Smith Boyd." Boyd also continued her active role in WMU, serving terms as WMUTS trustee and vice-president of Georgia WMU. Until his death in 1975, her husband fully supported her many involvements in mission work.

At the Centennial Annual Session in 1994, Mrs. Boyd participated, to the delight of the audience, in a panel of former Florida WMU executives. Her farewell statement in 1943 predicted her joy in returning to Jacksonville: "My interest in missions, and more particularly missions in Florida, will never end."

AN INTERVAL

1944

*W*hen Louise Smith Boyd resigned her position in November 1943, the WMU Executive Committee immediately appointed three of its members "to find out and to recommend, as early as possible, a successor to our secretary."[104] Until a new leader came, the committee placed responsibility in Elsie Renfroe's capable hands. For a year Renfroe carried the work of executive secretary as well as young people's secretary. Elizabeth Provence helped to shoulder the extra load in the field; Jo Withauer, in the office.

The immediate challenge was the 50th anniversary celebration of Florida WMU, scheduled for the First Baptist Church of Bradenton in January 1944. Cooperative efforts of the Executive Committee, staff, and local arrangements committee created effective sessions based on the Golden Jubilee theme.[105] The printed program, addresses, and decorations carried out the "golden motif." Opening each session with "Golden Incense of Prayer and Praise," Susan Adams Carden from Oklahoma City led the women "to mountain tops of inspiration and worship." As officers gave their 1943 reports and presented the Plan of Work for 1944, each added a link to "a Golden Chain reaching from a map of Florida to a world globe." Three women—Mrs. J. A. Lamb and Mrs. J. W. Willis, both of Palmetto, and Mrs. Lydia Hilley, Fort Meade—were recognized for 50 years of Florida WMU membership. Mrs. Hilley had welcomed delegates to the 1894 founding session in Plant City.[106]

Miss Elsie Renfroe
1940-1945

Young people helped to present "Golden Memories," a pageant depicting the history of Florida WMU. As an RA carrying a large American flag entered the auditorium, he touched a fuse box with the flag pole's metal tip, plunging the whole church into darkness just as the production began. The audience sat in stunned silence, some fearing an enemy attack, until men of the church found and corrected the problem. Despite the untimely interruption, the pageant won high praise from the audience.[107]

Among several "golden actions" in business session, the women voted to undertake a new "love project" for 1944. Dazzled by the success of their Mendoza efforts, they eagerly approved the raising of $10,000 for a boys' high school in the Niger Delta, Nigeria. They also made several significant changes in the WMU constitution by eliminating all divisional officers, adding a children's home chairman to the state officers, and deleting a reference to field workers. The historian was instructed to write an annual history each year. Kathleen Mallory, a regular Florida visitor, gave the closing address with "golden thoughts" on the topic "That the Generation to Come Might Know."

Light for Darkness in Africa

Missionary Louise Doyle Brantley, from Tallahassee, had traveled the state during much of 1943, telling of the work she and her husband Maurice were doing among the people of eastern Nigeria. Separate high schools for boys and girls ranked high among the needs of that area. The Florida WMU idea of building a boys' high school in the Niger Delta came in response to her effective presentations.[108] Mrs. Brantley's letter to Dr. George W. Sadler, Foreign Mission Board secretary for Africa, Europe, and the Near East, about the possibility of such a project, brought only a qualified "yes." Sadler reminded her that the FMB already had a girls' high school in the same area on its agenda and had been putting aside funds "from the Lottie Moon Over-and-Above" in preparation. He and Dr. Maddry preferred to pursue that undertaking first, he indicated, though they approved the concept of a boys' school. "Of course," concluded Sadler, "if some individual or some group insisted on making a contribution to this specific object, neither you nor we should decline such an offer."[109] Florida WMU must have "insisted."

With the successful Mendoza project in the record book, efforts to raise money for the boys' school took the character more of routine business than of an intense campaign. An additional $2,000 goal for youth raised the target to $12,000. Because Christian education would help to bring light and hope to the boys attending the school, promotion of the project focused on the theme "Light for Darkness." Efforts similar to the past year's publicity, prayer emphasis, and special program again motivated women and youth to respond enthusiastically. Affection for the Brantleys gave added incentive. As contributions gradually accumulated, Indian River Association women reached their apportionment and gained the WMS Honor Roll first. Youth from Lake County and Beulah Associations earned the first Young People's Honor Roll slots.[110] At the end of 1944, Mrs. Lassiter could report that both women and youth had surpassed their goals for the second "love project," giving a total of $14,711.90. She also noted: "Rev. Maurice Brantley, Supervisor of Education of the Nigerian Mission, assures us that every cent of this can be used profitably and that the Baptists of the Niger Delta are deeply grateful for our interest and love."[111]

Because of wartime restrictions, delays occurred in starting the project, but in 1949 the school opened to its first class. In May 1952, Brantley wired FMB leaders in Miami for the annual SBC meeting:

> GREETINGS TO CONVENTION FROM BAPTIST HIGH SCHOOL P[ORT] HARCOURT. SCHOOL RECEIVED GOVERNMENT RECOGNITION AND APPROVAL YESTERDAY.

Boys' Baptist High School in Port Harcourt, Nigeria. The building on left was gift of Florida WMU.

A remarkable achievement in only three years![112]

After the Biafran war in the late 1960s, the Nigerian government took over the school, but at the insistence of former students, allowed it to retain the name Baptist High School. The principal continued to be a Nigerian Baptist. In recent years, female students were allowed to attend upper grades. Many of the doctors, lawyers, civil servants, and other professionals in Nigeria in 1994 were graduates of the school.[113]

A Golden Opportunity

Money was certainly not the only means by which Florida WMU members could express their love of God and commitment to extend His kingdom. Prayer remained a basis for all their work. Study of world missions and the missionary message of the Bible was the key to engaging both women and youth in support of missions—"to know is to do." What the women had known as "personal service" became "community missions" in 1942, putting renewed emphasis on soul-winning and prompting more urgent efforts to reach service men with the gospel before they embarked overseas.

On the other hand, projects involving contributions, large or small, continually gave concrete evidence of WMU's effective stewardship education. A plea for gifts early in 1944 also illustrated the women's ability to squeeze every drop of impact out of a theme. Billed as "a *golden opportunity* for Florida Baptists," Willie King's desperate need of a new car gave occasion to "share in the work among our Seminole friends." Three or four articles in the *Witness* brought results. Soon there appeared on the WMU page an announcement that a 1939 Chevrolet "in excellent condition" had replaced King's "faithful Model 'A' Ford."[114]

An interval in WMU life became an interval in Florida Convention life as well when Dr. Bolton resigned to become pastor of Riverside Church, Miami. In only three years he had led the Convention to exceptional achievement in paying off all debts, beginning a Million Dollar Campaign for Stetson University, and instituting a program of rural and city missions.[115] Elsie Renfroe commended him as "friend, counselor, co-worker." Mrs. Rosser, WMU state president, declared: "He has shown himself so efficient generally, so genial in spirit, and so sympathetic in attitude toward the work of Woman's Missionary Union, that our organization sincerely regrets his decision to relinquish the post."[116] During the remainder of the year, Dr. Homer Lindsey, Sr., State Board of Missions president, acted as interim executive secretary of the Board.

A year of problems—"gas shortage, food shortage, leadership shortage"[117]—called for ingenuity from the WMU staff. While new members joined existing auxiliaries, Renfroe bemoaned the fact that of the more than 800 Baptist churches in Florida, over half had no organization for youth missions education. Although many faithful counselors persisted in youth work, others offered "an abundance of excuses and 'good reasons' for abandoning the task." Yet as the summer months passed, she could celebrate the results of 25 associational camps for GAs, RAs, and YWAs. Over 1,200 young people earned 1,347 mission study awards, 285 dedicated their lives for special Christian service, and 82 made professions of faith. The DeLand Assembly again filled its 600 spaces and touched those lives for missions. Growth in commitment to missions and gifts through the Cooperative Program also resulted from the 64 schools of missions organized by Renfroe and held in local churches during the year. Among those who led in camps, assemblies, and schools of missions were missionaries Mrs. M. E. Brantley and Rev. Charles Knight, Nigeria; Mrs. Cecil Moore, Chile; and Miss Rose Marlowe, China, as well as Mr. Edward Galloway, summer RA worker.[118]

As mothers continued to wave goodbye to their soldier "boys," Florida WMU realized as never before "the importance of capturing the youth of our state for Christ." A "special emphasis" on Royal Ambassadors brought the first male staff member of WMU, SBC, Royal Ambassador director J. Ivloy Bishop, to Florida for a series of five "fellowship suppers." Galloway, Florida's first RA field worker, spent the summer organizing new chapters, teaching counselors' courses, and working in camps. Camp work was never dull. At an RA camp in the Tampa Bay Association, a crowd of boys ran to a counselor, shouting that a snake had bitten one of the campers. The counselor quickly took him to the camp nurse. As she worked with his hand, cleaning it so that she could see the wound, she asked, "Do you know what kind of snake it was? What did it look like?" The patient brought his other hand around and said, "Here it is!" He had held the snake in his other hand the whole time. Before returning to Southern Seminary, Galloway took three Florida RAs to the first Young Men's Mission Conference at Ridgecrest.[119]

Mutual Trust, Shared Commitments

As Florida WMU leaders looked forward to the coming of a new executive secretary, they apparently wanted to have everything in order for the person to whom God would lead them. In September 1944, they petitioned the Executive Committee of the State Board of Missions "for a reaffirmation of the existing basis of co-operation between the Union and the State Mission Board."[120] What was that basis? How had that basis worked with the passage of time?

Although Florida WMU had declared an auxiliary relationship in 1894, until November 1946, SBM reports and Convention budgets routinely referred to WMU as a "department" of the Convention. Such references, rather than implying control, signified an inclusive spirit, shared commitments, and mutual trust. Dr. Brittain, as had State Board executive secretaries preceding him, often included "strong W.M.U. organizations in every church" in his Convention objectives for the coming year.[121]

Like Florida WMU, the Florida Baptist Convention had greatly enlarged its scope and organizational structure in the last two decades. Brotherhood and Student Work Departments were added. The Baptist Training Union Department separated from the Sunday School Department. Student Union, Stewardship-Promotion, and Christian Education Departments developed. As the number of Baptists grew and the areas of work expanded, Convention leadership continued to work cordially with the WMU staff.[122]

WMU staff members were considered employees of the Convention, and for a number of years the State Board of Missions had voted on the WMU secretary (actually approving what the women had already done), along with other paid Convention workers. At the Florida Baptist Convention meeting in January 1937, Dr. Brittain moved to amend the Convention constitution to provide for general Convention elections of both WMU and Brotherhood secretaries. Though not stated, his reason may have been to place the WMU secretary and the new Brotherhood Department secretary on the same public footing. Messengers affirmed the change.[123]

Partners in the Lord's Business

A key element in the relationship between WMU and the Florida Baptist Convention had always been money. In the beginning, WMU contributions designated for state missions provided the funds for the WMU budget. With the exception of the years 1911-1920, money from WMU members went straight to the Convention treasurer, with WMU origin indicated; credit was given to WMU on the basis of information provided.[124] From Dr. W. N. Chaudoin on, succeeding executive secretaries of the Convention quickly understood that, while WMU expenses might occasionally exceed those state missions contributions, WMU gifts to all missions causes far surpassed any expense to the Convention.

After the Cooperative Program (CP) structures were in place, WMU budget money came from CP contributions. The State Board of Missions annually set the percentages for division of CP income between Florida work, directed by the SBM, and Southern Baptist Convention causes, directed by the Executive Committee in Nashville. The struggle to remove state Convention debts in 1941 moved the original 55/45 percent split to 65 percent for Florida and 35 percent for the SBC, with a promise to work toward a 50/50 division.[125] Because the work of WMU was considered essential in promoting CP giving and mission offerings, WMU budget money was deducted *before* CP funds were divided.[126]

In summary, while Florida WMU chose its own staff and planned its own work, the Florida Union also submitted its budget to the State Board of Missions and received its operating money through the Convention. The SBM, however, did not always adopt the WMU budget precisely as the women had proposed it.[127] Although the women's organization held auxiliary status, records through the years show that Florida Convention leadership continued to view WMU as an integral part of Convention work and a partner in the Lord's business.

The responses of Convention leadership at the coming of the new WMU executive secretary demonstrated that attitude. In the October 12 *Witness*, the nominating committee placed the long-awaited announcement: Miss Josephine Jones would soon become Florida WMU's new executive secretary. Both Dr. Lindsey, State Board of Missions president, and Dr. Thomas Hansen, Florida Baptist Convention president, spoke for their organizations.[128] Dr. Lindsey said:

> I wish to join with the Florida Baptist Woman's Missionary Union in welcoming Miss Josephine Jones to our State. Nowhere will you find a more delightful fellowship of Christian people. We have no division in our midst. We have one of the most challenging opportunities to be found, and we trust that our State Mission program is one to match our opportunities.
>
> We trust that your stay with us will be a long one. From the very deep of our hearts we say, "Welcome."

From Dr. Hansen came other affirming words:

> I am delighted to welcome to our great State Miss Josephine Jones as W.M.U. Executive Secretary. We believe that Miss Jones has come into this part of God's Kingdom for "such an hour as this."
>
> Florida Baptists stand upon the threshold of unparalleled Kingdom undertakings; and to their accomplishment Miss Jones, through the W.M.U. department, will make a telling contribution.
>
> Our prayer is that God shall crown her labors with rich spiritual fruitage in the Gospel.[129]

Over the next 23 years, God would answer that prayer in abundance.

Lasting Legacies

1944 – 1967

"... serve the Lord your God with all your heart and with all your soul."
Deuteronomy 10:12

December 1943

The Lord told me that if I married David, you'd take my place in Florida," Louise Smith Boyd announced to her long-time friend, Josephine Jones.

Well, the Lord hasn't told me I'm supposed to go to Florida. I've been executive secretary in Illinois only a little over a year, and I'm not going to leave Illinois and go to Florida just because the Lord told you to get married," Jones responded firmly.

Josephine Jones
1944-1967

"Then I guess Florida will just have to wait for you," insisted Boyd. And she "doubled her prayer life over getting Jo from Illinois to Florida."[1]

When the nominating committee and Mrs. J. L. Rosser, state president, began the task of finding a new executive secretary for Florida WMU, the first person they considered was Josephine Jones. With high recommendations from Boyd and Elsie Renfroe, and the confidence which comes from prayerfully seeking the Lord's will, they invited Jones to direct Florida WMU.

Had the offer come before Jones left her job as Kentucky WMU young people's secretary, she would have seen it as providential, but feeling obligated to give Illinois WMU her best efforts, she turned down the invitation. As the months passed, the committee remained "active, prayerful, hopeful and confident that the one chosen of the Lord would be found."[2] Patience and faith obtained their reward unexpectedly.

The 1944 annual meeting of Woman's Missionary Union, Auxiliary to Southern Baptist Convention (WMU, SBC) occurred in Oklahoma City in September, rather than at the customary time of the Southern Baptist Convention meeting in May. Once again the war had disrupted normal procedures.[3] Almost nine months had passed since Jones and the committee had last corresponded. In the meantime, Jones continued thinking about the Florida women and remembering Louise's prayers. With more than 2,000 women attending the sessions in the Oklahoma City municipal auditorium, the possibility of a chance meeting between Mrs. Rosser and Josephine Jones was unlikely. Yet the two "ran into" each other. When Jones revealed that she still had Florida on her mind and was "only waiting for final light and leading," Rosser could only marvel at God's goodness.

Soon after the encounter in Oklahoma City, the committee received a telegram from Jones: "I am convinced God wants me to go to Florida." Louise Smith Boyd had known it all along!

Josephine Jones was a native of Lancaster County, Kentucky, where her

Frances Lyon, longtime friend and "family" to Jo Jones, poses on the running board of her assigned vehicle during World War II.

father worked a small farm. As a child, Jo moved into the home of her mother's twin sister and attended school in Danville, but in the summers she would return to the farm. Eventually she made a profession of faith and joined First Baptist Church, Danville. There a generous, missions-minded woman took an interest in Jo and encouraged her to consider attending the WMU Training School (WMUTS) and perhaps pursuing a missionary career. In fact, her mentor helped Jo to attend Centre College and then the WMUTS in Louisville.[4] She began work with Kentucky WMU at about the same time Louise Smith came to Florida. "Miss Smith and Miss Jones" became a familiar pair as they continued their close friendship from the Training School and managed to visit with each other at all kinds of WMU meetings.[5]

Later, while with Kentucky WMU in Louisville, Jones met the Lyon family, neighbors who resided in an apartment house across the street. When Jo's aunt moved to a nursing home, the Lyons invited Jo to live with them. At Jo's move to Illinois, their home and their hearts seemed empty. When Fran Lyon, Jo's contemporary, learned that Jo had accepted a job in Florida, Fran began formulating her own plan. During Christmas holidays 1944, she visited Jo in Jacksonville and applied for a teaching job. Before school began the next September, Fran and her mother moved to Jacksonville, bought a house when wartime conditions made that almost impossible, and again provided Jo Jones with the security of a loving family and a home from which she could continue her ministry.

*T*he "happy announcement" in the *Witness* bore the news: before the end of 1944, Josephine Proctor Jones would become the executive secretary for Florida WMU. "No one has been more highly recommended than Miss Jones," reported the nominating committee, "both as to her lovable character and her efficient work." During Jones' long tenure in Florida, they never doubted "that the right person has found the right place of leadership."[6]

Both realism and hope appeared in Jones' published farewell to 1944:

> The daily paper is filled with screaming headlines telling of new war fronts, increased bombing raids, home town boys who have paid the supreme sacrifice. . . . The radio cries out incessantly with the voices of many commentators, calling attention to the apparent hopelessness of the world situation.
>
> Against the dark background of [that] situation there arises the "Sun of righteousness with healing in His wings." We hear him saying, "If any man would come after Me he must deny himself and take up his cross daily and follow Me . . . whosoever would be great among you must be servant of all."
>
> We learn that the peace we are to know and have is the peace that comes from Christ, that which He promised when He said, "My peace I give unto you."[7]

Those words expressed several themes which would anchor Jones' relationships and her work in the state. For the women of Florida she became healer in relationships, servant model, and peacemaker.

Laborers Together

Dr. John Maguire, former pastor of Calvary Baptist Church, Birmingham, Alabama, had been executive secretary of the State Board of Missions exactly one week when the WMU annual meeting opened in Jacksonville on January 22, 1945. As he mounted the platform to speak, "the audience stood to express loyal cooperation" to the new state leader.[8] Beginning work in Florida at virtually the same time and later retiring in the same year, Jones and Maguire labored together through 23 years of Florida Baptist life. Differences of opinion occasionally strained the relationship, but generally they understood and respected each other, offering mutual support in working toward

Mrs. John Maguire

common goals. Maguire's wife, Clyde, unusually talented and deeply committed, invested herself alongside Jones, giving strong leadership wherever she was needed in Florida WMU.

Crowning a Century

A major emphasis in all denominational plans for 1945 was the Centennial Crusade, marking 100 years since the organizing of the Southern Baptist Convention on May 8, 1845, in Augusta, Georgia. "To complete, celebrate, climax, and crown this century of co-operative service for Christ,"[9] very high goals challenged every phase of Florida Convention and WMU activity, especially in the areas of evangelism and stewardship. Florida Baptists pledged to win 40,000 souls to Christ and to increase Cooperative Program (CP) gifts by $500,000. Including appropriate allocations, WMU targeted a 20 percent increase in almost everything statistical. The Florida Centennial Crusade committee expressed gratitude that "Miss Josephine Jones is here to help every Missionary Society and Circle in Florida to properly emphasize Community Missions this year." Mrs. J. E. Robinson, state Community Missions chairman, challenged the women to "enlist every W.M.U. member to be an evangelist and each member of the auxiliaries to be a Christian and then an evangelist."

A Time for War Drags On

As Jo Jones prepared the WMU *Witness* page each week, she made no mention of the world war that was building to a climax during her first year in Florida. Reports from state chairmen rarely mentioned the combat occurring in both Europe and Asia. Yet the "war effort" did more than touch the lives of Florida women; it pommeled them on every side.

For women the trauma of war took many forms: relatives in constant danger, disrupted family life, and employment outside the home, which was taken in part to keep industry going despite a manpower shortage, or to supplement income for families whose fathers and husbands served in the armed forces. For WMU members, more jobs and more money often translated into larger missions giving; but the pleas for generous mission offerings were echoed by appeals for the purchase of war bonds. They taught their children a double lesson: to give to missions in Sunbeams, GA, and RA, and to fill their savings stamp booklets to buy bonds. Rationing of "everything that tasted good or made life comfortable" required women's resourcefulness in the kitchen, in the clothes closet, and on the road.

Creativity Counts

"The road" held all sorts of challenges for WMU workers. Few could afford personal automobiles; gas rationing also forced more extensive use of trains and buses. On one such trip from Dade City to Jacksonville, Elizabeth Provence faced a travel predicament typical of the war years. Because she needed to be home by the next day, she took a train scheduled to leave Dade City at 11:00 p.m. and arrive in Jacksonville at 6:00 a.m. the next morning. She tried to buy a berth, but none was available. At that time trains were usually "full of troops on the move, service people going home on furlough, or families going to visit those in service." The conductor told her there were no seats in the coach cars and suggested she buy a seat in the club car. She bought the ticket, thinking that she would be "nicely situated in one of those overstuffed club car chairs where I could put my head back and sleep a little bit." When she got to the club car, however, no seats were left except straight chairs like those in a dining room. Provence recalled her solution:

> I knew I was not going to sit in a straight chair from 11:00 until 6:00 in the morning in a dimly lit club car where you couldn't even read because they had the lights out for people who wanted to sleep. I waited until the conductor had checked my ticket and gotten on his way. Then I took some straight chairs and built a little barrier so I wouldn't get stepped on, and I just lay down on the carpeted floor, put my purse under my head for a pillow, covered up with my coat, went to sleep, and didn't wake up until we got to Jacksonville![10]

The Word for the Day: Flexibility

In her gentle and diplomatic way, Josephine Jones gradually placed her seal on Florida WMU. Although she allowed herself time to learn the interests and observe the methods of the women with whom she worked, circum-

stances forced some immediate changes. Wartime travel difficulties often
were the culprit. For example, "the government regulation prohibiting
conventions of fifty or more delegates" required Jones to plan six smaller
conferences in different cities instead of the one large interracial institute
usually held at St. Augustine. Excellent attendance in each city indicated the
pressing need for such training sessions.[11] Once released from wartime
limitations, the interracial institute returned to the campus of Florida Normal
and Industrial Memorial College until 1950. Then the new format called for
smaller groups of Negro women leaders to visit Jacksonville for discussion
of "problems and needs."[12]

The April 12, 1945, *Witness* carried the announcement of another travel
complication: the Sunday School Board had canceled all Ridgecrest summer
conferences because of the "critical condition" of war-time transportation,
including "the necessity for transporting military personnel and materials to
meet the demands of war, and the imperative priority in the transportation of
wounded service men." For the same reason, all state and SBC summer
camps, conventions, and conferences, including SBC and WMU, SBC, annual meetings, were canceled. Once again Florida WMU proved its flexibility
and inventiveness, providing materials for "Y.W.A.-Camp-That-Stayed-at-
Home." Elsie Renfroe encouraged YWAs to get together for several days or
just one evening to "catch the importance of the Centennial celebration." A
number of "Stay-at-Home" camps were reported in the *Witness.*[13]

Even with wartime limitations, Florida's well-developed tradition of local
and associational camps provided missions education, recreation, and inspiration for 2,027 GAs and RAs.[14] Using an allocation from the State Missions
Offering, WMU employed another Southern Baptist Seminary student,
Robert Estes, to work in RA camps and promote RA work. After a successful summer, he challenged Florida Baptists:

> We consider Florida predominantly a missionary Baptist state. Yet of
> the approximately 835 Baptist churches there are only 183 reporting an
> organization for the purpose of training our future man-power along mis-
> sionary lines, meaning that 652 give no missionary training to our boys
> through the Royal Ambassador chapters. It is heartbreaking to think that a
> church could neglect such a vital part of God's program.[15]

And Now Abideth Love

Responsibility for the expansion and growing effectiveness of young people's work over the past five years had belonged to Elsie Renfroe. She had
successfully met every challenge. In the process she had also fallen in love.
When Rev. Charles Knight, missionary to Nigeria, came to Florida to speak
in 1944 summer camps and assemblies, he and Renfroe renewed a casual
acquaintance from their seminary and Training School days. In the meantime, he worked on his doctorate at Southern Seminary and accepted a call as
pastor of the Glasgow, Kentucky, First Baptist Church.[16]

Following in the steps of her mentor, Louise Smith, Renfroe sacrificed her WMU career for marriage. In December 1945, Renfroe presented her resignation to the Executive Board with the news that she and Knight were planning a wedding in January. Elizabeth Provence was soloist, and many other friends from Renfroe's WMU work were present for the ceremony in First Baptist Church, Tallahassee. Florida leaders and youth grieved over their "loss," but rejoiced in the happiness of one who had faithfully served God and Florida WMU.[17]

The Laborers Are Many

In June, July, and August 1945, Provence directed her second crew of summer field workers. The 16 college and WMUTS students worked in 43 rural or small town churches in 17 associations, plus 4 camps. Called "a summer, or Vacation, School of Missions," the week's program in each church combined "the characteristics of a School of Missions, a Bible School and a soul-winning campaign." Provence requested prayer "that people's eyes may be opened to the missionary responsibility that is theirs, that churches may become more loyal denominationally, and that souls may be born into the Kingdom of God."[18]

She probably should have suggested praying for physical stamina in the face of the strenuous schedule. From the intensive efforts, 1,637 mission study awards were earned; over 500 boys and girls, not yet Christians, were taught the plan of salvation; 140 individuals made professions of faith; 169 made rededications; and 58 committed to special Christian service. The work also resulted in 13 new missionary societies or auxiliaries.[19]

VICTORY! . . . and Failure

May 8, 1945, V-E DAY (Victory in Europe), brought great relief to those whose family members fought on the European front, but the war in the Pacific raged on. The detonation of two atomic bombs forced the unconditional surrender of the Japanese forces. Ironically, such enormous power to destroy human life, heretofore unimaginable by civilians, crashed the world scene while Southern Baptists were in the middle of their great Centennial effort to save souls.

Because V-E Day did not come in time to reschedule the SBC Centennial annual session, SBC leaders marked the occasion with a Centennial radio broadcast on the May 6 "Baptist Hour." Part of the program originated from Augusta. The Centennial Celebration actually took place during the 1946 SBC meeting in Miami.[20]

Whether the cause was war, or peace, or some other distraction, Florida Baptists heard a "report of failure" when they gathered in Jacksonville for the 1946 annual meeting. The Centennial Crusade report showed that the 875 Baptist churches in the state had baptized only 13,000 new members, fewer than half the 40,000 goal. It was, however, a 50 percent increase over the year before. Dr. Maguire challenged the Convention to a goal of 20,000 baptisms in 1946. He also championed the Cooperative Program, asking Baptists to visualize the causes supported by the whole denomination:

> To give **to** the Cooperative Program is rather a cold and abstract idea, but to give **through** the Cooperative Program to the various missionary, benevolent and educational causes dear to the hearts of Baptists, and the sake of Christ our Lord, is a heart-warming, spiritual act of worship and service.[21]

WMU, loyal CP supporter, also fell short in reaching goals but came closest in new tithers (18 percent) and increase in gifts (18.2 percent). Jo Jones encouraged the women, saying, "We know there were impressions and responses in the hearts of women and young people that we cannot tabulate but which do count for the Kingdom's advancement."[22]

A Friendly "Divorce"

At the January 1946 sessions, both the Florida Baptist Convention and WMU made significant decisions regarding annual meetings. FBC messengers voted to change the "State Convention year" to October 1 through September 30 and to set the FBC annual meeting regularly in November. Several months earlier Maguire and Jones had discussed the timing of WMU's annual meeting; he had asked her to present to the WMU Executive Board the question of selecting a separate time. Responding cooperatively, the WMU Board brought a recommendation to hold the "Annual W.M.U. Convention" at a time other than the "same week as the General State Convention." Maguire spoke for the recommendation, saying that it would give more time for the general Convention, provide pastors a better opportunity to attend the women's meeting "in order that they may get added inspiration," and solve the problem of finding hotel accommodations for the larger number attending the combined meetings.

Emerging from some dark corner every few years, the issue had sparked debate since the days of Miss Spalding, but separation had always been voted down. President Rosser reported:

> The majority of our women were reluctant to "divorce" ourselves, as one dear woman expressed it, from the general Convention; but, always ready to cooperate with our [FBC] Executive Secretary in any way possible, W.M.U. by a large majority accepted the recommendation.

She underscored the women's deep loyalty:

> Brother Solomon [*Witness* editor and publisher] in fun announces: "The women have divorced us." Who is "us"? Let it be remembered that we, as individuals, are members of the Florida Baptist Convention and are vitally concerned in everything that the Convention does, including its annual meeting. We do not "divorce" ourselves but plan to attend the Florida

Baptist Convention. Woman's Missionary Union, by its very name and Constitution, pledges itself to help carry out every plan made by the Florida Baptist Convention. Therefore, we, as loyal W.M.U. members and as Florida Baptists, must think now of attending two conventions.[23]

The first separate WMU annual meeting was held in Tampa in March 1947.

Miss Elizabeth Provence, hatless, young people's secretary; Miss Josephine Jones, executive secretary; Mrs. J. L. Rosser, president; Mrs. A. G. Chappell, vice-president at the first "annual meeting" held separately from the Florida Baptist Convention, Tampa, 1947.

Where Credit Is Due

Evidently "Dr. John" and "Miss Jones" held ongoing conversations about many aspects of WMU as they sought clearer definitions of relationship. Following the lead of the State Board of Missions, in March 1946 the Executive Board voted to change the WMU year to conform to the Florida Baptist Convention year, October 1 through September 30. That change made "by our blessed women" Maguire called "the most significant and far-reaching action that has been taken since I became Executive Secretary." In his *Witness* column, "The Secretary Says," he praised WMU:

> This means at long last we are ALL moving together; now the W.M.U. officers will be elected and installed along with all the other officers, teachers and leaders of the church.
>
> No agency of our church has meant more to the advancement of God's Kingdom than has our W.M.U. They have been foremost in their endeavor to keep missions in its proper place. We thank them for it.

Along with his praises, Maguire offered another proposal. Why not let Cooperative Program money given by the women "simply be credited from the church instead of crediting it as coming from the W.M.U."? Assuring the women that the Convention Bookkeeping Department kept "a strict account of what is credited to our W.M.U. in matters of mission money," he acknowledged the appropriateness of crediting foreign, home, and state missions offerings as instructed. "These specials can be so easily kept," he said, "for they really are 'over and above' the regular mission program of the church." He wondered, however, "if our noble women would not be putting forward the whole program of our Master, far more, if they would not insist on credit being kept for the W.M.U. monies sent in for the Cooperative Program."[24]

Maguire's concern was multiplied across the SBC. While WMU continued to urge support of the CP and WMU contributions grew in amount and percentage of total CP giving, even national WMU leaders lost their enthusiasm for the tedious recording of members' routine CP gifts. In 1947 the Florida Union acceded to Maguire's suggestion, voting to stop recording Cooperative Program gifts and report to WMU, SBC, an amount equal to one third the total Florida CP contributions.[25] In 1950 WMU, SBC, ceased tracking CP contributions, and most state Unions ended CP quotas as a motivational tool. In no way did those actions indicate diminished Cooperative Program support:

> WMU [SBC] tightened its Standard of Excellence to require that 75 percent of its members give regularly through the Cooperative Program. By 1957, a local WMU had to report 100 percent of its members giving through the CP in order to get top ranking.[26]

Who Is My Neighbor?

Southern Baptists in large numbers made their way to Miami in May 1946 for the first postwar meeting of the Southern Baptist Convention. WMU, SBC, held sessions in the Central Baptist Church, with Mrs. George Q. Holland, president of the Miami Association WMU, as general chairman of local arrangements. An ample supply of unrationed gasoline allowed 2,715 delegates and visitors to attend the WMU meeting.[27]

The matter on the hearts of many in Miami was the urgent cry for assistance from European and Asian countries left destitute by the war. In March, Josephine Jones had written Dr. M. T. Rankin, Foreign Mission Board executive secretary:

> I have been quite concerned that Southern Baptists are not doing anything in an organized way for World Relief. . . . It seems to me that the government and other relief agencies are ahead of the church in this and that we ought to be doing something about it. . . . I believe some of our people know that they *can* give to Relief if they are so inclined, but it does not seem that our people as a whole have been impressed with the urgent need for such help.[28]

SBC leaders, hearing such concerns from many directions, responded with a call to raise $3.5 million "for Relief and Rehabilitation in the war stricken areas of the world." Florida Baptists accepted a goal of $155,400. As WMU, SBC, took responsibility for raising one third of the national goal, Florida WMU set a goal of $51,800, one third that of the state.

Because of the emergency, the State Board of Missions and the WMU Executive Board voted to forego the State Mission Offering in 1946. "The objectives of our State Mission Offering will be provided for out of other funds," Jones explained in urging support of the relief offering. "May we go far beyond our goal! For this offering means life instead of death for millions of people—we must not fail!" The genuine concern of Florida Baptists, plus the cooperative promotion of the effort, produced the most successful offering in Florida Baptist Convention history. Leading the SBC, Florida surpassed the state goal on August 15. By November, with WMU also exceeding its portion of the goal, the offering had reached $245,000. Maguire patted his constituents on the back: "Certainly, every pastor, the members of our churches, our fine women through their W.M.U. and our great paper, have all had a great part in this glorious effort."[29]

Both WMS and auxiliary members also put a great deal of energy into the modern version of mite barrels—relief packages of food and clothing which might also contain towels, needles and thread, soap, pencils, and personal items like combs and toothbrushes.[30] Relief efforts continued for several years, with collections of children's toys, clothing, and money for medicine. Sunbeams raised money for Christmas candy to go overseas.[31]

A Basis of Cooperation

Almost two years after Florida WMU requested "a reaffirmation of the existing basis of co-operation between the Union and the State Mission Board," Dr. C. H. Bolton, former Florida Baptist Convention executive secretary and now a state Board member from Miami, brought the matter to the attention of the Board. At the June 1946 quarterly State Board of Missions meeting, he offered a resolution which first acknowledged the auxiliary status of WMU, "with its own Board and Convention, both in its Southwide and Statewide work." With that understanding, he proposed, first, the State Board of Mission's expression of appreciation for "the fine spirit of voluntary cooperation existing between the Union and the Convention" as they worked together "for the cause of Christ."

Second, he proposed:

> that the State Mission Board, which handles and is responsible for all monies sent through the Headquarters Offices in Jacksonville, recognize the expending of the amount of money set up in the annual budget for the operation of the Woman's Missionary Union to be the right of the Woman's Missionary Union Board.

Finally, he appealed for "voluntary cooperation" in three matters: 1) the election of two WMU Board members to membership on the State Board of Missions, with one of the two serving on the Budget Committee in order to present WMU's annual budget; 2) a "salary basis" for all employees, "jointly and satisfactorily worked out" on the basis of "similar salaries for similar work."; 3) unspent budget money not to be considered either a surplus retained "by the organization or department" or an amount to be added to the next year's budget.[32]

The State Board of Missions adopted the resolution. Except for similar salaries, the effects of the Board action soon began to appear. Eight years would pass before WMU staff would reach equality with Convention department staffs in the matter of pay. Then equality eroded year by year, even though at its August 1956 meeting, the SBM reiterated its previous action by adopting "recommendations related to W.M.U., setting salary scales and vacation policy the same as other departments."

Changing Titles, Changing Work

Although WMU had recently upgraded the field work position by renaming it "field secretary" and returning the field secretary to the Executive Board, Elizabeth Provence really wanted to concentrate on work with young people. For several months a selection committee had been looking for someone to take Elsie Renfroe's place, but apparently was making little progress. Suddenly, in August 1946, the Executive Committee unanimously elected the "well known and much beloved" Provence as the new Florida young people's secretary. How did committee members come to their decision?

Miss Hannah Reynolds, executive secretary of Louisiana WMU and Provence's good friend, invited her to consider the young people's job in Louisiana. Because Provence preferred to remain in Florida, she took the matter to her boss, whom she had grown to love and respect: "I really want to be a young people's leader. If the committee doesn't ask me to take the job here, then I'm going to Louisiana." Apparently, Jones had no intention of letting Louisiana have her excellent associate. Within a short time the announcement of Provence's selection as Florida Young People's leader appeared in the *Witness.*

In the same August 1946 meeting, the Executive Committee also changed the title of Jo Withauer's job from office secretary to assistant to the executive secretary. "Naturally gifted in the detailed work" of the WMU office, Withauer was "really 'a genius' with the mimeograph." She wrote articles, planned programs, and gave special attention to the development of Business Women's Circles. In July 1947, Florida WMU lost Withauer to the mission field when the Foreign Mission Board appointed her to work with the Baptist Publishing House in Rio de Janeiro.[33]

To Be or Not To Be a Department

Because of the calendar changes made in the January 1946 annual meeting, the state Convention met again in November 1946—that time without the companionship of WMU. Interesting differences occurred in Maguire's reports. In the January report, WMU headed the list of nine "Departments of Our Work." The WMU staff was also listed first under "Convention Employees and Salaries" for the past year. Jones' $2400 was only two thirds the salary of most other department heads.[34]

In contrast, after separation of annual meetings but affirmations, clarifications, cooperation, and praise during the year, WMU appeared in neither list in the November report. Maguire explained: "The Woman's Missionary Union is not a department of our work, but an auxiliary to the Florida Baptist Convention. Miss Josephine Jones is Executive Secretary of this Department." However, the recommendation to organize the State Board of Missions into committees for studying the needs of "each phase of our work" did include WMU.[35] Messengers may have felt somewhat confused by such seeming contradictions.

Most significant of all, perhaps, was the naming of three women—Mrs. Robert R. Walden, Mrs. Doak S. Campbell, and Mrs. C. G. Illingworth—as at-large members of the State Board of Missions.[36] For a period of 20 or so years just before and following the turn of the century, women regularly held Florida Baptist Convention committee posts. Gradually as Baptist work in the state strengthened, the number of women on committees decreased. Between World War I and World War II a woman on a Convention committee was an exception rather than a rule.[37] When appointments of a few women to FBC committees began to re-occur, there seemed to be little correlation with WMU. Neither the state WMU president nor other Executive Board members received routine State Board of Missions appointment, a request made as early as 1926 by the WMU and again in Dr. Bolton's resolution in 1946. However, the women certainly sensed progress and cooperation when the State Board of Missions named the at-large posts.

A-Camping We Will Go

With the help of Elizabeth Provence and RA summer workers, camping in Florida grew in statistics and in effectiveness. At first Josephine Jones thought the idea of state GA and RA camps was impractical because no central location was available. But her young people's secretary felt strongly about the need to sponsor such camps, especially in northwest Florida, where young people had almost no camping opportunities. When Stetson student Cecil Rathel began part-time RA work in 1947, Provence found an ally. "I learned early on that if there's a program or a project that is God's design and His will, then He's going to make everything fall into place," Provence said.

> I saw Him do it with our first camps. My associational young people's lead-
> ers and I had talked a lot about planning a state camp. Sam Renfroe, the
> business manager at Chipola Junior College, offered to let us use the col-
> lege's old army barracks.
>
> We didn't have much money—nobody had much money in those days—
> and we had to plan camp as cheaply as possible. We charged the campers
> $5.00 for Monday to Saturday. Of course, $5.00 wouldn't cover all the cost
> of food, so we asked the associations to ship us caseloads of #10 cans of
> vegetables and fruit, and some sent beef stew or canned chicken. Then we
> got a volunteer cook who helped us plan our menus around what we
> received. Cecil directed the RAs, and then I led the GAs and YWAs. That's
> the way we started camp.[38]

According to Provence's 1947 annual report, 87 boys and 147 girls attended those first camps. With 29 professions of faith and 54 dedications to special service, 35 percent of the campers made life-changing decisions.[39]

A Chariot Named Chip, Jr.

Provence's arrangement with Chipola Junior College resulted in more
than summer camp quarters. It put her "in the right place at the right time" to
purchase a much needed car:

> All the associational presidents and WMU folks in the smaller associa-
> tions knew what a time I was having with my traveling. Mother
> McCullough, president in St. John's Association, proposed at the Executive
> Board meeting that they open a fund and invite people to contribute to help
> Miss Provence get a car. Josephine Jones was just the most wonderful per-
> son that ever walked this earth and never hesitated to stand up for staff in
> their work, but she was very reluctant to ask people to do things for the
> staff, or for herself either. So when she didn't push for it, it was voted down.
>
> Well, Mother McCullough came to me and said, "Lib, open a savings
> account. You're going to be getting some money for a car." She went home
> and wrote every associational president, the very women that had turned
> down the request, and said, "Miss Provence needs a car. Let's get her one."
> Sure enough, the checks started coming in. I was very careful to keep a
> record and acknowledge every gift.
>
> New cars were still almost impossible to find, and I didn't know where
> I could locate a good used car. But while we were having camp, Sam
> Renfroe asked if I wanted to buy a car. I said, "Sure, if it's a good one." As
> it turned out, Chipola Junior College had just bought it for their president,
> but he had resigned suddenly, and Sam needed to sell it. So I bought this
> 1941 two-door black Ford and named it Chip, Jr., for the college.[40]

Later Provence wrote in the *Witness*: "To my many friends over the state I
want again to express my deepest gratitude for making this possible. I pray
that as a result of this gift His Kingdom may be extended with more effectiveness and greater rapidity."[41]

Happy Birthday to You

During the years of Josephine Jones' leadership, anniversary celebrations came rolling in with tidal regularity: the SBC centennial, 1945; WMU, SBC, 60th, 1948; Florida WMU 60th, 1954; WMU, SBC, 75th, 1963; and Baptist Jubilee Advance, multi-year emphasis leading to the sesquicentennial celebration of the founding of the Triennial Convention, forerunner of the SBC, 1959-1964. In addition, the missions education organizations—Sunbeams, GA, RA, and YWA—celebrated 40th, 50th, 60th, and 75th (Sunbeams) anniversaries. To some it may have seemed that growth and programs of work continually depended on the hype of anniversary goals and special agendas. To others the anniversary observances gave legitimate opportunity to learn from the past, evaluate the present, and invoke deeper levels of service for the future.

For the 60th year of WMU, SBC, planners chose the theme "For God and Home in Every Land," urging "re-emphasis of 'Family Worship' in establishing and maintaining a Christian home." Florida WMU goals called for 30 percent more tithers and additional units in all WMU organizations. When the statistics were tallied, Florida was far short in tithers, but reached or came very close to all enlistment targets.[42]

The 1948 "Commemoration Meeting" in Memphis not only looked with gratitude at the accomplishments of the past 60 years, but also ushered in a new era of leadership for the national Union. Kathleen Mallory, the embodiment of WMU since 1912, chose that historic moment to conclude her service as executive secretary. At the same time, Juliette Mather, who had been young people's secretary since 1921, moved into the "new and important position of editorial secretary." In the search for Mather's replacement as young people's secretary, the nominating committee sought the counsel of Alma Hunt, dean of women at William Jewell College in Missouri. She recommended Margaret Bruce of Tennessee. Three months later the committee went to Hunt again, that time to invite her to become the new executive secretary of WMU, SBC. Hunt began her 26-year tenure at the 1948 annual meeting.[43] Following in the tradition of strong servant leaders focused on the missions enterprise of Southern Baptists, Hunt added to the profile her own special blend of sharp intellect, smooth relational skills, and keen sense of humor, with just a touch of mischief.

Laying Strong Foundations

Florida WMU's "Commemoration" celebration in Ocala also brought a change of command with election of a new state president. During her five years in office, outgoing president Mrs. J. L. Rosser had guided the Florida Union through significant changes; her faithful, steady leadership had created smooth transitions in every instance. Now she passed her gavel to Mrs.

Roy L. Lassiter, who would take Florida WMU to the climactic celebration of its own 60th anniversary in 1954.

Lelia Boring Lassiter had already demonstrated her deep Christian character and her outstanding leadership qualities at every level of WMU work.

From steadfast service in her own church society and youth auxiliaries in Clermont, she had moved into associational leadership, even directing the associational youth camps for several years. On the state level, she had headed White Cross work and stewardship promotion. Her reward for service was greater opportunity to serve.

Living in a small house in the middle of an orange grove near Clermont, Lassiter maintained a simple life style; she had no telephone service until after the years of her presidency. She was "very careful with her money," so that she could support missions just as she encouraged others to do so. Even during the Depression, in the early years of their marriage, when her husband Roy gave her $6 a week for groceries, she set aside the first 60 cents as her tithe. Using the family car for WMU travel, she often brought missionaries or state staff home for the night. In all her many WMU involvements, she could always count on Mr. Lassiter's whole-hearted support. He seldom traveled with her, but he joined her in leading an RA group that at one time included their two sons.[44]

Mrs. Roy L. Lassiter
1948-1954

Waiting Before the Lord

To family members, it seemed that Lelia Lassiter "woke up each morning and waited for the Lord to give her instructions for the day." A deeply committed prayer warrior, she set the example for her family and early taught her sons to pray for missions.[45] To promote the 1948 Home and Family emphasis, Lassiter wrote in the *Witness:* "The greatest service which can be rendered Christ's Kingdom is to pray earnestly, constantly and intelligently. Parents can lead in this," using a prayer calendar to teach children to pray for missionaries. "To know, to care, to give, to pray! This is the part the family can have in world missions."[46]

Theo Thomas Lee (Mrs. Robert E.) recalled spending a week in the Lassiter home when she was a WMU field worker in 1938-39. Each day Mrs. Lassiter drove her to different churches in the association to lead mission studies or teach leadership courses. Lee remembered a morning when Lassiter and her two boys were having their devotional in the living room: "My room was right next to the living room, and I could hear what they were saying. That was the first time I'd ever heard somebody praying for me by name like that, and it really touched me."

Of Lassiter's leadership style, Lee said: "She was a hard worker, and she could work you, too! She was a pusher, but always sweet with it, never bossy. Mrs. Lassiter had a lovely spirit and made you feel good about what she was asking you to do."[47]

A High Point in Birmingham

As the Florida president, Lassiter also served as a vice-president of WMU, SBC, and attended the annual January Board meetings. "Those meetings were always a high point of each year," Lassiter wrote in an autobiographical sketch. "Working and sharing together with the officers of the Union and the other state presidents brought blessings and joy." She liked to recall that in 1951, she was the person who moved the adoption of the recommendation to buy a new WMU headquarters building, located at 600 North 20th Street, Birmingham.[48] Alma Hunt remembered Lassiter as "a person of real ability" who was frequently placed on Board committees. "I loved Mrs. Lassiter," Hunt said. "She was a faithful friend and continued to be, long after her term of service."[49]

Change, Challenge

Lassiter had already come to love Jo Jones, and the two of them made an exceptional pair as they led Florida WMU through the days of Lassiter's presidency, days of changing social conditions, general economic prosperity, and some re-working of WMU emphases on the national level. After World War II, when Rosie the Riveter was no longer needed, women found other

Ruby Milner

jobs "outside the home." Having made that break, they more readily broke with other feminine traditions such as styles of dress, "lady-like" behavior, and involvement in church activities. Perhaps women in Southern Baptist churches tended to change less rapidly or less drastically, but that trend would eventually challenge WMU's traditional methods.

One change for WMU was the rapid growth of Business Women's Circles. By the time Jo Withauer came to the WMU office in 1941, several BWCs had formed in Florida, and she took responsibility to work with them. The first BWC Conference met at Ridgecrest Baptist Assembly during the 1942 Foreign Missions Week. At the launching of an annual WMU Week at Ridgecrest in 1946, the BWC Conference aligned with that program.[50]

By 1948 Florida had 166 Business Women's Circles. Ruby Milner, Jo Withauer's replacement, planned the first Florida BWC camp, held at the new

Tampa Bay Assembly grounds in September 1948. "My Place in God's World Plan" was the theme. In the *Witness,* Milner appealed to her readers' business sense: "The cost is $5.50 per person for the entire time. You can't stay at home that cheaply." The 46 registrants organized a state BWC Federation, electing Milner president.[51] A change of pace for working women, the annual Labor Day weekend conferences grew in popularity, and a camaraderie developed among working women from all over the state. To encourage BWC attendance at WMU annual meetings, Milner planned a special BWC feature each year, usually a banquet. Milner continued to give strong guidance to BWC work until her retirement in 1968.

Mountain-Top Experiences

A "fine Florida delegation of about 75" attended Ridgecrest WMU week soon after the May 1948 election of Alma Hunt and Margaret Bruce. The Florida women found the two new leaders to be "gracious, charming, capable and devout handmaidens of the King," reported Mrs. R. Kelly White, West Palm Beach. Florida's Lelia Lassiter taught one class each day, and the women enjoyed conferences on the WMU Fundamentals: prayer, mission study, stewardship, community missions, and missionary education of young people.[52]

Well-planned conferences with excellent leaders and missionary speakers, and plenty of Nibble Nook ice cream, continued to draw Southern Baptist women to WMU week. Similar conferences at the new Glorieta Baptist Assembly in New Mexico met the needs of the growing Baptist population in the "pioneer" western states. In 1994, WMU, SBC, began a policy of alternating WMU weeks between Ridgecrest and Glorieta.

A Matter of Honor

Jones and Provence had become fixtures on the WMU staff, and Ruby Milner would add 20 years of office stability. But other staff came and went with disarming frequency. WMU, and particularly Lib Provence, played match-maker with young staff members. Cecil Rathel, who worked with RA, and Hazel Hodge, who in October 1949 began her job as field and office worker, were visiting Provence one evening. Provence suggested to Rathel that he "take Hazel somewhere."

"I don't have any money," Rathel bemoaned.

"Well, there's a Youth for Christ meeting. Go there. That won't cost you anything," Provence advised. That first date led to marriage a few months later. At the end of the ceremony, the couple exited under an arch of crossed swords held by Rathel's RAs, an impressive sight as they also displayed their RA shields.[53]

When the couple left for Southwestern Seminary in August 1950, Mrs. Lois Wells became the WMU office and field worker. The Rathels returned to Florida for summer RA work in 1951, and WMU had high hopes of employing Cecil full-time when he graduated in 1952. However, the State Board of Missions declined WMU's request for the position "because of financial commitments already made." In her annual report, Provence responded to that action:

> The keenest disappointment of my whole nine years of service with Florida [WMU] occurred when we failed to employ Mr. Cecil Rathel as our full-time Royal Ambassador Secretary. . . . I am praying that God will give us another chance to do for the cause of missionary education among our boys what we ought to do.[54]

Mission Coupons—Mission Dollars

Numerous successful projects pointed to the healthy condition of Florida's expanding WMU. Members continued their long-time commitment to the Children's Home. In 1948 the Home moved from Arcadia to a new campus in Lakeland. To furnish cottages, Florida WMU borrowed money from the State Board of Missions, then paid it back from State Missions Offerings. The women also collected coupons, by the hundreds of thousands, from soap and food products. Over a one-year period, coupons provided "three pianos, a deep freeze, sufficient blankets for the entire Home, a carpet for the new chapel, a power mower and a vacuum cleaner."[55] Boxes from WMU members and sponsorship of children remained important avenues of support.

Through both direct contributions and allocations from the State Mission Offerings, Florida WMU gave over $12,000 (goal $7,200) toward the purchase of the new WMU, SBC, headquarters building. In Birmingham for the annual planning meeting, Josephine Jones, Elizabeth Provence, and Lelia Lassiter represented Florida WMU at the building dedication on January 21, 1952. The national Union basked in the light of God's blessing: a recently constructed edifice, tailored perfectly to WMU's needs, at perhaps one third the cost of a new building.[56]

Restating the Case

Ever since Florida WMU, at the request of the State Board of Missions, promoted the first State Mission Offering in 1908, the Union had pushed the offering with unflagging zeal. The money had always supported causes important to the work of Florida Baptists. In recent years, the State Board of Missions had become more involved in directing and promoting the uses of the offering. At the February 1952 State Board of Missions meeting, a joint committee from the SBM and the WMU Executive Board unanimously presented a significant recommendation related to both WMU and the State Offering:

> We recognize the continued existence of the WMU as an Auxiliary. We request the Florida Baptist Convention, through the State Board of Missions, to consider and allocate a WMU operating budget to be taken

from the Cooperative Program funds.

It is clearly understood that a request is not a mandate to the Board.

We further request that 25% of the Special State Mission Offering be given to the WMU for special WMU projects.

The Accounting Department is to handle bookkeeping for the WMU. The WMU will conform to the voted policy of accounting of the State Board of Missions.

The recommendation was adopted. An effort to deal with salary inequities had failed in committee.[57]

Among causes receiving State Mission Offering funds from the WMU allocation were projects with the Seminole Indians, furnishings for the new William Sims Allen Hall at Stetson, and support for Negro education at Florida Normal and Industrial Memorial College in St. Augustine, a cause espoused by Florida WMU since the days of Louise Smith. College administrators and Negro Baptist denominational leaders greatly appreciated the women's support and showed it in part by electing first Smith and then Josephine Jones to the Board of Trustees. In 1954, at the college's "Sixty-second Anniversary Founder's Day," Mrs. Lassiter was one of four women to receive a "Meritorious Service Award." The program stated: "It is pleasant, now, to give recognition at this time to these leaders who are also servants to the best interests of all. It is hoped that this Award will in some small way express the gratitude of an appreciative community."

Standard or Style?

Miss Alma Hunt, executive secretary of WMU, SBC, made her first Florida appearance at the 1952 annual meeting in Orlando. She made a wonderful impression on the delegates; the women made a startling impression on her. Some 40 years later, she still recalled the event with a twinkle in her eye:

> I shall never forget those lovely women dressed in white who emerged from the doors at the back of the auditorium just before time to start the program. They walked down the aisles to the front pews and held up signs saying "Silence" or "Worship." Immediately they silenced all the talking and put us in the mood for prayer.
>
> I bowed my head to pray but kept my eyes open. When I looked down, I saw the women had on white sandals, and no hose! I had never seen a woman in a WMU meeting without hose.

For many years, WMU, SBC, had issued a guiding statement on a "Christian standard of dress." Each year as she and Margaret Bruce prepared the Yearbook, Hunt argued for doing away with the standard, which she considered unenforceable and undesirable because of changing styles. But Bruce resisted. "At that time," said Hunt, "we had never been to the WMU office in downtown Birmingham without heels, gloves, and a hat, much less barelegged."

When she returned to Birmingham, she reported to Bruce:

> Margaret, I've never been in a more worshipful meeting than the one in
> Florida. I've never seen women respond more quickly to the reminder of
> worship to come. The women who called us to worship were lovely and
> dignified. But they wore sandals and no hose. Well, Margaret, what do we
> do about the Christian standard of dress?

Some changes meet more resistance than others. Hats and hose disappeared
slowly from the WMU scene, but Florida did its part.

Planning Ahead for Looking Back

Committed to a celebration truly honoring the God who had blessed their
history, Florida WMU leaders began early to plan for the Union's 60th
anniversary in 1954. To guide the preparations, Mrs. Lassiter appointed an
anniversary committee: Mrs. Robert Walden, chairman, Mrs. G. Q. Holland,
Mrs. John Maguire, and Mrs. T. H. Hutchinson. Their detailed plans would
be presented at the final Orlando session.

Before the committee reported, however, another milestone was celebrated. After the young people's service, an "autographing reception" honored
Elizabeth Provence, author of *God's Troubadours*. Recounting the life story
of each of Florida's 42 foreign missionaries, the book made an appropriate
lead-in for a celebration of Florida WMU heritage. On Thursday morning,
the anniversary committee presented the theme, "Strengthen, O Lord, that
which Thou Hast Wrought." Psalm 90:17 provided the scripture: *And let the
beauty of the Lord our God be upon us; and establish thou the work of our
hands upon us; yea, the work of our hands establish thou it.* Members were
invited to submit entries in an anniversary hymn writing contest.[58]

The committee proposed that 1953 be a Year of Preparation, climaxing
with the 1954 celebration in Daytona Beach. They invited Mrs. Lassiter to
write a book of devotionals to be used throughout 1953 for personal spiritual preparation. They also recommended a 1953 special anniversary love
offering with a goal of $18,000. The money would be divided among foreign,
home, and state mission "objects," allowing $2,000 for a world tour for Jo
Jones. The 1952-53 Guide Book would include anniversary goals and plans,
as well as "suggestions for parties and banquets as stimulation for love offerings."

Goals were set for every aspect of the organization and work. Most used
"60%" or multiples of 60 in setting numerical targets. The goals were so
inclusive and so detailed that some women confused them with the Standard
of Excellence. State Mission Study chairman Mrs. John Maguire tried to
relieve the confusion on that point: "Remember that our Anniversary goals
are higher than the Standard. For example, the Standard requires 2/3 of the
enrollment reading a missionary book. Our Anniversary goal is **every** member reading a missionary book."[59]

1953: It Was A Very Good Year

The Year of Preparation demanded perpetual stamina. That staff members survived its demands was miraculous. Help came with the February arrival of Armand Ball, the first full-time RA secretary, but Lois Wells left on September 1 for a church staff position. Ball took a trainload of 210 RAs to the national RA Congress in Atlanta, held the first Young Men's Mission Conference, and in March 1954 led the Florida RA Congress with over 700 boys and leaders gathered in Ocala. Planned by Provence, Queen's Court banquets in five cities honored the Girls' Auxiliary 40th anniversary.

Six regional leadership conferences, 10 Days of Instruction (one-day training conferences for local officers and members), and the annual state leaders conference for associational officers provided multiple training opportunities. Of course, the regular programs of camps and assemblies also continued.

During those months women all over the state received spiritual blessings through Mrs. Lassiter's daily devotional book, *Search Me, O God.* Every Woman's Missionary Society had also received a copy of Lassiter's "Historical Highlights," containing information and instructions for presentation at a general meeting each month. There was just one problem: the president's five-year term would expire at the 1953 annual meeting. The women wanted her to finish what she had "so ably begun." Undaunted by the constitutional obstacle, the Executive Board simply asked that the constitution be changed to allow for the unusual circumstance. Delegates in Jacksonville in 1953 agreed, and by acclamation re-elected Lassiter as state president for a sixth year. Other changes made in offices and terms included eliminating the office of vice-president and its

Miss Josephine Jones, left, and Miss Juliet Mather saying goodbye to well-wishers as the two embark on the first leg of their around-the-world journey.

corollary, enlistment chairman, as well as the Margaret Fund chairman. The delegates also acknowledged the change of the WMU Training School to the

Carver School of Missions and Social Work, "now coeducational and inter-racial in its student body."[60]

Global Friendships

The anniversary love offering poured in during 1953. When Jo Jones was ready to begin her round-the-world tour with Juliette Mather, $2,000 await-ed her. Although those who worked with Jones observed her frugality, few knew she was a "double tither." Because they respected her leadership and admired her sacrificial life-style, providing their leader the four-month tour gave WMU members special pleasure.

While Jones visited Southern Baptist mission stations in Asia, Europe, and the Near East, Lassiter attended the first meeting of the North American Baptist Women's Union (NABWU), one of several continental unions mak-ing up the Women's Department of the Baptist World Alliance (BWA). Baptist women from all over the continent gathered in Columbus, Ohio. WMU, SBC, leaders had contributed to the development of both the BWA Women's Department and NABWU. Lassiter described the prevailing feeling at the inaugural meeting as "oneness in Christ," as the women "came to know each other better, to understand our problems, and to realize that 'our hopes, our fears, our aims are one, our comforts and our cares.' "[61]

That Which Thou Hast Wrought

Enjoying the 60th Anniversary Celebration of Florida WMU are, left, Mrs. Frances Crabtree, Mrs. Lelia Lassiter, Mrs. Mary Belle Holland, and Miss Josephine Jones.

With the Christian flag in the lead, 35 Royal Ambassadors carrying the flags of BWA nations led the dramatic processional opening the "Sixtieth Anniversary Annual Meeting of Florida Baptist Woman's Missionary Union." Following the flags came Dr. John Maguire, Florida Baptist Convention executive secretary; Dr. Harold Sanders, FBC president; former and present state WMU officers; associational presidents; representatives of societies and auxiliaries organized before or during 1894; and representatives of associations, societies, and auxiliaries that had attained the Standard of Excellence in the Year of Preparation.[62] The singing of the Doxology and the Anniversary Hymn, written by Mrs. C. L. Andrews of Westville, opened the meeting in the Peabody Auditorium, Daytona Beach, April 6, 1954. With Mrs. Lassiter presiding, pageantry and praise marked the entire meeting.

The keynote speaker was Louise Smith Boyd, former executive secretary. "We study the past," she said, "because of its bearing on the present and its promise for the future." Describing the kind of women needed to uphold the purposes of WMU, she challenged her listeners: "Today needs women who are steadfast in their convictions, flexible in their thinking, forward in their planning, courageous in their faith and who will work and get others to work."

Among many who spoke were Dr. Sanders; Miss Jones, who gave details of her recent world tour; Mrs. George Hayes, missionary to Japan; and Mrs. J. M. Dawson, renowned speaker and WMU leader from Texas and Washington, D.C. Deploring "the lost energy and talent of women who piddle their lives away on minor things," Dawson proclaimed, "What a divine thing it is to link our lives with that which engages the mind of God!" A central feature of the meeting was the presentation of the "Sixtieth Anniversary Pageant," written by Mrs. Maguire. Although 1,621 delegates registered for the meeting, over 2,300 attended the pageant session.

To commemorate the January 1894 inauguration of Woman's Baptist Missionary Union, Auxiliary to the Florida Baptist Convention, in Plant City, Lassiter presented a Memorial Plaque to Rev. L. Don Miley, pastor of Plant City First Baptist Church.[63] Miley gave to the president an anniversary gavel made by RAs in his church. When Mrs. George Q. Holland, Miami, took office as the new president, Lassiter passed that gavel to her.

Reports made during the meeting afforded interesting perspectives on the work of the preceding years. For the first time, an associational union, the Indian River Association WMU, had achieved 100 percent of the Associational Standard of Excellence. While few goals were met, large increases in most areas of work generated optimism. The number of societies climbed to 821 and auxiliaries to 2,457, with total membership of 61,458. Those numbers included 305 Business Women's Circles with 5,200 members. Surpassing the goal of $18,000, the Anniversary Offering went to the support of the anniversary celebration, including publishing of *Search Me, O God*; a medical clinic in Indonesia; the Baptist publishing house in Hong

Kong; Sunday School rooms for the Seminole Indian Mission; good will centers in Key West, Miami, Ybor City and the Italian work in Tampa; foreign mission volunteer and foreign student scholarships at Stetson; assistance for Negro women to employ a Negro field worker; Jones' mission tour; and Florida Normal and Industrial Memorial College (FNIMC).[64] Although names or places might have changed, those causes represented the heartbeat of Florida WMU over the previous six decades.

The Stetson Glee Club's singing of the "Hallelujah Chorus" from Handel's *Messiah* brought the 60th annual meeting to a stirring close. As many faithful servants stood to the magnificent music, no doubt they shared Lassiter's feelings: "My thoughts turned to the countless women, known and unknown, who had labored together with God to make that day possible, and my heart sang 'Hallelujah' as I praised God for every one of them."[65]

The Holland Era

Mary Belle Holland (Mrs. George Q.), another talented woman who had worked her way through WMU ranks, was the first president who had a Presbyterian background. Born in Charlotte, North Carolina, Holland grew up in Atlanta, Georgia. When she was 12 years old, she accepted Christ in a Presbyterian church. After her move to Florida, she was baptized in 1926 in the Haines City Baptist Church. Josephine Jones wrote of her:

> Her first service after becoming a Baptist was to organize a Girls' Auxiliary. Since that good beginning in W.M.U. leadership she has been W.M.S. president, associational president in South Florida and Miami, State mission study chairman and State vice-president.

In her "spare time," she earned an A.B. degree from Miami University, graduating Magna Cum Laude. Her husband, Dr. George Q. Holland, was a dentist.

Mrs. George Q. Holland
1954-1959

Holland also gave significant leadership as a vice-president of WMU, SBC. "One of the hardest co-workers I ever had was Mary Belle Holland," said Alma Hunt. "She was willing to undertake hard committee assignments and really difficult tasks. She was very devoted to WMU, SBC, as well as to Florida Baptists."

Closing the Gap

After the 60th anniversary celebration, would the women have energy for continuing the upward drive? Holland did not ask. She knew what she wanted to accomplish and expected others readily to do their part. She and Josephine Jones, together with Elizabeth Provence, Armand Ball, Ruby Milner, and the state Fundamentals chairmen, continued to push for growth in every area of the work.

In yearly reports, Jones and Provence challenged members to look beyond accomplishments and see what needed to be done. While 854 Woman's Missionary Societies represented 81 percent of Florida's Baptist churches in 1954, WMS membership was only about 20 percent of the approximately 150,000 women members in those churches. Recruiting remained a major challenge. Although the various Standards of Excellence had undergone subtle alterations, a major adjustment occurred in 1956 when the "Aims for Advancement" replaced the Standard of Excellence. Without changing the basics of WMU purpose and goals, the new Aims promoted by WMU, SBC, gave renewed incentive for achievement. Florida WMU received the Aims with enthusiasm. Much to Jones' satisfaction, annual reporting improved as did the level of accomplishment.[66]

To help with enlistment, leadership training, and promotion of work with young people, Provence enlisted "State Specialists": Mrs. Sam Renfroe, Graceville, Sunbeams; Mrs. Fletcher Dempsey, Palm Harbor, GA; and Mrs. Lois Wells, Tampa, followed by Mrs. Earl McGuire, Tampa, YWA.[67] "Lack of trained leadership continues to be our NUMBER ONE PROBLEM," said Provence.[68] Her "number one goal," therefore, was to provide training. She increased the number of training sites, enlisted more teachers with experience, and focused much of her energy on solving that problem. With a three-day Advanced Leadership conference in Ocala during the 1956 WMU Focus Week, Florida became one of the first states to initiate advanced training. The statewide GA House Parties, YWA Conferences, and RA Congresses, each attended by several hundred young people, added a zesty layer of missions awareness to the work of local auxiliaries.

No Place to Call Home

Primarily through WMU urging, the State Board of Missions seriously considered the question of a central camp site, but took no conclusive actions on purchasing camp property in the 1950s. As the number of weeks of GA and RA camping increased, camp staffs became virtual summer gypsies, moving camping equipment from place to place, wherever facilities were available.[69]

For several years, a one-week YWA summer camp, initiated by Lib Provence,[70] was held. At the heart, YWA camp was an experiment, and a successful one, in interracial relationships. One year campers included "a Christian Jewess from Jerusalem, Israel; a Hawaiian, two Brazilians, three Seminole Indians and eight Negroes," as well as one Negro on the staff. Another year there were "racial and national guests from Australia, Gaza, home mission points in New Orleans; Montgomery, Ala.; McIntosh, Ala., and our Florida fields in Tampa, Miami and the Seminole reservation."[71] Using the camping environment to study missions, pray together, and explore the meaning of God in one's life expanded genuine friendships beyond cultural boundaries.

In the adult world, however, race relations stirred volatile emotions. "Armand Ball and I took a lot of flak," Provence recalled. "We were called 'communist' on more than one occasion and received verbal abuse in anonymous letters and phone calls because of our efforts to help white youngsters learn better in matters of racial attitudes." Florida WMU lost the use of Tampa Bay Assembly grounds, an excellent home base, because of the racial issue.

Knowing that Josephine Jones supported their actions and believed in what they were trying to accomplish was important to Provence and Ball. More than once Jones stood up for them before the State Board of Missions, as well as the WMU Executive Committee. Despite obstacles, however, the number of campers and the number of life-changing decisions made during summer sessions encouraged Jones and her staff to continue the camping program and to push the State Board of Missions for purchase of camp property.

Provence and Ball also planned camps for Negro boys and girls on the St. Augustine campus of Florida Normal and Industrial Memorial College and for Seminoles on the Indian reservations. Ball usually recruited interracial staffs to work with the 170-200 campers in St. Augustine. At the Seminole camps, attendance fluctuated between 100 and 150, with "campers" ranging in age from small children to 90-year-old adults. Activities included campcrafts, recreation, WMU methods, preaching by Indian pastors, and even an RA Recognition Service. Genus Crenshaw, missionary to the Seminoles, praised the camps as very helpful to the Indians.[72]

Camping was only one extension of Josephine Jones' concern for the Seminole Indians. Like her predecessor, Louise Smith, she cared deeply about the Seminoles and Negroes in Florida. After the 60th anniversary offering provided money for new Sunday School space at the First Indian Church in Dania, she attended the dedication of the small educational building. On another occasion she flew with Crenshaw to Big Cypress Reservation, "camped out, and slept under church pews to teach the WMU study." With Jones' help, the women at Big Cypress achieved recognition as a standard WMS.

Cuba or Bust

In the 1950s, taking young people out of the country on mission trips was a bold innovation for stimulating missions awareness. Provence and Ball led a group of 10 GAs and RAs on a missions tour of Cuba. Each participant was

Armand B. Ball, Jr., and Beverly Jane Hodge Ball exit First Baptist Church Tallahassee, flanked by six Ambassador Plenipotentiaries. The two in the immediate front are: left, Roderick Conrad of Panama City and James Gross of Jacksonville. If their precision was somewhat less than military, their enthusiasm compensated. Note the RA shields held "heart high" by each boy. September 15, 1957.

at least 15 years old and working on an advanced step or rank. Both participants and leaders paid their own way. The group visited Southern Baptist mission points on the western end of the island and attended a citywide rally of GAs and RAs in Havana. A third chaperon, Beverly Hodge, became Mrs. Armand Ball. Like Cecil Rathel, Ball used an RA honor guard in the wedding.[73]

Under Ball's effective leadership, RA work in Florida made unusual progress. However, WMU, SBC, was moving rapidly toward transfer of Royal Ambassadors to the SBC Brotherhood Department. Florida WMU had contributed to that move. Louise Smith and Susan Adams, in 1939, had recommended that the Brotherhood become involved in training RA leaders who would then take leadership of RA organizations. The concept finally evolved into the transfer, on October 1, 1957, of work with boys nine years old and above.[74] Ball submitted his resignation effective September 30. In his final report, he advised:

> I trust that the transfer will be more in the spirit of the wife yielding the responsibility for the care of her favorite tree to her husband than in the spirit of transplanting a tree from one part of the yard to another. Through the years ahead Woman's Missionary Union must continue to show her interest, support, and sometimes gentle prodding in our Royal Ambassador work. We have nothing to fear in the transfer if we continue our interest and support on a local level.

The appreciations committee at the 1957 Annual Session wrote a lengthy commendation of Ball, praising him for his "rare combination of talents and abilities . . . used of God to build a state Royal Ambassador program equal to that of any state." They also prayed "that God may lead him into ever increasingly satisfying fields of service."[75] God honored that prayer as Ball continued to do outstanding work and eventually headed the American Camping Association, overseeing accreditation of camps throughout the nation.

Crossing the Borders

Other missions trips found a contingent of Florida YWAs crossing the country's northern border for a "once-in-a-youth-time gathering." When the

International students meet at Stetson.

Baptist World Youth Congress met in Toronto in 1958, 29 young women, 15 and older, made the trip, accompanied by Mrs. Earl McGuire. Expenses were about $6 a day for housing and food.[76]

In early 1959, Holland and Jones took their turn at missions touring outside the USA, visiting "Puerto Rico, San Blas, Colombia, Panama, and Guatemala." Jones spoke of her growing awareness of the greatness of God "as she saw His mighty works evidenced in the lives of individual Christians and in small but effective Baptist churches on the various mission fields."[77]

As Florida WMU members traveled to other nations, internationals came in increasing numbers to Florida. More and more foreign students enrolled in Florida colleges. The Baptist Student Union planned the first international student retreat for January 1958 on the Stetson campus. WMS members contributed $949.44 to help with expenses.[78] The plan was for each WMS to give $2 yearly for the Burney Fund and the International Student Retreat fund. The first $200 received would go to the Burney Fund, which ministered to children of foreign missionaries attending schools in America, and the remainder to the annual retreat, which as of 1994, was still taking place.

Walking in the Way

Baptists began in 1955 to plan for the 1964 sesquicentennial celebration of "the organization of Baptist work on a national scale in North America." Southern Baptists joined with several other major Baptist bodies in "adopting common goals and working together to accomplish long-range objectives." Although the SBC actually organized in 1845, its forerunner, the Triennial Convention, began in 1814. The Baptist Jubilee Advance, often referred to as the Third Jubilee Advance (a Jubilee year occurring every 50 years), was a multi-year commemoration involving every aspect of denominational activity.[79] WMU, SBC, leaders coordinated a plan of work in full support of the program. They added their own special twist, however, with goals for the national WMU 75th Anniversary coming in 1963.

In 1958, Florida WMU voted to aim for at least one WMU organization in every Florida Baptist Convention church by 1964 and to support the 30,000 Movement, an SBC effort to establish 30,000 new churches and missions by the end of 1964.[80] The women chose Mrs. John Maguire as Jubilee Advance Director. She wrote a program presenting Jubilee goals and plans, which the Radio and Television Commission recorded for presentation at the 1958 fall associational meetings. Finally, those goals became part of the Executive Board recommendations presented at the 1959 Annual Session. To help emphasize Baptist heritage, the Executive Board recommended that Mrs. Lassiter, state president 1948-54, "be secured" to write a history of Florida WMU.[81]

Tampa First Baptist Church entertained the April 1959 Annual Session of Florida WMU. Guest speakers included Mrs. R. L. (Marie) Mathis, WMU,

SBC, president; Dr. Baker James Cauthen, Foreign Mission Board executive secretary; and Dr. Arthur Rutledge, Home Mission Board division director. Dr. Maguire read the names of Florida foreign missionaries appointed since the 1958 session. As Bill Wester (Southern Rhodesia) and Bill Hickman (Argentina) unfurled the WMU missionary flag, a banner displaying a cross for each of the 61 Florida foreign missionaries in current service, the audience prayed for those taking Christ to foreign soil. Delegates and visitors gave $826.40 to the annual offering for distribution among "Flag" missionaries.[82]

Mrs. Umbelina de Landera, Cuban WMU president, in "excellent English" related "incidents in current Cuban life depicting the terrible persecution of the Batista regime, and the thanksgiving and faith of the Cuban people in the leadership of Castro." She spoke of "sacrificial victories and faithful progress in the Baptist life of Cuba, and pled for understanding and prayer in behalf of her people."

Youth work was featured several times during the two-day program. Conscious of the recently birthed Space Age, Elizabeth Provence challenged the women's commitment to guide youth in a spiritual direction:

> In a day when there is more known of the world of outer space than there is of the world of inner space, when there is scientific advance without Christian conscience, when materialism threatens to destroy us, youth looks for the way, and is often left confused and bewildered because there is no one who loves God and youth enough to be where she is needed to be, to say "this is the way. . . . walk ye in it."

As Mrs. Holland neared the end of her presidential term, according to State Board of Missions minutes, she "expressed her appreciation of having been the Board's guest."[83] Soon after her election in 1954, the SBM had voted to invite the state WMU president "to attend regular meetings of the State Board of Missions at our expense, without vote." She began the practice, still followed by the president in 1994, of regularly attending the State Board meetings. At the Annual Session Jo Jones voiced to Holland "the love and appreciation of all Florida WMU and presented her a sterling silver, diamond-studded WMU emblem, to be worn on a charm bracelet, as a remembrance" of her presidency.

Sufficient Grace

Many members of the host church, Tampa First Baptist, were present to congratulate their own Margaret Lockhart, (Mrs. J. H.), who received the gavel as the new president. Margaret Eckland Lockhart, whose father was a Norwegian immigrant, had grown up in Palm Avenue Baptist Church, a mission of Tampa First Baptist. She accepted Christ when she was an 11-year-old GA. After graduation from FSCW with a degree in music, she taught school and became an elementary principal. When she delivered art fees to the school system purchasing agent, J. H. Lockhart, she met her future husband. When they married, she became a "retired" school principal; he became a Baptist.

Mrs. J. H. Lockhart
1959-1964

The telephone call from Clyde Maguire and Jo Jones had startled Margaret Lockhart. She felt they must be desperate to ask her to take the state WMU presidency. Indeed, their first choice had been a retired missionary who had agreed to be nominated but backed out near the Annual Session date. No one, however, was better qualified than Lockhart. As an employed woman, she had come through the ranks of Business Women's Circles. An unusually effective associational WMU president, she had had several years' experience on the Executive Board. When she hesitated, her husband urged her, "Margaret, take it. I'm going to retire soon, and I'll travel with you." She wanted to obey God's leading, and with that encouragement she allowed her nomination.[84]

Mrs. Lockhart planned to attend the November 1959 annual meeting of the Florida Baptist Convention in Tallahassee. Since her husband could not accompany her, she decided to take the bus. About two hours out of Tampa a highway patrolman stopped the bus to give her the devastating news: Mr. Lockhart had died suddenly in his office. What would she do without him? How could she go on with her responsibilities? Every day God showed her that His grace is sufficient even in the most difficult circumstances.

The next year, at the 1960 Florida Baptist Convention meeting in Orlando, the Convention recognized Mrs. Lockhart's capabilities by electing her as second vice-president, making her the first woman to hold Convention office in Florida.[85]

On the Field

Lockhart and Jones worked closely in planning and carrying out training sessions. For the annual Days of Instruction, they divided the state and the other state officers between them. Each team led five or six training days, involving numerous classes. Total annual attendance at the instructional programs reached over 5,000 during Lockhart's presidency.

For other meetings, Lockhart and Jones often traveled together. To conserve both money and time for morning devotionals, they would save supper rolls and eat them for breakfast in their room the next morning. Prayer was very important. Often after especially intense programs, Jones would request quiet in the car as they moved to the next destination, so that they could meditate and pray for the results of what had been done.[86]

In the early 1960s, Jones opened the state leadership conference, held each fall at Stetson, to local leaders as well as to associational officers. In 1965 the conference offered advanced leadership training to local officers who had already completed the basic certificate. Mrs. G. M. Keene, Daytona Beach, and Mrs. C. L. Hargrove, Tavares, were the first two to complete the new program of advanced study.[87]

Love and Missions

Together Lockhart and Jones planned annual sessions. As they worked, if Lockhart felt insecure, Jones "took the lead and told [her] what to do." If the president felt confident, Jones freed her to follow her own ideas. Almost 30 years later, Lockhart's first Annual Session was still her most memorable one. For the 1960 meeting in Daytona Beach she chose a theme dear to her heart, "Love Never Faileth." The Stetson Verse Choir opened the session with a striking choral reading of 1 Corinthians 13.

Speakers' topics derived from the theme. Dr. Maguire managed to use his favorite phrase in declaring, "Love Never Faileth . . . in Favored Florida." Innovative thinking led to an interesting experiment: A World Missions Conference was held in combination with the Annual Session. Presenting the Baptist Jubilee Advance goals, Mrs. Maguire's pageant, "Love Triumphant," climaxed the three-day program."[88]

A Record of Faithfulness

Many Florida Baptists were startled when, three weeks after the Annual Session, Elizabeth Provence's letter of resignation appeared in the *Witness*. She had worked for Florida WMU more than 17 years. After spending almost three months in "prayerful consideration" of a Home Mission Board invitation, she shared her decision to accept the directorship of the Rachel Sims Mission in New Orleans. On several previous occasions, former director Gladys Keith had tried hard to entice Provence to work in the Crescent City. Now she felt certain it was God's will. She would leave September 15, 1960.[89]

Provence could look back with satisfaction at the results of her work. Statistics represented obvious successes: the annual GA House Party attendance had topped 1,000; the state YWA Conference was closing in on that number. Thirteen summers of camping in 11 different camps had touched the lives of a generation of Florida young people. Seminole camps were in their ninth year; Negro camps, their fifth. An outstanding YWA camp lasted seven summers. Hundreds of youth leaders all over Florida had received training because of her efforts.[90]

Yet, as many could attest from experience, at the core of Provence's work was always the special touch on individual lives. Before she left Florida, the *Witness* carried a page filled with tributes to her. As one GA camp staffer expressed her feelings, she may have unknowingly summarized Provence's personal and professional WMU goals:

"I appreciate Lib Provence because she is genuinely concerned for and
interested in young people; in the building of their character, the sharpen-
ing of their intellect, and in developing a growing Christian maturity aimed
at a Christ-controlled life."[91]

Florida WMU expressed appreciation in a tangible way with a pair of "handsome bookends," to remind her of their love, and a large gift of money, with
which Provence bought a car to carry her "hither 'n yon in New Orleans."[92]
A faithful servant of unusual insight, unique capabilities, and seemingly
inexhaustible energy, Elizabeth Provence left a special imprint on the lives of
thousands of Florida Baptists.

A Job Divided

For some time WMU, SBC, had advocated separate staff leadership for
YWA, GA, and Sunbeams. The Florida Executive Board thought in terms of
one person (Provence) to lead YWA and GA and one to lead Sunbeams and
even effected a constitutional change to reflect that arrangement. The State
Board of Missions budgeted for a Sunbeam leader to join Jones and Provence
in 1960, but no qualified person could be found. In the meantime, Provence's
resignation sent the WMU Board scrambling to find a replacement—or
replacements. The Lord had already been at work on that situation.

Miss Reda Copeland, of Wharton, Texas, was at that time youth director
at Southside Baptist Church, Jacksonville. To get there she had followed
God's pathway, which she first became aware of as an active YWA member
in Wharton First Baptist Church. One of the "WMU ladies" took a special
interest in her and led the church to send her to YWA Week at Ridgecrest
Baptist Assembly. During that week she felt God's call to special service.
That call led her to return to college to finish her bachelor's degree and on to
Southern Baptist Seminary, Louisville, Kentucky, for a Master of Religious
Education degree. From there she accepted Southside's invitation. After she
had worked two years at Southside, God made clear her WMU destination.
In August 1960 Copeland became Florida YWA director.[93]

Still a GA leader was needed. The women were delighted when the State
Board of Missions again cooperated by placing a "GA Secretary" in the 1961
budget. Almost immediately the personnel committee talked with Carolyn
Weatherford, a "Florida girl" who was YWA director on the Alabama WMU
staff. God had patiently guided her into WMU work, and she made her
Florida debut in Miami at the October state GA house party, which Provence
returned "home" to direct. Although Weatherford would not officially join
the Florida staff until January, Provence introduced "the new GA Director of
Florida" to the 1,500 girls attending the house party.[94]

The Sunbeams Also Rise

Next came the new Sunbeam director, who was introduced in a special recognition of Sunbeams at the 1961 Annual Session in Riverside Baptist Church, Miami. Mrs. R. D. Thompson led the Riverside Sunbeams in presenting a 75th anniversary observance of the beginning of Sunbeam Bands. Then came the anticipated announcement. Mrs. Leslie Sanders, chairman of the Executive Board's personnel committee, introduced Miss Carolyn Burnett, a Southern Seminary student, as the new director. She would begin her work on June 15, 1961, after completing her seminary degree. Welcoming her to Florida would be 1,144 Sunbeam Bands with 19,410 members divided among Beginner, Primary, and 8-year-old World Friends, as well as 75 Sunbeam Nurseries with 950 enrolled. Much work also awaited her, for 600 Baptist churches had no Sunbeam organization at all.[95]

The 1961 Annual Session also focused on Mrs. Lassiter's newly published Florida WMU history. Jo Jones and Margaret Lockhart "cooperated in a delightful presentation" of *On This Foundation: History of the Woman's Missionary Union, Auxiliary to the Florida Baptist Convention.* Jones' report of the book sounded like a fervent commercial:

> The first published history of Florida WMU since 1914, it throbs with the vision, devotion, and sacrifice of those who made this annual WMU report possible. Every woman must read this history. Every WMS will want a copy to keep with its WMU minutes and other historic materials. It should be studied in class and used as reference. Get your copy today. It will help us make today and tomorrow better than yesterday.[96]

Working Together

Staff complete! Seated, left, Ruby Milner, Jo Jones, and Anne Whatley. Standing, Carolyn Burnett, Carolyn Weatherford, Reda Copeland.

At last a complete staff filled the WMU office in the new Baptist Building at 1230 Hendricks Avenue. "We worked together really well," Carolyn Weatherford Crumpler recalled as she looked back over 30 years. "We all loved and catered to Jo and to Ruby Milner, Jo's assistant. She was the BWC promoter, and we all worked on 'Ruby's meeting,' which was the big social and missionary event of the year." "Ruby's meeting," the WMS Conference for Business Women held annually over the Labor Day weekend, had developed into an elaborate event held in plush hotels rather than the original campgrounds. In 1962 attendance climbed to 450, including a few men who accompanied their wives.[97]

From Present to Future

From the beginning of Florida WMU, the work with young people had been valued as the key to future support of missions. The new age-level directors pushed to reach ever larger numbers of Florida youth. As a special project to visit home mission sites and stimulate missions interest, Reda Copeland planned a trip to the 1961 YWA Week at Glorieta Baptist Assembly. She and Ruby Milner took three car-loads of YWAs cross country, stopping for a missions tour with Elizabeth Provence in New Orleans. Because most of the girls had never been out of Florida, every day of the trip produced a new and awesome adventure.[98]

Young women readily responded to Copeland's outgoing personality. The 1961 state YWA conference, Copeland's first, drew over 700 YWAs and counselors, the largest number ever. The words of Psalm 144:12—*that our daughters may be as cornerstones, polished after the similitude of a palace*—challenged the participants. Attendance at the 1962 DeLand conference reached 1,000. In 1963, Copeland decided to try two state conferences, one at Lakeland and one at Fort Walton Beach. Attendance at the two events equalled the previous year's 1,000.[99]

A House Party Divided

When the GA house party attendance reached 1,500, Executive Board members voted to hold two gatherings instead of one. That decision practically doubled the work, but Carolyn Weatherford heartily agreed. In her first year, she planned one house party for Seminole Heights Baptist Church, Tampa, and the other for First Baptist, Pensacola. "Now, Carolyn, you just have to forget West Florida," Dr. Maguire told her, but she wanted to try her strategy. The Tampa group reached the previous year's 1,500. The Pensacola gathering added another 700, demonstrating the value of bringing such programs to the distant panhandle.[100] Multiple house parties became a tradition.

Weatherford also picked up the camping program where Elizabeth Provence left off. "Lib really knew camping, and I inherited an excellent program from her," said Weatherford. However, the new GA director began to turn the program in a slightly different direction. After 1961 Weatherford dropped the advanced camping program to concentrate on more traditional Junior and Intermediate GA weeks at Camp o' the Suwanee and West Florida Assembly.

Burnett produced newsletters for local and associational Sunbeam Band leaders and developed a plan to train leaders on basic and advanced levels. In March 1963 she cooperated with the Church Music and Training Union Departments in presenting Children's Leadership Workshops. Held in eight different locations over the state, the workshops were the first such joint efforts.[101]

O Give Me a Home

After years of "roving camps" and unfulfilled attempts to find suitable property for purchase, WMU finally decided on an arrangement for a permanent camp site. In the 1960 Annual Session, delegates voted to establish a "permanent camp reserve fund" to receive contributions toward the purchase of camp property, and to request that the Florida Baptist Convention "purchase the Camp o' the Suwannee at Branford, Florida."[102] That recommendation finally convinced the State Board of Missions that WMU was serious about a camp site. The response of the SBM was in September to appoint a camp site committee, which included Mrs. Clyde Lipscomb, WMU camp committee chairman; Mrs. Edgar Cooper; Mrs. J. G. Hughes; and Mrs. Lockhart *ex officio*, along with six men, two *ex officio*. Committee chairman Tom Collins brought a recommendation to the November 1960 Florida Baptist Convention meeting in St. Petersburg: "The Camps and/or Assemblies Committee recommends that the Florida Baptist Convention purchase and establish a state camp, and that the particulars as to site, price, and means of financing be brought to the next annual session for approval." Although that move, which in effect rejected WMU's request, may have seemed discouraging to some of the women, it could also be viewed as the end result for which WMU was hoping. WMU members prayed for the committee and waited.

In 1961, the State Board of Missions put a binder on 340 acres of land near Clermont and recommended its purchase to the November Convention. However, further investigation showed the tract unsuitable for a camp,[103] and the search continued. Carolyn Weatherford and Rosella Lipscomb joined Oscar Bean, Florida Baptist Convention associate executive secretary, and James Graves, chairman of the State Board of Missions properties committee, in traveling the state to look for the best land available. "We trounced all over Florida," Weatherford said, "before we settled on the Lake Yale property."

At the 1962 Annual Session in Orlando, Lipscomb announced the Convention's purchase of a 155-acre tract of land at Lake Yale. She "encouraged local societies to continue gifts to the special 'Camp Fund'" to provide for "buildings and other facilities" on the campgrounds. Later the Convention would add 59 acres and set the order of development as "(1) Girls' Auxiliary Camp, (2) Royal Ambassador Camp, and (3) assembly facilities."[104] Behind the scenes, for 14 years Josephine Jones had prayed, encouraged staff members, and patiently reiterated the need for a permanent camp. Now she could rejoice at what the Lord had accomplished.

Cubans Also Seek a Home

The early optimism of Mrs. Landera, Cuban WMU president, concerning the Cuban government under Castro proved unfounded. Fleeing Castro's repressive government, Cubans in large numbers made their way to American shores. Rev. Milton Leach, Home Mission Board missionary to Spanish-speaking people in Miami, sought the help of Florida WMU.

Describing "the emergency situation which has arisen because of the staggering influx of Cuban refugees coming into our country through Miami," Leach appealed "to all WMU members" to assist in providing 1) scholarships for young people going into full-time Christian vocations; 2) resettlement of Cuban refugee families; and 3) assistance with food collections. Officially, delegates voted at the 1962 Orlando meeting to give one quarterly associational offering during that year to Cuban refugee work and "to cooperate with general associational committees" in finding ways to meet the emergency.[105] In addition, WMU members all over the state became involved in local church efforts to provide housing and find jobs, to set up English language and literacy classes, to minister to those held in refugee camps, and to share the gospel as part of their ministry.

The Diamond Challenge

Those attending the 1962 meeting in Orlando also were introduced to "Annie-Versary" (Mrs. Maguire) and her helpers, Margaret Lockhart and Jo Jones, who explained plans for celebrating the Diamond Anniversary of WMU, SBC. A pageant, "Making of the Diamond," presented Florida goals, which included large percentage increases in every phase of work. Mrs. Ralph Gwin, Palmetto, member at large of the Executive Board, was presented as the writer of program plans in the upcoming 1963 issues of *Royal Service*.[106]

For Jones, the "most significant and far-reaching" of the anniversary plans was the prayer emphasis: prayer retreats and 75 Days of Prayer. Florida WMU began with a retreat in March 1962 for 10 people: the president, four staff members, four Fundamentals directors, and the Jubilee chairman. "Spiritually refreshed," those 10 fanned out over the state to hold prayer retreats in 10 "strategic locations" for associational presidents and prayer and youth directors. Those in turn were to lead local organizations of all ages to have special times of prayer. "I hope that this is one plan that will become an annual event in the life of WMU," Jones said.

"Take the Night Train to Memphis"

To introduce the 50th anniversary of Girls' Auxiliary coming in 1963, a pageant, "GAs . . . Telling the Story," related events in GA history. Missionaries gave testimonies of GA influence on their lives. Mrs. James Monroe, Miami, state Stewardship director, was acknowledged as a writer for *Tell*, the GA magazine. Weatherford reported that more local churches were holding GA coronations and that the quality of Forward Steps work was improving. At that time, each girl sent her Forward Steps material for Queen rank and above to the state WMU office for grading. When "hundreds and hundreds" of girls sent their work to Jacksonville, Weatherford was "absolutely overwhelmed" and had to call for help. Mrs. W. G. Stroup, wife of the Florida Convention Music Department head, was one of many who came to her rescue.

Until the golden anniversary, Girls' Auxiliary had never held a national convention. Interest in the Memphis, Tennessee, meeting ran so high that registrations outgrew facilities, finally requiring three separate conventions. Weatherford chartered a special Atlantic Coastline train for the night-time trip. So many girls filled the 14 passenger cars that getting an accurate count was impossible until they departed the train in Memphis. Standing at the gate, two train officials and Weatherford counted the girls as they came off one by one. The final number was 649 girls and counselors. With others who traveled by car and bus, the Florida contingent reached nearly 1,000. Total attendance was 21,533. "It was a thrilling, never to be forgotten experience," Weatherford reported.[107]

On the other hand, such an enormous endeavor was also a very weighty responsibility for one person. Rather than make the Memphis trip with Weatherford, Jones had chosen to take her customary month-long vacation. As Weatherford came home, she found herself feeling somewhat abandoned. After completing the summer camp season, in September 1963 Weatherford resigned and returned to Alabama WMU as promotion division director and assistant to executive secretary Mary Essie Stephens.

Seeing the Results

At the same time that WMU activities moved toward the 1963 WMU, SBC, Diamond Anniversary and the 1964 culmination of the Baptist Jubilee Advance, Florida women were also seeing the fulfillment of an undertaking that had emerged from the state organization's 60th anniversary in 1954. First the anniversary offering, then the State Mission Offering had provided a scholarship for Samuel S. Ho, a Chinese student from Hong Kong. "Airsick from the long plane ride," the shy 18-year-old had arrived in Jacksonville

SAM HO GRADUATES FROM MEDICAL SCHOOL

Left to right: Miss Josephine Jones, Sam Ho, Mrs. H. C. Garwood

September 20, 1954. The next day he enrolled at Stetson University. Florida WMU asked Mrs. H. C. Garwood to be his campus "mother," and she and Ho developed "a fine friendship." After graduating from Stetson, Ho enrolled in Bowman Gray Medical School; Florida women continued his scholarship. In June 1962 Mrs. Garwood and Jo Jones attended Ho's second graduation. Jones reflected on the differences eight years had brought: "Now that boy was a man, able to comprehend difficult medical terms, able to converse on philosophy and other abstract ideas. How he had grown! And best of all, he had grown spiritually."[108]

Dr. Ho married Miss Patricia Kwa, a Christian young woman also from Hong Kong. After his residency in ophthalmology, Dr. and Mrs. Ho returned to Hong Kong, where he continued to practice ophthalmology in 1994. To Florida WMU Dr. Ho sent a special Centennial message:

> The overwhelming kindness, financial and moral support toward me by the Florida WMU made my college experience very memorable. Ms. Josephine Jones and Dr. and Mrs. Harry Garwood provided me rich spiritual inspiration and impetus for my academic and career achievements in later years.
>
> I would never forget the Florida WMU who so generously assisted and supported me in every way that I have become what I am now, able to continue to be a channel of blessings to humankind in the Orient. I hereby salute the Fla. WMU on this 100th anniversary and wish God's rich blessings upon her good work![109]

Dr. Ho, Hong Kong, 1994

A corollary program annually provided loan scholarships to a mission volunteer at Stetson and one or more Florida women enrolled in Southern Baptist seminaries.

More Pomp, Less Circumstance

After WMU Annual Sessions separated from Florida Baptist Convention annual meetings in 1946, the WMU meetings grew increasingly elaborate. Pageants, dramatic productions, presentations by youth groups, guest choirs, denominational leaders, mission board executives, other special speakers, and missionaries by the dozens inspired and challenged audiences; emphasis on business and reports decreased. A parallel development was the increasing assumption of decision-making responsibility by the Executive Board, and especially by the Executive Committee of the Board, which now included 10 "resident members" from the Jacksonville area, along with the president, recording secretary, and four state Fundamentals directors. Professional staff members were now *ex officio* participants without vote.

Panama City hosted the Florida Union's celebration of the WMU, SBC, 75th Anniversary in 1963. "Colored slides" presented the work of Florida WMU. Responding to the question, "Do you think Florida women can do that for which God has called them?" Jo Jones listed three components necessary to the task: "faith in God that is absolute," "sense of call or purpose," and "love for people." Jones gave little attention to goals in her annual report, and most were carried over to the 1964 Jubilee meeting. A pageant, "Women . . . Found Worthy," written by Mrs. James Monroe, now of Fort Walton Beach, and presented by the

Mrs. James (Laura) Monroe

Northwest Coast Association, concluded the 1963 session.[110]

Summing up the work of Florida WMU in the eight years leading to the national Diamond Anniversary, Jones observed: "Gains and trends are not always discernible, but in my limited judgment there is a trend in WMU to simplify methods, strengthen the missionary purpose and work with the entire church to bring about the will of God in all the world."[111]

Goings and Comings

Jo Jones must have felt as if her head were whirling by the time of the 1964 Annual Session in St. Petersburg. The swinging door of staff positions had seen all three of her staff members go out and a replacement for each come in. In June 1963 Reda Copeland resigned to marry William G. Stroup, Jr., minister of music at Live Oak. In September, at the same time that Carolyn Weatherford left Girls' Auxiliary for Montgomery and Alabama WMU, Mary Copes arrived to head Young Woman's Auxiliary work.

A native of the Eastern Shore of Virginia, Copes came to Florida from California Baptist College, where she had been dean of women. Mary came up through the ranks of Sunbeams, GA, and YWA—"the whole works," she said—and accepted Christ as her Savior in the Lower Northampton Baptist Church. With an associate degree from Radford College, she worked for a number of years in the business world, until a Bible study conference changed her life. During the weekend conference, she had "a fantastic experience with the Lord," and committed her future to His work.

Earning a bachelor's degree at Georgetown University and a master's degree at Southern Seminary prepared her to go through whatever doors the Lord might open. She had always loved missions, and now she wanted to go to the mission field, but her health prevented that course. After a year in California, she clearly heard the Lord's voice in the invitation to become Florida's YWA director.[112]

The personnel committee did not name a GA replacement until the spring of 1964, when Ruth Bagwell, former director of Religious Education at Eglin Air Force Base, accepted the position. In the same month, Carolyn Burnett announced her impending marriage to Rev. Bill Boyd, former Florida pastor. To fill the vacant Sunbeam slot, Jo Jones went in-house, recommending Elizabeth Painter, who had worked ten years in the Florida Training Union Department. Anticipating a complete staff once more, both Jones and Margaret Lockhart could contemplate with relief, as well as joy, the final Annual Session in the Baptist Jubilee Advance.

With Liberty and Light for All

The nation languished under a cloud of gloom. Only a few months earlier, the assassination of President John F. Kennedy had ushered in a time of national soul-searching. When Baptists looked objectively at the advances made over the past five years, they also saw an enlarging gap between their accomplishments and the spiritual needs of a lost nation and a lost world.

In Fifth Avenue Baptist Church, St. Petersburg, nearly 1,500 women gathered to proclaim "Liberty and Light" for that lost world. What was said may not have been remembered, but hardly anyone who was present forgot what she saw:

> The theme, "Liberty and Light for the World," was displayed over the baptistry. In the baptistry was a suspended globe which revolved at appointed times. On one side was an arm clasping a golden torch, which was designed to "burst into flame" when the program indicated. On the other side was a golden liberty bell which sounded at the beginning of each session "via the organ keyboard."[113]

A large replica of the Statue of Liberty in front of the baptistry completed the scene.

Jones' report emphasized the results of the last five years: 39 percent increase in total organizations (to 5,186); 1 1/2 percent increase in membership (1,238 increase); 67 percent of members receiving magazines; 27 percent increase in State Mission Offering to $57,766.66; 44 percent increase in Annie Armstrong Offering to $167,840.94; and 68 percent increase in Lottie Moon Christmas Offering to $490,165.87. The WMU of Warrington Baptist Church, Pensacola, reached the highest standard, attaining Honor achievement for four of the five years. The Florida missionary flag now displayed 93 crosses.[114]

From One Servant to Another

Mrs. Lockhart had faithfully led Florida WMU during five years of exciting multiple celebrations and somewhat hectic development of multiple staff. As she relinquished her post, she thanked the women for their prayer support and for the "rare privilege" of visiting in their homes and churches. Looking

Mrs. Clyde B. Lipscomb
1964-1969

back through the lens of 30 years, Lockhart reflected on a tendency often experienced by WMU leadership:

> I am afraid that while I was president, I put a great deal of energy into planning programs, keeping engagements, traveling—sometimes forgetting the reason for it all. I think I have honestly become more missions minded as I've grown older. The Lord has to educate us sometimes, I think.[115]

To take up the mantle of leadership, the women elected Rosella Herman Lipscomb of Jacksonville, whose husband, Dr. Clyde Lipscomb, was pastor of Hendricks Avenue

Baptist Church. Born in Erie, Pennsylvania, Rosella Herman grew up in St. Petersburg, Florida. After graduating from the University of Florida, she taught at Florida High School, the University's practice school. In 1943 Lipscomb came to Florida as BSU director. When he left his job in 1945 for a pastorate in Richmond, Virginia, he took his new bride, Rosella, with him. She left her Methodist affiliation to become a loyal Southern Baptist.

During the years since the family's 1953 arrival in Jacksonville, Mrs. Lipscomb had served as a resident member of the WMU Executive Committee and as state recording secretary. As chairman of the WMU camp committee, she had helped to guide the Florida Convention's purchase of the Lake Yale camp site. She had also served ably on the State Board of Missions; as a member of several State Board subcommittees, she had given strong leadership in planning and furnishing the new Baptist Building, which the Convention occupied in 1959.[116]

Jesus Wants Me for a Sunbeam

The new president had served on the personnel committee which interviewed Elizabeth Painter for her job with WMU. As Painter's friend, Lipscomb encouraged and guided the new Sunbeam Band director, who had already enjoyed life in Florida longer than she had lived in any other place.

As Elizabeth was growing up, her family had moved frequently because of her father's work in bridge construction. The last of nine children, she attended 18 grade schools in 10 different states.[117]

Elizabeth's first WMU memory came from her second-grade Sunbeam Band: "I remember singing, 'Jesus wants me for a TIGER, and a TIGER I will be.' When I sang it at home, they said the word was *TITHER.* Either one seemed to make equal sense." At age 10, as she visited her oldest sister in Wichita, Kansas, Elizabeth heard the wife of a visiting evangelist speak to the Junior Sunday School department:

Elizabeth Painter
1964 – 1988

She explained that Jesus wanted to come into our lives, to be our Savior and constant friend. I didn't have a best friend. I accepted Jesus as my Savior and went forward during the church service. My parents wanted me to wait until we settled permanently in Kansas to be baptized.

When Elizabeth's family moved to Charleston, South Carolina, she joined a GA organization for the first time. At age 16, the year she entered the College of Charleston, Elizabeth was recognized as the first GA queen in First Baptist Church, Charleston, the oldest Baptist church in the South. When she insisted on waiting no longer, she "was baptized at age 17 into the

First Baptist Church, Charleston, South Carolina."

Outlining the life of Paul in her Forward Steps had led Painter to hear God's call to special mission service. With degrees from Wichita University, she taught school and found her calling to be work with children. In 1954 she joined the Florida Baptist Convention Training Union Department as associate for nursery, beginner, and primary ages. In 1964 she felt especially excited about the move into WMU children's work.

We Want You Anyway

The second staff member welcomed at the 1964 Annual Session was Ruth Bagwell, the new GA director. "I've been a WMU member all my life," Bagwell said. Her second memory in life was being a Sunbeam (she did not reveal the first). At age 11, she "invited Jesus inside my heart." Because her church did not have a Girls' Auxiliary, as a 13-year-old Sunbeam she promoted straight to YWA.[118]

A graduate of Furman University and Southern Baptist Theological Seminary, Bagwell came to the Florida WMU staff from a position at Eglin Air Force Base. Following her interview with the personnel committee in Jacksonville, the chairman wrote her: "Although you don't know anything about camping, we want you anyway." After much prayer, Bagwell accepted the GA position and also spent 21 summers as Florida WMU camp director.

When she made the move, her WMU salary was so small, Bagwell recalled, that she shared an apartment with Anne Whatley, WMU office secretary, in the house of Anne's brother. Working with Anne and Ruby Milner made the WMU office a joy, Bagwell commented. "Their loyalty, commitment, and service were unequaled."

Fellowship and Missions

Race relations remained a sensitive topic in national life, often raising debate and sometimes causing divisions. In her personal life as well as in her public WMU life, Josephine Jones modeled the compassion and respect for those of other races which she encouraged among all WMU members. In her own church, Riverside Baptist, she worked diligently in the language ministry for Internationals.[119] Jones' Third Jubilee Advance report (1964) traced developments in work with Negroes over the preceding five years: In 1960 Florida WMU had assisted women from the three Negro Baptist Conventions in the state to employ Mrs. Corinne Watts as a field worker with their women's organizations and youth camps. Watts continued to do an excellent job. In November 1963 Jones had invited the presidents of the three Negro women's organizations in Florida, along with Mrs. Watts, Florida WMU president Mrs. Lockhart, and the WMU staff, to her home "for an all day meeting of prayer, fellowship and discussion of what we could do to bring understanding and mutual helpfulness to our work." Interracial prayer retreats in four areas of the state developed out of that meeting.[120]

Although the 1964 Civil Rights Act created some consternation, even among Christians, it could not deter WMS members from their commitments. Florida WMU responded to efforts by women of the National Baptist Convention to raise scholarship money for Florida Memorial College (formerly Florida Normal and Industrial Memorial College) by "purchasing" a

Dr. John Maguire at Florida Memorial College ceremony.

$100 membership in the scholarship fund and giving another $250 from WMU's regular scholarships. In addition WMU continued its annual $4,000 State Mission allocation for the St. Augustine school.[121] In 1967, Jones, Lipscomb, and several black leaders organized what became known as the Missions and Fellowship Conference. Dr. Julius Avery, the Florida Convention's director of work with National Baptists in the state, helped set up the first meeting at Lake Yale Assembly. The conference provided training and encouraged "interracial fellowship and understanding."[122] One long-term result of the conference was the organizing in Panama City of an interracial World Day of Prayer. Held in a black church one year and a white church the next, the meeting "helped open the way for better race relationships and became an enjoyable fellowship." Panama City women looked forward to the 28th annual gathering in 1994. [123]

Moving with Grace

As Josephine Jones advanced toward retirement, the years seemed to pass more quickly. Much of the work continued in routine fashion, accented by special projects and meetings. The year 1965 brought the Baptist World Alliance to Miami. Local WMU members assisted with preparations and hosting duties, while Florida WMU helped three women—from Jordan, Spain and Japan—to attend the international gathering.[124] GA camps were

held for the first time on the Convention camp property, which the State Board of Missions officially named "Lake Yale Baptist Assembly of the Florida Baptist Convention."[125]

In 1966 Dr. Maguire announced that he would retire at the end of the next year. Having preceded his arrival in Florida by only a few weeks, Jones decided that her retirement time had also arrived; she planned to leave by September 1967, allowing another leader to begin the new WMU year in October. Throughout the first eight months of 1967, Jones was in the spotlight which she had avoided for 22 years.

The program for the 1967 Annual Session carried Jones' picture and a tribute by Mrs. Lipscomb:

Miss Josephine Jones and Dr. John Maguire began and ended their Florida Baptist professional careers together. Mrs. Maguire, a close friend of Miss Jones, was a talented WMU leader.

> To the women of Florida, the name Josephine Jones is synonymous with missions. For twenty-two years her unselfish dedication has been a challenge and inspiration. Her leadership has helped us all grow in compassion and in the skills of mission service. She has loved the people with whom she has worked. They have responded to this love and dedication.

The Tuesday night session featured other tributes. Dr. Maguire "expressed his gratitude for the privilege of working with Miss Jones for more than 22 years." He also announced the naming of the "Josephine Jones Chapel" at the Lake Yale GA Camp and displayed for the audience the bronze dedication plaque to be mounted in the chapel. "Unsolicited love gifts" of $4,245.62 showed tangibly the affection of Florida women for their retiring leader.[126] As they spoke of her, they used such words as "strong and courageous," "visionary," "a saint," "gentle," "marvelous sense of humor," and "self-sacrificing."

Jo Jones knew how to move with grace from one phase of her life to another. Although she had dedicated more than a third of her years to Florida WMU, when she closed the door to her office on August 31, 1967, she never returned. She continued to go forward, knowing that her call remained "not to be served, but to serve."

Josephine Jones continued to live in Jacksonville, faithfully serving the Lord. Her death came December 4, 1974, during the Week of Prayer for Foreign Missions. Friends, knowing that she would not want to disrupt that important missions emphasis, waited until the end of the week to hold her memorial service. They encouraged gifts in her memory to the Lottie Moon Christmas Offering for Foreign Missions. Committed to helping other people through her death as she had helped them through her life, Jo Jones willed her body to medical science.

VII

All of One Accord

1967 – 1974

"Well done, good and faithful servant!"
Matthew 25:21

Autumn 1945

The new Junior Girls' Auxiliary leader in Frostproof has asked for training," said Josephine Jones to her two staff members, Elizabeth Provence and Elsie Renfroe. "Which of you is traveling in that direction soon?"

"I'm headed to Bartow and Haines City next week. I can just go a little farther," Provence volunteered. Only God knew that Jones was sending someone to begin the training of her successor.

Materials in hand, Provence exited the bus in Frostproof, ready to enlighten the First Baptist Church Junior GA leader about the fine points of the job. To her surprise, her trainee was a 15-year-old Intermediate GA! Undaunted, field worker Elizabeth Provence gave GA Carolyn Weatherford a serious course in Girls' Auxiliary leadership. That Provence valued the teenager as a person was an equally impressive lesson for young Carolyn.

The next time the two met, in the spring of 1946, Provence and her mother visited with Carolyn and her mother at an Orange Blossom Associational WMU meeting. Provence convinced Mrs. Weatherford that her now 16-year-old daughter should attend the Young Woman's Auxiliary Conference at Ridgecrest Baptist Assembly.[1]

Carolyn's church WMU provided conference scholarships for her and her best friend. A wealthy lady in the church gave each girl a new suitcase. "That was my very first suitcase," said Weatherford. "I've had many others since, of course, but none that I was as proud of." Before boarding the bus for her first trip to Jacksonville, Carolyn checked her luggage, including a second-hand bag holding shoes, camera, and other extras. In Jacksonville the girls joined 59 other YWAs traveling by chartered Greyhound bus to Ridgecrest.

Arrival at Ridgecrest brought a sobering moment—her extra bag did not arrive with her. In borrowed shoes Carolyn enjoyed an exhilarating week, soaking up the energy, inspiration, and poignant stories of the missionary speakers. At the last night's commitment service, Carolyn was one of eight Florida YWAs who dedicated their lives to foreign missions.[2] Later she reflected, "When I was sixteen, I thought if a woman were called, it was to be a missionary."

When Carolyn returned home, she did what the Foreign Mission Board had advised: she repeated in her church the commitment she had made at Ridgecrest. One month later her father drove her to Fort Pierce to reclaim the lost suitcase! Carolyn began to think of her many church involvements—including Vacation Bible School director, choir leader, Training Union director, and associational offices—as "getting ready" for the mission field.

In four years at Florida State University, Tallahassee, Carolyn Weatherford not only earned a degree in library science but also honed her leadership skills through work in Baptist Student Union, campus YWA, local church and associational activities, and summer GA camps. Not yet clear about the call she had experienced at Ridgecrest, Weatherford spent five years working as a school librarian, two in Eustis and three in Tampa. In Tampa, she joined Seminole Heights, "a very vibrant missionary church" with a number of former members serving around the world as Southern Baptist missionaries. During the school year, Weatherford did volunteer youth work at Seminole Heights; during the summer the church paid her. All the while she "kept remembering that commitment made at sixteen." Occasionally she thought about going to seminary, but "not really seriously."

It was a visiting evangelist who pierced her defenses, quoting David Livingstone's famous lines of commitment: "Send me anywhere, only go with me. Place any burden on me, only sustain me. Sever any ties, save the tie that binds my heart to yours." As those words struck home, her heart pounded and her face flushed.

"I've really let all this good stuff in Tampa tie me here," she thought. "If I'm serious about serving God where He wants me, I'm going to have to break away and go to seminary."

As Weatherford looked for direction on the question of seminary, she took the Seminole Heights YWAs to DeLand for the annual YWA spring conference on the Stetson University campus. The keynote speaker was Gladys Keith, director of the Rachel Sims Mission in New Orleans. Listening that weekend to Keith's dynamic testimonies about her work in the Louisiana city, Weatherford decided to attend New Orleans Baptist Theological Seminary (NOBTS). Even as she enrolled at NOBTS, Weatherford remained uncertain of her goal. "I don't think Carolyn has any interest in WMU work, but if you could get her in your classes, that would be good," wrote Lib Provence to the seminary's "WMU teacher."

"It's been 10 years since that Ridgecrest experience. I must have another call," Weatherford told herself repeatedly. Meanwhile, she took seminary classes, worked 40 hours a week as librarian and BSU director for Mather School of Nursing at Southern Baptist Hospital,[3] and began field work at Rachel Sims Mission. As persuasive speakers from the Home and Foreign Mission Boards urged seminary students to consider a call to missions, Carolyn listened intently, thinking, "Surely the Lord is going to call me this time," but she heard no new word from God.

During a visit home in Frostproof before her last summer semester, Weatherford received a call from Mary Essie Stephens, executive secretary of Alabama WMU. "Are you interested in state YWA work?" Stephens asked.

"No, not really." Weatherford replied, but she agreed to visit Montgomery. Replacing the receiver, Carolyn said to her mother, "That's where the Lord wants me to go." But it was not where she wanted to go. Baptist Student Union and church youth work drew her interest more than WMU. After a visit and an interview with the Alabama WMU personnel committee, Weatherford's answer remained, "I'm not interested." She interviewed for a job in Louisiana and accepted it, only to receive a telegram from Stephens saying, "It is not my custom to belabor a point, but we are so certain. Will you reconsider?" At that point Weatherford stopped running. She sent two telegrams, one withdrawing her acceptance of the Louisiana job and the other saying "Yes" to Alabama WMU.

While on the Alabama staff, Weatherford heard the challenge of Dr. Baker James Cauthen, Foreign Mission Board executive secretary: "If God is not calling you *not* to be a missionary, then you should consider appointment." Accepting that as her answer, she began the lengthy application process for FMB service.

An invitation to join the Florida WMU staff seemed providential. "I can have some time in my own state, and be close to my home and my family, before going overseas," Weatherford thought. During her two years, eight months as Florida Girls' Auxiliary director, she garnered friends all over the state as she promoted GA work. In the midst of her strenuous schedule she received word from the Foreign Mission Board that a potential high blood pressure problem would, in fact, prevent appointment. Now what? At last she understood what God's call to her had always been. Her favorite Bible verse, John 1:12, reminded her, *As many as received him, to them gave he power to become. . . .* She could become all that God had created her to be as she invested herself in serving Him through Woman's Missionary Union.

A four-year stint as Promotion Division director for Alabama WMU was the next step in Carolyn Weatherford's process of becoming. When the Florida WMU personnel committee contacted her about the executive secretary's position, she could see God directing her path. She would return again to her home state, a unique mission field in itself; she would answer the challenge of transition and testing; she would guide Florida WMU in its becoming.

he women of Florida did not elect Carolyn Weatherford to her new position. A personnel committee, formed out of the local Executive
Committee with Mrs. Carl Howell as chairman, selected her, and the Executive

Carolyn Weatherford
1967-1974

Board affirmed that action. But, she chuckled as she recalled, she was presented as the new executive secretary without official action at both the November 1967 meeting of the Florida Baptist Convention and the April 1968 WMU Annual Session. Despite the oversight, Florida Baptists applauded her selection!

Unlike Weatherford, Dr. Harold Bennett, the new Florida Baptist Convention executive secretary-treasurer, was "formally installed" in his job. Bennett began his Florida work in October, just four weeks after Weatherford arrived. A North Carolina native, he came to Florida from Texas, where he had headed the Missions Division of the Baptist General Convention of Texas.[4]

Bennett and Weatherford arrived to find "Favored Florida" Baptists riding the wave of unprecedented growth and development during the years of John Maguire and Josephine Jones (1945-1967). While the state population grew from 2.4 million to 6 million, church membership increased from 184,140 to 600,836, hovering near 10 percent of Florida residents. Total annual contributions enlarged from $3,360,000 to $41,880,000. Annual missions gifts increased from $585,000 to $5,933,000.[5] WMU organizations grew from 1,515 with 29,132 members to 5,598 with 88,635 members.[6] Now Bennett and Weatherford took up the challenge of keeping their organizations on track. That both followed long-term, much-admired, and successful predecessors served only to enhance their efforts.

Carolyn Weatherford's reentry into the Florida WMU scene coincided with the planning of the 75th Anniversary celebration. The Anniversary committee's emphasis on the future, rather than the past, was right in line with Weatherford's thinking. She adapted for her own planning the committee's list of goals challenging local organizations to earn special anniversary recognition. The celebration would run from April 1968 through the Annual Session in February 1969.[7] Two issues which had brought increasing frustration to WMU ranks claimed most of Weatherford's attention in the meantime.

Organizational Intricacies

While Weatherford was state Girls' Auxiliary director, Jo Jones had talked with her more than once about rank and file dissatisfaction with the perceived concentration of WMU decision-making power in Jacksonville. Lack of "ownership" had engendered growing apathy among members statewide. Weatherford wanted to reverse that trend. She and state president Rosella Lipscomb (Mrs. Clyde B.) pledged themselves to building strong grassroots loyalty to Florida WMU.

The Jacksonville power base had developed as a result of constitutional and bylaw changes over several decades. Although some variations had occurred, the basic organizational pattern of Florida WMU over the years called for an Executive Board made up of the officers (president, sometimes a vice-president, recording secretary, and committee chairmen or Fundamentals directors), plus the associational presidents (later called directors), and "resident members" as they were added through bylaw changes. Since the addition in the early 1920s of slots for two women residing "in or near Jacksonville," the number had grown to five and then to ten resident members.

In most years, the Executive Board met twice, acting for the state organization in the interim between Annual Sessions. At first the Executive Board worked with the executive secretary to plan annual meetings and draw up a budget. In time, the Board began to present at each annual meeting a plan of work for the coming year, and to make recommendations on other matters. A much later constitution gave the Executive Board responsibility for electing the professional leadership of the state organization. Ratifying such choices in Annual Session was customary.

The Executive Board, in turn, had an Executive Committee composed only of the officers and the "resident members," which acted as the interim body for the Board. It was the power of that "local" committee to which there was growing objection during Josephine Jones' years. For a number of years during Mrs. Peelman's tenure, the Executive Committee had met monthly; in the years of Louise Smith and Jo Jones it routinely met semi-annually or randomly when there was business to transact. In 1955 the governing articles of Florida WMU ceased to be called a "Constitution" and were referred to only as "By-Laws." At that time three members at large were added to the Executive Board, carrying over to the Executive Committee again if they lived "in or near Jacksonville," but that attempt at expanding the local committee did not satisfy long. In time, decisions on the annual budget moved from the Executive Board to the Executive Committee, as did the responsibility for allocating WMU's portion of the State Mission Offering. Election of WMU office workers was the province of the Executive Committee.

Certainly the women who served both the Executive Board and the Executive Committee acted in what they considered the best interests of

Florida WMU. Few actions were publicly questioned. Yet, the concentration of decision making in such a small group inevitably limited the involvement of a broader base of membership statewide. Thus came the desire of Weatherford and Lipscomb to see women all over the state reinvest themselves in making their organization "work."

Accomplishing that aim required redefining the organizational structure through changes in the bylaws. According to the new bylaws adopted in 1969, the Executive Board became the state WMU Council, made up of the president, vice-presidents, recording secretary, area representatives, and associational WMU directors. The vice-presidents were dropped in 1971, and a language representative joined the officers in 1973. The interim body of the Council was an Executive Committee made up of the officers, including the area representatives. Still in effect (with the addition of age-level committee chairmen) in the Centennial Year, 1994, that arrangement proved much more satisfactory in responding to the diverse interests of WMU members in general. Weatherford counted that change in organizational structure as one of the most effective and productive in Florida WMU history.

Taking Initiative

Jones had also shared with Weatherford her concern about the relationship of Florida WMU and the Florida Baptist Convention. During the tenure of Jones and Maguire, the destiny of Florida WMU had become even more intertwined with that of the Convention, but with more of the liabilities and fewer of the assets of the relationship. In 1960 Florida Baptist Convention president W. Hal Hunter had planted the seeds of change, suggesting that it was time "for the Convention to take initiative in inviting Woman's Missionary Union to full department status and fuller participation in Convention leadership."[8] Jones and Maguire had agreed, Jones explained, that the issue must be dealt with, but both had opted to leave the matter for their successors.

From the inception of the Cooperative Program (CP), Florida WMU had supported it, and WMU members had given a large percentage of the state's CP contributions. WMU program and salary requests, however, were often denied by those overseeing the Convention budget. In addition, the CP emphasis on unified giving allowed WMU less freedom for projects requiring extra gifts, such as the invigorating and unifying "love projects" of the 1940s. At the same time, as the State Board of Missions assumed more control over the State Mission Offering, WMU allocations declined to 25 percent of the annual goal. Adhering to Convention accounting policies, WMU also had diminishing freedom in using camp, conference, and house party fees.

Perhaps the issue most frustrating to the women pertained to WMU's professional leadership. Although the State Board of Missions had affirmed the principle of equal salary scales (1956), WMU salaries and benefits now lagged far behind. Nevertheless, WMU maintained a cooperative spirit, giving broad support to Florida Convention goals; working relationships and communication between WMU and Convention leadership remained cordial. To work through issues of mutual interest, the State Board of Missions appointed a WMU relationship committee composed of members from both groups. Supportive pastors and widespread respect for WMU accomplishments encouraged leaders to press on.

Dr. Harold Bennett

After Weatherford took office in 1967, Jones, Lipscomb, and she often discussed the relational issue. Having served on the State Board of Missions, Lipscomb possessed a good understanding of current problems. After consulting leadership of WMU departments in other states, Lipscomb and Weatherford decided to take the initiative. According to Bennett, Weatherford asked for an appointment after he had been in office only a short time. They visited "half a day," talking about "everything that had been going on" between the Florida Baptist Convention and "WMU auxiliary." As the conversation continued, Bennett asked, "Carolyn, do I hear you saying that you would like to become a department of the Convention?"

"Well, I didn't plan to say it at this point, but that's what I'm saying," she responded.[9] Later Weatherford recalled: "Dr. Bennett was absolutely floored. He said, 'Well, I would have wanted this to happen, but I certainly didn't dream that it would come without any initiative on my part.' " From that day, Bennett and Weatherford began laying groundwork for the move.

Growing Closer

At the January 1968 meeting of the WMU Executive Committee, Lipscomb, assisted by Weatherford, "presented the facts" regarding WMU status. "In essence," Lipscomb said, "we in Florida have been a 'department' working within the Convention's framework." The committee "looked with favor" on the possible change, urging "prayerful study and consideration." At the 1968 Annual Session in Gainesville, the WMU Executive Board approved and presented a recommendation:

> . . . that Florida Woman's Missionary Union move toward becoming a regular department of the Florida Baptist Convention by October 1969, and

God's Wonders

Martha Flowers Stroup

Martha Flowers Stroup

1. Through years of plen - ty, years of want, Our God sup - plies all need;
2. He gives com - pas - sion and con - cern, And makes us more a - ware
3. We con - tem - plate new won - ders for To - mor - row as to - day,

For noth - ing is too hard for Him Whose pow'r is great in - deed.
Of man - y souls whom we must win Through wit - ness, love, and prayer.
For God pro - vides new life in Christ Who is the Truth, the Way.

Oft times when paths are rough and steep, New cour - age He doth bring,
Be still and lis - ten as He speaks, Nor from His pre - cepts stray,
With grat - i - tude for won - ders wrought, Rich bless - ings we re - call,

He load - eth us with ben - e - fits, And makes our hearts to sing.
Stand still and see His acts di - vine, Go for - ward, Him o - bey.
For spe - cial ho - ly pur - pose, Lord, We of - fer Thee our all.

© Copyright 1968 by Martha F. Stroup

that an advisory Committee of the State WMU Executive Board work with the State WMU Leadership and the State Convention Leadership in establishing policies and a plan of work which will insure the continuing distinctiveness of Woman's Missionary Union.[10]

Approval by the women sent the recommendation to the State Board of Missions and on to the Florida Baptist Convention in November 1968, then back to WMU for final passage at the 1969 Annual Session.

The 1968 Gainesville meeting not only put into motion the WMU status change but also launched Florida's 75th Anniversary celebration. A "special feature" introduced the anniversary hymn "God's Wonders," by Mrs. W. G. Stroup. The SBC Radio and Television Commission produced a recording of the hymn, which was distributed free to local Unions. Prayer groups after the Tuesday evening session focused on the 1969 Crusade of the Americas, a great evangelistic effort involving 28 countries and 39 Conventions across two continents.[11] The presence of Carolyn Weatherford and Harold Bennett as new leaders of their organizations generated spirited response from the 700 registrants. Weatherford suggested that the low attendance was due "perhaps to the racial crisis" stemming from the assassination only a few days earlier of Dr. Martin Luther King, Jr.[12]

What? No Circles?

Having begun the processes to alleviate Florida's organizational problems, Weatherford turned her attention to those changes coming from the national level. In 1968 Florida WMU participated in "one of the most massive training efforts in WMU history," as leaders prepared women "for the major changes in missionary society operations."[13]

"What? No Circles? Fewer officers? No standing committees in WMS? Changes, changes, changes for 1968!"[14] If women had not already heard what was coming, the *Witness* article certainly caught their attention. Proposing a much simpler organizational plan for the Woman's Missionary Society, which in the opinion of some had become rigid and "top-heavy with officers and chairmen," the new plan gave flexibility in meeting the varied schedules and interests of women of the late 1960s and 1970s. The major feature was a move from circles to groups. Rather than being assigned to circles, members could choose groups focused on mission action (a major emphasis since 1965), prayer, mission Bible study, current missions, or other possibilities.[15]

Creating the new office of WMU director helped to clarify the separate identities of WMU, as the umbrella organization, and WMS, for women. "The new plan strengthens the relationship of Woman's Missionary Union to other parts of the church program," touted the WMU, SBC, promotional piece, *WMU Geared to Change*. "The WMU director is in a strategic place to work with the pastor, church staff, and church council." Youth organizations also had new manuals incorporating changes.

Four officers from each association—WMU president and YWA, GA, and Sunbeam Band directors—were urged to attend an interpretation meeting to learn about the plans, which were to take effect in October 1968.[16] They in turn led similar interpretation sessions in their associations, with over 5,000 attending. By the end of May, 3,369 women and "a few men" representing every Florida association had earned leadership cards for the new manuals, which were taught in eight area leadership schools.[17] The WMU staff and lay leadership expended tremendous energy in preparing leaders and members for the coming changes. The question now became, how would they respond to the changes?

Ruby Milner getting things in order before her departure after twenty years with Florida WMU.

The WMU staff had to adjust to a significant change when Ruby Milner, executive assistant and business women's promoter for 20 years, resigned in September 1968. The Lord soon sent Mrs. Nell Ganey to serve in Milner's place.

On That Foundation

In the spring of 1968, a resourceful missionary in Peru wrote to 30 universities offering, during a year's furlough, to exchange his services as a Spanish teacher for tuition in a Master of Education program. He received only one reply. A sensitive university president responded: "Come on. We'll make the arrangements when you get here."[18] In a few weeks, Alabama and Georgia natives Irvin and Mickey Northcutt with their two children arrived on the Stetson University campus in DeLand. President Paul Geren invited them to live in his garage apartment until he could "make arrangements."

Geren arranged for a house on campus, but it required a new foundation. After setting that work in motion, he sought help with furnishings from the best source he knew for mission support. Florida WMU immediately named a committee "to work out the details of furnishing the house and getting it ready" for the Northcutts. By opening day of fall semester, the missionary family had moved into their new home, and three of the four family members had registered as Stetson students. Only nine-year-old David did not matriculate. In addition to teaching Spanish and taking graduate courses, Irvin worked with international students on campus. He and Mickey also traveled 45,000 miles "all over Florida and Georgia" relating "the cause of Christ." After a busy, but happy year, the Northcutts returned to Peru with Irvin's degree in hand.

Carolyn Weatherford reported that the Northcutt family "blessed our hearts" during their year in the Stetson missionary residence. WMU named the residence the "Lulu Sparkman Terry House," in honor of the first Florida woman to serve in foreign missions.[19]

The Northcutts' association with the Terry House only began with that furlough. During the next 18 years, Irvin and Mickey moved to Cali, Columbia, and furloughed regularly in Gainesville, where he earned a Ph.D. degree at the University of Florida. He became a professor at the International Baptist Theological Seminary in Cali. While completing his doctorate, he wrote the degree plans for the Th.D. and Th.M. programs at the Cali seminary. In 1986 the couple spent another year on the Stetson campus, most of it in a different Terry House, as Irvin recovered from a near fatal heart attack. Again Florida WMU met their needs. After another medical crisis brought a ten-week stay on campus in 1988, they concluded their missionary career with a final year's furlough in a third Terry House. As Irvin and Mickey Northcutt moved to emeritus status in 1994, he reflected on the Terry House ministry:

> As I see it, the Terry House was the first step toward the existence of the valuable Th.D. program at the Cali seminary. The WMU stood by us and were so kind in helping provide for the house. We appreciated so much what the Terry House committee did during our last stay. We will be eternally grateful to Stetson for its kindness in so many provisions and to Carolyn Weatherford for her vision in seeing the utility of this ministry to missionaries.

Lulu Sparkman Terry House

Through the hospitality of the Terry House, Stetson University and Florida WMU continued their partnership in ministry to missionary families. The William Hickmans of Paraguay and the J. T. Owenses of Mexico were the next two families to occupy the missionary residence.

Go On Growing

Tallahassee First Baptist Church hosted the 75th Anniversary celebration of Florida WMU. The Annual Session theme, "Go On Growing," spotlighted growth in five areas: Knowledge, Understanding, Concern, World Vision, and Growing Together. Dr. Claude Rhea led the music; Mrs. Rhea opened each session with a special theme meditation. Through Dr. Rhea, Dr. Baker James Cauthen encouraged Florida WMU to go on growing and make the next 75 years "even more glorious" than the first 75. Mrs. Robert Fling, WMU, SBC, president and a pioneer missionary in New York state, spoke at two sessions and brought greetings from both Miss Alma Hunt, executive secretary of WMU, SBC, and former national president Mrs. R. L. Mathis.[20]

In her address, "Our Growing Knowledge," Weatherford lamented Woman's Missionary Society membership losses; even more, she regretted the " 'I don't care' attitude adopted by some toward the women who 'don't care.' " She challenged those present to grow in study, in prayer, in compassion, and in knowledge of Florida as a mission field. "We are not in the WMU business," Weatherford said, "but in the business of missions, using the tool of WMU."

"Carried."

The culmination of more than a year's work came at the Wednesday morning business meeting, when new bylaws were considered. A vote in their favor would approve a move to Convention department status. The vote carried. What the women had begun in Gainesville they finalized in Tallahassee. After 75 years of existence outside the Convention framework, Florida WMU returned to its roots as a department of the Florida Baptist Convention.

Dr. Bennett endorsed the action, saying, "I am convinced that Florida Baptists will be blessed by this new relationship. It is my prayer that we in return will be a blessing to the work of Woman's Missionary Union."[21] By June 1994, Bennett had not changed his mind. He reflected:

> I felt that the transfer of WMU to the Florida Baptist Convention staff would be a benefit to the Convention, and it proved to be so. I also thought it would elevate the visibility of WMU in the state and in our churches so that the WMU staff could do a better job in the churches. I think that happened, too.[22]

What therefore God hath joined together . . .

WOMAN'S MISSIONARY UNION
A DEPARTMENT OF THE FLORIDA BAPTIST CONVENTION

Members of Woman's Missionary Union worked hard at grasping the principles of the new relationship. The recently adopted bylaws contained several significant changes from preceding documents: now WMU put into writing what had always been its policy, pledging itself to "work with other departments in promoting the total program of Baptist work in Florida." The document introduced the WMU Council and area representatives. Officers included both Day and Night vice-presidents. The president and record-ing secretary were limited to five consecutive years of service; the vice-presidents and representatives, to three.

Associational WMU directors, who with the officers made up the WMU Council, served in rotating groups as the nominating committee. The presi-dent would appoint standing committees, at that time scholarship and camp. A key section stated: "The secretary of the WMU department of the Florida Baptist Convention shall be the executive secretary of this organization." Carolyn Weatherford often explained:

> *This organization* is like a club, with its officers, policies, goals, programs, etc. It operates side by side with the WMU department, which is governed by Convention policies, plans, and budget. The bridge between the two is the professional leader. No other Florida Convention department has such an arrangement.

Call Unto Me

As president, Rosella Lipscomb had successfully led Florida WMU through five years of significant change. Her insight and wisdom, strong leadership skills, and excellent sense of humor drew the admiration and love of women statewide, as well as of WMU staff. As his wife ended her presi-dential responsibility, Dr. Lipscomb prayed before the assembled women:

> Lord, we're thankful to have wife and mother back home. We pray for the new president's husband and daughter, that they will not tire of tv dinners and caring for themselves. Bless the Lenert family and all these women as they serve you. . . . [23]

With husband August A. Lenert, Jr., and daughter Earl Ann standing beside her, Cleota Lenert began her presidency with the challenge of Jeremiah 33:3, *Call unto me, and I will answer thee, and shew thee great and mighty things, which thou knowest not.*

Those words spoke *promise* to the Annual Session, but when the nomi-nating committee first contacted Mrs. Lenert, *which thou knowest not* meant, "You folks don't know what you're talking about." She described her response:

> I knew I had only worked with YWAs and children, and had just start-ed working with women in preparation for the WMU, SBC, changes. Besides, my husband had just gone through his first serious heart attack, and Earl Ann was just 14 years old and so involved in school. I thought, "I can't do this work," but something would not let me say no.
>
> Carolyn said, "Take your time and just pray about it."
>
> Once in a while I would start praying, and I would say, "No, Lord."
>
> Finally Carolyn called: "The committee's meeting next week, and we have to tell them 'yes' or 'no.'"
>
> I said, "Lord, these people need an answer. If you've got anything to say

Mrs. August Lenert
1969 – 1974

to me I want you to say it. I don't want to use your Word as a ouija board, but please help me see something special so I'll never forget it." I picked up the Bible and it just sort of fell open to Chapter 8 of 2 Corinthians:

Now therefore perform the doing of it; that as there was a readiness to will, so there may be a performance also out of that which ye have. For if there be first a willing mind, it is accepted according to that a man hath, and not according to that he hath not (11-12).

I sat there stunned, shut my Bible, and said, "Lord, you couldn't be much clearer, could you?"

Lenert immediately called Carolyn Weatherford with her answer: "I don't see that I have any of the ability you need, but the Lord said all I'm supposed to give you is a readiness, and He would take care of whatever I had and He wouldn't expect from me things I couldn't do." Lenert had occasion to go back to that scripture many times in the next five years.

The Sweet Work of the Church

Cleota Lenert, who grew up in Bryan, Texas, moved to Fort Walton Beach as a new bride in 1943. She and August joined a new Baptist mission, which became First Baptist Church, Fort Walton Beach. One of the 14 women members in the church later spoke to Lenert about WMU: "You know you want to get started in WMU work."

"Why, just tell me why," the young Lenert responded.

"Well," the lady answered, "because WMU is the sweet work of the church." Won by that answer, Lenert invested herself as WMU youth director, working with Sunbeams, GA, RA, and YWA. She became involved in work beyond the local church when she attended an associational meeting in Laurel Hill. Having lost their way, her group arrived late for the meeting and scattered to find seats in the packed auditorium. Lenert recalled what happened:

> Just as I reached the vacant seat, poised between heaven and earth, I heard the lady presiding—whom I had never laid eyes on, nor she on me— say, "The little lady with the brown hat on trying to sit down, would you be our youth director?"
>
> My pastor, just behind me, said in a stage whisper, "Take it, Cleota.

We'll help you."

Still not seated, I said, "I'll be happy to try if someone will tell me what to do."

The interview concluded with the presider's question, "Oh, yes, little lady, what is your name?" Little did that woman know that she was initiating the development of a future state president. Nor did Lenert think in such terms. She only knew that some time ago the Lord had called her to prepare for serving Him, and she was ready to follow His leading.[24]

Crusading in Cleveland and Buffalo

With the approach of the summer revivals for the 1969 Crusade of the Americas, outreach efforts moved into high gear. Teaming with New York and Ohio, Florida WMU arranged 93 sets of prayer partners between Florida and Buffalo; Carolyn Weatherford visited WMU groups in Buffalo and in Cleveland. In April, 15 Floridians, including Ruth Bagwell and Mary Copes, traveled to the Buffalo area, where they assisted in a telephone survey. Each caller needed to make 300 calls per day in order to reach the 800,000 telephone subscribers in the area. Working in a Niagara Falls church, Bagwell introduced herself over the phone to a young lady and expressed the interest of Baptists in her. She replied in surprise, "Are you for real?" After a lengthy conversation, she asked Bagwell to talk with her roommate also.[25]

When Cleveland Baptists requested help in following up on their phone survey, Elizabeth Painter and 22 others from Florida made visits and distributed literature. "This has been a very worthwhile undertaking, and expressions of gratitude have come from individuals and groups in both Buffalo and Cleveland," said Weatherford.[26]

Grouping and Grading

The 1968 organizational overhaul of WMU turned out to be only a tune-up for the new models of 1970. Earlier in the decade WMU, SBC, had voluntarily entered into a study of church organizations and the tasks most pertinent to each. Working with SBC leadership of Sunday School, Church Training, Church Music, and Brotherhood, the national Union cooperated in developing the new concept of "a unified, correlated, coordinated program" for churches. Because WMU age-level organizations did not fit precisely into the new age groupings—preschool, children, youth, and adult—WMU, SBC, was forced to redesign them.[27] New names, new periodicals, new programs, and reworded task statements offered new challenges for the 1970s, but the "unchanging purpose" of Woman's Missionary Union never wavered.[28]

Actually, the adult women's organization, Baptist Women, changed little from its immediate predecessor, the 1968 version of Woman's Missionary Society. *Royal Service* remained the periodical for women. The other groups, however, were restructured from their foundation. In seemingly hundreds of

"Shaping the Seventies" interpretation meetings, Florida WMU learned all about the new offerings: Baptist Young Women (BYW), married or single, 18-29 (later 34); Acteens, grades 7-12; Girls in Action (GA), grades 1-6; and Mission Friends, preschool girls and boys. Boys, ages 6-8, made the transition to RA under the SBC Brotherhood Department.

Staff assignments changed to match the new organizations: Carolyn Weatherford added responsibility for Baptist Women to her other work. Elizabeth Painter moved from Sunbeam director to Mission Friends and Girls in Action associate; Ruth Bagwell, from GA director to Acteens associate. Mary Copes moved to the Florida Sunday School Department in the spring of 1970. That vacancy was filled in October 1970, when Russell Drinnen became Florida's first Baptist Young Women associate.

Persistence Pays

A native of Knoxville, Tennessee, Drinnen had become a Christian as a child while attending a non-denominational church. Soon she and her family moved their memberships to Broadway Baptist Church. Although the teenager resisted, a dedicated Girls' Auxiliary leader persisted until she persuaded Russell to join GA. "Forward Steps and camps led me to want to help other girls have the same experiences I had," said Drinnen about her youthful decision to go into WMU work.

After graduation from Carson-Newman College, Drinnen earned a master's degree from Carver School of Missions and Social Work. In 1958 she began work as young people's leader for Illinois WMU. One day in 1970, as she was opening a letter inviting her to work for Alabama WMU, Carolyn Weatherford called. As Drinnen considered both job offers, she felt God directing her to accept the Florida invitation.[29]

Changes and Challenges

Helping their leaders and members make the transition to the new organizations called for every ounce of ingenuity Drinnen, Bagwell, and Painter could muster. "Some of the new concepts were hard to grasp," said Drinnen, reflecting on BYW in that era:

> Many of the smaller churches didn't have enough women to have two different organizations. The younger women with children found it hard to make BYW a priority, and when they did, childcare was often a problem. After that first year, though, the number of BYW organizations picked up, and we had over 300 by 1973.[30]

For Acteens, said Bagwell, "the traumatic change was in Forward Steps." Leaders and girls had to accustom themselves to the new plan for individual achievement called "Studiact." Despite increasing competition from secular activities that siphoned off the interest of teenage girls, Bagwell and a dedicated band of leaders maintained a fairly stable Acteens enrollment near 6,000.[31]

Painter now had two groups to guide through the process of change. She explained difficulties for Girls in Action:

> Many Girls' Auxiliary leaders who became Girls in Action leaders were very upset with the new individual learning plan called "Mission Adventures." It was easy to overlook the fact that Girls in Action members were much younger, for the most part, than Girls' Auxiliary members had been.
>
> Some leaders saw too many choices; others saw too little Bible material. A few continued to use the Girls' Auxiliary "Forward Steps" book, even duplicating the material because the books were no longer available. I often joked and said, "If I had had foresight enough to buy any of the copies, I could have made a fortune selling them. It's difficult to estimate how much some would have paid."

With fewer changes in methods, leaders of preschool Sunbeam Bands adjusted more easily to Mission Friends.[32]

Mission Friends learn about missions using Indian dress.

At the same time that the new organizational plans brought upheaval within the ranks, challenges from outside the organization also hit hard. Society was torn by the growing influence of drugs, the "hippie scene," struggles associated with the Vietnam War, and a general rebellion against authority and institutions, including the church. Within the church, special interest groups with no missions focus competed for the time and allegiance of women. The charismatic movement also created stress.[33]

Carolyn Weatherford was obviously God's chosen servant to guide Florida WMU through the maze of changes and challenges shaking WMU structures at all levels. In the midst of the tumultuous social climate, Weatherford had the sensitivity to meet women where they were, the enthusiasm to draw them toward where they needed to be, and the love to make them feel good about it.

Creating a Sense of Family

Because of her previous experiences on the Alabama and Florida WMU staffs, Weatherford had pledged herself to create a supportive, encouraging atmosphere for her associates. She described staff relationships as they developed:

> Elizabeth and Ruth had worked together for several years, but Russell had left her support system in Illinois. It was important for us to build a new system so she would have the confidence to let her super creativity work. Ruth was really good at enabling other staff, and very competent in her own work, too. She and I enjoyed cooking steaks occasionally out on the beach. And, of course, we all walked Elizabeth through her major back surgeries and helped her to adjust. I think we felt like family for each other.[34]

The training of staff to train others also took high priority with Weatherford. Partly out of Dr. Bennett's influence, she began regular staff meetings with Drinnen, Bagwell, and Painter, so that each one could be involved in larger planning while receiving support for her individual projects. The four of them planned numerous Leadership Training conferences at Lake Yale Assembly, West Florida Assembly, Baptist Bible Institute in Graceville, and various local churches. Studiact and Missions Adventures clinics, area Mission Friends workshops, and WMU mission action conferences punctuated their schedules. The staff often took training to the members, responding to as many invitations as possible from associational and local WMUs.

As a Convention department staff, all four attended a variety of training conferences on emphases such as lay evangelism, resort missions, church-related vocations, and human relations. Those conferences prepared them for participating in general Convention programs as well as their specific WMU assignments.

Building Team Spirit

At the same time that Weatherford worked on staff development, Bennett was building and restructuring the state Convention staff, which now included the WMU department. "WMU was totally accepted by the other departments. They were all a team," said Bennett, "and we had a tremendous team spirit." Keener Pharr led the new Education Division, while Woodrow Fuller headed the new Missions Division. Although education is one task of WMU, Bennett placed the new department in the Missions Division, because he understood missions—praying for missions, teaching about missions, and giving leadership to the special missions offerings—as its reason for being.[35] By the time Bennett had accomplished his staff goals, he had won for Florida the reputation of having one of the best state Convention staffs ever assembled. He had also won the gratitude of WMU staff members as he upgraded their salaries and benefits to match those of other Convention employees and provided Convention automobiles for their use. When Cleota Lenert took office, she quickly recognized that the Lord had placed her in state leadership at a choice time, "because of the relationships WMU enjoyed with the state Convention." She experienced the "openness," "camaraderie," and "marvelous team spirit" with which the men "welcomed us women as part of the missions team in Florida" and wherever Florida touched the world. "In spite of the problems WMU faced as an organization, that acceptance, as well as the spirit of enthusiasm and exuberance in the professional WMU staff, added to the joy of those years," Lenert reflected.[36]

Cleota Lenert's one goal was to help her fellow women "get our feet planted on level ground again and figure out where we were going." She explained:

> I was convinced that we had to help the women come back to basics. We had to help them become reconvinced and therefore recommitted to what WMU is all about. I thought if we could measure our personal lives and our WMU work against the fruits of the Spirit in Galatians 5:22-23, then we could see what we're supposed to be doing and go on with greater fervor to do it.
>
> I think that's why the Lord led me to use the fruits of the Spirit as the themes for the first four annual sessions while I was president. We used love, joy, peace, and faithfulness. Then at my last annual session, in St. Petersburg, we focused on "The Living Word." I wanted the women to really experience the Spirit and feel the stability that His love, joy, peace, and faithfulness can bring to us. Then we'd be better prepared to share the Living Word with our world.

Waging Peace

Among the Annual Sessions over which Lenert presided, she vividly remembered the 1972 meeting in Daytona Beach. A symbolic dove tied the program cover and decorations to the meeting's theme of "Peace."[37] Walker L. Knight, editor of *Home Missions* magazine, gave a devotional message, "Peacemakers," during each session.[38] "If peace is not within us, it is nowhere," Knight reminded more than 1,000 women in attendance.

Home and foreign missionaries and several Florida Convention leaders, including Bennett, brought reports under the heading "Peacemakers." Home missionaries on program included Mildred Womack and Ruby Miller, who ministered to the Spanish-speaking in Miami. Florida foreign missionaries Peggy Pemble of Brazil, Helen Masters of Nigeria, and Douglas Knapp of Tanzania, also spoke.[39]

Knapp had also spoken at the Annual Session on his previous furlough in 1968. At that time he had offered a challenge: "Oh, you are such beautiful women, and you wear such beautiful hats. I wish that I could ask you to give up your hats for missions." Then he told what he could buy in Tanzania with the money spent on those hats. Now, four years later, as he stood to speak in Daytona Beach, he saw that most of the women were bare headed. "You've given up your hats," he commented.

Later, as Fuller challenged those present to help with Florida Baptists' "People Search," he said, "I wonder if you would give up your shoes for state missions." Not to be outdone, Edgar Cooper, editor of the *Witness*, took the ploy one step further, saying, "I'm going to ask you to give up your girdles." His suggestion was greeted with hearty applause.[40]

Peace Offerings

Jesse Fletcher of the Foreign Mission Board brought the good news that the 1971 Lottie Moon Christmas Offering for Foreign Missions had already exceeded the $16,750,000 goal by $750,000. For the first time, the Annual Session offering taken for Florida-born missionaries was designated for magazine subscriptions. Mrs. Woodrow Fuller urged a generous offering to provide each missionary's magazine of choice.

Each session closed with "Peace Talk," a testimony of victory for missions through local churches. Pastors told of growth in missions offerings and bus ministries; women shared mission action victories in literacy work, beach ministries, psychiatric wards, and coffee houses. DeFuniak Springs optometrist Dr. Don Wennerberg and his wife Martha, a WMU area representative, spoke of victories in the Dominican Republic, to which they had traveled as volunteers "to help with eye problems and spiritual problems there."

For Tuesday afternoon Elizabeth Painter, with the host church, planned a special event called a "Missionary Attraction for Girls in Action." Over 700 GAs gathered in the church gymnasium to meet missionaries, obtain autographs, chat, and enjoy refreshments. One GA was heard to say to a home missionary, "You know, I learned something today. You're people just like me. I guess even I could grow up to be a missionary." That event, later called World Missions Discovery for Girls in Action, continued into the next decade.[41]

Peacing Lives Together

Reports for the previous year pointed to a variety of efforts to share the peace of Christ. Three of those involved support ministries for missionaries. Encouraging Baptist Women to provide a "home away from home" for the children of Florida-born missionaries attending colleges in the state, the recently appointed MK (Missionary Kid) committee advised sending cookies, inviting MKs into homes for weekends and holidays, and sending them money for phone calls to their parents.[42] In its fourth year of operation the

Terry House had provided a home for the Bryan Brasingtons. The Dottson Mills family was to arrive in the summer of 1972.

The third ministry to missionaries fulfilled a long-held dream of Cleota Lenert. With the help of the "Operation Extra Key" committee, WMU office personnel solicited vacation homes, apartments, even hotel space in off-season times, and through the mission boards coordinated their use for brief vacations by missionary families. Missionaries attested that those Florida vacations, otherwise unaffordable, relieved stress and created much-needed peaceful moments—as well as loads of fun![43]

Florida WMU had also provided a support ministry to the WMU of Alaska, sending Ruth Bagwell on a three-week trip to assist Judy Rice, Alaska WMU executive secretary. Bagwell reported that she had trained Acteens leaders, taught Acteens mission studies, and spoken at state Acteens meetings.

To close the 1972 Annual Session, Mrs. Robert Fling led "an earnest prayer for Peace," and the audience joined hands and voices in singing "The Lord's Prayer." Mrs. Maguire reported: "Those present left with a firm resolve to become, or to continue to be, God's peacemakers."

The Children's Home Connection

As Weatherford continued her efforts to involve more women in leadership statewide, the idea of promoting support of the Florida Baptist Children's Home surfaced. From the earliest days of "Mother Bean," Florida WMU had sustained unflagging interest in the Children's Home. With Lenert on the board of trustees, and the WMU department now a Convention partner of the Home, "Project Know-How" was a natural development.

The plan called for holding information meetings in each WMU area of the state, training women "to know how to tell the Children's Home story." The project gave opportunity to focus on the Home's needs and to promote the annual offering for the Children's Home ministries. Equally important, it also developed ties among women all over the state who could take the lead in that area of interest. By 1974, over 100 women had received the special training.[44]

The Lord's WMU Hitchhiker

Public transportation from Fort Walton Beach to anywhere beyond the western Florida panhandle was almost nonexistent and when available, costly. Cleota Lenert was frugal, especially when it came to spending the Lord's money. Combining WMU business into the same trip as meetings of the Children's Home Trustees helped to stretch her limited travel budget. On one of her "Pauline journeys," WMU had flown Lenert to Lake Yale for a meeting. From there the Children's Home took her to Lakeland for a Board meeting. Afterwards, when she asked for a ride to the airport, Roger Dorsett,

Children's Home administrator said, "Oh, I have a meeting at BBI [Baptist Bible Institute in Graceville], and I'm going to fly a plane up. Save your ticket and fly with me."

They were barely air-borne when Dorsett handed her a map, saying, "The person who sits in that seat gets to help me navigate." As the plane headed out over open water with the land fast fading from view, a voice over the radio said, "You are approaching a restricted flying area. Identify or else." Then the radio faltered! At first no one picked up their distress signal, but in a moment an operator in Georgia relayed the Panama City message: *the plane was invading military territory and they were going to shoot it down.*

"Can't we turn this thing around?" pleaded Lenert. "I'd rather get close to land and take my chance with the fish than be shot down by those gunners!"

Somehow they skirted the military zone. When they finally approached Destin, Dorsett banked sharply, coming in fast. The man in charge came running out of the hangar, absolutely furious, and he let them know. What an experience—and all for WMU! Vowing that she would never again take a private flight, Lenert "all but stood by the side of the road" to reach some meetings, but with the hat boxes and extra clothes she often carried, the Lord graciously spared her that![45]

Shrinking Numbers, Giant Steps

Through the 1960s, Florida WMU had continued its Jubilee emphasis on every Florida Baptist church having at least one WMU organization and every association having an organized WMU. Efforts to accomplish that goal became known as Operation 100%. By 1964, WMU enrollment nationwide had begun to decline, but, partly with the help of Operation 100%, Florida WMU bucked the trend until the late 1960s. Within five years, however, Florida lost approximately 35,000 members (including RAs, ages 6-8), or about 39 percent of its membership. Total Florida young people's enrollment declined by a significantly larger percentage than the women's membership. By the time WMU, SBC, renewed a consistent annual increase, the national Union had lost about 28 percent of its membership.[46] Those losses occurred in the context of a nationwide decline in church membership, attendance, and giving in the 1960s.[47]

Although membership statistics sometimes told a discouraging story, many good things were happening in Baptist life as a result of WMU efforts. Alma Hunt pointed to "churchwide involvement in record-breaking special missions offerings, increases in missions volunteers, increases in Cooperative Program gifts and attention to missions in denominational publications" as evidence of the effectiveness of WMU's missions education program.[48] An increasing number of native Floridians were volunteering for mission service, regularly crediting WMU missions education organizations with stimulating their missions commitments.

Some things WMU could not change. Many women, including pastors' wives who had been the backbone of local organizations, moved from the home into the business world, a trend that threatened WMU's very existence. Besides organizational and program changes devised to stem the life-threatening decline, WMU, SBC, designed a major enlistment emphasis called "GIANT STEP." Florida set goals of 25 percent increase in membership, in organizations, and in magazine subscriptions.[49] Enthusiastic promotion in the *Witness*, along with mail-out materials, urged every age-level organization to take a giant step by participating in an enlistment survey, then reaching every prospect. Russell Drinnen developed a GIANT STEP "buddy plan" for promoting Baptist Young Women growth.

Regaining Lost Ground

The WMU of Southside Baptist Church, Lakeland, set the standard for the state. In early 1973 members of Southside WMU met their goals of 25 percent membership increase, every member receiving the appropriate magazine, and at least one organization for each age level. Even though Florida WMU as a whole failed to achieve the GIANT STEP goals, the year 1973-74 brought an increase in membership and renewed a pattern of growth. Of the 47 associations, 45 elected WMU directors for that year.[50]

In Florida, camping provided a highly stable and effective avenue of youth missions education. Ruth Bagwell directed GA and Acteens camps at Lake Yale, while Drinnen led GA camps at West Florida Baptist Assembly, which the GAs called "Floridaga." Attendance averaged better than 1,800 during the summers of 1971-1974. Acteens Cometogethers drew almost 2,000 girls annually. BYW Happenings or area conferences began to build a steady following; the first BYW retreat was held at West Florida Baptist Assembly. By 1974, Florida ranked seventh in BYW membership and tenth in BYW organizations among Southern Baptist states.[51]

Florida's turn-around demonstrated that Weatherford and Lenert were on target in developing area dialogue sessions. Each area representative orchestrated a time for women to talk informally with the two leaders and to participate in formulating plans for another year. Expressing concerns and hearing words of encouragement from the executive secretary and the president generated increased loyalty and enthusiasm, which spread beyond the women who attended.

Sharing with WMU, SBC

Florida Baptist Women and Baptist Young Women continued contributing significantly through WMU, SBC. Active members, the mainstay of local organizations, published articles in WMU publications for every age group. Mrs. W. L. Pettis, Jacksonville; Mrs. D. L. Wennerberg, DeFuniak Springs; Mrs. Dan W. Maffett, Lakeland; Mrs. Thomas P. Zurflieh, St. Petersburg;

Mrs. John Maguire, Jacksonville; Mrs. Mark Yepes, Miami; Mrs. Fred Killam, Gonzalez; and Mrs. Robert Tremaine, Palm Court, were announced as writers for 1974 periodicals. Weatherford, Painter, Wennerberg, Lenert; Mrs. Glen Nations, Tampa; Mrs. Harold Epperson, Sarasota; Mrs. A. D. Dawson, Fort Lauderdale; and Mrs. Stanley Worsham, Panama City, led workshops during WMU weeks at Ridgecrest or Glorieta.[52]

The Florida staff and presidents consistently received major assignments of responsibility at the WMU, SBC, January Board meetings. Of Florida's presidents, Alma Hunt said:

> In the years that I was with WMU, SBC [1948-1974], when you take all of the Florida presidents together and think about their contributions to our committee work and to the shaping of plans and decisions about our work, I doubt that any state made a greater contribution to Woman's Missionary Union.[53]

Red, Brown, Yellow, Black, and White

While on vacation from her Alabama WMU job in the summer of 1967, Carolyn Weatherford had traveled with her parents to Lake Yale for the first interracial Missions and Fellowship Conference. After she returned to work in Florida, she expanded Jo Jones' dream for the annual conferences by emphasizing the "multiplicity and diversity of women in Florida."[54]

Weatherford's GA heritage had given her a special interest in Seminole women. In Frostproof, a scant 80 miles from the Everglades, she had grown up hearing about the Seminole Indians and as a GA had learned about Willie King, the Seminole mis-

Celestine Dixon, President, Woman's Convention, Auxiliary to the Baptist General State Convention of Florida, Inc., and Carolyn Weatherford, Florida WMU Director, attend Missions and Fellowship Conference.

sionary. Now she worked to involve Seminole women in the Missions and Fellowship Conference, as well as other WMU programs. She found that personal contact, along with training, made a big difference in their interest. One year she visited the Hollywood Reservation at Thanksgiving, attending the "All Indian Camp Meeting." On another visit to Brighton Reservation she stayed in the home of Alice Snow, a leader among Seminole women, who interpreted for her the next day as she took them through a WMU leadership training session. At Thanksgiving 1973 Weatherford and Alma Hunt visited Big Cypress Reservation, where they slept on church pews, then shared a Thanksgiving dinner of deer, killed by the men the day before.[55]

As Seminole women participated in local and state conferences, and some took classes at BBI, they felt more a part of WMU work and began to attend out-of-state meetings. Weatherford recalled an occasion at Glorieta:

> When we gathered in the auditorium for the first session of WMU week at Glorieta, Mrs. Mathis recognized different groups, stressing the fact that a lot of ethnics were present. She kept trying to get the Seminole women in their Seminole clothes to stand up. But Alice Snow, in her stoic way, said, "She hasn't asked for Florida Baptist Women to stand up. That's who I am. She keeps looking over here—but I'm not going to stand until she says Florida Baptist Women.

Por l'Amor de Cristo

Ten years had passed since Florida WMU had answered Milton Leach's call for help in ministering to Cuban refugees. As the Cuban population in Florida, along with various other language groups, had continued growing, local WMU organizations continued their support. In 1973, the state organization saw that the Spanish-speaking churches and missions needed guidance in establishing missions education for women and children. A bilingual woman trained in WMU work could reach out to language churches. Where could such a person be found?

The Lord had already been preparing for the time when Florida women would ask that question. He had placed His chosen servant in Hendricks Avenue Baptist Church, just down the street from the Baptist Building.

David and Gisela Torres had been active Baptist leaders in Cuba. A pastor, Rev. Torres had also edited a Cuban Baptist weekly similar to the *Witness*. He was one of many pastors who were imprisoned under Castro's regime. After his release in 1967, the Home Mission Board helped the Torreses to relocate in Jacksonville. They arrived with no possessions at all; Jacksonville Association churches provided their clothing and sufficient household goods to establish their home.

The couple joined Hendricks Avenue Baptist Church, which had significant involvement in language ministries. Working through Hendricks Avenue, Rev. Torres started a Spanish mission and eventually worked with a number of Spanish-speaking congregations in the Jacksonville Association.

A WMU leader on the national level in Cuba, Mrs. Torres had edited the Cuban WMU magazine. She began attending all kinds of WMU meetings with Carolyn Weatherford. Even though she understood little English, with the similarity of the Cuban and English organizations, she could understand what was happening. Soon she developed facility in English as well. A bilingual woman trained in WMU work. . . . [56]

An Answer to Prayer

In the 1973 Annual Session in Ft. Lauderdale, a language representative was added to the officers on the WMU Council and Executive Committee. Gisela Torres became the first woman elected to "serve as a liaison between the state organization and the various language WMU groups in the state." She would receive special training through language conferences during WMU week at Ridgecrest.[57]

Several other changes in the bylaws occurred at the same time the language representative was added: 1) Promotion of the Cooperative Program, which WMU had done from the CP's beginning, was articulated as a responsibility. 2) After two years of toying with four-year term limits for president and recording secretary, the five-year limit reappeared. 3) Area representatives were added on a rotating basis to the nominating committee. 4) The chairmen of age-level committees were added to the WMU Council and Executive Committee. 5) A quorum for the Executive Committee increased from five to seven.[58] Since the changes of 1973, the Florida WMU bylaws have remained essentially the same.

WMU Afloat

Cruising to the Bahamas was not a novel idea to Floridians, but a *missions* cruise to the Bahamas was another matter. Twice during her tenure in Florida, Carolyn Weatherford planned missions cruises to Nassau aboard the *Emerald Seas*, the first voyage after the 1970 Annual Session in West Palm Beach, the second following the 1973 meeting in Fort Lauderdale. Response surpassed expectations. Because they had personal contacts with SBC missionaries in the Bahamas, area director of missions Al Dawson and his wife Tanna of Fort Lauderdale, were asked to lead each cruise. On the 1973 trip, the group took a plaque for presentation to Bahamian Baptist Women, as well as library books and a gift of almost $300 to purchase others for the Nassau Bible Institute library. With the ship anchored in Nassau, the captain assigned the bar as the area for the Sunday morning worship service. A Bahaman choir came aboard to sing before Rev. Bill Billingsley preached in the unlikely surroundings. Nearly 500 persons on the two cruises learned firsthand about Southern Baptist mission work in the neighboring island nation.[59]

All in God's Plan

Weatherford's strenuous 1973 schedule also included speaking engagements at meetings of the Baptist Convention of New York and the North American Baptist Women's Union (NABWU) in Canada. Although to some people the enthusiastic Weatherford seemed tireless, she might not have worked the Canada trip into her schedule had she not been a featured speaker. Had Florida WMU known what that trip might lead to, the women undoubtedly would have discouraged her going.

The invitation to speak before a large audience of influential women had come from Alma Hunt. The speech was Weatherford's first occasion to earn wide public recognition. Later Hunt would recall: "A number of people said after Carolyn was elected to lead WMU, SBC, that they thought her NABWU speech was a real factor in her selection. She spoke so well, and people were really receptive to her."[60]

Alma Hunt announced in 1973 that, after 26 years at the head of WMU, SBC, she would retire in 1974. In early January 1974, while attending a United Christian Action advisory board meeting at Lake Yale, Weatherford and Lenert also worked on plans for the April Annual Session. In the back of Lenert's mind, however, other thoughts nibbled at her attention: the announcement of Hunt's successor had not come as expected at the WMU, SBC, January Board meeting. Who could take Alma's place in Birmingham? Even as Lenert retired for the night, she had trouble freeing herself of the question. Later she recounted what happened:

> The next morning I delayed going to breakfast because I tarried at prayer concerning WMU, SBC. Just as clearly as I would hear another person, not audibly but in my heart, I heard the Lord say, "I'm going to call Carolyn."
>
> I thought, "Lord, you and I have had some precious moments, but this is something I really don't want to hear. Let's look elsewhere." As I continued praying, I finally came to the point of saying, "Thank you, Lord, for the answer."
>
> In the dining room, I slipped into a seat beside Carolyn and said, "I think I need to talk to you a minute." As we moved off to ourselves, I said, "Carolyn, I don't know what to make of this, but I think you need to be getting your thoughts together. I believe the Lord is getting ready to tap you for Birmingham." That very night in Fort Pierce, where she had gone for another meeting, Carolyn received her first call from Christine Gregory, chairman of the WMU, SBC, nominating committee.[61]

Endings and Beginnings

For Lenert, finalizing the plans for the 1974 Annual Session, her last, was bittersweet. Because Weatherford was committed to secrecy, no mention could be made of her upcoming departure. Weatherford felt obligated to tell only two people: the woman chosen for nomination as the next state president and Woody Fuller, her Division director and close friend. She did not have to tell the prophetic Lenert.

In Fifth Avenue Baptist Church, St. Petersburg, 1,581 women registered for the 1974 Annual Session. Lenert's chosen theme, "The Living Word," interwove all program presentations, including staff reports. Alma Hunt spoke on "The Word Shared through Mission Support." In honor of her approaching retirement, Lenert presented Hunt with two gifts from Florida WMU, a prized conch shell, "large enough to serve a salad for many people," and a sea fan, both taken from the ocean off the coast of West Palm Beach.[62] In recognition of 10 years of faithful service with Florida WMU, Ruth Bagwell and Elizabeth Painter also received gifts, as well as bags of mail sent them "as a surprise from all over the state." Mrs. Henry Allen Parker, wife of the pastor of First Baptist Church, Orlando, and the first woman to serve as president of the State Board of Missions, spoke on "Sharing the Word, from a Woman's Point of View."[63]

At the presentation of the new president and her husband, Tanna and Al Dawson, Lenert challenged Tanna to "stir up all the Baptist Women of Florida" to share the Living Word, and Al to stand with her in love and support. The four past presidents at the meeting were on stage to share an

Cleota Lenert receives flowers from her pastor, James Monroe, and First Baptist Church, Fort Walton, upon completing five years as president. Husband August joins in.

encouraging word with Tanna Dawson.[64] Only Cleota and Tanna knew how much she was going to need it.

Carolyn Weatherford shared memories of working with Lenert over the past five years and expressed gratitude to her and her family for the sacrifices they had made. Words of appreciation for "Mrs. Lenert as the first WMU president to work in the relationship of a department" came from Dr. Fuller. Having been faithful to her vision, Cleota Lenert returned to Fort Walton Beach, once more to take up her mantle of service in her local church.

Becoming . . .

Spring—a time for new life, a time for annual associational WMU meetings. Each year the WMU staff worked together in planning and promoting the associational meetings. According to both Weatherford and her staff members, the brainstorming sessions were some of their most rewarding and enjoyable experiences

Although Weatherford's pending departure was unknown at the time, for the 1974 meetings the group chose the theme "You Can Become," based on her favorite scripture, John 1:12. "We used butterflies and the idea of moving from the cocoon to the butterfly in our suggestions for reports and other features of the program," she said. A highlight at each meeting was the appearance of a state WMU staff member, who brought a WMU message, and a missionary, who brought a missions message. Each speaker encouraged the women to see themselves as capable of their responsibilities. "We all spoke on the idea of God giving us the power to become His children and then enabling us to do what He asked," Weatherford said. "That was a high experience for all the staff and a high time of inspiration for me."[65] In 1974 members of the WMU staff attended 47 associational meetings with a total attendance of 4,200 women from 587 churches. [66]

Before the June WMU, SBC, meeting in Dallas, where Weatherford's new position would be announced, she told the news to Painter, Bagwell, and Drinnen. Drinnen also had news to share. For months the pastor of her church, San Jose Baptist, had talked with her about becoming director of a preschool program. She had decided to take the job and would leave WMU in August.

Becoming More

A front-page story in the *Witness* announced the news:

CAROLYN WEATHERFORD TO LEAD SOUTHWIDE WMU

In a *Witness* editorial entitled "Alabama Bound," Editor Cooper wrote:

> It is a long jump from Frostproof, Florida, Carolyn's home, to head woman of a 1,200,000 member organization. Expressing surprise over her unexpected opportunity Miss Weatherford said, "I started out as a Sunbeam and never in all the days I was a GA and YWA/er did I ever in my wildest imagination see myself walking in the footprints of people like Annie Armstrong, Kathleen Mallory and Alma Hunt." The statement is typical of the new

executive secretary who has not lost the wonder of God's leadership in her life.

[Carolyn] is friendly, orderly, neat, firm, decisive, cooperative, a hard worker and humble. If she will keep her same fine characteristics and personality traits she will go down in Southern Baptist history as one of the best in WMU leadership.[67]

Although the members of Florida WMU had seen their organization decline seriously in numbers, they had also seen an energetic young woman lead staff, officers, and grassroots membership to reverse the trend and find new commitments in teaching, supporting, and doing missions. Something very good had come out of Frostproof, and they were proud of their own Carolyn Weatherford.

To express their love, they sent gifts of money for presentation at a grand goodbye party at Lake Yale. The theme: "The Power to Become." New president Tanna Dawson planned the formal affair, attended by Florida Baptist Convention dignitaries and other friends from across the state. Cleota Lenert presented Weatherford a large hand-crafted butterfly with a check attached representing all the love gifts which had poured in. Later Weatherford wrote of her appreciation for the money; for the intangible gifts of friendship, cooperation, and support; and for the opportunities Florida Baptists had given her to speak in their churches, work in their associations, and visit in their homes.[68]

Carolyn Weatherford always looked to her Lord for guidance on the journey of becoming. At each stage of her life, as she served Him enthusiastically and faithfully, God rewarded her with larger challenges: *"You have been faithful with a few things. I will put you in charge of many things."*

Carolyn Weatherford served as executive director of WMU, SBC, until 1989, when she retired and married Rev. Joe Crumpler of Cincinnati. She continued to work in WMU at local and associational levels and became active in the Cooperative Baptist Fellowship. A new career as wife, mother, and grandmother offered still further challenges and joys in her journey of becoming.

VIII

Faithful to Missions

1974 – 1976

Fear the Lord and serve him with all faithfulness.
Joshua 24:14

August 1940

Come on, Bernice! Daddy's got Graymare hitched to the wagon!" Tears filled eight-year-old Bernice's eyes as she pulled on her scuffed oxfords. She was not sure which of her three older sisters had called, but she picked up the nickel she had saved for her offering and hurried to the front porch. When Daddy halted the wagon at the front steps on Sunday morning, he wanted Mother and all nine children ready to climb aboard—then!

The old wagon groaned with every turn of the steel-rimmed wheels as Graymare started the sharp climb out of the secluded Kentucky valley. Sometimes her older brother slid off the wagon to walk beside it, as if he could help Graymare. As they rounded a curve, Bernice could see both the Methodist and Baptist churches perched on the mountain slope ahead. She liked going to Sunday School at the Methodist church because almost every Sunday her teacher, Mrs. Lillie Burrell, talked about how much Jesus loves little children. When the class was over, Mrs. Burrell would slip a peppermint into each child's hand and say with a smile, "Be sweet this week, for Jesus' sake!"

Bernice especially liked the two Sundays a month when there was preaching at their Blue River Island Baptist Church. After Methodist Sunday School she and the other children usually scampered the 100 yards farther up the road to the Baptist service; today she ran to the wagon to claim a place on the bench beside her father, before her mother climbed in to ride the short distance. "I'm sorry I cried, Daddy," she said, referring to the day before, when he had brought in a neatly wrapped box from the drygoods store in Battletown.

Bernice had waited all Saturday afternoon for her father to arrive home with her new shoes. Proud to make his middle daughter happy, he had handed her the package. As she opened the box, she gasped at what she saw—two unmatched shoes! She burst into tears. Her father had deliberated between two pairs which he knew Bernice would like, but the clerk accidently packed one shoe from each pair. Knowing that he seldom made the 20-mile trip from their farm into Battletown, Bernice imagined that months might pass before she had new shoes to wear. The tears in her father's eyes, however, brought hers to a sudden halt.

Now she pressed her peppermint into his big hands lightly holding Graymare's reins, whispered her memory verse, *Be ye kind, one to another,* and gave herself a mental pat on the back: "Mrs. Burrell would be happy. I'm being sweet for Jesus."

By the time Bernice was 14, the men had torn down the one-room church house on the mountainside and reconstructed it in the valley. Now they had Sunday School classes in each corner of the room, and the preacher came every Sunday. Her younger sisters and brother fidgeted on the pew beside her during services, but she loved listening to Brother Harold Marsh. His words could transport her beyond the Kentucky borders, into a broader world than she had ever before imagined. Preaching often on missions, the pastor opened her mind to what Southern Baptists were doing in mission work around the world, what can happen when people really care about the lost, and how she could be a part of it.

Bernice looked forward to Vacation Bible School, especially because after that summer she would be too old for VBS. The Lord was planting an idea in her mind, a cloud small as a man's hand, which would eventually flood her life with the drumming rains of His call. With excitement she anticipated hearing the pastor teach the Intermediate Bible study in Acts. Just a few days beforehand, however, she was asked to fill in for the teacher of the Beginner class. What a disappointment! How should she respond? Remembering Mrs. Burrell's admonition, she said yes, for Jesus' sake.[1]

When Bernice left home to attend Georgetown Baptist College, she already was certain of her call to mission service. She had set her heart on working with Indians. That goal guided much of her thinking and preparation as she completed her college degree and entered the Carver School of Missions and Social Work. The Home Mission Board, however, would not appoint her to Indian work because the Indians would not respect a single woman. In the midst of her frustration, thinking of Mrs. Burrell's encouraging smile, Bernice asked God to show her where He wanted her to serve Him, for Jesus' sake.

God showed her the way to the Richmond, Virginia, House of Happiness, the oldest Baptist good will center in continuous service in the country. Five years later, she accepted an invitation to direct a good will center in North Carolina. After five years in that position, God led Popham into WMU work, as she accepted a call from North Carolina WMU to become state Sunbeam director. The year 1972 took her to California as director of the WMU

Department of the California Southern Baptist Convention.

When Carolyn Weatherford announced her approaching resignation in 1974, the Administrative Committee of the Florida Baptist Convention State Board of Missions, set out to find a replacement. Dr. Woodrow Fuller, Missions Division director, called Popham, inviting her to Jacksonville for an interview. "Lord, surely you don't want me to go to Florida," Popham prayed. "If there's any place I think I don't want to live, it's Florida." However, Popham had always felt that when a door opened, she should find out "if the Lord is in it." Remaining true to her commitment to God's direction, she arranged an over-night flight to Jacksonville. . . .

Bernice Popham
1974-1976

 he State Board of Missions elected Bernice Popham as Florida WMU Department director. For the first time in 80 years—since the women elected Jennie Spalding in 1894—WMU members had no part in choosing their state executive. For the first time they realized what they had given up in becoming a department, and, although they warmly welcomed Bernice Popham, the realization was painful. Even Carolyn Weatherford, who had made the preparations necessary for a smooth transition in department functioning, had not anticipated the shock created, not by the selection, but by the selection process. Bernice Popham began work in Jacksonville on October 1, 1974.

As a one-person WMU staff in California, Popham had originated the use of volunteer age-level directors, elected by and responsible to the state Convention but paid only expenses. In Florida, she found a quite different situation. Two full-time associates, Ruth Bagwell, Acteens, and Elizabeth Painter, Girls in Action (GA) and Mission Friends, awaited her coming. Having recently celebrated their tenth anniversaries with Florida WMU, Bagwell and Painter were walking encyclopedias of names, places, statistics, traditions, and broad acquaintance with WMU members and organizations throughout the state. They offered Popham excellent resources for quickly grasping the scope of WMU work in Florida.

She needed only to seek a Baptist Young Women (BYW) associate to complete the staff.

Elizabeth Painter, left, and Ruth Bagwell prepare a mailout.

Routine Matters

Under Popham's leadership, Florida WMU in the mid-1970s continued a strong focus on leadership training and on traditional events such as the Missions and Fellowship conference and the Baptist Women Labor Day conference for working women. Acteens Cometogethers, GA World Missions Discoveries, Acteens and GA camping, and Mission Friends day camps drew large numbers of participants. Ruth Bagwell took 380 Acteens to the National Acteens Conference in Memphis in 1975. That year, Painter's World Missions Discovery, held during the Annual Session in Orlando, drew 520 GAs. The youth organizations achieved a slight increase in members, but membership in Baptist Women and Baptist Young Women declined.

Ever since the earliest days of the Margaret Home and the Margaret Fund, Florida WMU had taken special interest in the families of Florida missionaries. In recent years that interest had extended to any missionary children attending school in Florida. At her election as president in April 1974, Tanna Dawson (Mrs. A. D.) had appointed the first Missionary Children committee. The new committee, chaired by former missionary to Nigeria Valda Long, was to initiate a ministry, "Home Away from Home," to MKs in Florida schools.

Committee members would also continue promotion of "an emergency fund to meet special needs of Florida MKs."[2] Each year the efforts to provide ministry to MKs brought special satisfaction to WMU members statewide.

An Avenue of Missions

In June 1975 Carrol Kelly joined the staff as Baptist Young Women associate. She came from St. Louis, Missouri, where she had been associational WMU Promotion director. A native of Hamilton, Texas, Kelly attended Southwest State College in San Marcos, Texas, and, after receiving her degree, taught school four years. Feeling called into a church-related vocation, she enrolled in the Master of Religious Education degree program at Southwestern Baptist Theological Seminary. After graduating in December 1973, Kelly went directly to St. Louis and after 18 months there, accepted Popham's invitation to work with Florida WMU. Kelly arrived in Jacksonville three days before the staff left for the national meeting of WMU, SBC, in Miami Beach. The drive to south Florida began her education in the geography of her new state.[3]

In addition to the commissioning of 18 new foreign missionaries, the Foreign Mission segment of the WMU, SBC, program focused on the plight of Vietnamese refugee families driven from home by the war in Vietnam. One of Florida's many Vietnamese refugees spoke of her own experiences. Mrs. Trinh Ngoc Thranh, former WMU president at Grace Baptist Church, Saigon, and now a resident of Orlando, said she and her family were blessed to be in the United States. "We had to escape," said Mrs. Thranh, "because Christianity under the Communist regime was a luxury." Former missionary to Vietnam, Lewis Myers, urged listeners "to continue among refugees the ministry and witness foreign missionaries started in Vietnam."[4]

Carolyn Weatherford came home to Florida to make her first report as national WMU executive secretary. In the Miami meeting, she commented on women in the SBC:

> In 1975, in the Southern Baptist Convention, the feminine segment of our denomination remains one of the great untapped resources. Woman's Missionary Union can offer women today an avenue through which they can give expression to their love for Christ and their concern for His people.

Elected to succeed Mrs. R. L. Mathis as president was Mrs. A. Harrison Gregory of Danville, Virginia. Christine Gregory described herself as "plain, earthy, but loving missions with all my heart."[5]

Preparing and Planting

When the WMU staff returned to the office, Bernice Popham put Carrol Kelly to work on a reading project. Realizing that Kelly, who was inexperienced on the state level, lacked both confidence and knowledge, Popham began remedying the first deficit by dealing with the second. She asked Kelly to study histories of WMU, SBC, by Ethlene Boone Cox and Alma Hunt, and the Florida WMU history, *On This Foundation*. Then the new Baptist Young Women associate studied the WMU and BYW manuals and made a teaching outline for fall BYW leadership training sessions. With more background information than she might have believed possible to absorb, Kelly felt better prepared to meet her responsibilities of training leadership and developing new BYW organizations. She recently reflected on that process:

> I had read most of those things before, but reading them with a purpose really made a difference. I had a better sense of the whole purpose of WMU and a better feel for our heritage. To know where we had come from gave me a solid foundation to build on.
>
> I've drawn on that knowledge many times as I've worked for WMU, SBC, and Tennessee WMU. And wherever I've managed staff, I've tried to give them some of that same kind of foundational understanding that Bernice wanted me to have.

The involvement of WMU department staff in the overall work of the Convention continued to draw positive response. Dr. Harold Bennett, Florida Baptist Convention executive secretary-treasurer, recalled Popham's cooperative involvement in Convention staff program discussions:

> When we sat around the staff table, it wasn't just a narrow "This is my task" approach. The whole task, everything, belonged to everybody, and then it was narrowed down and assigned out. Everybody helped to develop what we were doing.[6]

Carolyn Weatherford's "strong support" of Ruth Bagwell and Elizabeth Painter had already engendered Bennett's confidence in them. He said of Painter: "Her commitment to her task was unquestioned. She worked at it, and she did it well." Bagwell he knew not only as staff member but as his daughter's GA camp director: "Ruth was energetic to the hilt, you know. Our daughter Cynthia, who is a missionary, still remembers camp at Lake Yale and some of Ruth's famous sayings. She, too, was totally committed and did a good job."[7]

A mission adventure outside the walls of the Baptist Building brought a number of Convention staff together. Bennett, Popham, and Kelly were among those who worked to plant a church in the newly developing Deer Park area of Jacksonville. Sponsored by Southside Baptist Church, the Deermeadows mission began in an office building. Bennett preached occasionally, and Kelly served as youth Sunday School leader. The Bennetts and Popham were among the 16 founding members of the church. Having made phenomenal growth in its brief history, Deermeadows Baptist Church in 1994 hosted the Centennial Annual Session of Florida WMU.

Acceptance as a peer with other Convention staff and as a friend by Bennett and his wife Phyllis remarkably affirmed Kelly and partially accounted for her sense of blessing during her two-year stay in Florida. For Popham, helping to start Deermeadows Church was "one of the greatest experiences of my life."[8]

She Who Would Be Great Among You

Throughout its history the State of Florida has exhibited significant differences from other Southern states. Florida geography accounts, in part, for major distinctions in culture, life-style, and ethnic diversity. Florida WMU has reflected those differences. Although Florida was one of the ten founding states of Woman's Missionary Union, Auxiliary to Southern Baptist Convention (WMU, SBC), the state organization never claimed any of the "first families of WMU."[9] The WMU in numerous other Southern states had leaders from families well known in Southern Baptist circles and often interrelated with leading Baptist families in other states. In contrast, Florida WMU leaders have been primarily first generation Floridians without "connections." Florida records carry few references to a mother, aunt, or grandmother who had already established a reputation in state or national WMU. Leadership has always been open to the woman who commits herself to faithful service and works hard to promote the organization's goals.

Tanna Dawson's election to the presidency of Florida WMU was a good example of that principle. She had earned respect for her efficiency and dedication in local and associational offices, as state Mission Study director, and as one of the first area representatives. Dawson had also completed a term on the State Board of Missions before she became president.

Mrs. A. D. Dawson
1974 – 1979

Dawson was born Tatiana Temoshchuk in Philadelphia, Pennsylvania. Having emigrated from Russia in their late teens, her parents had met and married in Philadelphia. They first heard the gospel through the outreach of the Russian Baptist Church in the City of Brotherly Love. As members of the church held street meetings in the back alleys near their home, her father would sit on the doorstep, holding Tanna on his lap and listening to the preacher. When she was four years old, Papa became a Christian. Though at first her mother was afraid to listen to the preacher, the changes she saw in her husband convinced her of the truth of the Gospel. Six months later she, too, accepted Christ as her Savior. Her parents' strong Christian faith greatly influenced Tanna. Until she entered public school, Tanna spoke only Russian, and, although she began speaking and writing in English, the language in her home remained Russian.

Tanna made a profession of faith and was baptized at age 14. At 15 she felt called to be a missionary. While she attended the Philadelphia College of the Bible, she agreed to date Al Dawson only because he, too, was interested in mission work. They married in 1941. After Al completed work at Eastern Baptist Theological Seminary, he bought a tent. With the tent, the promise of $30 a month from each of their home churches, and a tremendous amount of faith, the coupled headed south to plant churches. After starting two churches in South Carolina, in the face of cold weather they continued south to Tampa. There local pastors were impressed with his ability to draw the lost to his tent meetings and recommended that the State Board consider hiring him. In 1944, he became one of the early area missionaries employed by the Florida Baptist Convention. For 36 years Dawson worked for the Convention, 26 of those years in Gulf Stream Association. WMU offered a major avenue through which Tanna served her Lord. The experience she had gained over the years before her election in 1974 helped her to keep an even keel as she led Florida WMU through an era of transition. Planning and guiding Annual Sessions became her special responsibility.[10]

Liberty in Christ

The nation's bicentennial birthday inspired the theme, "Proclaiming Liberty in Christ," as well as program details for the 1976 Annual Session of Florida WMU. Held in Southside Baptist Church, Jacksonville, each session opened with a Town Crier calling participants to order and a proclamation on some facet of Baptist history, prepared and read by Bernice Popham. Popham gave insights into the life of Roger Williams; Southern Baptist heritage in foreign missions; the faithful work of Florida's oldest WMU member, Mrs. Joel Gibson of Lakeland, born in 1874; and the history of the Jacksonville City Federation. "Stressing the importance of the association in proclaiming liberty in Christ," Popham gave brief details about the strong Jacksonville organization:

> The first recorded meeting was February 2, 1914, at the Riverside Church with Miss Kathleen Mallory, SBC, as one of the speakers. In January, 1915, the wife of the pastor of Riverside Church suggested the "circle plan" like they had used in Atlanta. In 1934, the Federation became the Jacksonville Association [WMU].[11]

Dawson congratulated Carolyn Crenshaw (Mrs. Genus) for "25 years of faithful service" in proclaiming liberty in Christ to the Seminole Indians. Several Seminole women—Mary Bowess, Alice Snow, Mary Louise Johns, and Daisy Butler—shared their testimonies, after which others attending the session joined them on the platform to present special music. Stirring patriotic renditions by a variety of musical groups interspersed devotional thoughts by former WMU presidents and presentations by missionaries, FBC personnel, and featured speaker Catherine Allen (Mrs. Lee N.), assistant to the executive director, WMU, SBC. The meeting closed with striking performances of "God Bless America" and the national anthem, giving the 1,004 registered messengers a vivid reminder that, after 200 years, the United States needed more than ever to hear the proclamation of liberty in Christ.

Family Matters

After WMU's welcome as a department into the Florida Baptist Convention family, there existed a happy, mutually beneficial relationship, reflecting the positive and cooperative relationship that had existed historically between the Convention and Florida WMU. One might liken the years following Carolyn Weatherford's departure to the period of time when young people struggle to understand their identities and the world in which they live. Tensions are inevitable at such a time, and they came to WMU. Two basic factors seemed responsible.

The first cause was a natural circumstance which might have been anticipated: following Carolyn Weatherford would have been difficult for anyone. But the 1974 newcomer faced an even greater challenge: she was following both Weatherford *and* Josephine Jones, a tandem accounting for 30 years of Florida WMU leadership. Although Jones had served for 23 years, hardly a tremor was felt as her mantle passed to Weatherford. After all, Weatherford was her protege; she had worked her way from GA on up under the tutelage of Jones and her co-worker Elizabeth Provence. In the minds of Florida women, serving on Jones' staff had solidified Weatherford's strong connections to her. Thus the women and the new leader, Bernice Popham, struggled with the transfer of a 30-year allegiance. No easy task on either side.

A second cause of tension was the different understanding of organizational priorities which Popham brought with her. California WMU had only a president elected by the women, with no other officers. Decisions on programming, staff, and promotion of WMU were the prerogative and the responsibility of the WMU department director under the authority of the California Convention. When the Florida State Board of Missions Administrative Committee interviewed and invited Popham to take the Florida position, she had every reason to assume that the Florida situation would be similar to that in California.[12]

Over its 80-year history, however, Florida WMU had developed an increasingly strong and effective leadership structure now centered in its Council, Executive Committee, and standing committees. The move to department status had not negated the importance of that structure to the ongoing work of WMU or to relationships with the women in Florida Baptist churches, who were the heart and backbone of that work.

Those different understandings led to some uneasiness throughout the state and particularly to some strain between Popham and Florida WMU's elected leadership. "I was called by the Convention, not WMU," said Popham, "and so there were times when we had to work those things out. We had some struggling to do, but we worked and planned together."[13] The same components that a young person needs to move through an identity crisis to a healthy self-concept enabled Florida WMU to do the same: prayer, patience, persistence, a servant spirit, and faithfulness to missions, its reason for being. God's hand held fast to Florida WMU, guiding, encouraging, enabling everyone concerned to emerge into the light of a new day.

Bernice Popham's professional life after seminary developed by decades. For the first ten years she worked in good will centers. As she approached the end of her tenth year in WMU work, the Lord again called her to make a change. When the South Carolina Baptist Convention invited her to join the staff as an associate in the Missions Ministries department, she followed her principle of exploring the situation "to find out if the Lord is in it." Convinced that the invitation was truly God's call, on December 31, 1976, Popham left Florida WMU, to begin a third decade of service to the Lord.[14]

After several years as an associate, Bernice Popham became director of the Missions Ministries Department of the South Carolina Baptist Convention. In a 1994 reorganization of Convention structure, she was promoted to director of the Missions Development and New Church Growth Team, overseeing missions ministries and new work and correlating those with the work of Woman's Missionary Union, Auxiliary to South Carolina Baptist Convention. God was stretching her third decade toward a score of years working in state missions.

Bringing Joy to Your Servants

1977 – 1991

"Serve one another in love."
Galatians 5:13

May 1938

Vanita Baldwin walked slowly out of the schoolyard toward the Baldwin Grocery and Mercantile Store. Normally she rushed to leave the schoolgrounds, but today she dawdled, sighing as she thought about Friday and the end of the school year.[1]

That night after she and her older brother had finished the dishes, Vanita headed to her mother's room. She could hear the sewing machine treadle clicking out stitches. Mrs. Baldwin carefully pulled the material back from the presser foot and laid it aside as Vanita asked to talk with her.

"And what is my Vanita so concerned about tonight?" Mrs. Baldwin asked.

Vanita adored her mother. No matter how busy Mrs. Baldwin was with the grocery store, the house, or her church work, she always had time when any of her children needed her. She sensed that Vanita needed her.

"Mother, I don't want school to be out," said Vanita.

"Well, I know you've always loved school. And we've never had to push you to do your lessons. But I'm surprised that you're not ready for vacation. Tell me about it," her mother responded.

"It's Miss Moore," Vanita said, her chin quivering. "I love her so, and I don't want to leave her class," Vanita explained.

"Oh, Dear Heart, I know Miss Moore is a wonderful teacher. She's made you feel very special, hasn't she?" Mrs. Baldwin understood Vanita's deep feelings. "But remember, you'll still be in her Sunday School class."

"Mother, she's the best teacher in the whole world!" Vanita insisted. "And you know what? I've decided that I want to be just like her. I want to be a teacher when I grow up and be just like Miss Moore!" Jean Moore was the daughter of Oak Hill Baptist Church pastor John Moore. As Vanita's seventh grade teacher and her Sunday School teacher, Moore modeled love, grace, gentility, and diligence in study, whether school books or God's Book. Besides attending Sunday School regularly, every Tuesday afternoon Vanita and her friends went to the Girls' Auxiliary meeting at the church. The leaders—her mother and her aunt—guided the girls to study about missionaries like Frank Fowler, Lulu Sparkman Terry, and Dr. and Mrs. D. F. Stamps in China.[2] The stories of Lottie Moon and Annie Armstrong stirred deep feelings in Vanita. Greatly influenced by Brother and Mrs. Moore, her teacher Jean Moore, and her GA leaders, Vanita asked Jesus to come into her heart as Lord and Savior when she was 13 years old. That experience only affirmed teaching as her chosen vocation.

After high school, Vanita enrolled at Stetson University, 40 miles away in DeLand. There for the first time she had opportunity to participate in Young Woman's Auxiliary. Again, involvement in mission study and participation in mission projects created a special feeling for Vanita. In addition to earning a bachelor's degree and teacher certification, she made a name for herself playing first base on the Stetson girls' baseball team. In 1946 she helped the Stetson team win the state championship, beating Florida State College for Women in the championship game.

Vanita Baldwin began her teaching career in a second-grade classroom in New Smyrna Beach. In a way, she was returning home, for all high school students from Oak Hill attended New Smyrna High School. Her father was happy that she had chosen to return to home territory. She was gratified that at last she could follow in Miss Moore's footsteps.

In the spring of her third year in New Smyrna Beach, Baldwin stopped by the post office one afternoon to check her box. As she glanced at the "Wanted" posters and the announcement board, an advertisement for a teaching position in the Panama Canal Zone caught her interest. Pausing to read it, she could not resist jotting down the information. The more she thought about going to Panama, the more viable it seemed. The application forms she requested came quickly; more swiftly than she had expected the process to culminate, she had received her teaching assignment at Fort Kobbe, Canal Zone, Panama. The rapidity of the whole process confirmed for her that God was leading the way.

"I don't know why my little girl wants to go so far away," Mr. Baldwin said occasionally, more to himself than anyone else. Yet he and Mrs. Baldwin did everything possible to help Vanita, because she was sure God wanted her to go. When the departure date arrived, they drove her to Miami for the flight to Panama. Even as they watched their daughter's plane take off in a heavy rainstorm, they found a sense of peace about her going. They believed that God would protect and bless Vanita as she followed His will. Good parents that they were, they did not stop at going the second mile. They went the

2000th mile, driving Vanita's car to New York City, and from there shipping it to Panama.

Baldwin quickly became involved in the life and ministry of the Cocoli Baptist Church in the Canal Zone. During her two years as a member, she served as the Woman's Missionary Union director and enjoyed working with home missionaries assigned to the area. The 1952 Week of Prayer for Foreign Missions did more than encourage her to give her money for foreign missions. Through that special missions emphasis she sensed that God was calling her "from the classroom of the children to the classroom of the church, from the school curriculum to the curriculum of God's Word."

Serving God through a church-related vocation meant a move back to the States and more education. Leaving Panama at the end of the school year, Vanita sailed with her car for the port of New York. Her parents rode the train to New York City to accompany her on the long drive back to Oak Hill.

God had taken Baldwin out of the country, away from friends and family, to reveal His will. He brought her back to receive their affirmation and support. Before Vanita left for Southwestern Baptist Theological Seminary in Fort Worth, Texas, Jean Moore promised her star pupil her constant prayers. "I wish you weren't going so far away," said her father, shaking his head but smiling, as he helped pack her car for the drive to Fort Worth and gave her his credit card.

At Southwestern, Baldwin met Mary Essie Stephens, a second-year student from Alabama. Stephens invited her to Young Woman's Auxiliary, then watched proudly as Baldwin took leadership of the group after Stephens had completed her term of office. Baldwin always looked the epitome of a lady, her prowess on the baseball field remaining a well-kept secret. One day, however, a group of campus friends gathered for an informal baseball game. As the leaders chose players for each side, Baldwin, appearing unlikely to contribute to either team's success, was the last to be chosen. In her first turn at bat she hit a home run! No one on campus ever again underestimated Vanita Baldwin.[3]

As she approached graduation in 1955, Baldwin contacted her friend, Stephens, who had become executive secretary of Alabama Woman's Missionary Union. Stephens invited her to meet a personnel committee seeking a field representative for Alabama WMU. After a successful interview, Baldwin moved to Montgomery to begin her WMU career. She learned quickly that all the qualities she had admired in Jean Moore were equally as important to WMU work as they were to teaching.

After six years traveling the state of Alabama, Baldwin moved to New Mexico as WMU Department director for the state Baptist Convention. There she established a reputation as a woman of vision and drive, completely devoted to the missions cause which she promoted. Over her 17 years in New

Mexico, she spoke during the worship service at almost every Baptist church in the state. "She's the best preacher in New Mexico," said many of the pastors. Yet she always created an aura of "genteel ladylikeness."[4]

When Carolyn Weatherford resigned in 1974 as Florida WMU Department director, Baldwin thought about the Florida job and what it could mean for her. She knew, however, that she could trust the Lord to direct her path at that stage of her life, just as He had graciously led her in the past. What she did not know was that her powerful prayer warrior, Jean Moore, was praying for God to call Vanita Baldwin back home to Florida.

r. J. Woodrow Fuller, director of the Florida Baptist Convention Missions Division, joined state president Tanna Dawson (Mrs. A. D.) in representing Florida WMU at the national Woman's Missionary Union Board meeting in January 1977. Fuller was not the first man from

Florida to attend such a meeting. Soon after Florida WMU became a Convention department in 1969, Dr. Harold Bennett, executive secretary of the Florida Baptist Convention, had visited the national Board meeting as Carolyn Weatherford's guest. Dr. Fuller's position was different, perhaps unique, for he went to Birmingham as interim director of the Florida Convention's WMU Department. While attending the meeting, he conversed with Vanita Baldwin, who was present as the New Mexico WMU Department director.[5] Jean Moore was praying.

Dr. J. Woodrow Fuller

Bernice Popham's resignation had become effective December 31, 1976. Carrol Kelly in March 1977 accepted the invitation of Missouri WMU to become Baptist Women/Baptist Young Women associate. Fuller wanted to make sure that the WMU programs continued as efficiently and effectively as possible. While the State Board of Missions sought a new department director, he worked with Tanna Dawson and staff members Ruth Bagwell, Acteens associate and WMU camp director, and Elizabeth Painter, Girls in Action (GA) and Mission Friends associate, to steady the state organization and maintain program promotion. Fuller asked Bagwell to work closely with Dawson on the April Annual Session in Titusville as well as other ongoing projects. Although Dawson's three years' experience had prepared her well for heavy leadership responsibilities, she was grateful for "the complete support of Dr. Fuller and Ruth Bagwell."[6]

Answered Prayers

During the spring Fuller and Bennett invited Vanita Baldwin to Jacksonville for an interview. The three discussed "the challenges of Florida, the program of Woman's Missionary Union, the department goals and objec-

tives, the staff members, the WMU Council, etc." She had questions for them, as they had for her. She wondered about the absence of women from the interview process. She asked Bennett, "If I am invited to speak in worship services in Florida churches, do I have your permission to do so?"

"Of course you have it," said Bennett, "if you get any invitations."[7]

Rumors had surfaced, but no one in WMU knew with certainty whom the State Board of Missions (SBM) might be seeking for the WMU director's position. Dawson, Bagwell, and Painter went to Lake Yale in May for the SBM meeting, not knowing that the Board was to act on Baldwin's election. Fuller had invited Baldwin to fly to Jacksonville, drive a Convention automobile on to Lake Yale, and meet with the Board. The three WMU

Miss Vanita Baldwin
1977-1991

leaders were surprised to see Fuller escorting Baldwin into the Board meeting. Realizing the implication of her presence, they felt somewhat disconcerted. Baldwin, who had worked with them in national WMU Board meetings, was chagrinned to recognize that they knew nothing of her coming. Yet they greeted each other cordially, and the moment passed. The SBM elected Vanita M. Baldwin as the new director of the Florida Baptist Convention WMU Department.[8] God had answered the prayers of Jean Moore.

Building Trust

Vanita Baldwin began her work in Jacksonville on June 10, 1977. Having studied the Florida WMU bylaws, she wanted to examine their significance, starting with the first statement under "Professional Leadership": "The director of the WMU department of the Florida Baptist Convention shall be the executive secretary of this organization." Thus one of her first priorities was the matter of her relationship with "this organization."

To explore that relationship, Baldwin invited Tanna Dawson to visit her in Jacksonville. For several days they probed the implications of the bylaws. One at a time, each read a bylaw to the other and articulated her understanding of that particular statement. How did each bylaw influence the role of the president? How did each one affect the status of the executive secretary? Then Baldwin and Dawson examined their expectations of each other and of their roles. Who held major responsibility for certain areas of work? What prerogatives lay with the president? With the executive secretary? Learning that Baldwin was committed to the WMU Council (Executive Board) system, so strong in Florida WMU tradition, greatly relieved any uncertainty Dawson may have felt. By the end of the week the two women had laid a strong foundation of trust for the years ahead and had become good friends in the process.[9]

Another priority of Baldwin's was the selection of a third staff member. Carolyn Weatherford and Bernice Popham had carried responsibility for Baptist Women along with the WMU Department. When Popham left, she recommended the combination of Baptist Women and Baptist Young Women for one associate. Baldwin also felt she could lead Florida WMU more effectively without the added responsibility of Baptist Women. Dr. Bennett agreed and told her to look for someone who could handle the combination position. Baldwin found that person working for Mississippi WMU in Jackson, but she did not accept Baldwin's first invitation to Florida.

Seeing Is Not Believing

While Baldwin continued to seek a third associate, the annual Baptist Women Labor Day Conference was held at Lake Yale in September 1977. The conference had begun in 1948 in a camp setting. Over the years it had evolved into an elaborate weekend program held in luxurious hotels, with attendance sometimes surpassing 400. In time, as Lake Yale became available, Carolyn Weatherford had reestablished a camp site for the conference and promoted it heavily for "night" Baptist Women. The Business Women's Circle movement had begun to phase out by the end of the 1950s, and WMU, SBC, was promoting flexible times for circle meetings. Night circles, of course, appealed to the businesswomen.[10] "A lot of working women didn't know anything at all about the Business Women's Circles which had begun the weekend retreat," Weatherford said, but they enjoyed the popular event. In the 1960s more couples and retired people attended the conference, which concentrated on missions and mission speakers.[11]

For the 1977 Labor Day conference, Weatherford returned to Florida as a featured speaker.[12] Just before she left Birmingham for Lake Yale, she got her first pair of tri-focal glasses. "Carolyn, I can hardly wait for you to speak with your tri-focals," the doctor had said, "because no matter where you look, you'll be able to see." Weatherford flew to Lake Yale a day early to finish her preparation; she was also working on a Bible study for another meeting the next weekend. She chuckled as she recalled what happened:

> I took my fat folder over to the dining hall and was sitting at the head table. When it came my turn to speak, I opened the folder and I had the Bible

study notes for the next week instead of my speech. Clyde Maguire was presiding, and when I had finished, she stood up and said, "Carolyn hasn't changed a bit. I never saw anybody with such a profundity of notes who never looked at them one time."

I stood again and said, "Oh, yes, I did look one time, only to find out they were the wrong notes!"

One long-term effect of the annual conference was played out in the life of Bobbye Spradley, from Perry, who was enlisted in WMU through the Florida Labor Day conference. Later, after a move to Kansas, she became the state WMU president and served on the WMU, SBC, Executive Board as vice-president from the Kansas/Nebraska Convention.[13]

Old Gold for BBI

A "loose end" which Baldwin treated as another priority was a WMU fund for Baptist Bible Institute in Graceville. Begun as a local effort in Lakeland in 1943, the school provided education for ministers unable to acquire educational qualifications through regular college and seminary channels. By 1948 BBI had caught the attention of the Florida Baptist Convention, and the State Missions Offering for that year included a $6,000 allocation for the school.[14] Similar allocations continued for several years. Still an independent institution, BBI moved to Graceville in 1953. "The people of Graceville, in cooperation with the First Baptist Church, acquired a tract of 160 acres inside the city limits and gave it to the new school for a campus." Immediately school trustees began to implement building plans for the new campus.[15]

In 1955 Florida WMU had voted to conduct an "Old Gold" campaign "for the purpose of erecting a WMU Building" on the BBI campus. The building would house missionary education and training for student ministers' wives and children. With an estimated cost of $25,000 to build and equip the structure, WMU hoped to begin construction "when $10,000 is available."[16] By November 1959 cash gifts and gold had amounted to $4,105.89.[17] In 1956 and 1957, the Florida Baptist Convention went through the process of taking ownership of the school.[18] Evidently in the course of events, the proposed WMU building was omitted from the campus master plan, and the fund raising was dropped.

When Baldwin checked on WMU funds, she found the "Old Gold" money still drawing interest in the Florida Baptist Foundation. In 18 years it had grown to more than $14,000. With the agreement of WMU, the State Board of Missions (SBM) in September 1977 authorized the release of the funds "being held in trust for the woman's building at Baptist Bible Institute," and designated them for married student housing at BBI.[19] Although Baldwin requested and the SBM adopted a recommendation that "an appropriately worded plaque acknowledging this gift be placed in the housing facility,"[20] by 1994 no plaque had been placed. With the assistance of Mrs. Jackie Draughon, area representative and college faculty member, and Dr. Tom Kinchen, college president, plans were made during the Centennial year to remedy the oversight.

Further Connections

Demonstrating Florida WMU's continuing interest in BBI, in 1978 president Tanna Dawson appointed the first WMU Baptist Bible Institute committee.[21] When BBI became Florida Baptist Theological College (FBTC) in November 1988, the name of the committee changed to match the new name of the institution. Committee members served as FBTC resource persons, finding ways to promote the school and encourage the student body. Another link between the college and WMU was the frequent use of WMU staff as guest teachers, especially in religious education classes. Vanita Baldwin often spoke in chapel, much to the delight of her student audiences. Yet another tie was the college's required course in WMU and Brotherhood methods. Taught by Jackie Draughon, the course was acknowledged as the only such required work in any upper-level institution in the nation. Although ambitious young pastors occasionally resented being required to take the class, more often than not, they thanked Draughon before the end of the semester.[22]

At the same September 1977 meeting in which the State Board of Missions released the WMU Old Gold fund to BBI, the Board also voted to accept an invitation from the SBC Foreign Mission Board and the Korea Baptist Mission of the FMB "to conduct a major city evangelization project in the Republic of Korea for the period of 1978-80."[23] The partnership project was an outgrowth of a new Southern Baptist Convention emphasis described as a "bold mission effort to evangelize the world by the close of the century." The visionary missions program, which came to be known as Bold Mission Thrust, was proposed at the 1976 SBC meeting in Norfolk, Virginia, and adopted by the SBC in Kansas City in 1977.[24] Florida WMU would soon become deeply involved in the Korea partnership.

GA Overnights

Elizabeth Painter chose Vanita Baldwin's first year as the time to begin an exciting new venture with Girls in Action members too young to attend summer camp. She planned two Mother-Daughter overnights, one at Lake Yale and one in west Florida. Painter arranged the schedule so that girls and their mothers (or their substitutes) did all activities together except for a 90-minute period on Saturday morning. At that time mothers attended a conference on parenting, while the girls participated in activities such as music, crafts, and games.

Each GA and her mother had a quiet time together, with a booklet giving guidance for a devotional. During the years she directed that type activity,

Painter recalled, "several mothers led their daughters to accept Jesus as Savior as a result of that quiet time." As Baldwin regularly attended at least one overnight each year, "[she] became a favorite missions speaker of both the girls and their mothers."[25]

Born for WMU

Frances Shaw, gifted and dedicated Baptist Young Women director for Mississippi WMU, had felt no inclination to move to Florida when Vanita Baldwin first contacted her. Several months later, however, when the two of them talked again, Shaw "began to feel that God was moving in my life and it was time for me to come to Florida."[26] She began her Florida

Frances Shaw

sojourn on June 10, 1978, a year to the day after Baldwin.

Shaw had first experienced God's movement in her life as a young child. Born in Galveston, Texas, she became a Christian when she was nine years old. The "closeknit fellowship" of Broadway Baptist, a small downtown church, nurtured Frances and taught her to care about missions. She eagerly entered into the activities of Sunbeams and Girls' Auxiliary and was crowned Queen in an associational coronation held in her church.

When Frances was in the seventh grade, her family moved to LaMarque, a small town near Galveston. In the LaMarque First Baptist Church, she progressed from Girls' Auxiliary to Young Woman's Auxiliary. "Probably my greatest growth in missions and even in my spiritual life began at that time," Shaw explained, "for YWA meant so very much to me." As a high school junior, she "felt God touch my life, calling me to do WMU work on the state level." Several persons suggested to Frances that she was being audacious: "You don't tell people that's your goal. You wait for WMU to contact you about serving," they said. The teenaged Frances did not feel audacious; she simply felt confident that God was leading her into missions education. Many obviously providential developments over her years of preparation continued to confirm Shaw's understanding of God's call.

Preparing for Service

A work scholarship at East Texas Baptist College, Marshall, allowed Shaw to go from high school directly to college. There she became acquainted with several Texas WMU staff members, including Joy Philips, Girls' Auxiliary director, and Eula Mae Henderson, executive director, who "made a tremendous impact" on Shaw's life. Those friendships led to summer opportunities to work at the Texas WMU leadership conferences, called house parties, on the Baylor University campus. She also continued active involvement in Young Woman's Auxiliary.

For eight years after her college graduation, Shaw worked in secular fields, first in an insurance firm, then in a public school near Dallas. Finally in 1967 she sensed God's timing for her to attend seminary. After graduating from Southwestern Baptist Theological Seminary in 1969, she joined the Mississippi Baptist WMU staff as YWA director. With the 1970 organizational changes, she became Mississippi WMU's first Baptist Young Women director. Mississippi's work with campus organizations had a strong tradition, and by the time Shaw left the state, she had helped to develop BYW on 25 college and junior college campuses.

The New Worker Comes

Shaw found her June 1978 move to Flordia difficult because of leaving her friends and other ties in Mississippi. "But it was also a very happy move," she said, "because I was going where God wanted me to be at that point in my life." To her surprise, she found the pine trees and rolling hills of north Florida much like the Mississippi terrain she had left. South Florida was a different story. Through Tanna and Al Dawson in Fort Lauderdale, she made her "first real contact" with the southern part of the state. Besides the different terrain, she quickly became aware of a rapidly growing ethnic population, which was already spreading into other areas of the state. The situation offered Shaw and Florida WMU a tremendous missions challenge.

For several weeks after Shaw began work, she traveled with Vanita Baldwin as part of an "orientation" program. During their trips, Shaw learned much about the state, her new boss, and the women of Florida. The strong "corps of workers already in place in Florida and their commitment to missions education" impressed "the new worker," as Ruth Bagwell and Elizabeth Painter called Shaw "for quite some time."

A lake house at Lake Wales was the setting for the 1978 WMU annual staff planning session, Shaw's first. Baldwin gave Bagwell and Painter responsibility for seeing that Shaw found her way to the meeting; subsequent schedules required them to go in two cars. While it was still dark, the three met for breakfast before traveling in tandem to Lake Wales. Having discussed possible routes from the restaurant to the interstate highway, Bagwell and Painter left in one car, while Shaw followed in another. Or so she thought. In the darkness and heavy traffic, she lost sight of them. "I went all the way to Lake Wales either driving very slow thinking it would give them time to catch me or speeding up trying to catch them," Shaw recounted.

Had she not been gawking at Circus World, she might have seen her friends as she turned south off Interstate 4. They had stopped at a service station and, having locked their keys in the car, frantically tried to flag her down to help them. But she never saw them. When they finally rendezvoused at Lake Wales, they all had a big laugh. Bagwell and Painter were quite relieved, because they were sure that Miss Baldwin was going to be upset with them for losing "the new worker." So much for experience, they agreed![27] The four staff members melded into a stalwart team who could work hard together. They also could laugh hard together.

New Leader for Florida Baptists

With all positions filled, the WMU state staff had just settled into a routine when Harold Bennett announced his resignation. He left Florida in April 1979 to assume leadership of the Southern Baptist Convention Executive Committee in Nashville. Florida Baptists had now contributed the top male and female leaders of the Southern Baptist Convention: Harold Bennett, directing the SBC Executive Committee, and Carolyn Weatherford, heading WMU, SBC. Bennett had walked beside Florida WMU through some strenuous days. He remained a friend of the organization and of its leaders. Even though he had not worked long with Vanita Baldwin, he spoke of her as both "strongly committed to what she was about" and also "a team player."[28] Despite his original skepticism, he probably was surprised but pleased to hear that in his last Convention year, 1978-79, Baldwin, with his permission, spoke in the worship services of 42 churches![29] That number continued to increase over the years.

Dr. Dan C. Stringer

The State Board of Missions set out to find the best possible replacement for Bennett. Satisfied that they had accomplished their mission, the Board elected Dr. Dan C. Stringer as the new executive director-treasurer of the Florida Baptist Convention. He began his Florida work November 1, 1979. A native of Cordell, Oklahoma, Stringer was a graduate of Baylor University and Southern Baptist Seminary in Louisville, Kentucky. Stringer's leadership style predicted an era of bold progress for Florida Baptists. Mrs. Stringer was a Florida native, born in Lisbon.[30]

Stringer had known Vanita Baldwin in New Mexico. He came to Florida with a high opinion of her speaking skills, and as they worked together on such projects as the state Disaster Committee and promotion of the State Mission Offering, he found her an "extremely effective" co-worker. "She wrote very excellent [State Missions Offering] material and presented it well," he said. "In Disaster committee meetings, Vanita had good ideas and did not back off from things that would be a challenge to accomplish in disaster relief."[31]

Welcome to Korea

Florida Baptists entered enthusiastically into the "Korea-Florida Special Project." Early efforts sent teams focusing on stewardship, church growth, and witness training into the five major cities of Korea. Mrs. Hei Do Lee, executive secretary of the Korea Baptist Convention WMU, attended as a guest the November 1978 meeting of the WMU Executive Committee. Much discussion in that meeting centered around a WMU project scheduled for March 1979. The project's purpose was "to provide leadership training and to seek to develop a deeper missionary concern among Korean Baptist church members and youth organizations." Whoever made the trip would also gather prayer requests for the 1980 evangelistic crusades in the five focal cities. Those prayer requests would in turn challenge Florida women to support the crusades through prayer.[32]

Baldwin, whose expenses for a Korea trip were already budgeted, suggested to the Executive Committee that, to accomplish those goals, she needed the help of "three other knowledgeable WMU leaders." The cost of the trip was estimated at $1,700. To provide for the expenses of three other persons would require a significant amount of money. After discussion of Convention policy in regard to fund raising, "the women voiced the opinion that enough money could be raised" through careful person-to-person efforts and through letters. As Baldwin requested, the group selected Tanna Dawson (Mrs. A. D.), June Fuller (Mrs. J. Woodrow), and Juanita Epperson (Mrs. Harold).[33]

The team left Jacksonville March 10, 1979. Missionary Lucy Wagner, associate general secretary, Korea WMU, planned itineraries for the four team members, who sometimes traveled in pairs. Through interpreters they spoke in "churches, mission meetings, prayer meetings, Bible study group meetings and associational and church WMU meetings,"[34] and with individuals, sharing their witness, giving encouragement, and gathering prayer requests. As they talked with Korean pastors, explaining their mission to take prayer requests home to Florida women, the pastors said, "The women are not coming?"

Because it was the intention of the project planners for women to remain at home and pray during the large crusades, team members responded, "No, only the men will come."

"Ah, no, this will never do," the pastors said. "Women must come. Men cannot go into the homes during the day to witness to the women while their husbands are at work."

After the team had heard those remarks on several occasions from different pastors, the next time a similar conversation began, Tanna Dawson said to June Fuller, "June, quick, get your tape recorder. Dr. Fuller needs to hear this!" They brought home not only many specific prayer needs but also the pastors' request that women be added to the crusade teams.[35] Florida Convention leaders, including Woodrow Fuller and Jim Ponder, Evangelism Department director, responded positively to the appeal from Korean pastors, and a large number of Florida women participated in the Korean evangelistic crusades of May-June 1980.

Soon after the completion of the Korean crusades, Dr. Fuller announced his retirement. Florida WMU said goodbye to a good friend and welcomed

1980 Evangelism Crusade in Korea. Lura Jean Hoss, left, and Pat Ford, far right, with Korean friends after a witnessing session.

Dr. James Goodson as a new friend and the new director of the Florida Baptist Convention Missions Division.

On a Pilgrimage to Florida

One WMU leader who went to Korea in 1980 was state president, Oma Dell Ely (Mrs. W. Mount) of Daytona Beach, who was elected at the 1979 Annual Session in Leesburg. Like Cleota Lenert, Ely was a gift from Texas to Florida WMU.

Oma Dell grew up in Lubbock, where she faithfully attended her church, participated in missions organizations, and made her profession of faith. While she was attending Wayland Baptist College in Plainview, Texas, she felt and responded to God's call to a full-time Christian vocation. Because of her father's death, she delayed going to seminary and instead spent a year with her mother, while at the same time earning a Master of Education degree at Texas Tech University.

Before entering seminary, Oma Dell had a significant spiritual experience when she visited an associational meeting with her cousin. As she listened to the missionary speaker, she also heard God speaking to her:

Mrs. W. Mount Ely
1979 – 1984

I felt He was saying to me, "Oma Dell, I want you to make a complete surrender of your life to me." I really thought I had done this because of knowing He wanted me in full-time Christian work, but He knew that I needed to make a complete surrender to do His will wherever He would lead me.

I remember saying specifically in my heart, "Lord, if you want me to be a foreign missionary, I'll go anywhere in the world."[36]

After her graduation from Southwestern Seminary, God tested that commitment by sending her on an overnight bus ride from Lubbock, Texas, to Georgetown, Kentucky. At Georgetown Baptist College, the 25-year-old Ely became a dormitory housemother and taught 10 hours a week of courses in worship, leadership, and church recreation. From Georgetown, she moved to Richmond, Virginia, where she worked for the Baptist Book Store as church library supervisor, setting up church libraries throughout the state.

The next leg of Oma Dell's pilgrimage took her to Lynchburg, Virginia, as a citywide Baptist Student Union (BSU) director. Lynchburg College, Randolph Macon Woman's College, Sweetbriar College, and two nursing schools in local hospitals offered a challenge she felt the Lord leading her to accept. After six years in Lynchburg, she spent three years as BSU director at Judson College in Marion, Alabama. During that time, as students repeatedly came to her for counseling, she realized a need for more insight into human dynamics. Seeking growth in that area of her life, in her second summer at Judson she took a 10-week course in Clinical Pastoral Education and worked as a student chaplain in the Birmingham Baptist Hospital system. The "powerful" summer experience affected her significantly:

> I went into it feeling that I was bound by inferiorities, not feeling free or strong enough to be the person that the Lord wanted me to be. When I came out of that experience, I saw other people differently. It wasn't that they had changed, but I realized that God had really changed me in that 10 weeks.

Contacts during that summer led Oma Dell to a new job as coordinator of social and religious activities for the Baptist School of Nursing in

Birmingham. There she met and married W. Mount Ely, again having a clear sense of God's direction. Because her husband's job required them to move every few months, she became accustomed to investing herself quickly in a local church. An unusual stay of more than two years in Fort Lauderdale gave opportunity for her involvement in Florida WMU on the associational as well as the local level. After a move to Daytona Beach, she became associational WMU director and continued regular attendance at Annual Sessions.

In early spring 1979, Ely and a friend went shopping at one of Florida's many Christmas specialty shops. She recalled what happened:

> Standing among the beautiful Christmas trees, some even snow covered, with an electric Santa waving endlessly, seemed a perfectly normal thing to be doing in early spring. However, suddenly hearing my name called over the loudspeaker wasn't normal. It was frightening. Who knew where I was? The voice on the other end of the line said, "This is Ouida Fults from Tampa. I'm chairman of the nominating committee for state WMU president. . . .
>
> That ended our shopping day. I was totally in shock.

After Oma Dell shared the conversation with her husband, Mount, who always encouraged his wife "to be faithful, to be obedient to God's will," they prayed about the situation. A few days later, Mount said, "Oma Dell, why are you waiting? You know what God wants you to do, so call that lady in Tampa, and give her your answer!" She did just that!

With never a complaining word, Mount faithfully supported his wife's WMU involvements. Throughout her five years as president, he kept Oma Dell's car constantly ready for travel, and travel she did, fulfilling a personal commitment to meet with women in all 48 associations. She was away so often that Mount said, "We don't have the money we would like to have to give to missions, but I give my wife!"

Besides going on the Korean mission, Ely also made several trips out of state. In 1981 she represented Florida WMU at the unveiling of a marker commemorating the founding of the national Union on May 14, 1888. One person from each state represented at the organizational meeting in 1888 was invited to attend the ceremony in Richmond, Virginia.[37] As state president, Ely was a vice-president of WMU, SBC, and a member of the Executive Board. During her tenure, the national WMU Board decided to move WMU headquarters from downtown Birmingham to a site southeast of the city called New Hope Mountain. In 1982 Ely represented Florida WMU at the site dedication service. There she received an engraved brass stake, which she later used as a gavel to open the 1983 Annual Session of Florida WMU. Ely and Vanita Baldwin participated at the 1984 laying of the new WMU building's cornerstone. The two of them had chosen several significant Florida WMU items for inclusion in the cornerstone.[38] WMU members could voluntarily contribute to a fund for paying the debt on the new headquarters property. The Florida WMU staff and president were recognized as the first professional staff to contribute $500 to the fund.[39]

Ely's strong commitment to prayer characterized every aspect of her leadership. "The president has a unique opportunity and responsibility," she said, "to be an intercessor, especially for the state WMU director. As we planned and traveled together, Miss Baldwin and I spent many hours sharing. Knowing more about the needs, I could pray more intelligently and specifically." Ely also observed with fascination the way "Miss Baldwin" prayed with each director of missions who visited with her at the annual Associational Leadership Planning Conference. After her years as president, Ely continued her faithful service both in her church WMU organization and on the state level. In 1992 she accepted chairmanship of a state Prayer Strategy Committee to lead Florida WMU into a second century of faithful praying.

The years of Ely's presidency saw the arising of new emphases and directions in the Southern Baptist Convention. The winds of change stirred some uneasiness on the part of Woman's Missionary Union, but in regular meetings at every level, women recommitted themselves to the support of Southern Baptist missions and the missions education of youth in Southern Baptist churches. At the heart of all WMU work, from the local church to the national Union, remained the WMU tasks: teach missions, engage in mission action, support world missions through praying and giving, and provide and interpret information regarding the work of the church and the denomination.

All the News . . .

Vanita Baldwin and the staff produced several publications that made important information available in associations and churches. *Viewpoint,* a quarterly bulletin which began publication in 1970, was distributed to the WMU director and the five age-level directors in each local church. Conceived by Frances Shaw and introduced in 1978, *Associational Focus* was sent quarterly to the same six officers of each associational WMU. A publication of which Baldwin was particularly proud was the Missionary Kids' Prayer Calendar. Each year an attractive booklet carried the names, addresses, and birthdays of children of Florida-born home and foreign missionaries, who were enrolled in colleges or seminaries in the United States. The WMU office also encouraged members to read the *Florida Baptist Witness.*

GAs in a Whirl

From the inception of the new WMU age-level organizations in 1970, Elizabeth Painter had planned statewide Girls in Action activities in connection with Annual Sessions only. In 1981, Painter, Vanita Baldwin, and the state GA committee decided to take "a bold new step," planning the first separate state event for GA leaders and members (girls, grades 1-6). First Baptist Church, Lakeland, agreed to host the first GA Whirl. A small registration fee from each girl would finance the event. Painter thought 200 participants would be a "reasonable response," and 400 would be a "GREAT response." About two weeks before the meeting, fewer than 100 had registered, but when more names began to come in, she decided to "add another section of missionary speakers to accommodate 400." Painter described the outcome:

> In Lakeland, the night before the Whirl, I enlisted four more speakers—that would be enough to take care of 600. The morning of the Whirl, people came and came and came. We ended up with between 800 and 900 attending, but the overflow crowd was not the only problem. Somehow I reserved the sanctuary and not the dining area. Someone else who was having a wedding reserved the dining area, but not the sanctuary. Thus we could not eat in the dining area, and they could not decorate the sanctuary until after we dismissed.
>
> We ate in the rooms, in the halls, on the stairs of the educational building. The conference rooms barely had enough space to get everyone in. However, those attending were all great. Everyone seemed to take the inconveniences in stride. Even years later, if something went awry, people would still say with a twinkle in their eyes, "This is no problem. Remember I was at the first Whirl."

The next year Painter planned two Whirls, limiting enrollment in each to 400. Eventually the number of Whirls climbed to four each year, with registration limited to 600 at each. Painter made special effort to move the locations around in order to reach as many different associations as possible.[40] In 1994 GA Whirls for grades 1-6 and Mother/Daughter Overnights for grades 1-3 continued to draw strong attendance.

STARTEAM on the Field

Recognizing that changing times bring changing needs and interests for women, the national Union sought to create a flexibility in organization and programming that would draw a variety of women—married/single, young/old, career/homemaker, for example. To convey the availability of a place for every woman and the need for WMU organizations in every church, in 1980 WMU, SBC, launched a National Enlargement Program, involving a STARTEAM in each state. Special training sessions in Birmingham equipped state teams to undertake the massive project. Five women composed Florida's original STARTEAM: Mrs. Rafael de Armas, Mrs. A. D. Dawson, Mrs. Maynard Roberts, Mrs. Roger C. Smith, and Mrs. James R. Thompson. Their assignment was to visit each of the 415 Baptist churches in Florida with no WMU organization, speaking with the pastor about the value of missions education, and identifying a woman in the church who might be enlisted to begin WMU. "All language and ethnic churches and missions in the Florida Baptist Convention" came under Mrs. de Armas' charge. The 48 associations were divided among the other four team members. The intensive efforts of STARTEAM members brought positive responses in 290 of the 320 churches visited.[41]

Because of the initial success, Florida WMU decided to continue the process. With Tanna Dawson as coordinator, new STARTEAM members were named and trained.[42] By the end of 1985 an additional 182 churches had received STARTEAM visits.[43] In 1986 a new national enlargement emphasis, VISION '88, took the spotlight.

Some called her "the best preacher in the state." Miss Vanita Baldwin.

Training the Leaders

Experience had taught Vanita Baldwin the importance of well-trained leadership and the necessity of training conferences that were accessible. Early in her tenure, with the help of staff, she planned multiple leadership training opportunities. In addition to the facilities at Lake Yale, local churches, including at least one in the panhandle section of the state and one in south Florida, hosted annual fall training conferences. North Florida especially welcomed the Florida Baptist Convention's purchase of property near Marianna and the subsequent construction of the Blue Springs Assembly conference facilities. The first WMU training session at Blue Springs was held in 1981, when five conferences over the state counted 1,610 attending. In 1983, seven conferences at scattered sites brought 2,000 leaders to hone their skills for associational and local work.[44] Another refinement came in 1987 when Baldwin and the staff began holding faculty training workshops to prepare those who would teach at leadership training conferences.[45]

One year as the staff discussed subjects which should be stressed at an upcoming leadership training conference, Bagwell remarked, perhaps facetiously, "Our ladies seem to have difficulty assembling and folding our wooden easels when they're setting up for our conferences or packing up afterwards." When Shaw and Painter said that they also had experienced the same problem, Baldwin agreed to give them a few minutes on the program for a demonstation. Painter recounted what happened in the conference:

> Ruth was in the front of the room with her easel. Frances and I were mid-way back on the sides of the conference room with ours—we reminded me of stewardesses. When Ruth began the instructions, it was as if her easel were possessed. As the wooden pieces flopped all over the place, we began laughing uncontrollably. We couldn't finish our demonstration. It wasn't long after that, that Miss Baldwin bought each of us a new metal easel, and the staff never again complained about hostesses who couldn't handle the equipment![46]

Language WMU Training Brings Results

A facet of training on which Baldwin and Shaw worked diligently centered on language churches. Training conferences for Indian, Spanish, and Haitian WMU leadership promoted growth in membership and effectiveness of the organizations.[47] Availability of language materials often posed problems, but WMU, SBC, provided several helpful products. As use of *Nuestra Tarea,* a Spanish-language complement of *Royal Service,* grew, editors increased the number of original articles in Spanish and included helpful suggestions for youth organizations as well as adults. Written in basic English, *Our Missions World* was designed for those who use English as a second language as well as for the deaf. With help from the Home Mission Board, WMU, SBC, also published materials, including special pieces for weeks of prayer, in Korean, Chinese, Japanese, and Romanian. With no Southern Baptist Convention agency ready to produce materials for the growing Haitian population, the Florida Baptist Convention began to reduce the language gap by preparing items for use in Haitian churches.[48]

The Florida WMU language committee from year to year included women of various language backgrounds, including Korean, Spanish, Haitian, and Indian. The report of the language committee at the April 1984 WMU Council meeting showed encouraging progress in language work. Mrs. Alice Snow, Seminole leader, shared developments in four Indian churches and two missions, one at Fort Pierce and one at Tampa. She reported Focus Week activities, Week of Prayer for Foreign Missions and plans for the Home Missions Week of Prayer, planned activities at quarterly meetings, and a Christmas program for senior adults presented by the children's choirs. Snow requested "prayer for the pastors and for more WMU training in the churches." Mrs. Jacques Dumornay, who "had contact with the Haitian churches from Fort Pierce to Miami," shared information about "GA Haitian Day, monthly pastor/wife meetings for training and fellowship, materials translated for WMU leadership, Acteens Haitian Camp, and monthly council meetings to plan for age level meetings in her church." She also asked for prayer "for pastors, wives and WMU leaders."[49]

Uneven responses to language WMU training sessions at Lake Yale led to some changes in the mid-1980s. By 1984, the staff and language committee had decided to try more local or regional training rather than centralized conferences. They had not yet made firm plans, when Ramon Martinez, Florida Baptist Convention director of ethnic education, called Clysta de Armas. He explained that he was planning an ethnic training conference, held annually in October with the Brotherhood Leadership Conference at Lake Yale. Some of the men wanted to bring their wives, and he requested that de Armas hold a conference for the women, any kind she wanted to. "Of course, I had WMU," said de Armas.

About eight women attended de Armas' WMU conference that year, nearly as many as had come to the traditional August training. Martinez wanted to hold similar sessions the next year. When about 40 women came, the successful response amazed everyone. The third year 60 women attended. Such large attendance allowed a division into age-level conferences and specialized sessions for Baptist Women officers. The meetings continued for several years. Exciting plans for a "really big" conference in October 1992 were under way when Hurricane Andrew struck. One of the hurricane's victims was the October meeting. After the forced cancellation in 1992, the conference, which took the new name Florida Baptist Men's and Wives' Conference, moved to a May meeting time which did not include ethnic training.[50]

Farewell to "Miss B"

April 1984 marked Ruth Bagwell's 20th year of service on the Florida

"Miss B"
Ruth Bagwell

WMU staff. A woman of remarkable spiritual depth, capacity for hard work, creative thinking, and concern for young people, "Miss B" never wasted words. Yet she became famous among campers and staff for her "sayings." She knew how to instill the highest values in her campers and how to draw the best efforts from her staffers. In the face of declining numbers in many areas of church life, she worked with leaders and girls to maintain Acteens membership above 6,000, even with fewer Acteens organizations. From 1977, the year when WMU, SBC, named the first National Acteens Panel, Florida Acteens under her leadership claimed a succession of outstanding panelists.

At the 1984 Annual Session in West Palm Beach First Baptist Church, Bagwell received special accolades in anticipation of her retirement at the end of the year. Present and former Convention staff, missionaries, WMU staff, and others, including Holly Hutson, 1984 National Acteens Panelist, and program guest Carolyn Weatherford, paid tribute to Bagwell.[51] Besides guiding the 1984 camping programs at Lake Yale and Blue Springs Assemblies, in June Bagwell climaxed her last months of Acteens leadership by taking 623 girls to Fort Worth, Texas, for the fourth National Acteens Conference. The Florida Acteens were part of 14,000 who gathered for the spectacular event. With over 800 decisions recorded, the effectiveness of the meeting was attributed to the prayer support of those committed to pray for the occasion. Florida had 1,996 persons who signed prayer commitment cards, second only to Texas.[52] Only God knows the count of Florida girls whose lives still carry the special imprint of Miss B.

A Persistent Call

As the 1984 Annual Session in West Palm Beach drew to a close, Oma Dell Ely turned the presidential gavel over to newly elected president Martha Wennerberg (Mrs. Don) of DeFuniak Springs. Born in Pelzer, South Carolina, Martha was only three days old when her mother died. She was raised by an aunt and uncle, who were the only parents she ever knew. Her cousin, whom she thought of as a sister, influenced Martha to attend church services. When Martha was 12 years old, she accepted Christ as her Savior in the First Baptist Church of Pelzer. After high school, she attended business school and worked for a large law firm in Greenville, South Carolina. During that time she went to Ridgecrest Baptist Assembly on summer vacation and there felt "the Lord was calling me to do something special." When she shared the good news with her family, they were not as enthusiastic as Martha had hoped they would be. They recognized that pursuing a Christian vocation would require a college education, and they felt unprepared to provide that for her. But she would not give up easily.[53]

As her sense of call persisted, Wennerberg spoke with one of the lawyers for whom she worked about leaving her job in order to attend college. He proposed that she attend nearby Furman University and continue working for the firm. "What an answer to prayer!" she thought, thanking God for his gracious provision. She continued to work for the same law firm even when she came home for the summer between her two years at Southwestern Seminary.

After seminary graduation Wennerberg served for two years as youth director for Congress Heights Baptist Church in Washington, D.C. When Carolyn Weatherford left Alabama WMU to become Florida Girls' Auxiliary director, Wennerberg accepted the invitation to fill Weatherford's slot as Young Woman's Auxiliary director in Alabama. After three years in Montgomery with Alabama WMU, Wennerberg sensed God leading her to accept the youth director's position with First Baptist Church, Montgomery.

Although she had "mixed feelings because I did enjoy what I was doing," she followed God's direction. Three months later she met Dr. Don Wennerberg, an optometrist from DeFuniak Springs, Florida, and a year later, in October 1965, they married. "Then I knew why the Lord had led me to First Baptist, Montgomery," said Wennerberg. "I never would have met Don if I had been traveling around all over Alabama as YWA director."

Modeling the Faith

Dr. and Mrs. Wennerberg made their home in DeFuniak Springs, where they were active members of First Baptist Church. Immediately finding her place in the church WMU, Martha entered Florida WMU work in time to participate briefly under Josephine Jones. Her previous experience in state work and her willingness to undertake large tasks with a servant spirit opened many doors to service. She was "flabbergasted," however, when the nominating committee asked to submit her name for the presidency in 1984. "I would never in my wildest imagination have dreamed that I would ever serve as president of any state WMU," she said as she described her response:

Marjorie McCullough, president of WMU, SBC, presents Martha Wennerberg, Florida WMU president, with the traditional "Jefferson Cup."

It had to be a family decision because our daughters were 13 and 11 at the time. I prayed about it a great deal and my decision to accept came one morning as I was reading my Bible. As I read a passage on the gifts God has given us, He helped me to see that I have gifts He wanted to use. And He really provided for my family. My mother-in-law next door helped with the girls, and God just seemed to work out my schedule so that I would be home for major events in their lives.

In the fall of 1984, the Wennerbergs suffered a great loss when lightning struck their home, setting it on fire. Martha was in Fort Lauderdale at the time, and the girls were home alone, with Don's mother next door. The family had to move out for five months, while the house was completely redone. After that, leaving home was more difficult for both her and the girls, but

Martha held fast to the words of Psalm 121:8, *The Lord will watch over your coming and going both now and forevermore.*

Looking at the lives of Florida WMU presidents reveals that often they faced great personal obstacles during their terms of office. Yet, without exception, each responded in faith and dependence on God's grace. Each modeled the inner strength which comes only by the Spirit's presence, enabling them to lead Florida women toward greater intimacy with their Lord and more faithfulness in service for Him.

Not only did Martha promote missions education and support of Southern Baptist missions through WMU, but she and husband Don also carried on a two-pronged mission ministry themselves. An article in the *Florida Baptist Witness* described their volunteer work:

> For nearly three decades, Don and Martha Wennerberg have been pro-viding "eyes" and "ears" to needy persons around the world through Southern Baptist foreign missionaries.
>
> For 30 years Don has operated Halo Net, a two-way radio system, from home. Each day, seven days a week, between 1 and 2:30 p.m., he checks in with missionaries [worldwide]. Through the years the system has grown to include more than just missionaries. Callers have learned that Halo Net has ears for any need and that they will get a response.
>
> Operating from a classroom at First Church, DeFuniak Springs, [the Wennerbergs also] have provided more than 50,000 pairs of eye-glasses and hearing aids to impoverished people around the world.[54]

New Acteens Associate

Cheryl Hebert began work on December 1, 1984, a month before Ruth Bagwell retired. A product of Florida WMU camps, she had camped at West Florida Baptist Assembly and worked on staff under Bagwell both there and at Lake Yale. Cheryl was born in Alexandria, Louisiana, while her father served as chaplain in a mental hospital in Pineville. After moves to churches in Alabama, Maryland, and north Florida, when Cheryl was nine years old, her father began a 12-year pastorate in Forest Heights Church, Tallahassee.[55]

One Sunday soon after the family had settled in Tallahassee, Cheryl made a profession of faith, not in the worship service, but while talking with her father after Sunday dinner. He explained in language she could understand about "the Lord's Supper, baptism, and the plan of salvation." Carefully he led her to understand each step: ✳ I am a sinner, and sin separates me from God. ✳ God loves me and has a wonderful plan for my life. ✳ God sent His only Son, Jesus, to die and come alive again for me, so my sins can be for-given. ✳ Jesus will forgive my sin and give me a new, clean life when I ask Him to be my Savior. When she understood what she "needed to do to become a child of the King," there at the kitchen table she accepted Christ as her Savior. Her father, who deeply loved people and the Lord, greatly influenced

Cheryl, as did Merle Cloud, a "dynamic Sunday School teacher and the epitome of a Christian example." Active in Sunbeams and Girls' Auxiliary, Cheryl missed the Acteens age group when WMU, SBC, restructured the youth organizations in 1970.

After high school, Hebert worked and attended college intermittently. In 1977, while on camp staff at Lake Yale, she sensed God's call into a full-time Christian vocation. She enrolled in Florida State University, completed a major in leisure services, and graduated in 1979. Much of the time after high school, Hebert also served on the staffs of small churches in north Florida and south Alabama. After earning a Master of Religious Education degree from New Orleans Seminary, she returned to Florida, working in the Crimes Compensation Department of state government.

In October 1984, Vanita Baldwin contacted her about the position Ruth Bagwell was leaving. After meeting with Dr. Dan Stringer, Florida executive director-treasurer, and Dr. Jim Goodson, Missions Division director, Cheryl Hebert in November was elected Acteens associate and WMU camp director. One of her early accomplishments, with the help of the state Acteens committee, was the establishment of a Florida Acteens Panel. The state panel recognized outstanding Acteens in similar fashion to the national panel. The six girls selected each year had opportunities to speak at state and associational Acteens meetings, to share suggestions about state Acteens programming, and to serve as pages for Florida WMU Annual Sessions and later Florida Baptist Convention annual meetings.

Hebert maintained a schedule of Acteens Cometogethers and added associational Lock-Ins; she promoted and trained girls as Acteens Activators—a national program for involving and training Acteens in missions projects within the country; and she planned the summer camping sessions. After holding two weeks of camp in the adult section of Blue Springs Assembly in 1985, with the completion of youth camp facilities, in 1986 Florida WMU began regularly holding camps there as well as at Lake Yale. Acteens membership, finally succumbing to the forces affecting some other church organizations, began a gradual decline. Lower attendance caused a cut in the number of camp weeks for GAs and Acteens.[56]

Rejoice!

One of Martha Wennerberg's first presidential duties was to appoint a committee for planning a 40th anniversary celebration of Florida WMU camping. She named faithful former president Tanna Dawson (Mrs. A. D.), as chairman, and to work with her, Pat Hutson (Mrs. Mel), Lura Jean Hoss (Mrs. W. L.), and Anne Tomyn (Mrs. Bill). The committee seemed to enjoy the planning, the hard work, and the results as much as any of the camping constituents. In preparation for the celebration, the committee commissioned a history, "Florida WMU Camping: 1946-86," which was written by

Elizabeth Provence and Ruth Bagwell and published by the Florida Baptist Convention in booklet form.

With the theme "Rejoice!" almost 200 former campers and staffers gathered at Lake Yale in late August 1986. Planners geared the two-day session to a typical camp schedule, including quiet times with a booklet of meditations, assembly times, campfires, singing, and watching old movies. Old friends and new, drawn by the bond of camp experiences, joined voices in camp songs long unsung but suddenly in the forefront of memory. Perhaps expanded by the passage of time, stories of great exploits during the days of "gypsy camping" (when no permanent campsite was available), drew roars of laughter, while poignant reminders of changed lives elicited tears.

Challenging Centennial goals reminded the celebrants that maintaining a highly effective camping program should be a priority for the future. Elizabeth Provence, Carolyn Weatherford, Ruth Bagwell, LuAnn Listebarger, the WMU staff, and the anniversary celebration committee all contributed to making the event a success on every count. Prior obligations forced both Weatherford and Bagwell to miss the happy occasion.[57]

The Wise Woman Builds Her House

Martha Wennerberg said, "I accepted the position of state president without an agenda that I wanted to accomplish. I was just a part of the total WMU

"The Florida Room," WMU, SBC, Building, Birmingham

program." Leadership of "the total WMU program," however, required extensive organizational skill, for Wennerberg's presidency covered the exciting years leading to the 100th birthday of WMU, SBC. Despite growing older, the national Union looked young and beautiful housed in the new headquarters building in Birmingham. Careful planning, unusual attention to functional detail, and exquisite furnishings made the new building a unique paean of praise to the mighty God served by Woman's Missionary Union. During Wennerberg's first WMU, SBC, January Board meeting, in 1985, she participated in the official dedication ceremony for the new building.[58]

With a count of Florida contributions to the building's cost showing $17,000, Carolyn Weatherford offered Florida WMU the opportunity to designate an area of the building as the "Florida Room." From a suggested list, Wennerberg and Baldwin chose the executive director's office space, desk, chair, and credenza. Weatherford "requested" that the designation honor Florida WMU executives Josephine Jones, Carolyn Weatherford, Bernice Popham, and Vanita Baldwin. The estimated cost of the project, $22,930, would require additional gifts of nearly $6,000. In April 1985 the WMU Council voted to undertake the project.[59] Beginning in June 1986, a Thank Offering was added to the opportunities for paying off the WMU, SBC, building debt. By April 1987 Floridians had contributed a total of $28,912.07, surpassing the goal for the Florida Room by nearly $6,000.[60]

To prepare Florida WMU for the 1988 national celebration, Wennerberg named Oma Dell Ely (Mrs. W. Mount) as the state Centennial chairman. Associational Centennial chairmen were chosen to promote Centennial goals, and area representatives accepted responsibility as "Special Enlistment Workers" for the VISION '88 enlargement emphasis. Plans were made for grand celebrations at the 1988 Annual Session in Lakeland as well as in special area and associational meetings. Responding to the request of WMU, SBC, for an up-to-date history of every state organization, Wennerberg also appointed Juanita Epperson (Mrs. Harold) to write a Florida WMU history for the years 1960 to 1988.[61]

Celebrate

The one-word theme *CELEBRATE* captured the spirit of the 1988 Annual Session, held in First Baptist Church, Lakeland. Over 1,000 women joined hearts in recalling the past and confronting the future. Each individual session was seasoned with quotations from early leaders of WMU, SBC, theme scriptures and hymns from bygone days, and words of recollection and wisdom shared by past Florida WMU leaders. Juanita Epperson, whose *On This Foundation, Part II* was ready for distribution, gave insights into episodes from Florida WMU history.[62]

Dr. Stringer commended the work of WMU and creative, dedicated, and courageous WMU leaders, past and present. "Woman's Missionary Union is a vital force within our denomination," he said. Disturbed by failure to meet the Lottie Moon Offering for Foreign Missions goal, and the slowdown in Cooperative Program giving, Stringer challenged his audience to "be faithful to the trust of those who have gone before us." Acknowledging the "tenuous times in the Southern Baptist Convention," he urged the women of 1988 to come to a new level of commitment despite obstacles, as their predecessors had done "in the testing times" of the past. "The answer," Stringer said, "is to remember that Jesus Christ is the same yesterday and today and forever."

Confronting women with the needs of the future, Carolyn Weatherford suggested that relevance, imagination, and "first class commitment to first class causes" will allow WMU to walk a sure-footed path into the second century. After 24 years of working on the Florida WMU staff, Elizabeth Painter chose the national centennial year to celebrate her retirement. During the Tuesday evening program, Vanita Baldwin recognized Painter's years of service and presented her with two dozen red roses. After several GA and Mission Friends leaders spoke on their work with Painter, she was presented notebooks of letters from friends and co-workers and a gift from Florida WMU. A unique individual of deep commitment to her Lord, Painter had played a significant role in introducing thousands of Florida children to the Kingdom of God. Her sensitive spirit and clever ideas would be missed.

Baldwin gave an enthusiastic and optimistic report for the past year. She celebrated new organizations in every age level, increased attendance in state and associational meetings, and great excitement in regard to mission study, mission support, and mission action. "But there is much more to be done to make missions come alive," she said. She urged the women to "be faithful in prayer," to "be diligent in enlisting girls and women," and to "move forward, united." In the only negative note of her address, Baldwin reported that at Elizabeth Painter's retirement at the end of 1988, the position of GA/Mission Friends associate would not be filled. Baldwin said: "Dr. Stringer told me that it relates to the department director's (me—Miss Baldwin's) retirement December 31, 1991. Leaving the position open and using contract workers he felt would be best for the administration and WMU."

The 1988 Annual Session closed with a "Litany on Celebration":

> *Leader:* As we depart from here, we join together in the name of Christ to be open to the future. We go to announce your presence among all the people of the world.
> *Congregation:* We go as members of the body of Christ, seeking ways to be instruments of your love.
> *All:* We go with the commission burned in our hearts: feed the people of God.

A Matter of Principle

The decision to delay the replacing of Elizabeth Painter caused a great deal of consternation among WMU membership, and, even with contract workers, placed an extra burden on staff. Later Stringer defended his decision, saying that he was applying the same principle in his own resignation as executive director. He would leave several administrative vacancies for his successor to fill.[63] In time some WMU leaders came to see the wisdom of waiting.

For the new executive director-treasurer, the
Florida Baptist Convention chose Dr. John Sullivan,
pastor of Broadmoor Baptist Church, Shreveport,
Louisiana. Sullivan, a West Virginia native, graduated from Grand Canyon Baptist College, Phoenix,
Arizona, and earned a Doctor of Ministry degree
from Southwestern Seminary. In his weekly *Witness*
column, "I Don't Mind Telling You," he did not
mind telling Florida Baptists that they needed to
give more money, plant more churches, and witness
more consistently in order to bring the Good News
to bear on the state's fast-growing and diverse population. Nor did he mind expressing his appreciation for the work of Florida WMU.[64]

Dr. John Sullivan

No Breathers for Shaw

With engaging humor, insightful planning, and the ability to relate to
women of varied backgrounds and interests, Frances Shaw continued to press
the development of Baptist Women and Baptist Young Women organizations.
Working with the state BW and BYW committees and Vanita Baldwin, she
developed the January Missions Retreats at Lake Yale and Blue Springs.
Those times of fellowship and learning later became the Women's Winter
Weekends. Shaw also advised and assisted the Language WMU committee in
planning training for women in language churches. In addition, she worked
to establish Campus BYW groups on the campuses of Chipola Junior College
and Palm Beach Atlantic College.

Shaw was also the driving force in founding a chapter of the Baptist
Nursing Fellowship (BNF) in Florida. "Closely tied to WMU," the BNF was
organized in Oklahoma City, Oklahoma, in 1983. State WMUs provide
"advisory and administrative support" for BNF chapters;[65] Florida also provided limited funding. In 1994, in response to Shaw's application, Florida
WMU received certification by the Florida Department of Professional
Regulation to offer continuing education credit at specified workshops and
conferences for nurses.

The Presidency Moves South

For the 1989 Annual Session, Martha Wennerberg chose a forward-look-
ing theme, "Our Future Bright as God's Promises." Though she was completing her final year as president, her consistently high level of work, yet
truly humble spirit, would lead to many opportunities for continued faithful
service, among them her election as WMU, SBC, recording secretary in
1992. To lead Florida WMU into the future, the women in Panama City elected Lois I. Walker (Mrs. Charles H.). The new president was born in

Knoxville, Tennessee. Living next door to the church property, her family was active in Central Baptist Church, Fountain City. Lois grew up in the missions organizations of Central Baptist and was the first Girls' Auxiliary queen crowned in her association. She was converted at age 13 in "a very real experience with the Lord."[66]

Mrs. Charles Walker
1989 – 1994

Lois attended Carson-Newman College, a Baptist institution in Jefferson City, Tennessee. There she met Charles H. Walker of Kentucky, who as a young boy had been one of Louise Smith's Royal Ambassadors. Although Charley had been called into service before he finished his last semester, they married in March 1944, immediately after Lois' graduation. After a year in Europe, much of it in the closing battles of World War II, he came home to his wife and baby daughter Ann in November 1945. After completing his education, in 1950 he moved his family to Tallahassee, where he became registrar of Florida State University. He and Lois were active members of Tallahassee First Baptist Church. At FSU they became acquainted with an outstanding Baptist college student named Carolyn Weatherford.

When the Walkers and their three children moved to Miami in 1960, they joined Miami Shores Church. Following their custom of local church involvement, Lois became the church organist; after almost 30 years, however, the WMU presidency led her to resign. She served as Girls in Action director and Baptist Women president; she was also elected director of the Miami Association WMU. She served on the state WMU Council as both associational WMU director and Area 12 representative.

Leading On

With varied experience at every level of WMU, Lois Walker was well prepared to guide the state organization into the last decade of the century. She also had an excellent support system. Giving her his full backing, her husband Charley traveled with her much of the time. "I thank God," Lois said fervently, "for such an understanding husband." From the beginning of her term of office, she also "rallied friends to pray for me." She gave them typed itineraries of her assignments, and as she traveled she sensed the support of their faithful prayers. In addition, Walker felt Baldwin's support: "Vanita took me by the hand and taught me so much as I began my presidency. She always addressed me as 'Madam President,' or 'My President.' She was dedicated to details and gave me much confidence. I knew exactly what was expected of me." As was the case with the presidents before her, prayer gave added depth to her relationship with Baldwin. The two often prayed together as they worked or traveled.

Walker's term of office included several "goodbyes" and "hellos," some of which were linked to WMU, SBC. Her first "official duty" was to represent Florida WMU at the August 1989 wedding of Carolyn Weatherford and Joe Crumpler in Birmingham. That same summer she flew to Albuquerque, New Mexico, to elect Carolyn's successor, Dellanna West O'Brien (Mrs. Bill). In her role as WMU, SBC, vice-president, Walker's skills were acknowledged by her fellow Executive Board members, who over her five years on the Board elected her chairman of both their finance and their nominating committees.

The years between Dan Stringer's 1988 announcement of Vanita Baldwin's approaching retirement and her 1991 departure from office brought recognition and reward for Florida WMU. Dedicated work by often unknown local members as well as state officers and staff had reversed a pattern of declining membership. For both 1989 and 1990, WMU, SBC, acknowledged Florida as the state with the largest percentage of increase in both membership and organizations. Baldwin and Walker received recognition plaques each year at the national annual meetings.[67]

At the same time Baldwin and Florida WMU faced some disturbing obstacles, among them the lack of leadership roles for women in the denomination, the need for a GA/Mission Friends associate, and non-Southern Baptist youth programs in a growing number of churches. Baldwin did not hesitate to express her concern "for Southern Baptist churches to use Southern Baptist curriculum in their missions education programs." She stated firmly, "Some non-Southern Baptist missions literature uses fictional missionary stories and claims that the missionary is the person who comes to the church to organize the program and workers. That's not a missionary nor missions."[68]

The Appointed Time

As 1991 neared, Walker and the four other most recent state presidents—Martha Wennerberg, Oma Dell Ely, Tanna Dawson, and Cleota Lenert—met with John Sullivan to consider ways of honoring their retiring director. "Dr. Sullivan was very gracious as we considered possibilities. He agreed that we might solicit monetary gifts from within WMU membership as one way of expressing our appreciation to Vanita," said Wennerberg. With that plan in operation, the next step was for the committee of presidents to design an evening of recognition for Baldwin at the 1991 Annual Session, which would take place in Southside Baptist, Jacksonville, her home church.[69]

With excitement and a bit of secrecy pervading the atmosphere, the audience gathered to honor Vanita Baldwin for 14 years of service as Florida WMU director. Guests for the special evening, several of whom completely surprised the honoree, included close friends from her childhood in Oak Hill and from her work in Alabama, New Mexico, and Florida. Several family members, including her 90-year-old mother, were also present.[70]

The tributes by those close to Baldwin paid signal honor to her personal and professional relationships. In addition, she received several special gifts. Recording secretary Virginia Fortner presented a check for $9,025.74, representing money given by Florida WMU organizations. Lois Walker and ladies from the Florida Association presented a quilt made of "squares [created individually by] the 49 associational WMU directors, area representatives and other WMU leaders and WMU Department Staff." Walker had sewn the squares together and the Florida Association women had then done the quilting. It was a labor of love for each person involved. Family and friends on the podium gave other gifts. The evening was emotionally demanding but superbly affirming for one who for 36 years had devoted her life to serving God through Woman's Missionary Union.

As much as any words spoken at the Annual Session, however, an editorial appearing that week in the *Florida Baptist Witness* honored Baldwin.[71] Editor Jack Brymer, friend and staunch advocate of Florida WMU, wrote:

> Soon after arriving in Florida in 1984 to assume the editorship of the *Florida Baptist Witness,* I found myself seated next to Vanita Baldwin at an annual associational meeting. I was scheduled to report on the work of the *Witness* immediately after Miss Baldwin's report. I felt fortunate to be following a layperson, particularly a woman, rather than a preacher.
>
> Was I ever in for a shock. I had never heard Miss Baldwin speak. She walked to the pulpit with a zing in her steps and excitement in her voice. As she spoke the audience perked up and began to respond with laughter and "amens."
>
> The longer Miss Baldwin "preached" the lower I sank in the pew. Why hadn't someone warned me about her, I thought. As I listened, however, my apprehension at having to follow such a dynamic speaker soon turned to respect and admiration, for I heard a message that made me thankful I was a Florida Baptist Christian and that challenged me to want to do more for the cause of Christ.

From her speaking powers, Brymer turned to Baldwin's strength as an administrator:

> During the last six years as editor of the *Witness,* I have observed her as the administrator of the work of Woman's Missionary Union. She is no less a dynamo there than in the pulpit.
>
> Miss Baldwin's tenure in Florida has not always been smooth sailing. During the 1980s, for example, membership in Woman's Missionary Union

declined not only in Florida but throughout the Southern Baptist Convention. Yet she remained optimistic and worked even harder until the downward trend was reversed.

Unwilling to fit into anyone's mold, Miss Baldwin has stood toe to toe with those she felt were unduly critical of WMU and its work during this difficult time. But she was always honest, up-front and cooperative.

Finally Brymer praised Vanita Baldwin's broader contribution to the denomination and to the place of women in Baptist life:

> With a prophetic voice . . . yet in her calm but forceful manner, Miss Baldwin has sought to keep the focus on the responsibilities of all Christians, male and female, to take the gospel into all the world. [She] has courteously but persistently called to the attention of Baptists the importance of women being involved in leadership at every level of Baptist life, not just WMU, and based not on their rights but on their responsibility.
>
> Vanita Baldwin has served Florida Baptists with courage and distinction. Her leadership during these tumultuous times has greatly enhanced the future of Woman's Missionary Union in Florida.

Amen and Amen.

Giving up work by which one has defined one's identity can be traumatic. By her own admission Vanita Baldwin found very difficult the process of leaving the work to which she had so wholeheartedly given herself. Those closest to her recognized her struggle. "Each final event was hard for her," said her friend Lois Walker, "so I tried to stand by and share those times." Yet Baldwin also realized that those 36 years with Woman's Missionary Union were a gift from God and that His richest blessings still lay before her. Although her pace might have relaxed a bit, a visit to Florida's northwestern partnership states, numerous speaking engagements, WMU events, and care of her mother filled her days. Jean Moore was now in heaven interceding for her, and God had much work for His faithful servant Vanita Baldwin yet to do.

"Miss Baldwin" became "Dr. Baldwin" in 1990 when Stetson University conferred on her the honorary Doctor of Divinity degree.

So Much to Celebrate, So Much to Do

1991 – 1994

. . . taking the very nature of a servant.
Philippians: 2:7

April 8, 1992

Hurrying to their seats on Wednesday morning of the 1992 WMU Annual Session, the audience quickly filled the auditorium of College Park Baptist Church, Orlando. Barbara Curnutt, the new director of Florida WMU, stood to make her first address before the women of the state. Poised, earnest, lovely in appearance, Curnutt wanted her first words to establish immediate rapport with her listeners. "I want to tell you how thrilled I am to be serving with you here in Texas!" she declared.

When the audience suddenly broke into laughter, Curnutt was stunned. "It took me 30 to 45 seconds to realize what I had said," she reported with a laugh, "and Florida women still tease me about 'working in Texas.' " The mistake was a natural one, more from habit than from nerves in her new situation, for Curnutt was a lifelong resident of Texas and came to Florida after 14 years on the staff of Texas Woman's Missionary Union.

Barbara Curnutt

A Missions Birthright

Barbara Curnutt was born into a "strong Southern Baptist, mission-minded family" in San Antonio, Texas. She described the shaping of her life by her family and her church:

> My parents were active laypeople in our church. My mother, who died of cancer when I was 10, was a very active WMUer, very much involved in missions and in the life of our church. It was a natural progression for me to come to an understanding of my need for a Savior, and I accepted Christ when I was nine.

WMU organizations played a large role in that process:

> Even when I was a baby, my mother took me with her to WMU meetings. I became involved in Sunbeams and then Girls' Auxiliary, going through all the Forward Steps before I moved into Young Woman's Auxiliary. The missions education organizations really shaped my perspective on the world and God's plan for all mankind.
>
> Besides the missions lifestyle of my parents and my involvement in WMU organizations, God helped me to see His activity in the world through the lives of a dedicated aunt and uncle, who were Southern Baptist missionaries in Brazil for 40 years.

Two retired missionaries from China also greatly influenced Barbara:

> Miss Hannah Sallee and her sister, Mrs. Robert Bryan, were in their nineties when I was a child. I remember as a GA looking forward to those unique opportunities when we girls, and sometimes the Royal Ambassadors, too, would be invited into their home to hear their stories of China, to eat with chopsticks, and to see some of their artifacts. I know those experiences greatly shaped my missions passion.
>
> Those ladies had known and worked with Lottie Moon. In fact, after Lottie Moon died in Kobe, Japan, the Foreign Mission Board commissioned Mr. Bryan, "Miss Mamie's" husband, to go to San Francisco and meet the ship carrying the urn with Lottie's ashes. I remember hearing those stories as a child, not even fully understanding the significance of those women and their lives in China, but they greatly affected my call to missions.

While at Girls' Auxiliary camp at age 13, Barbara sensed God calling her into missions, perhaps to be a foreign missionary. As she finished high school in San Antonio, she remained "open to God's leadership" and continued to seek His will concerning a missions vocation. Feeling led to pursue an education major, Barbara earned a bachelor's degree in elementary education at Texas Tech University and did graduate work in special education. Having completed her degree, she returned to San Antonio, where she taught special education.

A Journey of Discovery

After her first year of teaching, Curnutt accompanied her father and a tour group to the Holy Land. On that trip God gave her further direction: "God very distinctly communicated to me that there was something else he wanted me to do with my life other than teach school. I returned home to begin another journey, a journey to discover what God was calling me to do."

By the end of her second year of teaching, Curnutt knew that her next step was seminary. Still uncertain of where her training might lead, "in faith and obedience" she enrolled in Southwestern Seminary. There God continued to direct and shape her sense of call. When she graduated from Southwestern, she had opportunities to follow several different paths of ministry. At that point God clearly revealed His call to WMU leadership, and Curnutt accepted the invitation of Texas Woman's Missionary Union to serve as state Acteens consultant. After ten years, she became the associate executive director for Texas WMU.

A Burning Bush Experience

Curnutt's move to Florida hinged on a "dynamic encounter with God." For several years she had refused to consider invitations to other professional positions. In the spring of 1991, however, she began to feel a "holy restlessness" that led her to "deal with the possibilities of change." When the personnel committee of another state WMU contacted her about the director's position, she agreed to meet with committee members in June, then again in July. "Somewhere in the middle of that second meeting I began to sense that this was not God's will," Curnutt said, continuing the story of her call to Florida:

> At the end of the day, the committee unanimously asked me to take the position. They wanted a response, but because of the turmoil in my own heart, I could not respond. They agreed to give me time to pray through the matter.
> That was on Monday; I returned to Dallas that evening. The next day I continued to struggle with the situation. As I drove home from my office, I was almost overwhelmed with the need to find an answer. For some reason, I pulled into a McDonald's parking lot. I remember sitting in my car praying about the other state, and it was as if God were sitting in the car with me. It was as if I heard an audible voice. When He spoke to me, His words impressed upon me that I was headed, not to the other state, but to Florida.

Florida had not contacted Curnutt, but she knew the Florida Convention was also seeking a WMU director:

> I knew that night that it was a matter of time until I would hear from Florida. I knew. That experience in the parking lot was unique. I've never known something was going to happen before it happened, with that kind

of assurance. But that night it was solidified. It didn't matter what anyone else thought or said. Everybody had a lot of ideas about what I ought to be doing with my life, but that night it didn't matter anymore because I knew God wanted me in Florida, and it was settled.

Curnutt drove to the nearby home of a friend and co-worker who had been praying with her about the other state. As she walked into the house, she felt at peace.

"You've made a decision, haven't you?" said her friend.

"Yes, I have," replied Curnutt, "and you'd probably better sit down."

The friend sat. "Well?"

"I'm going to Florida," announced Curnutt.

Absolute silence. Then, "You're what?"

"I'm going to Florida," Curnutt repeated.

"Florida? That's wonderful," she said, though knowing that Curnutt had received no contacts from Florida.

On Wednesday morning Curnutt visited with a second co-worker and prayer partner. "The Lord has called me to Florida," she reported.

"Has Florida called you?" was the startled reply.

"No. I just know I'm headed there," Curnutt said, sharing confidentially with her friend her extraordinary experience on Tuesday evening.

Subsequent developments proved the accuracy of Curnutt's under-standing:

> Those were the only two people I told. That night, Wednesday night, I called the personnel committee chairman from the other state to decline their invitation. It was one more step of faith, because I knew what God had called me to do. After that I had complete peace. I have never looked back.
>
> The next day, Thursday, Dr. Jim Goodson, the Missions Division direc-tor for the Florida Convention, called me in the middle of the afternoon. I wanted to laugh, to say, "What took you so long?" But we talked for prob-ably an hour and a half on the phone, and then later for perhaps another hour. It all felt so right, and I knew that I would be where God wanted me.

Curnutt went through the interview process with Goodson and with John Sullivan, executive director-treasurer of the Florida Baptist Convention. In September she returned to meet with the administrative committee of the State Board of Missions for actual approval as a staff member:

> In that interview I told them about my experience. I didn't want to sound presumptuous, but I was confident. As I walked out of the room, I heard them all laughing. "You probably want to know what we were laughing about," said a former seminary classmate of Curnutt as he left the meeting. "As you left the room, one of the men on the committee said, 'Well, who are we to mess with the Holy Spirit?' " And that was that.

God in his wisdom and loving-kindness[2] knew Curnutt needed that kind of call. "It was a real gift to me," she reflected. "A number of times over the last three years I've drawn on the assurance of that experience."

Six Goals for Guidance

Barbara Curnutt began work in Jacksonville November 1, 1991. Her powerful sense of God's call to Florida included "a strong impression" that God wanted "to do something in and through the women of the state" and that the years ahead would be "a time of exciting adventure with Him." To get to know Floridians, Florida geography, and Florida Baptist churches, Curnutt needed to travel the state fast—while staying within the speed limit, mostly. As often as possible, she shared her goals for Florida WMU:

• to intensify emphasis on prayer and spiritual growth. "When I responded to God's call to Florida, I sensed that He was calling women to a renewed emphasis on prayer," she said.

• to increase personal involvement in ministry and witness. "Besides meeting significant needs in other people, this is one of the most effective entry points to involve young women in missions," explained Curnutt.

• to develop leaders who will become missions catalysts in churches and associations. "The leadership base is so critical to our future," she said. "We must develop future leaders as well as strengthen present ones."

• to strengthen and expand WMU in churches through age level organizations and churchwide activities. "Through our programming we will give a great deal of attention to this goal," said Curnutt.

• to design new approaches that will influence special audiences for the cause of missions. "Special audiences," she explained, "would include anyone who is not really involved in WMU. That might involve pastors or other church staff, ministers' wives, college students, ethnic groups, or fellowship organizations. We need to find new ways to interest and involve such groups in missions education."

• to involve ethnic leadership in determining effective missions education approaches and materials for language churches. "We have already begun special training emphases with our Haitian women," Curnutt said, "and we are giving a stronger emphasis to this priority in our Hispanic leadership training."[3]

As Curnutt shared those goals at the 1992 Annual Session in Orlando, she painted a disturbing picture:

> We live in a day unequalled by any other in history. There are more non-Christians who populate our world than any other time since the beginning of time. Over half of our nation is unchurched and growing more secular and ungodly every day, and 70 percent of our own state is lost without Christ.

At the same time, our denomination is struggling for its identity. And I fear the church is in danger of losing sight of God's missionary intention and our missions accountability.

She challenged her listeners to "let go of the familiar and the comfortable," to take risks, and to make new commitments in order to "claim new territory and inherit the future God has in store."[4]

A Visitor Named Andrew

The year 1992 found the WMU staff still short-handed. Since the retirement of Elizabeth Painter in 1988, the position of Girls in Action/Mission Friends associate had remained vacant. Former department director Vanita Baldwin and two other staff members—Frances Shaw, Baptist Women and Baptist Young Women associate, and Cheryl Hebert, Acteens associate and WMU camp director—had carried the work of that position as well as their own. Although funding had now been granted, until a new associate came, Curnutt, Shaw, and Hebert still carried the extra load. The burden seemed heavy, until August 24, 1992. Then it faded in comparison to the trauma spawned by Hurricane Andrew.

In the early morning hours of Monday, August 24, Andrew struck the east coast of Florida near Miami. No predictions had prepared the area for the devastation wreaked by the storm. Suddenly 250,000 people had no homes, 1.4 million people had no electricity, and the area had suffered $20 billion in property damage. The storm's fury caused at least 38 deaths.[5] By nine o'clock Monday morning a number of Convention staff members had gathered for an emergency meeting. "As we received assignments and responsibilities all around the table, we were getting some picture of the severity and magnitude of the disaster," recalled Curnutt. WMU was assigned responsibility for temporary emergency childcare. Curnutt explained how they proceeded:

> The Convention owned three disaster units, a feeding unit, a mobile medical unit, and a childcare unit. Prior to Andrew, Brenda Forlines, director of the Community and Migrant Missions department, had maintained the childcare unit, which is a huge trailer stocked with baby supplies, toys, teaching tools, and other equipment. We don't teach from the unit; it just carries the supplies. The idea is to find a safe structure, like a church, where we can set up everything. When Andrew hit, Brenda needed to give her attention to the migrants, and WMU was assigned the emergency childcare unit.
>
> As soon as we received our assignment, Frances Shaw and I, and the office secretaries, began mobilizing volunteers. I called Ann Coffman, because she had elementary school teaching experience and speaks Spanish, and Marie Smith, who is a retired nurse. I also called Elsie McCall from First Baptist, Lakeland. She had worked in childcare relief in a Texas disaster. The four of us headed to Miami not knowing what we would find

or where we would ultimately be. Frances stayed in the office lining up other volunteers.[6]

Learning Through Trials

Traveling together down Highway 95, Curnutt and Coffman made a list of items they would need. They stopped frequently to shop for supplies at Wal-mart and Sam's stores. "The Wal-marts were super," said Curnutt. "When they learned what we were doing, several stores donated items for the children. We literally put things together in motion towards Miami." The emergency childcare unit was assigned to Cutler Ridge Baptist Church, which had been severely damaged, yet was one of the least damaged churches in the area. "We learned through trial and error," Curnutt explained, "since we had never before experienced anything like this."

Quickly realizing that "the greatest need at that moment was for diapers and baby formula," Curnutt's group spontaneously opened up a baby supply distribution center. "I can't tell you how it all happened," said Curnutt; "God just provided. We kept clearing out huge rooms because the diapers kept coming in, the formula kept coming in. The volunteers really helped us get the thing organized." Keeping a sense of humor in the midst of material devastation and physical exhaustion helped the workers to cope. When people repeatedly referred to the WMU unit as the "baby distribution center," Curnutt emphatically denied ever having distributed even one baby. Besides dispensing baby supplies, they organized limited daytime childcare. The grateful responses of parents and children brought many tears to the eyes of volunteers.

Hispanic children explore "treasures" outside WMU-operated supply tent after Hurricane Andrew. Note bottles of water in background.

Curnutt described the progress of events:

> Florida Baptists developed one of the most respected and efficiently run disaster relief centers anywhere in that area. At first most of our donated items came from Baptist churches in Florida. Eventually all kinds of people outside Baptist life started funneling supplies through our units because they knew we would distribute them or use them to best advantage.
>
> A host of volunteers came and helped us with supply distribution and childcare. As the project grew, we continued to say we needed more volunteers, and they continued to come. When we moved the unit from Cutler Ridge to Florida City, they kept on coming.

Temporary childcare was one of the responsibilities of Florida WMU during the aftermath of Hurricane Andrew. See tents of Florida Baptist Convention in background.

One of those who came was Russell Drinnen, who was Florida WMU's first Baptist Young Women associate in 1970 and then director of a church preschool program. Drinnen later helped WMU evaluate the Andrew experience and organize for future responsibilities.[7] The response of women tremendously encouraged Curnutt:

> We'll never know the number of WMU members who were involved, not only in childcare but in feeding and in house repair. As a result of the Andrew experience, Florida WMU now has permanent responsibility for upkeep and restocking of the emergency childcare unit and also for temporary emergency childcare. We've already organized teams of women all over the state who can be ready to respond immediately in an emergency.

Cheryl Hebert, worked at Florida City, distributing baby food and supplies, administering first aid, and ministering to displaced persons.

A different stage in the recovery process found Frances Shaw and Curnutt assigned to a communications center in Pembroke Pines First Baptist

Church, near Fort Lauderdale. Working out of the center, Shaw enlisted volunteers to man the phone banks and organized housing for volunteers coming into the area. She also mobilized the Baptist Nursing Fellowship to staff the mobile medical unit located at Cutler Ridge Baptist Church.[8] Reflecting on her feelings during the experience, Curnutt said:

> Baptists in Florida experienced a sense of family in responding to the disaster. People from all over the state either gave resources or actually participated in the cleanup or reconstruction, or in food distribution. As all of us on the Convention staff worked together, we were so overwhelmed by the needs that everything else paled in comparison. We all felt pressure from the ongoing work—I was out of the office for six weeks—but dealing with people who had such tremendous needs, who had lost everything, made our programming seem insignificant. It was one of those periods in our history when nothing else mattered as much.

Discerning God's Plan

As time passed, filling the long-vacant position of Girls in Action/Missions Friends associate became an insistent priority for Curnutt. Week after week, month after month, she and the state GA and Missions Friends committees, as well as local age-level leaders throughout the state, prayed for God to reveal His choice, and for that person to respond to God's leadership. At the same time, He was preparing a woman born and raised in Miami to take the job.

Cindy Mallett Goodwin grew up in Miami Shores Baptist Church. Involved almost from birth in WMU missions organizations and other church activities, she experienced an awareness of her need for a Savior and accepted Christ at age seven. In a Sunbeam group led by Mrs. Douglas Knapp, who later went to Africa as a Southern Baptist missionary, Cindy encountered missions for the first time and learned about missionaries. Knapp's daughter Suzanne, who also became a missionary in Africa, was a fellow Sunbeam. As a small child, Cindy went to WMS circle meetings with her mother, Mary Mallett. Mrs. Mallett served as both church and association Girls' Auxiliary director while Cindy was growing up and also directed the Miami Association GA camp from 1960 to 1970. For that reason Cindy attended the association camp and later worked as a counselor under her mother's guidance. When she was a high school senior, she attended a Christian Vocation conference in St. Petersburg. Although she did not know specifically what God desired of her life, she responded there to what she understood as His call to a full-time Christian vocation.[9]

After high school graduation, Cindy entered Samford University in Birmingham. Two very special things happened during her Samford years: she had a growing sense of call to serve God through working with children, and she met Howard Goodwin. Immediately after graduation Cindy and Howard married in Miami and headed north to Southern Baptist Seminary in

Louisville, Kentucky. Howard earned a master's degree while Cindy earned enough money for them to live on. For the next 20 years, they served churches in Jacksonville, Florida; Decatur, Georgia; and Birmingham, Alabama. Often Cindy, as well as Howard, held a staff position, usually related to children's work. Two children of their own provided hands-on experience as well as great joy for their home.

In January 1993, at just the right time in Cindy Goodwin's life, Barbara Curnutt called her about the Florida WMU staff position. The Goodwins began to pray for God's specific direction. In April, at the WMU Annual Session in Tallahassee, Cindy and Barbara talked further. That conversation led to a meeting of the Goodwins with John Sullivan and Jim Goodson. In May the couple met with the State Board of Missions administrative committee at Lake Yale. There the committee elected Cindy Goodwin the WMU associate for Girls in Action and Mission Friends. The move from Birmingham was not without difficulties; both husband and wife exercised strong faith and a servant spirit in obeying God's call to Jacksonville. Cindy began her WMU work June 1, 1993.

Planning for a Bright Future

Although her parents had moved to South Carolina, Cindy Goodwin felt good about returning to Florida. After only a short time, she had a sense of being "at home" in the place where God wanted her. Her dark eyes sparkling, grinning broadly, she exclaimed, "I love it! Staff relationships are wonderful!" As she planned for the future of GA and Mission Friends in Florida, she began redeveloping a strong leadership base with leader training conferences for both age-level organizations. A successful innovation provided special fellowship times for Mission Friends and GA leaders at the 1994 Women's Winter Weekend conferences at both Lake Yale and Blue Springs Assemblies.

As Goodwin prepared church WMU leaders to work with changing formats in children's work, including coed missions activities, she said, "The exciting thing is that people are committed to teaching missions from a Southern Baptist viewpoint." She planned three GA Whirls for 1994 and Mother/Daughter overnights at both Florida assemblies. Dad/Daughter overnights were planned as a variation in connection with the camping season. Goodwin looked forward to a bright future in children's missions education:

> Children's ministers are seeing the need to make children aware of missions. They see that getting children involved in missions is important. The earlier we plant a missions vision in children, the more likely they are to become adult supporters of missions with their lives and their dollars. It's exciting to see churches grasp that principle and encourage children's mission organizations.

Barbara Curnutt, left, with staff, Frances Shaw, Sharon Thompson, Cindy Goodwin

Bienvenidos a Florida!

One of the challenges which most excited Curnutt as she came to Florida was the need for expanded WMU work in language churches. Florida's unique situation as a magnet, drawing immigrants not only from the Caribbean islands and Latin American countries but also from around the world, confronted the state's Baptists with unparalleled opportunities. State Convention leadership responded by making the development of language churches a major priority. Under Curnutt's direction the Florida language WMU committee developed subcommittees for guiding work with Hispanics and with Koreans. In January 1993, alongside the Women's Winter Weekend at Lake Yale, Frances Shaw planned and organized the first overnight retreat for Hispanic women. Positive response by the women led to a second retreat in 1994.[10]

To promote Haitian work, the language committee and staff designed two special events to train a select group of Haitian women, who in turn would train others in organizing WMU in local Haitian churches. WMU also initiated the request for 1994 State Missions Offering funds to provide a customized version of *Into All the World*, a missions education video feature produced by WMU, SBC. The plan called for sending the Florida version, done in French, without charge to Haitian churches. In 1994 two Haitian WMU members, Nathalie Balzora and Marilyn Delinois, were named to the first National WMU Ethnic Advisory Council.[11]

Bilingual Staff

Perhaps the most encouraging development in WMU language work was the addition of Sharon Thompson to the Florida WMU staff. Frances Shaw had generously shared her time and stretched her budget to include language WMU, but the work had grown beyond an appendage to other assignments. Recognizing the importance of the expanding language work in Florida, John Sullivan had stipulated that at least one WMU staff member must have fluency in a second language. The bilingual Thompson was elected by the State Board of Missions to serve in a multi-faceted slot—language associate, WMU camp director, and Acteens associate.

Sharon Thompson grew up in the missions organizations of Pensacola First Baptist Church. As a little girl, her enthusiasm in singing "Jesus Wants Me for a Sunbeam" led to a small crisis. Waving her arms expansively to create the sun, she knocked over the child on either side of her. With a little more control, but no less enthusiasm, she progressed into Girls in Action. Her mother, Mrs. Nannie Ruth Thompson, led her second-grade GA group. As a 13-year-old Acteen, Sharon accepted Christ during a week at Ridgecrest. Mrs. Pat Ford, an Acteens leader, gave her special encouragement in making her commitment genuine and living it out in her daily routine.[12]

Each year Sharon's Acteens group visited Mrs. Austin, a shut-in living near the church property. Thompson recalled a special visit with her:

One day after we had sung our songs and finished our program, Mrs. Austin

Florida WMU Acteens associate, Sharon Thompson, receiving her first GA award from leader Macklyn Fairchild at First Baptist Church, Pensacola

said she wanted to sing for us. This little 90-year-old black lady grabbed my hand and sang "He's Everything to Me." Then she looked at me with her dark piercing eyes and said, "And, Child, don't you forget—He's your everything."

Whenever I have felt inadequate to a task, God has said, "You don't have to be adequate. I'm your everything." And it all began when I was an Acteen visiting Mrs. Austin.

While in high school, Sharon was named a "National Top Teen," one of 20 Acteens chosen each year for the honor.

In Awe of "Miss B"

Although Sharon did not attend Florida WMU camps as a camper, when she was in high school she began six years on staff in GA and Acteens camps at Lake Yale and

Panama City. "Working in Florida WMU camps was one of the most exciting and life-changing experiences of my life," she said. "Camp was where I came into my own. It seemed to be the place where my gifts and abilities most fit." WMU camp director Ruth Bagwell influenced Sharon tremendously:

> I was always in awe of Miss B. When I first saw her at Acteens meetings and listened to her stories, I thought when God had a really big problem, He called on Miss B to solve it. The first summer I worked for her, before camp she called and said, "Miss Sharon, you'll be directing the choir at camp." I'd never even thought about doing such a thing, but I said, "Yes ma'am, I'll direct that choir." Because she said I would, I believed I could. Every time the staff left the campground, Miss B would say, "Remember who you are, whose you are, and who you represent." And now I say that to my staff, because it made such an impact on me.

One summer's camping theme gave Thompson a theme for life:

> We were studying soaring based on Isaiah 40:31, about soaring on wings like eagles. I decided I wanted to soar—to rise above the usual. One morning while the campers were having their quiet time, Miss B and I were walking. She looked across the campground at campers quietly reading their Bibles and praying, then turned to me and said, "And you, Miss Sharon, will teach them to soar." She walked away, and I wondered for a long time what that statement meant. Now I feel like that is my job as Florida WMU camp director—to teach girls to soar.[13]

Rebelling, Trusting

Thompson's aptitude for language became part of God's preparation for her future. As a high school junior, she felt God's call into a full-time Christian vocation, which she believed to be WMU work. Fearing that such a goal might be impractical, however, she enrolled in the nursing school at Samford University, Birmingham. Through various experiences, including camps and mission trips, she became convinced that her nursing studies represented a failure to trust God's wisdom and His plan for her life. Finally she exercised the faith which He required, left Samford only one semester away from receiving her Registered Nursing degree, and enrolled in Belmont College, Nashville. With an internship in child psychology as well as a Florida WMU scholarship to help with finances, she majored in psychology and Spanish.

While she was in college, her home church sent Thompson on several mission trips to Mexico. Those trips also made a profound impact on her life. In Mexico she experienced the foreign mission field for the first time and came to understand the importance of her prayers and her Cooperative Program gifts. Visiting a small Mexican village where almost no one spoke English and few had ever seen an Anglo, she entered the hut of a little old lady:

> She guided me to the back of her tiny hut, and we began to converse in
> Spanish. This lady had learned a little English from who knows where. In
> the middle of our conversation she stopped and said, "You, Sharon, remem-
> ber who you are, whose you are, and who you represent."

The adage of Ruth Bagwell now pervaded Thompson's language interests as
well as her camping experiences. God was clearing a pathway which
Thompson could not yet foresee.

After Belmont graduation, Thompson spent six months as a mission service corps volunteer, teaching English and Bible in a friendship house in
Kyoto, Japan. During her months in Japan, Thompson recognized once more
her calling "to be a caller of the called through WMU—to equip young girls,
teenagers, college students, and adults to do missions."

Back in the United States, she enrolled in Southwestern Seminary for a
degree in counseling. The Florida WMU scholarship fund again provided
financial help. While in seminary Thompson directed summer camps for
Alabama WMU; at her graduation, she went to Montgomery as resident
camping and GA consultant, later moving her age level emphasis to Acteens.

The Movement of God

When Cheryl Hebert resigned her position with Florida WMU, Barbara
Curnutt began to consider replacements. Thompson's Florida heritage, education, and experience made her a likely prospect for the position. Wanting
to be certain that such a choice was also God's plan, Curnutt waited and
prayed. As the language aspect of the position took form, Thompson's training and experience in that area, as well as in camping and Acteens work, confirmed for Curnutt that God was leading the selection process. Thompson,
approaching from a different perspective the question of leaving her Alabama
job, also became convinced that her invitation to join the Florida WMU staff
was God's call. She began her work in Jacksonville October 1, 1993. Plans
were made early for her to hone her language skills by attending the Spanish
Language Institute in Costa Rica after the 1994 camping season.[14]

As Thompson became acquainted with the increasingly diverse population
of the state, she saw that "the work with language WMU is inseparably intertwined with the movement of God in Florida." Her excitement about language work matched the excitement in language churches. Said Thompson:

> The women are growing in their missions vision. They are on mission, not
> only to win their own ethnic groups but to win the lost and develop mature
> Christians no matter their language or culture. They have counted the cost;
> they are committed to prayer; they want to move forward.

Wearing the hat of WMU camp director, in preparation for the summer
1994 camping season Thompson planned the construction of "ropes and

confidence" courses at both Lake Yale and Blue Springs camps. Volunteer ropes course experts from several states built the "high ropes" and "low ropes" outdoor courses. "The purpose of the courses," Thompson said, "is to build group cooperation, to provide elements of danger where there is no danger and opportunities to risk in a protected environment, in order to increase problem solving skills and to build trust—trust in each other, in self, and in God." Thompson planned for the new ropes and confidence courses to become "a significant part of the WMU camping program."

Ministers' Wives, Mentors, and Partners

As part of her vision for reaching out to women not involved in WMU, Curnutt introduced two special emphases. In November 1993 WMU initiated the "Just for Ministers' Wives" conference preceding the annual meeting of the Florida Baptist Convention. Covering half a day, special interest workshops addressed the unique needs of ministers' wives. Curnutt planned to make the "JMW" conference an annual affair.

Rather than an event, the second emphasis—mentoring and the development of mentors—was an ongoing program launched in 1994. Ann Coffman prepared a brochure, "Missionary Mentors: Investing in Lives," explaining the concept of one woman nurturing the spiritual development and missions involvement of another. A commitment form in the pamphlet encouraged every Baptist Woman and Baptist Young Woman to commit to mentoring another woman or girl.[15]

On the state level, Florida WMU enjoyed a relationship of mutual encouragement with the WMU organizations in Florida's partnership states. Developed as one avenue of Bold Mission Thrust emphasis, partnerships with Southern Baptists in Pennsylvania/South Jersey, Montana, and North and South Dakota had created bonds of friendship and opportunities for service through several departments of the Florida Baptist Convention. Florida WMU regularly provided materials for state-level WMU leadership and sent individuals to assist with leadership training, to speak at retreats, and to provide childcare during annual meetings.

Florida WMU received an invitation to become involved in another kind of "partnership" when Florida Baptist Theological College decided to provide a residence for furloughing missionaries. In 1992 the college remodeled and furnished a furlough home near the campus, naming it "Happynest." Through the FBTC committee, WMU worked with college officials to maintain supplies and keep the house in good condition. With Jewell Johns, area representative from Crestview, spearheading the project, Area One WMU members provided a washer and dryer for "Happynest."[16]

Redesigning Women

In the Centennial year, Florida WMU hardly paused to rest on its laurels. The staff planned extensive preparation for the organizational changes

Florida WMU joins in the cooperative effort of sponsoring Happynest, missionary residence at Florida Baptist Theological College, Graceville.

designed by WMU, SBC, to take place in October 1995. "Florida's theme for promoting the new design is 'Redesigning Women,' " said Curnutt, explaining:

> In fall 1994, the Florida staff will train 12 transition teams, one for each area. Each team has five persons, one trained especially for each organization: WMU (the "umbrella organization" comprised of all the others), Women on Mission (for all adult women), Acteens, Girls in Action, and Mission Friends. From January through December 1995, each area team will provide training to all leadership in the associations composing that area.
>
> We want to cover the state, to touch every church through training in every association, so that women at every level will know what should happen and will feel empowered to make it do so. The new structures offer exciting possibilities.

Preparing for Celebration

That Florida Woman's Missionary Union would soon celebrate a century of service surprised Barbara Curnutt, at her arrival in the state. She had no idea her friend was so old! Before Curnutt's move to Florida, Centennial committee members had been named but had not met. Sue Holladay, LuAnn Listebarger, Hazel Littlejohn, and chairman Martha Wennerberg wanted the new WMU director, along with state president Lois Walker and Frances Shaw, to participate with them in the planning process. Meeting at Ridgecrest in the summer of 1992, they made their first major decision, determining to publish a full-length history of Florida WMU.

Building on the 1993 theme, "Faithful Servants," committee members chose for the Centennial theme "Faithful Servants Fulfilling His Mission." As the supporting scripture, they selected 1 Corinthians 15:58b (NIV): *Always give yourselves fully to the work of the Lord, because you know that your labor in the Lord is not in vain.* The verse echoed WMU's historic scriptural motto, "Laborers together with God," while focusing on present and future commitment to faithful service. Former state president Oma Dell Ely wrote material for a Centennial prayer retreat in associations or local churches. Former WMU Department director Vanita Baldwin prepared a devotional guide for "100 Days of Prayer," beginning January 12, 1994, the 100th anniversary of the formation of Florida Woman's Missionary Union. The committee also challenged Florida WMU members with a set of associational, church, and personal goals. The goals supported three "priorities" centering on faithfulness servants in spiritual development, mission support, and expanded missions involvement.[17]

Faithful Servants

The 1993 Annual Session, held in the Thomasville Road Baptist Church, Tallahassee, heralded the approach of the Centennial Year. A major feature of the meeting was the recognition of five faithful servants in Florida WMU. Audiences listened expectantly as Saralyn Collins of Orlando, using dramatic monologues, introduced one of the five in each session.

• Honored as a "visionary servant," Juanita Guilliard, Riverview Church, Jacksonville, had worked with GAs for 40 years and was also involved in associational WMU work and literacy missions.
• Ninety-year-old Cora Fitzgerald received recognition as "the energizer—she just keeps going and going." A member of Parkview Baptist Church, Gainesville, Fitzgerald had served 33 years on the Santa Fe River Association WMU Council.
• Edith Keene, First Baptist Church, Daytona, was lauded as a "praying servant." Known as a prayer warrior, she had served as a leader in the Halifax Association WMU for 35 years and had taught Sunday School for 56 years.
• Harmony Association WMU director for 20 years, Ethel Bagley of Pine Grove Church, Trenton, was hailed as a "nurturing servant" who possessed the gift of hospitality.
• "Marching to the drumbeat of the faithful," Margaret Watson, Lebanon Baptist Church, Plant City, was praised as a "courageous servant." While caring for her critically ill husband and son, Watson had served as WMU director, church clerk, and pianist for her church, as well as WMU director for the Shiloh Association.[18]

Those five women represented the thousands of others, both present and past, who had faithfully labored together with God through more than 100 years of woman's mission work in Florida.

The Tuesday evening session included a feature on the impact of

Hurricane Andrew, "Found Faithful through the Storm," coordinated by Glenna Hegenbart. Carol Vandeventer, Tanna Dawson, Carol Wainwright, Norma Taylor, Helen Yates, and Marie Smith described their various avenues of service during the emergency situation. In recognition of his leadership of the Florida Baptist Convention relief efforts, Florida WMU honored Cecil Seagle, Florida Baptist Men Department director. President Lois Walker and Barbara Curnutt presented a plaque to Seagle and his wife Peggie in appreciation of their "untiring efforts" in relief work following Hurricane Andrew.

As Dr. John Sullivan, Florida Baptist Convention executive director, began a forceful address entitled "Find Us Faithful in Florida," he emphatically affirmed the role of Woman's Missionary Union in Southern Baptist life. Acknowledging "some unfortunate and unnecessary" criticism of WMU, he said:

> I'm not at all sure Southern Baptists recognize the great value of the work you do and have done. No missions support organization has prayed more, raised more money or taught more missionaries in the history of Christianity than has Woman's Missionary Union. You will be found faithful in Florida because of the great missionary challenge we have.

Fulfilling His Mission

In the months leading up to the Centennial Annual Session, the Centennial celebration took the spotlight in leadership conferences, associational WMU events, and local WMU organization plans. The *Florida Baptist Witness* carried news articles, editorials, pictures, and features on Florida WMU, current and past.

Florida WMU had accepted an invitation to hold the Centennial Annual Session in the lovely new Deermeadows Baptist Church sanctuary, Jacksonville. An appropriate choice, Deermeadows began as a mission in the mid 1970s and was constituted as a church in 1978. Several Florida Baptist Convention personnel, including WMU staff, were charter members. In a letter to "Members and Friends of Woman's Missionary Union," pastor Altus Newell reminded visitors: "The facilities in which you will meet are dedicated to reaching a lost world for Christ, beginning at our doorstep." General chairman of local arrangements

Martha Wennerberg, left, Centennial Committee chairman, with Barbara Curnutt.

Diane Newell, her husband, and many other members of the congregation and staff provided for every need of program participants and those in attendance. The pastor brought a ripple of laughter from the audience as he welcomed guests, saying, "Just let us know if there's anything you need, and we'll get it for you. Or, if we can't get it for you, we'll teach you to do without it!" Perhaps his words echoed the fact that for 100 years, Florida WMU members had often "done without" in order to provide support for Southern Baptist mission work.[19]

Over 1200 participants registered for the sessions in Deermeadows Baptist Church. High above the podium hung the maroon theme banner: "Faithful Servants Fulfilling His Mission, Florida WMU 1894 -1994." Smaller banners in shades of pink carried the names of individual session themes:

Risking, Dreaming, Mentoring, Persevering, Responding. Audiences were inspired, educated, amused, and challenged by dynamic Bible teacher Esther Burroughs; WMU, SBC, executive director, Dellanna O'Brien; top Southern Baptist and Florida Convention leaders, and beloved Florida missionaries. Mother and daughter Laura Monroe and Saralyn Collins dramatized significant WMU moments from the past 100 years.

Lois Walker, having served faithfully for five years, introduced newly elected president Ann Coffman. A former missionary, Coffman's bilingual skills and experience in WMU leadership had prepared her well for that moment in Florida Baptist history.

Mrs. Bill Coffman,
Florida WMU President
elected 1994

The thorough planning and preparation of Lois Walker, Barbara Curnutt, and associates Frances Shaw, Cindy Goodwin, and Sharon Thompson moved the program smoothly through each session. The unpredictable took over only when three former executive secretaries—Vanita Baldwin, Carolyn Weatherford Crumpler, and Louise Smith Boyd—joined Barbara Curnutt for a panel discussion of WMU in their eras. A prepared format became lost in the process, as each of the esteemed former leaders shared insights and incidents from her tenure. The 94-year-old Boyd, who had led Florida WMU as young people's secretary 1931-1936 and as executive secretary 1936-1943, especially delighted the audience with her exuberant and animated responses.

While the panel focused on the joy of past experiences, Barbara Curnutt, in her director's report, addressed the future. Acknowledging the immense challenges of the days ahead, she urged a compelling faith in the God who goes before us to prepare the way:

Barbara Curnutt, far right, enjoys, along with the audience, the comments of three former directors of Florida WMU, Vanita Baldwin, left, Carolyn Weatherford Crumpler, and Louise Smith Boyd.

As we gather in this place, we are remembering. We have built memorials, and memorials are important; but God is doing a new thing. He is calling us to be what we have never been before. He is calling us to new levels of faith.

As we embark on a new century, we walk by faith into unfamiliar, untrodden territory. But we walk with the assurance of God's presence and promise: *I will lead the blind by ways they have not known, along unfamiliar paths I will guide them; I will turn the darkness into light before them and make the rough places smooth* (Isaiah 42:16 NIV).

As the Centennial Celebration moved to a dramatic crescendo, the challenge of bringing light to a world groping in darkness gripped the audience. Inspired by their predecessors and empowered by God, the women of Florida WMU committed themselves to another century of faithful service to a faithful God.

EPILOGUE

As Florida Woman's Missionary Union moves into a second century of missions leadership, many are asking the question, "What does the future hold for WMU?" Three 1994 leaders shared their responses for readers of *Faithful Servants*.

Dellanna O'Brien
in Florida Room

DELLANNA O'BRIEN

I see an exciting, challenging future for WMU. I feel a genuine excitement about the new organizations and publications. Membership may be smaller in the future, but the impact will be greater. It will require greater commitment. I couldn't be more optimistic. We have our best years ahead of us.

JOHN SULLIVAN

Woman's Missionary Union continues to be one of our best hopes to thrust us into the missionary movement of the twenty-first century. We will need to find new paradigms without scrapping old principles. We will need to concentrate on flexibility without scrapping facilitation. We will need to preserve the past not as a shrine, but as a stewardship—not as a museum, but as a momentum—not as our glory, but as our guide—not as praise only to past generations, but as our promise to a new generation.

Missions education is absolutely essential to the ongoing work of winning the world to faith in Christ. No one does missions education and action better than the WMU. Those who imagine that we can promote mission offerings without

WMU do not understand the history or the future of our missionary endeavors. The Florida Baptist Convention will seek in every possible way to ensure the future of this wonderful organization.

BARBARA CURNUTT:

If I could design a future for WMU, it would consist of very strong ongoing missions organizations in all age levels. Churches would look to WMU for strong missions leadership. I want others to see WMU as catalytic people, people who are involved in pro-active ways, advocates of missions, doers of missions. I think the future is bright and I'm excited to be a part of it.

For you created my inmost being; you knit me together in my mother's womb. I praise you because I am fearfully and wonderfully made; your works are wonderful, I know that full well. . . . All the days ordained for me were written in your book before one of them came to be.

Psalm 139:13-14, 16b

"Conceived in the hearts of women devoted to the cause of Christ, from the womb of sacrifice and service was born the Woman's Baptist Missionary Union of Florida" (p. 46). As the Father created and knows the days of each individual who is a part of Florida Woman's Missionary Union, so He created and knows the days of that organization birthed in Plant City, January 12, 1894. Florida WMU was fearfully and wonderfully formed to serve the Lord. Before all time and eternity, God knew the days He planned for our existence and our mission. Our response cannot be gauged by what the future may hold. It must be measured only by our obedience to God's call to service.

Let us not fear the future, Florida WMU. Rather, with confidence in the promises of God, let us make known the name of Jesus as we walk toward Calvary . . . and Resurrection.

MPT

On the following pages...

ABBREVIATIONS

BB	*Baptist Basket*
BW	Baptist Women
BYW	Baptist Young Women
CP	Cooperative Program
FMB	Foreign Mission Board
FBC	Florida Baptist Convention (*never First Baptist Church*)
FNIMC	Florida Normal and Industrial Memorial College
FWMU	Florida Woman's Missionary Union
GA	Girls' Auxiliary (1913-1969)
	Girls in Action (1970 on)
HH	*Heathen Helper*
HMB	Home Mission Board
LMS	Ladies' Mission (or Missionary) Society
NBC	National Baptist Convention
RA	Royal Ambassadors
SBC	Southern Baptist Convention
SBM	State Board of Missions
WMS	Woman's Missionary Society
WMU, SBC	Woman's Missionary Union, Auxiliary to Southern Baptist Convention
WMUTS	Woman's Missionary Union Training School
YWA	Young Woman's Auxiliary

NOTES

Chapter I
Are Ladies Entitled...?

[1]Foregoing vignette is based on known facts about the Baileys. Sources are indicated in subsequent endnotes.

[2]*History of the Baptist Denomination in Georgia* (Atlanta: Jas. P. Harrison, 1881), 16.

[3]*Baptist Denomination in Georgia*, 16.

[4]S. B. Rogers, *A Brief History of Florida Baptists, 1825-1925: A Century of Service and Progress* (Jacksonville, c. 1925), 12. On January 9, 1895, an article by Dr. Chaudoin entitled "Origin of the Witness" appeared in the *Florida Baptist Witness*. He mentions this abortive attempt at a state paper but does not identify the two men involved. See also Edward Earl Joiner, *A History of Florida Baptists* (Jacksonville: Florida Baptist Convention, 1972), 83-84.

[5]Joiner, 48-49.

[6]Joiner, 49-50.

[7]*Baptist Denomination in Georgia*, p. 16.

[8]Baptist Denomination in Georgia , 16-17.

[9]Walter Belt White, *A History of the First Baptist Church, Talladega, Alabama: Its Pastors, People, and Programs Through One Hundred Fifty Years, 1835-1985* (Talladega: First Baptist Church, 1985), 26.

[10]Catherine B. Allen, *A Century to Celebrate: History of Woman's Missionary Union* (Birmingham: Woman's Missionary Union, Auxiliary to Southern Baptist Convention, 1987), 25.

[11]Allen, 25-26.

[12]Allen, 26.

[13]Allen, 27. [Quoted from William Heth Whitsett Address delivered at the SBC Annual Meeting, 1895.]

[14]Hermione Dannelly Jackson and Mary Essie Stephens, *Women of Vision, Centennial Edition* (Montgomery, Alabama: Woman's Missionary Union, Auxiliary to Alabama Baptist State Convention, 1988), 4-7.

[15]Ethlene Boone Cox, *Following in His Train* (Nashville: Broadman Press, 1938), 47-50. The formation of Central Committees [state organizations] occurred in the following order: South Carolina, 1875.

Virginia claims to have been either the first or second state with a Central Committee. Records are unclear, but by 1878 the work in Virginia was well organized.

Central Committees in other states were organized as follows:

Missouri, 1876.
North Carolina, 1877 [Allen, 28, indicates 1876]. Women met with so much opposition that they worked behind the scenes and held no more elections until 1886.

Texas, committee linked to Home Mission Board, 1878; committee linked to Foreign Mission Board, 1879.

Georgia, 1878.
Kentucky, 1878.
Mississippi, 1878.
Tennessee, 1882. Work of the committee was interrupted but reorganized in 1887.
Arkansas, 1883.
Alabama, 1884.
Louisiana, 1884.
Florida, 1894.

[16]White, 48.

[17]White, 48.

[18]White, 48.

[19]Kate Ellen Gruver, *From This High Pinnacle: One Hundred Years with Georgia Baptist Woman's Missionary Union* (Atlanta: Woman's Missionary Union, Auxiliary to Georgia Baptist Convention, 1983), 10, 12.

[20]Gruver, 17.

[21]Mrs. Stainback [Martha Eleanor Loftin] Wilson, *Pioneer Work and Progress of the Woman's Baptist Missionary Union of Georgia*, 1893), 8. In Mrs. Harvey Hatcher, *History in Georgia: Woman's Baptist Mission Work, Its Origin and Object* (Atlanta: Woman's Baptist Mission Union of Georgia, 1902), 12, Hatcher also recognizes the contribution of Mrs. Bailey, "a co-worker at Quitman, Ga."

[22]Florida Baptist Convention (FBC) Annual, January 1880, 15. In John Leonidas Rosser, *A History of Florida Baptists* (Nashville: Broadman Press, 1949), 56-57, the author clarifies the counting procedure: "We should remember that the early membership included both races and that in many of the churches the colored exceeded the white members. After the War Between the States, there

was a gradual separation of the races, and that separation was officially declared in 1880."

[23]Rogers, 10.

[24]See FBC Annual 1870s. See also Rosser, 50.

[25]Rosser, 55. According to Joiner's later history of Florida Baptists, attendance became so discouraging that the effort to meet was abandoned from 1877 through 1879. He also records no names of convention officers for those years. See Joiner, 59.

[26]FBC Annual, January 1880, 3.

[27]Rosser, 56.

[28]Rosser, 61. See also Joiner, 59-60, for recognition of a "new spirit" in a number of areas of state life.

[29]Rosser, 64. Rosser adds that the list of pledges made at the December 1880 convention "had been 'so carefully put away as never to be found.'"

[30]This society, the oldest one in the state in continuous existence, is still serving the Master's cause as Florida Woman's Missionary Union celebrates its centennial anniversary.

[31]FBC Annual 1882, 24.

[32]FBC Annual 1881, 25. (Quoted in the introductory section of Chapter 1, p.4.)

At that same annual session N. A. Bailey was also elected as one of two secretaries of the State Board of Missions. Even though he held paid Convention positions, often full-time, during many of those years, he was reelected every year until his death in 1897. See Joiner, 304-305.

An interesting mystery is presented by the listing of Bailey as a convention secretary in 1873, supposedly the year the Baileys moved from Georgia to California. Since it was not unusual for south Georgia pastors to participate in the Florida Convention [in 1857 the annual meeting was even held in Thomasville, Georgia; Joiner, 302], this is not an impossibility. However, it would probably require an adjustment of the time frame presented in Bailey's biographical sketch in *History of the Baptist Denomination in Georgia*, 16-17. See William Cathcart, ed., *The Baptist Encyclopedia* (Philadelphia: Louis H. Everts, 1881), 58, for a time line that might allow for Bailey's holding this office in 1873.

[33]Allen, 32.

[34]Allen, 32.

[35]FBC Annual 1882, 23-24.

[36]FBC Annual 1882, 24. All quotations from George Allen's report, 24-26.

[37]FBC Annual 1882, 24-25.

[38]FBC Annual 1883, 10.

[39]FBC Annual 1883, 10. Italics added.

[40]Mimeographed sheet from typed history of the Bethlehem/Campbellton church, n.p.

[41]FBC Annual 1883, 7.

[42]*Heathen Helper* (HH), June 1884.

[43]FBC Annual 1885, 23. Many ladies of that day used their own initials instead of their full names or their husbands' names. After her marriage, Mrs. Bailey's name occasionally appeared in print with her own initials rather than her husband's. Mrs. L. B. Telford, the second corresponding secretary of Woman's Work in Florida, always used her own initials, standing for Lucina Beach, rather than her husband Robert's name. Mrs. Chipley, another outstanding early WMU leader from Pensacola, sometimes used her husband's initials in referring to herself as Mrs. W. D. (Walter Dudley) Chipley. At other times she preferred to be called Mrs. B. B. (Bettie Billups) Chipley. She also used the initials A. E., for Ann Elizabeth.

[44]Louise Porter Hood, *History of Woman's Missionary Union, Auxiliary to Florida Baptist Convention*, 1911, 12.

[45]Wilson, 8.

[46]Allen, 37.

[47]Wilson, 8.

[48]Wilson, 9.

[49]Allen, 38-39.

[50]FBC Annual 1885, 37. All references to Mrs. Bailey's 1885 report, 37-39.

[51]FBC Annual 1885, 47.

[52]Allen, 40.

[53]Wilson, 9.

[54]FBC Annual 1886, 13-15.

[55]FBC Annual 1886, 43-44.

[56]FBC Annual 1886, 14-15.

Chapter II
A Place Beside Their Brethren

[1]Lynda Skaddan, great-great granddaughter of Robert Telford, possesses Lucina's original journal as well as copies of Robert's letters and notes written during missionary service in Siam and China.

[2]Robert Telford to Rev. S. Peck, November 25, 1854. Original letters and notes of Robert Telford are located in American Baptist Archives Center, Valley Forge, Pennsylvania. That was the same king whose difficult behavior was recorded by Anna Leonowens and later portrayed in the fictional "Anna and the King of Siam" and "The King and I."

[3]Skaddan described the journal in a letter to Ms. Francendese, March 27, 1989: "[Mrs. Telford] wrote

in a notebook with a quill pen in a difficult-to-read script using old English spellings, abbreviations, and phonetical spellings for Siamese names and places. It is a simple, emotional, personal diary relating a story of a long ocean voyage, homesickness, hardship, strength, love for her husband, companionship of fellow missionaries, exasperation with the native people, the birth of two sons and the death of one. Through it all she puts her trust in the power of prayer."

[4]John Leonidas Rosser, *A History of Florida Baptists* (Nashville, Tennessee: Broadman Press, 1949), 68-69.

[5]Rosser, 68.

[6]Jesse Earle Bowden, "Colonel Chipley Builds a Railroad" in *Iron Horse in the Pinelands: Building West Florida's Railroad: 1881-1883,* ed. Virginia Parks (Pensacola: Pensacola Historical Society, 1982), 29.

[7]FBC Annual 1884, 27.

[8]Harry C. Garwood, *Stetson University and Florida Baptists: A Documentary History of Relations Between Stetson University and the Florida Baptist Convention,* ed. Edward A. Holmes, Jr. (Deland, Florida: Florida Baptist Historical Society, 1962), 17-41.

[9]E. Earl Joiner, *History of the First Baptist Church, DeLand, Florida,* 1975, 1-9.

[10]South Florida Baptist Association Annual Minutes 1885, 1.

[11]FBC Annual 1886, 12.

[12]Lelia Boring Lassiter, *On This Foundation: History of the Woman's Missionary Union, Auxiliary to the Florida Baptist Convention* (Jacksonville, Florida: Convention Press, 1961), 19.

[13]FBC Annual 1901, 59.

[14]FBC Annual 1888, 12. During the school year, 1888-1889, a yellow fever scare "delayed the opening of [Stetson University] till December" and forced some students to give up school for the entire year (FBC Annual 1895, 64). Jacksonville also experienced a severe outbreak of the mysterious and often fatal disease. Unaware of its cause, many people fled the city. Rembert W. and Eleanor B. Patrick and Hester G. Fisackerly, *The Story of Florida* (Austin: Steck-Vaughn Company, 1959), 244-45.

[15]FBC Annual 1888, 12.

[16]FBC Annual 1888, 8. Further references to this meeting can be found in the 1888 Annual.

[17]FBC Annual 1888, 11.

[18]FBC Annual 1885, 10-13.

[19]FBC Annual 1888, 12.

[20]Toni Moore Clevenger, *On the Bay—On the Hill: The Story of the First Baptist Church of Pensacola, Florida,* ed. Martha Pope Trotter (Pensacola: First Baptist Church, 1986), 69, 70, 73, 77. See index for numerous other references to the Chipleys and their relationship to the church and Woman's Missionary Union.

[21]Catherine B. Allen, *A Century to Celebrate* (Birmingham: Woman's Missionary Union, Auxiliary to Southern Baptist Convention, 1987), 41.

[22]Allen, 44.

[23]*The Baptist Basket* (BB), June 1888, 100. Mrs. Telford's remarks were summarized in the minutes of the meeting, and that summary has been quoted many times subsequently. However, the direct quotation makes a stronger statement.

[24]"Special Days Program," The Salinon Corporation, Dallas, Texas, 1980.

[25]BB, 100. Italics added.

[26]"Minutes of The Woman's Meeting, Richmond,Virginia, May 11,14, 1888" in *Minutes of Woman's Missionary Union, 1888-1897,* 8. Located in President's File, WMU Archives, Birmingham, Alabama.

In 1890 a revision of the Constitution changed the name to Woman's Missionary Union, Auxiliary to Southern Baptist Convention. "Report of Second Annual Meeting of the Woman's Missionary Union, Auxiliary to Southern Baptist Convention, held in Fort Worth, Texas, May 9-12, 1890" in *Minutes of Woman's Missionary Union, 1888-1897,* 27. WMU, SBC, Minutes after 1890 will be referred to as WMU, SBC, Annual Report (WMU, SBC, AR).

[27]WMU, SBC, Minutes, 1888; BB, June 1888; Allen, 119.

[28]Perhaps she visited family in New York state after leaving Richmond.

[29]FBC Annual 1889, 20.

[30]FBC Annual 1889, 58.

[31]FBC Annual 1889, 22.

[32]"Report of Sixth Annual Meeting of the Woman's Mission Societies, and First Annual Meeting of the Executive Committee of Woman's Mission Societies, auxiliary to Southern Baptist Convention, held in Memphis, Tenn., May 10-13, 1889." In *Minutes of Woman's Missionary Union, 1888-1889,* President's File.

[33]WMU, SBC, Minutes, 1889, 18.

[34]WMU, SBC, Minutes, 1889, 11-12.

[35]WMU, SBC, Minutes, 1889, 22.

[36]Cited in Allen, 118-119. Italics added.

[37]FBC Annual 1890, 22-23. Dr. Forbes was president of that institution when it opened as DeLand College in 1885 in the facilities of the DeLand Academy. In 1887 the name was changed to DeLand University; in 1889 it became the John B. Stetson University. See Garwood, 17-41.

[38]FBC Annual 1890, 12.

[39]FBC Annual 1890, 12. Italics added.

[40]See Joiner, 87-90, for summary of relationships between Negro Baptists in Florida and the Florida Baptist Convention, 1880-1901.

[41]FBC Annual 1889, 17. In Guild's last report he said: "I had misgivings in going to Florida from the extreme North, that meeting those in the extreme South might cause unpleasant friction. In this I have been agreeably disappointed. . . . I am glad to say I never saw brethren work more harmoniously and lovingly."

[42]Although FBC Minutes do not record Telford's name in connection with the work before 1891, Lynda Skaddan's information on her great-great grandfather indicates that he "conducted Institutes for colored Baptist Ministers 1889-1893."

[43]FBC Annual 1891, 16. In the same report (p. 36), Chaudoin lauded another friend of Woman's Mission Work, Brother N. A. Bailey, who was then serving not only as a state missionary but also as his Assistant Corresponding Secretary. The position was elective but unofficial in the first years Bailey held it. At that session it was authorized through an amendment to the FBC constitution.

[44]FBC Annual 1891, 36.

[45]Allen, 121.

[46]Clevenger, 94. Cooperation on this scale was a new experience for the two churches and probably contributed to the eventual reuniting of the two congregations as First Baptist Church.

[47]FBC Annual 1891, 55. Further references to this meeting and Mrs. Telford's report are from same source.

[48]Mrs. John [Clyde] Maguire, "Woman's Missionary Union, Auxiliary to the Florida Baptist State Convention," *Encyclopedia of Southern Baptists* (Nashville: Broadman Press, 1958), 2:1530.

[49]WMU, SBC, AR, 1891.

[50]WMU, SBC AR, 1891, 34.

[51]Cf. Mrs. Bailey's plea in the *Baptist Basket* for "no invidious comparisons."

[52]FBC Annual 1892, 42-43.

[53]FBC Annual 1892, 65.

[54]FBC Annual 1892, 64-65.

[55]Allen, 193-194.

[56]BB, May 1892, 69.

[57]Cited in Allen, 148. See also Catherine B. Allen, *The New Lottie Moon Story* (Nashville: Broadman Press, 1980), the definitive biography of Miss Moon.

[58]Allen, *Century,* 148, 149. In 1918, at the suggestion of Annie Armstrong, the offering was named for Lottie Moon, who conceived it.

[59] E. S. Broadus, "Woman's Missionary Union in Atlanta," *Western Recorder,* 26 May 1892.

[60]Allen, 148.

[61]FBC Annual 1893, 100.

[62]FBC Annuals, 1889 - 1893. See also Lassiter, 23.

[63]FBC Annual 1893, 97.

[64]FBC Annual 1893, 93.

[65]FBC Annual 1893, 98.

[66]FBC Annual 1893, 99.

[67]FBC Annual 1893, 101.

[68]FBC Annual 1893, 119.

[69]FBC Annual 1894, 50.

[70]FBC Annual 1894, 55.

[71]FBC Annual 1894, 22.

[72]FBC Annual 1894, 20-21.

[73]FBC Annual 1895, 26.

Chapter III
An Uncharted Path

[1]Florida Baptist Convention (FBC) Annual 1894, 55.

[2]Louise B. Porter, "Woman's Work in Florida," *Florida Baptist Witness,* 29 November 1899, 6.

[3]FBC Annual 1894, 55. Showing a different understanding, Louise Porter later wrote: "Miss Spalding *offered her services* to the board to carry on the work until the next convention, or until such a time as the board saw fit to choose another secretary." Porter, 6. Italics added.

[4]FBC Annual 1894, 56.

[5]Catherine B. Allen, *A Century to Celebrate: History of Woman's Missionary Union* (Birmingham: Woman's Missionary Union, Auxiliary to Southern Baptist Convention, 1987), 289, 322-24.

[6]WMU, SBC, Annual Report (WMU, SBC, AR), 1893, 34.

[7]FBC Annual 1894, 57.

[8]FBC Annual 1894, 73-74; 23, including response.

[9]FBC Annual 1894, 51.

[10]FBC Annual 1894; Spalding's complete report, 54-58.

[11]*Book of Remembrance,* Ruby Anniversary, WMU, SBC. This hand-written book is kept in the Florida WMU offices, Baptist Building, Jacksonville.

[12]The constitution as adopted was printed in FBC Annual 1895, 80-83.

[13]Edward Earl Joiner, *A History of Florida Baptists* (Jacksonville: Florida Baptist Convention, 1972), 96, 301.

[14]Lelia Boring Lassiter, *On This Foundation: History of the Woman's Missionary Union, Auxiliary to the Florida Baptist Convention* (Jacksonville: Florida Convention Press, 1961), 33.

[15]FBC Annual 1895, 41, 36.

[16]WMU, SBC, AR, 1894, 35-36.

[17]Rembert W. and Eleanor B. Patrick and Hester G. Fisackerly, *The Story of Florida* (Austin: Steck-Vaughn Company, 1959), 268.

[18]FBC Annual 1895, 36.

[19]FBC Annual 1895, 43.

[20]FBC Annual 1895, 41.

[21]FBC Annual 1896, 27.

[22]History of Marion Baptist Association W.M.U.," 3.

[23]FBC Annual 1896, 27. Catherine Allen traces the evolution of this offering emphasis: The Week of Self-Denial for Home Missions was observed annually. In 1903 it became known as a Week of Prayer and Self-Denial. Gradually the term "thank offering" replaced the original self-denial offering "out of shame that so few were practicing the idea." In 1934, Annie Armstrong's name was added to the offering and in 1969, WMU changed the name to Annie Armstrong Easter Offering for Home Missions. *Century to Celebrate,* 155.

[24]FBC Annual 1893, 96.

[25]FBC Annual 1896, 28.

[26]Lassiter, 33.

[27]Patrick, 269.

[28]FBC Annual 1896, 24, 25; FBC Annual 1895, 35.

[29]*Witness*, 14 January 1915, 10.

[30]FBC Annual 1897, 24. See also FBC Annual 1896, 28.

[31]FBC Annual 1897, 22.

[32]Allen, 101.

[33]Allen, 101, 102.

[34]FBC Annual 1897, 22. This appears to be the first reference to "Sunbeams" in FBC minutes, several years earlier than previously thought.

[35]*Witness*, 19 January 1997; FBC Annual 1897, 61.

[36]FBC Annual 1897, 18.

[37]*Witness*, 19 and 26 May 1897.

[38]FBC Annual, January 1898. Complete Minutes of the Woman's Missionary Union meeting, 69-75.

[39]FBC Annual, January 1898, 22. Searching for any arrangement which would promote better work and greater contributions, delegates at the January 1898 state Convention voted to change the time of Annual Meetings to the end of the year. Thus a second annual session was held in 1898, beginning on Wednesday before the fourth Sunday of November, in Madison.

[40]FBC Annual, January 1898, 52.

[41]*Witness*, 19 January 1898.

[42]*Witness*, 15 June 1898.

[43]FBC Annual 1899, 39.

[44]Porter, 6; Lassiter, 33.

[45]FBC Annual 1899, 62-63; FBC Annual 1900, 37.

[46]FBC Annual 1900, 38.

[47]FBC Annual 1900, 54-55.

[48]FBC Annual 1900, 37.

[49]Joiner, 99.

[50]FBC Annual 1901, 32. In the SBM report Dr. Chaudoin reported 288 ministers, "including the super-annuated, the secularized, the lazy, the young men preparing for the work, the anti-missionaries and all others."

[51]*Witness*, 8 June 1898.

[52]FBC Annual 1901, 41.

[53]FBC Annual 1905, 97-98.

[54]FBC Annual 1906, 57-58.

[55]Fannie E. S. Heck, *In Royal Service: The Mission Work of Southern Baptist Women* (Nashville: Broadman Press, 1913), 187-188; Allen, 103-04.

[56]Lassiter, 41.

[57]FBC Annual 1903, 33, 66.

[58]Allen, 46.

[59]*Witness*, 26 February 1902.

[60]Catherine B. Allen, *Laborers Together with God: 22 Great Women in Baptist Life* (Birmingham: Woman's Missionary Union, 1987), 170.

[61]FBC Annual 1904, 47.

[62]FBC Annual 1905, 94. Catherine Allen to author, 26 August 1994: "The 'Chautauqua Salute' is the waving of white handkerchiefs by all in the audience. It must have originated at Chautauqua, New York, where many of the early WMUers and other SBC leaders went to spend the summers hearing lectures. In those days it would have been unthinkable to applaud in a religious meeting, and everybody had a nice white hankie. Voila! The salute was born."

[63]FBC Annual 1905, 98-100.

[64]Jane Moon Thorpe, compiler, As the River Flows . . . : Santa Fe River Baptist Association Minutes 1857-1940 (Santa Fe River Baptist Association, 1978), 38.

[65]Franklin Fowler, taped interview with author, October 1993.

[66]*Witness*, 19 July 1984.

[67]FBC Annual 1904, 46. Italics added.

[68]FBC Annual 1904, 48.

[69]*Witness*, 3 March 1904. The newspaper article is apparently the only extant copy of Mrs. Chipley's work.

[70]*Witness*, 7 February 1907.

[71]FBC Annual 1905, 36, 41.

[72]FBC Annual 1905, 106.

[73]*Witness*, 11 November 1909. In this article, for the first and only time Spalding cautions the women to use the correct name of the organization— Woman's Baptist Missionary Union or W.B.M.U., saying, "it is a mistake to refer to the State Union as W.M.U." However, she herself was not consistent in using the name, and the women did not seem troubled by using WMU and WBMU interchangeably.

[74]*Witness*, 11 November 1909.

[75]FBC Annual 1907, 101.

[76]FBC Annual 1907, 107, 110. Italics added.

[77]FBC Annual 1907, 94, 96.

[78]FBC Annual 1908, 27.

[79]FBC Annual 1908, 126.

[80]*Witness*, 20 May 1909. Letter dated 21 December 1908.

[81]FBC Annual 1909, 15.

[82]*Witness*, 30 April 1908.

[83]*The Florida Handbook, 1963-1964,* compiler, Allen Morris (Tallahassee: The Peninsula Publishing Company, 1963), 294. The state automobile registration law was enacted in 1905. In the first two years, 296 automobiles were registered.

[84]FBC Annual 1909, 8, 54, 84.

[85]FBC Annual 1910, 77.

[86]FBC Annual 1909, 87.

[87]FBC Annual 1909, 8, 54, 92.

[88]FBC Annual 1910, 11, 16.

[89]*Witness*, 18 November 1909.

[90]*Witness*, 23 December 1909.

[91]FBC Annual 1910, 86.

[92]FBC Annual 1908, 126.

[93]FBC Annual 1910, 92-93, 78, 45, 91.

[94]*Witness*, 3 February 1910.

[95]FBC Annual 1910, 93.

[96]FBC Annual 1910, 93.

[97]FBC Annual 1910, 94.

[98]WMU, SBC, AR 1910, 12.

[99]*Witness*, 19 May 1910.

[100]WMU, SBC, AR, 1910, 37.

[101]*Witness*, 23 June 1910.

[102]*Witness*, 2 June 1910.

[103]*Witness*, 12 January 1911.

[104]FBC Annual 1911, 104. Minutes of WMU annual meeting, 92-119.

[105]*Witness*, 7 January 1915.

[106]Ashville, North Carolina, City Directory, vols. 17-29; *Witness*, 29 October 1931.

Chapter IV
Advancing the Cause

[1]Marion Peelman Crews, taped conversation with her daughter Dorothy, circa 1974. Also Dorothy and Frances Crews, taped interview with author, 6 February 1993. Further details about the Peelmans' move to Florida and the personal experiences of the Peelman and Crews families are taken from these sources.

[2]Florida Baptist Convention (FBC) Annual 1900, 55.

[3]FBC Annual 1905, 105.

[4]FBC Annual 1906, 108.

[5]*Florida Baptist Witness,* 7 February 1907.

[6]FBC Annual, January 1912, 97.

[7]Mrs. R. M. (Rosa) Hunter, "Trip to Jacksonville—1911," transcribed notes in WMU, SBC, Archives, Catherine Allen Papers, Box 1D, Annual Meeting, 1907-1915.

[8]Woman's Missionary Union, Auxiliary to Southern Baptist Convention, Annual Report (WMU, SBC, AR), 1911, 73-74.

[9] WMU, SBC, AR, 1911, 74.

[10] FBC Annual, January 1912, 95.

[11]Louise Porter Hood, *History of Woman's Missionary Union, Auxiliary to Florida Baptist Convention,* 1914, 33.

[12]FBC Annual, January 1912, 118-119.

[13]FBC Annual, January 1912, 121.

[14]*1928 Book of Remembrance,* WMU Office, Jacksonville, Florida, n.p.

[15]FBC Annual, December 1912, 121.

[16]Catherine B. Allen, *A Century to Celebrate: History of Woman's Missionary Union* (Birmingham: Woman's Missionary Union, 1987), 430 [Eljee Bentley, Chronology].

[17]FBC Annual, December 1912, 80. Italics added.

[18]FBC Annual, December 1912, 50.

[19]FBC Annual, December 1912, 26-27.

[20]Ethlene Boone Cox, *Following in His Train* (Nashville: Broadman Press, 1938), 83-84; *Witness,* 17 April 1913.

[21]FBC Annual 1914, 74; *Witness,* 3 May 1928.

[22]FBC Annual, December 1912, 35.

[23]*Witness,* 27 February 1913.

[24]*Witness,* 27 February 1913.

[25]*Witness,* 27 February 1913.

[26]Moses Nathaniel McCall, *A Baptist Generation in Cuba* (Atlanta: Home Mission Board, Southern Baptist Convention, 1942), 73-74. See also Louie D. Newton, *Amazing Grace: The Life of M. N. McCall, Missionary to Cuba* (Atlanta: Home Mission Board, Southern Baptist Convention, 1948), 66-68.

[27]Margaret McRae Lackey, *Decade of W.M.U. Service, 1913-1923* (Nashville: Sunday School Board, Southern Baptist Convention, 1923), 6.

[28]*Witness,* 29 May 1913.

[29]Cox, 84.

[30]Allen, 109. According to Allen, the organization received the name "Girls' Auxiliary" in 1914. The GA pin was designed in 1915; the watchword (Isaiah 60:1), the hymn ("We've a Story to Tell"), and the colors (white and nile green) were chosen in 1924.

[31]Cox, 85.

[32]FBC Annual 1914, 72.

[33]FBC Annual 1914, 76.

[34]Lelia Boring Lassiter, *On This Foundation: History of the Woman's Missionary Union, Auxiliary to the Florida Baptist Convention* (Jacksonville: Convention Press, 1961), 50.

[35]Hood, 62,63.

[36]Edward Earl Joiner, *A History of Florida Baptists* (Jacksonville: Florida Baptist Convention, 1972), 121-22.

[37]FBC Annual 1915-1916, 70, for example. In 1915 the Columbia College group was one of two honor college YWAs in the entire SBC.

[38]FBC Annual 1916-1917, 80.

[39]FBC Annual 1915-1916, 69.

[40]FBC Annual 1916-1917, 61-63. Other references to report are from same source.

[41]"[Heck's] final official words became the most quoted lines in WMU history," said Catherine B. Allen in *Laborers Together with God: 22 Great Women in Baptist Life* (Birmingham: Woman's Missionary Union, 1987), 34.

[42]Allen, Laborers, 35.

[43]*Home and Foreign Fields (Fields),* February 1917, 24.

[44]Allen Morris, comp. *The Florida Handbook,* 1963-1964 (Tallahassee: The Peninsular Publishing Company, 1963), 364.

[45]*Witness,* 12 April 1917.

[46]*Witness,* 15 November 1917.

[47]FBC Annual 1916-1917, 74.

[48]Allen, *Century,* 98.

[49]FBC Annual 1915-1916, 83.

[50]*Witness,* 30 May 1918.

[51]FBC Annual 1916-1917, 80, 91.

[52]FBC Annual 1917-1918, 83.

[53]FBC Annual 1916-1917, 89-90; FBC Annual 1924-25, 95.

[54]FBC Annual 1916-1917, 93.

[55]Morris, 19.

[56]*Fields,* March 1918.

[57]*Fields,* December 1916, 28.

[58]*Witness,* 18 April, 1918.

[59]FBC Annual 1919, 92.

[60]*Witness,* 13 June 1918.

[61]Allen, 168.

[62]*Witness,* 30 May 1918.

[63]Allen, *Century,* 185-188; Cox, 186-192; FBC Annual 1917-1918, 85; *Witness,* 30 May 1918.

[64]FBC Annual 1919, 93.

[65]FBC Annual 1919, 31.

[66]*Witness,* 21 August, 23 October, and 4 December 1919.

[67]*Witness,* 8 January 1920.

[68]See Allen, 125-129; Rosser, 95-96; FBC Annual 1924-1925, 100.

[69]FBC Annual 1921, 116-117; 33-34.

[70]*Witness,* 25 July and 7 November 1918.

[71]*Witness,* 29 January 1920.

[72]The FBC moved there from the Heard Building in 1916; in 1921 Convention headquarters moved to 205 Peninsular Building. Lassiter, 52.

[73]On another visit, Frances saw a pile of letters on her grandmother's desk. Wanting to help, she gathered them in her arms and deposited them in the mail box. That was not exactly the kind of help Mrs. Peelman needed—they had not been stamped.

[74]FBC Annual 1920, 103, 98, 99.

[75]*Witness,* 2 September 1920.

[76]FBC Annual 1920, 95.

[77]FBC Annual 1921-22, 110.

[78]FBC Annual 1921-22, 34.

[79]"Society Methods," *Royal Service,* May 1922, 30.

[80]FBC Annual 1921-22, 116, 117, 113. Printed lists of officers and references to offices did not always reflect decisions made during annual

business sessions. As the organizational chart became more complex, the women sometimes seemed to disregard their own actions.

[81]FBC Annual 1923-24, 107, 112.

[82]*1928 Book of Remembrance.*

[83]Hood, 33.

[84]See FBC Annuals, 1912-1923, for Wamboldt's addresses.

[85]FBC Annual 1923-24, 98, 117. The two-year limit was removed after Mellon's presidency. In 1926 a five-year limit was placed on a president's service.

[86]FBC Annual 1925-26, 121.

[87]FBC Annual 1924-25, 106.

[88]*Witness*, 3 September 1924.

[89]FBC Annual 1925-26, 14.

[90]See Allen, *Century,* 132-141, for details of WMU, SBC, involvement in development and progress of CP.

[91]FBC Annual 1929-30, 130-132.

[92]FBC Annual 1925-26, 126, 110.

[93]Crews Interview.

[94]Joiner, 176.

[95]FBC Annual 1928-1929, 141.

[96]FBC Annual 1926-27, 130.

[97]*Witness*, 20 May 1926.

[98]*Witness*, 15 September 1927.

[99]Cox, 91-92.

[100]FBC Annual 1927-28, 130.

[101]FBC Annual 1927-28, 114-158, random pages.

[102]FBC Annual 1928-29, 139.

[103]FBC Annual 1928-29, 14, 21.

[104]FBC Annual 1928-29, 139.

[105]FBC Annual 1929-30, 124.

[106]*Witness*, 31 May 1928.

[107]Mildred Bennett Golden, *Through the Years with the Woman's Missionary Union of Wekiwa Association,* Orlando, Florida, c. 1945.

[108]FBC Annual 1927-28, 132; FBC Annual 1928-29, 139-140.

[109]FBC Annual 1891, 16.

[110]*Thy Neighbor—Thyself* (Richmond: Woman's Missionary Union of Virginia, n.d.), 34.

[111]Mrs. Peelman to Fletcher, 8 February 1928. All correspondence between Mrs. Peelman and Fletcher referred to in text is located in the Fletcher file, Virginia Baptist Historical Society, University of Richmond.

[112]Rees Watkins, VBHS, interview with author, 29 October 1993.

[113]See correspondence between Storer and Fletcher, April-May, 1928, Fletcher file, VBHS.

[114]Louise Fletcher, notebook for April 1928. In several small (some 2 inches by 3 inches) note-books, Fletcher carefully articulated details of her travels, visits, daily work, and personal activities. All notebooks referred to are located in Fletcher file, VBHS.

[115]Louise Fletcher, notebook: "Report of Work in Graves Association for month of October [1928]."

[116]"Tenth Annual Session of the West Florida Association," Fletcher file, VBHS.

[117]Undated article, Pensacola News, Fletcher file, VBHS.

[118]*1928 Book of Remembrance.* After months of convalescence, Fletcher became director of the Stony Lonesome Good Will Center, located in a mining camp near Norton, Wise County, Virginia. That position began her long career in Virginia mission work. Louise Fletcher, *The Diary of a State Missionary* (Richmond: Woman's Missionary Union of Virginia, 1967), 15.

[119]Peelman to Fletcher, 14 July 1929.

[120]Allen, *Century,* 130.

[121]FBC Annual 1930-31, 18, 23.

[122] FBC Annual 1931, 124.

[123]Eloise Glass Cauthen, taped interview with Toni Clevenger and author, Richmond, Virginia, October 1993. Interview is source of all information from Mrs. Cauthen referred to in text.

[124]FBC Annual 1934-35, 120.

[125]FBC Annual 1930-31, 24, 26, 99.

[126]FBC Annual 1930-31, 106.

[127]FBC Annual 1930-31, 99.

[128]*Witness*, 18 December 1930.

[129]Christine McConnell Rousseau, *Turquoise Path: Cherished Memories of My Father F. C. McConnell* (Nashville: Broadman Press, 1943), 213. F. C. McConnell and George W. Truett were cousins; McConnell was the pastor who baptized Truett.

[130]Gideon Jacques Rousseau, *Ex Angustam Portam (Through the Strait Gate): Reminiscences of G. J. Rousseau, 1952.* Bound carbon copy of unpublished memoirs, First Baptist Church library, Pensacola, Florida. Among Baptist leaders on Rousseau's ordination council were J. B. Tidwell, L. R. Scarborough, S. M. Provence, Pat M. Neff, and his father-in-law. Martha Trotter, "The Real Aristocracy of Gideon Jacques Rousseau, 1880-1969," a paper written for the Florida Baptist Historical Society, 1990.

[131]*Witness*, 6 February 1930.

[132]FBC Annual 1930-31, 98.

[133]FBC Annual 1930-31, 103-104.

[134]FBC Annual 1930-31, 119.

[135]*Witness*, 18 December 1930.

[136]*The Commercial Dispatch,* Columbus, Mississippi, 6 April 1932.

[137]FBC Annual 1933, 49-50.

[138]Frank Tripp, "Baptist Hundred Thousand Club and the W.M.U.," *Royal Service,* October 1933, 5.

[139]*Witness*, 14 December 1933.

[140]FBC Annual 1933, 50-52.

[141]*Witness*, 14 December 1933.

[142]Mrs. Peelman to Fletcher, 29 December 1931.

[143]Theo Thomas Lee, taped interview with Vanita Baldwin and author, Jacksonville, Florida, February 1993.

[144]FBC Annual 1935-36, 149.

[145]FBC Annual 1935-36, 189-90.

[146]FBC Annual 1935-36, 198-199.

[147]FBC Annual 1935-36, 122.

[148]*Witness*, 9 April 1936.

[149]Recommendation to annual session, 1937. FBC Annual 1936-37, 177.

Chapter V
They are Precious in His Sight

[1]Louise Smith Boyd, assisted by Dorothy Pryor, taped responses to questionnaire, Atlanta, Georgia, 3 March 1993; Louise Smith Boyd and Dorothy Pryor, taped interview with author, Ridgecrest, North Carolina, 23 August 1993. Information used throughout chapter on Boyd's family relationships, education, and personal experiences is taken from these sources.

[2]Woman's College Annual, 1930.

[3]*Florida Baptist Witness,* 9 July 1931.

[4]Florida Baptist Convention (FBC) Annual 1931, 99.

[5]Inabelle Coleman, who became an editor with the FMB and later a missionary to China.

[6]Alma Hunt, taped interviews with TC and author, Ridgecrest, North Carolina, 25 August 1993; Roanoke, Virginia, 24 October 1993.

[7]Etter Turner, taped interview with author, DeLand, Florida, 12 March 1993. Further details regarding Turner-Smith/Boyd friendship are from same source.

[8]FBC Annual 1932, 41.

[9]FBC Annual 1932, 43, 128.

[10]The university conferred the honorary doctor of laws degree upon Turner in 1983. In 1994, Florida WMU's Centennial year, Stetson established "an outstanding student award in honor of the first woman dean of students at the university—Etter McTeer Turner." The award goes to the graduating senior with " 'the highest standards of excellence in academic performance, leadership, community service, personal character and integrity.' " Those characteristics reflect not only present university goals but also the aims of Louise Smith and Etter Turner as each in her turn worked with the young people of Florida.

[11]FBC Annual 1932, 43.

[12]FBC Annual 1932, 43.

[13]FBC Annual 1934-35, 124-25.

[14]FBC Annual 1934-35, 121.

[15]*Witness*, 13 July 1933.

[16]*Witness*, 24 January 1935.

[17]*Witness*, 14 December 1933; FBC Annual 1934-35, 68.

[18]*Witness*, 4 July 1935.

[19]FBC Annual 1934-35, 119, 145.

[20]FBC Annual 1934-35, 141.

[21]FBC Annual 1934-35, 141. [See *Witness*, 11 April 1935, for good picture of Fisher and another of a Grace McBride YWA.]

[22]FBC Annual 1934-35, 142. Personal details of trip are from Smith tapes.

[23]Spellings of names of countries are taken from contemporary records. For account of Eastern European segment of trip by Everett Gill, missionary to Rumania, see *Witness*, 17 January 1935.

[24]FBC Annual 1934-35, 140, 142.

[25]Sunbeam, 7 February; YWA, 11 April; GA, 4 July; RA, 7 November 1935.

[26]*Witness*, 4 November 1943.

[27]*Witness*, 16 April 1936.

[28]FBC Annual 1936-37, 141; FBC Annual 1943-44, 97.

[29]Boyd Interview.

[30]Boyd Interview.

[31]FBC Annual 1936-37, 139.

[32]FBC Annual 1936-67, 41, 138.

[33]FBC Annual 1936-37, 41, 127.

[34]*Witness*, 28 April 1938. As a young student, Carver had attended the Southern Baptist Convention in Richmond when WMU was formed in 1888.

[35]*Witness*, 19 May 1938; FBC Annual 1938-39, 196.

[36]*The Alabama Baptist,* 19 May 1938.

[37]*Witness*, 19 May 1938.

[38]FBC Annual 1938-39, 199.

[39]FBC Annual 1938-39, 195, 198.

[40]FBC Annual 1938-39, 211-213.

[41]FBC Annual 1938-39, 222. "Theo" is her real name, given to her by her father, who wanted a boy baby.

[42]*Witness*, 23 February 1933.

[43]Theo Thomas Lee (Mrs. Robert E.), taped interview with Vanita Baldwin and author, Jacksonville, Florida, November 1992.

[44]FBC Annual 1939-40, 170.

[45]FBC Annual 1940-41, 189; 1943-44, 123.

[46]Catherine B. Allen, *A Century to Celebrate: History of Woman's Missionary Union* (Birmingham: Woman's Missionary Union, 1987), 131-32.

[47]Louise Smith (LS)to C. E. Maddry (CEM), 14 February 1940, "General Correspondence 1940-1949," Box 931, Foreign Mission Board Archives, Richmond, Virginia. All FMB correspondence referred to in this chapter is found in same file.

[48]FBC Annual 1940-41, 206; FBC Annual 1941-42, 134-45.

[49]Allen, 132.

[50]FBC Annual 1942-43, 102-103.

[51]FBC Annual 1942-43, 100. Because of ill health, Lee could not continue in office.

[52]Joiner, 46-47, 50-51, 87-90, 133-34, 167-68.

[53]FBC Annual 1926, 120-21.

[54]FBC Annual 1937-38, 142.

[55]FBC Annual 1936-37, 56.

[56]FBC Annual 1936-37, 123-25, 141; *Witness*, 3 September 1936.

[57]*Witness*, 8 October 1936.

[58]Allen, 249.

[59]*Witness*, 8 October 1936.

[60]*Witness*, 29 October 1936.

[61]*Witness*, 4 March 1937.

[62]FBC Annual 1940-41, 187.

[63]Allen, 251.

[64]FBC Annual 1941-42, 138; *Witness*, 24 July 1941.

[65]FBC Annual 1943-44, 106.

[66]FBC Annual 1943-44, 100.

[67]The HMB, the FBC, and Oklahoma Indians cooperated in efforts to reach the Florida Seminoles. Having made several trips to the state, in 1917 Rev. H. M. Harjo, a Creek Indian from Oklahoma, returned "at his own cost" to live in Stuart and try to establish work with the Seminoles. The effort did not last long, and the results are unknown. *Home and Foreign Fields,* February 1917, 19.

[68]Joiner, 100-101.

[69]FBC Annual 1935-36, 28-29, 190.

[70]FBC Annual 1936-37, 125.

[71]FBC Annual 1936-37, 125; FBC Annual 1937-38, 157.

[72]FBC Annual 1939-40, 17, 209; *Witness*, 25 January 1940.

[73]*Witness*, 7 November 1940.

[74]FBC Annual 1941-42, 101-102.

[75]*Witness*, 12 November 1942.

[76]*Witness*, 21 January 1943.

[77]*Witness*, 11 November and 9 December 1943.

[78]*Witness*, 3 August 1939.

[79]Franklin Fowler, taped interview with TC and author, Richmond, Virginia, 26 October 1993.

[80]*Witness*, 22 March 1934.

[81]*Witness*, 20 January 1944.

[82]Wilson had begun her career with WMU as Helen Moore. In 1929 she married G. E. Wilson in a unique morning ceremony in the Peelman home.

[83]FBC Annual 1940-41, 36, 183, 196. Susan Adams Carden later became the executive secretary of Oklahoma WMU.

[84]FBC Annual 1940-41, 183, 195.

[85]FBC Annual 1933, 117.

[86]Elsie Renfroe Knight (Mrs. Charles), taped response to questionnaire, Atlanta, Georgia, March 1993.

[87]FBC Annual 1936, 175; 1937, 174.

[88]FBC Annual 1941-42, 155-56.

[89]Rosser, 108-109; FBC Annual 1941-42, 130.

[90]Elizabeth Provence, taped interview with TC and author, Ridgecrest, North Carolina, August 1993.

[91]Elizabeth Provence, interview. This and other personal incidents and biographical data found in this chapter are taken from Provence's interview.

[92]For example, LS to CEM, 14 February 1940; LS to Everett Gill, Jr. (EG), 12 December 1942; and EG's response, 16 December 1942.

[93]FBC Annual 1942-43, 134, 136.

[94]LS to CEM, 22 April 1943.

[95]Ann Rosser King, typed copy of her mother's obituary, January 15, 1970. Dr. Rosser's *A History of Florida Baptists,* the first book-length history of the Convention, was published in 1949.

[96]FBC Annual 1942-43, 105. White Cross work continued until 1946. When Dr. M. T. Rankin, FMB secretary, wrote that hospital needs on foreign fields could be met through Cooperative Program and Lottie Moon Offerings, Florida WMU ceased to promote the work and deleted the White Cross

chairman from the list of state officers. FBC Annual 1945-46, 126.

[97] *Witness*, 22 and 29 April 1943.

[98] *Witness*, 17 June 1943; FBC Annual 1943-44, 101.

[99] See random letters dealing with this project in "General Correspondence 1940-1949," Box 931, Foreign Mission Board Archives, Richmond, Virginia.

[100] FBC Annual 1943-44, 97; Franklin Fowler, interview. The first medical consultant for the FMB, Dr. Fowler served in that position 25 years, retiring in 1985.

[101] "Report of the Andean, or Cuyo, District, River Plate Mission," circa 1949, HMB files, SBC Historical Commission, Nashville, Tennessee.

[102] *Witness*, 11 November 1943.

[103] *Witness*, 4 November 1943.

[104] *Florida Baptist Witness*, 28 October 1943.

[105] Elsie Knight Renfroe, taped response to questionnaire, Atlanta, Georgia, March, 1993. Renfroe praised the helpful spirit of local churches in hosting a variety of WMU meetings.

[106] *Witness*, 27 January 1944. Further references to this meeting are from Florida Baptist Convention (FBC) Annual 1943-44, 83-135.

[107] Knight Questionnaire. Also Provence, interview.

[108] *Witness*, 27 April 1944.

[109] Louise Brantley to George W. Sadler, 2 January 1944; GWS to LB, 15 January 1944.

[110] *Witness*, 9 March, 17 February, 4 May, 18 May 1944.

[111] FBC Annual 1944-45, 135.

[112] Maurice Brantley to Southern Baptist Convention, Western Union Wire, Miami, Florida, May 1952.

[113] Dale Moore and Ralph Davis, Nigeria missionaries emeriti, telephone interviews with author, August 1994.

[114] *Witness*, 13 January and 13 July 1944. Italics added.

[115] W. G. Stracener, "A Sketch of Florida Baptist History" in *Centennial Celebration: Florida Baptist Convention,* program booklet, Daytona Beach, November 16-18, 1954.

[116] *Witness*, 13 July 1944.

[117] FBC Annual 1944-45, 121.

[118] FBC Annual 1944-45, 114-116, 121-124.

[119] Snake episode from Knight questionnaire; Allen 435; FBC Annual 1944-45, 124.

[120] *Witness*, 27 June 1946.

[121] For example, see FBC Annual 1936, 39.

[122] When asked about working relationships with the men on the Florida Convention staff, Louise Boyd said, "They were wonderful to me!"

[123] FBC Annual 1936-37, 14.

[124] Sometimes mistakes were made and the women complained about inaccurate record keeping. For example, Miss Spalding and Mrs. Peelman referred to state records which were not in line with their own. Most of the time, however, every effort was made to be completely fair, as in Dr. Brittain's actions to straighten out some confusion over contributions to the $75 Million campaign.

[125] FBC Annual 1936-37, 57; FBC Annual 1940-41, 22.

[126] FBC Annual 1938-39, 54. The SBC Executive Committee in 1931 had recommended this consideration of state WMU expenses (Allen, 136). For several years, funds supporting other entities charged with CP promotion, including the budgets of the Brotherhood Department and the *Florida Baptist Witness*, were treated similarly by the FBC. See FBC Annual 1941-42, 184, for another example.

[127] For example, see *Witness*, 12 March 1936.

[128] *Witness*, 14 December 1944.

[129] *Witness*, 14 December 1944.

Chapter VI
Lasting Legacies

[1] Frances Lyon, taped interview with Toni Clevenger, (TC) Elizabeth Provence, and author, Jacksonville, 4 April 1994.

[2] *Florida Baptist Witness*, 12 October 1944.

[3] Because of the war, no WMU, SBC, annual meeting was held in 1943.

[4] Lyon Interview.

[5] Louise Smith and Dorothy Pryor, taped interview with TC and author, Ridgecrest, North Carolina, 23 August 1993.

[6] *Witness*, 12 October 1944.

[7] *Witness*, 28 December 1944.

[8] Florida Baptist Convention (FBC) Annual 1944-45, 143.

[9] J. E. Dillard, Southern Baptist Promotion Director, *Witness*, 24 August 1944.

[10] Elizabeth Provence, taped response to questionnaire, April 1993.

[11] FBC Annual 1945-46, 135, 125.

[12] FWMU AR 1949-50, 22.

[13] *Witness*, 21 June 1945. For camp report example, see *Witness*, 6 September 1945.

[14]FBC Annual 1945-46, 146.

[15]*Witness*, 13 September 1945.

[16]Elsie Renfroe Knight, taped response to questionnaire, Atlanta, Georgia, March 1993.

[17]*Witness*, 27 December 1945; Knight Questionnaire. Eventually Elsie returned to Nigeria with Charles for one term of mission service. The illness of a son forced their resignation. They returned to serve a Florida church before moving to Atlanta, where they still live in 1994.

[18]*Witness*, 21 June 1945.

[19]FBC Annual 1945-46, 150. Provence directed students in that intensive summer work for several more years. In 1946, WMU planned 143 regular schools of missions, the largest number for any one year. The next year the new FBC Community Missions Department took over direction of schools of missions. FBC Annual 1947, 25.

[20]R. Paul Caudill, "Centennial, Southern Baptist Convention," *Encyclopedia of Southern Baptists* (Nashville: Broadman Press, 1958), 1: 243-44.

[21]FBC Annual 1945-46, 17, 18, 38.

[22]FBC Annual 1945-46, 133.

[23]FBC Annual 1945-46, 39, 121; *Witness*, 21 February 1946.

[24]*Witness*, 4 April 1946.

[25]*Witness*, 10 April 1947.

[26]Catherine B. Allen, *A Century to Celebrate: History of Woman's Missionary Union* (Birmingham: Woman's Missionary Union, 1987), 139-40.

[27]*Witness*, 23 May 1946.

[28]Jones to Rankin, 7 March 1946, General Correspondence Files, FMB Archives, Richmond, Virginia.

[29]FBC Annual 1946, 33-34.

[30]*Witness*, 28 November 1946; FBC Annual 1946, 14.

[31]*Witness*, 17 June 1948.

[32]SBM Minutes, 7 June 1946.

[33]*Witness*, 15 August 1946; 21 August 1947. Withauer married Dr. T. B. Stover, head of the Publishing House, after the death of his first wife. The two continued mission service in Brazil.

[34]FBC Annual 1945-46, 32, 36.

[35]FBC Annual 1946, 34, 41, 42.

[36]FBC Annual 1946, 118.

[37]Mrs. Alfred I. Dupont of Jacksonville, long time trustee of Stetson University, was the most notable exception.

[38]Provence Questionnaire.

[39]FWMU AR 1946-47, 26.

[40]Provence Questionnaire.

[41]*Witness*, 11 September 1947.

[42]*Witness*, 9 October 1947; FWMU AR 1947-48, 16, 20, 24.

[43]Alma Hunt, *History of Woman's Missionary Union* (Nashville: Convention Press, 1964), 158.

[44]Lelia Boring Lassiter, hand-written autobiographical sketch in Lassiter papers.

[45]Betty Lassiter (Mrs. Richard), taped interview with author, Orlando, Florida, March 1993.

[46]*Witness*, 12 August 1948.

[47]Theo Thomas Lee (Mrs. Robert E.), taped interview with Vanita Baldwin and author, Jacksonville, November 1992.

[48]Lelia Boring Lassiter, "Mrs. Roy L. Lassiter, President Florida W.M.U. 1948-54," undated autobiographical sketch in Lassiter papers.

[49]Alma Hunt, taped interview with TC and author, Ridgecrest, North Carolina, 25 August 1993.

[50]Mary Christian, WMU, SBC, to Dr. G. W. Sadler, FMB, March 15, 1943: The Executive Committee voted "to alternate the B.W.C. Conference between Home and Foreign Mission Weeks thus giving those who attended several years in succession the opportunity of hearing the foreign missionaries one year and those under the Home Mission board the next." The 1943 conference was planned for HM Week. General Correspondence, FMB Archives.

[51]FWMU AR 1947-48, 18, 22; *Witness*, 5 August 1948.

[52]*Witness*, 19 August 1948.

[53]Provence Questionnaire; *Witness*, 4 May 1950.

[54]SBM Minutes, September 1951; FMWU AR 1950-51, 30.

[55]*Witness*, 22 March 1951.

[56]Hunt, *History*, 164.

[57]SBM Minutes, February 1952.

[58]FWMU AR 1950-51, 17-19. Succeeding details on plans are from same source.

[59]FWMU AR 1951-52, 31. WMU, SBC, had ceased to give mission study awards, instead setting standards encouraging individual members to read mission books. Missionary Round Tables, challenging readers to move beyond the basics, promoted group discussions of books from a list specified by WMU, SBC. Allen, 198, 199.

By 1954, Florida had over 400 Round Tables. FWMU AR, 1952-53, 36.

[60]FWMU AR 1951-52, 3-9; *Witness*, 2 April 1953.

[61]*Witness*, 5 November 1953. Mrs. R. L. [Marie] Mathis, "North American Baptist Women's Union" in *Baptist Advance: The Achievements of the Baptists*

of North America for a Century and a Half (Nashville: Broadman Press, 1964), 485-487; *Witness*, 5 November 1953.

[62]FWMU AR 1952-53, 7-19; *Witness*, 8 and 15 April 1954. Further details of meeting are also taken from these sources.

[63]The Presbyterian Church building in which the 1894 meeting was held was no longer in existence.

[64]FBC Annual 1954, 85, updated list.

[65]Lassiter, "President."

[66]FWMU AR 1956-57, 24.

[67]FWMU AR 1953-54, 20, 24.

[68]FWMU AR 1954-55, 30.

[69]See *Florida Woman's Missionary Union Camping 1946-1985*, by Elizabeth Provence and Ruth Bagwell, 1986, for a detailed history of the Florida WMU camping program.

[70]Many persons throughout the state knew Elizabeth Provence as "Lib." Especially was she called Lib by those in camping.

[71]FWMU AR 1952-53, 29; FWMU AR 1955-56, 31.

[72]Genus Crenshaw, taped response to question-naire, Fort Lauderdale, Florida, May 1993.

[73]Provence Interview; *Witness*, 30 September 1954; FWMU AR 1954-55, 35-36; Armand Ball, interview with TC, August 1994.

[74]Susan Adams to Juliette Mather, 4 February 1939, in Brotherhood Commission files. Also Carolyn Weatherford Crumpler, taped interview with author, Jacksonville, February 1993. Crumpler was shown a letter in the Brotherhood Commission files, written by Smith and making the recommendation for transfer, but recent efforts to locate the letter failed. The transition for boys in grades 1-3 came later.

[75]FWMU AR 1955-56, 35, 16-17. The constitution of 1955 for the first time uses the term "annual session," rather than "annual meeting."

[76]*Witness*, 20 March 1958; FWMU AR 1957-58, 26.

[77]*Witness*, 30 April 1959.

[78]FBC Annual 1958, 89.

[79]Davis Collier Woolley, "Introduction," *Baptist Advance: The Achievements of the Baptists of North America for a Century and a Half* (Nashville: Broadman Press, 1964), ix.

[80]FWMU AR 1956-67, 14.

[81]*Witness*, 2 October 1958; FWMU AR 1957-58, 15.

[82]FWMU AR 1957-58, random pages; *Witness*, 30 April and 7 May 1959. Further references to 1959 Annual Session are from same sources. The list of Florida foreign missionaries, with their addresses and birthdays, appeared for the first time in that annual report. The list also included home missionaries serving in the state.

[83]SBM Minutes, 21 October 1954 and 9 December 1958.

[84]Margaret Lockhart (Mrs. J. H.), interview with author, July 1994. Other autobiographical data also taken from interview.

[85]*Witness*, 28 November 1960.

[86]Cleota Lenert (Mrs. August), taped interview with author, Fort Walton Beach, Florida, February 1993.

[87]FWMU AR 1959-60, 24; FWMU AR 1960-61, 27; FBC Annual 1966, 97-98.

[88]*Witness*, 24 March 1960; FBC Annual 1960, 108.

[89]*Witness*, 28 April 1960.

[90]FWMU AR 1958-59, 26-30.

[91]*Witness*, 11 August 1960.

[92]*Witness*, 10 November 1960.

[93]Reda Copeland Stroup, interview with author, July 1994.

[94]*Witness*, 10 November 1960; Carolyn Weatherford Crumpler (Mrs. Joe), taped interview with author, Jacksonville, February 1993. To avoid confusion, references to Crumpler's interview may refer to "Weatherford." Additional biographical details and personal experiences of Crumpler are from same source.

[95]FWMU AR 1959-60, 18-19.

[96]FWMU AR 1959-60, 25-26.

[97]FBC Annual 1962, 92.

[98]FBC Annual 1961, 93.

[99]FWMU AR 1960-61, 29-30; 1961-62, 24; 1962-63, 28.

[100]FWMU AR 1960-61, 32.

[101]Elizabeth Painter, taped response to question-naire, Jacksonville, March 1993; FWMU AR 1962-63, 29.

[102]FWMU AR 1958-59, 15.

[103]FBC Annual 1961, 65; SBM Minutes, May 1964. The property was purchased and later sold at a profit, with proceeds going to construction at the Lake Yale property.

[104]FWMU AR 1960-61, 16. FBC Annual 1963, 63; SBM Minutes, May 1964.

[105]FWMU AR 1960-61, 13.

[106]FWMU AR 1960-61, 11-24. Further details from 1962 Orlando meeting are from same source.

[107]Crumpler interview; FWMU AR 1962-63, 26.

[108]*Witness*, 28 October 1954 and 2 August 1962; FWMU AR 1961-62, 23.

[109]Samuel Ho, M.D. to Florida WMU, 4 August 1994.

VI

[110]FWMU AR 1961-62, 20-21; *Witness*, 30 May 1963.

[111]*Witness*, 2 May 1963.

[112]Mary Copes, interview with author, July 1994.

[113]FWMU AR 1962-63,10.

[114]FWMU AR 1962-63, 23-25, 21.

[115]*Witness*, 30 April 1964; Lockhart to author, 5 July 1994.

[116]*Witness*, 30 April 1964.

[117]Painter Questionnaire. Further biographical details on Painter are from same source.

[118]Ruth Bagwell, taped answers to questionnaire, Lake Yale, Florida, March 1993. Further biographical references are from same source.

[119]Lyon Interview.

[120]FWMU AR 1962-63, 27.

[121]FWMU AR 1963-64, 28.

[122]*Witness*, 1 June 1967; Painter Questionnaire.

[123]Mildred Worsham (Mrs. Stanley), interview with author, August 1994.

[124]Juanita Epperson, *On This Foundation, Part II: History of Florida Woman's Missionary Union 1960-1987* (Jacksonville: Florida Baptist Convention, 1988), 5.

[125]SBM Minutes, November 1965.

[126]*Witness*, 7 May 1967.

Chapter VII
All of One Accord

[1]Carolyn Weatherford Crumpler (Mrs. Joe), taped interview with author, Jacksonville, February 1993. To avoid confusion, references to Crumpler's interview usually refer to "Weatherford." Unless otherwise noted, additional biographical details and personal experiences of Crumpler are from same source.

[2]*Florida Baptist Witness*, 2 May, 20 June, and 8 August 1946.

[3]The Mather School of Nursing is now part of William Carey College, Hattiesburg, Mississippi.

[4]Edward Earl Joiner, *A History of Florida Baptists* (Jacksonville: Florida Baptist Convention, 1972), 247.

[5]Joiner, 310-13.

[6]FBC Annual 1944-45, 120-21; FWMU AR 1965-66, 31.

[7]*Witness*, 4 January 1968.

[8]*Witness*, 24 November 1960.

[9]Harold Bennett, taped interview with Toni Clevenger, Orlando, Florida, June 1994.

[10]*Witness*, 25 April 1968.

[11]*Witness*, 28 November 1968.

[12]Florida Woman's Missionary Union Annual Report (FWMU AR) 1967-68, 29.

[13]Catherine B. Allen, *A Century to Celebrate: History of Woman's Missionary Union* (Birmingham: Woman's Missionary Union, 1987), 210.

[14]*Witness*, 22 February 1968.

[15]Allen, 100.

[16]*Witness*, 25 January and 4 January 1968.

[17]*Witness*, 13 June 1968; FWMU AR 1967-68, 28-29.

[18]Irvin Northcutt, taped response to questionnaire, Gainesville, Florida, June 1994. Further information on the Northcutts is from same source.

[19]FWMU AR 1967-68, 30.

[20]FWMU AR 1967-68, random pages. Other details of 75th Annual Session are from same source.

[21]*Witness*, 15 May 1969.

[22]Bennett Interview.

[23]Cleota Lenert (Mrs. August), taped interview with author, February 1993. All details of Lenert's election to the presidency are from the same source.

[24]Lenert Interview. All biographical details are from same source.

[25]Ruth Bagwell, taped response to questionnaire, March 1993.

[26]*Witness*,1 May and 19 June 1969; FBC Annual 1969, 115.

[27]Allen, 110

[28]*WMU '70*, Promotional pamphlet (Birmingham: Woman's Missionary Union, Auxiliary to Southern Baptist Convention).

[29]Russell Drinnen, taped interview with author, Jacksonville, February 1993.

[30]See *Witness*, 15 March 1973.

[31]The 1970-71 Annual Report showed 806 Acteens organizations with enrollment of 6,972. The report for 1983-84, Bagwell's last year, showed 661 Acteens units with 6,905 enrolled.

[32]Elizabeth Painter, taped Interview with author, Jacksonville, Florida, February 1993.

[33]In her interview Lenert discussed in detail the effects of those problems on women in general and on WMU.

[34]Crumpler Interview.

[35]Bennett Interview.

[36]Lenert Interview.

[37]Crumpler Interview. According to Crumpler, the cost of the dove cut-out on the front of the program took most of Lenert's budget for the Annual Session. That decision may have created more stress than peace.

[38]Knight later published those segments in the "Christmas issue of *Home Missions Magazine.* During the historic moment in America's history when Anwar Sadat and Menaham Begin signed the treaty of peace at Camp David, President Carter in his speech quoted one of the segments." Juanita Epperson, *On This Foundation, Part II: History of Florida Woman's Missionary Union 1960-1987* (Jacksonville: Florida Baptist Convention), 1987, 11.

[39]*Witness*, 11 May 1972. Other details of session are from same source.

[40]Crumpler Interview.

[41]*Witness*, 11 May 1972; FWMU AR 1972-73, 24; Painter Questionnaire. GA quotation from *Witness*, 3 March 1973.

[42]See also Executive Committee Minutes, December 1973.

[43]Lenert Interview.

[44]*Witness*, 11 April 1974.

[45]Lenert Interview.

[46]See membership statistical chart in Allen, 474-77.

[47]E. Earl Joiner, Curator, Florida Baptist Historical Society, interview with author, August 1994.

[48]*Witness*, 14 March 1974.

[49]*Witness*, 31 May 1973.

[50]*Witness*, 12 April and 20 September 1973.

[51]FWMU AR 1970-71 through 1973-74; FWMU Council Minutes (Council), April 1974.

[52]*Witness*, 26 April and 13 December 1973.

[53]Hunt Interview. Presidents during the years 1948-1974 were Lelia Lassiter, Mary Belle Holland, Margaret Lockhart, Rosella Lipscomb, and Cleota Lenert.

[54]Crumpler Interview.

[55]Crumpler Interview.

[56]Clysta de Armas and Gisela Torres, taped interview with author, Jacksonville, April 1994.

[57]*Witness*, 14 June 1973.

[58]FWMU AR 1971-72, 5-8.

[59]Crumpler Interview; FBC Annual 1970, 155, and 1973, 122; FWMU Executive Committee Minutes , December 1973.

[60]Hunt Interview.

[61]Lenert Interview.

[62]Council Minutes, April 1974.

[63]FWMU AR 1972-73, 10-16. Other details of meeting are from same source.

[64]They were Mrs. Robert E. Lee, Mrs. R. L. Lassiter, Mrs. George Q. Holland, Mrs. Clyde B. Lipscomb, and Mrs. Lenert.

[65]Crumpler Interview.

[66]FBC Annual 1974, 123..

[67]*Witness*, 13 June and 1 August 1974.

[68]*Witness*, 3 October 1974.

Chapter VIII
Faithful to Missions

[1]Preceding vignette based on Bernice Popham, taped interview with Toni Clevenger (TC) and author, Columbia, South Carolina, November 1993. Further biographical and personal data are from same source.

[2]Florida WMU Annual Report (FWMU AR) 1972-73, 13; Florida WMU Council Minutes (Council Minutes), April 1974.

[3]Carrol Kelly, taped interview with author, Jacksonville, Florida, April 1994. Furhter biographical details and statements by Kelly are from same source.

[4]*Witness*, 19 June 1975.

[5]*Witness*, 19 June 1975.

[6]Harold Bennett, taped interview with TC, Orlando, Florida, June 1994.

[7]Bennett Interview.

[8]In individual interviews, Bennett, Popham, and Kelly all related the planting of Deermeadows Church and commented on the significance of that experience.

[9]Neither of Florida's representatives at the founding meeting had descendants who followed them in WMU leadership. Mrs. Bailey's daughter, Mrs. Willis, was active in WMU only at the local level. Mrs. Telford's remaining son, Robie, lost touch with the family. The circumstances of his later life and death are uncertain.

[10]Tanna Dawson (Mrs. A. D.), taped response to questionnaire, March 1993.

[11]FWMU AR 1974-75, 8-16. All subsequent details of annual session are from same source.

[12]Popham Interview.

[13]Popham Interview.

[14]Popham Interview.

VII

VIII

Chapter IX
Bringing Joy to Your Servants

[1]Vanita M. Baldwin, interview with author, August 1994; also Baldwin, response to questionnaire, Jacksonville, June 1993. Other biographical and professional data concerning Baldwin are from same sources unless otherwise noted.

[2]See Chapters 3 and 4.

[3]Baldwin's seminary classmate Ada Mae Smith shared this story at the Florida WMU Annual Session, Jacksonville, 9 April 1991.

[4]Christine Gregory (Mrs. A. Harrison), Florida WMU Annual Session, Jacksonville, 9 April 1991; also, Gregory, taped interview with Toni Clevenger (TC) and author, November 1993.

[5]Carolyn Weatherford Crumpler (Mrs. Joe), taped interview with author, Jacksonville, Florida, February 1993. To avoid confusion, Crumpler is referred to in this chapter as "Carolyn Weatherford" prior to the time of her marriage in 1989.

[6]Tanna Dawson (Mrs. A. D.), taped response to questionnaire, Fort Lauderdale, Florida, March 1993.

[7]Baldwin Interview.

[8]Baldwin Questionnaire; Dawson Questionnaire.

[9]Baldwin Questionnaire; Dawson Questionnaire.

[10]Catherine B. Allen, *A Century to Celebrate: History of Woman's Missionary Union* (Birmingham: Woman's Missionary Union, 1987), 100.

[11]Crumpler Interview.

[12]*Florida Baptist Witness*, 28 July 1977.

[13]Crumpler Interview.

[14]Edward Earl Joiner, *A History of Florida Baptists* (Jacksonville: Florida Baptist Convention, 1972), 191-93.

[15]Joiner, 224-25.

[16]*Witness*, 8 March 1956.

[17]Lelia Boring Lassiter, *On This Foundation: History of the Woman's Missionary Union, Auxiliary to the Floriday Baptist Convention* (Jacksonville: Convention Press, 1961), 111.

[18]Joiner, 225.

[19]*Witness*, 29 September 1977.

[20]Florida WMU Annual Report (FWMU AR) 1976-77, 25-26.

[21]FWMU AR 1976-77, 32.

[22]Jackie Draughon (Mrs. Walter, Jr.), taped interview with author, Graceville, Florida, December 1992.

[23]*Witness*, 29 September 1977.

[24]*Witness*, 20 June 1977.

[25]Elizabeth Painter, taped response to questionnaire, Jacksonville, Florida, July 1993.

[26]Frances Shaw, taped response to questionnaire, Jacksonville, Florida, March 1994. Further biographical and professional details are from same source unless otherwise indicated.

[27]Shaw Questionnaire.

[28]Harold Bennett, taped interview with TC, Orlando, Florida, June 1994; FBC Annual 1979, 157.

[29]Florida Baptist Convention Annual (FBC Annual) 1979, 157-58.

[30]*Witness*, 20 September 1979.

[31]Dan C. Stringer, interview with TC, June 1994.

[32]Florida WMU Executive Committee Minutes (EC Minutes), November 1978.

[33]EC Minutes, November 1978.

[34]Florida WMU Council Minutes (Council Minutes), April 1979.

[35]Dawson Questionnaire.

[36]Oma Dell Ely (Mrs. W. Mount), taped interview with author, DeLand, Florida, May 1994. Further biographical details are from the same source.

[37]Ely Interview.

[38]Ely Interview.

[39]Juanita Epperson, *On This Foundation, Part II: History of Florida Woman's Missionary Union 1960-1987* (Jacksonville: Florida Baptist Convention, 1987), 17.

[40]Painter Questionnaire.

[41]FWMU AR 1980-81, 21.

[42]Council Minutes, April 1984.

[43]BC Annual 1984, 151-52; FBC Annual 1985, 138-39.

[44]FBC Annual 1981, 134-35; FBC Annual 1983, 145-46.

[45]FBC Annual 1987, 133-34.

[46]Painter Questionnaire.

[47]Baldwin Questionnaire.

[48]Allen, 440; Clysta de Armas (Mrs. Rafael) and Gisela Torres (Mrs. David), interview with author, Jacksonville, Florida, April 1994.

[49]Council Minutes, April 1984.

[50]de Armas/Torres Interview.

[51]FWMU AR 1983-84, 17-18.

[52]EC Minutes, November 1984.

[53]Martha Wennerberg (Mrs. Don), taped interview with author, Pensacola, Florida, July 1994. Further biographical details are from same source.

[54]*Witness*, 9 April 1992.

[55]Cheryl Hebert, interview with author, August

1994. Further biographical details are from same source.

[56]See WMU AR for 1986 through 1992.

[57]EC Minutes, November 1986.

[58]Wennerberg Interview.

[59]Council Minutes, April 1985.

[60]Council Minutes, April 1987.

[61]EC Minutes, November 1985; Council Minutes, April 1985.

[62]WMU AR 1987-88, 10-36. Further details of 1988 Annual Session are from same source.

[63]*Witness,* 26 May 1988.

[64]John Sullivan, resume; *Witness* columns; Remarks, 1993 WMU Annual Session, for example.

[65]Allen, 183.

[66]Lois I. Walker (Mrs. Charles H.), interview with author, August 1994; also Walker, response to questionnaire, February 1993. Further biographical details and comments are from same sources.

[67]Walker Questionnaire.

[68]*Witness,* 11 April 1991.

[69]Wennerberg Interview.

[70]FWMU AR 1990-1991, 13-17. All 1991 Annual Session details are from same source.

[71]*Witness,* 11 April 1991.

[8]Frances Shaw, taped response to questionnaire, March 1994.

[9]Cindy Mallett Goodwin (Mrs. Howard), interview with author, August 1994. Further biographical details are from same source.

[10]Curnutt Interview; Clysta de Armas (Mrs. Rafael) and Gisela Torres (Mrs. David), taped interview with author, April 1994.

[11]Curnutt Interview; de Armas/Torres Interview.

[12]Sharon Thompson, taped response to questionnaire, Montgomery, Alabama, November 1992.

[13]Sharon Thompson, interview with author, August 1994.

[14]Curnutt Interview; Thompson Interview.

[15]Curnutt Interview.

[16]Curnutt Interview.

[17]Centennial Committee minutes, 1992-93.

[18]Florida Woman's Missionary Union Annual Report (FWMU AR) 1992-93, 10-24. Other details of the 1993 Annual Session are from same source.

[19] Details of 1994 Annual Session are from author's personal observation.

Chapter X
So Much to Celebrate,
So Much to Do

[1]Barbara Curnutt, taped interview with Toni Clevenger (TC) and author, August 1994. Further biographical details are from same source.

[2]Jeremiah 31:3.

[3]Curnutt Interview.

[4]Barbara Curnutt, "Cross Over People," speech manuscript, April 1992. See also *Witness,* 16 April 1992.

[5]*Florida Baptist Witness,* 27 August, 3 September, and 10 September 1992; *Florida Baptist Leadership News,* November 1992.

[6]Complete story of response to Hurricane Andrew is from Curnutt Interview. Roles of WMU staff, along with other convention personnel, were described in letter form from Cecil W. Seagle, Convention Coordinator of relief efforts, to author, 27 July 1994.

[7]Russell Drinnen, interview with author, Jacksonville, Florida, February 1993; Curnutt Interview.

IX

X

MEETING LOCATIONS
1882-1994

"The Ladies' Meeting of the Baptist Convention of the State of Florida"

1882 - Lake City
1883 - Lake City
1884 - Orlando
1885 - Jacksonville
1886 - Gainesville
1887 - DeLand

1888 - no meeting
1889 - Ocala
1890 - Monticello
1891 - Pensacola
1892 - Kissimmee
1893 - Lake City

Annual Meetings of Florida Woman's Missionary Union held in connection with the annual meeting of the Florida Baptist Convention

1894 - Plant City
1895 - Leesburg
1896 - Pensacola
1897 - St. Augustine
1898 - Tampa (January)
1898 - Madison (December)
1899 - DeLand
1900 - Arcadia
1901 - Marianna
1902 - no meeting
1903 - Lake City
1904 - Kissimmee
1905 - Jacksonville
1906 - Bartow
1907 - Live Oak
1908 - Plant City
1909 - DeFuniak Springs
1910 - Gainesville
1911 - DeLand
1912 - Ocala (January)
1912 - Lakeland (December)
1913 - Arcadia
1914 - Pensacola
1915 - no meeting
1916 - Live Oak

1917 - Orlando
1918 - Tallahassee
1919 - Tampa
1920 - Jacksonville (January)
1920 - Kissimmee (December)
1921 - Miami
1922 - Gainesville
1923 - DeLand
1924 - Lakeland
1925 - Tampa
1926 - Lake City
1927 - Bradenton
1928 - Miami
1929 - Jacksonville
1930 - Tampa
1931 - Orlando
1932 - Daytona Beach
1933 - Pensacola
1934 - no meeting
1935 - DeLand
1936 - Arcadia
1937 - Ocala
1938 - Jacksonville
1939 - West Palm Beach
1940 - Lakeland

1941 - Gainesville   1946 - Jacksonville (January)
1942 - Panama City   1943 - Jacksonville
1945 - Jacksonville   1944 - Bradenton

**Annual Sessions of Florida Woman's Missionary Union
held separately from the annual meeting
of the Florida Baptist Convention**

1947 - Tampa   1971 - Lakeland
1948 - Ocala   1972 - Daytona Beach
1949 - Daytona Beach   1973 - Fort Lauderdale
1950 - Winter Haven   1974 - St. Petersburg
1951 - Panama City   1975 - Orlando
1952 - Orlando   1976 - Jacksonville
1953 - Jacksonville   1977 - Titusville
1954 - Daytona Beach   1978 - Pensacola
1955 - Lakeland   1979 - Leesburg
1956 - St. Petersburg   1980 - Hollywood
1957 - Gainesville   1981 - Gainesville
1958 - Tallahassee   1982 - Tampa
1959 - Tampa   1983 - Tallahassee
1960 - Daytona Beach   1984 - West Palm Beach
1961 - Miami   1985 - Cocoa
1962 - Orlando   1986 - Orlando
1963 - Panama City   1987 - Daytona Beach
1964 - St. Petersburg   1988 - Lakeland
1965 - Jacksonville   1989 - Panama City
1966 - Leesburg   1990 - Merritt Island
1967 - Orlando   1991 - Jacksonville
1968 - Gainesville   1992 - Orlando
1969 - Tallahassee   1993 - Tallahassee
1970 - West Palm Beach   1994 - Jacksonville

CHRONOLOGY

1845 - Southern Baptist Convention (SBC) was organized.

1848 - Records show that by this date, the Female Missionary Society was meeting in Bethlehem (later Campbellton) Church, Jackson County. This was probably the first such society in the state.

1854 - Florida Baptist Convention (FBC) was organized.

1871 - Woman's Mission to Woman was organized in Baltimore, Maryland.

1873 - Lottie Moon was appointed as missionary to China by SBC Foreign Mission Board (FMB).

1875 - South Carolina organized a Central Committee to direct woman's mission work in the state.

1880 - Florida Baptist Convention delegates organized the State Board of Missions (SBM) and elected W. N. Chaudoin corresponding secretary.

1881 - The SBM appointed Rev. N. A. Bailey one of two state missionaries.
- Mrs. N. A. Bailey organized the Ladies' Mission Society of the Micanopy Baptist Church, the oldest society still in existence in 1994.
- Florida Baptist Convention approved women as delegates to annual meeting with the same privileges as men.
- Dr. Chaudoin appointed Mrs. N. A. Bailey "Sister secretary" for Woman's Mission Work, the first FBC department.

1884 - Mrs. Bailey attended the first organized meeting of women held during an annual SBC meeting.
- *Florida Baptist Witness* was established.

1885 - Minutes of the Ladies Mission Meeting were included in the FBC annual report.

1887 - Mrs. L. B. Telford was elected corresponding secretary for Woman's Mission Work in Florida.

1888 - Florida was one of ten founding states when women meeting in Richmond, Virginia, organized Executive Committee of the Woman's Mission Societies, Auxiliary to SBC.
- The new national organization promoted the first Christmas Offering for Foreign Missions.

1890 - Women changed the name of the national organization to Woman's Missionary Union, Auxiliary to Southern Baptist Convention (WMU, SBC).

1894 - Women delegates organized Woman's Baptist Missionary Union of Florida and elected a Central Committee to direct the work of the Florida Union. They elected Jennie Lucena Spalding corresponding secretary and treasurer.

1895 - WMU, SBC, instituted the first Week of Prayer and Self-Denial Offering for Home Missions.

1899 - WMU, SBC, recommended graded system of missionary education for all age levels.

1901 - Rev. L. D. Geiger was elected corresponding secretary of Florida State Board of Missions.

1906 - Florida WMU auxiliary status was clarified.
- *Our Mission Fields* became first WMU, SBC, periodical.

1907 - Florida Baptists established Columbia College in Lake City as state Baptist school.
- WMU Training School opened in Louisville, Kentucky. WMU, SBC, organized Young Women's Auxiliary (YWA).

1908 - At the request of the State Board of Missions, Florida WMU promoted first State Missions Week of Prayer and State Mission Offering. WMU, SBC, organized Royal Ambassadors (RA).

1909 - Dr. S. B. Rogers was elected third corresponding secretary of the State Board of Missions.
- Two Jacksonville churches began the first RA chapters in Florida.

1910 - Florida WMU adopted the Standard of Excellence for local organizations.
- Florida WMU appointed first field secretary.

1911 - Women delegates elected Mrs. H. C. Peelman corresponding secretary of Florida WMU.
- Foreign Mission Board appointed Mrs. A. J. Terry (Lulu Sparkman) to Brazil. She was Florida's first woman foreign missionary.

1912 - Statewide summer assemblies began at Columbia College.

1913 - Mrs. Peelman assisted in organizing WMU in Cuba. Columbia College students began first college YWA in Florida.
- WMU pin, permanent hymn, and watchword were adopted in recognition of WMU, SBC, 25th anniversary.

1914 - Florida WMU published *A History of Florida Baptist Woman's Missionary Union* by Louise Porter Hood.
- State Convention offices were established in Jacksonville.
- WMU, SBC, changed the name of *Our Mission Fields* to *Royal Service*.
- First Girls' Auxiliary chapter in Florida was organized.

1917 - WMU, SBC, recommended the Circle plan for all societies and published a manual of WMU methods.

1918 - Prayer Calendar was printed in *Royal Service*.
- Christmas offering was renamed the Lottie Moon Christmas Offering for Foreign Missions.

1919 - SBC launched the $75 Million Campaign.
- Florida WMU cooperated with the Home Mission Board (HMB) in establishing the Seaman's Institute in Jacksonville

1920 - White Cross work was begun.

1925 - SBC launched the Cooperative Program.

1926 - Dr. C. M. Brittain was elected executive secretary and treasurer of the State Board of Missions.

1928 - Ruby (40th) anniversary of WMU, SBC, was celebrated.

1933 - SBC launched the Hundred Thousand Club.

1934 - "Thank Offering" was renamed the Annie Armstrong Offering for Home Missions.
- Children's Home Auxiliary was formed.
- Florida WMU observed 40th anniversary.

1935 - Focus weeks for auxiliaries began.
- Graded mission study books were published by the FMB and HMB.

1936 - Florida WMU elected Louise Smith as executive secretary.

1938 - WMU, SBC, celebrated Golden Jubilee anniversary.
- Florida WMU sponsored a state YWA house party and RA camps.

1940 - Florida WMU pledged $35 thousand toward helping erase a denominational debt of $3 million.

1941 - State Board of Missions elected Dr. C. H. Bolton executive secretary and treasurer.

1942 - Florida WMU conducted a state GA house party and a RA conclave.

1943 - Florida WMU raised money to build a church in Mendoza, Argentina, as a memorial to Rev. Frank J. Fowler.

1944 - Florida WMU observed Golden anniversary.
- Florida WMU raised money to build a Boys Baptist High School in Nigeria.
- Josephine Jones was elected executive secretary of Florida WMU.
- State RA worker was employed.
- State Board of Missions elected Dr. John Maguire executive secretary-treasurer.

1945 - Southern Baptist Convention observed centennial anniversary.

1946 - Florida WMU voted to hold the Annual Session at a different time from the Florida Baptist Convention annual meeting.

- WMU week at Ridgecrest Baptist Assemby was introduced by WMU, SBC.
- Florida WMU heavily promoted war relief efforts.
- Three women were named "at large" members of the Florida State Board of Missions.

1947 - Florida WMU began its summer camping program.

1948 - Business Women's Circles Federation of Florida was organized.

1950 - Camps were held for Seminole Indians and Negro children.

1952 - WMU was organized at Big Cypress Indian Reservation.

1954 - State Board of Missions invited Florida WMU president to attend meetings.
- Florida's first RA Congress was held in Ocala. Group of GAs and RAs made a mission trip to Cuba.

1956 - Aims for Advancement replaced Standard of Excellence.

1957 - WMU, SBC, transferred RA above third grade to the Brotherhood Department.

1958 - International Student Retreat was held at Stetson University.

1959 - State WMU president, Mrs. J. H. Lockhart, was elected second vice-president of the Florida Baptist Convention.

1960 - Florida WMU expanded position of young people's secretary to create three new staff positions.

1961 - Florida WMU published *On This Foundation: History of the Woman's Missionary Union, Auxiliary to the Florida Baptist Convention* by Lelia Boring Lassiter.

1962 - Florida Baptist Convention purchased land at Lake Yale for use as a state camp site.

1963 - Girls' Auxiliary 50th Anniversary convention was held in Memphis, Tennessee.

1964 - Florida WMU carried out "Operation 100%" enlargement campaign.
- Florida WMU provided personal and financial help to Cuban refugees.

1965 - Girls' Auxiliary camp for the first time was held at Lake Yale Baptist Assembly.

1967 - Josephine Jones organized interracial Missions and Fellowship Conference at Lake Yale.
- Florida Baptist Convention dedicated GA camp chapel at Lake Yale as the "Josephine Jones Chapel."
- Carolyn Weatherford was elected Florida WMU executive secretary.
- Florida Baptist Convention elected Dr. Harold Bennett executive secretary-treasurer.
- Rosella Lipscomb (Mrs. Clyde), state WMU president, was elected second vice-president of Florida Baptist Convention.

1968 - WMU, SBC, implemented changes in WMU's organizational structure.
- Florida WMU worked with Stetson University to provide a campus missionary residence, which was named the Lulu Sparkman Terry House.

1969 - Florida WMU moved from an auxiliary to a department of the Florida Baptist Convention.
- New bylaws established the WMU Council.

1970 - WMU age-level organizations experienced major changes in structure, programs, and resources.
- Florida WMU sponsored missions cruise to the Bahamas.
- RAs in grades one through three were transferred to the SBC Brotherhood.

1971 - BYW Happenings, Acteen Cometogethers, and statewide GA events at Annual Sessions replaced house parties.

1972 - Florida WMU implemented WMU, SBC, "Giant Step" enlistment emphasis.
- Annual Session Offering for Florida-born missionaries was used to provide a yearly subscription to each missionary's magazine of choice.
- "Operation ExtraKey" provided vacation housing for missionaries on furlough.
- "Project Know-How" was initiated in support of Children's Home.

1973 - WMU Council added language representative and age-level committees.

- Florida WMU sponsored second missions cruise to Bahamas.

1974 - Carolyn Weatherford resigned to become executive director of WMU, SBC.

- Bernice Popham was elected Florida WMU Director.

1975 - First Missionary Kids committee was appointed.

1977 - Vanita Baldwin was elected Florida WMU Director.

- SBC launched Bold Mission Thrust.

- FBC began a three-year Evangelism Project with Korea.

- First GA Mother/Daughter Overnights were held.

1978 - First WMU Baptist Bible Institute committee was appointed.

- Acteens began a volunteer missions program called Acteens Activators.

- WMU, SBC, and Home Mission Board employed a WMU consultant to work with black Baptists.

1979 - Florida WMU sent a training team to Korea.

- Dr. Dan C. Stringer was elected executive director-treasurer of FBC.

1980 - Florida WMU STARTEAM was appointed and trained.

1981 - First GA Missions Whirls were held.

- Mission Retreats began at Lake Yale and Blue Springs.

1982 - WMU, SBC, held ground breaking for new headquarters building in Birmingham.

1983 - State WMU leadership conferences attracted over 2,000 women.

1985 - Florida WMU voted to finance a Florida Room (Executive Office) in new national headquarters building.

1986 - "Vision 88" enlargement emphasis began.

1988 - Florida WMU published *On This Foundation Part II, History of Florida Woman's Missionary Union 1960-1987,* by Juanita Epperson.

- Florida WMU observed Centennial of WMU, SBC.

1989 - John Sullivan became executive director-treasurer of the Florida Baptist Convention.

1991 - Barbara Curnutt was elected Director of Florida WMU.

1992 - Florida WMU assisted in relief efforts for victims of "Hurricane Andrew."

- Florida WMU Centennial committee commissioned Martha Pope Trotter to write a complete history of Florida Woman's Missionary Union.

1993 - Mission Retreats were renamed Women's Winter Weekends.

- First overnight retreat for Hispanics was held at Lake Yale during Winter Weekend.

- Five Florida WMU members were presented as "Faithful Servants" at WMU Annual Session in Tallahassee.

- Florida WMU initiated a "Just for Ministers' Wives" Conference at the annual FBC meeting.

1994 - First Dad/Daughter Overnights were held at Lake Yale and Blue Springs.

- Two Haitian members of Florida WMU were named to the first national WMU Ethnics Advisory Council.

- Mentoring emphasis was launched at Florida Centennial Celebration.

- Florida WMU observed 100 years as "Laborers Together with God." Centennial theme was "Faithful Servants Fulfilling His Mission."

LEADERSHIP OF FLORIDA WOMAN'S MISSIONARY UNION

OFFICERS AND COMMITTEE CHAIRMEN

Names throughout roster are styled according to Florida WMU Annual Reports.

Presidents:

Mrs. T. D. Crawford	1894-1896
Mrs. J. E. Oates	1896-1897
Miss Caroline Palmer	1897-1904
Mrs. B. M. Bean	1904-1905
Mrs. M. B. Harrison	1905-1906
Mrs. W. C. Powell	1906-1907
Mrs. M. B. Harrison	1907-1911
Mrs. N. C. Wamboldt	1911-1923
President Emerita	1923-1933
Mrs. J. A. Mellon	1923-1925
Mrs. E. C. Bostick	1925-1929
Mrs. G. J. Rousseau	1929-1936
Mrs. Robert R. Walden	1936-1941
Mrs. Robert E. Lee	1941-1943
Mrs. J. L. Rosser	1943-1948
Mrs. Roy L. Lassiter	1948-1954
Mrs. George Q. Holland	1954-1959
Mrs. J. H. Lockhart	1959-1964
Mrs. Clyde B. Lipscomb	1964-1969
Mrs. August A. Lenert	1969-1974
Mrs. A. D. Dawson	1974-1979
Mrs. W. Mount Ely	1979-1984
Mrs. Don L. Wennerberg	1984-1989
Mrs. Charles Walker	1989-1994
Mrs. Bill Coffman	1994-

Mrs. J. A. Mellon	1912-1916
Mrs. S. B. Rogers	1916-1926
Mrs. Brinson McGowan	1926-1927

Beginning in 1927 the state president automatically became the Florida vice-president of WMU, SBC.

Recording Secretaries:

Mrs. E. D. Beggs	1894-1897
Mrs. J. C. Porter	1897-1906
Mrs. H. C. Peelman	1906-1911
Mrs. Porter Van Hood	1911-1913
Mrs. J. A. Lamb	1913-1916
Mrs. W. M. Bashlin	1916-1918
Mrs. A. P. Montague	1918-1920
Mrs. W. M. Bashlin	1920-1925
Mrs. J. A. Prater	1925-1926
Mrs. O. T. Moncrief	1926-1939
Mrs. A. E. Lightfoot	1939-1944
Mrs. B. D. Locke	1944-1945
Mrs. E. J. Driskell	1946-1951
Mrs. R. Kelly White	1951-1952
Mrs. John M. Crabtree	1952-1957
Mrs. Ladislau Biro	1957-1962
Mrs. Clyde B. Lipscomb	1962-1964
Mrs. E. B. Kirkpatrick	1964-1966
Mrs. Orrin W. Stites	1966-1971
Mrs. Tom Perrin	1971-1974
Mrs. Ernest Campbell	1974-1979
Mrs. J. C. Grimm	1979-1984
Mrs. F. H. Mallett	1984-1989
Mrs. W. C. Fortner	1989-

Florida Vice-Presidents of WMU, SBC:

Mrs. W. D. Chipley	1888-1889
Mrs. L. B. Telford	1889-1892
Mrs. W. D. Chipley	1893-1910
Mrs. C. A. Carson	1911-1912

Advisory Board:

Mrs. N. A. Bailey	Mrs. J. C. Newman	Mrs. John McKinney
Mrs. E. W. Agnew	Mrs. Ida I. Bruce	Mrs. T. W. Wilder
Mrs. M. F. Hood	Mrs. J. C. Porter	Mrs. S. A. Standley
Mrs. B. M. Bean	Mrs. W. D. Chipley	Mrs. J. E. Oates
Mrs. M. B. Harrison		

District and Divisional Vice-Presidents:

Mrs. S. R. Skinner	Mrs. H. H. McDonald	Mrs. J. F. Chapman
Mrs. W. A. Burns	Mrs. Mell Leonard	Mrs. Agnes McLeonard
Mrs. E. Porter Van Hood	Mrs. D. W. Burke	Mrs. Walker Blair
Mrs. O. K. Reaves	Mrs. D. U. McGinnis	Mrs. Cora Chapman
Mrs. L. H. Calkins	Mrs. J. Sidney Morris	Mrs. J. Ray Arnold
Mrs. Porter E. Webb	Mrs. W. O. Butler	Mrs. S. J. McMorris

Mrs. O. T. Moncrief
Mrs. W. T. Gary
Mrs. E. C. Bostick
Mrs. Frank Wilson
Mrs. H. C. Garwood
Mrs. A. J. Moncrief
Mrs. F. J. Lavendar
Mrs. N. B. O'Kelley
Mrs. E. A. McDowell
Mrs. Ed Williams
Mrs. W. R. Jones
Mrs. J. Harrison Griffin
Mrs. E. O. Thompson
Mrs. J. G. Asher
Mrs. Jack Stevens
Mrs. W. L. Maige
Mrs. C. A. Moore

Mrs. G. J. Rousseau
Mrs. J. A. Mellon
Mrs. W. H. Bixby
Mrs. W. M. McDonald
Mrs. J. C. McGhee
Mrs. M. A. Love
Mrs. P. C. Berkley
Mrs. Louise Hill
Mrs. A. E. Gammage
Mrs. J. W. Thorne
Mrs. F. G. Almon
Mrs. A. C. Kerby
Mrs. W. P. Head
Mrs. T. H. Edney
Mrs. W. M. Vines
Mrs. L. E. Womack
Mrs. C. C. Cook

Mrs. O. W. Byrd
Mrs. C. H. Bolton
Mrs. G. A. Fellows
Mrs. J. S. Bookhardt
Mrs. U. E. Reid
Mrs. M. H. Massey
Mrs. C. M. Brittain
Mrs. G. H. Morthland
Mrs. A. V. Freeman
Mrs. R. B. Mayfield
Mrs. Ray Walden
Mrs. Amzie Wilson
Mrs. J. E. Robinson
Mrs. Ira D. S. Knight
Mrs. H. H. Link
Mrs. Frank Bamberg
Mrs. W. M. Tillman

District and Divisional Young People's Leaders:

Mrs. Robert Sandford
Mrs. E. A. Milton
Miss Louise Bouie
Mrs. Vivian McGeachy
Miss Rosa Lee Schumann
Mrs. O. T. Moncrief
Miss Helen Chase
Miss Constance Chase
Mrs. James Cook
Miss Nethelma Locke
Mrs. U. E. Reid
Mrs. Ira Larkins
Mrs. S. J. McMorris
Miss Rutella Cook
Mrs. J. H. Matthews
Mrs. W. Q. Bartlett
Mrs. Frank Wilson
Mrs. W. B. Martin
Mrs. W. A. Burns
Mrs. C. V. McMurphy
Mrs. James S. Day, Jr.
Mrs. W. O. Byrd
Mrs. R. V. Carraway

Mrs. L. H. Bingham
Mrs. Martha Starling
Miss Ellen Stakemiller
Miss Eloise Mosely
Mrs. J. N. Daniel
Mrs. W. W. Stallings
Mrs. G. T. McRae
Mrs. C. C. Tooke
Mrs. W. L. Maxwell
Mrs. C. C. Cook
Miss Katherine Vincett
Miss Katherine Rawls
Miss Eva Ford
Mrs. H. C. Meador
Mrs. M. S. Penton
Mrs. A. E. Lightfoot
Mrs. Leo Thompson
Mrs. D. H. Yawn
Miss Myrtle Lee Bell
Mrs. J. E. Turlington
Mrs. R. H. Thompson
Miss Margaret Moore
Mrs. LeRoy Jones

Mrs. J. F. Vagts
Miss Ally Sue Frink
Mrs. H. M. Langston
Mrs. L. B. White
Miss Marguerite Lumpkin
Miss Genevieve Barry
Mrs. Reed Edmunds
Mrs. J. C. Holly
Mrs. J. J. Cater
Miss Vermel King
Mrs. H. C. Bentley
Mrs. H. B. Jamieson
Mrs. A. J. Reenhart
Mrs. W. B. Shores
Mrs. J. L. Meeks
Mrs. T. M. Smiley
Mrs. Fred Smith
Mrs. H. M. Leichty
Mrs. Lewis Haines
Mrs. A. V. Freeman
Mrs. L. B. Register
Mrs. W. H. Wells

Margaret Fund Chairmen:

Mrs. W. D. Chipley	1909-1910
Mrs. H. C. Peelman	1911-1912
Mrs. W. W. Weekley	1912-1914
Mrs. J. M. Vesey	1914-1916
Mrs. J. S. McLemore	1916-1918
Mrs. R. A. Burford	1918-1919
Mrs. W. C. Thacker	1919-1920
Mrs. J. L. White	1920-1930
Mrs. E. R. List	1930-1931
Mrs. C. A. Waller	1931-1940
Mrs. A. S. Corley	1940-1943
Mrs. Robert R. Walden	1943-1948
Mrs. J. W. Norman	1948-1949
Mrs. S. D. Wallace	1949-1952
Mrs. J. Powell Tucker	1952

WMU Training School Chairmen (Trustee):

Mrs. W. D. Chipley	1909-1910
Mrs. B. W. Blount	1911-1941
Mrs. C. R. Pittard	1941-1944
Mrs. A. E. Lightfoot	1944-1949
Mrs. W. B. Thirlwell	1949-1954
Mrs. Charles W. Knight	1954-1957

Social Service Chairman:

Mrs. E. C. Angell	1916-1917

Personal Service Chairmen:

Mrs. E. C. Angell	1917-1929
Mrs. Selwyn Chalker	1929-1932
Mrs. W. F. Brown	1932-1936
Mrs. C. M. White	1936-1940
Mrs. J. R. Black	1940-1942
Mrs. J. L. Booker	1942-1943

Community Missions Chairmen:

Mrs. J. E. Robinson	1943-1947
Mrs. Clifford Walker	1947-1952
Mrs. Waldo Wood	1952-1954
Mrs. J. Titus Aldrige	1954-1959
Mrs. Waldo Wood	1959-1964
Mrs. Phil Maxwell	1964-1968

Chairman Yang Chow Hospital Supplies:

| Miss Eliza Powell | 1920 |

White Cross Chairmen:

Mrs. C. C. Long	1926-1936
Mrs. P. L. Tucker	1936-1941
Mrs. John B. White	1941-1942
Mrs. Roy L. Lassiter	1942-1943
Mrs. J. J. Cater	1943-1944
Mrs. Frank Bamberg	1944-1945

Press Chairmen:

Mrs. Julien S. Rogers	1918-1919
Mrs. A. R. Montague	1919-1920
Mrs. W. M. Bashlin	1920-1921
Mrs. H. M. Wilson	1921-1923

Publicity Chairmen:

Mrs. H. M. Wilson	1923-1924
Mrs. Waldo Willis	1924-1927
Mrs. J. W. Mitchell	1927-1928
Mrs. E. A. McDowell	1928-1932
Mrs. E. D. Solomon	1932-1933
Mrs. Grace Pillsbury	1933-1936
Mrs. E. J. Driskell	1936-1941
Mrs. F. L. Dykes	1941-1945
Mrs. John E. Busey	1945-1946

Assistant Publicity Chairman:

| Mrs. C. Slade | 1929-1940 |

Circle Plan Leader:

| Mrs. M. M. Taylor | 1927 |

College Correspondents:

Miss Maud Montague	1912-1913
Miss Sue Simpson	1913-1916
Mrs. H. W. Markham	1916-1920
Mrs. R. A. Rasco	1920-1921
Miss Virginia Bow	1921-1925
Miss Margaret Stern	1925-1926
Mrs. W. L. Harrell	1926-1928

Superintendents of Young Women's Auxiliary:

Mrs. Lee MacDonell	1911-1912
Mrs. H. W. Markham	1912-1916
Mrs. P. P. Arnold	1916-1918

Superintendents of YWA and Girls' Auxiliary:

Mrs. P. P. Arnold	1918-1919
Mrs. J. G. Edwards	1919-1920
Miss Cecelia Nolan	1920-1921

Superintendents of Royal Ambassadors and Sunbeam Bands:

Mrs. S. B. Rogers	1911-1912
Mrs. W. M. McDonald	1912-1913
Mrs. P. P. Arnold	1913-1916
Mrs. C. W. Perkins	1916-1918
Mrs. O. E. TeBow	1918-1919
Miss Jennie Camp	1919-1921

Stewardship Chairmen:

Mrs. Ralph Ferrel	1925-1926
Mrs. J. Sidney Morris	1926-1927
Mrs. Stewart Long	1927-1931
Mrs. Allen S. Cutts	1931-1940
Mrs. J. L. Rosser	1940-1943
Mrs. Roy L. Lassiter	1943-1948
Mrs. R. Kelly White	1948-1951
Mrs. Waldo Wood	1951-1952
Mrs. S. D. Wallace	1952-1957
Mrs. W. B. Thirlwell	1957-1960
Mrs. James L. Monroe	1960-1965
Mrs. John Maguire	1965-1968

Mission Study Chairmen:

Mrs. R. L. Bonsteel	1917-1918
Mrs. C. M. Brittain	1925-1927
Mrs. F. L. Porter	1927-1929
Mrs. W. M. Vines	1929-1931
Mrs. Alfredo Diaz	1931-1939
Mrs. C. R. Pittard	1939-1941
Mrs. E. J. Driskell	1941-1943
Mrs. George Q. Holland	1943-1946
Mrs. Earl B. Edington	1946-1950
Mrs. John Maguire	1950-1955
Mrs. Ralph Gwin	1955-1960
Mrs. John Mein	1960-1961
Mrs. James Thomspon	1961-1966
Mrs. A. D. Dawson	1966-1968

Historians:

Mrs. Porter Van Hood	1914-1921
Mrs. B. M. Bean	1921-1923
Mrs. H. C. Garwood	1923-1928
Mrs. B. A. Inglis	1929-1943
Mrs. E. J. Driskell	1943-1944
Mrs. George Q. Holland	1946-1948
Mrs. Robert R. Walden	1948-1953
Mrs. W. H. Moncrief	1953-

Jubilee Director:

Mrs. John Maguire	1961-1964

WMU, SBC, Centennial Chairman

Mrs. W. Mount Ely	1986-1988

Second Century Fund Coordinator and
Florida Centennial Committee Chairman:

Mrs. Don Wennerberg	1989-

President, Children's Home Auxiliary:

Mrs. J. A. Lamb	1934-1943
Mrs. T. M. Johns	1943-1944

Children's Home Chairmen:

Mrs. Ira D. S. Knight	1944-1946
Mrs. Robert E. Lee	1946-1948
Mrs. Roy Amidon	1948-1953
Mrs. M. D. Oates	1953-1955

Prayer Chairmen:

Mrs. Earl B. Edington	1955-1960
Mrs. S. D. Wallace	1960-1965
Mrs. Ralph Gwinn	1965-1968

Area Representatives:

AREA 1:

Mrs. James Monroe	1969-1973
Miss Carolyn Brooks	1973-1976
Mrs. August A. Lenert	1976-1979
Mrs. Hollis E. Smith	1979-1980
Mrs. Robert Jernigan	1980-1983
Mrs. Clark Doll	1983-1986
Mrs. Carldean Watson	1986-1989
Mrs. Cleota Lenert	1989-1992
Mrs. Jewel Johns	1992-

AREA 2:

Mrs. Walter Draughon, Jr.	1969-1971
Mrs. Stanley Worsham	1971-1974
Mrs. D. L. Wennerberg	1974-1977
Mrs. Addison Pressley	1977-1980
Mrs. D. L. Wennerberg	1980-1983
Mrs. J. W. Owens	1983-1986
Mrs. George Edens	1986-1987
Mrs. Shirley Ulmer	1987-1990
Mrs. LaVerral Fox	1990-1993
Mrs. Bobby Surber	1993-

AREA 3:

Mrs. R. A. McInnis	1969-1971
Mrs. Walter Draughon	1971-1973
Mrs. Teman Gandy	1973-1976
Mrs. E. L. Scruggs	1976-1979
Mrs. Roger C. Smith	1979-1982
Mrs. Walter Draughon, Jr.	1982-1985
Mrs. Roger C. Smith	1985-1987

Mrs. Mary Knight	1987-1990
Mrs. Mary Dawkins	1990-1993
Mrs. Jackie Draughon	1993-

AREA 4:

Mrs. W. E. Boyd	1969-1970
Mrs. Paul Melin	1970-1971
Mrs. T. J. Fletcher	1971-1974
Mrs. Charlie Webb	1974-1977
Mrs. Max Hart	1977-1980
Mrs. Louie Grubbs	1980-1983
Mrs. Robert Palmer	1983-1986
Mrs. T. J. Fletcher	1986-1989
Mrs. Marintha Howard	1989-1992
Mrs. Eleanor Grubbs	1992-

AREA 5:

Mrs. Clyde Lipscomb	1970-1973
Mrs. Robert Staver	1973-1974
Mrs. W. G. Stroup	1974-1978
Mrs. James Thompson	1978-1981
Mrs. F. H. Mallett	1981-1984
Mrs. Mary DeLoach	1984-1987
Mrs. Judy Koivisto	1987-1990
Mrs. Ann Coffman	1990-1993
Mrs. Madelyne Temoshchuk	1993-

AREA 6:

Mrs. James L. McKinney	1969-1970
Mrs. Stephen Zakor	1970-1971
Mrs. Paul Melin	1971-1974
Mrs. H. G. Thorpe	1974-1977
Mrs. Clyde Harless	1977-1978
Mrs. P. G. Stafford	1978-1980
Mrs. Charles Van Alstine	1980-1982
Mrs. Ernest R. Campbell	1982-1983
Mrs. Kenneth Langdon	1983-1986
Mrs. Anne Tomyn	1986-1989
Mrs. Sue Holladay	1989-1992
Mrs. Carol Vandeventer	1992-

AREA 7:

Mrs. John B. White	1969-1971
Mrs. M. K. Langston	1971-1973
Mrs. Paul Melin	1973-1974
Mrs. Richard Brown	1974-1977
Mrs. Connie Hargroves	1977-1980
Mrs. Thomas Broomall	1980-1983
Mrs. Nolan Kennedy	1983-1984
Mrs. Mildred Langston	1984-1987
Mrs. Cleon Spence	1987-1990
Mrs. Ruby Smith	1990-1991
Mrs. Cleon Spence	1991-1994
Mrs. Carolyn Sellers	1994-

AREA 8:

Mrs. J. H. Jacobs	1969-1971
Mrs. Raymond Brothers	1971-1974

Mrs. Ivan Farrens	1974-1977
Mrs. Norman Bennett	1977-1980
Mrs. G. M. Keene	1980-1983
Mrs. W. O. Lott	1983-1986
Mrs. Dottson Mills, Sr.	1986-1989
Mrs. Oma Dell Ely	1989-1992
Mrs. Doris Haynes	1992-

AREA 9:

Mrs. A. D. Dawson	1969-1971
Mrs. James McKinney	1971-1974
Mrs. O. L. Haynes	1974-1977
Mrs. James McKinney	1977-1980
Mrs. Harold Epperson	1980-1983
Mrs. James Smith	1983-1986
Mrs. Adelene Clemons	1986-1988
Mrs. Juanita Epperson	1988-1990
Mrs. Delta Jordan	1990-1993
Mrs. Jane McKinney	1993-

AREA 10:

Mrs. J. B. White	1971-1973
Mrs. Randy Madanian	1973-1974
Mrs. Joseph Folds	1974-1975
Mrs. James Sledge	1975-1977
Mrs. William Robinson	1977-1979
Mrs. Maynard Roberts	1979-1982
Mrs. Betty Lambert	1982-1985
Mrs. T. Irven Lawhorn	1985-1988
Mrs. Lady Ham	1988-1991
Mrs. Jewel Faye Roberts	1991-1994
Mrs. Margaret Watson	1994-

AREA 11:

Mrs. J. H. Jacobs	1971-1973
Miss Valda Long	1973-1976
Mrs. Mabel Bigelow	1976-1979
Mrs. James Slater	1979-1982
Mrs. Statia McAlister	1982-1985
Mrs. Mel Hutson	1985-1988
Mrs. Gloria Dupree	1988-1991
Mrs. Betty Gibbs	1991-1994
Mrs. Helen Yates	1994-

AREA 12:

Mrs. A. D. Dawson	1971-1973
Mrs. F. H. Mallett	1973-1976
Mrs. W. L. Hoss	1976-1979
Mrs. Willard Green	1979-1980
Mrs. Genus Crenshaw	1980-1982
Mrs. W. L. Hoss	1982-1985
Mrs. A. D. Dawson	1985-1988
Mrs. Charles Walker	1988-1989
Mrs. John Crabtree	1989-1991
Mrs. Lynn Sloan	1991-1992
Mrs. Lucille Elliott	1992-

Language Representatives:

Mrs. David Torres	1973-1976
Mrs. Aguedo Sanchez	1976-1977
Mrs. Rafael de Armas	1977-1980
Mrs. Pedro Pared	1980-1981
Mrs. Jorge Comesanas	1981-1983
Mrs. David Torres	1983-1984
Mrs. Rafael de Armas	1984-1988
Mrs. Becky Arango	1988-1989
Mrs. Nancy Acosta	1989-1992
Mrs. Clysta de Armas	1992-1994
Mrs. Mirian Lopez	1994-

Age Level Committee Chairmen:
Baptist Women:

Mrs. A. D. Dawson	1972-1974
Mrs. Harold Epperson	1974-1976
Mrs. James Thompson	1976-1977
Mrs. Stanley Worsham	1977-1978
Mrs. Harold Epperson	1978-1979
Mrs. Conrad Willard	1979-1980
Mrs. Clinton Pons	1980-1981
Mrs. Jackie Stephens	1981-1982
Mrs. Nolan Kennedy	1982-1983
Mrs. James H. Ham, Jr.	1983-1984
Mrs. Timothy Linn	1984-1985
Mrs. Doris Cummins	1985-1986
Mrs. Shirley Ulmer	1986-1987
Mrs. Ginger Fortner	1987-1988
Mrs. Sue Holladay	1988-1989
Mrs. Carldean Watson	1989-1990
Mrs. Michele Pelham	1990-1991
Mrs. Betsy Brown	1991-1992
Mrs. Helen Yates	1992-1993

Baptist Women Leadership Team Leader:

Mrs. Sarah Fitzgerald	1993-1994
Miss Anna Guy	1994-

Baptist Young Women:

Mrs. Tom Roote	1972-1974
Mrs. Jimmy Jackson	1974-1976
Mrs. Charles Hendricks	1976-1977
Mrs. Gary Dobbs	1977-1978
Mrs. Charles Hendricks	1978-1979
Mrs. Steven Hegenbart	1979-1980
Mrs. Silas Bryant	1980-1981
Mrs. Larry Grantham	1981-1982
Mrs. Russell Clemons	1982-1983
Mrs. Robert Richardson	1983-1984
Mrs. Marilou Grimes	1984-1985
Mrs. Marcia McKinney	1985-1986
Mrs. Helen Yates	1986-1987
Mrs. Deena Pate	1987-1988
Mrs. Marcia McKinney	1988-1989
Mrs. Delta Jordan	1989-1990
Mrs. LuAnn Listebarger	1990-1992
Mrs. Sue Reed	1992-1993

Baptist Young Women Leadership Team Leader:
Mrs. Nancy Grigsby	1993-1994
Mrs. LuAnn Listebarger	1994-

Acteens:
Mrs. Mel Hutson	1972-1974
Mrs. Celia Perry	1974-1975
Mrs. David Rocker	1975-1976
Mrs. H. E. Smith	1976-1977
Mrs. William Wall	1977-1978
Mrs. Mel Hutson	1978-1979
Mrs. Richard Mullins	1979-1980
Mrs. Alvin Ford	1980-1981
Mrs. David Rocker	1981-1982
Mrs. Bonnie Young	1982-1983
Mrs. James Godwin	1983-1984
Mrs. Mel Hutson	1984-1985
Mrs. Pat Ford	1985-1986
Mrs. Susan Courtney	1986-1987
Mrs. LuAnn Listebarger	1987-1988
Mrs. Patti Kaswinkel	1988-1989
Mrs. Lynn Gager	1989-1990
Mrs. Linda Ballard	1990-1991
Mrs. Betty Lee	1991-1993

Acteens Leadership Team Leader:
Mrs. Sonja Roberson	1993-1994
Mrs. Linda Ballard	1994-

Girls in Action:
Mrs. Nan Green	1972-1973
Mrs. Harrison Edinger	1973-1974
Mrs. W. L. Pope	1974-1975
Mrs. Owen Hunt	1975-1977
Mrs. Billy Brown	1977-1978
Mrs. James Newman	1978-1979
Mrs. Don Joneycutt	1979-1980
Mrs. Carol Richelieu	1980-1981
Mrs. Bobby Ludlum	1981-1982
Mrs. Ron Mensinger	1982-1983
Mrs. Don Morgan	1983-1984
Mrs. Gerald Edwards	1984-1985
Mrs. Carol Ann Wilkinson	1985-1986
Mrs. Vonnie Shaklee	1986-1987
Mrs. Marsha Beasley	1987-1988
Mrs. Vonnie Shaklee	1988-1989
Mrs. Ruth Gray	1989-1990
Mrs. Mary Elizabeth Semple	1990-1991
Mrs. Pat Honeycutt	1991-1992
Mrs. Ruth Gray	1992-1993

Girls in Action Leadership Team Leader:
Mrs. Melissa Sipek	1993-1994
Mrs. Linda Belz	1994-

Mission Friends:
Mrs. Henry Clay Hooter	1972-1973
Miss Dale Mooneyham	1973-1974
Mrs. Ina Crawford	1974-1975
Mrs. Edwin C. French, Jr.	1975-1976
Mrs. Anthony Kay	1976-1977
Mrs. Genus Crenshaw	1977-1978
Mrs. J. Oscar Lumpkin	1978-1980
Mrs. James Smith	1980-1981
Mrs. George Kasyan	1981-1983
Mrs. Elbert H. Walker	1983-1984
Miss Cindy Lumpkin	1984-1985
Mrs. Natalie Lightsey	1985-1986
Mrs. Nancy Lee	1986-1987
Mrs. LaVerral Fox	1987-1988
Mrs. Roblyn Wood	1988-1989
Mrs. Linda Kasyan	1989-1990
Mrs. Roblyn Wood	1990-1991
Mrs. Joyce Fortner	1991-1992
Mrs. Nancy Lee	1992-1993

Mission Friends Leadership Team Leader:
Mrs. Joyce McCartney	1993-1994
Mrs. Christine McCauley	1994-

WMU Leadership Team Leader:
Mrs. Ginger Fortner	1993-1994
Mrs. Melanie Clubb	1994-

Committee Chairmen:
Scholarship:
Mrs. John Maguire	1961-1968
Mrs. S. O. Bean	1968-1969
Mrs. Don L. Wennerberg	1970-1971
Mrs. Walter Draughon, Jr.	1971-1972
Mrs. T. J. Fletcher	1972-1974
Mrs. Teman Gandy	1974-1976
Mrs. August A. Lenert, Jr.	1976-1978
Mrs. Mabel Bigelow	1978-1979
Mrs. Max Hunt	1979-1980
Mrs. James Slater	1980-1981
Mrs. Louie Grubbs	1981-1982
Mrs. Robert Jernigan	1982-1983
Mrs. Statia McAlister	1983-1984
Mrs. W. O. Lott	1984-1985
Mrs. Mildred Langston	1985-1986
Mrs. Adelene Clemons	1986-1987
Mrs. Helen Lawhorn	1987-1988
Mrs. Shirley Ulmer	1988-1989
Mrs. Mary Knight	1989-1990
Mrs. Frances Crabtree	1990-1991
Mrs. Cleota Lenert	1991-1992
Mrs. LaVerral Fox	1992-1993
Mrs. Jewel Faye Roberts	1993-1994
Mrs. Helen Yates	1994-

Children's Homes (1971-1988)
Florida Baptist Family Ministries (1988-):
Mrs. J. B. White	1971-1973
Mrs. James McKinney	1973-1974
Mrs. Joseph Folds	1974-1975
Mrs. F. H. Mallett	1975-1976
Mrs. W. O. Hoss	1976-1979

Mrs. Roger Smith	1979-1980	**Baptist Bible Institute (1978-1989)**	
Mrs. Maynard Roberts	1980-1981	**Florida Baptist Theological College (1989-):**	
Mrs. James Slater	1981-1982	Mrs. E. L. Scruggs	1978-1979
Mrs. W. L. Hoss	1982-1984	Mrs. Addison Prescott	1979-1980
Mrs. Betty Lambert	1984-1985	Mrs. Roger Smith	1980-1981
Mrs. James Smith	1985-1986	Mrs. D. L. Wennerberg	1981-1982
Mrs. T. Irven Lawhorn	1986-1987	Mrs. Walter D. Draughon	1982-1985
Mrs. Tanna Dawson	1987-1988	Mrs. Clark Doll	1985-1986
Mrs. Anne Tomyn	1988-1989	Mrs. Carldean Watson	1986-1987
Mrs. Lady Ham	1989-1990	Mrs. Mary Knight	1987-1988
Mrs. Gloria Dupree	1990-1991	Mrs. Carldean Watson	1988-1989
Mrs. Mary Dawkins	1991-1992	Mrs. Shirley Ulmer	1989-1990
Mrs. Jewel Faye Roberts	1992-1993	Mrs. Oma Dell Ely	1990-1991
Mrs. Eleanor Grubbs [North Area]	1993-1994	Mrs. LaVerral Fox	1991-1992
Mrs. Doris Haynes [Central Area]	1993-1994	Mrs. Mary Dawkins	1992-1993
Mrs. Jane McKinney [South Area]	1993-1994	Mrs. Jewell Johns	1993-1994
Mrs. Margaret Watson	1994-		

Terry House:

Mrs. Raymond Brothers	1971-1974
Mrs. Ivan Farrens	1974-1977
Mrs. James McKinney	1977-1980
Mrs. G. M. Keene	1980-1981
Mrs. Charles Van Alstine	1981-1982
Mrs. F. H. Mallett	1982-1984
Mrs. James Smith	1984-1985
Mrs. Gertrude Langsdon	1985-1986
Mrs. Mary DeLoach	1986-1987
Mrs. Betty Mills	1987-1988
Mrs. Dot Spence	1988-1989
Mrs. Judy Koivisto	1989-1990
Mrs. Sue Holladay	1990-1991
Mrs. Oma Dell Ely	1991-1992
Mrs. Dot Spence	1992-1993
Mrs. Carol Vandeventer	1993-1994
Mrs. Carol Vandeventer	1994-

Missionary Kids:

Mrs. James Monroe (Study)	1971-1972
Miss Valda Long	1973-1975
Mrs. James Sledge	1975-1976
Mrs. O. L. Haynes	1976-1977
Mrs. Clyde Harless	1977-1978
Mrs. C. Norman Bennett	1978-1980
Mrs. James Thompson	1980-1981
Mrs. Genus Crenshaw	1981-1982
Mrs. Tom Broomall	1982-1983
Mrs. Betty Lambert	1983-1984
Mrs. Mary DeLoach	1984-1985
Mrs. J. W. Owens	1985-1986
Mrs. A. D. Dawson	1986-1987
Mrs. Judy Koivisto	1887-1988
Mrs. Mary Knight	1988-1989
Mrs. Dot Spence	1989-1990
Mrs. Lady Ham	1990-1991
Mrs. Sue Holladay	1991-1992
Mrs. Betty Gibbs	1992-1993
Mrs. Lucille Elliott	1993-1994
Mrs. Madelyne Temoshchuk	1994-

PROFESSIONAL STAFF

Corresponding Secretaries/Executive Secretaries/Directors:

Mrs. N. A. Bailey	1881-1886
Mrs. L. B. Telford	1887-1893
Miss J. L. Spalding	1894-1911
Mrs. H. C. Peelman	1911-1936
Miss Louise Smith	1936-1943
Miss Josephine Jones	1944-1967
Miss Carolyn Weatherford	1967-1974
Miss Bernice Popham	1974-1976
Miss Vanita Baldwin	1977-1991
Miss Barbara Curnutt	1991-

Assistants to Executive Secretary:

Miss Jo Withauer	1946-1948
Miss Ruby Milner	1948-1968

Field Secretaries:

Mrs. Carrie Hobson Baer	1921-1922
Miss Cecelia Nolan	1922-1923
Mrs. W. L. Harrell	1923-1924
Mrs. Lucile Brown	1926-1928
Miss Louise Fletcher	1928-1929
Miss Theo Thomas	1938-1939
Miss Mary Wilson	1940-1943
Miss Elizabeth Provence	1943-1946

Young People's Secretaries:

Miss Cecelia Nolan	1921-1924
Mrs. W. L. Harrell	1924-1930
Miss Louise Smith	1931-1936
Miss Marguerite Lumpkin	July 15-Sept. 1, 1936
Miss Susan Adams	1936-1940
Miss Elsie Renfroe	1940-1946
Miss Elizabeth Provence	1946-1960
YWA-GA Secretary	1960

Royal Ambassador Directors:

Mr. Cecil Rathel [part-time]	1947-1951
Mr. Armand Ball	1953-1957

Young Woman's Auxiliary Directors:

Miss Reda Copeland	1960-1963
Miss Mary Copes	1963-1969

Baptist Young Women Associates:

Miss Russell Drinnen	1970-1974
Miss Carrol Kelly	1975-1977

Baptist Women/Baptist Young Women Associate:

Miss Frances Shaw	1978-

Girls Auxiliary/Camp Directors:

Miss Carolyn Weatherford	1961-1963
Miss Ruth Bagwell	1964-1970

Acteens Associate/Camp Directors:

Miss Ruth Bagwell	1970-1984
Miss Cheryl Hebert	1985-1992
Miss Sharon Thompson	1993-

Sunbeam Band Directors:

Miss Carolyn Burnett	1961-1964
Miss Elizabeth Painter	1964-1970

Girls in Action/Mission Friends Associates:

Miss Elizabeth Painter	1970-1988
Mrs. Howard Goodwin	1993-

100 Years of Florida Woman's Missionary Union

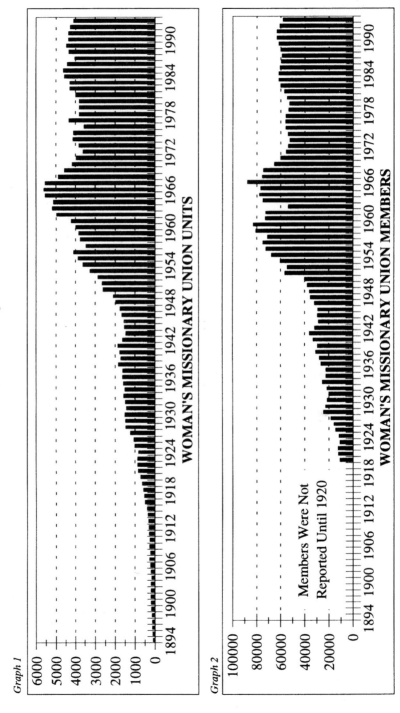

Graph 1

WOMAN'S MISSIONARY UNION UNITS

Graph 2

Members Were Not
Reported Until 1920

WOMAN'S MISSIONARY UNION MEMBERS

Development of Age-level Organizations, Florida WMU

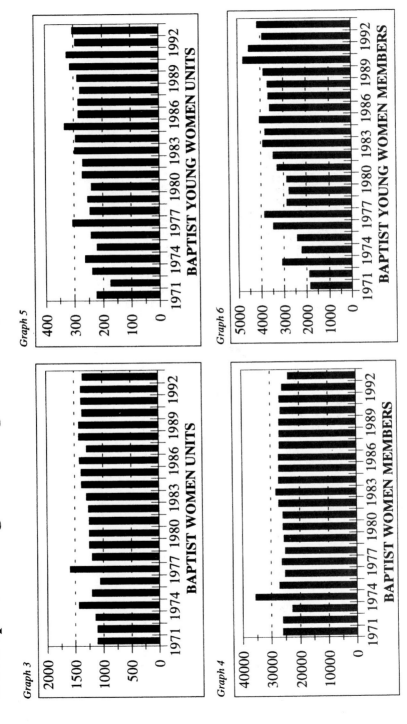

Graph 3

Graph 4

Graph 5

Graph 6

BAPTIST WOMEN UNITS

BAPTIST WOMEN MEMBERS

BAPTIST YOUNG WOMEN UNITS

BAPTIST YOUNG WOMEN MEMBERS

Development of Age-level Organizations, Florida WMU

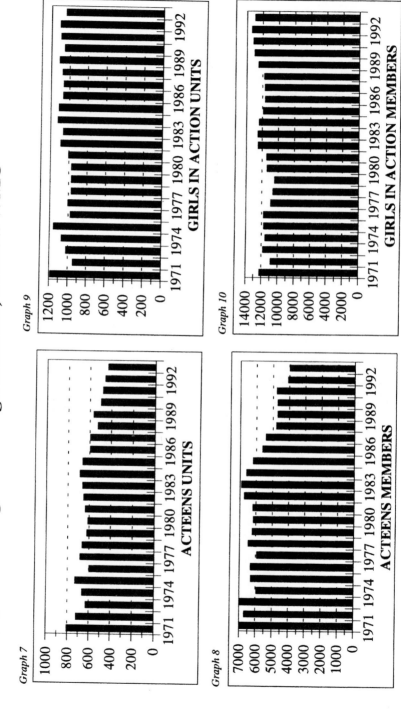

Graph 7

Graph 8

Graph 9

Graph 10

Development of Age-level Organizations, Florida WMU

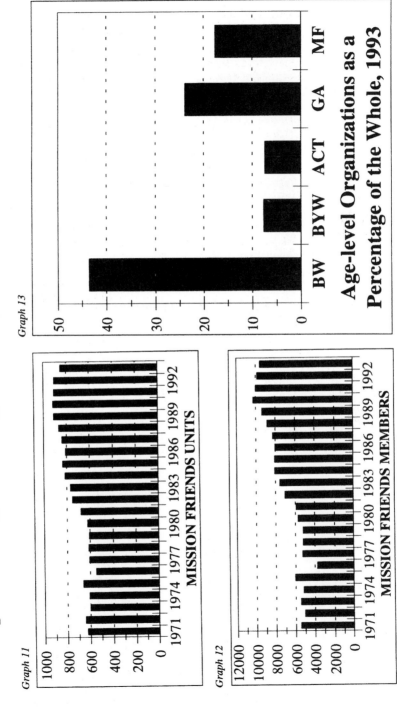

Graph 11

Graph 12

Graph 13

MISSION FRIENDS UNITS

MISSION FRIENDS MEMBERS

Age-level Organizations as a
Percentage of the Whole, 1993

BW BYW ACT GA MF

INDEX

MARTHA POPE TROTTER

Martha Pope Trotter graduated Magna Cum Laude from the Mississippi University for Women. She did graduate study in English at Emory University, Atlanta.

Since moving to Pensacola in 1979, Martha has focused her energies in serving God through First Baptist Church, Pensacola. Her writing experience, coupled with her involvement in Florida Woman's Missionary Union, led to her selection by the Florida WMU Centennial committee as the author of the Centennial history.

For 33 years, Martha was married to Dr. Robert W. Trotter, pastor, licensed psychologist, and Clinical Pastoral Education Supervisor. At the time of his death in July 1993, he was Director of Pastoral Care and Counseling at Baptist Hospital, Pensacola.

Martha has served as chairman of the Board of Directors of the Florida Baptist Historical Society and has written for *Christian Single* and *Royal Service* magazines. She has two children and two grandchildren.

TONI MOORE CLEVENGER

Journalism and television are lifelong interests of Toni Moore Clevenger. After marrying Dr. Charles E. Clevenger, Toni settled into being career wife, mother, and now grandmother.

During her college years at Samford University she was a well-known television personality at Channel 13 the NBC affiliate in Birmingham. She worked for the *Mobile Press Register* and the *Birmingham News*. In 1964 the Clevengers moved to Pensacola, where they became active in First Baptist Church.

Toni's earlier media experience and training came to be seen as gifts God could use in her church and denomination. Serving 12 years on the *Florida Baptist Witness* Commission, Toni was chairman, vice-chairman, and chair of the three-person committee that wrote the Editorial Policies of the *Witness*. She serves as a trustee of the Radio and Television Commission of the Southern Baptist Convention and has worked with the local ACTS affiliate for the entire 10 years of its existence.

Toni is the author of *On the Bay—On the Hill*, the history of First Baptist Church, Pensacola, published in 1986.

ABOUT THIS BOOK

The production of *FAITHFUL SERVANTS* was by PEC Printing & Publishing, Pensacola, Florida, under the direction of Willie E. Small. Kelly L. Bexley, graphic arts manager, supervised the printing process. Gilbert J. Coté, copy editor, and Paula Reilly, typographer, set the text from WordPerfect files prepared by the author. Overall production control was provided by Toni Clevenger. Florida Woman's Missionary Union, Jacksonville, Florida, served as publisher. We gratefully acknowledge the assistance and cooperation of PEC personnel in the publication of this volume.

No Mysteries Out of Ourselves

No Mysteries Out of Ourselves

Identity and Textual Form in the Novels of Herman Melville

Peter J. Bellis

upp

University of Pennsylvania Press
Philadelphia

MIDDLEBURY COLLEGE LIBRARY

Copyright © 1990 by the University of Pennsylvania Press
All rights reserved
Printed in the United States of America

Library of Congress Cataloging-in-Publication Data

Bellis, Peter J.
   No mysteries out of ourselves : identity and textual form in the novels of Herman
Melville / Peter J. Bellis
      p.   cm.
   ISBN 0-8122-8229-9
   1. Melville, Herman, 1819–1891—Criticism and interpretation. 2. Identity (Psychology) in
literature. 3. Body, Human, in literature. 4. Self in literature. I. Title.
PS2388.I35B4 1990
813'.3—dc20   89-29797
                                                                                CIP

*This book is for my parents
and, above all, for Miriam*

Contents

Acknowledgments

THIS BOOK has taken a good number of years to write. It has worked its way from seminar papers into a dissertation, and from there into its present form. At every stage of the process, there have been teachers, colleagues, and friends who have offered support, intellectual incitement, and good advice, and I owe them all my thanks.

At the University of Texas, I was introduced to Melville by Wayne Lesser, and to deconstruction by Gayatri Spivak. At Johns Hopkins, my dissertation was given its initial impetus by the late Laurence Holland and much of its final shape by its directors, John T. Irwin and Larzer Ziff. At the University of Miami, I have been aided by the receipt of a Max Orovitz Summer Research Award, but even more by the support of John Paul Russo and Zack Bowen, chairmen of the department during my time here. And I am also indebted to Zachary Simpson and the editorial staff of the University of Pennsylvania Press.

A briefer, somewhat different version of Chapter V appeared in *American Literature* 59 (1987): 548–69.

Ultimately, though, I owe the most to my first and most important teachers, my parents, and to my closest colleague and best friend, my wife. So it is to them that this book is dedicated, with love and gratitude.

I Introduction

IN CHAPTER 60 OF *MOBY-DICK*, Ishmael speaks of "the magical, sometimes horrible whale-line."[1] What follows is characteristically Melvillean, a dense passage that moves swiftly from the smallest technical details to the largest of philosophical questions. If "The Line" begins as a literal description of its subject, it ends with the transformation of fact into figure, as Melville returns to one of his primary themes, the nature and limits of the self. Embedded in this chapter are three different versions of identity: bodily identity, genealogical or inherited identity, and autobiographical or textual identity.

The main thrust of "The Line" is the *physical* peril of whaling—the threat it offers to the *bodily* self. Arranged in the whale-boat before the chase begins, the line

> folds the whole boat in its complicated coils, twisting and writhing around it in almost every direction. All the oarsmen are involved in its perilous contortions . . . [no one can] be thus circumstanced without a shudder that makes the very marrow in his bones to quiver in him . . . (240)

The seaman is made intensely aware of the shape and bulk of his body, forcibly reminded that he exists only *in* his body. His shudder is both a psychological and a physical response, as fear literally fills and convulses the space of the self; the involuntary quiver indicates the inseparability of mind and body.

When the harpoon is darted, the line is pulled out of the boat at an incredible speed:

> to be seated then in the boat, is like being seated in the midst of the manifold whizzings of a steam-engine in full play, when every flying beam, and shaft, and wheel, is grazing you. It is worse; for you cannot sit motionless in the heart of these perils, because the boat is rocking

like a cradle, and you are pulled one way and the other, without the slightest warning . . . (240)

The body normally serves as a vehicle of self-expression, in movement or gesture (even if only the involuntary movement of a shudder); here, on the other hand, bodily constraint immobilizes and silences the sailor. He is confined inside a machine, a deadly engine to which he must become a passive accessory. Any movement may be fatal now—embodiment itself is dangerous.

This threat is implicit even in "the graceful repose of the line, as it silently serpentines about the oarsman before being brought into actual play" (241). It is like "the deadliest [of] snakes"—a "twisting and writhing" symbol of the oarsman's perilous implication in the Fall and the physical vulnerability that is its consequence (240). The body that identifies him also marks him for death.

Original sin is, of course, a matter of inheritance, a component of one's *genealogical* identity. The whaleman is, inescapably, a "son" (240): "All are *born* with halters around their necks" (241, my emphasis). The genealogical chain is, obviously, made of births *and* deaths, structured by both a father's authorizing, identifying power and his inevitable absence or loss. If the line of genealogical progression links father and son through shared or repeated guilt, the punishment for that guilt—death—leaves a temporal gap between them, a gulf that deprives the son of the authority by which he would define himself.

Later in the chapter, Ishmael compares the static, silent whale-line to "the profound calm which only apparently precedes and prophesies of the storm" (241). "The calm," he continues, "is but the wrapper and envelope of the storm; and contains it in itself." The movement here is from temporal images ("precedes and prophesies") to spatial ones ("wrapper and envelope"). The shift is noteworthy because Ishmael's comments apply not only to his subject, but also to the workings of his autobiographical text. For one of "The Line's" primary functions is proleptic, to "prophesy" and "contain" the end of Ishmael's narrative: "a very little thought," he says, will "enable you to account for those repeated whaling disasters—some few of which are casually chronicled—of this man or that man being taken out of the boat by the line, and lost" (240). "Repeated disasters," only "casually chronicled," involving "this man or that man"—it is, of course, Ishmael who will be thrown out of Ahab's boat by the line, tossed aside by the narrative line at the end of *Moby-Dick*.

Ishmael's goal as autobiographer is to establish a *textual* identity for himself, but that identity is at once defined and threatened by the events of his story. He establishes the circumstances of his own survival, but displaces them from narrative into exposition; he anticipates events in order to preempt a narrative closure that will abandon him. For the line of autobiographical narrative, as he will discover, always ends with a gap between the writer and his earlier, now written self. No autobiography can be adequate to its subject; none can be more than a "draught of a draught" (128).

I.

"The Line" stands at the center of *Moby-Dick*, itself the central text of Herman Melville's career. But its different models of selfhood—bodily, genealogical, and textual—are the alternatives that Melville explores throughout his work, from *Typee* through *Billy Budd*.

In a sense, Melville's career *begins* with the problem of identity, with John Murray's reservations about the authenticity of *Typee*. Melville's English publisher doubted at first that the "practised writer" responsible for the book could have been the ordinary seaman whose experience it purported to describe.[2] Murray's suspicions may have been misplaced, but they were not unjustified—author and adventurer were indeed one and the same, but Melville had both fictionalized his experience and incorporated material from other sources. The resulting text could be said to represent or embody Melville's experience only indirectly at best.

A few years later, it is Melville himself who makes self-representation an issue. He does not wish to "go down to posterity," he tells Hawthorne in 1851, as "a 'man who lived among the cannibals.'"[3] He no longer sees himself as either the sailor of 1842 or the writer of 1845; he distances himself from both his earlier self and the text that ostensibly represents it. What was once an external challenge to the authenticity of his work has become an internal dilemma, a problem that troubles both the author and his texts.

It should be no surprise to find self-definition as a major subject in Melville's work, for the contradictions in his social, political, and family relations all worked to problematize rather than confirm his sense of self. Second son of a once-wealthy family, he first left home to serve as a common sailor. An ardent democrat despite his Dutch patrician ancestry, he married the daughter of a conservative Massachusetts jurist. Writing might have seemed the only way in which to mediate between or fuse these widely differing roles, to define a self that could be all (and none) of the above.

My intent is not, however, to read Melville's fiction as simply veiled autobiography. What I describe in the following pages is instead a career driven by its own internal dynamic, by a continual examination and reexamination of a single complex of issues—the problem of identity, of defining and representing the self. In so doing, I will, I realize, be deemphasizing the shaping force of Melville's historical and cultural context. Melville does turn away from that context, I would argue, but not in a simple flight from hard facts and material realities. What he seeks is a position from which to reengage the world more forcefully, a place to stand and a sense of self on which to build.

When Melville begins to consider questions of identity and self-definition, in *Typee*, he focuses primarily on the bodily self. In the South Seas, it is the white man's body that marks his social, cultural, and political difference from the Polynesian. But for Melville's narrator, the body is first and foremost a determinant of *individual* identity. This is true in two senses: first, human existence *is* the experience of embodiment. The spatial extension of the body serves as the basis for the distinction between self and other; the body's surface is a limit, enclosing the self and excluding all other selves and objects. Second, if embodiment is something experienced from "within," the outline and surface of the body also function as outward signs of identity, the only ones from which an individual cannot be separated or detached. Bodily form, as it is perceived by others, is the primary ground of social relations, the external evidence by which the self is "recognized" or "known."

The first of these claims implies a rejection of Cartesian dualism, a refusal to ground identity solely in the mind's consciousness of its own processes. The Cartesian ego is constituted by a series of divisions—between the mind and the body as an object of sense perception, and between the mind as subject and as object of its own self-observation.[4] For Melville, however, the individual's awareness of his body precedes the disjunctive operations of reflective thought: "no man can ever feel his identity aright except his eyes be closed," Ishmael says in *Moby-Dick*, invoking a sense of *felt* embodiment that is both distinct from other sense perceptions and more fundamental than cognition or self-consciousness.[5] In neurological terms, the awareness of one's body as one's own is indeed a kind of perception distinct from all others—proprioception.[6] The body is not simply the first member of the class of objects; its existence is not established through the five senses rejected by Descartes, and thus is not open to doubt in the same way that other objects are.[7]

The uniqueness of the link between body and self appears most forcefully in the experience of pain. Pain cannot be shared by others; it cannot be experientially "known" by any but oneself.[8] Beyond this, intense pain almost transcends representation—it cannot be accurately described and so cannot, except in the most rudimentary sense, be communicated to others. In this case, bodily sensation is inescapably and exclusively "proper to" the self.

Consciousness of oneself as a being distinct from others is also first established in terms of the body—in an infant's first awareness of himself as *physically* separate from his mother, for example. Even in the Lacanian model, in which the "self" is a purely linguistic or symbolic entity, the child gains access to language through an internalization of this sense of difference—through the perception of himself as a *visual* object.[9] The very conception of a self thus begins with the fact of "being in" or "having" a body.[10]

In *Typee*, the bodily self is regarded as a defining feature of Western identity, to be defended against the external force of native culture. *White-Jacket*, on the other hand, describes a "civilized" naval order that undermines the link between body and self; it is now society that generates a radical self-alienation. Western culture offers ideological support for such alienation, in the Christian opposition between the immortality of the soul and the mortality of the body, but this is a distinction that Melville rejects outright: if we begin with or in our bodies, he holds, we enter eternity with them as well. The human body is, after all, made in God's image; the human countenance is a "'face divine.'"[11] And when the sailors of the *Neversink* "rise at the Last Day," they do so *in their bodies*, each an "image of his Creator."[12] In its original or natural form, the body is a link between man and God, not a sign of their separation.

If man is made in God's image, however, any change in the shape or surface of the body is a sign both of his mortality, his distance from God, and of a division within the self, a loss of self-identity. The individual thus becomes a stranger to himself and others, radically different from what he has been. Whether such a bodily alteration be a tattoo, a scar, or the loss of a limb, physical mutilation precipitates a rupture in proprioception and a drastic psychological dissolution. Where Descartes asserts that "body is by nature always divisible, and the mind is entirely indivisible" (Meditation VI, 196), Melville argues in *Mardi* that the *human* body cannot be altered or divided and still remain itself, precisely because of its privileged link to the self.

While Melville's early novels are concerned with preserving the integrity of the bodily self, *Mardi* and *Moby-Dick* struggle to comprehend and accept the consequences of its loss. *Moby-Dick* in particular is the point at which Melville turns on the assumptions of his earlier novels: as Ishmael probes the link between Ahab's physical and psychological wounds, his examination reveals a dizzying, self-multiplying fragmentation within the self, as oppositions between self and other, inside and outside, are collapsed and deconstructed.

If Ahab's crisis of identity would have been merely anomalous in *Typee*, by this point in his career, Melville has come to suspect that it may be paradigmatic.[13] Even in its "normal," undamaged state, the body bears within it and depends upon *internal* differences. Neither can it remain in a single, constant state; if it were to do so, it would be reduced to the status of an inanimate object. Bodily alteration and decay are inescapable, functions of the temporal nature of human existence—in religious terms, the consequences of man's fallen state. The integrity and stability of the body can never be more than an ideal, a conceptual stay against its eventual but inevitable dissolution. This is the truth represented for young Redburn in his dying shipmate Jackson, for Pierre in his family portraits, and reiterated for Melville and his readers in the metamorphoses and disguises of *The Confidence-Man*.

Melville's concern, I should note here, is almost exclusively with the *male* body.[14] Any number of "threats" to the integrity of a man's body are "normal"—although perhaps no less traumatic—for women: in sexual intercourse, the woman's body is penetrated by the male; in the course of pregnancy, it contains within it another body that is and is not distinct from its own; and in childbirth, that second body is cut away from its mother's into an independent existence. Melville uses images of pregnancy and childbirth only rarely—briefly in *Moby-Dick*'s "The Grand Armada" and as part of a satiric allegory in "The Tartarus of Maids"—but the female body remains largely excluded from his work.

When Melville turns to an examination of genealogical identity, his focus is again on the dynamics of *male* intergenerational relations. A son's genealogical link to his father would seem both to approximate the immediacy of bodily identity, through the son's physical resemblance to his father, and to add the permanence of an external order stretching between and beyond individual generations. But even though the son may resemble the father, resemblance is not identity—it is instead an ambiguous fusion of likeness and difference. Within the family structure, the father is the primary source of both physical and linguistic authority: it is he who links these two orders in giving the son his name. But the son's name again both unifies and differentiates: his last or family name identifies him with the father, while his first name marks the difference between them. For Melville's fictional sons, however, the last name is crucial, since in the father's absence it is his *name* that remains as a sign of his lost authority.

The father's very ability to name his son is, however, based on his temporal priority. It is their distance in time that structures the father/son relation, not the repetition or continuity implicit in the family name. The son cannot repeat or replace his father, Redburn discovers, for he can never turn back time and assume his father's position of temporal priority.

It is the irreversibility of paternal absence that is most important for Ishmael, Ahab, and, finally, Pierre. Each wavers between nostalgia and rebellion, with Ahab and Pierre driven toward the latter. Where Ishmael sees himself as an orphan, cast out of patriarchal structures of authority, Ahab must reestablish such structures and insert himself within them if he is to define himself in opposition to his absent father. And Pierre, in attempting to escape from genealogy altogether, finds that he has done away with the very ground of self-definition; he too must resurrect and internalize patriarchal authority, even if it means his own destruction.

My emphasis here is on a *linear* relationship between father and son rather than on the triangular structure of the Oedipus complex. For the incestuous and parricidal aspects of the Oedipal conflict are, in Melville's novels, most often preempted, on the literal level at least: the son's drive to fill the father's position in the family is a desire not to supplant him but to fill his *already empty* place. The mother is not an object of the son's desire, but only an inadequate father-supplement, herself a sign of paternal absence.

This lack of an immobilizing Oedipal structure has a clearly destabilizing effect, for without its repressive regulating force, the son's relation to language remains tangled and confused. The loss of the father is, on the one hand, an incitement to speech—it is the need to fill a linguistic void that compels the son to assert his position as his father's namesake. At the same time, however, the father's absence deprives the son of the authority required to ground the act of naming and initiate narrative. The name of the father remains both the key to language—no son can define himself except in genealogical terms—and the sign of the loss of the authoritative ground for self-definition.

Melville's fictional sons cannot escape from the paternal discourse that defines them as *merely* sons; they can never progress from a position of secondariness or belatedness. They undertake their autobiographical texts as self-conscious and reluctant inheritors of paternal authority, only to discover that linguistic authority cannot be inherited, but must be constructed within and by their texts themselves.

Beyond the problem of temporality that divides father and son, Melville's narrators also discover temporal gaps *within themselves*, both discontinuities in their remembered experience and a gulf between its written record and their continuing lives. The central premise of autobiography, however, is that the self is defined through the continuity of memory, a continuity that can be established and inscribed in a text.

The most famous definition of identity as based on the continuity of memory is John Locke's: a "person," he says, "is a thinking intelligent being, that has reason and reflection, and can consider itself as itself, the same thinking thing, in different times and places; which it does only by that consciousness which is inseparable from thinking, and . . . essential to it."[15] Locke's position thus builds on Descartes', as he makes self-consciousness the basis of the self, and uses it to establish the terms of identity:

> since consciousness always accompanies thinking, and it is that which makes every one to be what he calls self, and thereby distinguishes himself from all other thinking things: in this alone consists personal identity, i.e., the sameness of a rational being; and as far as this consciousness can be extended backwards to any past action or thought, so far reaches the identity of that person; it is the same self now it was then; and it is by the same self with this present one that now reflects on it, that that action was done.[16]

For Locke, it is the potential continuity between thought in the present and thought or action in the past that establishes the self as a distinct and stable entity. The self is what it can *remember* itself as being, thinking, or doing.

David Hume and Thomas Reid both offer sharp critiques of Locke's view, however. "When I enter most intimately into what I call *myself*," Hume says, "I always stumble on some particular perception or other. . . . I can never catch *myself* at any time without a perception, and can never observe any thing but the perception."[17] "They are the successive perceptions only, that constitute the mind," he claims, "nor have we the most distant notion of the place where these scenes are represented, or of the materials of which it is composed" (253). Memory, according to Hume, can yield only distinct and "particular perceptions," and we can have no access to any unifying stratum beneath them. He insists that *all our perceptions are distinct existences*, and *that the mind never perceives any real connexion among distinct existences*" (636). We only "feign the continued existence" of such perceptions, and rely on "the notion of a *soul*, and *self*, and *substance*, to disguise the variation" in them (254).[18] Reid extends Hume's argument to the "consciousness" invoked by Locke, claiming that "Consciousness, and every kind of thought, are transient and momentary, and have no continued existence; and therefore, if personal identity consisted in consciousness, it would certainly follow, that no man is the same person any two moments of his life."[19]

Melville's writing moves toward a view of memory and identity that resembles Hume's and Reid's far more than it does Locke's. White-Jacket, for example, keeps track of his experience only in terms of disconnected moments: "there is a particular day," he says, "which, from my earliest recollections, I have always kept the run of, so that I can even now tell just where I was on that identical day of every year past" (173). His pride in his memory here only serves to emphasize the amount that he cannot recall—364 days out of every year. In such a context, the continuity of memory and identity can be no more than a retrospective projection, one that Melville's narrators, from Tommo to Ishmael, all hesitate to acknowledge or accept. Redburn, for example, explicitly refuses to connect his "*first* voyage" with his present existence as remembering writer.[20]

The fragmentary nature of remembered experience is readily acknowledged by contemporary theoreticians of autobiography. The autobiographer's task, according to Georges Gusdorf, "is to reassemble the scattered elements of his individual life and to regroup them in a comprehensive sketch."[21] Such a "regrouping" involves, however, not the recovery of an experiential unity but the creation of a *textual* unity. And the creation of a new textual identity only divides the individual once again, into writing and written selves. "Every autobiography," Jean Starobinski remarks, "is a self-interpretation," and as such it reinstitutes the Cartesian split between the self as subject and as object of consciousness.[22] This gap between writing and written selves is emphasized even more strongly by Louis A. Renza: "how," he asks, "can [the autobiographer] keep using the first-person pronoun, his sense of self-reference, without its becoming in the course of writing something other than strictly his own self-referential sign—a de facto third-person pronoun?"[23] For Renza, "the autobiographer's split from his persona . . . denominates the autobiographical act *as such* to the writing self" (386).

This interpretive distance also marks an ineradicable temporal distance: just as the son cannot recapture the father's presence, so the writing self can only confirm its difference from the earlier self it "re"-creates in words. "When a narrator recounts what has happened to him," according to Roland Barthes, "the *I* who recounts is no longer the same *I* as the one that is recounted. . . . the *I* of discourse can no longer be a place where a previously stored-up person is innocently restored."[24] The "I"'s linguistic nature as a "shifter," a signifier whose referent changes with each use, must thus subvert the project of textual self-creation at the very moment it begins.

On an even more basic level, the self cannot be enclosed in a first-person narrative, for that narrative can never include the writer's present. Both the act of composition and the moment afterward must remain unrecorded, making the ostensibly *external* boundary of the text an *internal* boundary within the life it would encompass. For Paul de Man, the specularity of self-understanding indicates "the tropological structure that underlies all cognitions, including knowledge of self"; autobiography "demonstrates . . . the impossibility of closure and of totalization."[25]

In several senses, then, the autobiographical project can "succeed" only by sacrificing the integrity and continuity of the self it would define. Memory can neither recover nor reconstitute a stable and continuous selfhood—in de Man's words, autobiography "deprives and disfigures to the precise extent that it restores" (930). The autobiographical text is essentially epitaphic, a memorial to a self (or selves) it designates as already lost or "other than" the writer.

These temporal problems inherent in first-person narrative are confronted directly by Redburn, White-Jacket, and Ishmael as each struggles to recover and give form to his experience. Each acknowledges, and then dodges, the temporal distance between his experience and his act of writing; each deliberately leaves his text open-ended, refusing to solidify the link between the writing and the written self. It is only in *Pierre*, with its third-person narration, that Melville provides a conventional closure—but he does so at the cost of his hero's life, and with an admission that biographical narrative must remain at an even greater distance from its subject.

James Olney suggests an alternative conception of identity, one that offers an escape from the difficulties of temporal self-definition: "Life," he argues, "does not stretch back across time but extends down to the roots of individual being; it is atemporal, committed to a vertical thrust from consciousness down into the unconscious rather than to a horizontal thrust from the present into the past."[26] Such images of spatial penetration do indeed appear in Melville's work; Ishmael considers them as part of Ahab's epistemological project. But for Ishmael, Pierre, and Melville himself, the drive toward a postulated interior essence is also doomed—it can yield only a void or an endless series of textual surfaces.

Melville's investigation of identity and its representation leads him, on the one hand, to the frantic, phantasmagorical verbal flux of *The Confidence-Man*, and, on the other, to the stoic dramatic economy of *Billy Budd*. The former proclaims the impossibility of ever knowing or representing identity: "'Nobody knows who anybody is,'" says the "mystical" Mark Winsome.[27] Bodies, texts, and even the Paternal authority of God's Word are all thrust into the cauldron of ceaseless interpretation and reinterpretation, all deprived of any ultimate status or relation to the self. The latter work seems to offer a set of clear moral coordinates, but they map only a portion of a shifting textual surface; beneath it remain innumerable mysteries of both iniquity and goodness.

2.

What I offer here, then, is an attempt to couple the thematic and formal aspects of Melville's work. Critics have most often dealt with these topics separately: many have treated particular themes or subjects in Melville's texts, from religion (Lawrance Thompson, T. Walter Herbert) to race (Carolyn L. Karcher) to male sexuality (Robert K. Martin);[28] others have pursued stylistic or formal issues (F.O. Matthiessen, Walter Bezanson, Warner Berthoff).[29] My claim, in the other hand, is that narrative form takes on far more than just technical importance for Melville; insofar as it becomes the vehicle for self-representation, it carries an immense thematic weight as well.[30]

Readers such as Charles Feidelson and Richard Brodhead have discussed Melville's efforts to fuse intellectual and formal concerns—successfully, for Feidelson, unsuccessfully, for Brodhead.[31] Neither, however, has fully considered the stakes Melville plays for when he tests the possibilities and limits of representation. It is only when one acknowledges Melville's primary interest as *self*-representation that the intensity and persistence—even the obsession—of his pursuit begin to make sense.

From a different perspective, Edgar Dryden has focused on the question of fictional form in Melville's work, but he disassociates it from the psychological and epistemological problems to which it is a response. According to Dryden, the Melvillean narrator

> fictionalizes his earlier experience in an attempt to define its truth or meaning to himself and to his reader. . . . By the act of turning his experience into a story, he places himself outside of that experience—in effect, treats it as though it belonged to someone else.[32]

To assume, as Dryden does, that Melville's narrators are willing to accept such a fictionalization of their own identities is both to misjudge the tone and to beg the most crucial questions raised in his novels. It is, in a way, to read *Typee* as if it were *The Confidence-Man*, to read the despair of Melville's last novel into his first.

The pivotal point between those two books, and in my argument, is the completion of *Moby-Dick*. For it is here that Melville exhausts the possibilities of autobiographical representation that he had methodically examined in *Redburn* and *White-Jacket*. It is here, too, that he begins to attack definitions based on bodily and genealogical identity—the terms he had sought to assert and defend in *Typee*.

Pierre marks an abandonment of Melville's earlier project, offering the first of a series of bleak and deeply ironic critiques of individual selfhood. I have not discussed *Israel Potter* or Melville's short fiction here, because I see them as elaborating the critique of selfhood in *Pierre* and foreshadowing that in *The Confidence-Man*. In Melville's work of the mid-1850s, selves remain either inaccessible ("Bartleby") or "knowable" only through ironized or alienated *mis*representation ("The Paradise of Bachelors and the Tartarus of Maids," "Benito Cereno," *Israel Potter*), precisely the alternatives elaborated at greater length in *Billy Budd* and *The Confidence-Man*.

Earlier I described Melville's work as internalizing and deepening issues that initially appear as merely external ones. It is this interiorizing movement that will shape my argument in the chapters that follow. Just as the bodily self is first perceived as threatened by external forces, so the genealogical self is initially seen as defined by an external structure of patriarchal authority. In both cases, however, Melville and his heroes find the difficulties of bodily and genealogical self-definition to be ultimately internal (Chapters II and III). On a different level, Melville's increasing focus on textuality itself marks a subordination of thematic (external) issues to the process of autobiographical representation, to the privileged "interiority" of self-knowledge and the internal workings of his novels themselves (Chapter IV). In Chapter V, I consider *The Confidence-Man*, and, briefly, *Billy Budd*, as summarizing and concluding Melville's exploration of these issues.

My argument thus leads me away from Melville's social and historical context toward a focus on narrative and textual form. Such an image of Melville's career is accepted even by those critics who emphasize his political and cultural concerns: Michael Paul Rogin, for example, speaks of Melville's "absorption into texts that were increasingly self-referential—in their private meanings for Melville . . . and their isolation from a realistic social world."[33] But this concern with problems of textuality and literary form is, I would suggest, hardly an escape from politics and ideology. It is an indirect but powerful response to a political and cultural impasse that is itself, in part, a crisis of representation.

Problems in literary or autobiographical representation are, at the very least, continuous with those in the larger realms of politics and culture.[34] What was the slavery crisis of the 1850s, for example, but a breakdown in political "representation" because of society's inability to define what a "person" is—to determine what it is that constitutes a "self"? Allen Grossman has called this a "crisis of the establishment of the person"; he describes Whitman, Melville, and their contemporaries as writers entering "a new territory where the worth of persons was subject to the risk of finding a form."[35] What I take Grossman to mean here is that the search for new forms of representation is "risky" because of what is to be entrusted to those forms—the worth or definition of "personhood" itself. It is the "refounding of personhood," he says, that is the "deferred business" of American literature of the period (192).

Melville's search for self-definition may be shaped primarily by internal factors, but it does speak to the cultural context Grossman describes. Melville's long examination of bodily and genealogical identity, for example, when brought to bear on the slavery issue in "Benito Cereno," yields a thorough deconstruction of the category of race as determining or representing moral character.

Donald Pease has spoken in broader terms of a "crisis in self-legitimation" that generated a search for "visionary compacts," "forms of cultural agreement" more lasting than the negative "Revolutionary mythos" of opposition.[36] Melville may well have begun his career with just such an objective. In *Typee*, for instance, he begins by defining American society as "home," a cultural matrix that fully defines the self. In that novel, Melville's narrator reasserts his identity by recovering and returning to his place in family, society, and history.

For Melville, however, a true "compact" must be a bond between individuals, not, as Pease seems to suggest, a transcendence of selfhood. I read Melville's attempt to define and ground individual identity as the first step in a process of social reconstitution or redefinition. The process founders at that first step, however—in later, darker works like *Israel Potter*, Melville defines his heroes through their *alienation* from American society and history. The past, he concludes, can be made "usable" only by turning it into fiction; history appears not as a framework that confers or defines identity, but as itself a fiction that swallows up and obscures the "truth" of individual experience.[37] In this sense, *Israel Potter* and *The Confidence-Man* both renounce the possibility of a Melvillean "visionary compact," a textual or narrative order adequate to the task of national self-definition.

It might be argued that such an emphasis on the individual is an unproductive or false basis on which to begin a process of social or cultural reconstruction. For Pease, at least, the separation and distinction required for self-definition would correspond to what he calls the merely "negative freedom" valued by literary modernism.[38] And, given the ideological centrality of individualism in American culture, Melville's project might seem trapped within the system it would revise, simply reinforcing the "self-interest" Pease describes as undermining "civic relations" (x).

I would respond to the first of these points by citing the example of Michel Foucault, whose work has shaped the aims and methods of today's New Historicism. The "general theme of my research," Foucault says, is "the subject"—how the subject is "objectivized" by the "dividing practices" of economic, social, and political institutions, and how "a human being turns him- or herself into a subject."[39] He describes his texts as taking part in a number of different "struggles," all of which "revolve around the question: Who are we? They are a refusal of these abstractions, of economic and ideological state violence which ignore who we are individually, and also a refusal of a scientific or administrative inquisition which determines who one is" (781). Foucault's terms are obviously "negative" (his emphasis on "refusal," for example), but the result is hardly the mystification or suppression of ideology so often decried and "counteracted" by recent reevaluations of nineteenth-century American literature.

Foucault concentrates on the way in which the self is acted upon by social and institutional power; in my reading, Melville seeks an absolute ground that will place it beyond the reach of such forces. The versions of identity at stake here are obviously very different, but for both writers, it is the *self* that is the point of resistance, the standpoint from which society and culture must be analyzed and judged. I can think of no more powerful refusal of a psychological or "administrative inquisition" than Bartleby's simple "I would prefer not to."[40]

If Melville's demand for an *absolute* selfhood differentiates him from Foucault, it also puts him at odds with the Emersonian individualism that dominated 1850's America. If the early Emerson privileged the self as the point at which Spirit works upon the world, *Conduct of Life* (1860) describes it as the site of a Nietzschean power struggle between the amoral forces of will and fate. Such a selfhood is ultimately little more than the creation of the social, economic, and political forces that act upon it—it is this view of the self as malleable, negotiable commodity that Melville rejects and resists throughout his career.

For Melville, a problematic or unstable selfhood simply means a loss of essential, meaningful identity. In my view at least, he stands outside and against the tradition that Richard Poirier, Harold Bloom, and others see as central to American culture. For Poirier, "the great line of American literature from Emerson to Adams to Stevens" begins with an acceptance of human identity as "nearly always problematic"; he goes on to describe both Emerson and Stevens as contemplating the "dissolution" or "eradication" of the self.[41] Whatever Melville's texts may ultimately succeed or fail in representing, they are a passionate embodiment of the *desire* for a secure identity on which to ground social and personal relations. Fictionality is, to him, always a limit, a condition to be confronted and overcome; we must come to know our "selves" as more than merely fictitious or illusory mystifications. There must be something there that cannot be "written off," explained or interpreted away by either ideological or linguistic analysis.

Melville's work finally presents a picture of the self as always thrown back on its own physical, psychic, and verbal resources. "[S]ailing with sealed orders, we ourselves are the repositories of the secret packet, whose contents we long to learn," he says in *White-Jacket*, "There are no mysteries out of ourselves" (398).

II Bodily Identity: The Changing Shape of the Physical Self

TOMMO, THE NARRATOR OF *TYPEE*, introduces his reader to the Marquesans through a pair of anecdotes. In both cases, the contrast between white and native cultures turns on their different views of the body and its relation to the self. Melville presents these as merely "amusing incident[s]" (6), but behind his comic tone lie issues that will become central to his text.

In the first of these episodes, a group of natives encounters a white woman for the first time, in the person of a missionary's wife. At first they admire this "new divinity," but "becoming familiar with its charming aspect, and jealous of the folds which encircled its form, they sought to pierce the sacred veil of calico in which it was enshrined" (6). For Europeans, be they missionaries or military men, the body is an essentially private and interior space, a "shrine" whose limits cannot be pierced without putting the self at risk. Clothing reinforces this by converting the body's "exterior," the skin, into an interior; the body's outline may be represented or suggested by the "veil" of clothing, but it is not to be directly revealed.

For the Marquesans, on the other hand, the body has no special privilege or private status:

> [The lady's] sex once ascertained, their idolatry was changed into contempt; and there was no end to the contumely showered upon her by the savages, who were exasperated at the deception which they conceived had been practised upon them. . . . she was stripped of her garments, and given to understand that she could no longer carry on her deceits with impunity. (6–7)

To the natives, clothing that obscures the form of the body is a "deceit"; representing instead of revealing the body is withholding, and thus *mis*-representing, the self. For them, the human body is the basis of a shared, communal identity; to hide one's body from view is to deny a primary social bond. Since they do not regard an individual's body as something private, a unique and inalienable attribute of the self alone, they cannot understand the Western desire to withhold it from public scrutiny.

In the second of Tommo's anecdotes, it is the body's *surface* that comes into question. The king and queen of Nukuheva are ushered onto an American ship by a group of French officers, who have dressed them in European clothing befitting their "elevated station" (7). There is, however, "one slight blemish" in the king's appearance, "a broad patch of tattooing" across his face that makes him look "as if he wore a huge pair of goggles" (7–8). The natives adorn themselves not by covering the body but by marking it directly, permanently altering it. Unlike a pair of goggles, a tattoo does not remain external to and detachable from the body; it becomes an inseparable part of the body.

The queen's legs, visible below the hem of her dress, are also "embellished with spiral tattooing"; Western clothes cannot fully conceal these tattoos or the view of the body they suggest.[1] Neither can "civilized" conventions prevent a "shocking . . . catastrophe," as the queen, much to the "consternation" of the French, shows her delight in one of the sailors' tattoos—"all at once the royal lady, eager to display the hieroglyphics on her own sweet form, bent forward for a moment, and turning sharply round, threw up the skirts of her mantle, and revealed a sight from which the aghast Frenchmen retreated precipitately" (8). The term "hieroglyphics" is a telling slip on Melville's part, for the Marquesans have no written language, not even a pictographic one. It is only from the European perspective that tattoos take on the status of signs, inscriptions independent of the body that bears them. It is for Westerners that the tattooed body becomes a text, a signifying object deprived of its link to an interior and private self. For the Marquesans, the body does not yield a self-knowledge distinct from one's public identity; it thus need not be withheld or preserved from external alteration. It may be embellished, and thus changed, with the embellishments becoming part of an undivided, essentially public or social self.

In beginning with these examples, Melville's narrator indicates the importance of bodily identity in *Typee*. He positions his text squarely between these opposing cultural views, in a way that outraged Melville's American publishers, who cut both passages from their "revised edition" of the novel.[2] But in the events of the narrative, it is Tommo's body, not his text, that is the point of intersection between white and native cultures, and he finds himself forced to defend it as the privileged and private ground of identity. If his identity is to remain the same—if he is to remain himself—he believes that his body must retain its spatial integrity, its "wholeness." If a part of the body is lost or its surface marked (tattooed), this will create a visible discontinuity in its appearance, marking it as no longer in its original state, no longer self-identical. And a temporal discontinuity in the form of the body in turn implies a fundamental discontinuity within the self; Tommo will no longer be able to know or recognize himself. He may undergo an external change of costume among the Typees, but a tattoo would be a far more radical change, one that would threaten his very identity.

The desire to preserve the body, and thus the self, from external change or discontinuity is the point from which Melville begins his consideration of bodily identity. The narrators/protagonists of *Typee* and *White-Jacket* both regard threats to the shape or surface of their bodies as threats to their sense of self. But where *Typee* places such threats outside the limits of Western culture, *White-Jacket* locates them at the heart of "civilized" order. In *Mardi* and *Moby-Dick*, this interiorizing movement shifts from the cultural level to that of the body itself, as Melville sketches the disastrous philosophical and psychological consequences of the marking or loss of a part of the body. Even if the body could be preserved from external violation, he concludes, it is always already divided, differing from and within itself over time—the internally corrupt and self-consuming body is the nightmare image that haunts *Redburn* and leads Melville from defense to critique and finally to abandonment of the notion of bodily identity.

As should be clear by now, I take Melville to be speaking primarily of bodies *as bodies*, as literal, physical objects rather than symbolic ones. In so doing, I am departing from a long line of critics—from Richard Chase and Newton Arvin in the late 1940's through Michael Rogin and Neal Tolchin in the 1980's—who have sought the symbolic or psychological "meaning" of Tommo's leg injury, for example, or of White-Jacket's garment.[3] Instead, I am aligning myself with readers like Sharon Cameron, who has emphasized the brute literalness of the "disembodiments" of *Moby-Dick*. She and I stake out the same territory, if you will, but we approach it from opposite directions: in Cameron's reading, birth itself is a disembodiment, a cutting away of the self from nurturing mother and world; the body exists only as a fragment, incomplete as long as it is withheld from relations with others. She sees Melville and his characters as struggling to overcome that incompletion through fantasies of fusion with or incorporation of both external objects and other persons.[4] I, on the other hand, approach *Moby-*

Dick not in isolation, but as a culmination and critique of Melville's earlier work. From my perspective, the yearning to transcend the limits of the body appears only as a *response* to the breaching of those limits, to the loss of Melville's earlier faith in the bodily self as an integral and independent unit. The line between self and other remains, for him, an essential demarcation.[5]

I.

Tommo's first fear is of a fate far worse than tattooing, for the Typees are notorious cannibals; indeed, the very word "Typee" means "a lover of human flesh" (24). "The thought of voluntarily throwing ourselves into the hands of these cruel savages, seemed to me an act of mere madness," he says (51). Tommo conflates "selves" and bodies here; his "panic" comes from the recognition of his body as a physical object, one that may be possessed by—fall into the hands of—another.

Cannibalism is a particularly terrifying form of death because it involves the complete destruction of the body—both its fragmentation and its absorption into another body. Both Christian burial and native ritual designate a space belonging to the body, and the coffin suggests, and symbolically preserves, the body's shape.[6] But cannibalism's intent is to destroy the spatial integrity of the body, to obliterate its *difference from* other bodies by literally making it part of them.[7]

Even before Tommo enters the Typee valley, he is thus conscious of his body as a crucial but vulnerable determinant of his identity. By the time he and Toby make their descent from the mountains, one of Tommo's legs has become painfully swollen—he "half suspect[s]" that he has been bitten by a snake, even though the islands are supposedly free of them (48). It is after this wound, this reminder of his "fall" into embodiment, that he first glimpses a landscape he compares to "the gardens of Paradise" (49). This symbolic estrangement from his surroundings is soon internalized; twenty-four hours later, "I could not look at the limb which had pained me so violently . . . without experiencing a sense of alarm" (55). Tommo's body may *look* as if it remains a continuous whole, but he *feels* it as sharply divided: the pain makes his leg seem something alien, something other than the "me" on which "it" is inflicting pain.[8] Proprioceptive self-consciousness is no longer coextensive with the body; Tommo now finds his perceiving "self" defined *in opposition to* part of his body—this is what produces his "sense of alarm."

Once among the Typees, Tommo feels immobilized by his injury, "cut off . . . from all intercourse with the civilized world" (104). "It was idle for me to think of moving from the place," he laments (97). At first, his native attendant Kory-Kory carries him about, like a "porter" shouldering a "trunk" (89). His body is reduced to the status of an object without motive power, and Tommo is thereby returned to a state of childlike dependence— he is shown how to eat and wash himself as if he were indeed "a froward, inexperienced child" (89).

The Typees' "medical practice" only reinforces this split between body and self, treating Tommo's leg almost as a separate object. A native "leech" begins by "manipulating" the leg, and then, "on the supposition probably that the complaint had deprived the leg of all sensation, began to pinch and hammer it in such a manner that I absolutely roared with the pain" (80). The "old wizard" acts as if Tommo's leg were no longer connected to the rest of his body, and continues his "treatment" despite Tommo's pleas and screams (80). The "patient" has to be held down, like "a struggling child in a dentist's chair," until this "torture" has run its course (80). The healing Tommo desires becomes a torture he cannot prevent; he cannot control either the pain in his leg or what others may do to increase or diminish it. The only link between mind and leg is a pain that cannot even be ver- balized: he can only "roar" helplessly. "My unfortunate limb," Tommo concludes, "was now left much in the same condition as a rump-steak after undergoing the castigating process that precedes cooking" (80). It is now simply a piece of flesh to him—that Tommo can compare a part of his own body to edible meat suggests a drastic alienation from it, to say the least.

What is for Tommo an *internal* "disorder" (98), a dual rupture of both the body's space and the link between body and self, the natives seem to treat only *externally*, with "poundings" followed by the application of "herbal remedies"—the "doctor" leaves the leg "swathed in leafy ban- dages" (80, 97).[9] These "mild applications" can, however, only "soothe the pain" (98), diminishing Tommo's awareness of his body. And insofar as they do so, they also diminish his sense of himself as a white man from outside the valley.

When ships are sighted approaching the bay, Tommo's reaction is immediate and physical: "It sent a thrill of joy through my whole frame" (119). He is prevented from going to the beach, however, and gradually sinks into a state of "apathy," losing track of time and giving up all hope of escape. It is at this point that "My limb suddenly healed, the swelling went down, the pain subsided" (123). This "healing" takes place because he has

begun "to bury all regrets, all remembrances of my previous existence"—
because he no longer tries to preserve the connection between his present
existence in the valley and his past outside it (144). In forgetting his earlier
life, Tommo enacts a metaphorical suicide and "burial" of his former self.

With this act of self-forgetting, Tommo also becomes less fearful of the
Typees' cannibalism, but this threat is soon replaced by that of tattooing.[10]
All the natives are tattooed in some manner; not even "the beauteous form
of Fayaway was altogether free from the hideous blemish" (86). The most
extreme form of tattooing is represented by the old guardians of the Ti,

> on whose decrepit forms time and tattooing seemed to have obliter-
> ated every trace of humanity. Owing to the continued operation of this
> latter process, which only terminates among the warriors of the island
> after all the figures sketched upon their limbs in youth have been
> blended together . . . the bodies of these men were of a uniform dull
> green color. (92)

When the tattooing process is complete, the shape and color of the body are
completely obliterated, and with them "every trace of humanity"—these
"repulsive-looking creatures" have become "fixtures," both immobile and
apparently unconscious of events around them (93, 158, 129). The unmarked
human form is, for Tommo, the ground of individual and human identity.
Tattooing, whether partial or complete, means that the body is no longer in
its original state; the body, and thus the self, is now something other—
something less—than itself.[11]

Tommo compares the tattoo artist Karky to a "stone-cutter," a "dentist," and an "army surgeon," implying that he breaks off, removes, or
excises part of the body (217–18). He later speaks of Karky as an "artist,"
filled "with all a painter's enthusiasm" at the prospect of working on
Tommo's white skin (219). But even if the artist "adds to" the body, he
nevertheless treats it as an object, and would have others do so as well—as a
two-dimensional surface whose only value is as the ground for his designs.
Karky wishes to "distinguish *himself* in his profession" (my emphasis), but
he would so by making his "client" no longer distinguishable in the same
way—as the same person—he was before.

In Tommo's image, the tattoo "artist" treats the skin as a painter treats
the surface of a canvas, denying its inseparable link to the rest of the body
and to the self. But tattooing in fact works by puncturing the skin, breaking
into the space of the body and inserting an alien substance, the dye.[12] The

tattoo is at once "on" and "in" the body, external and internal to it. Tattooing introduces into/onto the body some*thing* distinct from the self, violating both its spatial integrity and its exclusive relation to the self. The body as a "whole" is thereby distinguished from the self, and this, in Melville's terms, is a radical self-alienation: "What an object he would have made of me!" Tommo exclaims (219).

Karky wishes to inscribe a set of "parallel bands which were to encircle my countenance," a design like one that Tommo has earlier compared to "the grated bars of a prison window" (219, 83). This tattoo will destroy the relation between self and body, imprisoning its bearer in a body, behind a face, that has become alien to him. As Karky traces the design across Tommo's face with his finger, "the flesh fairly crawled upon my bones"— his body turns against itself, its component parts separating in revulsion (219).

"Horrified at the bare thought of being rendered hideous for life," Tommo tries to escape from Karky (218). "This incident opened my eyes to a new danger," he says, the possibility that "I should be disfigured in such a manner as never more to have the *face* to return to my countrymen" (219). A tattooed face is a particularly traumatic disfigurement, for the face is the part of the body's surface that is revealed in identifying oneself to others. The face is also a part of the body that cannot be seen except in a reflected, mediated fashion—Tommo will not be able to see his tattooed face except as the face of another, or as the effect of his transformation is reflected in another's facial expression. He will always be known—and, in a literal sense, *seen*—as "a 'man who lived among the cannibals.'" The tattoo that inscribes his entry into Typee society will be reinscribed by every white man's glance, marking him as estranged from his own "civilized" world.

Tommo often speaks of the natives' "physical strength and beauty," but his emphasis is on the unmarked, "natural" body and the absence of any "natural deformit[ies]" or "blemishes" among the Typees (180). He links their physical health to a natural morality, a "sort of tacit common-sense law which . . . has its precepts graven on every breast" (201). The echo here is of St. Paul's distinction between the letter written "in tables of stone" and the Spirit written "in fleshy tables of the heart" (2 Cor 3:3). If God's spiritual Law is written on the human breast (for the skin is continuous with the body as a whole, and thus with the heart), man's marking of the body must therefore be like the letter that Paul says "killeth" (2 Cor 3:6). Tommo often calls a tattoo a "blemish" (7, 86), and his choice of words is instructive: it is those with "blemishes" whom the Old Testament prohibits from "coming nigh" to make an offering to the Lord (Lev 21:16–24). A tattoo will be "the utter ruin of my 'face divine,'" he says (220).[13]

"From the time of my casual encounter with Karky the artist, my life was one of absolute wretchedness," Tommo laments (231). This new threat makes him more keenly aware of his "state of captivity," of the external constraints that separate him from civilization, and it is at this point that his "painful malady," "after having almost completely subsided—began again to show itself, and with symptoms as violent as ever. This added calamity nearly unmanned me" (231–32). The consciousness of his outward vulnerability is internalized in his wounded leg, which Tommo associates with the loss of a defining physical and psychological characteristic, an "unmanning."[14]

A different set of "fearful apprehensions" now begins to "consume" him, as he discovers more evidence of the Typees' cannibalism—three shrunken heads, including that of a white man (232–33). "I shuddered at the idea of the subsequent fate his inanimate body might have met with. . . . Was I destined to perish like him—like him, perhaps, to be devoured, and my head to be preserved as a fearful memento of the event?" (233). Such a "preservation" of the body in fragmented, diminished form is only a further desecration, a parody of preservation. A week later, Tommo finds the bones of an enemy warrior, the remains of a cannibal feast (238).

Given his redoubled sense of physical danger, Tommo is now determined to escape, regardless of his physical weakness. When ships enter the harbor, he leaps up, "insensible to the pain that had before distracted me," and goes down to the beach in spite of the natives' opposition (245). He clambers into a boat and, in fighting off his pursuers, dashes a boat hook at one of them—wounding or scarring him in the process (253). He has seen the natives' wish to tattoo him only as a desire to do violence to his body. The violence of tattooing is for them only secondary, however; here Tommo inflicts violence for its own sake, with no thought of the scars or marks it will leave. The contrast is a paradigmatic one, symbolizing the violence inherent in the Western drive to "civilize" native cultures, the violence on which the very notion of "civilization" is constructed.

If the tattoo is the mark that *separates* white and native cultures in *Typee*, the mark of the lash *integrates* and unifies the "civilized" naval order of *White-Jacket*. Bodily punishment—flogging and death—is the basis of the officers' authority aboard the *Neversink*. That authority is demonstrated in two complementary ways: in the placement and regulation of the sailors' bodies within the limited space of the ship, and in the spectacular display of physical force that leaves its trace in the scars from the cat.[15] In both cases, the body is reduced to the status of an object—either a mechanism carrying out a specific function or a surface whose markings will testify to the efficacy of the power structure that contains it.

White-Jacket describes the captain's power in terms of his metaphorical presence throughout the vessel: "his subordinates are disintegrated parts of himself, detached from the main body on special service" (217). The officers ostensibly form a single "body," whose authoritative presence is coterminous with the physical limits of the frigate. Even as White-Jacket invokes the metaphor, however, he discredits it as a mere "fiction," for the organic unity of a living body cannot be recreated or "magnified" through "disintegration" and "detachment." This symbolic body is ultimately only a grotesque parody, for the captain's power is expressed on and against the bodies of the sailors.[16]

The ordinary seaman, on the other hand, cannot move beyond the reach of the captain's authority; in his strictly defined role and place, he is "immured" in "a sort of sea-Newgate, from which he can not escape" (176). The order of shipboard life is defined in terms of physical position—"every man of a frigate's five-hundred-strong, knows his own special place, and is infallibly found there. He sees nothing else, attends to nothing else, and will stay there until grim death or an epaulette orders him away" (8). His "place" and function come to shape a seaman's character: "the gunner's gang of every man-of-war are invariably ill-tempered, ugly featured, and quarrelsome," White-Jacket says, "their being so much among the guns is the very thing that makes a gunner's gang so cross" (44–45). The "topmen," on the other hand, are "more liberal-hearted, lofty-minded, gayer," because their work lifts them high above "the petty tumults, carping cares, and paltrinesses of the decks below" (47). But even they cannot escape a degree of dehumanization; when White-Jacket praises the sailor's character, his language turns body into machine: "Let them feel of our sturdy hearts, beating like sledge-hammers in those hot smithies, our bosoms . . . let them feel of our generous pulses, and swear that they go off like thirty-two-pounders" (77).[17]

In this closed and microcosmic system, men become interchangeable: when the ship's cooper falls overboard, for example, there are thirteen sailors who can "supply [his] place" (74). White-Jacket himself is called upon to replace an oarsman on the Captain's gig—until, that is, he can procure a substitute (161, 163). He especially detests the charade of training for combat; the call to general quarters "amounts to a general drawing and quartering of all the parties concerned," he says (64). What irks him most is his assigned post on the quarter-deck, where enemy sharpshooters may hit him instead of the officers they are aiming at: he has an "invincible repugnance to being shot for somebody else. If I am shot, be it with the express understanding in the shooter that I am the identical person intended so to be served" (66). But individuality, in life or death, is precisely what naval order denies as it reduces the sailor's body to mere physical mass, an object with a function but no "self." The officers use "man-of-war's-men," White-Jacket says, "as the sailors used their checker-men" (173).[18]

There is no escape from this physical regimentation, no private space or time, aboard the *Neversink*: "It is almost a physical impossibility, that you can ever be alone" (35). A sailor's belongings are kept in his bag or hammock, but he has access to his bag only once a day, and the hammocks are stowed away from eight in the morning until sunset. There are no "secret nooks" in a man-of-war: "Almost every inch is occupied; almost every inch is in plain sight; and almost every inch is continually being visited and explored" (41).

This rigid spatial order is based upon the Articles of War and the authorized violence that lies at their center. The Articles are read aloud to the crew once a month, "the burden of nearly every Article" being the possible sentence for the offense described: "*Shall suffer death!* The repeated announcement falls on your ear like the intermitting discharge of artillery" (293). The reading of the Articles, in which the seamen are threatened with corporal or capital punishment, is itself a dramatized act of violence, a series of "minute-guns" fired at the crew (294). White-Jacket may well "recoil" at each discharge, for he is trapped "in a sad box," unable to escape from the "gripe" of Martial Law (294, 295).

But it is the public administration of punishment—flogging—that most forcibly demonstrates the captain's absolute physical power. It is the cat that extends the spatial regulation of the sailor's body onto and into the body's surface, turning the body itself into the record of its powerlessness and dehumanization. All hands must "witness punishment," and the sailor knows that he, too,

> is liable at any time to be judged and condemned. And the inevitableness of his own presence at the scene; the strong arm that drags him in view of the scourge, and holds him there till all is over; forcing upon his loathing eye and soul the sufferings and groans of men . . . of his

own type and badge—all this conveys a terrible hint of the omnipotent authority under which he lives. (135)

The threat of the lash cannot be avoided and cannot be forgotten—White-Jacket even compares the call to witness punishment to "the Last Trump" on the Day of Judgment (135).

Naval officers defend such corporal punishment by saying that "it can be inflicted in a moment . . . when the prisoner's shirt is put on, *that* is the last of it" (139). But White-Jacket distinguishes between the momentary infliction of punishment and its lasting and fundamental effect: "the body [is] scarred for the whole term of the natural life" (142). The seaman carries the "traces" of his punishment to the grave and beyond—"with these marks on his back, this image of his Creator must rise at the Last Day" (142). Flogging, like tattooing, destroys the original form of the body, eradicating the sailor's resemblance to his God and thus denying his fundamental humanity.

"True dignity" may remain "untouched" by the lash, but this

> is one of the hushed things, buried among the holiest privacies of the soul; a thing between a man's God and himself; and forever undiscernible by our fellow-men, who account *that* a degradation which seems so to the corporal eye. But what torments must that seaman undergo who, while his back bleeds at the gangway, bleeds agonized drops of shame from his soul! (142)

The sailor's "true dignity" is "buried" in his soul; the "privacy" of the self is no longer the space *of* the body but instead a space *within* and *other than* the body.[19] His self-knowledge is now at odds with the judgments of others, which are based on the altered appearance of the body's surface.[20] The lash establishes an opposition between surface and depth, the inside and outside of the body, redefining the "true" self as interior and hidden, no longer coextensive with the body. But the act of demarcation must cut across the line it would establish: since body and soul begin as one, physical wounds are necessarily also psychological ones, outer scars also inner ones. The extreme punishment of "flogging through the fleet" may or may not lead to the victim's death, but it always means the death of his earlier, innocent self: "he never is the man he was before, but [is] broken and shattered to the marrow of his bones" (371).

One of the crucial moments in the novel comes when White-Jacket is himself threatened with flogging for not being at his assigned post during a maneuver. His fear and rage have an instantaneous physical effect on him; he *feels* his body with a new and sudden intensity, as if it is already a corpse instead of a "self." "My blood seemed clotting in my veins," he recalls, "I felt icy cold at the tips of my fingers, and a dimness was before my eyes" (280). "I felt my man's manhood so bottomless within me," White-Jacket says, "that no word, no blow, no scourge of Captain Claret could cut me deep enough for that," but he nevertheless thinks of rushing at the captain and throwing them both overboard, to let Jehovah "decide between us" (280). "I but swung to an instinct in me," he says, "the privilege, inborn and inalienable, that every man has, of dying himself, and inflicting death upon another . . . the last resources of an insulted and unendurable existence" (280). White-Jacket, like Tommo, finds himself forced either to suffer or to inflict violence, to kill or be killed, as he sees it. But several men step forward to vouch for him, and the captain allows him to go unscathed.[21]

Only one man—the ship's Surgeon—can limit the exercise of the captain's violent authority. He can prevent or delay a flogging or excuse sailors from duty by consigning them to the sick bay—confining them to a different place in the ship. But the *Neversink*'s surgeon, one Cadwallader Cuticle, uses his authority only to take this institutionalized violence to a new and grisly "scientific" extreme. As a surgeon, he exposes both the body's surface and its interior to public view; his objective is not to heal the body or restore its integrity, but to leave his own mark—the sign of his professional authority and power—upon it. He may play "the part of a Regenerator of life," but it is "Morbid Anatomy [that is] his peculiar love"—he has a collection of casts "representing all imaginable malformations of the human members" (259, 249).

When a seaman is shot in the leg while trying to sneak off the ship, Cuticle calls in other surgeons for a consultation. Despite his protestations that " 'I feel no professional anxiety to perform the operation,' " Cuticle ignores their advice and proceeds to amputate the leg, even though the patient may " 'be entirely made whole, without risking an amputation' " (253–54). The Surgeon takes a cool and perverse pleasure in creating his own malformations: " 'how much better,' " he says, " 'to have the contusions and lacerations' " of a wound " 'converted into a clean incision' " (256). He is reminiscent less of the Typee "doctor" than of Karky or their unseen cooks: the table on which his surgical instruments are placed is, in fact, compared to "a dinner-table." For White-Jacket, the operation is only "scientific" cannibalism; it turns a living body into an anatomical specimen, an object of knowledge, but an object nonetheless. The surgery ends with the sailor "parted in twain at the hip" (262); the loss of a part of the body is not merely a quantitative change, but a qualitative one, as radical a fragmentation as if the body had been sawn in half. Such a loss cannot be survived—the sailor dies, and Cuticle exhibits both leg and body the following morning (264).[22]

If Tommo can escape from his threatening confinement, White-Jacket cannot: he can only respond to the conditions aboard the *Neversink* by trying to protect his body. Nothing can save him from the unnatural violence of the captain's lash or the surgeon's knife, but he makes his white jacket as a "shelter" against the weather (3). It is nothing more than a shirt, an "interior" garment folded over on itself, but once it has been slit open lengthwise, it undergoes a "metamorphosis" into an exterior covering (3). The metamorphosis remains incomplete, however, for even though White-Jacket pads the inside of the jacket, he is not allowed to waterproof it with a coat of paint.

From the moment of its creation, the jacket is doomed to failure. In the cold weather off Cape Horn, the seamen lie "in a state of half-conscious torpidity," almost "freezing alive, without the power to rise and shake themselves" (119). But when White-Jacket tries to move around, "to break the icy spell," "[t]he first fling of my benumbed arm generally struck me in the face, instead of smiting my chest, its true destination. . . . in these cases one's muscles have their own way" (119). Even with the protection of the jacket, his body escapes from his control, with the uncontrolled violence of its movements turned against itself. The penetrating cold creates an anesthetizing split between mind and body: "In such weather any man could have undergone amputation with great ease, and helped take up the arteries himself" (101). The body becomes both alien and unreliable, almost dangerous: "our hands and feet were so numb that we dared not trust our lives to them" (108). Protecting the body is at once essential and impossible; mittens, for example, are no help at all—aloft, the sailors "literally carry their lives in their hands, and want nothing between their grasp of the hemp, and the hemp itself" (36). Protecting the body's surface means blurring the sailor's sense of his own body and thus endangering his life.

In a storm, the sailor's awareness of his body as a defined and limited space seems to drift away completely: "You become identified with the tempest; your insignificance is lost in the riot of the stormy universe around" (108). If the differentiation between the body and what lies outside it, between self and other, breaks down, death is the inevitable result, as

Ishmael will discover on the mast-head in *Moby-Dick*. No jacket can adequately insulate the body's surface as a boundary or maintain the body as a single, functioning unit.

The jacket's whiteness becomes a sign of its vulnerability to both cold and rain:[23] "in a rain-storm I became a universal absorber . . . long after the rain storms were over, and the sun showed his face, I still stalked a Scotch mist; and when it was fair weather with others, alas! it was foul weather with me" (4). Instead of keeping out moisture, the jacket seems to attract it, shrinking into a "soaked and heavy . . . burden" (4).

The garment's permeability leads to the failure of its other major purpose—as a storehouse or private space. The only "thing" that the sailor has with him all the time, the only "space" he can call his own, is that defined by his body. White-Jacket intends, in making his jacket, to create an extension of his body and its privileged space:

> I proposed, that not only should my jacket keep me warm, but that it should also be so constructed as to contain a shirt or two, a pair of trowsers, and divers knickknacks . . . I had accordingly provided it with a great variety of pockets, pantries, clothes-presses, and cupboards. . . . my jacket, like an old castle, was full of winding stairs, and mysterious closets, crypts, and cabinets; and like a confidential writing-desk, abounded in snug little out-of-the-way lairs and hiding-places. (36)

As White-Jacket's imagery suggests, the jacket is designed as an alternative to the dehumanizing spatial organization of the ship, as a "castle" or second body constructed to enclose, to both defend and hide, the self. This is a gesture of rebellion against the captain's authority—his comparison of the jacket to a "confidential writing-desk" connects it with the activity of writing, which the officers (and White-Jacket himself) regard as implicitly mutinous.[24]

White-Jacket is at first elated by the apparent success of his plan: "I fairly hugged myself, and reveled in my jacket; till alas! a long rain put me out of conceit of it. I, and all my pockets and their contents, were soaked through and through, and my pocket-edition of Shakspeare was reduced to an omelet" (37).[25] The jacket's permeability makes it a poor storehouse; and when White-Jacket "discharges" his "saturated cargo" in order to dry it in the sun, his fellow sailors discover the garment's "hidden" purpose (37). He finds himself dogged by pickpockets, who make off with several items that very night. "So, in the end, I masoned up my lockers and pantries; and

save the two used for mittens, the white jacket ever after was pocketless"
(37). Despite his efforts, White-Jacket finds himself unable to extend or
protect his body as the essential constituent of his identity aboard ship.

The jacket is, in fact, *worse* than a failure. Originally intended to encase
and protect the body, it is taken by others to stand for and replace the body.
White-Jacket's nickname, after all, refers neither to his body nor to his
history or genealogy but to the secondary, exterior garment. The jacket is
used by the officers to identify him against his will; while the other men are
"secure from detection—their identity undiscoverable" at night, "my own
hapless jacket forever proclaimed the name of its wearer. It gave me many a
hard job, which otherwise I should have escaped. . . . how easy, in that mob
of incognitoes, to individualize '*that white jacket*,' and dispatch him on the
errand" (120–21). The jacket that was to provide an escape from the officers'
control only places him more firmly within it. The garment that was to
protect the integrity of the body is given a metonymic status, made not to
represent but to replace the body as a sign of identity. Turning the jacket
into a sign for the self implicitly denies both the primacy and the integrity of
the body, making it dependent on the sign/jacket if it is to be known or
identified. An inanimate object, whose primary feature—its color(less-
ness)—is beyond White-Jacket's control, thus displaces his body as the
sufficent and unmediated ground of identity. It is a paradigmatic instance of
his self-alienation on board the *Neversink*.

White-Jacket eventually tries to separate or distinguish himself from
his jacket. He attempts to exchange it for another sailor's (121), and then to
have it auctioned off (201–02):

> But no, alas! there was no getting rid of it, except by rolling a forty-
> two-pound shot in it, and committing it to the deep. But though, in
> my desperation, I had once contemplated something of that sort, yet I
> had now become unaccountably averse to it . . . If I sink my jacket,
> thought I, it will be sure to spread itself into a bed at the bottom of the
> sea, upon which I shall sooner or later recline, a dead man. So, unable
> to conjure it into the possession of another, and withheld from bury-
> ing it out of sight forever, my jacket stuck to me like the fatal shirt on
> Nessus. (203)

Although White-Jacket had at first resisted giving the jacket even a metonymic relation to the self, he has, despite his efforts to detach himself from it,
come to view the jacket as synecdochally linked to his body, an ultimately

inseparable part of it. Discarding the jacket means losing a part of his body; "burying" it implies his own death and burial. His attempts to dissociate himself from his garment soon become merely rhetorical: "'Blast my jacket you may,'" he tells his messmates, "'I'll join you in *that*; but don't blast *me*'" (333). "Jacket! jacket!," he cries, "thou hast much to answer for" (334).

In the end, however, and in the hindsight of narration, the jacket is revealed to be inimical to the self, threatening rather than preserving the body. The jacket is "white, yea, white as a shroud. And my shroud it afterward came very near proving" (3). On two occasions, it "came near being the death of me" (76). He is asleep one night "high up on the main-royal-yard . . . the white jacket folded around me" (77). The sailors, taking him for the dead cooper's ghost, suddenly drop the yard down to the deck, "to test my corporeality" (78). The jacket is taken not as a sign for his body but as a mark of *bodilessness*.

White-Jacket "tears off" his garment and throws it on the deck:

> "Jacket," cried I, "you must change your complexion! you must hie to the dyers and be dyed, that I may live. I have but one poor life, White Jacket, and that life I can not spare. I can not consent to die for *you*, but be dyed you must for me. You can dye many times without injury; but I can not die without irreparable loss, and running the eternal risk." (78)

He first personifies the jacket, giving it a "complexion," but then reasserts its inanimate status in the pun that follows. The jacket can be dyed or altered without a radical change in its status; its original form or color has no special privilege. The body, on the other hand, is not a "made" object; it cannot be changed and still remain itself—dyeing and dying would be one and the same.

The jacket once again comes "near proving [its owner's] shroud" when White-Jacket is sent aloft one night. The wind blows its skirts over his head, and he is thrown into the sea in trying to free himself. His limbs "involuntarily threw themselves out," and when "some fashionless form brushed my side, . . . the thrill of being alive," the sensation of embodiment itself, "tingled in my nerves, and the strong shunning of death shocked me through" (393). It is the body itself that first instinctively responds to and resists the threat of death; only then does "an agonizing revulsion" come over him as he begins to sink (393). He tries to swim toward the ship, but instantly I was conscious of a feeling like being pinioned in a feather-bed, and, moving my hands, felt my jacket puffed out above my tight girdle with water. I strove to tear it off; but it was looped together here and there, and the strings were not then to be sundered by hand. I whipped out my knife, that was tucked at my belt, and ripped my jacket straight up and down, as if I were ripping open myself. With a violent struggle I then burst out of it, and was free. (394)

The jacket imprisons the body, and threatens it with drowning. White-Jacket must cut it open, repeating and undoing the gash by which it was created. It is "as if I were ripping open myself"—he must inflict violence on the object that has usurped the privileged position of the body. This symbolic murder of the false body is required for the true body, the true self, to "burst out" and be "free." The jacket, slowly sinking, is taken for a shark by the sailors on deck, and "the next instant [a] barbed bunch of harpoons pierced through and through the unfortunate jacket, and swiftly sped down with it out of sight" (394). The jacket has threatened to engulf, to consume and replace the body, and it must be metaphorically killed if White-Jacket is to survive and write his book.[26]

Even in the "civilized" world, bodily identity can never be adequately enclosed or defended. A garment or covering may seem to protect the body, but in doing so it either displaces the body as the primary ground of identity or proves antithetical to it. The disciplinary order of a man-of-war—and, by extension, that of society as a whole—is built upon the transformation of the body into a physical, mechanical mass; no exterior barrier can avert this radical alienation of self from body. The bodily self is always vulnerable; the dangers of embodiment are inherent and inescapable.

2.

As early as *Mardi*, published a year before *White-Jacket*, Melville has begun to consider the altered or *internally* damaged body: the "original" and "unmarked" body has already become a nostalgic ideal rather than a reality for him. Embodiment itself is described as a *limit*: "Though your ear be next-door to your brain, it is forever removed from your sight. . . . It is because we ourselves are in ourselves, that we know ourselves not" (296–97).

In *Mardi*, Melville examines not a symbolic self-mutilation or suicide but a quite literal one. Samoa's arm has been mangled and "shattered" in a fight, and it is soon "in such a state, that amputation became necessary" (70, 71, 77). But in Polynesia, unlike aboard the *Neversink*, "every man is his own barber or surgeon, cutting off his beard or arm, as occasion demands" (77). "The warriors of Varvoo," according to Melville's narrator Taji, are forced by the clumsiness of their instruments to perform such operations in stages, over a period of days: "Hence it may be said, that they amputate themselves at their leisure, and hang up their tools when tired" (77). The identity of surgeon and patient seems to make the loss of a body part less traumatic, for the process of amputation is integrated into the temporality of daily life and made dependent on the strength and stamina of the body itself. This may *seem* to be the case, but Melville's wording ("they amputate *themselves*") insists that it is the *self*, not just a physical object, that is being divided.

Samoa in fact consigns the task of amputation to his wife, but the process is quick, and the wound heals fast. The philosophical consequences of the operation are no less radical, however. "Three strokes, and the limb . . . was no longer Samoa's," Taji says; it has lost its integral relation to the rest of the body, and thus can no longer be said to "belong" to it (78). But Samoa is "superstitiously averse to burying in the sea the dead limb of a body yet living; since in that case [he] held, that he must very soon drown and follow it; . . . equally dreading to keep the thing near him, he at last hung it aloft from the top-mast-stay" (78). Samoa, like White-Jacket, has a "superstitious" belief that the body will somehow reunite with its lost part, even if it means the death of the whole. But if he cannot throw the limb overboard, neither can he bear its presence near him as a continual reminder of his bodily incompletion, his physical difference from his earlier self.

The narrator takes up the question of this difference within the self from another perspective:

> Now, which was Samoa? The dead arm swinging high as Haman? Or the living trunk below? Was the arm severed from the body, or the body from the arm? The residual part of Samoa was alive, and therefore we say it was he. But which of the writhing sections of a ten times severed worm, is the worm proper? (78)

If identity is vested in the body's "original" integral state, in its "whole-ness," then no part of the body, large or small, living or dead, can serve to define the self. The consequences of amputation and self-amputation are the same—Samoa is no longer himself. He is "but a large fragment of a man, not a man complete" (78). "A man complete" is a tautology here, for "a man *in*complete" is no longer a man, and certainly no longer "the same man."[27]

Samoa's loss of an arm is, however, only one of a series of bodily mutilations he has undergone. Not only does he wear "a well polished nail" through his nose, "but he wore his knife in the lobe of his dexter ear, which, by constant elongation almost drooped upon his shoulder" (98). Such an incorporation of external objects into the body destroys its spatial integrity, disfiguring Samoa for life. "In other respects," the narrator adds,

> he was equally a coxcomb. In his style of tattooing, for instance, which seemed rather incomplete; his marks embracing but a vertical half of his person, from crown to sole; the other side being free of the slightest stain. Thus clapped together, as it were, he looked like a union of the unmatched moieties of two distinct beings; and your fancy was lost in conjecturing, where roamed the absent ones. When he turned round upon you suddenly, you thought you saw some one else, not him whom you had been regarding before. (98–99)

Samoa's tattoos are a spatial representation of the *temporal* disjunction created by tattooing. He is a living embodiment of the contrast between "before" and "after" that divides the self from its previous bodily existence. He is in this sense an imperfect union of the fragments of two men, a union that cannot even simulate the integrity of a whole, but can only mark its absence. Samoa is both himself and "some one else" at the same time. The marking of the body's surface and the loss of its spatial integrity are here combined—the result is a radical and irreversible fragmentation of the self.

Melville's narrator does assert that one essential feature of Samoa's body remains unchanged: "his eye; which in civilized man or savage, ever shines in the head, just as it shone at birth" (99). "My Islander had a soul in his eye," he says, "looking out upon you there, like somebody in him" (99). The eye may contain the soul and indicate its permanence, but this soul, this "somebody," is an unidentified and separate "body" *within* the body, distinct from and finally alien to it. And even the eye is "brilliantly changeful as opal," constant and constantly changing at the same time (99).

The assertion that the self can remain intact despite bodily change or mutilation is sharply undercut, however, by Taji's frequent comparisons between Samoa and the Roman general Belisarius (73, 86, 98). For the rebellious Belisarius did not lose an arm—according to legend, he lost his sight.[28] The allusion suggests that Samoa's loss is at least analogous to the loss of his eyes, the supposed signs of the self's continuous existence within the body. The narrator's final, damning comparison is with Lord Nelson, who lost both an arm and an eye, and was thus "but three-quarters of a man" (78). However much Taji may wish to minimize the effects of Samoa's bodily fragmentation, his comparisons consistently imply a drastic loss of self-identity.

If Melville describes the disintegration of the bodily self in *Mardi*, it is not until *Moby-Dick* that he fully explores its psychological consequences— in his characterization of Captain Ahab. Ishmael, Melville's narrator, certainly senses the vulnerability of the body; he echoes White-Jacket in his desire to insulate or protect his body when he is aloft on the mast-head. It is a spot, he laments,

> destititute of anything approaching to a cosy inhabitiveness, or adapted to breed a comfortable localness of feeling . . . you may carry your house aloft with you, in the shape of a watch-coat; but properly speaking the thickest watch-coat is no more of a house than the unclad body; for as the soul is glued inside of its fleshly tabernacle, and cannot freely move about in it, nor even move out of it, without great risk of perishing . . . a watch-coat is not so much of a house as it is a mere envelope, or additional skin encasing you. You cannot put a shelf or chest of drawers in your body, and no more can you make a convenient closet of your watch-coat. (137)

The passage serves as a quick summary of White-Jacket's attempts to reshape his surroundings as an extension of his body. Ishmael differs from his predecessor, however, in that he accepts a distinction between soul and body, even as he insists on their inseparability. His narrative hindsight allows him to repeat and reject White-Jacket's image of jacket as house, emphasizing instead the impossibility of encasing and protecting the body.

It is the inseparability of self and body that now becomes the primary focus of "The Mast-Head," as Melville again reworks ideas from *White-Jacket*. Just as White-Jacket "give[s] loose to reflection" when he is aloft, and feels himself fused with the universe, "a part of the All" (76), philosophical reverie may lead the "absent-minded youth" on the mast-head to take "the mystic ocean at his feet for the visible image of that deep, blue, bottomless soul, pervading mankind and nature . . . In this enchanted mood, thy spirit ebbs away to whence it came; becomes diffused through time and space" (*Moby-Dick*, 140).[29] But such an apparent transcendence of the body is simply a loss of self: the young man "loses his identity." Even the dream of an escape from embodiment may well be fatal: "while this sleep, this dream is on ye, move your hand or foot an inch; slip your hold at all; and your identity comes back in horror" (140). The sleeping White-Jacket is suddenly dropped to the deck, but the "young Pantheist" risks dropping into the sea. The fusion of self and other leads to a potentially deadly fall, not a rebirth.

Like White-Jacket, Ishmael faces a series of challenges to his desire for a constant and self-contained physical identity on board ship. In Chapter 72, "The Monkey-Rope," he and Queequeg are bound together as part of the process of cutting into a dead whale: "should poor Queequeg sink to rise no more, then both usage and honor demanded, that instead of cutting the cord, it should drag me down in his wake" (271). Here it is not an object—a jacket—whose attachment to the body threatens it with drowning, but another body. Queequeg becomes Ishmael's double or twin, but they are "Siamese" twins—each of their bodies is incomplete, each dependent on its "inseparable twin brother" for survival (271). Chief among the "dangerous liabilities" of the bond is that it violates the integrity and wholeness of the body, and thus of the self: "my own individuality was now merged in a joint stock company of two," Ishmael says, "my free will had received a mortal wound" (271). The "marriage bond" between the two men has been turned into a "wedding" as unnatural and "detestable" (104) as a "joint stock company," a fictitious union that can only threaten the self with a "mortal wound" (271).[30]

In Chapter 94, "A Squeeze of the Hand," it is not Ishmael's body that is at risk, but rather his consciousness of its form and limits. He is assigned to squeeze the lumps out of the newly extracted sperm, but "after having my hands in it for only a few minutes," his fingers seem to lose their shape, to metamorphose into "eels," alien creatures that "serpentine and spiralize" away from him into the vat of sperm (348). The blurring of bodily sensation soon becomes a more radical loss of self-consciousness:

for the time I lived as in a musky meadow; I forgot all about our horrible oath; in that inexpressible sperm, I washed my hands and my heart of it . . . I squeezed that sperm till I myself almost melted into it; I squeezed that sperm till a strange sort of insanity came over me; and I found myself unwittingly squeezing my co-laborers' hands in it, mistaking their hands for the gentle globules. (348)

Just as Tommo "forgets" his troubles and "buries" his "sorrow" when native girls anoint his body with "fragrant oil" in *Typee* (110), Ishmael's self-forgetting also links diminished physical self-awareness to a surrender of memory and responsibility. Such a loss of self-consciousness is a "sort of insanity," a dissolution of the self to the point where hands and sperm, self and other, become indistinguishable in their fluidity and formlessness. It is the physical counterpart of the the the mast-head-stander's dream.[31]

This moment of visionary fusion is, however, sharply and immediately reversed, as Ishmael breaks off to describe a very different operation.[32] Down in the blubber-room, large pieces of blubber are cut into "portable horse-pieces" (350). The cutting-spade, Ishmael says, "is sharp as hone can make it; the spade-man's feet are shoeless; the thing he stands on will sometimes irresistibly slide away from him . . . Toes are scarce among veteran blubber-room men" (350). From an image of blending identities, Ishmael shifts abruptly to "a scene of terror" and self-mutilation (350). The diptych clearly links the two processes as opposite but equally radical threats to the body and the self.[33]

One of the things Ishmael forgets in squeezing sperm is "our horrible oath"—he forgets Ahab and the physical wound that lies behind his quest. If Ishmael's primary concern has been with fixing the body's outer limits, the cutting-spade returns him to the problem of maintaining its *internal* integrity—it brings him back to Ahab. In a sense, it is Ahab's loss of a leg that generates the action of the novel, for it dramatically alters his character, making him a different man in psychological as well as physical terms. "It is not probable," Ishmael says, that Ahab's monomania

> took its instant rise at the precise time of his bodily dismemberment. Then, in dashing at the monster, knife in hand, he had but given loose to a sudden, passionate, corporal animosity; and when he received the stroke that tore him, he probably but felt the agonizing bodily laceration, but nothing more. Yet, when by this collision forced to turn towards home, and for long months of days and weeks, Ahab and anguish lay stretched together in one hammock . . . then it was, that his torn body and gashed soul bled into one another; and so interfusing, made him mad. (160)

Like the scar left by the lash, Ahab's "bodily laceration" has direct psycho-logical consequences: when the body is "torn," the soul is "gashed." Here Ishmael expands his distinction between body and soul, describing them as different in *kind*, albeit inseparable and equally vulnerable. The self, he suggests, is structured by an *internal* difference; body and soul are an inseparable pair of interdependent terms. If the internal barrier between them is breached, the result is an "interfusing," a blending of inside and outside that is the germ of Ahab's madness.

This process of physical violation and psychological destabilization does not end when the captain's leg "heals," however. For Ahab cannot replace his lost leg, cannot repair the "tear" in his body and soul: as Elijah puts it, "'when Captain Ahab is all right, then this left arm of mine will be all right'" (87); recovery is a *physical* impossibility. "I lost *this* leg," Ahab says (147, my emphasis). But he cannot point to the leg itself; he can only indicate the ivory stump that marks its absence. The new leg can never be more than a mark of Ahab's physical incompletion, the sign of a lost wholeness. It can never become a part of his body, but must remain an alien object, essentially opposed to the body to which it is forcibly attached.[34] This fact is demonstrated with the utmost possible force when, shortly before the *Pequod* is to sail, Ahab is "found one night lying prone on the ground, and insensible; by some unknown, and seemingly inexplicable, unimaginable casualty, his ivory limb, having been so violently displaced, that it had stake-wise smitten, and all but pierced his groin" (385). The leg that was to "complete" the body *from without* becomes a stake driven *into* the body; the loss of a limb becomes a more essential loss, an emascula-tion.[35]

This undoing—both external and internal—of the opposition be-tween inside and outside becomes increasingly pervasive as the novel pro-gresses. It is the defining feature of Ahab's injury and his ensuing madness, so it must inevitably shape his "fiery hunt" as well. The inversion of inside and outside, surface and depth, becomes visible in "The Quarter-deck": just as the planks are "all over dented . . . with the peculiar mark" of Ahab's walk, so on his "ribbed and dented brow . . . you would see still stranger foot-prints—the foot-prints of his own unsleeping, ever-pacing thought" (140). The surface of the deck is marked from above by Ahab's leg, but his brow is marked from within by his thoughts. And on this occasion,

> those dents looked deeper, even as his nervous step that morning left a
> deeper mark. And, so full of his thought was Ahab, that at every

uniform turn that he made . . . you could almost see that thought turn
in him as he turned, and pace in him as he paced; so completely
possessing him, indeed, that it all but seemed the inward mould of
every outer movement. (141)

"Those dents" is necessarily ambiguous, referring to both the marks on the
deck and those on Ahab's brow. Ahab's thought and body are differentiated
here, the former within but almost coextensive with the latter. Cut into by
the jaws of the whale from without and molded by the mind from within—
the body seems little more than a hollow shell, the line of intersection
between outside and inside. When Ahab smites his chest, Stubb thinks "'it
rings most vast, but hollow'" (144).

This oscillation between inside and outside, this opposition between
soul and body, is described in greater psychological complexity in Chapter
44, "The Chart." Its final lengthy paragraph is a tortuous one, riddled with
pronouns whose referents remain unclear; this instability of reference suggests an indeterminacy and flux within Ahab himself:

[The captain's dreams,] resuming his own intense thoughts through
the day, . . . whirled them round and round in his blazing brain . . . and
when, as was sometimes the case, these spiritual throes in him heaved
his being up from its base, and a chasm seemed opening in him, from
which forked flames and lightnings shot up, and accursed fiends beckoned him to leap down among them; when this hell in himself yawned
beneath him, a wild cry would be heard through the ship; and with
glaring eyes Ahab would burst from his state room. (174)

The inner whirl of nightmare opens a chasm in, and at the same time
beneath, the space of the self. Ahab's "blazing brain" contains or generates
an unconscious realm of hellish disorder, a region that is and is not "part
of" or "within" the self.

Ishmael does, however, try to clarify the shifting relations between
these mental fragments:

crazy Ahab, the scheming, unappeasedly steadfast hunter of the white
whale; this Ahab that had gone to his hammock, was not the agent that
so caused him to burst from it in horror again. The latter was the
eternal, living principle or soul in him; and in sleep, being for the time
dissociated from the characterizing mind, which at other times em-

ployed it for its outer vehicle or agent, it spontaneously sought escape from the scorching contiguity of the frantic thing, of which, for the time, it was no longer an integral. (174–75)

The "eternal, living principle or soul" had earlier been opposed to the body; here it is also distinguished from the conscious mind. Ahab's mind, Ishmael says, uses his soul as its "outer vehicle"; the soul itself, it seems, is manipulated *from within*, by the "contiguous" mind. This, however, is an inversion of the true relation between mind and soul: "to the purely spiritual, the intellectual but stands in a sort of corporeal relation" (183)—the mind "embodies" the soul as the body does the mind.

Both the place and the meaning of "agency" undergo a shift here; Melville uses "agent" to designate first a primary and then a secondary, merely apparent cause. The notion of a "self" to which a single intention or desire can be attributed is being stripped away as Ishmael's description proceeds. The destruction of the link between soul and body is mirrored by the disintegration of that between mind and soul; Ahab's bodily self-alienation is reduplicated on the psychological level as well.[36]

"But as the mind does not exist unless leagued with the soul," Ishmael continues,

[Ahab's] purpose, by its own sheer inveteracy of will, [must have] forced itself . . . into a kind of self-assumed, independent being of its own. Nay, could grimly live and burn, while the common vitality to which it was conjoined, fled horror-stricken from the unbidden and unfathered birth. Therefore, the tormented spirit that glared out of bodily eyes, when what seemed Ahab rushed from his room, was for the time but a vacated thing, a formless somnambulistic being, a ray of living light, to be sure, but without an object to color, and therefore a blankness in itself. (175)

Mind and soul, like soul and body, cannot exist apart, but Ahab has forced them apart. Whether it is his "disembodied" soul or his mind that glares out of Ahab's eyes, it is pure emptiness, a "blankness" as terrifying as the whiteness of the whale. The complex and interdependent relationship among body, soul, and mind has been irretrievably ruptured as a result of Ahab's maddening wound. The loss of physical self-identity leads inexorably to the dissolution of psychological identity; the absence of Ahab's leg is followed and paralleled by an absence within the self.

Ahab recognizes the irreversibility of both his physical loss and the process of psychological fragmentation it has set in motion. No blacksmith can "smooth" the "seam" on his "ribbed brow": "'though thou only see'st it here in my flesh, it has worked down into the bone of my skull—*that* is all wrinkles!'" (403). He describes his monomania as "madness maddened! That wild madness that's only calm to comprehend itself!" (147), acknowledging the self-multiplying power of his psychological disintegration. There is no way to combat this internal process, no calm island within the self that is not already possessed by his madness. He has made himself into a "Prometheus," Ishmael says: "thy thoughts have created a creature in thee . . . a vulture feeds upon that heart for ever; that vulture the very creature he creates" (175).

Paradoxically, however, the violence of the conflict between Ahab's "special lunacy" and his "general sanity" only gives his madness "a thousand fold more potency" (161). His monomania turns this self-fragmenting force outward, identifying the absence within him with its polar opposite outside him, with the inscrutable and massive plenitude of the white whale:

> he at last came to identify with [Moby Dick], not only all his bodily woes, but all his intellectual and spiritual exasperations. The White Whale swam before him as the monomaniac incarnation of all those malicious agencies which some deep men feel eating in them, till they are left living on with half a heart and half a lung. (160)

For Ahab, Moby Dick is at once the object whose fullness corresponds to his own incompletion and the external embodiment of the divisive force he feels within him.[37] The white whale represents divisiveness itself, the "subtle demonisms of life and thought" that undermine and intermix the differential terms on which self-knowledge, and knowledge in general, can be based: "All that most maddens and torments; all that stirs up the lees of things; all truth with malice in it . . ." (160).

The captain does not wish to simply appropriate the whale's physical completeness. The whale's body is consumed and annihilated as it is transformed into sperm oil—an almost ritual process in which its potency is appropriated and absorbed (see Chapter 95, "The Cassock"); in this sense, a whaler is indeed a "cannibal of a craft" (67). Ahab's objective is not, however, to transform or consume the whale: his aim is simply destruction, to "dismember my dismemberer" (147), to become the agent rather than the victim of physical fragmentation.[38] But he can only become such an agent through an act of further *self*-victimization; in his attack on the whale, "as if his chest had been a mortar, he burst his hot heart's shell upon it" (160).[39] Ahab's hunt is inevitably suicidal.

This external projection of his own decay, with its repeated inversions of inside and outside, is clear in Ahab's speech to Starbuck in "The Quarter-deck," when he declares his aim to "'strike through the mask'" (144). "'How can the prisoner reach outside except by thrusting through the wall?'" he asks, "'To me, the white whale is that wall, shoved near to me. Sometimes I think there's naught beyond. But 'tis enough'" (144). The captain's desire to "strike through the mask" and into the body of the whale is at the same time a desire to break out of the prison of his own body.[40] The physical limits of the body are, for him, no longer a positive defining characteristic to be defended; the surface of the body is only a negative, imprisoning limit, the point at which the "outside" world, in the fullness of its otherness, presses in upon the self with annihilating force.[41]

Once the notion of bodily integrity has been abandoned, Ahab insists that fragmentation become the norm—he will dismember the whale (the world) as it has dismembered him, doing the violence that has been done to him. Where Tommo uses violence to defend his body and White-Jacket is prepared to do so, Ahab cannot strike out except to strike *back* in revenge. The result will be either the fragmentation of the whale's body or the discovery of the "naught beyond"; in either case, the production of a division or absence within the whale will mean that he is no longer Ahab's opposite but his mirror image. The internalization of difference at once multiplies and annihilates it, yielding an identity.

The one character who has confronted the absence at the heart of fullness is the castaway, Pip, but such knowledge, "heaven's sense," is "man's insanity" (347). "The sea," Ishmael says, "had jeeringly kept his finite body up, but drowned the infinite of his soul" (347), and this absolute disjunction between body and soul becomes the defining feature of Pip's madness. "'Pip? whom call ye Pip?'" he asks, "'Pip's missing'" (427). Body has been completely sundered from self, identity redefined as disembodiment.

It is Pip who provides the clearest image for Ahab's self-destructive pursuit. The doubloon Ahab has nailed to the mast as a prize for the first man to sight the whale is, the cabin-boy says, "'the ship's navel . . . and they are all on fire to unscrew it. But, unscrew your navel, and what's the consequence?'" (363). The consequence, of course, is that one's bottom falls off. "Unscrewing" a part of the body—in this case, the part that is a sign of the body's very existence as an independent entity—is only the first step in a process of disintegration that cannot be stopped.[42]

Ahab in turn places Pip "'in my own screwed chair'" in the captain's cabin, telling him "'another screw to it, thou must be'" (436). The cabin-boy replies that "'ye have not a whole body, sir; do ye but use me for your one lost leg . . . I ask no more, so I remain a part of ye.'" He offers his soulless body as a substitute for Ahab's lost leg, himself as the captain's complementary opposite. But Ahab knows that Pip can never be a part of him, knows that his physical and psychological wounds are irreparable even in metaphorical terms.[43] Pip remains at the center of the ship, in the captain's place, becoming another symbolic "navel," a sign of Ahab's own self-alienation and madness.

In Ahab's case, the alienation of self from body does approach the limit represented by Pip. With the destabilization of the opposition between inside and outside, Ahab loses the sense of his body as a distinct and inviolable space. His body's space has already been violated, and is continually reviolated by the sign of that violation—his ivory leg. For Ahab still feels his "old lost leg" as if it were present: "Look," he says to the carpenter, "put thy live leg here in the place where mine once was; so, now, here is only one distinct leg to the eye yet two to the soul. Where thou feelest tingling life . . . there to a hair, do I" (391). Ahab's internal, proprioceptive sensation of embodiment no longer corresponds to his intellectual and visual sense of his body, but now stands opposed to it as a mere delusion.[44]

If two legs—old and new, real and artificial—can seem to occupy the same space at the same time, it is no longer possible to identify the self with the body, for the body has ceased to exist as a spatial unit. "How dost thou know," Ahab asks the carpenter, "that some entire, living, thinking thing may not be invisibly and uninterpenetratingly standing precisely where thou now standest; aye, and standing there in thy spite?" (391). The captain's body has undergone a radical alteration, so that it is no longer self-identical in temporal terms, but now he suggests that the body may never have been spatially self-identical, that its space can be its own and another's at the same time. His anguished question, "'Is Ahab, Ahab?'" (445), can be read in several ways: Is Ahab *still* the same man as the Ahab who had not yet encountered the white whale? Was the bodily being identified as Ahab *ever* the same as Ahab the man?

What Ahab comes to realize is that the body cannot, even in its ostensibly "original" and unaltered form, be taken as an integral and inviolable whole. The division between self and other may be located along the line of the body's surface, but that surface is radically permeable,[45] and the self-definition it provides must remain arbitrary and vulnerable, haunted by "that old Adam"—the temporal and physical fragility of human life (391). Ahab's ivory leg is only an external sign of the body's inevitable internal decay and death. Ishmael's comparison of feeding whales to "mowers" (234) is not a casual one; he deliberately makes them part of the natural cycle of growth and harvesting. The white whale's ferocity represents that of Time itself: "sweeping his sickle-shaped lower jaw beneath him, Moby Dick had reaped away Ahab's leg as a mower a blade of grass in the field" (159–60). The whale can take part of the captain's body only because the entire body will one day be "reaped away."[46] Ahab's rage against the whale is indeed "the general rage and hate felt by his whole race from Adam down" (160), man's rage against his own mortality, against the *curse* of embodiment itself. "'Accursed fate!'" he cries, "'that the unconquerable captain in the soul should have such a craven mate'" in the subordinated but vulnerable otherness of the body (458).

This sense of the body as a sign of human limitation, both physical and moral, has already appeared as a secondary theme in *Redburn*. Here Melville moves beyond the possibility that the body may suffer a violent alteration from without, suggesting that it may remain apparently intact and still be possessed or consumed by something within but other than itself.

On the *Highlander*'s first night at sea, a man rushes on deck, "trembling and shrieking in the most frightful manner, so that I thought one of the sailors must be murdered below" (50). Redburn first thinks the man's terror is a response to external violence, a murder, but it is actually a prelude to violence of a different sort—"almost before we knew what it was, the shrieking man jumped over the bows into the sea" (50). This is one of the sailors who had been brought aboard unconscious, "dead drunk": "He must have suddenly waked up, I suppose, raging mad with the delirium tremens . . . and finding himself in a strange silent place, and knowing not how he had got there, he had rushed on deck, and so, in a fit of frenzy, put an end to himself" (50). Delirium tremens is a physical reaction with psychological effects—hallucinations. Here it leads to a "raging madness" that results in suicide. The body is, in a sense, "possessed" by a hallucinatory delirium of its own making, a delirium that leads to bodily self-destruction. The young Redburn does not understand how the body can thus turn on itself—but he finds that it is his bunk that the dead man had occupied, and that he now lies in the dead man's place.

In a later chapter, "A Living Corpse," the boy is shown a parallel instance of the body consuming and destroying itself. One of the men carried aboard ship in Liverpool, supposedly "in a state of intoxication" (243), turns out to be a corpse. A sailor holds a light to the man's face, and when "the yellow flame wavered for a moment at the seaman's motionless mouth," this is taken as a sign of life:

> But hardly had the words escaped, when, to the silent horror of all, two threads of greenish fire, like a forked tongue, darted out between the lips; and in a moment, the cadaverous face was crawled over by a swarm of worm-like flames. . . .
>
> The eyes were open and fixed; the mouth was curled like a scroll, and every lean feature firm as in life; while the whole face, now wound in curls of soft blue flame, wore an aspect of grim defiance, and eternal death. Prometheus, blasted by fire on the rock. (244)

The flame that at first seems to detect life only reveals "eternal death," as the body burns, consuming itself. Redburn's description of the flames as "worm-like" links the incident to a traditional image of bodily corruption and decay. And all the while the man's features remain intact, "firm as in life." If the allusion to Prometheus suggests that this physical destruction is a neverending punishment for mortal presumption, Redburn soon provides an explicitly religious comparison: "I almost thought the burning body was a premonition of the hell of the Calvinists, and that Miguel's earthly end was a foretaste of his eternal condemnation" (245). Physical corruption is inseparable from spiritual corruption, the inevitable mortal consequence of man's fallen state.

The image of mortality and corruption that "haunts" the narrator "to this day" is, however, embodied in his shipmate Jackson (57). According to Redburn, he is "as yellow as gambodge," his hair has fallen out, and his nose is "broken down the middle" (56). But it is Jackson's eye, like Samoa's, that is the main outward sign of his spiritual condition: "he squinted with one eye, and did not look very straight out of the other . . . one glance of his squinting eye, was as good as a knock-down, for it was the most deep, subtle, infernal looking eye, that I ever saw lodged in a human head" (56, 57). Jackson's eye manifests the internal violence of physical and psychological decay—he is clearly no longer the image of his Creator. Rather than bearing the mark of an immortal origin, "he carried about with him the traces of [his own vicious career], and the mark of a fearful end at hand"— he is "a Cain afloat" (58, 104). Redburn also compares him to Milton's Satan, who "dilutes our abhorrence with admiration . . . only because he is not a genuine being, but something altered from a genuine original" (276). Jackson's physical decay is an "alteration" of God's image, and it is the alteration that Redburn finds so terrifying, for every man is, to one degree or another, changed by his experience, "marked" as fallen from God's immortal perfection.

"Nothing was left of this Jackson but the foul lees and dregs of a man," but the loss is an internal one: he "was being consumed by an incurable malady, that was eating up his vitals" (58). His interior decay is visible only indirectly—Redburn sees something in his eye like the "forked tongue" of flame issuing from the burning corpse (60). This inner contagion manifests itself more clearly in psychological terms: "He seemed to be full of hatred and gall against every thing and every body in the world; as if all the world was one person, and had done him some dreadful harm, that was rankling and festering in his heart" (61). Jackson is "consumed" by hatred, regarding the world outside him as "one person," a single healthy "body" that is responsible for his own disease; he is a two-legged forerunner of Ahab. And his ill-will may be contagious: Jackson's hatred sets the crew against Redburn as well, making him "a sort of Ishmael in the ship," and he begins "to feel a hatred growing up in me against the whole crew—so much so, that I prayed against it, that it might not master my heart so completely, and so make a fiend of me, something like Jackson" (62). Redburn's fear of Jackson implies that he sees his own potential—every man's potential—for such spiritual estrangement and decay.

As his illness worsens, Jackson becomes more clearly demonic, "such a hideous looking mortal, that Satan himself would have run from him" (57). "[T]he malady which had long fastened its fangs in his flesh, was now gnawing into his vitals," permeating the space of his body:

> His cheek became thinner and yellower, and the bones projected like those of a skull. His snaky eyes rolled in red sockets . . . The weaker and weaker he grew, the more outrageous became his treatment of the crew. The prospect of the speedy and unshunable death now before him, seemed to exasperate his misanthropic soul into madness; and as if he had indeed sold it to Satan, he seemed determined to die with a curse between his teeth. (275, 276)

Jackson becomes a *memento mori*, his "snaky" eyes resting in the blood-red sockets of an empty skull. He is a riveting image of death in life, another "living corpse." When he comes on deck for the last time, after a month of inactivity below, "the blue hollows of his eyes were like vaults full of snakes; and issuing so unexpectedly from his dark tomb in the forecastle, he looked like a man raised from the dead" (295). The only life in his body is that of deadly snakes; otherwise it is an empty "vault," a tomb.

Redburn has feared that Jackson will "do some terrible thing" (61), but as in the case of the drunken suicide, Jackson's latent violence emerges only in one last self-destructive climb into the rigging, which leads to a final bloody cough and a fall into the sea. Afterwards, the sailors "never made the slightest allusion" to him, seeming "to repress the recollection" of his tyranny over them (296, 297). With the dissolution of his body, even the memory of Jackson disappears into silence. He becomes "a nameless vagabond without an epitaph" (276). "None, but I," Redburn says, "narrate what he was" (276). It is Redburn's text that now gives Jackson renewed life, in an act of preservation that troubles him: "in historically canonizing on earth the condemned below," in giving them eternal life in the canon of historical texts, "we do but make ensamples of wickedness; and call upon ambition to do some great iniquity, and be sure of fame" (276).

Here Redburn hints at the dark side of his own narrative project. If the body is internally divided and decaying, the inevitability of this dissolution reveals the instability and inherent vulnerability of the identification of self with body; his response as writer has been to replace the mortal body with an immortal text. But no textual representation can have the ideal unity and immediacy of the body itself; it must remain divided and incomplete, reproducing within it facts and images that threaten and undermine the self it would preserve.

Redburn, White-Jacket, and Ishmael all attempt such a textual self-creation. For White-Jacket and Ishmael, it is an explicitly defensive project, one designed to escape or deflect the bodily dangers to which their narratives expose them. Ishmael will confront the whale in a different spirit than Ahab; he will seek to appropriate its bodily integrity in shaping his text. He prepares for this project by turning his own body into a text, by having the dimensions of the whale's skeleton tattooed onto his arm. "In my wild wanderings," he says,

> there was no other secure way of preserving such valuable statistics. But as I was crowded for space, and wished the other parts of my body

> to remain a blank page for a poem I was then composing . . . I did not
> trouble myself with the odd inches. (*Moby-Dick*, 376)

Such tattoos alter the body, to be sure, but the shape of the body also determines the tattoos, as "the odd inches" of the whale's measurements are lost. The "poem" Ishmael "composes" is, of course, Ishmael himself. He surrenders the integrity of his body in preserving such data, but only because he has already conceived the project of writing *Moby-Dick*, of substituting a textual body for the whale's body and an autobiographical text for his own. "Methinks my body is but the lees of my better being," he proclaims, "take my body who will, take it I say, it is not me" (41). But just as the exact dimensions of the whale are lost in transcription, so must the exact dimensions of the writer's experience be lost—autobiographical texts must also be fragmentary, haunted by images of an idealized, unified self that is beyond recovery or recreation.

III Genealogical Identity: Filial Repetition and Rebellion

IN A LETTER OF MARCH 3, 1849 to Evert Duyckinck, Melville discusses Ralph Waldo Emerson, one of whose lectures he had just attended. My interest here is not so much in Melville's estimate of Emerson as in the terms of his response. These terms are *genealogical*, but the literary genealogy Melville invokes is also one that he himself resists.

"I think Emerson is more than a brilliant fellow," he says:

> Be his stuff begged, borrowed, or stolen, or of his own domestic manufacture he is an uncommon man. . . . Lay it down that had not Sir Thomas Browne lived, Emerson would not have mystified—I will answer, that had not Old Zack's father begot him, Old Zack would never have been the hero of Palo Alto. The truth is that we are all sons, grandsons, or nephews or great-nephews of those who go before us. No man is his own sire. (*Letters*, 78)

Emerson, Melville says, can write only from within a literary tradition, from a particular point in a textual genealogy. No writer can escape the influence of his predecessors, for it is from them that he derives his own language and authority. They are his literary fathers, and he their son. Melville would thus deny to Emerson, and to himself, a primary or "original" relation to the world. Our fathers always "go before us"; their temporal priority is, finally, what defines us as their sons.

But Emerson wishes to escape this genealogy, to recover an unmediated and primary position of pure originality. This Melville describes as his "gaping flaw": the "insinuation, that had he lived in those days when the world was made, he might have offered some valuable suggestions" (79). For Melville, Emerson's desire to return to an ultimate point of origin, to be present at the creation, is both self-contradictory and self-defeating. For to recreate the universe is also necessarily to recreate oneself, to become

one's "own sire." And the return to a beginning is first and foremost a
return, a beginning again. The very notion of a return depends upon the
existence of a prior beginning, an original moment whose lost authority
remains unquestioned and unrecovered. "Never will the pullers-down be
able to cope with the builders-up," Melville remarks (79); never, in other
words, can one overcome the accumulated force of history and escape one's
genealogical inheritance.

On the other hand, Melville begins by claiming just such a position of
originality. His letter opens, in fact, with a gesture of violent resistance:
"Nay, I do not oscillate in Emerson's rainbow," Melville declares, "but
prefer rather to hang myself in mine own halter than swing in any other
man's swing" (78). His desire to escape from Emerson's influence seems
almost suicidal in its intensity. A page later, this image of death by stran-
gulation takes on a new resonance, for Melville goes on to say that "I love all
men who *dive*. Any fish can swim near the surface, but it takes a great whale
to go down stairs five miles or more" (79). If Emerson is a "thought-diver,"
an intellectual whale, Melville casts himself as an artistic Ahab, a whale-
hunter who will die entangled in his own line. He too would rewrite
history, the same history of which he insists Emerson is a part.

In his closing paragraph, Melville turns from Emerson to Shakespeare.
"I would to God," he says,

> Shakspeare had lived later, & promenaded in Broadway. Not that I
> might have had the pleasure of leaving my card for him at the Astor, or
> made merry with him over a bowl of the fine Duyckinck punch; but
> that the muzzle which all men wore on their souls in the Elizabethan
> day, might not have intercepted Shakspers [sic.] full articulations. For
> I hold it a verity, that even Shakspeare [sic.], was not a frank man to the
> uttermost. And, indeed, who in this intolerant Universe is, or can be?
> But the Declaration of Independence makes a difference. (79–80)

Melville does not wish to master or to have preceded Shakespeare. On the
contrary, he asserts that his position as nineteenth-century American son is
freer than that of his English literary ancestor. But he does long for the
presence, in New York, in 1849, of a figure of Shakespeare's indisputable
authority. He would make his literary forefathers his *contemporaries*, be-
stowing upon them his freedom as he claims a share of their authority.
Rather than yearning to be "his own sire," Melville would overcome the

distance between father and son by abolishing paternity altogether, replacing it with a democratic brotherhood of equals.[1]

Melville thus takes several different and contradictory positions in this two-page letter. At one point he expresses a desire for a union with his "fathers"; at another he acknowledges his inevitable distance from them; and at a third he seems driven to rebel against their influence. All these different attitudes toward paternal authority reappear in his novels: in *Redburn*, *Moby-Dick*, and *Pierre*, Melville explores the relationship between father and son, investigating the consequences and limits of a genealogically defined identity.[2] His protagonists all describe themselves as sons of absent or lost fathers, and their differing responses to this loss mark the trajectory of Melville's thought.

After touching on the subject in *Typee*, Melville begins to examine genealogy directly in *Redburn*: here the young hero tries to imitate his father, to repeat his actions and thus assume his experiential and linguistic authority. In *Moby-Dick*, Ishmael also longs for a father's presence, but recognizes that no unifying repetition is possible, that the "paternal secret" on which he would base his identity is beyond recovery. Ahab's response to his absent father, on the other hand, is to project an irreducible antagonism between father and son, to define himself *in opposition to* his father. Pierre finally discovers paternal authority to be itself a fiction, but one that every son must simultaneously expose and internalize in his own self-destructive rebellion.

A recurrent problem for psychoanalytic readings of Melville has been his repeated emphasis on *absent* fathers and father figures. In order to speak of Oedipal conflicts, critics must often project paternal figures into the novels for Melville's narrator/sons to rebel against. Readers from Newton Arvin through Eric Sundquist have, for example, identified Moby Dick as a paternal symbol, only to qualify the judgment almost immediately, granting the whale female qualities as well.[3] In a way, such critical projections simply echo those of Ahab and Pierre; Melville himself has already thematized the interpreter's need for father figures to struggle against.

Among more recent writers, Neal Tolchin and Régis Durand have chosen to begin with the question of paternal absence. Tolchin reads the novels in terms of Melville's unresolved grief for his own father; Durand uses Lacan's concept of the "name-of-the-father" to link the absent father to problems of linguistic authority and narrative form.[4] My vocabulary is neither Oedipal nor Lacanian, but my focus is also on problems of naming and verbal mastery—both are attributes of the lost father throughout Melville's fiction. It is language that at once links and separates father and son, identifying and enabling the son while reserving ultimate authority and meaning as the property of the dead patriarch.

I.

Paternity appears as a secondary concern in *Typee*, where it is one of a cluster of issues that define the cultural differences between Tommo and the islanders. The absence of patriarchal family structures among the natives is closely linked to their lack of both a temporal or historical consciousness and a written language. Just as Tommo tries to preserve his body as an unmarked whole, he clings to his language and sense of history; just as life among the Typees threatens his bodily identity, it also undermines his temporal identity, his position in a written paternal history.

The book begins outside the Typee valley, in a larger world that Tommo presents as the realm of history, in which the colonization of the Pacific proceeds apace. As the story opens, his ship is approaching the Marquesas, and Tommo spends a paragraph describing his "jumbled anticipations": "Naked houris—cannibal banquets—groves of cocoa-nut," etc. (5). His curiosity is, he says, "to see those islands which the olden voyagers had so glowingly described" (5). Tommo's images come from written descriptions of earlier voyages; he sets out to place his experience in the context of a preexisting history of exploration and colonization, and devotes the rest of his first chapter to historical comments and anecdotes.

This combination of temporality and authorship will be reasserted in genealogical terms at the novel's end, for Tommo will come to see the timeless, repetitive life of the Typees as a fundamental threat to his identity as son and writer. Time passes "almost imperceptibly" among the natives, and Tommo gradually loses "all knowledge of the regular recurrence of the days of the week" (97, 123). "I gave myself up to the passing hour," he says, and "sought to bury all regrets, and all remembrances of my previous existence" (124, 144). His primary accommodation to Typee culture is this "forgetting": he forgets the passage of time and his own previous existence in time. In "burying" his "regrets" and "remembrances," he abandons the continuity of memory that defines the self. He "gives himself up" in accepting the atemporal, antihistorical world of the Typees.

"[W]ith these unsophisticated savages," Tommo remarks, "the history of a day is the history of a life" (149). The days succeed one another, each indistinguishable from its predecessor, each forgotten in its turn. The Typees' "time" is repetitive rather than cumulative, mythical rather than historical.[5] At the base of one of the island's mountains there stands a massive temple, now overgrown and crumbling:

> These structures bear every indication of a very high antiquity, and Kory-Kory . . . gave me to understand that they were coeval with the creation of the world; that the great gods themselves were the builders; and that they would endure until time shall be no more. Kory-Kory's prompt explanation, and his attributing the work to a divine origin, at once convinced me that neither he nor the rest of his countrymen knew anything about them. (154–55)

The temple's beginning and its end both lie outside human time, according to Tommo's guide, but such a mythic explanation is, for Tommo, only historical ignorance. "There are no inscriptions, no sculpture, no clue, by which to conjecture [the temple's] history," he laments (155).

But "how many generations of those majestic trees which overshadow them have grown and flourished and decayed since first [these structures] were erected!" Tommo exclaims (155). For him, history is a matter of "generations," a line of succession that depends on the concepts of ancestry and paternity.[6] The Typees are, however, a matriarchal rather than patriarchal society, lacking precisely the sense of paternal ancestry that might connect them with the builders of the ruined temple.

"A regular system of polygamy exists among the islanders," Tommo notes, but it involves "a plurality of husbands, instead of wives . . . No man has more than one wife, and no wife of mature years has less than two husbands" (191). The Typees, as a result, have only a loose family structure, with no clear sequence of generations and no particular authority vested in the familial elders. Tommo describes the entire tribe as "one household": "The love of kindred I did not so much perceive, for it seemed blended in the general love . . . it was hard to tell who were actually related to each other by blood" (204). Without a patriarchal line of descent, the basis of a historical consciousness, the temporal and authoritative difference between generations cannot exist.

Other aspects of Typee culture also militate against the formation of genealogical identity: Tommo sees a small boy who "bore a marvellous resemblance to" the Typee chief, "whom I should certainly have believed to have been the father, were it not that the little fellow had no triangle upon his face—but on second thoughts, tattooing is not hereditary" (190). Tattooing, a primary social ritual for the natives, works to obscure or destroy the link between father and son. Along with their matriarchy and polyandry, it reinforces the Typees' lack of temporal or historical awareness.

A primary constituent of any historical consciousness would, of course, be written language. But the Typee language is completely oral, and heavily reliant on gesture (142). It is "very difficult to be acquired," Tommo claims, the main difficulties being its "duplication of words," and the "different senses in which one and the same word is employed . . . the particular meaning being shown chiefly by a variety of gestures and the eloquent expression of the countenance" (224–25). Acts of speech are ephemeral, entirely dependent on the presence and performance of the speaker—lost at the moment of utterance.

The Typees' existence in an eternal present is thus inseparable from their lack of both a patriarchal or generational consciousness and a written language. For Tommo, history and paternity remain identified with written English. His final disillusionment with life in the valley comes when he finds that "[t]here was no one with whom I could freely converse; no one to whom I could communicate my thoughts" (231). Tommo never admits to having learned the Typee language—as if the ability to speak it would deprive him of his linguistic inheritance as a speaker of English.[7] The power of language is finally attested to during Tommo's escape, as Marheyo assents to his departure by pronouncing "the only two English words I had taught him—'Home' and 'Mother'" (248). Given the maternal and atemporal basis of Typee culture, these are perhaps the only English words he could have taught Marheyo—although "Time" and "Father" are crucial for Tommo, they must remain incomprehensible abstractions for the natives. But even if Tommo cannot explain these concepts, he has nevertheless established the authority of a language that depends on them and forced Marheyo to translate Typee values into Western terms. It is from this position of linguistic superiority that he returns to "civilization" to write his book.

When Tommo does finally escape, he escapes back into history and back to an identity defined and expressed in terms of paternity and writing. His Appendix begins: "The author of this volume arrived in Tahiti the very day that the iniquitous designs of the French were consummated" (254). He describes himself as "the author of this volume," not "Tommo." For "Tommo" is the Typee chief's corruption of "Tom," and "Tom" is not even "my real name" (72). Outside the Typee valley, Tommo goes by his "real name," the name given him by his father, the name that is also his father's. And this return to his father's name, to his place in a patriarchal line of descent, is also a return to Western history, on "the very day" that other more important events take place. History, paternity, and the act of writing are affirmed as intimately related and inseparable components of identity.

If *Typee* assumes the existence of a stable genealogical identity to which its narrator can return, *Redburn* begins with its hero's departure from the family circle. Paternal authority is again most forcefully manifested as linguistic or literary power, but in the father's absence, the son's ability to assume that power becomes a critical problem. The novel opens, in fact, by invoking the father's experiential and linguistic mastery—its first words are those of Redburn's older brother, who first speaks the boy's name and begins the movement of the plot: " 'Wellingborough, as you are going to sea, suppose you take this shooting-jacket of mine along . . .' " (3).[8] It is the voice of a father-surrogate that enables Redburn to begin his own narration, identifying him and authorizing the tale that is to follow.

The presence of a paternal *surrogate* is, however, insufficient to disguise or compensate for the father's absence. It is Redburn, not his brother, who has decided that he will go to sea, and the decision has been prompted by the rupture of the family structure upon his father's death.[9] The father brings the son into the world of language by giving him a name—this is the linguistic authority toward which the son must strive, the authority Redburn claims to have attained as he begins to write the story of his life. But the indirection of his opening suggests more than childhood dependence on a father's authority; it implies a continuing anxiety about the grown man's claim of mastery.

It is precisely his inability to construct a "life story" that drives the young Redburn to sea: he speaks of "[s]ad disappointments in several plans which I had sketched for my future life," disappointments springing from his father's bankruptcy and death (3). If the father's presence had assured the boy of his identity, his absence leaves the son unable to envision a future for himself. His response is to leave his family and travel to Europe—to repeat his father's journey—in pursuit of both experience and the ability to turn it into narrative.[10]

The boy's "taste for the sea" is first awakened by the exotic language of shipping advertisements: "To my young inland imagination every word . . . suggested volumes of thought" (4). His imagination is in turn "assisted by certain shadowy reminiscences," memories of life in a seaport during his father's career as an importer (4). The father's authority is both derived from and manifested in his ability to travel, to leave his family; within the household, it is embodied in the paintings and books he has brought back from Europe. Among them are "two large green French portfolios of colored prints," but they are "more than I could lift at that age" (6). Even more inaccessible are the books locked in a tall library case, one being "a copy of D'Alembert in French": Redburn wonders "what a great man I would be, if by foreign travel I should ever be able to read straight along without stopping, out of that book, which was now a riddle to everyone in the house but my father" (7). Both French and the paternal knowledge it symbolizes are "riddles" to the boy, riddles whose solution requires a mastery of language through travel.

Just as Redburn longs to read the books locked behind the glass of the library case, he is fascinated by the hidden interior of his father's glass ship, brought from Europe as a present for the boy's great-uncle and namesake, Senator Wellingborough. If he could pry it open and "break the glass all to pieces," he thinks, "I would infallibly light on something wonderful" (8). The ship is "*La Reine*," the queen that is the father's possession, withheld from the son (9). It is only long after his father's death—at the time he writes his book—that the older Redburn will be able to claim the ship as his own.

Travel gives his father more than a set of mysterious texts and objects, however: it gives him the authority of a storyteller. The boy hopes to return from his travels and imitate his father, to "hereafter be telling my own adventures to an eager auditory" (7). This vision of himself as storyteller recurs as Redburn's ship, the *Highlander*, leaves the port of New York. He looks forward to his return, when he will be "telling my adventures to my brothers and sisters; and with what delight they would listen, and how they would look up to me then, and reverence my sayings; . . . even my elder brother would be forced to treat me with great consideration" (32–33). Experience will bestow on him his father's narrative power; he sees himself taking his father's place in the family circle, forcibly supplanting his brother. He will become a man who can tell his own story—the man who writes *Redburn*.

But as the ship heads out to sea this fantasy gives way, and Redburn finds himself unable to imagine his return. Even the memory of his father fails to reassure him: "how could I credit it, that he, my own father, whom I so well remembered, had ever sailed out of these Narrows, and sailed right through the sky and water line, and gone to England . . ." (34–35). His father has not, of course, sailed out of *these* Narrows, for the Narrows have changed in the years since his departure. Even if Redburn follows his father's path, he will always come *after* him, to places that are no longer the same. This lesson, as yet only implicit, will be driven home when the boy reaches Liverpool.

One aspect of the Narrows does seem unchanged, though—an old fort that Redburn remembers visiting with his father and a sea-captain uncle. Inside its walls lies a pastoral enclosure, the exact opposite of the expanse of ocean before him. "It was noon-day when I was there, in the month of June," he recalls, "and I was so glad and happy then" (35, 36). But those were the "delightful days, before my father became a bankrupt, and died" (36). His father's death means a loss of innocence, an expulsion from Edenic enclosure into the fallen world of the ocean and the *Highlander*.

On board ship, Redburn encounters a social system very different from the land society he knows, but he still believes its authority and structure to be fundamentally patriarchal, similar in this respect to the family he has left behind. The objects he brings with him from his life ashore do him little good, however: he has been forced to sell his brother's gun for very little, and his shooting jacket, with its oversized buttons, draws only comic remarks from the sailors (22, 19). It soon shrinks in the rain, becoming "unspeakably unpleasant" and constricting (74). The familial objects that Redburn has regarded as signs of inherited social position quickly lose their meaning at sea, becoming worse than useless.

The shooting jacket does, however, provide the boy with a new name: "'I'll baptize you over again,'" the chief mate says, "'henceforth your name is *Buttons*'" (28). The jacket is now no more than a private relic, a sign of Redburn's nostalgia for the authorizing, identifying power of a paternal order. The absence of such an order aboard ship is evidenced by his new nickname: "Wellingborough," his great-uncle's name, is replaced by "Buttons," a comic deflation of the inherited object, the jacket that has linked him to his family.

The boy's initiation is in great part a linguistic process, and the rebaptized "Buttons" must now begin to learn both the language of the sea and its rules for speech. The mate orders him to "'slush down the main-top mast,'" but the phrase is "all Greek to me," a foreign language that Redburn must admit he does not know (30). Throughout the first section of the novel, learning this new language is equated with learning the skills the words describe. Where the boy's father had mastered French, he must now learn the "Greek" of sailing terminology.

He must also learn the rules according to which language is used aboard ship. When Redburn disobeys an order, piling some shavings in a different spot from the one indicated by the mate, he is rebuked, and asks for an explanation. But the mate "without explanation reiterated his order like a clap of thunder" (29). This, Redburn comments, "was my first lesson in the discipline of the sea . . . sea-officers never gave reasons for any thing they order to be done. It is enough that they command it" (29). Shipboard authority is manifested in linguistic prerogatives; the mate speaks and the "boy" Redburn is bound to silent obedience.

The ship's hierarchy is not, however, a hereditary order, based on a paternal or genealogical model. Redburn only begins to comprehend this when he tries to pay a "social call" on the captain (67). At first, he thinks that "sea-captains are fathers to their crew" and that the captain will treat him kindly as a gentleman's son, a younger equal (67). He imagines that Captain Riga will "ask me questions concerning my parents, and prospects in life; besides obtaining from me some anecdotes touching my great-uncle, the illustrious senator" (67). The boy expects to be treated as a son, a descendant of his father and great-uncle who is thus entitled to tell their stories. But his attempt to speak to Riga yields only a furious rebuff, which leads Redburn to "put him down as a sort of impostor," "no gentleman" after all (71). Rather than surrender the notion of a social and economic order modeled on the patriarchal family, young Redburn simply views the captain as a false father, one whose authority is based on false pretensions to social rank. The boy still thinks of the world as governed by genealogical or familial structures, in which, he believes, identity and authority are conferred rather than created or earned.

The adult narrator consistently distances himself from the boy's attempts to recapture a lost paternal presence. This is nowhere more evident than when young Redburn tries to use his father's guidebook, an inherited paternal text, as a "key" to the city of Liverpool. The narrator begins this section with a return to his father's library and a survey of the travel books it contained. He quotes several titles in full: the first are in French, reminders of the father's linguistic superiority over the boy; the last is "*THE PICTURE OF LIVERPOOL*," a book that the narrator sets out to "immortalize," to "paint . . . from the life" (143). The older man still has the volume before him, and for a moment the book does link father and son in an illusory repetition: he turns "the very pages which, years and years ago, my father turned" (143). But the book is now no more than a "relic" from the past, "spotted and tarnished with time" (143). He proceeds to open the volume and read it, finding various marginal notes and drawings he himself had made as a boy. He also discusses his father's memoranda of his trip to Liverpool, and although he says they are difficult to "decipher," he copies "a few at random," reproducing his father's record of expenses and appointments (144). For the adult Redburn, the text is "a piece of antiquity," a historical artifact (148); its signficance is now only self-referential—it is not the timeless "picture" its title claims but rather a record of its owners and readers in the decades since its publication.

The narrator hints at the book's temporal vulnerability when he comments on the map included in it. One corner is "yellowish white," marked in crayon by him as a boy, but "the space designated by that spot is now, doubtless, completely built up in Liverpool" (145). He goes on to describe the passage of time in spatial, architectural terms: "as St. Peter's church was built in great part of the ruins of old Rome, so in all our erections . . . we but form quarries and supply ignoble materials for the grander domes of posterity" (149). The guidebook can no longer be accurate; the father's text is invalidated by the very history indirectly inscribed in its margins.

The boy, however, sees the book as "the infallible clew" to all the "intricacies" of Liverpool (151). For him, his father's use of the book makes "its fidelity proved beyond a peradventure"—"Dear delusion!" the narrator remarks (152). As the boy follows the route traced on his father's map, "So vivid was now the impression of his having been here . . . that I felt like running on, and overtaking him . . . But I soon checked myself, when remembering that he had gone whither no son's search could find him in this world" (155).[11] Now the young Redburn begins to see the impossibility of recapturing his father's presence, of "overtaking" him by following his earlier travels. His father's absence is not spatial but temporal; the boy cannot simply follow his father into death.

His disillusionment with the guidebook is not long in coming, for he finds that the places marked in it—those visited by his father—no longer exist: "the Liverpool my father saw, was another Liverpool" entirely (152). "This precious book," he concludes, "was next to useless . . . the thing that had guided the father could not guide the son" (157). It is time itself, he finds, that makes the recovery of a guiding paternal presence impossible: "This world . . . is a moving world . . . it never stands still; and its sands are forever shifting" (157). Geographical sands are also the sands of time; the physical world is necessarily a *temporal* world. The narrator elaborates, speaking to his younger self: "Guide-books, Wellingborough, are the least reliable books in all literature; and nearly all literature, in one sense, is made up of guide-books" (157). Those of Redburn's generation will be inadequate for the next, and his own text will be no different from the old book he would "immortalize": "Every age makes its own guide-books, and the old ones are used for waste paper" (143, 157). All those texts that assert a paternal authority over the actions of readers/sons must be "unreliable," for no son can overcome the passage of time and stand in his father's place. "I am not the traveler my father was," young Redburn admits (160). He cannot be the *man* his father *was*—the past tense marks the ineradicable gulf between absent father and living son.

Redburn is also forced to acknowledge his father's temporal *priority* as he imagines his father's Liverpool visit. "I was not born then," the boy realizes, "when he walked this flagging, I was not so much as thought of . . . My own father did not know me then; and had never seen or heard, or so much as dreamed of me" (154). The son cannot exist without the father, but the father must have existed *without* and *before* the son. "Poor, poor Wellingborough," he thinks, "Here you wander a stranger in a strange town, and the very thought of your father's having been here before you, but carries with it the reflection that, he then knew you not, nor cared for you one whit" (154). His journey to Liverpool, rather than bringing him closer to his father, has only revealed the distance between them and reinforced the father's position of inaccessible temporal authority. Like any other sailor, Redburn seems no more than "a neglected step-son of heaven" (140).

Redburn may have begun to acquire the linguistic power that, years later, will enable him to write his own autobiographical text. But such authority comes only at a price. The problem is not that a stable familial identity cannot be transferred to the shifting and unstructured "real" world; the difficulty lies in the very notion of inheritance. For just as Redburn cannot be "the man my father was," so his words cannot derive their authority from his father's. That authority is temporally grounded and temporally limited—it cannot be passed from father to son. It is not the father's death that problematizes the son's identity; the split between them lies within the genealogical relation itself, in the temporal division that provides its essential structure. As Redburn writes his own life story, he must acknowledge its difference from, not claim its identity with, his father's. Nevertheless, his text must still be haunted by his father's, based now upon their separation rather than their unity, upon the father's absence rather than on his recovery or return.

2.

Unlike Redburn, Ishmael does not go to sea in search of a missing father, but both he and Ahab still rely on genealogical imagery, defining themselves as sons whose fathers must and always will be absent. While Redburn is first named and then renamed, Ishmael opens his text by asserting his power to name himself. "Call me Ishmael," he says, assuming a name that may or may not be his real one (*Moby-Dick*, 12). "Ishmael" is, of course, an Old Testament name. Ishmael's self-naming is at once an assertion (or usurpation) of paternal authority and a gesture dependent on the authority of the ultimate Paternal Text, the Bible.

The Biblical reference, however, undermines rather than reinforces Ishmael's claim to narrative authority. The "Ishmael" of Genesis 16–17 is Abram's illegitimate son, a "wild man," whose "hand *will be* against every man, and every man's hand against him" (Gen. 16:12). The Lord changes Abram's name to Abraham as part of His covenant with him and his son Isaac; Ishmael's name, however, remains the same, for the Lord's covenant is not with him. In turning to the Bible for his authority, Melville's Ishmael thus takes upon himself a double illegitimacy, one that is both physical and spiritual.

Such an ambivalence toward physical and spiritual paternity runs throughout Ishmael's narration.[12] He proclaims himself an outcast but still clings to the authority that has disowned him and cast him out. At the very end of the novel, in the Epilogue, he describes himself as "another orphan," rescued by the *Rachel* "in her retracing search after her missing children" (470). The captain of the *Rachel* has taken his sons with him to sea, so that they may follow him in a whaling career. One of the ship's boats, with the captain's younger son aboard, had set out in pursuit of Moby Dick, never to be seen again. Here it is not the son who searches for a lost father, but the father who searches for a son. Ishmael does not mention this inversion, however—he says that he is rescued by the ship, the maternal *Rachel*, not by the paternal figure of the captain.

Ishmael's image of fatherhood, human or divine, is one of strength rather than weakness, of a power that absents itself rather than a weakness that may suffer loss:

> When Angelo paints even God the Father in human form, mark what
> robustness is there. And whatever they may reveal of the divine love in
> the Son, the soft, curled, hermaphroditical Italian pictures . . . hint
> nothing of any power, but the mere negative, feminine one of submis-
> sion and endurance . . . (315)

Ishmael's God is the Old Testament Father; his response to the Son is
ambivalent at best. Ishmael's emphasis is on the Father's power; the Son's
virtues are only "negative" and "feminine"—opposite characteristics that
may be seen as complementary to those of the Father, or merely as signs of a
lack of "masculine," paternal authority.[13]

This vision of God the all-powerful Father is reminiscent of Father
Mapple's. The preacher ends his sermon with the claim that,

> "eternal delight and deliciousness will be his, who coming to lay him
> down, can say with his final breath—O Father!—chiefly known to me
> by Thy rod—mortal or immortal, here I die. I have striven to be
> Thine, more than to be this world's, or mine own. . . . I leave eternity
> to Thee; for what is man that he should live out the lifetime of his
> God?" (51)

Ishmael may not accept the Christian self-surrender espoused by Mapple,
but he does long for a reunion with a Father who has been "chiefly known"
to him as an absent or lost source of power. If it is not for man to "live out
the lifetime of his God," it is the lot of every son to outlive his human father
and to struggle against his loss.

Ishmael's friendship with Queequeg at first seems to offer an alternative to such nostalgia for a lost father. The essence of their friendship/
marriage is a doubling that allows for the substitution of one friend for the
other in the face of death.[14] But the bond between them is, from the very
start, overshadowed or haunted by genealogy. Queequeg's embrace reminds Ishmael of an event in his childhood—"whether it was a reality or a
dream, I never could entirely settle" (32). Ishmael had been "trying to crawl
up the chimney," but his stepmother "dragged me by the legs out of the
chimney and packed me off to bed, though it was only two o'clock in the
afternoon of the 21st June, the longest day in the year" (32).[15] For trying to
fill the empty phallic space of the chimney, Ishmael is sent to bed, enclosed
in his dark and womblike "little room" (32). He sees this as an entombment
or death, to be followed by a "resurrection" (32).

After falling into "a troubled nightmare of a doze," Ishmael wakes, "half steeped in dreams," to find himself in darkness: "nothing was to be seen, and nothing was to be heard; but a supernatural hand seemed placed in mine. My arm hung over the counterpane, and the nameless, unimaginable, silent form or phantom, to which the hand belonged, seemed closely seated by my bed-side" (33). The memory of this phantom hand—that of his stepmother or his absent (dead?) father—returns to Ishmael at this moment. Queequeg's "bridegroom clasp" (33) reminds him of the touch of a ghostly parent.

Ishmael takes Queequeg's part against Bildad, countering the captain's demand that the savage be baptized—renamed within the paternal order of the church—by affirming that Queequeg is a "deacon" in the "great and everlasting First Congregation" to which "every mother's son and soul of us belong" (83). But the link between the two friends nevertheless remains a shifting and vulnerable one. In "The Monkey-Rope," as we have seen, the possibility of substituting a double for the self is radically undermined. Both whaling procedure and the events of Ishmael's story come to bind him to Queeuqeg in a fashion that is at once natural and unnatural.

It is, however, genealogy—paternity rather than brotherhood—that indirectly enables the final substitution of Queequeg for Ishmael that allows the latter to survive. As the son of a "High Chief," with "excellent blood in his veins—royal stuff" (56), Queequeg had been tattooed by a now dead "prophet and seer," who,

> by these hieroglyphic marks, had written out on his body a complete theory of the heavens and the earth, and a mystical treatise on the art of attaining truth; so that Queequeg in his own proper person was a riddle to unfold; a wondrous work in one volume; but whose mysteries not even himself could read, though his own live heart beat against them; and these mysteries were therefore destined in the end to moulder away with the living parchment whereon they were inscribed, and so be unsolved to the last. (399)

Queequeg is himself a sacred text, the bearer of a paternal wisdom that is to mean to span the generations. But not even he can read his "hieroglyphic" tattoos—he preserves the markings by copying them onto the coffin that will become the ship's lifebuoy, but they remain a set of empty signs, inscribed on a hollow, lifeless text. And with Queequeg's death they are doubly sundered from their paternal origin. The sign that marks Ishmael's survival, the accomplished substitution of friend for friend, brother for brother—the coffin/lifebuoy—is another sign of paternal absence.[16]

At key points throughout his text, Ishmael is forced to return to the image of the father in describing the ground or original basis from which "true" identity is derived. He tells the story of Ahab's dismemberment and ensuing madness in Chapter 41, "Moby Dick," but concludes:

> Ahab's larger, darker, deeper part remains unhinted . . . But vain to popularize profundities, and all truth is profound. Winding far down within the very heart of this spiked Hotel de Cluny where we stand . . . take your way, ye nobler, sadder souls, to those vast Roman halls of Thermes; where far beneath the fantastic towers of man's upper earth, his root of grandeur, his whole awful essence sits in bearded state; an antique buried beneath antiquities, and throned on torsoes! So with a broken throne, the great gods mock the captive king . . . question that proud, sad king! A family likeness! aye, he did beget ye, ye young exiled royalties; and from your grim sire only will the old State-secret come. (161)

The truth of Ahab's character, the truth of all character, lies at the bottom of a winding descent into darkness and the ruins of the past. This spatial movement downward is a movement back in time, to the origin of the self, a movement that will overcome the temporal distance between father and son. The whole, essential character of the exiled son is an "old State-secret," the secret of the Father/King.

There are, however, notes of hesitation or ambivalence in Ishmael's description. "We" stand in the Hotel de Cluny, but it is "ye nobler, sadder souls" who are to undertake the search for the Father/King—Ishmael himself will not risk the descent. And he describes the Father as "an antique buried beneath antiquities," a "captive king" on a "broken throne" mocked by the gods. The "whole awful essence" of the Father remains, but it is at the same time buried, broken, and held captive. This is, finally, a psychological rather than a physical journey, a descent into the self that reveals both the ruins of the father's lost authority and the son's desire to recover or project an integral paternal presence.

Ishmael's ambivalence toward paternal authority does have its rebellious side: "I myself am a savage," he says, "owning no allegiance but to the King of the Cannibals; and ready at any moment to rebel against him" (232). His attitude toward the father differs from Ahab's in degree rather than in kind—if nostalgia outweighs anger in Ishmael, rage overwhelms longing in his captain.

Ahab too has an Old Testament name, that of a "'wicked king'" who died a bloody and gruesome death, as Ishmael recalls (77). But Peleg tells him "'never [to] say that on board the Pequod. Never say it anywhere. Captain Ahab did not name himself'" (77). No son names himself (unless, of course, he is an Ishmael creating his own pseudonym), but Ahab's name is "'a foolish, ignorant whim of his crazy, widowed mother,'" a name arbitrarily bestowed in the father's absence (77). If a first name differentiates between father and son, in Ahab's case it also exemplifies the loss of paternal and linguistic authority. And Ahab's last name, which would identify him with his father, is never once mentioned in *Moby-Dick*. In a sense, his struggle is to escape his name, to show himself to have been misnamed, to prove his name not to have been prophetic.

To ensure his absolute control over the *Pequod*, Ahab creates a ritual bond between himself and his crew. He appropriates the language of paternal authority in doing so, but his real aim is to break with and subvert, rather than extend and support, the claims of historical and genealogical precedent. In "The Quarter-deck," he says that he will "'revive a noble custom of my fisherman fathers before me'" (145). In this ceremony, Ahab inverts the ship's hierarchy by appointing the mates as "cupbearers" to their inferiors, the harpooneers. "'Disdain the task?'" he asks, "'What, when the great Pope washes the feet of beggars, using his tiara for ewer? Oh, my sweet cardinals! your own condescension, *that* shall bend ye to it'" (146). The mates are "*my* sweet cardinals"—Ahab is, by implication, their Pope, their Holy Father. His ritual undermines rather than confirms conventional authority, subordinating the *Pequod*'s legitimate objectives to his own absolute power and his rebellious pursuit of the white whale.[17]

If Ahab is willing to make use of paternal metaphors and images in presenting himself to his crew, he forces himself to reject the demands of actual, physical paternity. He refuses to aid the captain of the *Rachel* in his search, and, finally, denies his own paternity when Starbuck summons up a vision of his wife and child in Nantucket: "'Let us home!'" the mate pleads, to "'the wife and child of thy loving, longing, paternal old age! . . . See, see! the boy's face from the window! the boy's hand on the hill!'" (444). Starbuck's appeal is to Ahab *as a father*, but the captain turns away, casting aside the thought of wife and son. "[L]ike a blighted fruit tree he shook, and cast his last, cindered apple to the soil" (444)—Melville's image is desexualized and barren.

" 'What is it,' " Ahab asks, " 'what nameless, inscrutable, unearthly thing is it; what cozening, hidden lord and master, and cruel, remorseless emperor commands me . . . against all natural lovings and longings . . . to do what in my own proper, natural heart, I durst not so much as dare?' " (444–45). Rather than a powerful father, Ahab sees himself as the powerless subject of an "inscrutable" and "hidden" master, whose power is, by implication, improper and unnatural. Ahab does not describe this master as a "father"; he goes even further—this unnatural ruler is God Himself, the ultimate Father. " 'Is Ahab, Ahab?' " he asks,

> "Is it I, God, or who, that lifts this arm? . . . [How] can this one small heart beat; this one small brain think thoughts; unless God does that beating, does that thinking, does that living, and not I. By heaven, man, we are turned round and round in this world, like yonder windlass, and Fate is the handspike." (445)

Ahab's conjunction of God and Fate brings us back to his Biblical name, the name taken from God's Word that may well prophesy the captain's fate—he may be like the Biblical Ahab, condemned to a violent death for his rebellion against God, the Old Testament Father. Ahab, finally, cannot see himself as a father, but only as a victimized son.[18]

The primary form of Ahab's victimization has, of course, been his dismemberment by the whale, a symbolic castration that may have become a literal one. "All the anguish of [his] present suffering" is, for Ahab,

> but the direct issue of a former woe . . . as the most poisonous reptile of the marsh perpetuates his kind as inevitably as the sweetest songster of the grove; so, equally with every felicity, all miserable events do naturally beget their like. Yea, more than equally, thought Ahab; since both the ancestry and posterity of Grief go further than the ancestry and posterity of Joy. . . . some natural enjoyments here shall have no children born to them for the other world, but, on the contrary, shall be followed by the joy-childlessness of all hell's despair; whereas, some guilty mortal miseries shall still fertilely beget to themselves an eternally progessive progeny of griefs beyond the grave. (385)

Ahab describes the chain of causes and effects as a genealogy, a paternal line that extends throughout this world and into the next. For him, the genealogical chain is a universal lineage of grief and punishment that cannot be escaped, not even when the son becomes a father in his turn: "To trail the genealogies of these high mortal miseries," Ahab concludes, "carries us at last among the sourceless primogenitures of the gods . . . The ineffaceable, sad birth-mark in the brow of man, is but the stamp of sorrow in the signers" (386). There is, for Ahab, no ultimate legitimating source of paternal power; even the gods are fatherless sons, their power derived from "sourceless primogentitures." Not even they can escape the sorrow of sonship, a sorrow reinscribed upon the brow of every man at birth. Every man thus bears the mark of his father's grief; each is the text that confirms the father's paternity and gives the son his place in the genealogy of grief and loss.

For a moment, Ahab may entertain the thought of life as circular, an endless "'round'" in which we are "'infants, boys, and men, and Ifs eternally'" (406).[19] But this is not a perspective that he can finally accept: "'Where lies the final harbor,'" he asks, "'whence we unmoor no more?'" (406). His desire for an end, a resting place, is in fact a desire for a beginning, a lost paternal origin—"'Where is the foundling's father hidden? Our souls are like those orphans whose unwedded mothers die in bearing them: the secret of our paternity lies in their grave, and we must there to learn it'" (406). Ahab describes "our souls" as illegitimate, abandoned by their fathers and born only at the cost of their mothers' lives. "The secret of our paternity," the name of the father, is "the foundling's" goal; it is the missing father who is responsible for both the death of the mother and the identity of the orphan son. But that secret lies in the grave, and the son can only learn it there.

Ahab, like Ishmael, knows the absent father to be beyond recovery. But where Ishmael hesitates to project his desire for a paternal presence onto reality, Ahab does so in explicit and violent terms. In Chapter 119, "The Candles," lightning sets the *Pequod*'s yardarms and masts aflame with static electricity, the masts burning "like three gigantic wax tapers before an altar" (415). And before this "altar," Ahab enacts a terrifying ritual of fire- and father-worship. "'Oh! thou spirit of clear fire,'" he cries,

"whom on these seas I as Persian once did worship, till in the sacramental act so burned by thee, that to this hour I bear the scar; I now know thee, thou clear spirit, and I now know that thy right worship is defiance. . . . I own thy speechless, placeless, power; but to the last gasp of my earthquake life will dispute its unconditional, unintegral mastery in me. . . . of thy fire thou madest me, and like a true child of fire, I breathe it back to thee." (416–17)

Simple worship of the fire-father yields only a further sign of alienation, a scar; Ahab thus declares, paradoxically, that "thy right worship is defiance," that to be a "true child of fire," he must "breathe it back to thee." The true son must defy his father; the fullest worship of paternal power is the son's self-destructive resistance to it.

Ahab thus defines himself in opposition to the ground from which he claims to spring. If embodiment is the crucial fact of his maimed existence, his image of the father is of a bodiless force, one that cannot be wounded or divided. Both fire-father and white whale represent everything that Ahab is not. But both are also projections from within him—it is from the chasm of Ahab's own unconscious that "forked flames and lightnings [shoot] up" (174) to form a father against whom he may rebel. His monomaniac project of revenge is, and is meant to be, an "unfathered birth" (175)—it is the whale, after all, who faithfully " 'worships fire' " (409).

The whale-hunter willingly embraces his own destruction, for it will testify to his ultimate difference from that which consumes him:

> "Thou canst consume; but I can then be ashes . . . Light though thou be, thou leapest out of darkness; but I am darkness leaping out of light, leaping out of thee! . . . now I do glory in my genealogy. But thou art but my fiery father; my sweet mother, I know not. Oh, cruel! what hast thou done with her? There lies my puzzle; but thine is greater. Thou knowest not how came ye, hence callest thyself unbegotten . . . I know that of me, which thou knowest not of thyself, oh, thou omnipotent. There is some unsuffusing thing beyond thee, thou clear spirit, to whom all thy eternity is but time, all thy creativeness mechanical. Through thee, thy flaming self, my scorched eyes do dimly see it. . . . Here again with haughty agony, I read my sire." (417)

Ahab defines himself as "darkness leaping out of light," turning the loss of continuity between father and son into the purest of oppositions. In doing so he inverts the figure/ground relationship between light and darkness, turning himself into the reciprocal ground of his father's being. But as Ahab confronts and defies his fire-father, he glories in his own self-conscious estrangement. He at least knows that he stands in irreducible opposition to his father, while the fire cannot know its own ground or source. Ahab knows what the fire cannot, that it, too, springs from a source beyond itself, that it, too, participates in a genealogy of opposition, loss, and self-destruction. The fire may blind him, but he can nevertheless see through it and "read my sire." The father is now the son's text. But the writing is, after all, only Ahab's—this genealogy is his construction, and it reveals only his own ultimate powerlessness, his continued desire for and dependence on the father.

Ahab's ultimate gesture of rebellion against the father, and against God, comes, perhaps, with the forging of the new harpoon that he intends for Moby Dick. The harpoon is tempered not in water but in the blood of his harpooneers, and Ahab performs a ritual baptism: " 'Ego non baptizo te in nomine patris, sed in nomine diaboli!' " (404). "I do not baptize you in the name of the father, but in the name of the devil"—not in the name of God the Father, but in the name of the first rebellious son, the Son of Light who made himself the Father of Darkness.

But Ahab's defiance of paternal authority has not escaped, and cannot escape, its force. Subversion and defiance remain the most powerful forms of worship, gestures of opposition that only confirm and strengthen the power of the father himself. Ahab may pervert the Christian sacrament of baptism, but his black baptism can be no more than a perversion, dependent on the language and form of the original for its own power. What returns, with redoubled force, is Ahab's desire for a paternal presence on or against which to ground his identity.

Even Ahab's image of a *fire*-father may in fact be an echo of his Biblical namesake. In 1 Kings, it is as fire that God reveals Himself, when Elijah calls upon Him to accept his offering (1 Kings 18:38). King Ahab, however, sees only this violent, self-consuming sign of God's power. The Lord is not present in the fire as He is in the "still small voice" that speaks to Elijah alone (1 Kings 19:12). As Captain Ahab knows only too well, he can escape neither paternal absence nor the genealogy that both defines and destroys him.

3.

In *Pierre*, Melville both recapitulates and extends the progression from an unquestioned structure of genealogical authority to one that exists only as a self-destructive projection of the son's desire. The novel begins not with a son's attempt to be a repetition of his father, but with an achieved *illusion* of repetition. And it concludes, not with a son's expression of defiance and rebellion, but with an examination of the way in which rebellion against paternal authority must finally subvert and destroy itself. In denying the legitimating power of the father, the son must lay claim to that power even as he undermines it, internalizing the father's absence and depriving himself of the terms of a possible self-definition.

The story opens in the timeless world of Saddle-Meadows, the Glendinning family estate. It is a "trance-like . . . green and golden world" that seems to "defy Time's tooth."[20] In this landscape, Pierre's family history is spatialized and "sanctified" (8). The manor is named in memory of a battle in which his paternal great-grandfather, "mortally wounded, had sat un-horsed on his saddle in the grass" (5–6). The horizon itself is for Pierre "a memorial ring" (8). In a sense, he does dwell among his ancestors; their lives are commemorated and preserved in the living landscape that surrounds him.

Pierre quite literally stands in his forefathers' place, living in their house and using their possessions as if they were his own. He now drives his grandfather's phaeton, "reining steeds, whose great-great-great-grand-fathers grand old Pierre had reined before" (32). " 'The quaint old arms on the panel, always remind me who it was that first rode in it,' " he tells his mother, and, he adds, " 'who it was that *next* rode in it' " (19). Her response is a blessing and an injunction: " 'God bless you, my dear son!—always think of him and you can never err; yes, always think of your dear perfect father, Pierre' " (19). The son is to take his father as a model, to strive to reach and repeat his godlike perfection. But such a generational fusion yields a disturbing confusion of reference in his mother's words: the antecedent of "him" is "God," not "your father," and "Pierre" refers to both father *and* son.

This Pierre is "not only the solitary head of his family, but the only surnamed male Glendinning extant" (7), the namesake of both his father and grandfather and "the likeness, and very soul" of his father "transformed into youth once again" (73). Pierre does not, however, see his position in generational or temporal terms; his imagery is spatial: he hopes to "cap" the "fame-column, whose tall shaft had been erected by his noble sires" (8). His father's memory is a marble shrine in Pierre's heart, "a niched pillar, deemed solid and eternal . . . which supported the entire one-pillared temple of his moral life" (68). The boy has "marbleized" the image of his father—"things which in themselves were evanescent, thus became un-changeable and eternal" (68).

This narrative comment echoes an earlier critique of Pierre's imagined "fame-column," which is compared to a "crumbling, uncompleted shaft" among the ruins of Palmyra, said to have been built by Solomon himself: "These Time seized and spoiled; these Time crushed in the egg; and the proud stone that should have stood among the clouds, Time left abased beneath the soil. Oh, what quenchless feud is this, that Time hath with the sons of Men!" (8). It is Time, and its destructive, fragmenting power, that has been excluded from Pierre's enclosed, "marbleized" world. His "proud stone," the narrator suggests, will also be "left abased beneath the soil"—a buried and broken symbol of his ancestors' mortality. Time's "feud" is not, however, with men in general, but with "the sons of Men": it is *genealogical time* that will fragment the paternal column on which Pierre would build.

Pierre sees his life as an "illuminated scroll," a "sweetly-writ manu-script," but his image is of a completed object—he does not as yet imagine the (sexual) act of creation or think of his father as an absent author/progenitor (7). He relies upon the passive voice in describing the "one hiatus" in his life: "A sister *had been omitted* from the text" (7; my em-phasis). His is only a muted lament, however; grief is only a "ghost story" to him (60). But once the story—the tale of his father's guilty authorship—is told, it will indeed come back to haunt and mock him.

The father's absence does have its consequences, however, even in the static, "sanctified" realm of the family estate. It is, after all, what makes the gap in Pierre's life story apparently permanent. And his father's death also destabilizes Pierre's relationship with his mother. Mary Glendinning sees "her own graces," "her own curled and haughty beauty," in her son; she regards him as her double, a confirmation of her own youth, not as his father's son (5, 90). Her vanity and narcissism lead her to substitute for the terms "mother" and "son" those of "sister" and "brother" (5). But his mother's merely "fictitious title" cannot, for Pierre, fill the gap in his father's text (7). The incestuous overtones of "Sister Mary" (14) only extend and deepen genealogical and generational disorder, as the most overtly fictional and illusory element in the timelessness of Saddle-Meadows.[21]

Historical or narrative time enters Pierre's world with his first sight of Isabel, the woman who will claim to be his illegitimate half-sister. Her face is "vaguely historic and prophetic; backward, hinting of some irrevocable sin; forward, pointing to some inevitable ill" (43). As if to emphasize the temporality suggested by Isabel's face, the narrator describes Pierre's first vision of her in a flashback, in a chapter entitled "The Presentiment and the Verification" (43). As the title implies, the novel's movement forward in time will now be linked to a movement of investigation and interpretation, its narrative progression based on Pierre's discovery, reconstruction, and fulfillment of paternal narrative.

Just as Isabel's shriek at her first sight of Pierre "split[s] its way clean through his heart, and leave[s] a yawning gap there" (45), the receipt of a letter from her leaves him internally divided, "half alarmed, and half bantering with himself" (62). This self-division is frighteningly literalized when Pierre reenters his room: he "started at a figure in the opposite mirror. It bore the outline of Pierre, but now strangely filled with features transformed, and unfamilar to him" (62). He thinks of destroying the note unread, but "[h]ardly had this half-crazy conceit made itself fully legible in his soul, when he was conscious of his two hands meeting in the middle of the sundered note" (62). Pierre becomes conscious of his decision *not* to read by "reading" it in his own soul—interpretation is internalized even as it is rejected. So, too, do his hands meet in the act of "sundering" the note; even before he reads the letter, Pierre is already entangled in a network of splittings and doublings.

Isabel's letter begins hesitantly, anticipating that Pierre will not recognize its authorizing signature: "'The name at the end of this letter will be wholly strange to thee'" (63). Her anxiety is not misplaced, for naming is precisely what is at stake here—whether Pierre will "recognize" her as his sister and give her the family name. Isabel makes her claim succintly and directly: "'Pierre Glendinning, thou art not the only child of thy father . . . the hand that traces this is thy sister's; yes, Pierre, Isabel calls thee her brother—her brother! oh, sweetest of words. . . . Pierre, my brother, my own father's child!'" (63–64). Her primary concern is with what she is entitled to "call" Pierre—"my brother"—and she does so seven times in the course of the note. "Pierre Glendinning" is synonymous, she asserts, with "my brother," and she calls upon the paternal "eye of the sun" to witness her right to redefine, by verbal apposition, both him and herself (63, 64). She signs herself "'THY SISTER, ISABEL'" (64).

Isabel at once divides and doubles the Glendinning line, but if a family tree can branch out, Pierre's marble "fame-column" can only split and crumble. Her claim is that she and Pierre have the same father, a single origin; the effect of her letter, however, is to divide Pierre's image of his father as its receipt has divided him.

Pierre goes from his bedroom into a closet next door, "whither he had always been wont to go, in those sweetly awful hours, when the spirit crieth to the spirit, Come into solitude with me, twin-brother . . . a secret have I; let me whisper it to thee aside" (71). In this place, in which the divided self whispers secrets to its own "twin-brother," there hangs a portrait of Pierre's father. It is a picture of him as a bachelor, an image "strangely dissimilar" to the one displayed in the drawing room of the house, a portrait commissioned years later by Pierre's mother (72). The latter painting is of the father Pierre remembers, "therefore, he himself could not but deem it by far the more truthful and life-like presentation of his father" (72). But Pierre does not follow his mother in rejecting the earlier "chair portrait": "[I]n the first place, there was a difference in time, and some difference of costume to be considered, and the wide difference of the styles of the respective artists" (72). It is the temporal difference that is primary, however. Pierre's acceptance of the chair portrait comes after he compares two portraits of himself, one made at age four, the other at sixteen:

> Except an indestructible, all-surviving something in the eyes and on the temples, Pierre could hardly recognize the loud-laughing boy in the tall, and pensively smiling youth. If a few years, then, can have made in *me* all this difference, why not in my father? thought Pierre. (73)

The difference between the son's portraits is a *repetition* of that between the father's. But it is a repetition of a *difference*, an internal temporal split, an inherited self-division that must undermine the possibility of repetition itself. For which image of his father can Pierre be said to resemble or repeat? And which Pierre is the repetition? Pierre is also, after all, projecting his own divided selfhood onto his father, in a self-contradictory attempt to unify himself.

He has, until now, tried to reconcile these contrasting images of his father—the chair portrait "sometimes seems to say" to him, "believe not the drawing-room painting; that is not thy father; or, at least, is not *all* of thy father" (83). "Consider," it asks,

> whether we two paintings may not make only one . . . In mature life, the world overlays and varnishes us . . . then, we, as it were, abdicate ourselves, and take unto us another self, Pierre; in youth we *are*, Pierre, but in age we *seem*. Look again. I am thy real father, so much the more truly, as thou thinkest thou recognizest me not. (83)

The ostensibly comforting words of the portrait are in fact subversive and threatening, for if the earlier bachelor portrait is the truer one, the father is most himself before fatherhood, when he cannot be "recognized" by the son who does not yet exist. The father's identity not only contains within itself a temporal difference, but is defined by his temporal priority, the distance in time between father and son that makes him finally unknowable.

Even when confronted with "the no longer wholly enigmatical, but still ambiguously smiling" chair portrait, Pierre still tries to evade the divided paternal image he has created (87). He turns the picture's face to the wall, but this is not enough:

> "Oh, symbol of thy reversed idea in my soul," groaned Pierre; "thou shalt not hang thus. Rather cast thee utterly out, than conspicuously insult thee so. I will no more have a father." He removed the picture wholly from the wall, and the closet; . . . But still, in a square space of slightly discolored wall, the picture still left its shadowy, but vacant and desolate trace. (87)

Pierre rejects this image of his father, but here, as in his actions toward Isabel, he "casts out" paternal authority only to resurrect it in another form. The "shadowy, but vacant and desolate trace" of the father remains—but now only as a tormenting absence within the son.

Pierre does not here reject the concept of paternal authority, but only its divided representation in his father's portraits. Later, he displaces his anger onto the chair portrait itself, attacking the representation instead of its "original": "since in his own memory of his father, Pierre could not recall any distinct lineament transmitted to Isabel, but vaguely saw such in the portrait; therefore, not Pierre's parent, as any way rememberable by him, but the portrait's painted *self* seemed the real father of Isabel" (197). If he cannot fuse his father and Isabel's, he must destroy one in order to preserve the other. He burns the picture that links his father to Isabel. "'It shall not live,'" he says,

> "Hitherto I have hoarded up mementoes and monuments of the past; been a worshiper of all heir-looms . . . but it is forever over now! If to me any memory shall henceforth be dear, I will not mummy it in a visble memorial . . . never more will I play the vile pygmy, and by small memorials after death, attempt to reverse the decree of death, by essaying the poor perpetuating of the image of the original." (197–98)

Pierre rejects all "heir-looms," all representations that would pretend to stand for their lost originals. He will accept the passage of time and its "decree of death." But Pierre himself is a "visible memorial" of his father; the essence of genealogical identity is the son's *representation of* the father. He cannot destroy the image of the father without destroying his own "representative" status, the basis of his own authority and identity.

When Pierre and Isabel meet, she says that he is " 'entitled to my tale' " (114). The first thing she remembers is a dark, half-ruined house: " 'No name; no scrawled or written thing; no book, was in the house; no one memorial speaking of its former occupants . . . no trace then to me of its past history' " (115). Her story also begins in a timeless space, a place she cannot identify for the same reason that she cannot yet identify herself—it and she are both nameless, lacking the legitimation of a father's text.

The key point in Isabel's narrative is her discovery of the one piece of evidence on which she bases her identity—the name of her father. A man had visited her for a time during her childhood, a man " 'called by us *the gentleman*, and sometimes *my father*' " (145). On what will be his last visit, he " 'chanced to leave his handkerchief behind,' " and Isabel finds on it " 'a small line of fine faded yellowish writing' " that she cannot yet read (146). When her "father" never returns, and " 'the impression of his death became a fixed thing to me,' " Isabel hides her " 'precious memorial' " of him:

> "I folded it in such a manner, that the name was invisibly buried in the heart of it, and it was like opening a book and turning over many blank leaves before I came to the mysterious writing, which I knew should be one day read by me . . . I resolved to learn my letters, and learn to read, in order that of myself I might learn the meaning of those faded characters." (146)

In the absence of the father himself, Isabel makes the handkerchief into a sacred text, in which is hidden the father's name. It is this forced substitution of the name for the father himself that leads her into the world of language; she learns to read in order to "learn *my* letters," the letters of the " 'talismanic word—Glendinning,' " her name as her father's daughter (147). It is the language of paternity that Isabel would use to define herself, and it is in this language, in the name of the father, that Pierre responds, as " 'thy leapingly-acknowledging brother, whom thy own father named Pierre!' " (66).

Pierre's response to Isabel's story is again a divided one. On the one hand, his duty does not "consist in stubbornly flying in the marble face of the Past, and striving to reverse the decree which had pronounced that Isabel could never perfectly inherit all the privileges of a legitimate child" (174). It is his father's silence, the silence of death, that has "decreed" Isabel's illegitimacy, and Pierre's temporal position as son will not allow him to reverse the passage of time and openly recognize her as his sister. The silence of the dead father binds the son, even though the father, "unrecallably dead and gone from out the living world, [has] returned to utter helplessness" (177). Pierre decides to "hold his father's memory untouched; nor to one single being in the world reveal the paternity of Isabel" (177). On the other hand, he feels driven to act upon this secret knowledge, in a private act of recognition. He will, by "the *nominal* conversion of a sister into a wife," give Isabel the family name—by entering into a "fictitious alliance," a pretended marriage (177, 175; my emphasis).[22]

"'I stand the sweet penance in my father's stead,'" he tells Isabel, "'thou, in thy mother's'" (154). He will take his father's place, and Isabel her mother's; together they will repeat the actions of their parents. Isabel agrees, saying that "'more than ever filled my mother toward thy father, Pierre . . . upheaved in me'" when she first saw him (155). This repetition is at once an assertion of filial identity and a sacrifice of it, for they propose to merge their identities with those of their parents. Pierre asks Isabel to bring food and drink, so that they may share "'the real sacrament of the supper'" (162). He will take into himself the symbolic body of the father, and with it the father's power to recognize his daughter. But if father and son become one, the father's power over the son is destroyed, for the differential relation between them is denied. Pierre's gesture is simultaneously suicidal and parricidal.[23]

The marriage can only be a flawed or corrupted repetition at best: it must be either a desexualized union or an incestuous one—in either case a genealogical failure. Symbolically, the marriage becomes triply incestuous, a union of brother and sister, father and daughter, mother and son. Pierre can escape his incestuous relation to his mother only by resurrecting it with Isabel. His assumption and internalization of the father's authority only reconfirms its collapse.

Pierre may publicly preserve the family line, but he privately extends and divides it. His marriage will reunify the Glendinning line by ending or perverting it; it is in this ironic sense that he succeeds in "capping" the family "fame-column." He takes upon himself the father's linguistic authority, his power to bestow the "talismanic word" of the family name, but only to ensure than it can never be used again. Pierre asserts the power of genealogical temporality in his public silence, only to deny and abolish it in his private recognition of Isabel.[24]

Pierre's action also forces his mother to acknowledge genealogical and generational time. Her response to his evasiveness is to drop the pretense of her sisterhood: "'Sister me not, now, Pierre;—I am thy mother'" (95). When he tells her of his marriage, she responds as the head of the family, a paternal surrogate, and disowns him: "'Beneath my roof, and at my table, he who was once Pierre Glendinning no more puts himself'" (185). This is both a statement of fact and assertion of power—"he who was once Pierre Glendinning," Pierre's father, is now dead, and in his absence, Pierre's mother exercises his power to deprive her son of the family name. It is the name that is all-important for her: "'He bears my name—Glendinning. I will disown it; were it like this dress, I would tear my name off from me, and burn it till it shrivelled to a crisp!'" (193). "Glendinning" is, of course, her name in a different sense than it is Pierre's or his father's, and it is precisely this difference that Pierre has insisted upon in his recognition of Isabel.

Mrs. Glendinning's power, like Isabel's illegitimacy, is ultimately based in her husband's silence and death. Pierre's father had died insane, without "framing a new will to supersede one made shortly after his marriage, and ere Pierre was born" (179). By that will, "all the Glendinning property was declared his mother's" (179). Pierre is unnamed in his father's will, because he is as yet unborn—the father's temporal priority over the son is asserted once again. Pierre, however, feels bound by his father's silence in this matter, too—he feels "an invincible repugnance to dragging his dead father's hand and seal into open Court" (180). So he leaves his mother to repeat and confirm his father's silence, to leave him unnamed, and thus disinherited, in her own will (285).

Pierre now comes face to face with the signs and consequences of paternal absence. For him the controlling power that is "so significantly denominated The Finger of God" is rather "the whole outspread Hand of God; for doth not Scripture intimate, that He holdeth all of us in the hollow of His hand?—a Hollow, truly!" (139). Instead of the Finger that inscribes the Law, Pierre finds only hollowness. "Silence," the narrator remarks, "is the only Voice of our God," and no man can "get a Voice out of Silence" (204, 208). For Pierre, the voice of the father has been reduced to silence, a silence he cannot fill without an authority derived from the absent father himself.

But it is Pierre who has fragmented and cast out that authority; this vacancy and silence is of his own making:

> The old mummy lies buried in cloth on cloth; it takes time to unwrap this Egyptian king. . . . By vast pains we mine into the pyramid; by horrible gropings we come to the central room; with joy we espy the sarcophagus; but we lift the lid—and no body is there!—appallingly vacant as vast is the soul of a man! (284–85)

Pierre has himself emptied his father's tomb, despoiled it of its moral and linguistic authority. And in doing so, he has deprived himself of the ground of his own identity; his soul is now as "appallingly vacant" as the father's sarcophagus—"nobody" is there as well as "no body." Pierre has made himself into another "Ishmael" (89). But unlike the Ishmael of *Moby-Dick*, he can no longer conceive of even a broken or captive king from whom he may obtain the "old State-secret" of his identity. For he has taken his father's power into himself, leaving only an emptiness in the father's place, and it is against this emptiness that he must finally struggle.

He tells Isabel that "'thou wantest not the openness; for thou dost not pine for empty nominalness, but for vital realness'" (192). He promises her a relation beyond naming, more real than his possible bestowal of the father's name. But that relation will be made possible only by a self-conscious corruption and fictionalization of the family name in their pretended marriage. Their union is *nothing but* nominal; it exists only in words and is no more substantial than "a web of air" (175). Pierre tears the language of genealogy loose from its referents, emptying it of its claims to truth just as he has emptied his father's tomb.

Isabel tells him that she knows of Virtue and Vice only "by hearsay" (274). "'What are they, in their real selves, Pierre?'" she asks (274). "'A nothing is the substance,'" he replies, "'it casts one shadow one way, and another the other way; and these two shadows cast from one nothing . . . are Virtue and Vice'" (274). Virtue and Vice are no more than verbal shadows; behind them lies "nothing," no authorizing ground or paternal presence. Pierre's torment comes, he says, from "'the law . . . That a nothing should torment a nothing; for I am a nothing'" (274). Identity is "nothing" and names only shadows, groundless and arbitrary signs, inherently fictitious. When Isabel addresses him as "'my brother,'" his response is simple but ambiguous: "'I am Pierre'" (274). Their genealogical relation is also "nothing," another empty fiction.

Ironically, Pierre's intention has been to support himself by writing a piece of popular fiction. He has contributed a series of poems to magazines, and is confident that his "name" will bring him an immediate audience.

Writing has been a gesture of independence for him, a demonstration that he can earn money beyond his "noble patrimony" (260). "A proud man," the narrator comments, "likes to feel himself in himself . . . He likes to be not only his own Alpha and Omega, but to be distinctly all the intermediate gradations" (261). This Godlike self-creation and self-enclosure amounts to a rejection of all "patrimonies," an act in which Pierre will constitute himself as the author of his own being, "his own sire."

But time—and God Himself, the narrator suggests (261)—will hardly allow for such an integral self-sufficency. Both "divinity and humanity . . . cruel father and mother . . . even the paternal gods themselves did now desert Pierre" (296). He finds himself less and less able to write; the temporal divisions within him now become physical ones:

> the only visible outward symbols of [his] soul—his eyes—did also turn downright traitors to him . . . they absolutely refused to look on paper. He turned them on paper, and they blinked and shut. The pupils of his eyes rolled away from him in their own orbits. He put his hand up to them, and sat back in his seat. Then, without saying one word, he continued there for his usual term, suspended, motionless, blank. (341)

The narrator's imagery suggests more than the separation of the soul from its "outward symbols"; it implies a literal fragmentation of the body. When his eyes close, Pierre is left "blank": he can see only blankness; the unwritten page of his manuscript is a blank; and, unable to read or write, he is himself a blank.

In stripping himself of genealogical identity and denying paternal authority as the ground of linguistic truth, Pierre has made himself and his text into a blank. He has nothing to define himself with or against, and no terms in which to do it. The self-destructive, fruitless nature of his task is allegorized in Pierre's dream vision of Enceladus. In his dream, "the actual artificial objects around him" are replaced by "a baseless yet most imposing spectacle of natural scenery . . . the phantasmagoria of the Mount of the Titans, a singular height standing quite detached on a wide solitude not far from the grand ridge of dark blue hills encircling his ancestral manor" (342). Pierre returns to Saddle-Meadows, but not to its encircling, once "sanctified" hills. The Mount of the Titans stands apart, solitary and forbidding.

On the slope beneath it lie a number of "recumbent sphinx-like shapes thrown off from the rocky steep"—its broken and fragmented offspring, the foremost of which is

> a form defiant, a form of awfulness . . . Enceladus the Titan, the most potent of all the giants, writhing from out the imprisoning earth . . . still turning his unconquerable front toward that majestic mount eternally in vain assailed by him, and which, when it had stormed him off, had heaved his undoffable incubus upon him, and deridingly left him there to bay out his ineffectual howl. (345)

Enceladus is "both the son and grandson of an incest" seeking "to regain his paternal birthright even by fierce escalade" (347). But he has been mutilated, deprived of speech—immobilized and silenced by his mountain father.

In Pierre's dream, Enceladus and the other stone Titans come to life, and renew their assault upon the "invulnerable" steep:

> "Enceladus! it is Enceladus!"—Pierre cried out in his sleep. That moment the phantom faced him; and Pierre saw Enceladus no more; but on the Titan's armless trunk, his own duplicate face and features magnifiedly gleamed upon him with prophetic discomfiture and woe. (346)

Pierre now sees himself as doubly illegitimate, the son of a double incest, with no hands to write or tongue to speak, throwing himself against the blank rock of his own genealogy. "It is according to eternal fitness" (347) that sons assail their fathers, worshiping them in defiance, but Pierre has already stripped his father of his authority and made meaningless the "paternal birthright" he would assert. His rebellion against genealogy is revealed as only a self-destructive and barren repetition.

Pierre, finally, has no other opponent than the blankness of the Mount, the "vacant and desolate" space on the wall that marks his father's absence. He has forced himself to "wrestle . . . on the nakedest possible plain" (297), but unlike Jacob, he cannot hope for a blessing—a renaming by God the Father. For Pierre wrestles only with himself: "Concentrating all the remaining stuff in him, he resolved by an entire and violent change, and by a willful act against his own most habitual inclinations, to wrestle with the strange malady of his eyes, this new death-fiend of the trance, and this

Inferno of his Titanic vision" (347). Pierre, like Enceladus, has no recourse but violence—a violence directed against himself and his own literal and imaginative vision.[25]

The final, damning event that precipitates Pierre's self-destruction is his discovery of a painting closely resembling the chair portrait of his father. It hangs among a collection of European forgeries, "wretched daubs . . . christened by the loftiest names known to Art," but it is doubly nameless: "*No. 99. A stranger's head, by an unknown hand*" (349–50). "The pervading look of it, the subtler interior keeping of the entirety, was almost identical," Pierre concludes, to that of the chair portrait: "still, for all this, there was an unequivocal aspect of foreignness, of Europeanism, about both the face itself and the general painting" (351). The face is the same, yet different; it is an uncanny return of the dead father's image, but one that undermines rather than confirms the authority of the "original": "the original of this second portrait was as much the father of Isabel as the original of the chair-portrait. But perhaps there was no original at all to the second portrait; it might have been a pure fancy piece" (353). Perhaps there is no "original" for the chair portrait either; perhaps Pierre's image of his father is just a "fancy piece," his own projection against the blankness and vacancy of the father's absence.

Pierre's struggle now turns outward, as he confronts and murders his cousin, Glendinning Stanly. Glen and Pierre had once been joined in a boyish "love-friendship" (217). But just as Time has divided Pierre from his father and against himself, so it has separated the cousins and turned "boy-love" into hatred. It was Glen whom Pierre had supplanted as Lucy Tartan's suitor, but it is Glen who replaces Pierre in his mother's will as the heir to Saddle-Meadows (287). Earlier, when Pierre had imagined Glen replacing him in Lucy's affections, he had thought that "Glen would seem all the finest part of Pierre, without any of Pierre's shame; would almost seem Pierre himself—what Pierre had once been to Lucy" (288). He "conjured up this phantom of Glen transformed into the seeming semblance of himself" (289); Glen is, for him, a threatening double.

Now, in his frustration and despair, Pierre abandons language entirely, taking the insulting letter in which Glen has "given him the lie" and using it as top-wadding for a brace of pistols: "'I'll send 'em back their lie, and plant it scorching in their brains'" (358). When Pierre meets his cousin, Glen shouts "'Liar! Villain!,'" and strikes him with his glove, leaving "a half-livid and half-bloody brand" (359). This is marking or writing as an act of violence, and Pierre responds in kind—he fires both pistols, with their textual top-wadding, at Glen: "Spatterings of his own kindred blood were upon the pavement; his own hand had extinguished his house in slaughtering the only unoutlawed human being by the name of Glendinning" (360).

Pierre's rebellion against his own genealogy has come to its inevitable suicidal conclusion. In his last prison cell soliloquy, he says that both this and the other world will be "hell" for him: " 'Well, be it hell. I will mold a trumpet of the flames, and with my breath of flame, breathe back my defiance' " (360). Pierre's defiance echoes Ahab's, but he is no longer capable of projecting a father's image outside himself—these are flames within him, consuming him in his battle against himself.

In his dedication to *Pierre*, Melville speaks of the "old times" when "authors were proud of the privilege of dedicating their works to Majesty. A right noble custom, which we of Berkshire must revive" (vii). But Melville, like Ahab, invokes paternal authority only to ironize and subvert it. His novel is not dedicated to any human majesty, but to Mount Greylock.

Melville describes the "majestic mountain" as "my own more immediate sovereign lord and king," who has bestowed "his most bounteous and unstinted fertilizations" upon the writer (vii). The mountain is here a figure of male authority and potency, the paternal source of Melville's own imaginative power. But he gives Greylock the title of "his Imperial Purple Majesty," and purple is the color of Pierre's Mount of the Titans when seen from a distance. Behind this mountain's "Most Excellent Purple Majesty" lies only the rocky desolation and blankness of paternal absence.

These ironic tensions suggest Melville's own ambivalence toward paternal authority. In his dedication, written after the completion of the novel, one assumes, Melville indicates that Pierre's project—and Ahab's—have been his own. If "ego non baptiso te in nomine . . ." is the "secret motto" of *Moby-Dick*, as he suggested to Hawthorne (*Letters*, 133), it is the impulse behind *Pierre* as well.

But it is an impulse that can never be fulfilled, as *Pierre* itself demonstrates. With the loss or destruction of paternal authority, the son's text can no longer derive its legitimacy from a source outside itself. Each text must demonstrate the adequacy of its own language and form to the experience it claims to embody—genealogical identity is supplanted by *textual* identity, and the integrity of the self becomes a function of the integrity and continuity of an autobiographical text.

IV Textual Identity: Autobiography and the Fiction of Self-Creation

"UNTIL I WAS TWENTY-FIVE, I had no development at all," Melville wrote to Hawthorne on June 1, 1851, "Three weeks have scarcely passed, at any time between then and now, that I have not unfolded within myself. But I feel that I am now come to the inmost leaf of the bulb" (*Letters*, 130). Melville's image of an organic "unfolding" has often been noted, but beneath it lies another rather different image of the self. The "development" he describes is, after all, not merely physical or genealogical—for it was at twenty-five that Melville became a writer. The leaves unfolding within him are the pages of his texts. Melville's novels are full of images of hidden writing; here it is the inner text of the self that unfolds in the pages of the work.

The latent tension in this image between the organic and the textual introduces a discordant note into an almost feverishly exuberant letter, written as *Moby-Dick* was about to go to press. If the self is revealed on or in its leaves, is that self exhausted in the unfolding of the "inmost" leaf? If, on the other hand, the self is what lies beneath the leaves, then it can never be revealed *on* them; it may be revealed, but never represented. The self must either be exhausted by its textual representation or escape it altogether. Even in Melville's excitement over the completion of *Moby-Dick*, one can already glimpse the despair and frustration that will shape *Pierre*.

The identity Melville discovers as he writes and reads is a discontinuous one at best, one only partially or momentarily embodied in language: it is in this same paragraph that he speaks of his "horrible" reputation as "a 'man who lived among the cannibals'" (130). The sailor/author of *Typee* is not the author of *Moby-Dick*, he implies.[1] But neither can the Melville of 1851 succeed in adequately representing himself in his work: "What I feel most moved to write, that is banned,—it will not pay. Yet, altogether, write the *other* way I cannot. So the product is a final hash, and all my books are botches" (128).

Melville's dissatisfaction begins with *Redburn*, at the point where he starts to question both genealogical and textual identity. That novel shows Melville's increasing awareness of both the act of writing and the assumptions about knowledge and representation implicit in narrative form. Once a text has been desacralized, stripped of the father's external authority, it becomes dependent on its own internal structure and language to adequately embody and recreate its subject. And when the text is an autobiographical (or pseudo-autobiographical) one, it is the possibility of self-knowledge and self-representation that is at stake.

Textual self-creation is, however, threatened by the same force that ultimately undermines bodily and genealogical identity—the passage of time. For the very temporality that structures autobiographical narrative also distances the writer from both his earlier experience and the embodiment of that experience in a text.[2] A simple recapitulation of events cannot, as Redburn discovers, join writing and written selves; it can only objectify the gap between them.

In *White-Jacket* and *Moby-Dick*, Melville and his narrators try to escape the temporal constraints of narrative by inserting alternative textual structures: in *White-Jacket*, a spatial investigation of the ship as microcosm, and in *Moby-Dick*, both a spatial analysis of the whale's body and a dramatic rendering of events themselves. These expository and dramatic counter-structures are attempts to achieve a different kind of textual order and verisimilitude, but they have their own uncontrollable and threatening implications. The self cannot, finally, be given adequate textual form, for the writer himself always remains outside the closure of his text, a living challenge to his own self-representation, caught between his distance from and his dependence on his own "life story." Such formal issues are openly thematized in *Pierre*, as Melville abandons first-person narrative and sharply distances himself from both his protagonist and the autobiographical project itself.

For too long, critics accepted Melville's own self-deprecating description of *Redburn* and *White-Jacket* as merely "two *jobs*, which I have done for money" (*Letters*, 91). Even today, the emphasis remains on their thematic contents, with occasional mention of formal "flaws" like *Redburn*'s shifts in narrative perspective. My reading, on the other hand, emphasizes the *thematic and formal* continuity between these works and *Moby-Dick*, treating them as a sequence of deliberately increasing formal complexity.

Many writers make no attempt to connect *Moby-Dick* with the rest of Melville's work, treating it instead as an isolated masterpiece.[3] Others see only external or biographical causes for Melville's technical development as a writer—his encounters with Shakespeare and Hawthorne, his growing alienation from his readership, etc. Melville's shifts in subject matter and tone in *Pierre*, for example, are seen by Hershel Parker and Brian Higgins as his reply to the critical and popular reception of *Moby-Dick*.[4] Such explanations, however, have little to say about either the formal changes in Melville's texts or his decision to abandon first-person narration in *Pierre* (and most of his work thereafter).

An exclusively formal reading like Edgar Dryden's, on the other hand, cannot explain the radical shift in tone between *Moby-Dick* and *Pierre*. If, in Dryden's terms, Ishmael succeeds in constructing a *fictional* world, why is that world so emphatically rejected in *Pierre*? The answer, I think, is that neither Ishmael nor Melville seeks a fictional selfhood, and that *Moby-Dick* is Melville's final, unsuccessful attempt to create an autobiographical self that will be more than fictional. These are the stakes that Melville plays for in his increasingly complex, increasingly desperate formal experiments. It is the failure of autobiographical form as a mode of self-definition or creation that generates both the bitterness and the third-person detachment of Melville's narration in *Pierre*.

I.

The first half of *Redburn*, as we have seen, is structured by the memory of the hero's absent father. The father serves as a mediating, enabling figure: the difference in perspective between man and boy is stabilized and represented by the ability or failure of each to recognize the irreversibility of paternal absence. But after the boy's disillusionment with his father's guidebook, the ironic distance between narrator and character collapses,[5] and it is left to the narrator to create a textual—rather than genealogical—order that will both link and distinguish between boy and man. It is *Redburn*, not *The Picture of Liverpool*, that must now identify him as its author.

This slippage, in which the voices of boy and man become indistinguishable, also reveals a more basic tension. Just as time must separate the boy from his father and make the latter's actions unrepeatable, so it must separate the older narrator from his boyhood self. They are, in one sense, identical, but in another, they remain utterly different. Just as history strips *The Picture of Liverpool* of its referential value, demonstrating the gulf between father and son, so the boy's crayon marks in the margins contrast with the adult's description of the volume, suggesting a comparable gap within Redburn himself. It is this difficulty—this temporal division *within* the self—that Melville and his narrator attempt to address in the second half of the novel.

The adult Redburn has defined himself throughout as a narrator, as the storyteller whose knowledge and linguistic authority differentiate him from his younger self. He thus maintains a steadily ironic distance from the boy's linguistic inexperience; it is he, after all, who cites the terms that he now understands, the language he has mastered since the events of his story. He describes going to sea for the first time as "like going into a barbarous country, where they speak a strange dialect . . . sailors have their own names, even for things that are familiar ashore" (65). And beyond this, there is also "an infinite number of totally new names of new things to learn" (65). The narrator, unlike the boy, revels in this proliferation of names: "It is really wonderful how many names there are in the world," he says (65–66). He assumes that language can be stabilized and mastered, just as the "mixed and entangled" ropes in the ship's rigging can be disentangled into separate lines, each with its own name (65). The man's knowledge of sea language and procedure is the standard that defines the boy's ignorance and naiveté and establishes his own narrative authority.

The mature Redburn is still vulnerable to a nostalgia for the innocence and security of childhood, but he checks himself by reasserting his position as narrator. Just as the boy longs for the days when his father had taken him to the fort in New York harbor, the older narrator wishes to "build a little cottage . . . and live there all my life" (35). He must repress this desire, however, "for when I think of those days, something rises up in my throat and almost strangles me" (36). Such a renewed dependence on paternal authority would undermine, not strengthen, his authority as narrator, effectively silencing him. Here Redburn uses his authorial role as a defense against his desire for the father's return; patriarchal authority and textual control are now described as antithetical, the latter conceived as an escape from the mystification and failure of the former.

The boy is confronted with a series of purportedly authoritative texts aboard ship: first the Bible, then *The Wealth of Nations*, and finally Jack Blunt's *Bonaparte Dream Book*. Each proves either uninterpretable or use- less. Their failures, which foreshadow that of his father's guidebook, are all registered by the narrator, though not by the boy himself.[6] The *Dream Book*, for example, is satirized through direct narrative manipulation. Blunt "revered, adored, and worshiped" his book, believing it to contain "all the secrets of futurity" (90). But he can barely read, and the text leaves him "perplexed and lost in mazes" (90). He does manage to escape, however, arriving "at a conclusion satisfactory to him" by projecting the meaning he desires onto the text he cannot interpret (90–91). Young Redburn does not comment on Blunt's "reading," but the narrator's ironic distance is evident as he juxtaposes his description of the book with a near collision at sea: "This Dream Book of Blunt's reminds me of a narrow escape we had . . ." (92). The near accident occurs just as the sailor is busily interpreting a dream, before his book can "predict" it.

Blunt, as we shall see, is far from an atypical reader. He believes that his book contains "the secrets of futurity," that the principle of temporal order can be hidden "inside" a text. But such secrets can be uncovered in only two ways: by entanglement in an interpretive "maze" or the projection of meaning onto the textual surface. Texts are not composed of easily separable strands like those of the *Highlander*'s rigging. Compounding the problem is the fact that interpretation is a *temporal* process, one that must insert itself between a prediction and its fulfillment. The narrator knows that time has undermined the authority of his father's text, but he does not yet realize that the lesson applies to all texts, his own included.

Redburn's objective is, ultimately, to control narrative time—to overcome the temporal distance between boy and man by creating a textual order that will act as a link between them. His self-conscious narrative ordering becomes increasingly apparent as the ship nears Liverpool. He carefully regulates his description of the boy's treatment by the sailors, discussing each "bitter lesson" at the appropriate moment, "all in good time" (48). He mentions geographical points not when they are reached by the ship, but according to his own authorial convenience (97)—the temporal and geographical structure of the voyage is clearly subordinated to that of narration itself.

His narrative interventions in the temporality of the voyage are soon openly acknowledged, as he compresses the remainder of the outward trip: "we have not got to Liverpool yet; though, as there is little more to be said concerning the passage out, the Highlander may as well make sail and get there as soon as possible" (114). This narrative compression increases still further when the ship reaches port:

> as I do not mean to present a diary of my stay there, I shall here simply record the general tenor of the life led by our crew during that interval; and will then proceed to note down, at random, my own wanderings

about town, and impressions of things as they are recalled to me now, after the lapse of so many years. (136)

What is foregrounded here is the text's status as a made object, one whose order is created rather than given. And Redburn presents his narrative rearrangement as the necessary result of the lapse of time between his experience and his act of writing. The temporal gap that gives him his narrative authority also prevents a systematic representation of events—it makes his experience inaccessible except in a truncated, random form, defined by the limits of his present memory. The man can never fully reproduce (repeat) the boy's experience in his text. "[S]o many years have elapsed," he laments, "ere I have thought of bringing in my report" (200).

The second half of the novel, however, is marked by the attempt to fashion just such a repetitive structure, one that will enable Redburn to maintain a relation of simultaneous identity with and difference from his earlier self. As before, this relationship depends on the mediating presence of a third term—in Chapter 44, Redburn introduces Harry Bolton to the reader.

Harry, like Redburn, is fatherless, but unlike his friend, he has squandered a substantial inheritance—a crucial and characteristic difference, as it turns out. Redburn sets out to initiate Bolton into life at sea, but he does not wish to make Harry's voyage a simple repetition of his own. He wants to help Harry avoid his own earlier mistakes, to make his friend's shipboard experience parallel to but different from his. But despite his vow that Captain Riga, "that *gallant gay deceiver*,'" will not "altogether cajole" Harry, his warnings prove ineffectual (219). The captain dons "that same bland, benevolent, and bewitchingly merry expression, that had so charmed, but deceived me," and Bolton returns from his interview "full of admiration at so urbane and gentlemanly a sea-captain" (219, 220). Redburn's paradoxical desire for repetition "with a difference" cannot be satisfied; as both boy and man discover, neither difference nor repetition can be fully controlled, on either the level of action or that of narration. In this case, Harry's repetition of Redburn's mistake undermines both the value of initiation and the boy's claim to a position of narrative superiority. Harry remains irreducibly different from his friend, and this difference prevents his assimilation into a triangular structure (boy/Bolton/narrator) that will parallel that of the outward journey (boy/father/narrator).

The main obstacle to such a repetitive structure is, in fact, not so much that Harry and Redburn are different, but that Harry seems to embody the very principle of difference itself, to represent an element of disorder inimical to any narrative structure. Under cross-examination, Harry shows himself to be another possible "deceiver." He describes his previous experience as a sailor with an "off-hand and confident air," but Redburn notes that "even in conversation, Harry was a prodigal; squandering his aristocratic narratives with a careless hand; and, perhaps, sometimes spending funds of reminiscences not his own" (220, 221). If Redburn's initiation began with a training in the proper use of sea language, Harry's speech is characterized by its irresponsibility, its resistance to the very notion of "truthful" representation.

One of Bolton's first actions is to carry his friend off to London, in flagrant violation of the ship's regulations. But before they leave, he changes into a "perfectly plain suit" (225) and then slips away to don false whiskers and a mustache. " 'It's *me*,' " says the stranger who rejoins Redburn, "and who was *me* but Harry, who had thus metamorphosed himself. I asked him the reason; and . . . expressed a hope that he was not going to turn gentleman forger" (226). Harry's identity is unstable, liable to metamorphose before his friend's eyes; he looks, in fact, like one of those "perfectly formed beings . . . who seem to have been born in cocoons" (216). Such changeableness makes Redburn fear that Bolton will turn into a forgery, a false gentleman, or turn to forgery, the misuse of language to misrepresent identity. If this were the case (and it is), Harry would become an outright threat to linguistic order, unassimilable into either nautical or narrative structure.

Bolton takes his companion to a gambling house, whose atmosphere of unreality reminds Redburn of the fairy-tale palace of Aladdin. Fantasy and reality are inseparable here, however; the name of the *actual* house is the same as that of the *fictional* "Aladdin's Palace" (231). And this real/fictional palace is built of illusions: its floors sound hollow, mocking the magnificent decor, and its "walls [are] painted so as to deceive the eye" in the artificial gaslight (228).

The primary illusion in this "Aladdin's Palace" is, of course, the gambling that takes place there. Chips are substitutes for money, which is itself a substitute for real goods; and these signifiers, doubly removed from their referents, are then surrendered to the play of chance. Gambling, in this sense, represents a fundamental dissolution of the signifying order, and Harry, as a compulsive gambler, embodies this instability. "His conduct was unaccountable," Redburn says, he "seemed almost another person" (233). The apparent inconsistency of Bolton himself makes a narrative "account" of his character impossible.

The artificial and illusory timelessness of the gambling house is profoundly disorienting for Redburn, too. He finds it hard to think of his friends and relatives in America, to connect his life there with his presence in such a house (229). He begins to lose his sense of his own continuous identity over time. Finally, a "terrible revulsion" comes over the boy, and the place begins to seem corrupt and "infected" (233). Harry eventually sweeps him back to Liverpool again, making him swear never to ask about "'this infernal trip,'" placing its unauthorized and indescribable events outside the realm of discourse, beyond all linguistic control (235).

The trip has, in fact, taken them into a subversive territory, where actions become unnarratable and "unaccountable," and identity and self-consistency no more than illusions. The episode undermines the very possibility of self-representation in art or language; it cannot be spoken of or repeated if narrative order is to be maintained. Silence, on the other hand, is also insufficient; even though Harry flees the gambling house in near-suicidal despair, he remains a linguistic gambler, "spending" his words as if they, too, were empty signifiers and threatening to "infect" or corrupt the text that would enclose him.

The narrator responds by attempting to integrate Harry into the order of linguistic authority on which his text depends. "It was destined that our departure from the English strand, should be marked by a tragical event, akin to the sudden end of the suicide, which had so strongly impressed me on quitting the American shore," he says at the opening of Chapter 48 (243). One of the newly shipped men, as I described earlier, turns out to be a corpse, which bursts into phosphorescent flames, terrifying the crew and Redburn himself (244–45). The narrator thus tries to counter the nightmarish dissolution of order on the trip to London with another nightmare vision, one that *reconstitutes* narrative order, by describing the event as a repetition of an earlier one, another beginning.

But before the older Redburn even begins to describe "how my friend, Harry, got along as a sailor" (252), he breaks off his narration in an attempt to anticipate, and thus defend against, the failure of initiation that is to follow. He does so by collapsing narrative time and announcing Bolton's eventual death:

Poor Harry! a feeling of sadness, never to be comforted, comes over me, even now when I think of you. For this voyage that you went, but carried you part of the way to that ocean grave, which has buried you up with your secrets, and whither no mourning pilgrimage can be made. (252)

His friend, like his father, is now dead, gone beyond the reach of any earthly journey. The proleptic narrative intrusion both acknowledges and preempts Harry's failure to be another Redburn, to repeat his process of initiation and maturation. The unbridgeable temporal distance between Redburn and the Bolton he remembers has, however, always existed; it is only reemphasized and reified by Redburn's survival.

The narrator struggles against this loss, exclaiming, "But Harry! you live over again, as I recall your image before me. I see you, plain and palpable as in life; and can make your existence obvious to others. Is he, then, dead, of whom this may be said?" (252). A moment later, however, he admits that the Harry he remembers is not the Harry who once lived: "you are mixed with a thousand strange forms, the centaurs of fancy" (252). Memory cannot bring the dead back to life; it can only reconstitute them as creatures of the imagination, fictions similar in kind to the illusions of "Aladdin's Palace."[7]

The narrator's preemptive interruption thus calls into question its own claims for the re-presentational power of memory. For now the instability and unreality of "Aladdin's Palace" are shown to be inevitably reproduced by the very operations of memory on which Redburn's text depends. Harry represents not so much an *external* threat to textual order as an element of *internal*, constitutive disorder that must undermine the stability of any narrative structure. There is no clear opposition between the "illusion" of the gambling house and the "reality" of Redburn's text; the two are inextricably intertwined. If the first half of the novel culminates in a revelation of the paternal absence at its center, the second half illustrates the inevitable breakdown of its own narrative and textual order.

When Harry first appears on the deck of the *Highlander*, his outlandish dress leads Redburn to suspect once again that his friend has lied about his experience at sea. Where Redburn had been simply ignorant of shipboard language and custom, Harry flaunts his disregard for them with a sartorial pun: "'Is not this the morning watch, and is not mine a morning gown?'" (254). He will not admit his ignorance, and only sets out to provoke the crew even further. "Thus," says the narrator, "Harry, from the very beginning, was put down for a very equivocal character" (254). Bolton is labelled by the crew, but also put down in the text as "equivocal"; such equivocality or inconsistency of character will be the norm of *The Confidence-Man*, but here it is simply unassimilable—for Redburn and Melville himself—into the orders of either ship or narrative.

Harry tells his friend that "*his nerves would not stand*" going aloft into the rigging (255–56). Going aloft for the first time and returning safely began Redburn's integration into the life of the ship, but it has the opposite effect on Bolton. Ordered at last to climb the rigging, he complies, but "came down pale as death" and refuses to do so again—"For the residue of the voyage," Harry "became an altered person" (257). Neither boy nor man can understand the change: "Perhaps his spirit, for the time, had been broken. But I will not undertake to explain . . . there are passages in the lives of all men . . . so seemingly contradictory of themselves, that only He who made us can expound them" (258). This is a radical admission on the narrator's part. Harry has been lost to him not simply because of his death, but because there is no linear or structural consistency by means of which the development of character can be understood or represented. And if Harry is finally an inaccessible mystery to both character and narrator, Redburn the boy must then be a similar mystery to Redburn the man.

The narrator's attempt to create a triangular structure that will link him to his boyhood self thus collapses long before it can be completed. The character on whom the pattern depends—Harry Bolton—not only proves unreliable and inconsistent but also reveals the instability and disorder inherent in all written narrative. If Redburn's memories of Harry are matters of "fancy" rather than fact, so must his memories of his own experience be either fragments or fictionalized reconstructions. Memory cannot yield more than a fragmented, discontinuous selfhood, and Redburn's text cannot do more than confirm the loss.

Once the repetitive structure linking boy and man has given way, the narrator's adult perspective comes to dominate the text—his narrative responsibilities and present memory determine its structure. He carefully selects his details—about the fever that sweeps through the steerage, for example: "scenes ensued," he says, "over which, for the most part, a vail must be drawn; for such is the fastidiousness of some readers, that, many times, they must lose the most striking incidents in a narrative like mine" (286). The narrator's primary relationship is now with his text and its readers in the present, not with his own experience in the past. He locates his book in relation to other texts: several chapters begin with Biblical or classical allusions (277, 267), and his description of the epidemic is designed to fill in the blanks left in newspaper reports (292).

The ship reenters the Narrows outside New York harbor at midday on a Sunday (298). The *Highlander* is becalmed, but this pseudo-pastoral moment does not coincide with the moment of return; the pastoral security earlier associated with the father is not reinvoked as the voyage ends. When the ship docks the following morning, Harry and Redburn remain on deck, "for the scene of suffering is a scene of joy when the suffering is past; and the silent reminiscence of hardships departed, is sweeter than the presence of delight" (301). Here the passage of time brings joy at the *loss* of the past, more joy than the present delight that will itself be lost in a moment. The boy's desire to repeat the past has been replaced by an acceptance of his (safe) distance from it, just as the narrator's attempt to recapture his childhood experience has given way to an assertion of his present narrative role.

Once ashore, Redburn finds letters whose "purport compelled my departure homeward" (304). He leaves his friend, remarking tersely that "I never saw Harry again" (311). He passes over his reception at home—the boy had longed for this moment, in which he would return as a storyteller like his father, but for the older narrator it is only "compelled" and remains overshadowed by Harry's absence. "I pass over this," he says, "and will conclude *my first voyage* by relating all I know of what overtook Harry Bolton" (311). It is again Bolton who prevents the closure of a repetitive structure, leaving the text to end in a series of fragmented, second-hand reports of his fate.

Redburn's description of Bolton's death does, however, allow him to obscure the discontinuity between the end of *"my first voyage"* (rendered twice in italics) and his act of writing. After a row of asterisks, the narrator adds an epilogue: "Years after this, I found myself a sailor in the Pacific," he begins (312). Another sailor tells him of an Englishman who had died on a whaling cruise, a gentleman's son, who, like Harry, "'sang like a bird'" (312). "Trembling with expectation," Redburn asks the man's name— "'Harry Bolton was not your brother?' cried the stranger, starting" (312). In a sense, their relationship has indeed been fraternal, for both Harry and young Redburn have been participants in a repetitive structure designed to replace and supersede a lost paternal authority. But the same temporality that divides father and son and makes a resurrection of the father's presence impossible now separates Redburn and Bolton.

Time also divides Redburn from his younger self, and this distance is forcibly restated by the novel's last words: "But yet I, Wellingborough Redburn, chance to survive, after having passed through far more perilous scenes than any narrated in this, *My First Voyage*—which here I end" (312). Between the end of Redburn's "first voyage" and the composition of his text lie "far more perilous scenes," moments of experience that must remain discontinuous, temporally distinct from one another even as the boy's experience remains irrecoverably distant from the man's act of writing. Redburn's closing is an emphatic reassertion of that act—the book is his narration, which here he ends. But he can, finally, define himself only indirectly, as the man whose experience extends beyond the limits of this (or any) autobiographical text.

2.

Unlike Redburn the boy and Redburn the man, the narrator and central character of *White-Jacket* are not distinguished by a sharp difference in age. The temporal gap between them is instead represented symbolically, by the white jacket whose possession identifies the sailor/character and whose surrender enables the writer to survive and begin his text. And while Redburn treats the temporal structure of his voyage as a necessary organizational principle, the narrator of *White-Jacket* tries to escape the self-division inherent in narrative temporality by juxtaposing his voyage with a second, expository structure, a spatial investigation of the "geography" and hierarchy of a man-of-war. These two modes of recapturing and ordering experience—temporal narrative and spatial exposition—alternate as organizational patterns throughout the novel, but neither can satisfactorily identify its creator. Melville's text ends by abandoning them both, first suspending narrative temporality and then redefining the microcosmic status of the *Neversink*: instead of an external structure in whose terms the self is to be defined, the ship becomes an image of the larger, transcendent—but still problematic—self.

White-Jacket begins in mid-voyage and ends before the *Neversink* reaches its final destination. Melville's narrator invokes the temporality of a voyage, but only to divest it of its power to determine the beginning and end of his text. The novel opens in the port of Callao in Peru, identified in Melville's Preface to the English edition as "the frigate's last harbor in the Pacific, just previous to weighing her anchor for home."[8] The narrator has not joined the *Neversink* at this point in its cruise—he often refers to events earlier on the voyage (91, 207, 223, 290). This initial divergence from his voyage frame is at once an assertion of his power over the materials of his story and an admission that temporal narration yields only a contingent and inadequate structure, not a necessary or unchallengeable one.

The event with which the narrator begins is part of a personal history—the making of the jacket that will give him his nickname. The jacket itself is the subject of the first sentence: "It was not a *very* white jacket, but white enough, in all conscience, as the sequel will show" (3). Its color is introduced as the course of a symbolic narrative order, to be demonstrated in a series of events ("as the sequel will show"). Almost immediately, however, a tension is established between character and narrator—the former is identified by means of his jacket while the latter, who no longer has the jacket, remains an unnamed "I." He may refer to himself as "White-Jacket," but in doing so he is closer to creating a pseudonym than establishing a single identity.

We have seen how the jacket, at first intended as a device to insulate and protect the body, soon becomes an identifying mark, much against its owner's will. The transformation of an object external to the self into an ostensible synecdoche for it suggests White-Jacket's loss of freedom and identity aboard ship. The narrator's very ability to speak either in the first person or as "White-Jacket" thus indicates the power he assumes *as writer*.

Authorial power, however, is again predicated upon the narrator's difference from, not his identity with, his earlier self. The assertion of narrative control only reinscribes and confirms this internal limit, as when the narrator describes the abandonment of his jacket in the penultimate rather than the final chapter of the book. If the temporal structure of the voyage need not enclose the text, neither can that defined by the making, wearing, and discarding of the jacket. Indeed, the narrator has from the very beginning spoken of the jacket as something he will have to *outlive*: "my shroud it came very near proving . . ." (3). Narrator must necessarily be distinct from character, and his textual authority must inevitably depend upon and recreate the self-division he seeks to remedy.

Such temporal discontinuities have, in fact, already been described as inherent within the self. The narrator speaks of his memory in terms of a series of distinct and separate moments: "[T]here is a particular day of a particular month of the year, which, from my earliest recollections, I have always kept the run of, so that I can even now tell just where I was on that identical day of every year past" (173). Such a temporal fragmentation of the self is implicit in the workings of memory itself; just as different moments of selfhood must be distinct from each other in space and time, so "White-Jacket" is no longer identical with the narrator's "I."

Melville's narrator turns to a spatial survey of the *Neversink* in the hope that this expository mode will give his text, and thus his experience, a spatial, rather than temporal, integrity. The importance of this second structure is indicated both in his subtitle, "The World in a Man-of-War," and in his Preface: "The object of this work," he claims, "is to give some idea of the *interior life* of a man-of-war" (487, my emphasis). His method, he says, will be to "paint general life in the Navy" through "illustrative scenes"—to open and display the ship's interior on the surface of the page (487, 386). The *Neversink* has neither a "Directory" nor a "*Handbook*"— *White-Jacket* is to be the "reliable guide," the inventory and map the reader needs (127).

The frigate does seem to offer the possiblity of textual closure, for it functions as a tightly closed, microcosmic system, "a state in itself," with the captain as its absolute despot (23). Its order is, however, built not only on physical confinement—for the men, the ship is a "sea-Newgate," a floating prison (176)—but also on a comparable psychological constriction. Its spatial organization is designed to obliterate the seaman's sense of identity, to abolish his past and future and redefine him in purely spatial terms, through his present place aboard ship. To escape the scourge, one sailor is driven to "isolate and entomb himself," locking up his past as in a bank vault (52). White-Jacket himself withholds the fact of his previous service on a whaler, suppressing his own earlier identity (16). Remembering moments from his past becomes no more than a way of "*killing* time" (173, my emphasis).

The "or" that links Melville's title and subtitle actually marks the temporal and spatial orders as mutually exclusive, for the spatial regime of the *Neversink* is specifically designed to exclude the temporality of individual lives. "Before" and "after" are reconceived as periods outside the world of the ship and beyond the captain's reach. In this sense, then, White-Jacket the writer must be an "outsider" in relation to his own experience as a sailor: the roles of narrator and sailor are once again shown to be incompatible.

Authority on the *Neversink* is, as I have suggested, manifested through the management of the space of the ship. Officers are distinguished from men in that they have access to the entire vessel. For them, "almost every inch is in plain sight" (41); their supervisory power directly corresponds to the sailors' lack of privacy. Much of the ship is hidden from and "completely inaccessible to the sailor": the cabins of Commodore and Captain are, of course, "sealed volumes" to White-Jacket (127, 128). But if he is to complete his survey of the man-of-war as microcosm, these are precisely the areas he must include, for they will be excluded from the narrative proper. His "*Handbook*" is thus written in violation of the order it represents and can only be written from outside it.

White-Jacket breaks the temporal progress of his story in Chapter 30, to discuss the "Subterranean Parts" of the ship (123). He begins his survey only hesitantly, from the outside, as "A Peep through a Port-hole," but then takes the reader "under the lee of my white jacket," reasserting his sailor's perspective to examine the "depths" of the ship's hold (123). This, however, is the most dehumanizing station for a sailor; the "holders" are "a lazy, lumpish, torpid set," "pale as ghosts," nameless men with "contracted souls" (10, 11, 47). Here is yet another reason for White-Jacket's hesitation, for the images that dominate his "picture" are, again and again, those of violence and death. The "gloomy apartment" of the Yeoman's store-room, accessible only through a "dim, devious corridor," contains the "vaults and catacombs" of the *Neversink*'s armory (124). For White-Jacket, these store-rooms are a "bottomless hole," and he has a "peculiar dread" of the "goggle-eyes" of the Yeoman, fearing that he may "drag me down into tarry perdition" (125, 126).[9]

The narrator next moves up from the hold to the main-mast, the center of both the ship and the disciplinary order by which it is ruled. Equidistant from the hold and its opposite, White-Jacket's main-top, the base of the main-mast is "the only place where the sailor can hold formal communication with the captain and officers" (131). It is "the Police-office, Court-house, and yard of execution," the point at which floggings are administered before the assembled crew (131). Here White-Jacket's geographical exploration stops abruptly, as both character and text are called to "witness punishment."

White-Jacket returns to explicitly spatial terms only in Chapter 76, "The Chains," where he describes the one spot to which a sailor may "steal away, and, for a few moments, almost be private" (322). "The chains designates the small platform outside of the hull," he explains, a point on the margin of the ship, on the *Neversink* and outside it at the same time (322). Here one can look out over the sea and remain unobserved from the main deck, outside naval order for a moment.

The "tranquillizing" effect of the chains (322) is short-lived, however—the next chapter takes White-Jacket below decks again, to the ship's hospital, the sick-bay. This is yet another "subterranean vault," presided over by the surgeon's steward, "a small, pale hollow-eyed young man, with [a] peculiar Lazarus-like expression" (326). He has "buried himself below," and "his countenance ever wore an aspect of cadaverous resignation to his fate" (326). It is here, in this poorly ventilated "furnace" of a death chamber, that White-Jacket ends his expository survey and joins it to his narrative, as he watches over his dying messmate Shenly (336).

Where Redburn had been tempted to smash his father's glass ship to reach the treasure he imagined hidden in its interior, White-Jacket has managed to penetrate into the interior of the *Neversink*. What he finds there is not an "interior life," but only death. The world of the frigate can neither enclose the text nor absorb it; it does not define White-Jacket, but instead excludes him and his writing.

Enclosure within the spatial system of the ship means both physical constraint and a psychological oppression that is tantamount to the death of the self. The sailor's personality is inevitably obscured or absorbed by his place and function aboard the man-of-war. Seamen are no more than interchangeable pawns: at best, they "harmoniously dove-tail into each other, and, by our very points of opposition, unite in a clever whole, like the parts of a Chinese puzzle" (164).

The key to this "puzzle" is, of course, the Articles of War, the set of "arbitrary laws" upon which its structure of command depends (138). White-Jacket, confined by the physical limits of the ship, is also covered and enclosed by the terms of the Articles, from which there is no escape either: "Afloat or wrecked the Martial Law relaxes not its gripe" (295). The Articles are an unholy Text, based on un-Christian violence, which sets officers, marines, and crew in "incurable antagonism to one another" (374).

Most important, however, the Articles are the *only* text granted authority aboard the *Neversink*. There is no space allotted for a chapel or a library, for example, no place in the ship's structure for either Biblical or literary authority. Neither is there any "liberty of expression" allowed to White-Jacket or his comrades (65): the sailor's tongue is "treble-knotted by the law" (218). The symbolic order White-Jacket would appropriate cannot, ultimately, structure his autobiographical text, for that order defines itself by suppressing individuality and writing. If the *Neversink* were indeed a microcosm of the world as a whole, *White-Jacket* could never have been written. The temporal self-division of narrative, he discovers, carries with it both a physical and, more important, an authorial freedom that he is ultimately forced to reassert.

The act of writing, even when it does not directly attack naval customs, is the creation of a countertext, and thus an act of independence, a defiant assertion of individuality.[10] One sailor keeps a journal, reading from it to other sailors, but the captain, hearing that it "contained reflections somewhat derogatory to the dignity of the officers," orders it nailed shut and thrown overboard, on the ground that it contravenes "a certain clause in the Articles" (43). *White-Jacket* is a similar text, one whose existence depends upon and testifies to its author's escape from the enclosure of the *Neversink* and its laws. The narrator even likens his act of writing to an act of mutiny, declaring himself willing to "fight you—Commodores and Captains of the navy—on your own quarter-deck" (147).

White-Jacket offers his text, along with art and fiction in general, as antidotes to the dehumanization brought on by the reduction to place and function on board ship: "perhaps the best of all" remedies is "a shelf of merrily-bound books" (46). *White-Jacket* in particular counteracts the force of the Articles by historicizing them, placing then within a larger narrative. Naval customs, according to the narrator, are perpetuated because of "the prevailing mystification that has been thrown about" them, making them immune to historical change (231). His strongest argument against the Articles involves a tracing of their "genealogy" back to the Restoration, when they originated as a "tyrannical" reaction against the freedom within the Cromwellian navy (297–98). The writing of *White-Jacket* thus leads him back to a renewed assertion of the power of history, of time itself, against the static spatial order of the man-of-war. The text's very existence must, in fact, deny the validity of the microcosmic order it attempts to create; it must assert its own temporal incompletion, its own lack of closure and inability to encompass its author's experience, as the price of individual freedom.

The tension between White-Jacket's two roles thus remains an inescapable structural difficulty, a necessary strain within the text. For all of "White-Jacket's" limitations as common sailor, it is *his* experience that gives the narrator access to the *Neversink*. The narrative persona thus must oscillate between the distanced "I" and the involved but constrained "White-Jacket," just as the novel swings between the two formal poles of spatially organized exposition and temporally structured narrative. The narrator has not been unaffected by his experience; it has not left him "unhardened" (345). And his narrative must, to be true to its subject, retain the stamp of the "man-of-war world" (345).

At times, the narrator openly manipulates the gap between sailor and writer, often using "White-Jacket" to define the limits of his knowledge and his text: it is "White-Jacket" who must evade the matter of incompetent officers, "White-Jacket" whose "understanding is limited" (112, 194). In discussing the Articles of War, on the other hand, the narrator uses the first person to emphasize his present power and freedom, *addressing* "White-Jacket," speaking to an earlier self who cannot himself speak out (294–95).

Just after one of the novel's climactic moments, in which White-Jacket is driven to the point of open rebellion when he is to be unjustly flogged (for not being at his assigned post), the narrator retreats from the event into the editorial "we":

> Let us forget the scourge and the gangway a while, and jot down in our memories a few little things pertaining to our man-of-war world. I let nothing slip, however small; and feel myself activated by the same motive which has prompted many worthy old chroniclers, to set down the merest trifles . . . which, if not preserved in the nick of time, must infallibly perish from the memories of man. (282)

His detachment as narrator gives him a safe distance from his own harrowing experience, but it also preserves that experience; it allows him, paradoxically, to forget and record at once—to forget, perhaps, because he has done the recording. He responds by placing his faith in the passage of time itself, which will invalidate his picture of naval life, rendering it no more than an archaic text, an outdated historical fragment. His "guidebook" will become like Redburn's, a relic rather than an authoritative text. He imagines a time when nothing of White-Jacket the man will remain; there will only be a book, *White-Jacket*, to be "quoted to show the people in the Millennium what [or who] a man-of-war was" (282).

The book's last numbered chapter is set on the main-top, a marginal spot like the chains, seemingly above and beyond the authority of the ship's officers. For White-Jacket, it becomes an ideal space of freedom and brotherhood: "We main-top-men were brothers," he says, a "fraternity of fine fellows . . . and we loaned ourselves to each other with all the freedom in the world" (15). He longs to recapture this freedom, in fact, contrasting it with the "martial formalities and thousand vices" of the ship below (77). He associates the "lofty masthead" with "eternal principle" (147); falling from the "royal-yard" is "like falling as Lucifer from the well-spring of morning down to the Phlegethon of night" (196). He says he feels "persuaded in my inmost soul" that it is "the fact of my having been a main-top-man" that enables him to give an "account of our man-of-war world; withholding nothing; inventing nothing" (47). The main-top-man's perspective is, for him, analogous to the writer's.

The rigging is also a timeless, eternal space, close to the unchanging stars (76). It is here that White-Jacket would wish to close his text—on the main-top, outside both space and time. He deliberately suspends his description of the cruise, refusing to recount the *Neversink*'s arrival in Norfolk. "Let us leave the ship on the sea—still with the land out of sight," he says, shifting into the first person plural and the present tense:

We main-top-men are all aloft in the top; and round our mast we circle, a brother-band, hand in hand, all spliced together. . . . Our last death-denouncing Article of War has been read; and far inland, in that blessed clime whitherward our frigate now glides, the last wrong in our frigate will be remembered no more; when down from our main-mast comes our Commodore's pennant, when down sinks its shooting stars from the sky. (396–97)

As the world falls away from this visionary tableau, the "ever-noble . . . matchless and unmatchable Jack Chase" has the last word, quoting Camoens (397).

The narrator thus attempts to close *White-Jacket* on the idyllic, mythical heights of the main-top—a illusory realm that would allow for both spatial unity and temporal freedom. But this is simply to evade the difficulties of the relationship between "White-Jacket" and the narrator's "I" by breaking the temporality of narration before the gap between character and narrator must be acknowledged at the voyage's end.

The question of identity does reemerge in the book's epilogue, "The End." This section extends the ambiguity of the novel's title: the book does not simply contrast history (*White-Jacket*) with a spatial microcosm (*The World in a Man-of-War*); it also describes the world in a *man*-of-war, a man-of-war's man. The narrator restates his image of the ship as a world, a microcosm, with its destination "a secret to ourselves and our officers" but then goes further, turning the ship/world into a body, collapsing it into the self: "Thus sailing with sealed orders, we ourselves are the repositories of the secret packet, whose mysterious contents we long to learn. There are no mysteries out of ourselves" (398). What remains at the end of *White-Jacket* is the mystery of the self, a mystery whose solution is blocked by the temporal gap between experience and its representation; identity can be textualized only metaphorically, as a "secret packet" within the self, an inner Text that is its fate.

3.

Redburn ends by simply acknowledging the distance between its narrator and the events it has described; *White-Jacket* reasserts this temporal disjunction as preferable to the silence and imprisonment implied by the man-of-war as microcosm. To some extent, these novels take up the problem of self-representation only as a philosophical or technical issue; it is not depicted as a psychological crisis for the autobiographer. In *Moby-Dick*, Melville raises the stakes considerably, intensifying his narrator's desire for self-definition and pushing his text up to and beyond the limits of first-person narrative. For Ishmael, the gap between experience and its representation is indeed traumatic, for it coincides with his abandonment at sea, an event that throws his very identity and sanity into question. His efforts to create an alternative to temporal narrative are thus more complex and more compulsive, leading him not only to an expository analysis of the whale but also into the dramatic mode, to recapture the immediacy of his experience by breaking through the past tense of his narration.[11]

Ishmael's predicament as writer springs from the very fact of his survival, from his need to find a meaning in his experience that will justify his continued existence. The best place to enter the novel, then, may be at the point where Ishmael realizes that he *has* survived, in the novel's epilogue. The epilogue acts as a pivot or seam in the text, an endpoint that Ishmael tries to present as another beginning. Its logical function is to establish the provenance of the preceding tale, to authenticate it by confirming his survival as a potential narrator.[12] For Ishmael, it is the logical precondition for *Moby-Dick*'s existence as a text, and he presents the epilogue as the first step in his process of "telling": "And I only am escaped alone to tell thee," reads its epigraph (*Moby-Dick*, 470). In the epilogue, Ishmael seeks to close his story and begin his storytelling in a single gesture.

But experience does not, as we have seen in *Redburn* and *White-Jacket*, transform itself smoothly into memory and narration in this way. Like the closing chapters of *White-Jacket*, the epilogue is an attempt to construct such a continuity, to bridge or obscure the temporal gap between action and text. In Ishmael's case, this gap coincides with his period of immersion in the ocean, a terrifying, possibly maddening experience. Pip, the *Pequod*'s cabin-boy, returns from a similar abandonment as a madman, speaking of himself in the third person and the past tense (397). It is an experience Ishmael never describes directly, from which he returns as an obsessive, anxious narrator, speaking of himself in the past tense of his narration.[13]

Ishmael sees himself surviving only as the bearer of a tale; in the epilogue, we find him clinging to a lifebuoy that is also a coffin and a text. He is "drawn towards the closing vortex" that has devoured the *Pequod*: "When I reached it, it had subsided to a creamy pool. Round and round, then, and ever contracting towards the button-like black bubble at the axis of that slowly wheeling circle, like another Ixion I did revolve" (470). The "black bubble" is the lifebuoy/coffin/text, but it lies at the center of a vortex, at the heart of a maddening, deadly swirl. His primary concern as writer is to establish his narrative and interpretive mastery over his experience, to give his text an integrity of meaning that will make it more than a mere repetition of the events it describes, more than a cyclical return to this vortex. (In a sense, this is the same desire Redburn reveals in his treatment of Harry Bolton—to create a repetition with, in this case, a saving differ-ence.) By stabilizing and reshaping the temporal linearity of events into a text, he aims to overcome their divisive force and thus make character and narrator temporally continuous, identical once again.[14] Both Ishmael's survival and his identity depend upon his ability to textualize his experi-ence: his quotation from Job (1:14–19) implies that he has escaped for a single reason, "only . . . to tell thee."[15]

Ishmael prefaces his text with an impressive array of etymological and textual precedents, but the Etymology and Extracts only indicate his anx-iety about the status of texts in general and his own in particular. Their randomness and inaccuracy display only his lack of confidence and desire for textual authority. He masks his worries, however, with a grand but ambiguous rhetorical gesture: "Call me Ishmael" (12). The name may or may not be a pseudonym like "White-Jacket," but Ishmael consciously appropriates its double-edged biblical connotations. By commanding the reader to address him and at the same time precluding any possibility of address, he establishes himself as another outcast, one whose relation to his reader depends upon tension and difference.[16]

The defensiveness behind Ishmael's self-presentation becomes obvious almost immediately, as rhetorical force gives way to evasion: "Some years ago—never mind how long precisely—having little or no money in my purse, and nothing particular to interest me on shore, I thought I would sail about a little and see the watery part of the world" (12). Ishmael conspic-uously avoids any attempt to date the events of his story—to establish their beginning—and dissuades the reader from any inquiry of his own ("never mind how long"). He displays a studied nonchalance, presenting himself as motiveless and his journey as without direction ("I would sail about a little").

The rest of the paragraph, however, systematically undermines this assumed casualness. Ishmael, it reveals, has gone to sea as an escape from his own uncontrollable and self-destructive violence:

Whenever I find myself growing grim about the mouth; whenever it is a damp, drizzly November in my soul; *whenever I find myself involun-*

tarily pausing before coffin warehouses, and bringing up the rear of every funeral I meet; and especially *whenever my hypos get such an upper hand of me,* that it requires a strong moral principle to prevent me from deliberately stepping into the street, and methodically knocking people's hats off—then, I account it high time to get to sea as soon as I can. (12, my emphases)

Ishmael's fall into depression and morbidity is marked by a detached self-observation ("I find myself"), a division of the self into powerless observing subject and violent, irrational object. Such a split is inherently self-destructive—his journey is begun as an effort to repress and redirect a suicidal fragmentation of the self.[17]

The passage is, however, written in the present tense. These dangerous internal divisions remain even after Ishmael's voyage; they are still present as he begins his narration. If going to sea was a deflection and an escape, Ishmael hopes that reengaging with his experience—writing *Moby-Dick*—will be a restorative and unifying process. He sees his text as a means by which to reconcile and integrate his narrative consciousness (subject) with his experiential, acting self (object). He refuses to provide a date for the beginning of his story because, as his choice of tense and his repetitive verbal patterns ("whenever . . . whenever . . .") imply, it is still, or is again, beginning.

Ishmael claims that all men are, like him, drawn to the water, and to the meditation that is and always will be "wedded" to it (13). "Surely all this is not without meaning," he concludes,

And still deeper the meaning of that story of Narcissus, who because he could not grasp the tormenting, mild image he saw in the fountain, plunged into it and was drowned. But that same image, we ourselves see in all rivers and oceans. It is the image of the ungraspable phantom of life; and this is the key to it all. (14)

If self-scrutiny divides the self into observer and observed, the subject and the object of reflection, water-gazing reproduces and images the process in a doubling of self and reflected image. It is thus that "meditation and water are wedded," joined in difference forever (13). This splitting/doubling is "tormenting," however, because the self and its image, its ungraspable surface reflection, can never be reunified.[18]

The passage also suggests two responses to this dilemma, two different ways in which it may provide "the key to it all." The pursuit of identity and truth may be represented as a direct penetration: the key may open a door into a hidden inner space—the interior of a ship or of a body, or the space beneath a reflecting watery surface. These are the terms in which Ahab describes his pursuit of Moby Dick. Or the search may take the form of a decoding, an interpretation of the surface itself, based upon a *written* key. Ishmael's text experiments with both possibilities: the first in its dramatic chapters, whose images are those of a spiralling descent into pure action, a vortex; the second in its expository chapters, which analyze the body of the whale by dispersing its three-dimensional space over a two-dimensional surface, as a picture/text for interpretation.

For Ishmael, both options represent escapes from the difficulties of narration. He describes his voyage as "part of the grand programme of Providence" drawn up by "those stage managers, the Fates" (15–16). His language blends both textual and dramatic imagery (written program and actual performance), but the Fates also determine events by spinning and measuring out the thread of a mortal's lifeline, establishing a *narrative* line as they do so. It is in response to the linearity of time and fate that Ishmael undertakes his experiments in form, each dominated by an image in which forward, linear movement is deflected or transformed. Such one-dimensional movement, when turned downward in an attempt at spatial penetration, yields a spiral—the vortex of the novel's dramatic chapters. And when dispersed over a two-dimensional plane, it yields the atemporal woven surface of the expository sections. Both structures are attempts to resist the linear progression that enforces and reiterates the temporal split within Ishmael's narration, culminating in his abandonment, his isolation on the edge of death and madness.[19]

These experiments in form are foreshadowed—obliquely thematized, one might say—at several points early in the narrative. Images of surface interpretation are repeatedly played off against images of reality as a depth to be reached or possessed.[20] The oscillation between these perspectives is at its most complex in Chapters 7–9, in which Ishmael visits the Whaleman's Chapel, and Chapters 23–24, which yield Ishmael's first direct commentary on whaling in general.

At the beginning of "The Chapel," Ishmael notes the silent isolation of each of the worshipers. Their grief is muffled and "incommunicable"; it is only the storm outside that "shrieks" (39). All sit "steadfastly eyeing several marble tablets, with black borders, masoned to the wall" (39). Their gaze leads Ishmael to describe three of the tablets, which memorialize whalemen lost at sea, their bodies unrecovered and unburied. It is their focus on these "frigid inscriptions" that isolates the worshipers; the illiterate Queequeg is the only one to notice Ishmael's entrance (40).

Ishmael assumes that many of the congregation are mourning lost relatives, and responds with a self-conscious, openly rhetorical address to his readers:

> ye whose dead lie buried beneath the green grass; who standing among flowers can say—here, *here* lies my beloved; ye know not the desolation that broods in bosoms like these. What bitter blanks in those black-bordered marbles which cover no ashes! What despair in those immovable inscriptions! What deadly voids and unbidden infidelities in the lines that seem to gnaw upon all Faith, and refuse resurrections to the beings who have placelessly perished without a grave. As well might those tablets stand in the cave of Elephanta as here. (41)

Nothing lies behind these tablets; they are inscribed surfaces that cover no depths, hide no remains. Their inscriptions refer to men who are doubly absent: both dead and placeless. The location of the tablets in New Bedford is completely arbitrary. They may be, in this sense, paradigms of textuality—like Redburn's guidebook, with its descriptions of places that no longer exist, they bear the traces of absent referents, inscriptions that at once promise and deny the possibility of resurrection and return. Interpreting these surfaces yields only a sense of loss, for Ishmael here associates meaning with the filling of an interior space, the presence of a body.

Ishmael's discomfiture is evident in the next two paragraphs. The first is another series of questions, syntactically disguised, but questions nonetheless:

> In what census of living creatures, the dead of mankind are included; why it is that a universal proverb says of them, that they tell no tales, though containing more secrets than the Goodwin Sands; how it is that to his name who yesterday departed for the other world, we prefix so significant and infidel a word, and yet do not thus entitle him, if he but embarks for the remotest Indies of this living earth . . . (41)

No text—no census or proverb, no word—can be adequate to the reality of death. Death in the whale fishery, Ishmael says, is "a *speechlessly quick* chaotic bundling of a man into Eternity" (41, my emphasis). The dead may "contain" secrets, but these are not "tales" to be easily or safely told. The dead are excluded from language, "hushed" by the living (41). "All these things," Ishmael says again, "are not without their meanings" (41). But such "meanings" are too troubling for words—Ishmael cannot even ask such questions about absence and death openly; they must be masked as statements or exemplary citations.

Ishmael's evasiveness only increases when he comes to describe his own response to the scene:

> It needs scarcely to be told, with what feelings, on the eve of a Nantucket voyage, I regarded those marble tablets, and by the murky light of that darkened, doleful day read the fate of the whalemen who had gone before me. Yes, Ishmael, the same fate may be thine. (41)

The first sentence, like "all these things are not without their meanings," assumes that something has already been said or discovered, rather than acknowledging it as perhaps unsayable. Ishmael now casts himself in the role of reader, one who deals with texts about death, not death itself. Such a distinction is at work in the second sentence as well: Ishmael speaks there as *narrator*, addressing Ishmael the *character*; his use of the second person ("thine") reaffirms the gap between action and narration, and in doing so, the fact of his survival.

It is this textual distance that lets Ishmael grow "merry" again, and discuss the possibility of death more jovially, claiming that

> We have hugely mistaken this matter of Life and Death. Methinks that what they call my shadow here on earth is my true substance. . . . Methinks my body is but the lees of my better being. In fact take my body who will, take it I say, it is not me. (41)

Here Ishmael speaks as narrator, in the present tense. His "shadow," he suggests, is his "true substance." As Ishmael writes he creates a shadow, a double made of black and white, his autobiographical text. In drawing back from the possibility of his own death, Ishmael is forced to reverse himself, now *affirming* the idea of self-perpetuation in a text.[21]

After the anxieties and maneuverings—in tense, person, and syntax—of "The Chapel," "The Pulpit" quietly returns to the past tense: "I had not been seated very long ere a man of a certain veritable robustness entered . . ." (42). The narrative restraint is as significant as the tense, for

Father Mapple, not the observing Ishmael, is the central figure of the next two chapters; his movement and speech dominate the narrative. Ishmael swings uneasily back and forth between the roles of character/observer and narrator, the temporal distance between them acknowledged even in his language: "At the time I now write of," he says, "Father Mapple was in the hardy winter of a healthy old age," distinguishing the "now" of his writing from the "then" of his story (42).

The narrative description follows Mapple as he climbs into his pulpit, pulling its rope ladder up after him. Ishmael admits to having "pondered some time without fully comprehending" this, for Mapple has "such a wide reputation for sincerity and sanctity, that I could not suspect him of court-ing notoriety by any mere tricks of the stage" (43). Ishmael denies that the pulpit is a theatrical prop, but the terms of his denial reflect the dramatic quality of both this chapter and the next. This proto-dramatic form is a response to the inadequacy of the Chapel's inscriptions: Ishmael's interpre-tive presence, first as character and then even as narrator, disappears, replaced by Mapple and images of a descent or fall *into* meaning. Ishmael does speculate about the pulpit for the rest of the paragraph, but this is the last appearance of the first person and of Ishmael as character until Chapter 10, eight pages later.

Chapter 8 ends with Ishmael speaking as narrator about the pulpit: "What could be more full of meaning?—for the pulpit is ever the earth's foremost part; all the rest comes in its rear; the pulpit leads the world. . . . the world's a ship on its passage out, and not a voyage complete; and the pulpit is its prow" (43–44). This is as much an introduction as a conclusion. Ishmael asserts the the pulpit's position ahead of and above the rest of the world, a point to which Mapple ascends in order to preach. His sermon, Ishmael implies, will stand at the prow of the text, anticipating and encap-sulating its meaning. Here Ishmael's narrative presence ends; the following chapter, "The Sermon," contains almost no narrative description. Mapple's words are quoted in their entirety, his sermon a self-contained and essen-tially dramatic moment.22

Mapple first kneels and offers "a prayer so deeply devout that he seemed kneeling and praying at the bottom of the sea" (44). The pulpit/ prow has now become the sea floor—height and forward position are now depth. He takes as his text Jonah 1:17: "'this book, containing only four chapters—four yarns—is one of the smallest strands in the mighty cable of the Scriptures Yet what depths of the soul does Jonah's deep sea-line sound!'" (45). The preacher begins with "chapters," then, punning on "yarns," turns them into "strands"—segments of a narrative line are re-figured, twisted into strands in the larger "cable" of the Scriptures. Horizontal narrative progression is transformed into a vertical "sounding" of spiritual depths.

Mapple's retelling of the story of Jonah is full of images of downward movement. His cabin aboard ship is a "'contracted hole, sunk . . . beneath the ship's waterline'" (47). Despite "'the whirl of woe he feels,'" his "'prodigy of monstrous misery'" at last "'drags him drowning down to sleep'" (47–48). But Jonah's repentance only comes after a further, literal descent into the sea, as "'the eddying depths sucked him ten thousand fathoms down'" into "'the whirling heart of . . . a masterless commotion'" (50, 49). The descent is a whirling, eddying movement, carrying him down to the bottom of the sea and inside the whale—for him, salvation lies in the dark and violent depth at the center of a vortex.

But Mapple says that the lesson of the book of Jonah, the truth within the vortex, is "'two-stranded'": it is "'a lesson to us all as sinful men, and a lesson to me as a pilot of the living God'" (45). Even the one Word of the Bible yields a divided or double lesson when it is unwound, "opened" by the preacher's explication.

Mapple's distinction is between living, sinning men and himself as a speaker, a division disturbingly parallel to Ishmael's sense of himself as split into actor and narrator. The lesson for all men is that "'if we obey God, we must disobey ourselves,'" that salvation requires an abnegation and denial of the self (45). This self-surrender, the loss of the self as an independent willing agent, is what Jonah finds at the heart of the vortex. But the lesson for Mapple as preacher seems particularly appropriate to Ishmael: "'Woe to him who would not be true, even though to be false were salvation! Yea, woe to him who, as the great pilot Paul has it, while preaching to others is himself a castaway!'" (50). Ishmael has literally been a castaway and is only able to tell his story, his "truth," because of it. Has he been cast away from the truth, out of the vortex that consumes the self? Is his text therefore a false one?

Instead of the surface texts of the tablets on the Chapel wall, which can only indicate their own absence of meaning, Mapple's sermon offers the vortex, a downward, circling penetration beneath waterline and storyline towards truth. But it is both a truth achieved at the cost of the self and a double lesson, divided within itself. Ishmael's form also registers these characteristics: the chief feature of the dramatic mode is its surrender of narrative mediation for the sake of representational force. In a sense, this loss of interpretive distance and control also means a loss of *narrative* identity.

This surrender is evidenced by Ishmael's complete lack of response to the sermon. He does not even mention his own departure from the Chapel afterward; Mapple is described as "kneeling, till all the people had departed, and he was left alone in the place" (51). Mapple's words are never integrated into the forward movement of Ishmael's tale, for he has removed all trace of himself as observing character and, as far as possible, as recording narrator as well.[23] One step further and narrative description becomes stage directions, yielding the explicitly dramatic form of Chapters 37-40.

An opposite shift—away from narrative toward exposition—occurs in Chapters 23 and 24, again in response to the subject of death. Ishmael stops his narration and reasserts his control over the text at the opening of "The Lee Shore": "Some chapters back," he says, "one Bulkington was spoken of" (97). Not some *time* back, but "some chapters back"—Ishmael's reference is to a point in his text, not a moment in narrative time.

Ishmael recognizes Bulkington at the *Pequod*'s helm and, looking forward (but, more important, backward from his position as survivor and narrator), alludes to his shipmate's death: "Wonderfullest things are ever the unmentionable; deep memories yield no epitaphs; this six-inch chapter is the stoneless grave of Bulkington" (97). Here the link between the tablets in the Chapel and Ishmael's book becomes explicit. The length of the chapter (six inches) is spatial rather than temporal; its anticipation of Bulkington's death departs from and escapes the forward movement of the narrative line, dispersing its temporal force into textual space. The depths of memory and the grave are not *reduced to* but are instead *transformed into* the surface of the page. Unlike the inscriptions in New Bedford, the words on Ishmael's page do not mark the absence of a grave—they are the unmarked grave itself. Ishmael here suggests the possibility—his objective—of recovering or reestablishing a textual *presence*. He implies that the body of a man, or of the whale, may be reconstituted in the body of his text.

But Ishmael seems to relinquish this desire almost as soon as he has voiced it, returning to a valorization of penetration and depth. He compares Bulkington to a ship in a storm, driven back out to sea in fear of running aground. He addresses Bulkington (or the reader—the second person does not distinguish between them) directly:

> Know ye, now, Bulkington? Glimpses do ye seem to see of that mortally intolerable truth; that all deep, earnest thinking is but the intrepid effort of the soul to keep the open independence of the sea. . . .

But as in landlessness alone resides the highest truth, shoreless, indefinite as God—so, better is it to perish in that howling infinite, than be ingloriously dashed upon the lee, even if that were safety! (97)

The "highest truth" lies only in the "howling infinite" of the sea. It, like God Himself, must be indefinite, impossible to fix or claim. The risk in the soul's "intrepid effort" to find truth and God—the threat of the vortex, of the loss of the self—is what makes such knowledge "mortally intolerable." Intolerable because it is mortal, deadly.

But "bear thee up grimly," Ishmael advises Bulkington, "Up from the spray of thy ocean-perishing—straight up, leaps thy apotheosis!" (98). If death is the result of Bulkington's "deep, earnest" searching, it will be followed by a spiritual countermovement, the leap upward of his apotheosis. This is Mapple's lesson, delivered in Ishmael's voice this time. Ishmael's survival cannot have been such an apotheosis; his chapter is, after all, entitled "The Lee Shore," not "The Open Sea." If truth can only be discovered in the moment of perishing and apotheosis, Ishmael's efforts must be either self-destructive or fruitless, leading to either a loss of the self or a reassertion of its temporal fragmentation.

In the course of this chapter, Ishmael has already pulled back from Bulkington and the thought of his eventual death, speaking again as narrator rather than character. His narrative role itself now becomes the subject of "The Advocate." "As Queequeg and I," he begins, "are now fairly embarked in this business of whaling," a business regarded as "rather unpoetical and disreputable," I am "all anxiety to convince ye, ye landsmen, of the injustice hereby done to us hunters of whales" (98). The first "I" is Ishmael the character, with whom Queequeg has embarked on the *Pequod*; the second is Ishmael the narrator, anxious to make his reader respect whalemen in general. An experiential, decidedly mortal relationship with Queequeg is relinquished in favor of a safer textual link to the reader.[24]

Ishmael is soon immersed in whaling history again, mining his reference texts for citations. He carries on a mock dialogue with the reader, defending the dignity of whales and whaling by providing various historical examples. He appends a footnote, however—"See subsequent chapters for something more on this head" (101)—referring to Chapters 82 and 90. Such thematic links imply another textual structure independent of narrative; the note reminds us that texts are always "spatializations" of subjects or events, spreading them across surfaces and throughout volumes. Books have shapes of their own—in later chapters, Ishmael will seek to identify the massive body of his text with that of the whale itself.

But the last paragraph of this chapter concerns Ishmael himself as writer:

> if, by any possibility, there be any as yet undiscovered prime thing in me . . . if hereafter I shall do anything that, upon the whole, a man might rather have done than to have left undone; if, at my death, my executors, or more properly my creditors, find any precious MSS. in my desk, then here I prospectively ascribe all the honor and the glory to whaling. (101)

Here Ishmael, for the first time, mentions his text as something that will survive him. His story is that "as yet undiscovered prime thing" that is still within him; completing the work will be the thing better done than left undone; and the "precious MSS." to be found in his desk—that will be *Moby-Dick*, the book that will give him his reputation and perpetuate his memory. Both the interior "contents" of the self and its potential activity are, in this proleptic vision, transformed into a text. The "secret packet" of *White-Jacket*, individual (and authorial) identity itself, is what Ishmael seeks to represent or recover in the pages of *Moby-Dick*.

If Ishmael toys uncertainly with alternatives to narration in these early chapters, he goes on to examine them in greater depth—fully dramatized representation in a series of chapters beginning with "The Quarter-Deck" and self-conscious exposition in his cetological chapters. The former privilege Ishmael's role as observing character, drawn toward the vortex and Ahab's pursuit of the whale, and the latter his position as narrator and survivor, preoccupied with textual surfaces. Both seek a meaning outside or beyond the limits—the fragmented selfhood and preordained end—of narrative, but both will founder, just as Ishmael's earlier efforts have done.[25]

Chapter 35, "The Mast-head," illustrates both the perils of Ishmael's storyline and the narrative defenses he erects against them. First of all, it is not Ishmael but *you*, "a dreamy meditative man," who faces danger atop the mast-head: "There you stand, a hundred feet above the silent decks . . . lost in the infinite series of the sea" (136). As "the tranced ship indolently rolls [and] the drowsy trade winds blow," it is "you," not Ishmael, who lose yourself in the infinite sea, resolved into languor and passivity (137). Ishmael, as before, has reasserted his position as narrator, taking advantage, for the moment, of his safe distance from events. For the loss of consciousness, implicit here, will later in the chapter become loss of identity and death.

Ishmael does gradually move back into the first person, speaking of "we Southern whale-fishers," and then admitting that "I kept but sorry guard. With the problem of the universe revolving in me, how could I—being left completely to myself at such a thought-engendering altitude" (139). But when it comes to the consequences of such high-altitude thought, he again slides out of the first person, admonishing "ye shipowners of Nantucket" not to hire "any lad with lean brow and hollow eye; given to unseasonable meditativeness" (139). Such a lad is Ishmael himself, but he will not acknowledge the fact.

For such a "sunken-eyed young Platonist" (139), gazing inward, will spot few whales:

> [L]ulled into such an opium-like listlessness of vacant, unconscious reverie is the absent-minded youth by the blending cadence of waves with thoughts, that at last he loses his identity; takes the mystic ocean at his feet for the visible image of that deep, blue, bottomless soul, pervading mankind and nature . . . In this enchanted mood, thy spirit ebbs away to whence it came; becomes diffused through time and space. (140)

The young man "loses his identity," as waves blend with thoughts, and he takes the sea to be one with his own soul. He sees the ocean as a surface, an image of bottomlessness that reflects his own thought, not a real and dangerous depth. Ishmael has already mentioned the lack of physical barriers between self and other on the mast-head, but it is ultimately mental barriers that must constitute and preserve the self.

Identity can only be known as a difference, the product of the opposition between self and other: "[W]hile this sleep, this dream is on ye, move your hand or foot an inch; slip your hold at all; and your identity comes back in horror. Over Descartian vortices you hover" (140). The self cannot rise above events and merge with sea and sky; it will only plunge into "Descartian vortices," to its own death. The reason for Ishmael's use of the second and third person is now obvious—it is a grammatical displacement of his own terror, his own moment of peril on the mast-head, onto "ye Pantheists," his readers (140). He has evaded the possibility of his own death by reestablishing both this "external" difference and an "internal" one—between himself as character and mast-header, and as narrator and shaper of the text.

Ishmael does, however, surrender his narrative distance once again, on a much larger scale, in the drama of the next five chapters. "The Quarter-Deck" opens with a set of stage directions: *"Enter Ahab: Then, all"* (140). The following chapters move downward, away from Ishmael as character (he never appears) and away from him as narrator as well, into the dramatic form. As in "The Chapel," the formal movement toward drama is accompanied by a shift in imagery: from a surface, through a series of circles, into a downward penetration—a fall into the vortex.

"The Quarter-Deck" opens with Ahab as its central, enigmatic figure, pacing back and forth across the deck. Near the close of day, the captain halts and orders the entire crew aft and down, the mast-headers in particular. Ahab, like Mapple, will stand above his audience, subordinating them (and Ishmael's narration) to his own dramatic presence. Just as with the sermon, Ishmael reproduces Ahab's speech with no comment or mention of his own participation.

After a series of questions to the crew, Ahab speaks directly to the mast-headers: " 'ye mast-headers have before now heard me give orders about a white whale. . . . d'ye see this Spanish ounce of gold'—holding up a broad bright coin to the sun—'it is a sixteen dollar piece, men,—a doubloon' " (142). The scene has begun with the downward movement of the mast-headers to the deck; now Ahab's thought breaks through his enigmatic silence into speech and action, emerging in a set of circular images. He "revolves" on his ivory leg in its pivot-hole and displays one golden circle, the coin, against another, the sun (142).

Ahab next describes Moby Dick in terms of its surface features: " 'a white-headed whale with a wrinkled brow and a crooked jaw . . . with three holes punctured in his starboard fluke' " (142). The harpooneers recognize the whale, and Queequeg adds another detail:

> "And he have one, two, tree—oh! good many iron in him hide . . . all twiske-tee betwisk, like him—him—" faltering hard for a word, and screwing his hand round and round as though uncorking a bottle . . .
>
> "Corkscrew!" cried Ahab, "aye, Queequeg, the harpoons lie all twisted and wrenched in him." (142–43)

Queequeg's gesture, "screwing his hand round and round," is a narrowing series of circles, a corkscrew. Surface details are superseded by another circular image: the whale's movement, which has twisted the harpoons this way, takes the form of a vortex. This is also the image Ahab uses to describe his hunt: "'I'll chase him round Good Hope, and round the Horn, and round the Norway Maelstrom, and round perdition's flames before I give him up'" (143).

No dissenting voice remains, only the "long face" of Starbuck. He requires, Ahab says, "'a little lower layer,'" a deeper explanation, one closer, in Ahab's terms, to the truth:

> "All visible objects, man, are but as pasteboard masks. But in each event—in the living act, the undoubted deed—there, some unknown but still reasoning thing puts forth the mouldings of its features from behind the unreasoning mask. If man will strike, strike through the mask!" (144)

Visible surfaces mask an inner truth, a deep reality to be encountered only in a violent confrontation, a penetration that breaks through the mask. Ahab will not be content to interpret surfaces; he will pursue the whale down into the vortex of action and reveal its hidden truth in an "undoubted deed," a moment of uninterpretable discontinuity and rupture.[26]

At the end of his speech, Ahab acknowledges Starbuck's acquiescence in an aside. Here Ishmael's narrative voice makes its last appearance, as the wind dies and a laugh comes from the hold:

> Ah, ye admonitions and warnings! why stay ye not when ye come? But rather are ye predictions than warnings, ye shadows! Yet not so much predictions from without, as verifications of the foregoing things within. For with little external to constrain us, the innermost necessities in our being, these still drive us on. (145)

Ishmael here moves from the *temporal* authority of warnings and omens to the *spatial* force of inner necessities and drives, following Ahab. So too does his dramatic form privilege action over interpretation, in an attempt to reproduce the reality and truth of "undoubted deeds."

The captain's presence and imagery now effectively control the text, and he takes full advantage of the dramatic moment he has created.[27] He ranges the harpooneers and mates before him, all within the circle formed by the rest of the crew. Ahab inverts the hierarchy of command, ordering the crew to drink first: "'Round with it, round! . . . it goes round excellently. It spiralizes in ye'" (145). As the flagon circles around Ahab, the drink "spiralizes" within each sailor, each internalizing the captain's vortex. The mates now cross their lances, and Ahab touches the "axis," grasping the "level, radiating lances at their crossed center," again placing himself at the center of a series of circles (145). He next appoints his mates as "cup-bearers" to their inferiors, the harpooneers, and in the last act of his demonic sacrament, this swirling, maddening compact, the harpooneers invert their weapons, turning the sockets of the harpoons into "murderous chalices" from which they drink (146).

Ahab now retires within his cabin, going below decks. The next chapter, "Sunset," in form a dramatic soliloquy, continues and internalizes "The Quarter-deck's" circling downward movement.[28] Ahab gazes out his window and describes the horizon as "the ever-brimming goblet's rim," a circle; the sun is another golden circle that "plumbs the blue" as it "dives" into darkness (147). The series of downward-moving circles narrows further until it reaches Ahab's own head: "Is, then, the crown too heavy that I wear?" he asks, "this Iron Crown of Lombardy. . . . 'Tis split, too—that I feel; the jagged edge galls me so, my brain seems to beat against the solid metal" (147). Ahab himself is caught, as the narrowing vortex presses in upon him, even as his "one cogged circle fits into all [the] various wheels" of his crew, making them "revolve" with him (147).[29]

Not even the gods, Ahab says, can swerve him: "Over unsounded gorges, through the rifled hearts of mountains, under torrents' beds, unerringly I rush! Naught's an obstacle, naught's an angle to the iron way!" (147). Again, the progress is downward—over, then through, and finally under. Ahab's "iron way" is down, through the surface, into the whirling, fragmenting violence of the vortex.

This, of course, is one of the alternatives suggested by the story of Narcissus in "Loomings," a penetration into truth figured as depth. Ishmael, too, is tempted by this escape from narrative temporality, an escape represented in his text by the dramatic form. His effort, in these chapters, is to privilege his perceiving consciousness as character, and through an assumed transparency of perception and transcription, to represent action and speech unmediated by narrative structure. His aim is to recapture the integrity and immediacy of his experience by abolishing the temporal distance between narration and event, a distance that can only be recreated and reenforced by linear narrative.

But Ishmael's drive through the narrative surface, like Ahab's, yields only further conflict and fragmentation. After Ahab's soliloquy comes a series of short chapters leading into the confused and broken dialogue of

Chapter 40, "Midnight, Forecastle." It begins with a curtain, the foresail, rising to reveal "the watch standing, lounging, leaning, and lying in various attitudes"—a theatrical chorus (149). Most of the sailors remain unnamed and uncharacterized, identified only as national types; the exceptions are Tashtego, Daggoo, and, most important, Pip.

The cabin-boy stands at the heart of the scene, beating time on his tambourine so the sailors can dance. The tambourine is, of course, a circle, with a set of circular "jinglers" around its circumference (151). It is the beat created by striking the tambourine that is important to the men—their dance is no more than a rhythmic violence that threatens to destroy both Pip and the tambourine. An Azore sailor tells Pip to "bang it . . . Make fire-flies; break the jinglers!" (151). When the boy protests that they are already dropping off, a China sailor tells him to "rattle thy teeth, then," and "pound away" at himself (151). "Merry-mad!" cries a third, "Hold up thy hoop, Pip, till I jump through it! Split jibs!," calling on his fellows to "tear yourselves" in the dance (151).

But the dancing soon ceases as the ship heads into a squall. A Manx-man describes the lightning as "lurid-like . . . all else pitch black"—the storm throws the *Pequod* and the action on deck into a swirl of black and white (153). Daggoo, the black harpoonneer, seizes on the Manxman's remark: "Who's afraid of black's afraid of me! I'm quarried out of it!" (153). A Spanish sailor taunts him, calling his race the "dark side of mankind— devilish dark" and describing the lightning as "Daggoo showing his teeth" (153, 154). The harpooneer's reply is again in terms of black and white: "White skin, white liver!" (154). They fight; both gods and men, Tashtego says, are "brawlers" (154). One man tells the fighters to "plunge in"; another calls for the crew to form a "ring" around them (154). This is God's work, "sweet work, right work," the Manxman comments, "In that ring Cain struck Abel" (154). Within this circle black and white collide in a primeval opposition, in a conflict that echoes the first act of violence and yields only death or perpetual estrangement.

The mate, however, calls the crew to the rigging as the squall hits, and they scatter. Left alone, center stage, is Pip: "what a squall!" he exclaims,

But those chaps there are worse yet—they are your white squalls, they. White squalls? White whale, shirr! shirr! Here have I heard all their chat just now, and the white whale—shirr! shirr!—but spoken of once! and only this evening—it makes me jingle all over like my tambourine—that anaconda of an old man swore 'em in to hunt him!

> Oh, thou big white God aloft there somewhere in yon darkness, have mercy on this small black boy down here; preserve him from all men that have no bowels to feel fear. (155)

Pip links white men, white squalls, white whale, and, finally, "thou big white God." All, even God himself, are in pure opposition to Pip—"this small black boy down here." At the center of the white swirl—the dance, the fight—at the bottom of the dramatic vortex, there stands a black boy, who can know himself only as fundamentally different and distant from other men and from the ground of his existence, God Himself.

Ishmael's experiment with the dramatic mode, his foray into the vortex of unmediated action, leads to this point. Its lesson is, like Mapple's, a double one: that the self can be known only be means of differences and oppositions, ultimate contrasts of black against white; and that it can only know itself as estranged from its origin and source of being. And the purveyor of this knowledge is Pip, the soon to be maddened and self-divided castaway, a figure with whom Ishmael will directly compare himself.[30]

The final images of "Midnight, Forecastle" are those of the Epilogue—white circles, black center, the isolated and fragmented self. Ishmael's dramatic mode has repeated, rather than escaped, the self-division inherent in his narrative. Neither narrative line nor dramatic vortex can be fully subjected to authorial control; the uncontrollable repetition of imagery threatens Ishmael's mastery over both his text and himself, making knowledge inseparable and indistinguishable from madness.

It is this failure of the dramatic form that compels Ishmael's reassertion of narrative distance and control at the start of Chapter 41, "Moby Dick": "I, Ishmael, was one of that crew" (155). Both Ishmael's narrative "I" and his name as character have been completely absent from the preceding chapters, but now they are desperately reasserted. It is a rhetorical gesture reminiscent of "Call me Ishmael"—its ostensible purpose is to locate Ishmael within the previous scenes, but by the sheer forcefulness of the act of naming, it reestablishes his temporal distance from them as narrator. "I, Ishmael," although it assumes an identity between "I" and "Ishmael," actually repeats and reinforces the difference in an "I" writing about "Ishmael's" experience.[31] This renewed self-fragmentation is, however, a reaction to a loss of self equally extreme: "A wild, mystical, sympathetical feeling was in me; Ahab's quenchless feud seemed mine" (155). Ishmael, in other words, had become indistinguishable from Ahab, had lost his identity in his plunge into the captain's vortex.

This is the most extreme of the novel's oscillations in form, swinging from an immersion in drama directly to exposition and interpretation. Ishmael picks up the thread of his narrative for only a moment, to look backward without advancing the story.

"Moby Dick," like "Loomings," pulls back immediately from its initial rhetorical force; the next few pages are riddled with hesitations and qualifications. "For some time past," Ishmael says, "though at intervals only," the White Whale has haunted the seas "mostly frequented" by Sperm Whale fishermen: "But not all of them knew of his existence; only a few of them, comparatively, had knowingly seen him; while the number who as yet had actually and knowingly given battle to him, was small indeed" (155). Ishmael here establishes as much distance as possible between himself and Ahab's obsession, broadening and blurring his focus by discussing the Sperm Whale fishery in general and its lack of substantive knowledge of Moby Dick. He concludes by making others responsible for the stories he has recounted: "to some minds it was not an unfair presumption, I say, that the whale in question must have been no other than Moby Dick" (155). The "I" here merely comments on the probability of others' belief in the existence of Moby Dick; he places their stories between himself and the whale, restricting his responsibility to narratives, to texts alone.

Before long Ishmael has again made his way back to the safety of his whaling texts. The first person briefly reappears—"we find some book naturalists" (157)—but when he must admit that some captains "even in the face of these things were ready to give chase to Moby Dick," Ishmael's language becomes tangled and defensive once again: there are "a still greater number who, chancing only to hear of him distantly and vaguely, without the specific details of any certain calamity, and without superstitious accompaniments, were sufficiently hardy not to flee from the battle if offered" (157–58).

The same evasiveness characterizes Ishmael's treatment of those who believe

> that Moby Dick was ubiquitous; that he had actually been encountered in opposite latitudes at one and the same instant of time.
>
> Nor, credulous as such minds must have been, was this conceit altogether without some faint show of superstititous probability. . . .

the hidden ways of the Sperm Whale when beneath the surface remain, in great part, unaccountable to his pursuers; and . . . have originated the most curious and contradictory speculations regarding them. (158)

The whale cannot be tracked, the story of its movements cannot be told, once it is beneath the surface. By diving it escapes temporal calculation— dives out of time and into hidden depths. These "conceits" imply that the whale can be pursued only in the way that Ahab intends, that the vortex from which Ishmael has escaped is one he must reenter if he is ever to know the whale. Ishmael's hesitation and refusal to commit himself to anything beyond the textual surface are, at this point, essential defenses.

In discussing Moby Dick's "ferocity" and its effects on "the minds of his more desperate hunters," Ishmael mentions the reaction of "one cap- tain, [who,] seizing the line-knife from his broken prow, had dashed at the whale . . . blindly seeking with a six inch blade to reach the fathom-deep life of the whale. That captain was Ahab" (159). It has taken almost four pages, but at last Ishmael can return, circuitously, to the material of his narrative.

By the end of the chapter, Ishmael has recovered himself sufficiently, reestablishing his distance from events as survivor and narrator, so that he can pass judgment on Ahab and his crew: "this grey-headed, ungodly old man, chasing with curses a Job's whale round the world, at the head of a crew . . . of mongrel renegades, and castaways, and cannibals" (162). Ishmael's language here achieves a directness and compression totally un- like—because it is seven pages away from—the evasiveness with which he began. But it is still not entirely honest. Ishmael, of course, was one of those "castaways," but he makes no mention of his own presence. Instead, he speaks of the crew as an inexplicable alien group:

> How it was that they so aboundingly responded to the old man's ire— by what magic their souls were possessed, that at times his hate almost seemed theirs . . . what the White Whale was to them, or how to their unconscious understandings, also, in some dim, unsuspected way, he might have seemed the gliding great demon of the seas of life,—all this to explain, would be to dive deeper than Ishmael can go. (162)

This is a calculated refusal on Ishmael's part. He suggests reasons for the crew's obedience and at the same time rejects the possibility of "diving" into their unconscious desires, even though he, too, has shared them: "The subterranean miner that works in us all, how can one tell whither leads his shaft by the ever shifting, muffled sound of his pick? . . . For one, I gave myself up to the abandonment of the time and the place" (162–63). Ishmael can again speak of how he "gave himself up" to Ahab only now that he has rejected (and survived) the captain's quest. In a sense, he has given himself up as a character, as one who dives into experience; his concern as narrator will be with surfaces, with interpreting and writing texts. He will only attempt to trace the miner's movement from the surface, listening for the "muffled sound of his pick." Ishmael will pursue the second option suggested by the Narcissus story, and attempt to discover meaning by turning the whale into an interpretable surface.

When Ishmael does return to the dramatic mode, in Chapters 107–09 and 119–23, each sequence is built around a scene with Ahab as its physical and psychological center. The second of these groups is clearly parallel to Chapters 36–40: both end in a midnight storm, and in Chapter 119, "The Candles," Ahab concludes his ritual fire worship by reinvoking the oath of "The Quarter-Deck" (418). But these later dramatic chapters have a different status in Ishmael's text. By this point, he has already distanced himself, as both character and narrator, from Ahab's fiery hunt. The dramatic form is a concession to the force of Ahab's presence, but it no longer represents a surrender of the *text* to his epistemology and aims.

If Ishmael reacted against the events and images of "Midnight, Forecastle" with a violent reassertion of his narrative role, in these later chapters he offers no such response. In both Chapters 109 and 123, it is Starbuck who confronts Ahab. The first episode comes to a climax when Ahab threatens the mate with a musket, the second when Starbuck holds the same musket over his sleeping captain (394, 421–22). In both cases, the conflict is confined within the narrative proper; it does not extend onto the level of textual structure. If Ishmael took it upon himself to interpret omens in "The Quarter-Deck," it is Starbuck who performs this role in "The Candles" (145, 418).

The drama has been revealed as Ahab's mode of self-representation, and its images linked to his drive toward an interior truth. His dramatic mode *rejects* the mediation of a narrative presence or voice; in this respect, it is the formal counterpart of his drive toward a direct and immediate contact with reality. Ishmael's rejection of Ahab thus forces him to surrender the dramatic mode as well.[32]

"What the white whale was to Ahab, has been hinted; what, at times, he was to me, as yet remains unsaid"—so Ishmael begins Chapter 42, "The

Whiteness of the Whale" (163). But what it is that "remains unsaid" may in fact be unsayable. It was a

> vague, nameless horror . . . so mystical and well nigh ineffable was it, that I almost despair of putting it in a comprehensible form. It was the whiteness of the whale that above all things appalled me. But how can I hope to explain myself here; and yet, in some dim, random way, explain myself I must, else all these chapters might be naught. (163)

Both the whiteness of the whale and Ishmael's reaction to it are formless, almost incomprehensible. Whiteness is the whale's primary surface feature, the ground against which all others are distinguished; if the whale's body is to provide the spatial form for Ishmael's text, he must find a way to describe its whiteness, to bring it into language. But he also feels driven to explain and master his own response, to "explain myself," for it is upon his view of the whale and upon his identity that "all these chapters" depend. In the last sentence, however, Ishmael defines himself not in relation to the whale, but in relation to "these chapters," to his text. His project, here and in his other cetological chapters, grows out of this double gesture: by textualizing the whale, he will again attempt to represent the essence of his experience, and thus himself.

Ishmael begins with whiteness as a positive or beautiful attribute, approaching his subject by way of examples and citations, as usual. But the primary connective in his list is "though"—these are all *counter*examples. Ishmael piles them into his page-long, one-sentence paragraph in order to delay its final clause and his admission that "there yet lurks an elusive something in the innermost idea of this hue, which strikes more of panic to the soul than that redness which affrights in blood" (164). He cannot help but return to the image of an inner meaning in describing the "elusive something" that cannot be found on white surfaces themslves, but only in the "innermost idea" of the color.

Eventually Ishmael does come back to whiteness as a source of terror, citing instances from "the common, hereditary experience of all mankind" that "bear witness to the supernaturalism" of the color:

> the one visible quality in the aspect of the dead which most appals the gazer, is the marble pallor lingering there; as if indeed that pallor were as much the badge of consternation in the other world, as of mortal trepidation here. And from that pallor of the dead, we borrow the

expressive hue of the shroud in which we wrap them. . . . while these terrors seize us, let us add, that even the king of terrors, when personified by the evangelist, rides on his pallid horse. (166)

Ishmael has at last begun to discuss whiteness as associated with death, the absence of color marking the absence of life. Whiteness is the ghostly trace of lost color, a sign of "consternation" and terrifying disorder. He speaks not of his own reaction here, but of "common, hereditary" responses ("while these terrors seize *us*, let *us* add"). The editorial "we" again links writer and reader, reaffirming Ishmael's immediate concern with his textual surface.

Ishmael stays on an abstract, universal level as he pauses to consider his own method as writer. "How," he asks, "is mortal man to account for" the supernatural force of whiteness?

> To analyse it, would seem impossible. Can we, then, by the citation of some of those instances wherein this thing of whiteness— though for the time either wholly or in great part stripped of all direct associations calculated to impart to it aught fearful, but, nevertheless, is found to exert over us the same sorcery, however modified;—can we thus hope to light upon some chance clue to conduct us to the hidden cause we seek? (166–67)

The object of our search is "hidden," but Ishmael says it is not to be discovered through an analysis, an opening up, of whiteness. He will instead cite instances of the power of whiteness and "hope to light upon some chance clue." His model is neither a spatial penetration nor a linear narrative progression; it is instead a pattern of examples displayed across the surface of the text. Ishmael's chain of examples—Whitsuntide, White Friar, White Tower, White Mountains—quickly degenerates into wordplay, however (167). The only pattern it reveals is linguistic, words used to fend off direct consideration of their original referent. Ishmael's reliance on chance is only another way of deferring the problem.

Ishmael's next move is to create and introduce the voice of a reader to whom he may respond: "thou sayest, methinks this white-lead chapter about whiteness is but a white flag hung out from a craven soul; thou surrenderest to a hypo, Ishmael" (168–69). By splitting his narrative voice into two antagonistic personae, by redividing himself, Ishmael is at last able to confront his fear of whiteness. It is, he says, an instinctive reaction to the "demonism" in the world: "Though in many of its aspects this visible world seems formed in love, the invisible spheres were formed in fright" (169). Whiteness straddles the line between the visible and the invisible; it is, as Ishmael will shortly suggest, the ground against which other colors can be seen, but once they have been differentiated from it, whiteness becomes an unperceived background, invisible.

"[N]ot yet," Ishmael admits, "have we solved the incantation of this whiteness . . . why, as we have seen, it is at once the most meaning symbol of spiritual things, nay, the very veil of the Christian's Deity; and yet should be as it is, the intensifying agent in things the most appalling to mankind" (169). He has at least isolated the problem in this, the last paragraph of the chapter, focusing on the extreme nature of the emotions prompted by whiteness. What follows is another of Ishmael's strings of questions:

> Is it that by its indefiniteness it shadows forth the heartless voids and immensities of the universe, and thus stabs us from behind with the thought of annihilation, when beholding the white depths of the milky way? Or is it, that as in essence whiteness is not so much a color as the visible absence of color, and at the same time the concrete of all colors; is it for these reasons that there is such a dumb blankness, full of meaning, in a wide landscape of snows—a colorless, all-color of athe-ism from which we shrink? (169)

Here the opposition between depth and surface appears once again. On one hand, the "indefiniteness" of whiteness is a "shadow," a representation as formless as "the heartless voids and immensities," the "white depths" that cast a paradoxical, impossible, white shadow. Whiteness represents an underlying depth that is pure chaos and emptiness, absolute meaningless-ness and death. On the other hand, whiteness is both the absence of color on a surface and that which makes other colors visible in their difference from it. Such differentiation is what makes signification possible; whiteness is thus an absence of signification that contains the potential for all significa-tion. It is absence as pure generative possibility, a blankness that Ishmael describes in religious terms as both the "very veil" of the Christian deity and the "most appalling" sign of His irrecoverable absence.

Whiteness as the sign of depth can yield no meaning, only death; surface whiteness is both the lack and the possibility of meaning. Given this opposition, Ishmael's embrace of a technique of surface interpretation is almost inevitable.[33] He will take the whiteness of Moby Dick as an analogy for the whiteness of his own empty page, which he will seek to fill with the features of the whale.

Ishmael has already laid out the terms of his expository project in Chapter 32, "Cetology." "Already we are boldly launched upon the deep," he says,

> soon we shall be lost in its unshored, harborless immensities. Ere that come to pass; ere the Pequod's weedy hull rolls side by side with the barnacled hulls of the leviathan; at the outset it is but well to attend to a matter almost indispensable to a thorough appreciative understanding of the more special leviathanic revelations of all sorts which are to follow. (116)

"We" are at once the crew of the *Pequod*, now at sea, and Ishmael and his readers, now well into the story. What lies ahead are "unshored, harborless immensities," the boundless space of the sea, and, implicitly, the formlessness of the action yet to come. Even though both voyage and text have already begun, he tries to establish this point as a new "outset," a moment at which another kind of form can be enunciated.

It is a "systematized exhibition of the whale in his broad genera" that Ishmael would "put before" the reader (116). He describes his project as an "exhibition," a spatial display instead of a narrative, emphasizing surface extension rather than depth or temporal progression. He will classify "the constituents of a chaos" by turning them into a visible, interpretable surface (117).[34]

Ishmael lists dozens of authors who have written about whales, but their texts finally add up to nothing: the sperm whale "lives not complete in any literature. . . . his is an unwritten life" (118). Instead of a life story, a narrative, Ishmael sets out to provide a grouping, a "popular comprehensive classification" of "the various species of whales" (118).

"[I]t is a ponderous task," he says, "to grope down into the bottom of the sea after them; to have one's hands among the unspeakable foundations, ribs, and very pelvis of the world" (118). But he will nevertheless try to "grope down" into the "unspeakable" depths of the world's body, bringing the whales up to the textual surface where he may display them. In keeping with this emphasis, Ishmael defines the whale "by his obvious externals"— his surface rather than internal features—as "*a spouting fish with a horizontal tail*" (119).

Ishmael does more than make the whale his text, however; he treats the whales themselves as "books" in his classification, grouping them under the headings "Folio," "Octavo," and "Duodecimo" according to size (120). In his "Bibliographical system," he will take hold of them "bodily, in their entire liberal volume, and boldly sort them that way" (123). Ishmael's pun on "volume" identifies the three-dimensional space of the whale's body with that of his text—Moby Dick becomes *Moby-Dick*. By incorporating the physical integrity of the whale into the fabric of his book, he will give it a shape and unity beyond the scope of temporal narrative.

But Ishmael has already acknowledged his system to be partial and fragmentary: he will promise nothing complete, he says, "because any human thing supposed to be complete, must for that very reason infallibly be faulty" (118). His object is "simply to project the draught of a systemization of cetology" (118). The natural unity of the living whale cannot, he admits, be directly reconstituted in language. He closes the chapter by returning to this point:

> It was stated at the outset, that this system would not be here, and at once, perfected. You cannot but plainly see that I have kept my word. . . . small erections may be finished by their first architects; grand ones, true ones, ever leave the copestone to posterity. God keep me from ever completing anything. This whole book is a draught—nay, but the draught of a draught. (127–28)

That which is true must be left unfinished. Truth, Ishmael has said, is "shoreless, indefinite as God"; it cannot be enclosed or ordered by any verbal architecture. He now moves beyond his classification system to describe his "whole book" as necessarily a "draught of a draught." It is not a narrative to be brought to a close, but a text to be written and rewritten, in an endless process of revision and expansion. Even at this delayed outset, Ishmael anticipates the failure of his cetological project.

Nevertheless, his effort in the expository sections of *Moby-Dick* remains to generate a textual countermodel to Ahab's quest. If Ahab wishes only to dismember the whale, to destroy its bodily integrity, Ishmael seeks to incorporate and appropriate its natural unity. He hopes to create a spatial rather than temporal structure for his text, to project the figure of the whale across the two dimensions of its pages in order to preempt, or at least defer, the linear progression of his narrative.

Ishmael provides an image for this approach in Chapter 47, "The Mat-Maker." One sultry afternoon, he and Queequeg are "mildly employed" weaving a sword-mat, and Ishmael drifts off into speculation, taking his imagery from the weaving:

> it seemed as if this were the Loom of Time, and I myself were a shuttle mechanically weaving and weaving away at the Fates. There lay the fixed threads of the warp subject to one single, ever returning, unchanging vibration . . . This warp seemed necessity; and here, thought I, with my own hand I ply my own shuttle and weave my own destiny into these unalterable threads. Meanwhile, Queequeg's impulsive, indifferent sword, sometimes hitting the woof slantingly, or crookedly, or strongly, or weakly . . . this easy, indifferent sword must be chance—aye, chance, free will, and necessity—no wise incompatible—all interweavingly working together. (185)

Necessity is a "straight warp . . . not to be swerved from its ultimate course," a linear progression, a narrative line (185). Ishmael describes his free will as perpendicular to it, intersecting it in an opposition that, modified by the blows of chance, turns its single line into a two-dimensional surface, narrative into exposition, temporal forward movement into spatial expansion.[35]

Ishmael applies the image of writing as weaving directly to his text in Chapter 54, "The Town-Ho's Story," as he inserts a tale he heard as a result of the *Pequod*'s gam with the *Town-Ho*. The story, first passed on to Tashtego with "Romish injunctions of secrecy" (208), is to be kept among the seamen, never to be divulged to the ship's officers; its very possession is a challenge to their authority—telling this story aboard the *Pequod* is as implicitly rebellious as on the *Neversink*. Ishmael's retelling of the *Town-Ho*'s story thus reemphasizes his distance from and independence of Ahab. As narrator/weaver, he again challenges and delays the movement of his large tale, "Interweaving in its proper place this darker thread with the story as publicly narrated on the ship" (208).

In "The Town-Ho's Story" Moby Dick appears as an agent of retribution and violent justice; by inserting a tale that prefigures the end of his own, Ishmael hopes to anticipate, and thus reduce, its traumatic force.[36] Beyond this, his private, "lasting" narration is an exercise of his narrative free will, an act of self-assertion made even more flagrant by its insistence on his own survival: "For my humor's sake," he says, "I shall preserve the style in which I once narrated it at Lima, to a lounging circle of my Spanish friends" (208). What follows is a transcript of that narration, one that took place, obviously, after the end of the *Pequod*'s cruise. The proleptic framing allows Ishmael to once again identify himself as both narrator and *survivor*, and, in this case, to describe "the *Pequod*'s story" as a interruption of the *Town-Ho*'s, one he can easily dispense with as "too long a story" (221).[37]

Ishmael's next chapter, "Of the Monstrous Pictures of Whales," shifts abruptly to a new subject—not texts about whales, but pictures of them: "I shall," he says, "ere long paint to you as well as one can without canvas, something like the true form of the whale as he actually appears to the eye of the whaleman when in his own absolute body the whale is moored alongside the whale-ship" (224). Just as Ishmael began, in his Extracts, by placing his text amongst other books about whales, he now locates it in relation to pictures of whales, "those curious imaginary portraits of him which . . . challenge the faith of the landsman" (225). The comparison implies that he will not only be weaving a two-dimensional surface, but also projecting (painting or embroidering) a figure on that surface—the image of the whale.

"The living whale, in his full majesty and significance, is only to be seen at sea in unfathomable waters," Ishmael claims, "and afloat the vast bulk of him is out of sight" (227). The fullness of the whale's true shape lies hidden beneath the surface, he says, implying a link between truth and a hidden depth. But he withdraws this privileging of interior meaning almost immediately, asserting that the whale's skeleton, the hidden center of its hidden body, "gives very little idea of his general shape" (228). The whale cannot be understood or represented synecdochally—"the only mode in which you can derive even a tolerable idea of his living contour, is by going a whaling yourself; but by so doing, you run no small risk of being eternally stove and sunk by him" (228). The only alternative to the two-dimensional surfaces of pictures and texts is physical confrontation—Ahab's vortex.

Ishmael spends two more chapters discussing representations of whales in various media, closing his survey with figures of whales to be seen in nature, "defined along the undulating ridges" of mountains or outlined in the stars: "[W]hen expandingly lifted by your subject," he says, you will "trace out great whales in the starry heavens, and boats in pursuit of them . . . Thus at the North have I chased Leviathan round and round the Pole with the revolutions of the bright points that first defined him to me" (233). This is Ishmael's comic reply to Ahab's vow to chase the whale around the globe. He describes himself standing at the Pole and projecting the figure of the whale (the constellation Cetus) onto the revolving visual surface of the sky. Rather than simply telling the story of Ahab's hunt, following the line of his pursuit, Ishmael stops and traces the shape of the whale onto his text, giving it the spatial order of the whale's body.

But if the whale cannot be safely encountered as a living whole, Ishmael must build his picture from descriptions of its constituent parts. In Chapter 68, "The Blanket," he begins with a description of the skin. Here Ishmael the narrator is squarely in the spotlight, speaking confidently in the first person and the present tense: "I have," he says, "given no small attention to that not unvexed subject, the skin of the whale" (259). It is hard, however, to identify the "skin" of the whale: its blubber may be eight to fifteen inches thick, but "you cannot raise any other dense enveloping layer from the whale's body . . . from the unmarred dead body of the whale, you may scrape off with your hand an infinitely thin, transparent substance," but this "is not so much to be regarded as the skin of the creature, as the skin of the skin, so to speak" (259). Ishmael's aim is to find the surface of the whale, but he discovers only a "surface" a foot thick or one infinitely thin and transparent. In order to invoke the spatial integrity of a body, one must first define its boundaries, but Ishmael's analysis begins by undermining rather than confirming the distinction between inside and outside, blurring the outline of the figure he would establish.

His response is to read one surface, the blubber, through the other, the thin, transparent one. He uses this isinglass-like material, he says, "for marks in my whalebooks . . . laid upon the printed page, I have sometimes pleased myself with fancying it exerted a magnifying influence" (259). The "visible," rather than the transparent surface of the whale, is what he now takes as his text, his whalebook:

> it is all over obliquely crossed and re-crossed with numberless straight marks in thick array, something like those in the finest Italian line engravings. But these marks do not seem to be impressed upon the isinglass substance above mentioned, but seem to be seen through it, as if they were engraved upon the body itself. . . . In some instances, to the quick, observant eye, those linear marks, as in a veritable engraving, but afford the ground for far other delineations. (260)

Ishmael's impression is that these marks should form part of an engraving—a picture. And, he concludes, the delineations for which they are the ground are "hieroglyphical"—picture writing (260). But it is a writing for which Ishmael has no key; like the hieroglyphic characters carved into rocks by American Indians, "the mystic-marked whale remains undecipherable" (260).

If the whale's body is already a text or picture, however, if the whale represents itself in or on its own body, Ishmael's efforts may simply be redundant. On the other hand, it is only the "quick, observant eye" that sees these "marks" as signs. It is Ishmael who distinguishes figure from ground, projecting these "delineations" onto the surface of the whale. In either case, Ishmael's textual project is off to a rather inauspicious start.

"The Prairie" is yet another example of Ishmael's insistence on surface interpretation. He sets out not to go inside the whale's head or ask it to speak (as Ahab has in "The Sphynx") but to "scan the lines of his face" and "feel the bumps" on its head (291). The whale is "an anomalous creature" in that it "has no proper nose" (292). Its "god-like dignity" is manifested in its brow:

> gazing on it . . . you feel the Deity and the dread powers more forcibly than in beholding any other object in living nature. For you see no one point precisely; not one distinct feature is revealed; no nose, eyes, ears, or mouth; no face; he has none, proper; nothing but that one broad firmament of a forehead, pleated with riddles, dumbly lowering with the doom of boats, and ships, and men. (292)

The whale's forehead is an expanse of whiteness; no features can be distinguished upon it or differentiated from its white background. Yet again, the examination of individual features of the whale's body blurs rather than clarifies Ishmael's picture.

The whale's wrinkles are "riddles," containing the doom of boats and men. But these are riddles, not stories or pictures, and they remain insoluble except in death. The whale's "genius" lies not in books or speeches, but is "declared in his pyramidical silence" (292). Unable to read the surface of the whale's skin and brow, Ishmael is forced to return to the image of a secret, inner chamber, like the tomb at the heart of the silent pyramid, in which its true being and meaning lie. If "there is no Champollion to decipher the Egypt of every man's and every being's face," he says, "how may unlettered Ishmael hope to read the awful Chaldee of the Sperm Whale's brow?" (292, 293).

"If the Sperm Whale be physiognomically a Sphynx," Ishmael says in "The Nut," its brain is a "circle which it is impossible to square" (293). The brain is "at least twenty feet" from the whale's "apparent" forehead:

> So like a choice casket is it secreted in him, that I have known some whalemen who peremptorily deny that the Sperm Whale has any other

brain but that palpable semblance of one formed by the cubic-yards of his sperm magazine. Lying in strange folds, courses, and convolutions, to their apprehensions, it seems more in keeping with the idea of his general might to regard that mystic part of him as the seat of his intelligence. (293)

Instead of the tiny hidden casket of the whale's real brain, whalemen treat the larger, folded and convoluted sperm magazine as the mystic "seat of his intelligence": they do so to preserve a link between the whale's internal and external features, to keep inside consonant with outside. But Ishmael rejects such physiological mystifications: "the head of this Leviathan, in the creature's living intact state, is an entire delusion. As for his true brain, you can see no indications of it, nor feel any. The whale, like all things that are mighty, wears a false brow to the common world" (293). He almost claims that the whale's featureless brow is a mask, with no connection to its inner being. But he pulls back from this, Ahab's position, suggesting that even if the whale's head and brain cannot be read, its spine and hump may signify its "indomitableness." Like the whalemen he criticizes, he is finally driven to read a single feature as a synecdoche that connects the whale's physical appearance to its "character."

Ishmael returns to the contrast between his act of writing and the whale's silence in "The Fountain." His narrative first person is very much in evidence, as he dates the moment of composition—"fifteen and a quarter minutes past one o'clock P.M. of this sixteenth day of December, A.D. 1850" (310). This, of course, is a point in human and textual history. The whale's respiration, on the other hand, has its own regularity, a rhythm that has remained constant across the centuries, as much a mystery as the contents of the spout itself. This aspect of the whale eludes textualization as well. Ishmael goes on, in fact, to suggest that writing and speech are only signs of human weakness: "what has the whale to say?" he asks, "Seldom have I known any profound being that had anything to say to this world, unless forced to stammer out something by way of getting a living" (312). The bodily presence of the living whale relegates language to a secondary role at best, as no more than an inadequate substitute for the presence it would reconstruct.

In "The Tail," Ishmael concludes his cetological survey for the time being, by celebrating the beauty of the whale's tail. When he comes to describe its movements—three-dimensional "gestures" that he cannot "express" directly—he reduces them to a list, a textual array (317, 315). But he

still laments his inability to understand these "mystic gestures," these unreadable signs:

> Dissect him how I may, then, I go but skin deep; I know him not, and
> never will. But if I know not even the tail of this whale, how under-
> stand his head? much more, how comprehend his face, when face he
> has none? Thou shalt see my back parts, my tail, he seems to say, but
> my face shall not be seen. But I cannot completely make out his back
> parts; and hint what he will about his face, I say again he has no face.
> (318)

Ishmael here recapitulates the interpretive failures of the preceding chapters, describing the limits of his surface reading of the whale's body. For he
has found the whale as inscrutable as God, indefinable and faceless. His
"dissection" has yielded no unified form, but only a fragmentation; again
and again, Ishmael's analysis has blurred the clarity and destroyed the
integrity of the figure it would present. The hyphen that indicates the
transformation of Moby Dick into *Moby-Dick* is, ultimately, the sign of a
cut, a *dis*figuring scar. In a sense, Ishmael has performed the very dismemberment called for by his monomaniac captain.

"The Cassock" marks the final moment in Ishmael's dissection, and
here he offers a closing image for his project. The whale's phallus is "a very
strange, enigmatical object," identified only rather coyly and indirectly
(350). Ishmael describes how the mincer removes and dries the skin of the
phallus, turning the tip inside out and "slip[ping] himself bodily into it"
(351). He appropriates the phallic power of the whale in order to annihilate
it, slicing the blubber into pieces thin as "bible leaves"—into his tub "the
minced pieces drop, fast as the sheets from a rapt orator's desk" (351).
Ishmael, too, has sought to invoke the power of the whale in shaping his
text, creating his own "bible leaves." But his "leaves" remain only disconnected fragments, without the unifying authority of a sacred text. His
writing has cut apart the body whose integrity he would appropriate—it is
ironically fitting, perhaps, that it ends with a castration.

Ishmael returns to the whale's body for the last time in "A Bower in the
Arsacides." He has by now exhausted the anatomy of the living whale; the
figure he would impose on the body of his text has failed to do more than
interrupt or defer his narrative. Ishmael has "chiefly dwelt upon the marvels
of [the whale's] outer aspect . . . But to a large and thorough sweeping
comprehension of him, it behoves me now to unbutton him still further,

and . . . set him before you in his ultimatum; that is to say, in his unconditional skeleton" (373). He had earlier claimed that the whale's skeleton does
not suggest its outward shape; it cannot therefore be taken as a synecdoche
for the whole. The whale's "ultimatum" must be a meaning of a different
order, coming not from mere dissection but from "breaking the seal and
reading all the contents" of the whale (373). Ishmael's language implies a
penetration, an opening—but one that reveals another, textual surface.
And his biblical overtones imply that it will be a visionary text, an apocalyp-
tic revelation.

Ishmael devotes the rest of this chapter to the whale's skeleton. This is
knowledge acquired on another voyage, part of another story—the insertion again moves Ishmael outside *this* narrative, suggesting his life after it.
The skeleton lies in an island temple, overgrown with vegetation:

> Through the lacings of the leaves, the great sun seemed a flying shuttle
> weaving the unwearied verdure. Oh, busy weaver! unseen weaver!—
> pause!—one word!—whither flows the fabric? . . . Speak, weaver!—
> stay thy hand! but one single word with thee! Nay—the shuttle flies—
> the figures float forth from the loom; the freshet-running carpet for
> ever slides away. The weaver-god, he weaves; and by that weaving is he
> deafened. (374)

Standing within the whale/temple, Ishmael does have a vision—of God as a
deafened and oblivious weaver and nature as a ceaselessly changing tapes-
try. This is much closer to Pip's maddening vision of God's foot upon the
Loom of Time than to Ishmael's own reverie in "The Mat-Maker." His free
will as weaver/writer has been replaced by his bafflement as an interpreter.
Ishmael cannot perceive a pattern in this fabric, let alone claim that his free
will can alter it. The skeleton itself seems to be the weaver: "Life folded
Death; Death trellised Life; the grim god wived with youthful Life, and
begat him curly-headed glories" (375). Life and Death are inextricably
interwoven in a continual generative embrace; neither is distinguishable as
primary or secondary, figure or ground. The process of figuration itself
seems threatened here—Ishmael's conception of a woven surface, carried
to its limit, is as terrifying and uncontrollable as the vortex.

Ishmael enters the skeleton itself, "and with a ball of Arsacidean twine,
wandered, eddied long amid its many winding, shaded colonnades and
arbors. But soon my line was out; and following it back, I emerged from
the opening where I entered" (375). He treats the skeleton as a Cretan

labyrinth, a telling comparison. For the simplest or most primitive form of the labyrinth is a narrowing series of circles—the 1851 edition of *Webster's Dictionary* lists "maze" as derived from the Saxon "mase," meaning whirlpool.[38] Ishmael's expository mode has, despite his efforts, led him back to the vortex.

The whale cannot be understood by "poring over his dead attenuated skeleton," Ishmael concludes: "Only in the heart of quickest perils; only when within the eddyings of his angry flukes; only on the profound unbounded sea, can the fully invested whale be truly and livingly found out" (378). The whale cannot be textualized, cannot be interpreted; Ishmael returns to images of eddying violence and depth, images like Ahab's. Only in the formless profundity of the sea, in the dangerous action of his narrative, can the whale be encountered in its living fullness.

Such an encounter does take place in "The Grand Armada," when the *Pequod's* boats attack a herd of whales. Ishmael's boat is drawn into the center of the herd, away from "the circumference of commotion" where the others are at work (324). The boat reaches the "innermost heart" of the shoal, "that enchanted calm which they say lurks at the heart of every commotion. . . . in the distracted distance we beheld the tumults of the outer concentric circles, and saw successive pods of whales, eight or ten in each, swiftly going round and round" (324). The boat remains upon the surface, but far beneath it, "suspended in those watery vaults," float "the nursing mothers of the whales, and those that by their enormous girth seemed shortly to become mothers" (325). "Some of the subtlest secrets of the seas seemed divulged to us in this enchanted pond," Ishmael says, "We saw young Leviathan amours in the deep" (326). Beneath the center of the herd, at the heart of its concentric circles, there lies a space of pure and peaceful fecundity.

Ishmael can only watch these whales from a distance, but he does, for a moment, appropriate and internalize the image, linking knowledge of the whale with self-knowledge:

And thus, though surrounded by circle upon circle of consternations and affrights, did these inscrutable creatures at the centre freely and fearlessly indulge in all peaceful concernments; yea, serenely revelled in dalliance and delight. But even so, amid the tornadoed Atlantic of my being, do I myself still for ever centrally disport in mute calm; and while ponderous planets of unwaning woe revolve round me, deep down and deep inland there I still bathe me in eternal mildness of joy. (326)

He postulates an internal, central space where his true selfhood lies: an "inland" spot, an island in the "tornadoed Atlantic of my being." It is also an *atemporal* center—Ishmael turns to the present tense, emphasizing the word "still" in an attempt to fight off the temporality that threatens such a unified identity. For this vision of an inner, silent self, joyful in its calm integrity, can last only for a moment.[39]

One whale, maimed by a cutting spade, has broken the line and entangled itself in it; it dashes through the herd with the spade flying loose, "wounding and murdering" its comrades (327). The whale line both entangles and cuts, disrupting the peaceful circles of the herd. Just so do the events of the narrative line break into the inner space of Ishmael's reverie and cut it short:

> the whales forming the margin of our lake began to crowd a little, and tumble against each other . . . then the lake itself began faintly to heave and swell; the submarine bridal-chambers and nurseries vanished; in more and more contracting orbits the whales in the more central circles began to swim in thickening clusters. . . . the entire host of whales came tumbling upon their inner centre. (327)

The whaleboats can only enter the herd as a disruption, their linear movement in direct conflict with its circular shape. The temporal movement of penetration to a center closes off the depths beneath, turning the circles of whales into a whirling, narrowing vortex from which Ishmael's boat must escape if he is to survive. His conception of an inner, central self is equally vulnerable—the awareness of having reached a center must also be an awareness of the self as divided, both tornadoed and calm at once. The calm center, like the internal features of the whale, can never be a synecdoche for the whole; it is only a metonymy that, under the pressure of temporality and self-consciousness, reiterates the divisions within the self.[40]

Having returned to narration, Ishmael is repeatedly forced to confront such internal divisions. In Chapter 93, "The Castaway," he describes "a most significant event [which] befell the most insignificant of the Pequod's crew . . . providing the sometimes madly merry and predestinated craft with a living and ever accompanying prophecy of whatever shattered sequel might prove her own" (344). The event is Pip's abandonment at sea and his resulting madness. But this is less a prophecy of what may happen to the *Pequod* than a reminder to Ishmael of what will happen (has happened) to him. He, like Pip, will be abandoned at sea, and if the prophecy is fulfilled, he, too, will be "shattered" by the experience.

Pip is put into Stubb's boat as a temporary replacement, as Ishmael will be assigned to Ahab's. In his panic, Pip jumps out and is left behind: the ocean "stretch[es] flatly away, all round, to the horizon . . . Out from the centre of the sea, poor Pip turned his crisp, curling, black head to the sun, another lonely castaway, though the loftiest and the brightest" (346–47). Pip is at the center of this ocean circle, his black head contrasted with the whiteness of the sun above him—the absolute difference he had spoken of in "Midnight, Forecastle" is now realized.

But "the awful lonesomeness" of such isolation, "the intense concentration of self in the middle of such a heartless immensity," is "intolerable," Ishmael says (347). Pip is rescued at last,

> but from that hour the little negro went about the deck an idiot . . . The sea had jeeringly kept his finite body up, but drowned the infinite of his soul. Not drowned entirely, though. Rather carried down alive to wondrous depths, where strange shapes of the unwarped primal world glided to and fro before his passive eyes . . . [Pip] saw God's foot upon the treadle of the loom, and spoke it; and therefore his shipmates called him mad. So man's insanity is heaven's sense; and wandering from all mortal reason, man comes at last to that celestial thought, which, to reason, is absurd and frantic; and weal or woe, feels then uncompromised, indifferent as his God. (347)

Pip's abandonment divides him into finite body and infinite soul. The latter is carried down from the center of the ocean to the "wondrous depth" of a timeless "primal world," where Pip sees "God's foot upon the treadle" of the Loom of Time, the true source of both temporal and spatial order. He has penetrated to the generative depth of "The Grand Armada," and returns from the vortex feeling himself "uncompromised," invulnerable to experience, to the pull of the narrative line, as "indifferent as his God."

"The thing is common in that fishery," Ishmael concludes, "and in the sequel of the narrative, it will then be seen what like abandonment befell myself" (347). He minimizes the strangeness and importance of such an abandonment but leaves the relation between it and his narrative ambiguous—will it take place within the sequence of events comprised by the narrative line or after it, in a separate "sequel" to the story? Is Ishmael's isolation an inevitable outcome or an escape from the predestined end of the tale?

Ishmael moves to disassociate himself from Ahab, and from the story itself, in "The Try-Works," where he suffers a comparable, though temporary, loss of self.[41] He takes the *Pequod*'s helm at midnight, with the try-works in full operation, its "fierce flames" licking up the surrounding blackness (353). "Wrapped, for that interval, in darkness," he slides into an "unaccountable drowsiness," awakening to find that "a strange (and ever since inexplicable) thing" has happened (354). He is "horribly conscious of something fatally wrong," for where the binnacle lamp had stood a moment before, now

> Nothing seemed before me but a jet gloom, now and then made ghastly by flashes of redness. Uppermost was the impression, that whatever swift, rushing thing I stood on was not so much bound to any haven ahead as rushing from all havens astern. A stark, bewildered feeling, as of death, came over me. Convulsively my hands grasped the tiller, but with the crazy conceit that the tiller was, somehow, in some enchanted way, inverted. My God! what is the matter with me? thought I. Lo! in my brief sleep I had turned myself about . . . (354)

Ishmael discovers the ship to be "rushing from all havens astern," not toward a harbor or safe conclusion, but away from safety in a movement of pure opposition that can find no haven but death. This is where the fiery vortex of the try-works, of the captain's hunt, will lead. It is a fatal inversion that cannot be righted by another inversion—Ishmael cannot simply reverse the ship's direction, that of the narrative line, without capsizing the vessel.

Ishmael deflects and universalizes his moment of terror with a burst of narrative rhetoric: "Look not too long in the face of the fire, O man! . . . believe not the artificial fire, when its redness makes all things look ghastly" (354). For the contrast between fire and darkness is a false one: "the glorious, golden, glad sun [is] the only true lamp—all others but liars" (354). The *Pequod*'s fire is, of course, Ahab's; it is Ahab to whom Ishmael had, if only temporarily, given himself up. The fiery chasm within Ahab is a sign of his madness, for it has obliterated and replaced the white light of his soul.

"Give not thyself up, then, to the fire," Ishmael advises,

lest it invert thee, deaden thee, as for the time it did me. There is a
wisdom that is woe; but there is a woe that is madness. And there is a
Catskill eagle in some souls that can alike dive down into the blackest
gorges, and soar out of them again and become invisible in the sunny
spaces. And even if he for ever flies within the gorge, that gorge is in
the mountains; so that even in his lowest swoop the mountain eagle is
still higher than other birds upon the plain, even though they soar.
(355)

Ishmael's image suggests a mode of self-preservation, a response to Ahab's
"fiery hunt." The eagle's flight is a perpetual oscillation, diving into blackness and then soaring into invisibility in the whiteness of the sun. This is a
fundamental and necessary opposition, but death and madness lie at either
extreme, in a penetration into either ultimate depth and darkness or ultimate height and light. The pattern of the eagle's flight makes him superior
to the "other birds upon the plain" in that it recognizes both the necessity of
the extremes and the impossibility of their attainment.[42]

The image also describes Ishmael's technique in writing *Moby-Dick*.[43]
He has dived into the vortex of action in its dramatic sections, only to
withdraw into exposition. His text is a series of engagements and disen-
gagements; his relation to his experience, and to the images within his own
writing, continually fluctuates. Here he suggests the impossibility of a final
resolution in either black or white, drama or exposition—the endlessness of
his own storytelling, with its necessary interplay of words on the page, of
black on white. But this is only one moment in the novel, a tentative
statement, not a normative one. It only images the text's oscillation between forms; lying within the text, it cannot itself conclude the process.

Three chapters later, in "The Doubloon," Ishmael reestablishes his
concern with interpretation, with reading surfaces. But now he brings both
the dramatic mode and images of circularity and centrality into the interpretive process. The doubloon, nailed to the mainmast, is a circle at the
center of the ship, but it is also covered with letters and images, an inscribed
surface. In "The Quarter-deck," the coin is Ahab's symbol, to be claimed
when his hunt has been completed; here Ishmael reintroduces it as the
object of an *interpretive* pursuit. He uses the doubloon as a touchstone,
with which he recharacterizes the major figures of the book, before his
narration is finally swallowed up by Ahab's quest.

Ahab has often stopped before the coin, but one morning he seems
newly attracted by its "strange figures and inscriptions," as though "for the

first time beginning to interpret for himself in some monomaniac way whatever significance might lurk within them. And some certain significance lurks in all things, else all things are little worth, and the round world itself but an empty cipher" (358). Once again, Ahab seeks a meaning hidden "within" the figure, and Ishmael's narration echoes his terms—there must be significance "in" things, or the sphere of the "round world" will be "but an empty cipher," either a linguistic sign without a referent or the flat and empty circle of a zero sign.

Before the coin, "Ahab, not unobserved by others, was now pausing" (359). Ishmael moves to the present tense and establishes a dramatic situation of characters observing one another. Ahab's speech is quoted in its entirety, with no gloss or narrative comment:

> "The firm tower, that is Ahab; the volcano, that is Ahab; the courageous, the undaunted, and victorious fowl, that, too, is Ahab; all are Ahab; and this round globe is but the image of the rounder globe, which, like a magician's glass, to each and every man in turn but mirrors back his own mysterious self." (359)

Faced with the task of interpretation, Ahab can see only himself; every surface is for him a mirror. The coin is for him an image of the "rounder globe"—the eye—that mirrors back each man's "mysterious self." Such a conflation of earth and eye, that which is seen and that which sees, makes the object and the subject of perception one and the same. If the surface of reality only mirrors the surface of the eye, no interpretation is possible; the mirror can only be penetrated, seen through, once it has been broken through. It is thus that Ahab has been forced to define meaning as depth and the self as an inner mystery.[44]

In the absence of a narrative frame, Stubb now "soliloquize[s]" (360), noting Ahab's act of reading before examining the doubloon himself and introducing and commenting on the speeches of Flask, the Manxman, Queequeg, Fedallah, and Pip. Each reading adds another possible interpretation, each "reflecting" the character of the reader. Even though Queequeg and Fedallah do not speak, Stubb provides interpretations of their actions, readings of their readings: Queequeg, he says, is "comparing notes; looking at his thigh bone; thinks the sun is in the thigh, or in the calf, or in the bowels . . . here comes that ghost-devil, Fedallah . . . What does he say, with that look of his? Ah, only makes a sign to the sign and bows himself" (362). Both texts and interpretations proliferate here: Queequeg compares the inscriptions on the coin with his tattoos, his own body/text, and Fedallah "makes a sign to the sign." And, of course, Stubb's speech (and Ishmael's text) includes and interprets them all.

Pip comments on this multiplication of readings: "'I look, you look, he looks; we look, ye look, they look,'" he says (362). Each "look," each act of reading, both repeats and differs from its predecessors, reconstituting the coin. As the framing perspectives widen, the movement of interpretation expands outward on the textual surface. The dramatic form is here not a penetration—it widens rather than narrows the possibilities of interpretation, generating more surfaces, more texts.

Pip is the first of these readers to notice Stubb, and the mate, unnerved, withdraws. If Stubb has taken on a pseudo-narrative role within the dramatic framework of the scene, Pip is now left with the last word, as in "Midnight, Forecastle": "'Here's the ship's navel, this doubloon here, and they are all on fire to unscrew it. But, unscrew your navel, and what's the consequence?'" (363). He characterizes the others' desire to find meaning in the coin as their being "on fire to unscrew it"; the false and self-consuming light of fire is again linked to a corkscrewing, self-destructive movement toward a postulated inner truth.[45]

It is Ahab's terms that govern the last thirty chapters of the text. Along with the vortex, the most powerful images are of an increasingly rigid, "monomaniac" linearity as the captain's quest nears its end (171). In "The Chart," Ishmael had described the way in which Ahab plots his course, "study[ing] the various lines and shadings" on his charts "and with slow but steady pencil trac[ing] additional courses over spaces that before were blank" (171). The captain charts the whale's habitual travels, tracing its movement from point to point on the surface of the ocean, and thus plotting the Pequod's cruise, the narrative line. His objective is "the Line" of the equator (173), the circumference of a circle that is visible only as a horizontal line on the surface of the ocean or a chart. Ahab's aim is, of course, to break through such surfaces, to turn forward movement in time into a downward penetration out of time: "with the charts of all four oceans before him, Ahab was threading a maze of currents and eddies, with a view to the more certain accomplishment of that monomaniac thought of his soul" (171).

The captain's pursuit, earlier imaged as a descent into a vortex, is here described as "*threading a maze* of currents and eddies." Just as the Minotaur stood at the center of the Cretan labyrinth, so Moby Dick lies at the center of Ahab's maze/vortex. And just as Theseus carried a thread into the labyrinth, Ahab attempts to "thread" his way toward the whale, turning both the line of the *Pequod's* voyage and the thread spun out by the Fates, the narrative line, to his own "monomaniac" ends. But unlike both Theseus and Ishmael, Ahab will not follow his line back out of the labyrinth/vortex; his confrontation with Moby Dick will result in death for himself and his crew.

As Ahab nears his quarry, he deliberately narrows the dimensions of his pursuit. He first destroys the quadrant, which locates the ship in three-dimensional space (412); then makes himself "lord over the level lodestone" by remagnetizing the compass, subordinating its two dimensions to his own "iron way" (425); and finally turns to the log and line to measure the ship's speed along the single line of its course (426). But the line breaks—it cannot withstand the force of Ahab's drive into the vortex.

This rigid linearity is dramatized in "The Forge," in which the blacksmith forges the captain's new harpoon. Ahab cools the finished arrow of the point not in water but in the blood of his harpooneers, and goes on to "baptize" it in the name of the devil (404):

> A coil of new tow-line was then unwound . . . and stretched to a great tension . . . At one extremity the rope was unstranded, and the separate spread yarns were all braided and woven round the socket of the harpoon; the pole was then driven hard up into the socket; from the lower end the rope was traced half way along the pole's length, and firmly secured so, with intertwistings of twine. This done, pole, iron, and rope—like the Three Fates—remained inseparable. (405)

Ahab "unstrands" the different "yarns" that make up the rope—this is the language Mapple uses to describe his interpretation of Scripture, but Ahab's purpose is, of course, both demonic and decidedly *anti*-interpretive. The "intertwistings" of the text—of Ishmael's shifts in form—are fused into the inflexible and deadly line of the harpoon. Ahab's weapon and his revenge are now the Fates that measure out—and cut—the narrative line.

This is the line that will toss Ishmael aside, a castaway. By this point in the book, his withdrawal as character and narrator is already well underway. He last speaks as character in "The Pacific" (399), and his final narrative comment comes in "The Symphony," Chapter 132. Here he describes Ahab as "tied up and twisted; gnarled and knotted with wrinkles, haggardly firm and unyielding . . . lifting his splintered helmet of a brow to the fair girl's forehead of heaven" (442). The contrast between the twisted, tortured old man and the bright blue day produces Ishmael's burst of rhetoric:

> Oh, immortal infancy, and innocency of the azure! . . . Sweet child-hood of air snd sky! how oblivious were ye of old Ahab's close-coiled woe! But so have I seen little Miriam and Martha, laughing-eyed elves, heedlessly gambol around their old sire; sporting with the circle of singed locks which grew on the marge of that burnt-out crater of his brain. (442–43)

Ahab will unleash his "close-coiled woe" in his attack upon the whale, releasing and straightening it like the coiled whale line as his harpoon is darted. But Ishmael responds with a counterimage of children circling round an old man. He presents another circle, the man's "singed locks," that radiates outward in a generative genealogical progression.[46]

For a moment, Ahab can see his own wife and child in Starbuck's eyes, but he says that he feels driven "*against* all natural lovings and longings" (445, my emphasis). "We are turned round and round in this world, like yonder windlass," he laments, "and Fate is the handspike" (445). Turning back to the image of the vortex, he finds Fedallah's eyes, not Starbuck's, reflected in the water.

At last come the three days of the chase. Pursued by the whaleboats on the first day, Moby Dick dives, and Ahab must wait for the whale to surface, his eyes "whirling round in his head as he swept the watery circle" (448). When the white whale does reappear, it is as pursuer rather than pursued, destroying Ahab's boat and then swimming "swiftly round and round the wrecked crew" in "ever-contracting circles" (450). Ahab's head is the center of this "direful zone"; he has reached the center, but not yet the bottom of the vortex (450).

At the start of "The Chase—Second Day," Ishmael slows his narration to point out that the "pursuit of one particular whale, continued through day and night, and through night into day, is a thing by no means unprece-dented" (453). Nantucket captains can anticipate a whale's movements, his "future wake through the darkness": for them, "the proverbial evanescence of a thing writ on water, a wake, is . . . as reliable as the steadfast land" (453–54). Ishmael's image emphasizes the mortal limits of Ahab's linear pursuit, his challenge to the evanescence of human life in time. Here he withdraws, refusing to follow in the *Pequod*'s wake as "the ship tore on" (454).

Ishmael now vanishes entirely. The crew are now "one man, not thirty," striving "through that infinite blueness to seek out the thing that might destroy them" (454, 455). This time Moby Dick appears as pure whirling force, twisting the harpoon lines, "corkscrewing" them into "mazes" (456), and then diving in "a boiling maelstrom" (457). Starbuck again challenges Ahab: "'Shall we keep chasing this murderous fish till he swamps the last man? Shall we be dragged by him to the bottom of the sea? Shall we be towed by him to the infernal world?'" (459). But Ahab has sworn to "'ten times girdle the unmeasured globe; yea and dive straight through it'" in pursuit of the whale (459).

When Moby Dick is sighted on the morning of the third day, Ahab cries, "'Forehead to forehead I meet thee'"—he will come "face to face" with the faceless whale, throwing himself and his men against the whiteness of its inscrutable blank forehead, meeting it not in an act of interpretation but in an act of violence (461). And this time Ahab's drive into the vortex is completed. He darts his harpoon into the whale, but "the line . . . ran foul. Ahab stooped to clear it; he did clear it; but the flying turn caught him round the neck, and voicelessly . . . he was shot out of the boat" (468). Ahab is strangled by his own line, and as Moby Dick dives, he is taken down as well, in the dive, the penetration, that he has so long desired. The *Pequod* and then Ahab's whaleboat both go down: "concentric circles seized the lone boat itself, and all its crew, and each floating oar, and every lance-pole, and spinning, animate and inanimate, all round and round in one vortex, carried the smallest chip of the Pequod out of sight" (469).

All, of course, except Ishmael, who is left where he began, "floating on the margin of the ensuing scene," fragmented and orphaned by his own tale (470). His narrative voice reemerges in the epilogue, but he must struggle to reestablish his identity and authority as writer: "It so chanced," he says, "that after the Parsee's disappearance, I was he whom the Fates ordained to take the place of Ahab's bowsman, when that bowsman assumed the vacant post; the same, who, when on the last day the three men were tossed from out the rocking boat, was dropped astern" (470). The actors here are "chance" and the Fates, not Ishmael the weaver/writer. He can only identify himself retrospectively, as the powerless victim of the Fates, tossed aside and dropped out of the narrative.

Ishmael is, as we have seen, finally drawn into "the closing vortex" as the *Pequod* goes down (470). He is, once again, caught within the vortex and the fundamental opposition between the whiteness of its "creamy pool" and the "button-like black bubble" at its center (470). He compares himself, not to the Catskill eagle, but to Ixion, bound to a ceaselessly turning wheel as a punishment, and likens his task as writer to Ixion's ceaseless agony. He has struggled to reconstruct both himself and his tale in the hope that his completed text, like Orpheus' song, may stop the wheel, the vicious circle of experience lived and relived in memory. But the telling has repeated the events of the tale without reshaping them to establish an overarching unity or meaning, without recovering the integral selfhood Ishmael had sought.

Ishmael clings to his story as he had to Queequeg's coffin. The savage's body has become a text that outlives its author and saves another, Ishmael. But the coffin is, of course, empty, indicating only the absence of a body, the loss of interior meaning. And its figures are "an interminable Cretan laby-rinth" (32), an unreadable surface whose truth cannot be recovered without another surrender to an interpretive vortex. As weaver and writer, Ishmael must always stand outside and beyond his text, living on to relive his story, forever at the mercy of the Fates and the linearity of Time itself.

Moby-Dick is Melville's most direct confrontation with the limits of first-person narration, his most forceful exploration of the possibility of creating a purely textual identity. The effort to escape bodily decay and genealogical separation from the father by writing oneself into a new, timeless existence will become the explicit subject of *Pierre*, but there Melville shifts from first- to third-person narrative, distancing himself from his hero and making the novel a critique of Pierre's suicidal project.

4.

Pierre, like *Moby-Dick*, begins with the twin oppositions of surface and depth, interpretation and penetration. Unlike Ishmael, however, Pierre does not willingly move from the image of meaning as depth to that of meaning as a surface or fabric—the shift is forced upon him as both character and writer. One of the novel's primary themes is the dissolution of form and meaning; neither self nor reality can be grasped or imaged as a stable unity. Each remains tangled and ambiguous, frustrating and en-tangling the interpreter or writer. Where Ishmael finally turns back out of his textual labyrinth, Pierre is denied the possibility of return—his life itself becomes an entanglement, and the only potential closure lies in an act of suicidal violence.

The novel begins, as we have seen, in the ostensibly timeless paternal space of Saddle-Meadows. Here all is open and unambiguous, the "truth" of character a simple unity to be apprehended directly, without the mediation of either representation or interpretation. The primary example of such psychological clarity is Pierre's fiancée, Lucy Tartan: blonde and fair, with the light blue of "the heavens" as her color, she appears bathed in "golden loveliness and light," the "transparency of her clear Welsh complexion" glowing (33, 58).

Lucy is not a writer but an artist, her sketches contained in a blue portfolio: "'Open it!'" she tells Pierre, "'what secret thing keep I from thee? Read me through and through. I am entirely thine. See!'" (40). She offers her art as an object not for interpretation but for immediate visual possession. In so doing, she claims, she offers *herself*—not just an adequate self-representation, but her essential being.

Lucy asks precisely this kind of self-revelation from Pierre, but the very terms of her demand reveal the mystification on which it depends:

> "'tis Love's own self that now speaks through me—only in unbounded confidence and interchangings of all subtlest secrets, can Love possibly endure. Love's self is a secret, and so feeds on secrets, Pierre. . . . Thou must be wholly a disclosed secret to me." (37)

It is Love itself that ostensibly speaks here, as Lucy surrenders her voice and self to the emotion. Love, however, is defined as both antithetical to secrecy and dependent on it at the same time: Love itself is a secret and "feeds on" secrets, consuming them but also deriving its strength from them. If disclosure is the expression of Love, secrets must remain for disclosure to take place. Relations between lovers are not, after all, a matter of transparent self-revelation, but of an interplay between disclosure and secrecy. "Love is built upon secrets," the narrator later remarks (81).

It should come as no surprise, then, that Pierre cannot swear to "'never keep a secret'" from his fiancée (37). The secret he keeps from Lucy and the "mystery" he hides from his mother (47) are one and the same—his response to his first sight of Isabel's face. As Pierre begins to discover the secrets of paternity, he enters the world of time and language, of storytelling, interpretation, and self-conscious deception. The suitor ready to "utter the magic word of marriage to his Lucy" instead finds himself lying to both mother and fiancée for the first time (61, 50).

If Lucy's sketches present the self as a clearly visible surface, Isabel's music is a depth that transcends rather than preempts representation: it is "incapable of being translated into words; for where the deepest words end, there music begins with its supersensuous and all-confounding intimations" (282). The "stringed tongue" of her guitar produces music that is "the deep voice of the being of Isabel"; its melody, "by an apparent magic . . . touche[s] the secret monochord in [Pierre's] breast" (173). This is a communication deeper than language, beyond rational interpretation—it only "confounds" and mystifies. Isabel claims, however, that "'better, a million times, and far sweeter are mysteries than surmises: though the mystery be unfathomable, it is still the unfathomableness of fullness; but the surmise, that is but shallow and unmeaning emptiness'" (153). She thus presents herself in terms directly opposite to Lucy's, describing the self as an unfathomable depth of meaning.

But just as all of *Moby-Dick*'s epistemological approaches lead to the vortex, this opposition crumbles as the novel progresses. If Lucy's open surface is inseparable from secrecy, so Isabel's depth depends on surfaces— in *Pierre* all forms of meaning collapse into an ambiguous textuality.

Isabel's "mystery" is displayed only as a *veiled* depth; a veiling or partial covering is required for it to be revealed. Her "concealed emotion," for example, is visible only as a movement beneath her dress: the "velvet shows elastically; contracting and expanding, as though some choked, violent thing were risen up there within from the teeming region of the heart" (46). What is it, Pierre asks, "'that thou has veiled in thee so imperfectly, that I seem to see its motion, but not its form? It visibly rustles behind the concealing screen'" (41). Pure depth is invisible; it can only be discerned indirectly, as imperfectly hidden beneath the surface of a veil or that of the body itself.

Isabel's first sense of her own identity comes through a similar combination of revelation and concealment: "'weeks and years ran on, and my hair began to vail me with its fullness and its length; and now often I heard the word beautiful, spoken of my hair, and beautiful, spoken of myself'" (123). The natural growth of her hair at once hides her features and generates a characterization of them as "beautiful." So too does the "fullness" of Isabel's hair cover her guitar: "her long dark shower of curls fell over it, and vailed it; and still, out from the vail came the swarming sweetness, and the utter unintelligibleness, but the infinite significancies of the sounds of the guitar" (126). It is the veil itself, the "dark tent of hair" enclosing the kneeling girl (150), that releases both her identity and her music, turning face and guitar into hidden depths.

When Isabel begins to sing, however, Pierre hears

the tones above deftly stealing and winding among the myriad serpen-
tinings of the other melody:—deftly stealing and winding as respect-
ing the instrumental sounds, but in themselves wonderfully and aban-
donedly free and bold—bounding and rebounding as from multitudi-
nous reciprocal walls; while with every syllable the hair-shrouded form
of Isabel swayed to and fro with a like abandonment, and suddenness,
and wantonness. (126)

What comes forth from beneath the veil is not a single sound, but two
contrasting sets of sounds. The two progressions remain distinct, "stealing
and winding," bouncing off each other—the "deep voice" of Isabel's being
is this "serpentining" interplay of music and voice, not a single sound at all.

Even though Isabel may present herself, through her music, as a
mystery beyond interpretation, she identifies herself to Pierre by telling her
tale, first offering him the written text of her letter and then a verbal
narrative as evidence for him to interpret. If Pierre takes Lucy's " 'sweet
heart' " to be directly visible, a " 'dear missive to me from heaven,' " Isabel's
first address to him is mediated by a folded letter written in an "irregular
hand, and in some places almost illegible" (62, 64). "Such a note," the
narrator says, "can be easily enough written . . . impostors are not unknown
in this curious world; or the brisk novelist, Pierre, will write thee fifty such
notes" (69–70). The letter is another veil, asserting and at the same time
withholding Isabel's identity and legitimizing presence. Her hair may be an
organic extension of her physical being, but her letter is designed to
function in her absence. Texts have no organic or essential link to their
authors; insofar as they attempt to substitute for or counterfeit the presence
of the writer, any or all may be impostures.

The two key events in Isabel's narrative both involve the uncovering of
hidden depths. These moments are paradigmatic ones, however, because
they disclose not bottomless depths but interior *surfaces* to be interpreted as
texts. The first of these "deep" texts is the name Isabel finds embroidered on
her father's handkerchief. She folds the handkerchief "in such a manner,
that the name was invisibly buried in the heart of it, and it was like opening
a book and turning over many blank leaves before I came to the mysterious
writing" (146). The girl takes a flat surface and folds it over on itself to
produce an inner hiding place, but this depth is only a series of surfaces,
pages to be turned over in sequence. In one sense, this is an ominous
gesture, for Isabel's "book" is created as a hiding place; textualizing evidence of one's identity here means hiding or obscuring, not revealing or

confirming it.[47] If this is the case, Pierre's autobiographical project must be doomed to failure.

The second text is not hidden by Isabel herself; it is the name "Isabel," which has been gilded onto the interior of her guitar. The writing has been deliberately hidden by someone, though, " 'because the lettering could only have been put there before the guitar was put together' " (148). The instrument that creates Isabel's mysterious music has also been constructed as a hiding place—it reveals that which lies beyond interpretation but conceals its own interpretable textual contents.

Isabel's proclamation of meaning as depth is thus contradicted by the textual surfaces upon which she bases her identity. It is not only an interior depth that may hide the self; a surface, visible or hidden, may also function as a hiding place.

At first, however, Pierre is unwilling to surrender the notion of a single, unitary meaning, possession of which will make interpretation unnecessary: "mysteries," he decides, are "best and soonest unraveled by the eventual unraveling of themselves" (53). His image—of mystery as entanglement—suggests that the complexity of a three-dimensional mass will "unravel" into the single line or thread of an intelligible narrative. Linearity, he assumes, is a natural or primary state, to which events will inevitably return—without interpretive intervention.

It is Isabel's letter that forces interpretive choice upon him:

> [He] seemed distinctly to feel two antagonistic agencies within him; one of which was just struggling into his consciousness, and each of which was striving for the mastery . . . One bade him finish the selfish destruction of the note; for in some dark way the reading of it would irretrievably entangle his fate. The other . . . seemed mildly to say— Read, Pierre, though by reading thou may'st entangle thyself, yet may'st thou thereby disentangle others. (63)

In reading the letter and then listening to Isabel's story, Pierre will be forced to accept, at least provisionally, the image of meaning as a tangle that the interpreter must himself unravel—at the price of his own fragmentation and entanglement.

It is the interpreter's loss of freedom, his involvement in an *unending* process of unraveling, that frightens Pierre most. Faced with the "unchangeable" yet inescapably "ambiguous" smile of the chair portrait of his father, Pierre tries to use a story—his aunt's tale of his father's love for "a lovely young Frenchwoman"—as a "wedge" to force open the "crack" of his father's smile and "probe" into an inner depth (84). Isabel's letter is, for him, another wedge, another anti-interpretive weapon: "now, *now*! Isabel's letter read: swift as the first light that slides from the sun, Pierre saw all preceding ambiguities, all mysteries ripped open as if with a keen sword" (85). If meaning is tangled and ambiguous, Pierre would treat it as a Gordian knot to be "ripped" apart in an act of violence. The echo of Ahab and his drive to penetrate beneath the "mask" of reality is clear: "'Thou Black Knight, that with visor down, thus confrontest me, and mockest at me: Lo! I strike through thy helm, and will see thy face, be it Gorgon! . . . From all idols, I tear all veils; henceforth I will see the hidden things; and live right out in my own hidden life'" (65–66). This exclamation comes, however, before Pierre's first meeting with Isabel, before his encounter with her veiled truth and the serpentining mystery that emerges from beneath her hair.

After their first interview, Pierre returns to this opposition between untangling and cutting, but it leads him to a different conclusion. In Isabel's life, he says, "there was an unraveled plot; and he felt that unraveled it would eternally remain to him" (141). (I take "unraveled" to mean "tangled" here. The narrator's use of the word fluctuates in the following passage: in the first and last sentences "unravel" means "untangle"; in the third, "unravelable" means "beyond untangling.") Pierre has read many novels, but

> their false, inverted attempts at systematizing eternally unsystemizable elements; their audacious, intermeddling impotency, in trying to unravel, and spread out, and classify, the more thin than gossamer threads which make up the complex web of life; these things over Pierre had no power now. Straight through their helpless miserableness he pierced . . . He saw that human life doth truly come from that, which all men are agreed to call by the name of *God*; and that it partakes of the unravelable inscrutableness of God. . . . while the countless tribes of common novels laboriously spin vails of mystery, only to complacently clear them up at last . . . the profounder emanations of the human mind, intended to illustrate all that can be humanly known of human life; these never unravel their own intricacies, and have no proper endings; but in imperfect, unanticipated, and disappointing sequels (as mutilated stumps), hurry to abrupt intermergings with the eternal tides of time and fate. (141)

Life is here a "complex web," not a single narrative line. The unraveling of interpretation can have "no proper ending"; its conclusions can only be arbitrary "mutilations." But when Pierre "pierces through" such attempts to unravel the web of reality into narrative, he finds no inner face or meaning. Such knowledge belongs to God alone and must remain forever "inscrutable" and inaccessible to men. There is now no alternative to unraveling, no escape from the endless instability of interpretation.

An earlier narrative passage confirms this insight. It begins with a description of the "casket, wherein we have placed our holiest and most final joy, and which we have secured by a lock of infinite deftness" (69). "[C]an that casket," the narrator asks, "be picked and desecrated at the merest stranger's touch, when we think that we alone hold the only and chosen key?" (69). Here a key opens the hidden space of joy, but a page later, this "key" becomes an interpretive device—the double meaning is the same as in "Loomings," but here there is a *progression* in which the second meaning *displaces* as well as opposes the first. "[F]athers and mothers!" the narrator exclaims,

> give heed! Thy little one may not now comprehend the meaning of those words and those signs, by which, in its innocent presence, thou thinkest to disguise the sinister thing ye would hint. Not now he knows . . . but if, in after-life, Fate puts the chemic key of the cipher into his hands; then how swiftly and how wonderfully, he reads all the obscurest and most obliterate inscriptions he finds in his memory; yea, and rummages himself all over, for still hidden writings to read. (70)

These hidden secrets are those of paternal sexuality, of a primal cipher that is "inscribed" in the memory to be remembered and "read." Pierre's struggle to understand Isabel's story involves just such a retrospective examination of his own memory, using the interpretive key that she has given him. "Tear thyself open," Pierre exclaims to himself, "and read there the confounding story of thy blind doltishness" (171). Textualizing the self can only be superfluous and repetitive if the memory that defines the self is already a "confounding story," an interior text.

Having lost the key to his travelling chest, Pierre forces it open, only to find the chair portrait, "with its noiseless, ever-nameless, and ambiguous, unchanging smile" (196). "'[S]nake's nest!'" he cries—inside this casket, there is only another surface, another dangerous, serpentining interpretive tangle (196). He may destroy the portrait, but he cannot stop the regress of interpretation once it has been set in motion:

because Pierre began to see through the first superficiality of the world, he fondly weens he has come to the unlayered substance. But, far as any geologist has yet gone down into the world, it is found to consist of nothing but surface stratified on surface. To its axis, the world being nothing but superinduced superficies. (285)

Beneath these surfaces lies no coherent meaning—only the empty sarcophagus of the father's tomb and the blank "inscrutableness" of God. In *Pierre*, there is finally no firm "depth" of meaning; there is nothing but slippery textual surfaces.

Truth, Pierre discovers, does not stabilize and unify; it "steal[s] on us, and rob[s] us," manifesting itself only as fragmentation and loss (65). For him, Isabel's face and his father's "reciprocally identified each other, and, as it were, melted into each other . . . interpenetratingly uniting" (85). The result is not a stable unity, however; it is an instability that undermines the very possibility of unity, even within each individual face. As "the physical world of solid objects now slidingly displaced itself from around him," Pierre quotes a verse from Dante, "descriptive of the two mutually absorbing shapes in the Inferno":

"Ah! how dost thou change,
Agnello! See! thou art not double now,
Nor only one!" (85)

The faces are neither separate nor unified, neither "double now,/ Nor only one." Opposition and unity are both only moments in a continual flux, always subject to "sliding" or displacement.

Such shiftiness and reversibility is implied by the title of Book IX, "More Light, and the Gloom of that Light. More Gloom, and the Light of that Gloom" (165). There is no "Ultimate of Human Speculative Knowledge" at which the seeker may abide (167). "Ultimate" positions must always be unstable, points at which "the most immemorially admitted maxims of men begin to slide and fluctuate, and finally become wholly inverted" (165). The explorer is continually assailed by "sudden onsets of new truth . . . irruptions of those barbarous hordes which Truth ever nourishes in the loins of her frozen, yet teeming North" (167).[48] Truth is ever-changing, ever-fragmenting and multiplying, impossible to fix or describe; its essence is an "everlasting elusiveness" that leaves a "lurking insincerity . . . [in] even the greatest and purest written thoughts" (339).

When Pierre moves from interpretation to action, he sets out to become Isabel's "champion," to defend her against "all conceivable contingencies of Time and Chance" by "map[ping] out his and her young life-chart" (106). He will "make a sacrifice of all objects dearest to him, and cut himself away from his last hopes of common happiness"—the conventions that tie him to his mother are "light as gossamer, and thinner and more impalpable than airiest threads of gauze" (106). Just as Pierre has wished, like Ahab, to break through surfaces rather than enmesh himself in interpretation, he will now, he says, cut and break away from the contingent threads of Time and Chance. But if truth is shifting and elusive, it belongs to the realm of the contingent. And a "life-chart" is just another text, a fabric of contingent signs—writing or "mapping out" is the mirror image of interpretation, an equally destabilizing self-entanglement.

Pierre's pretended marriage to Isabel will "entangle him in a fictitious alliance, which, though but in reality a web of air, yet in effect would prove a wall of iron" (175). He is involving himself in "such an inextricable twist of Fate, that the three dexterous maids themselves could hardly disentangle him, if once he tie the complicating knots about him and Isabel" (175). "[T]hou rash boy!" the narrator exclaims, "are there no couriers in the air to warn thee away from these emperilings, and point thee to those Cretan labyrinths, to which thy life's cord is leading thee?" (176). The single "cord" that links a son to his mother at birth, once broken, splits and twists (unravels?) into a labyrinth as the fetus's "life-line" becomes the man's fate. The attempt to shape one's life is both an interpretive act, as one tries to solve the puzzle of a labyrinth, and an act of writing, as one retraces that maze with linguistic thread. The conscious construction of an identity makes the self into the object of its own interpretation; giving form to the self means textualizing it, opening it to the vagaries of interpretation.

Pierre persists, however, in seeing his action as a tearing free rather than an entanglement: "'thy true heart,'" he tells Isabel, "'foreknoweth not the myriad alliances and criss-crossings among mankind, the infinite entanglements of all social things, which forbid that one thread should fly the general fabric, on some new line of duty, without tearing itself and tearing others'" (191). The narrator, however, echoes Dante in his description of Pierre and Isabel's subsequent embrace: "Then they changed; they coiled together, and entangledly stood mute" (192).

Pierre's resolve entangles not only himself and Isabel—"he turned round and tied Lucy to the same stake" (178). The mapping or plotting that makes Lucy "so intimately interwoven . . . in his extraordinary scheme," is, according to the narrator, "at bottom" only a matter of linguistic "juggling" and arbitrary substitution: "like an algebraist, for the real Lucy he, in his scheming thoughts, had substituted but a sign—some empty x—and in the ultimate solution of the problem, that empty x still figured; not the real Lucy" (181). In constructing his "life-chart," Pierre reduces its terms to empty signs, each arbitrarily chosen and applicable to a number of interchangeable referents. He tries, for example, to substitute Isabel for Lucy in accepting his cousin Glen's offer of a house in the city for the use of "Mr. and Mrs. Pierre Glendinning" (228). In so doing, he turns "Mrs. Glendinning" into another "empty x," emptying the sign on which he would bestow a crucial importance. When Lucy finally joins them at the Apostles it is, for Isabel, only one more "thread" weaving itself "into the general riddle" (314).

If Pierre's life has already become a matter of manipulating empty signs, his career as writer reflects rather than escapes this process of entangling and fictionalization. Writing yields neither a deep and timeless meaning nor a stable identity for the writer. Texts must remain ambiguous and inadequate, unable to represent either their subjects or their authors. Even before Pierre begins his new career, he encounters a paradigmatic text, whose shiftiness and uncertain relation to its "author" foreshadow the fate of Pierre's own efforts; on the stage from Saddle-Meadows to the city, he reads Plotinus Plinlimmon's pamphlet, "EI"—"If."

The pamphlet itself is "a thin, tattered, dried-fish-like thing; printed with blurred ink upon mean, sleazy paper"—the "waste paper" of a previous traveler (206). If the pamphlet is only a physical fragment, it is a fragment in terms of its contents, too; it is only the first of "Three Hundred and Thirty-Three Lectures, . . . being not so much the Portal, as part of the temporary Scaffold to the Portal of [the author's] new Philosophy" (210). This text marks a beginning, but it establishes only a temporary position, one to be discarded, like scaffolding, once Plinlimmon's philosophical edifice is complete. For the author, too, it will eventually be "waste paper."

Plinlimmon begins with a qualification, describing all human wisdom (including, presumably, his own) as "provisional" (211). The rare souls that "'give Heaven's own Truth'" are, he says, like "'sea chronometers (*Greek*, time-namers),'" which remain set to Greenwich time wherever they may be (211). But no sooner has he provided this image of "true naming" than he admits its inadequacy: even the best chronometers "'will gradually more or less vary from Greenwich time'" (211). Plinlimmon tries to salvage his simile by claiming that chronometers can be "rated," their inherent inaccuracies measured and discounted (211). But this is only to reestablish a *relative* accuracy, not an absolute correspondence. Indeed, the rhetorical figure Plinlimmon employs itself claims only a relative accuracy; in choosing the resemblance of simile rather than the identity of metaphor, he undercuts his own claim in the act of making it.

Nevertheless, Plinlimmon continues to use the image of the chronometer, making it one term of an opposition between "chronometrical" or absolute Truth and "horological" or relative human wisdom (212–13). It is this oppositional structure that gives both terms their meaning, but while horological or relative time can be realized and described, absolute or Heavenly Time must lie beyond the provisional realm of language, as the failure of Plinlimmon's simile implies. God's Time and Truth can only be posited as a necessary but absent pole of his opposition.

Plinlimmon goes on, however, to claim that truth must be practically realizable in horological terms—it must be capable of representation in language and action if it is to be regarded as "true" for men. And " 'so far as practical results are concerned—regarded in a purely earthly light—the only great original moral doctrine of Christianity . . . has been found (horologically) a false one; because . . . it has proved entirely impracticable' " (215). He here defines a set of terms for the establishment of truth, but those terms are explicitly horological. The result is that the relative is made into an absolute standard; the opposition between "absolute" and "relative" is itself inverted and undermined.

The philosopher's next move must be, he recognizes, to establish the real correspondence, rather than the apparent contradiction, between the chronometrical and the horological, but this, he says, " 'will be further elucidated in subsequent lectures . . . ' " (212). His pamphlet, however, has already demonstrated the radical incommensurability of Heavenly Truth to its relative, provisional expression in language. Language can only posit the existence of absolute truth as a necessary and constitutive absence, one that can only be represented through the approximation of a simile or the conjecture of an "if." And "if" is the word with which the torn pamphlet ends—"a most untidy termination" (215).

If, as Plinlimmon's text suggests, language cannot claim to express absolute Truth, neither can it be said to express its author's identity or "original intention"—again, the pamphlet is an exemplary case. Plinlimmon "never was known . . . to write with his hands" or even open a book;

"the sleazy works that went under his name" are "nothing more than his verbal things, taken down at random, and bunglingly methodized by his young disciples" (290). Texts here have no more than a "random, and bunglingly methodized" status. The "sleazy works that went under his name" have no inherent link to Plinlimmon himself; no text, this example implies, has any necessary link to the posited intention or identity of the author whose name it bears.

Pierre may or may not understand the lessons of Plinlimmon's pamphlet, but they will be those of his own literary career. A would-be publisher suggests that his poems be issued in "Library form" and sends him a sample title page, on which Pierre is described as "GLENDINNING / Author of / *That world-famed production, 'The Tropical Summer: a Sonnet.' / 'The Weather: a Thought.' . . .*" (247). Pierre feels a momentary elation upon seeing "the imposing enumeration of his titles—long and magnificent as those preceding the proclamations of some German Prince" (249). The titles of his poems here become his titles as a poet. His name does not identify their origin; instead, their names identify him. Publication, rather than establishing the authority of the writer's name, only devalues and replaces it with those of the printed texts themselves.

It is not that Pierre wishes to escape the process of literary canonization, by which author is turned into text, his physical body transformed into a body of work, a "canon." He only seeks to retain control over the process. He thus declines to have his poems published in "Library form," because he believes "that his future productions might at least equal, if not surpass, in some small degree, those already given to the world" (250). His body of work will change, just as "his boyish features and whole expression were daily changing" and, indeed, as his signature changes, "owing to the very youthful and quite unformed character of his handwriting" (253). Pierre's goal is to leave a single image and signature, to establish a unified textual corpus that will, unchanging and unchangeable, identify him forever.

Pierre's objective, in other words, is to replace his own ever-changing temporal existence with the timeless unity of a text. In one sense, this is only a nostalgic desire to return to the illusions of Saddle-Meadows. He writes in order to escape from temporal and interpretive instability, to reestablish a spatially defined "essential" self. The narrator, however, soon notes the inescapable temporality of composition. A writer, he says, builds a "temple" out of the marble "quarries" within himself (257). But Pierre is both "very young" and "very unarchitectural," and as in digging for precious metals in the mines, much earthy rubbish has first to be troublesomely handled and thrown out; so, in digging in one's soul for the fine gold of genius, much dullness and common-place is first brought to light. Happy would it be, if the man possessed in himself some receptacle for his own rubbish of this sort: but . . . No common-place is ever effectively got rid of, except by essentially emp-tying one's self of it into a book. (258)

The priceless depth of the soul may be embodied in a text, but this process of substitutive representation is neither instantaneous nor certain. The instability of writing arises from its nature as a temporal process: surfaces must be penetrated *before* depths can be reached and "rubbish" unearthed *before* the "gold of genius" is found. What begins as the author's attempt to transform the depth and fullness of the self into a textual double becomes an effort to "empty" the self of its superficial rubbish. His text comes to be defined as what the self *is not*—or is no longer—it "embodies" only that which the self has rid itself of. The only benefit of writing, the narrator concludes, is that a "book can be put into the fire" (258).

It is not long before Pierre finds this to be true of his own work. He can no longer bear to even read his poems, and is driven to reject his own published writing as an inadequate representation of both its subject and its author:

"in the hour of composition, I thought the very heavens looked in from the windows at astonishment at their beauty and power. Then, afterward, when days cooled me down, and again I took them up and scanned them, some underlying suspicions intruded; but when in the open air, I recalled the fresh, unwritten images of the bunglingly written things; then I felt buoyant and triumphant again; as if by that act of ideal recalling, I had, forsooth, transferred the perfect ideal to the miserable written attempt at embodying it . . . now, the ten thousand universal revealings brand me on the forehead with fool! and like protested notes at the Bankers, all those written things of mine, are jaggingly cut though and through with the protesting hammer of Truth!" (272–73)

Pierre's texts cannot serve as signs of the self that may rectify his sense of self-division; they only reproduce and deepen it, invalidating his signature and destroying the value of his name. In "disowning" his previous work

(282), Pierre abandons his hope of "surpassing" and building onto it—he himself divides his proposed textual corpus, declaring his earlier writing to be unconnected to his present self and his new project.

"[R]enouncing all his foregone self," Pierre undertakes "a comprehensive compacted work"—he wishes to begin both himself and his writing anew, to produce a work that will "comprehend" both author and subject (283). Pierre's intent is again to "tear himself free" from "entanglements," but now the entanglements are his own writings and his public image as an author. He sees himself as "transplanted into a new and wonderful element of Beauty and Power," but this is the same illusion he fell victim to as a poet—he is, "in fact, but in one of the stages of the transition" (283). He remains enmeshed in time—trapped within the temporality of his own development as writer, as he "immaturely attempts a mature work" (282).

Pierre describes the act of writing as a circling movement that brings forth and encloses the depths of the self. His enterprise is an "advancing and concentring" one that will produce a "great, deep book" (338, 341). "[M]ost grand productions of the best human intellects," he believes,

> are built around a circle, as atolls (*i.e.* the primitive coral islets which, raising themselves in the depth of profoundest seas, rise funnel-like to the surface, and present there a hoop of white rock, which though on the outside everywhere lashed by the ocean, yet excludes all tempests from the quiet lagoon within), digestively including the whole range of all that can be known or dreamed. (283)

Pierre thinks of his text in the terms in which Ishmael speaks of an "island self"—for him, it is a defensive enclosure, in which "the whole range of all that can be known or dreamed," the self included, can be given a calm and stable form. Just as nature forms the atoll, Pierre is "elementalizing" the "strange stuff, which in the act of attempting [his] book, has upheaved and upgushed in his soul" (304).

If Pierre's book is indeed the exteriorization of his soul, its "depth" requires the emptying of his "gold of genius," the surrender of his identity (338). Given the anti-genealogical, atemporal terms of his project, he must "have directly plagiarized from his own experiences" (302). Is this, the narrator asks, "creation, or destruction? Builds Pierre the noble world of a new book? or does the Pale Haggardness unbuild the lungs and the life in him?" (304). He is being "devoured by the all-exacting theme of his book" (308); as he "give[s] himself up" to his work, he finds that he has "less and less to bring to it" (339, 338). Such creation must be self-destruction, an exhaustion of the self that amounts to a "rehearsing [of] the part of death" (305).

Pierre eventually loses control over his text: "like a vast, lumbering planet, [it] revolves in his aching head"; rather than creating an encircling text, he is soon circling himself, revolving in *its* "troubled orbit" (305, 298). He is diving deeper and deeper into a "whirlingness" in pursuit of Truth—his attempt to escape a labyrinth leads him to the vortex of self-annihilation (339).

The creation of a text out of the "strange stuff" of the author's own experience cannot but fail. For the self that Pierre would express in his book has already been fragmented and radically undermined by that experience. Pierre writes because he desires to make a ground or unity for the self; "impostor philosophers" may pretend to "get a Voice out of Silence" (208), but he is attempting a creation *ex nihilo*, a getting a self out of silence. "'I am a nothing,'" he tells Isabel, and "'From nothing proceeds nothing'" (274). God is the only "original author," and He speaks to man only as "Silence" (259, 204).

Pierre is finally forced to break off his writing. "'I render no accounts,'" he proclaims, "'I am what I am'" (325). He cannot, finally, enclose his life in a text because he cannot write his own death: "'Death [will steal] the last leaf, and [rub] it all out, to scribble his own ineffaceable *hic jacet* there'" (309). "'[E]re that vile book be finished,'" Pierre realizes, "'I must get on some other element than earth'" (348). The most he can accomplish is to bring about his own death, to enable someone else to write his life story. "'Life's last chapter well stitched into the middle!'" he exclaims in his last prison-cell soliloquy, "'Nor book, nor author of the book, hath any sequel, though each hath its last lettering'" (360). His writing or "lettering" must cease before he ceases to live; the "last chapter" of his life must come in the middle of his text. Pierre has no sequel, as his text will have none, but neither can that text be Pierre's "sequel." It remains but a fragment, "replete with errors," only "randomly corrected" (340), its language incommensurate to its subject and falling far short of its author's intentions. Both Pierre and his book end in blankness, broken off prematurely in "a most untidy termination."

The "someone else" who is able to complete Pierre's story is, of course, the narrator of the novel. It is he who turns Pierre into *Pierre*, writer into text, in a necessarily posthumous process. But if Pierre's life has called into question the possibility of self-representation, it has also undermined the possibility of an adequate third-person representation. The gulf between language and truth that makes autobiography impossible must also make biography impossible.

This is, in fact, a lesson of which the narrator seems very much aware. His text is self-consciously unstable and self-contradictory, never for a moment suggesting the possibility of an adequate or "natural" language or form. Its opening chapters, for example, describe the apparently secure and open world of Saddle-Meadows in a language that is consciously antiquated and excessive, constantly calling attention to itself and to the narrator's shaping, mediating presence. On the summer morning on which the story begins,

> The verdant trance lay far and wide . . . As touched and bewitched by the loveliness of this silence, Pierre neared the cottage, and lifted his eyes, he swiftly paused, fixing his glance upon one upper, open casement there. Why now this impassioned, youthful pause? Why this enkindled cheek and eye? Upon the sill of the casement, a snow-white glossy pillow reposes, and a trailing shrub has softly rested a rich, crimson flower against it.
>
> Well mayst thou seek that pillow, thou odoriferous flower, thought Pierre; not an hour ago, her own cheek must have rested there. "Lucy!"
>
> "Pierre!" (3–4)

The passage moves from the narrative past tense, through a pair of rhetorical questions, into the present tense, and thence into Pierre's thoughts, which are reproduced without quotation marks. The rhetorical questions indicate a conspicuous act of narrative withholding, as does the introduction of the characters in an ostensibly dramatic fashion, before they are identified for the reader. The narrator at once asserts his omniscience, in reproducing Pierre's thoughts, and hints at a lack of omniscience, in his questions. The claim of omniscience also implies a distance between narrator and character; the absence of quotation marks around Pierre's thoughts, on the other hand, suggests a complicity or at least a proximity between them. Such initial instabilities or ambiguities make *Pierre*'s third-person narrative problematic from the very start. For Melville, the third person clearly has no special authority or security, only a different set of limitations.

What the passage conveys most clearly perhaps, is the fact of narrative intervention itself, the necessity for the narrator to come between readers and characters in order to give his text coherent form.[49] Again and again, the narrator interrupts his story to comment on his own storytelling activity and describe the text itself. He speaks up, for example, in defense of his own asides: "to the observant reader the sequel will not fail to show, how important is this circumstance. . . . Nor will any man dream that the last chapter was merely intended for a foolish bravado, and not with a solid purpose in view" (12). His book does have "a solid purpose," he claims, a unity of intention to which his apparent aside in fact conforms.

Such discursiveness may, the narrator later admits, "seem [a] rather irregular sort of writing" (25). "By immemorial usage," he says, he feels "bound to celebrate" Lucy Tartan, constrained by the conventions within which he writes (25). His wandering is in this case an attempt to avoid the standard list of a heroine's charms, which he characterizes as a "vile inventory" (25). "My proper province," he argues, "is with the angelical part of Lucy," but readers have a "prejudice against angels," and "therefore I shall martyrize myself, by letting such gentlemen and ladies into some details of Lucy Tartan's history" (25). He is clearly dissatisfied with such narrative conventions and resists the readerly expectations that he himself invokes.[50]

It is not long before the narrator mounts a direct critique of the linear causality implied by his own narrative form:

> In their precise tracings-out and subtle causations, the strongest and fieriest emotions of life defy all analytical insight. . . . the most impressive, sudden, and overwhelming event, as well as the minutest, is but the product of an infinite series of infinitely involved and untraceable foregoing occurrences. Just so with every motion of the heart. . . . Idle then would it be to attempt by any winding way so to penetrate into the heart, and memory, and inmost life, and nature of Pierre. (67)

This is reminiscent of Pierre's attack on novels' "'impotency, in trying to unravel . . . the complex web of life'" (141).[51] The narrator acknowledges that "tracing out" the lines of causation will yield only an "infinitely involved" textual web. Like Ishmael rather than Pierre himself, he will not attempt to "wind" his way into a depth, into the heart and "inmost life" of his subject.

In the very next chapter, however, he describes himself as again constrained, but now "bound to Truth, liege lord" (107). And Truth bids him "steal yet further into Pierre," which he proposes to do by following "the endless, winding way,—the flowing river in the cave of man; careless whither I be led, reckless where I land" (107). This is an opposite form of narrative self-sacrifice, not an abandonment *to* narrative, but an abandonment *of* narrative for the sake of an interior penetration.

The image of a river again appears as the narrator describes two conflicting modes of writing history: "By the one mode, all contemporary circumstances, facts, and events must be set down contemporaneously; by the other, they are only to be set down as the general stream of the narrative shall dictate" (244). Here, however, it is the temporality of narrative that is a "stream." But "I elect neither of these" modes, he concludes, "I write precisely as I please" (244).

The narrator will not, it seems, valorize either textual depth or temporal progression. Instead, he combines and shuffles these two possibilities in another river image: a "quiet retrospective little episode in the career of my hero" is "this shallowly expansive embayed Tappan Zee of my otherwise deep-heady Hudson" (259). The flow of the narrative is linked to the deep Hudson; retrospective, discursive interruptions are only "shallowly expansive." He ends with the equivalent of a despairing shrug:

> There is infinite nonsense in the world on all of these matters; hence blame me not if I contribute my mite. It is impossible to talk or write without apparently throwing oneself helplessly open . . . Still, it is pleasant to chat; for it passes the time ere we go to our beds. (259)

Speech and writing are always inadequate and vulnerable, regardless of their form; his storytelling is no more than a "chat" to "pass the time," a deferral of the silence of sleep or death.

The narrator's inconsistencies soon take on a note of bitterness, as he refuses to try to overcome the necessary incompleteness of his perspective:

> As a statue, planted on a revolving pedestal, shows now this limb, now that . . . continually changing, too, its general profile; so does the pivoted, statued soul of man, when turned by the hand of Truth. Lies only never vary; look for no invariableness in Pierre. Nor does any canting showman here stand by to announce his phases as he revolves. Catch his phases as your insight may. (337)

Just as Pierre discovers that Truth exists only as a continual flux, the narrator finds "no invariableness in Pierre." And it is this continual change in both particular and abstract truth that the text will reflect; the narrator will not mislead his readers by "announcing" or regulating its variations.

This instability in the narrator's view of his text also characterizes his relationship to his hero, which vacillates between an ironic distance and a sympathetic desire for proximity. A degree of narrative detachment is a necessary structural element in *Pierre*, for the text is, after all, written after the events it describes. The narrator's knowledge of Pierre's fate is, like Ishmael's, based upon the temporal fact of his survival to tell the tale; just as Ishmael the writer is temporally distant from his earlier experience, the narrator of *Pierre* begins at a distance from Pierre himself.

This narrative distance is highlighted by an insistent, almost obsessive use of foreshadowing that begins very early in the novel. In the first chapter, for example, the narrator says that Pierre and his mother "flowed on the pure joined current of life. But as yet the fair river had not borne its waves to those sideways repelling rocks, where it was thenceforth destined to be forever divided into two unmixing streams" (5). He even seems to establish an agenda for his text: "we shall see," he says, if the "blessing" of the countryside

> pass from [Pierre] as did the divine blessing from the Hebrews; we shall yet see again, I say, whether Fate hath not just a little bit of a word or two to say in this world; we shall see whether this wee scrap of latinity be very far out of the way—*Nemo contra Deum nisi Deus ipse.* (14)

With the repetitive rhetorical structures of a sermon, the narrator here lays down the terms in which the events of the story are to be understood; his distance from the characters is openly ironic, his authority manifested in his invocation of this "wee scrap of latinity."

Literary allusions appear as important indicators throughout *Pierre*, with their naive use by the characters forcefully ironized by the narrator's hindsight. Pierre and his circle are shown to be trapped, not in the history they would write, but in an already written *literary* history beyond their comprehension or control. In a playful exchange with his mother, for example, Pierre demurs from her description of him as a "Romeo." He is " 'far from being [Shakespeare's] Romeo,' " he says, and Mrs. Glendinning agrees, noting that he will not disobey his parents by marrying against their wishes: " 'you, Pierre, are going to be married before long, I trust, not to a Capulet, but to one of our own Montagues' " (18). The obedient Pierre, she says, will marry "one of our own," in an act of figurative incest; he will, however, in an act of disobedience, enter into a (perhaps) literally incestuous marriage with Isabel. Both characters treat Shakespeare's tragedy in a comic fashion, but events to come will cast an ironic light on their interpretation and reveal the true relevance of *Romeo and Juliet*. The novel ends, in fact, with a melodramatic echo of the play's death scene, as Pierre and Isabel take poison in his prison cell.

Dante's *Inferno* functions in a similar fashion. It is the text that Pierre at first refuses to interpret, but it is also the one to which his mind and arm, "wandering and vague," will later lead him (42, 168). And the book he writes will also be an "Inferno" (317). His image of a "concentring" penetration into depth fits the geography of Dante's Hell quite neatly, but in a way that Pierre himself can never realize. The narrator consistently employs both Shakespeare and Dante to confirm the limits of his characters' knowledge and establish his own (and the reader's) interpretive superiority and distance.

The narrator's ironies are too easy, however, for he, too, is constrained—by the retrospective nature of his narration itself. It may give him the benefit of hindsight, but it also deprives him of an unmediated knowledge of his subject. And while the story's completion may make possible a complete knowledge of its events, it also determines and limits the act of narration. The inclusiveness of the narrator's knowledge is, in fact, directly proportional to his powerlessness to change or reshape what he knows. At moments he even seems to feel trapped by his own story, tortured rather than enabled by his knowledge: "Are there no couriers in the air," he cries out to Pierre, "to warn thee away from these emperilings . . . Where now are the high beneficences? Whither fled the sweet angels that are alledged guardians to man?" (176). This outburst, this lament that he is powerless to "warn" Pierre, manifests the narrator's only partly repressed desire to *change* Pierre's story as he repeats it. Like Pierre himself, the narrator would rewrite Pierre's life and struggle with him against his fate. He would abandon the distance that makes his narration possible, if such an abdication of narrative power could be paradoxically transformed into an accumulation of power sufficient to reshape the story.

In the end, the narrator cannot claim an absolute, omniscient distance from his characters. At one point he may insist that "the thoughts we here indite as Pierre's are to be very carefully discriminated from those we indite concerning him," implying both that he knows Pierre's thoughts and that he "knows better than" his hero (167). But at another point, he admits that "we know not Pierre Glendinning's thoughts" (162). And elsewhere he equivocates, saying only that "Pierre *might have seemed* to see" a resemblance between Isabel's face and the chair portrait, or that "he *seemed somehow* to derive some general vague inkling concerning" Plinlimmon's pamphlet (197, 209; my emphases). What these formulations "seem to suggest" is that the narrator's knowledge comes only indirectly, through his own interpretation rather than simple omniscience.

At moments, in fact, the narrator finds himself forced to "draw a vail" over Pierre's thoughts and abandon any attempt at representation: "Some nameless struggles of the soul can not be painted, and some woes will not be told. Let the ambiguous procession of events reveal their own ambiguousness" (181). Here he surrenders to the temporal "procession of events," even though he knows that it will lead to no revelation of meaning, but only to further "ambiguousness." By the end of the novel, the narrator comes to admit his inability to represent the inner life of his characters: "With such bewildering meditations as these in him, running up like clasping waves upon the strand of the most latent secrecies of his soul . . . the feelings of Pierre were entirely untranslatable into any words that can be used" (353). He finally pulls back, like Ishmael, from the attempt to confront and depict the "latent secrecies of the soul."

The last words spoken in the novel are Isabel's: "'All's o'er, and ye know him not!'" (362). She speaks to Frederic Tartan and Charlie Millthorpe, but she might as well be addressing the narrator and the reader, too. If first-person narrative cannot enclose or give form to the self and its experience, the third person obtains narrative closure only by excluding the inner life of its protagonist. The self lies beyond representation—both the initial and the final mystery for Melville and the characters and narrators of his fictions.

V In Confidence: Identity as Interpretive Construction

AMONG THE SURVIVING MANUSCRIPT FRAGMENTS of *The Confidence-Man* are Melville's drafts of Chapter 14, "Worth the consideration of those to whom it may prove worth considering." Here his narrator defends the inconsistency of his characters:

> that author who draws a character, even though to common view incongruous in its parts as the flying-squirrel, and at different periods as much at variance with itself as the butterfly is with the catterpillar from which it proceeded; may yet, in so doing, be not false, but faithful, to facts. . . . it is with man as with his maker; for just as by the contrasts obvious in the workings of Providence, the pious mind is forced into a confession of ignorance; so, by the inconsistencies in human conduct, the philosophic intellect is driven to exclaim 'I know it not.'[1]

The self, Melville suggests, is "at much at variance with itself" as if it existed only in a state of continuous bodily transformation. The discontinuity of such a metamorphosis is not foreign or threatening to the self—it is its only possible mode of being. If man's external appearance is an image of his maker, God either manifests Himself inconsistently or is Himself continually changing. Human identity is finally as inscrutable as the divine; both lie beyond rational understanding, their self-consistency a matter of belief rather than knowledge. Just as Pierre resembles his father in his internal self-division, so every man resembles his Heavenly Father in his inscrutability.

"[I]f reason be judge," the narrator continues,

> no author has produced such inconsistent characters as Nature herself has. So that the worst that can be said of any author in this particular is that he shares a fault if fault it be, with the author of authors. And it

must call for no little sagacity in a reader, unerringly to discriminate in a book between the inconsistencies of conception & those of life.[2]

If "the author of authors" can create only inconsistent creatures, a mortal author can create only a self-contradictory and inconclusive text, not an adequate or complete representation of human character. The accuracy and truthfulness of a text are finally impossible to judge; here, as in *Pierre*, interpretation is a labyrinthine entanglement that yields no firm or definite result.

In the published version of *The Confidence-Man*, as in this early draft, the distinctions between bodily, genealogical, and textual identity are continually blurred and confused. Melville encapsulates and replays his earlier attempts to define and represent the self, but only to discredit and discard them: bodies and texts become interchangeable and inconclusive evidence of identity, and presumably authoritative paternal texts, both literary and religious, are stripped of their special status. No evidence—bodily, genealogical, or textual—can yield accurate knowledge of the self; all collapse, as in *Pierre*, into shiftiness and ambiguity. Human nature, like the divine nature, can only be a matter of faith, of "confidence."

This, however, is a conclusion doggedly resisted by what Hershel Parker has termed the "standard line" of Melville criticism.[3] Ever since Elizabeth Foster's 1954 edition of the novel, commentators have been attempting to fix and stabilize the contents of Melville's text, to "discover" a central character and narrative thread and to identify the "good" and "evil" elements.[4] Many of the equivocal characters who flit in and out of *The Confidence-Man* are declared to be "avatars" of a single ubiquitous figure— usually described as the Devil himself.[5] This longing for interpretive and moral certainty springs, I would suggest, from the reader's desire for textual order and consistency, a desire that Melville encourages, manipulates, and finally mocks.

In a way, the "standard line" is an attempt to turn *The Confidence-Man* into its opposite or mirror image—into a text like *Billy Budd*. On one level, that novel does seem to offer clear moral oppositions—goodness in Billy, evil in Claggart. But as the tangled and disputatious critical history suggests, *Billy Budd* is exactly like *The Confidence-Man* in at least one respect: it deliberately opens itself to any number of incompatible readings, without valorizing any one of them. It is at once a testament of acceptance, resistance, and ambiguity;[6] it is, at one and the same time, essentially a story of political, psychological, and religious conflict.[7] Barbara Johnson has explored the way in which *Billy Budd* problematizes interpretation itself;[8] what I shall attempt here, much too briefly, is to suggest how this breakdown in representation bears on the problem of understanding and defining the self.

I.

From the outset of *The Confidence-Man*, physical appearance and textual evidence are played off against each other as a basis for identifying the self. Each is in turn cited as the ground for the other, in a whirl of references and cross-references that ultimately calls the possibility of all self-knowledge into question. This process begins in Chapter 3, with the appearance of Black Guinea, a character at first described in purely physical terms: "a grotesque negro cripple, . . . who, owing to something wrong about his legs, was, in effect, cut down to the stature of a Newfoundland dog" (10). This "cutting down" makes him something less than human, "'der dog widout massa,'" as he puts it (10). He goes about collecting pennies by catching them in his mouth, like a dog catching objects thrown to him: and, "as in appearance he seemed a dog, so now, in a merry way, like a dog he began to be treated" (11).

If Guinea's deformity seems to determine both his character and others' behavior towards him, his legs are nevertheless described as if they were mere objects, possessions rather than integral parts of the body and the self. Guinea even speaks of his legs as if they were somehow transferable to another body: "'What ge'mman want to own dese here legs?'" he asks, almost as if offering them for sale (10). The narrator says that the cripple's good humor amuses "some of that crowd, whose own purses, hearths, hearts, all their possessions, sound limbs included, could not make gay" (10). "Hearths" and "hearts" fall into the same category here, as do "purses" and "limbs."

The integral relation between body and self is further questioned by "a limping, gimlet-eyed" man with a wooden leg, who claims that Guinea's deformity is "a sham, got up for financial purposes": "'He's some white operator, betwisted and painted up for a decoy'" (12, 14). The skeptic questions Guinea's two primary, and presumably unchangeable, physical characteristics, his color and his deformity. If the most basic of bodily features are indeed subject to alteration and counterfeiting, then the man with the wooden leg may be right to say that "'Looks are one thing, and facts are another'" (14).

Once the cripple's bodily appearance has been challenged, the crowd turns suspicious, asking him for "documentary proof," a "plain paper . . . attesting that his case was not a spurious one" (13). Bodily form is no longer self-evident proof of identity; now "a plain paper," a document, is invoked as definitive evidence. Guinea has "'none o' dem waloable papers,'" but he does provide a list of passengers who can "'speak a good word'" for him (13). With Guinea's list, though, we return to the realm of physical appearance, for he identifies his "ge'mman" friends with only fragmentary descriptions: a "'ge'mman wid a weed, and a ge'mman in a gray coat and white tie . . . a ge'mman wid a big book, too; and a yarb-doctor; and a ge'mman in a yaller west; and a ge'mman wid a brass plate; and a ge'mman in a wiolet robe . . .'" (13). All but one are distinguished through the possession of an object or a piece of clothing—these incidentals of dress are to identify them, and they are in turn to identify the cripple. They know him, in fact, "'as well as dis poor old darkie knows hisself'" (13). Guinea's blackness, his deformity, his own self-knowledge—all essential features of his identity—become dependent on accidentally chosen external objects: "a weed," "a gray coat," and "a yaller west."

A Methodist minister suggests that one should "'put as charitable a construction as one can upon the poor fellow'" (14). Such a "charitable" view also denies the immediacy of Guinea's physical being, making it dependent on interpretation, something "constructed" by the onlooker or reader. Even the "ge'mman in a gray coat and white tie," when he later appears, says that "'nature has placarded the evidence of [Guinea's] claims'" upon him (29)—that his body is a *text* whose interpretation will establish its reality as a *body*. Bodies and texts are here inseparable, indistinguishable, and equally inconclusive: "'You can conclude nothing absolute from the human form,'" the Cosmopolitan later remarks (226).

In *The Confidence-Man*, the body can no longer serve to define the self as a simple physical presence; it requires an authenticating text or narrative in order to be "believed." But credibility need have nothing to do with truth, as is demonstrated by the case of "a soldier of fortune" (93). He is "a singular character in a grimy old regimental coat," whose "interwoven paralyzed legs, stiff as icicles, [are] suspended between rude crutches" (93). An herb-doctor offers to help him, if he will only "'Give me your story'" (94).

The man says that his illness began while he was imprisoned as a witness in a murder case, but the doctor refuses to believe him. "'That don't surprise me,'" replies the cripple, "'Hardly anybody believes my story, and so to most I tell a different one'" (97). The true story of his paralysis is not believed, while a false one—that he was wounded in the Mexican War— yields "a pretty good harvest" of coins when he begs from the other passengers (98). A true story is not enough to authenticate the man's disability, but a fiction does the trick. As narratives or texts displace bodies as evidence of identity, rhetorical effectiveness—"exchange value," in the monetary terms of the *Fidéle*—comes to replace truth.

The ship's barber agrees with the Cosmopolitan on the unreliability of physical appearance; the barber, in fact, takes this as the ground for a general distrust of mankind: "'can one be forever dealing in macassar oil, hair dyes, cosmetics, false moustaches, wigs, and toupees, and still believe that men are wholly what they look to be?'" he asks (232). The Cosmopolitan suggests that a wig is no different from the roof of a house, but the barber replies that "'His coat and his roof no man pretends to palm off as a part of himself, but the bald man palms off hair, not his, for his own'" (233). His distinction is between what is acknowledged to be an addition to the body and what is falsely displayed as a *part* of the body, but the Cosmopolitan attacks this argument, asking, "'Not *his*, barber? If he have fairly purchased his hair, the law will protect him in its ownership, even against the claims of the head on which it grew'" (233). Here he suggests that the body is "possessed" like any other object—that Guinea's blackness, for example, is *equivalent to* another man's "yaller west." Beyond this, the self and the objects it purchases may even stand *opposed to* the body as determinants of identity. A disguise may represent the self more truly than the body it conceals.

The barber relies instead on texts to guarantee the veracity and reliability of others. In agreeing to take down his sign, which reads "'No Trust,'" and to have "confidence" in his customers, he insists "that the agreement should be put in black and white," especially the Cosmopolitan's offer to provide security against any possible losses (234). The Cosmopolitan comments that paper is "'such flimsy stuff,'" and suggests a merely verbal agreement (234–35). "'But your memory may be none of the best,'" the barber responds, "'Well for you, on your side, to have it in black and white'" (235). A text is unchangeable, human memory inherently unreliable. Once the agreement has been written and signed, however, the barber asks for a "'money-pledge'" to back it up (237). He wants another set of printed texts (paper money may be counterfeited, too, of course) to "insure" (237) the text that will insure against a lapse of memory. This second demand opens up the prospect of an endless succession of texts, each validating its predecessor, each requiring authentication in its turn.

This infinite regress of textual "insurance" has been suggested earlier by the herb-doctor, who warns a sick man against counterfeit versions of his "Omni-Balsamic Reinvigorator" (82–83). "'I have adopted precautions,'" he says:

> "Take the wrapper from any of my vials and hold it to the light, you will see water-marked in capitals the word *'confidence,'* which is the countersign of the medicine . . . But if still any lurking doubt should remain, pray enclose the wrapper to this address," handing a card, "and by return mail I will answer." (83)

The name on the wrapper is the primary evidence for the "true" identity of the medicine. But that text requires a "countersign," a watermark within the paper itself. And if the countersign is ambiguous, the doctor offers a card, whose text is an address to which the wrapper may be sent for validation. Each text depends upon another, and none can possibly be said to establish the medicine's authenticity or efficacy.

The novel will eventually close on this note of undecidability, as an old man tries to use a pamphlet entitled *"Counterfeit Detector"* to test his money (246). Once again one text is called upon to validate another, but it leaves the old man perplexed: "'there's so many marks of all sorts to go by, it makes it a kind of uncertain'" (248). The pamphlet lists various signs, but in the case of the old man's three dollar bill, the "sign" woven into the paper on which the bill is printed "'is not always to be relied on'" (248). The man is left wondering whether his bill is too old to be evaluated, "'or else it's a counterfeit, or else—I don't see right—or else . . . I don't know what else to think'" (248). The search for conclusive textual evidence of identity is, as the Cosmopolitan suggests, "'a wild-goose chase,'" an endless process of interpretation and reinterpretation that can never reach any ultimate ground or close (249). *The Confidence-Man* begins with one "'wild goose chase'" (14)—the search for the figures on Guinea's list—and ends with another.

The movement from bodies to banknotes is characteristic of *The Confidence-Man*. On board the *Fidéle*, "essential" features of the self are either dependent on or indistinguishable from objects only accidentally associated with it. No one form of self-representation can be privileged over any other; bodies and texts are both simply interpretive objects, pieces of evidence whose "truth" can never be determined.

2.

One of the few characters to have shown "confidence" in Black Guinea is a country merchant, who gives him a half dollar and in the process drops one of his business cards (17). The merchant's encounters with a "man with a weed" and the "transfer-agent" of the Black Rapids Coal Company also call individual identity into question; but here the focus is different—not so much on the unreliability of external evidence as on the internal divisions that deprive the self of unity or stability. The merchant is accosted by "a man in mourning" with "a long weed in his hat" (18), who addresses him as "Mr. Roberts," implying that since he knows the merchant's name, "Mr. Roberts" must know him. " 'Is it possible,' " he asks, " 'that you do not recall my countenance? . . . Can I be so changed?' " (18, 19). He thus shifts the grounds of identification from names to faces and asserts that his appearance cannot have changed beyond recognition. When this tack also fails, "John Ringman" reverses himself, putting the merchant's identity into question rather than his own:

> "Are you not, sir, Henry Roberts, forwarding merchant, of Wheeling, Virginia? Pray, now, if you use the advertisement of business cards, and happen to have one with you, just look at it, and see whether you are not the man I take you for."
>
> "Why," a bit chafed, perhaps, "I hope I know myself."
>
> "And yet self-knowledge is thought by some not so easy. Who knows, my dear sir, but for a time you may have taken yourself for somebody else?" (19)

Roberts is to turn to the text of his own business card, not in order to identify himself to others but to verify his identity for himself. Self-knowledge, his companion says, is not to be taken for granted. The merchant may, in fact, have "taken himself for someone else" for a time, felt estranged from or other than himself. His sense of self may not have been continuous over time, as the merchant assumes.

Ringman goes on to describe their "meeting," some six years before.

"'[Y]ou have a faithless memory,'" he says, implying that Roberts' memory may be somehow distinct from and antagonistic to him (19). The gap he has described in Roberts' temporal self-consciousness is now a division within his present self, a split that the merchant himself seems to recognize: "'I don't like this going dead against my own memory,'" he objects (19). At this point the man with the weed again changes his terms, describing Roberts' memory as both a physical object and a text, a "tablet" from which the record of their meeting has been "erased" (20). And the cause of this "erasure," he suggests, is physical—an "'injury on the head,'" perhaps. All that is "'register[ed] . . . in the memory'" may be "'bruised out'" by such an injury, he claims (20). Eventually, the merchant does admit to having been "taken with a brain fever, losing his mind completely for a considerable interval" (20). The result of the conversation is not that Roberts "recognizes" Ringman, but that he comes to admit the discontinuous nature of his own memory and sense of self.

Before Ringman departs, he tells the merchant that an agent of the Black Rapids Coal Company is aboard the *Fidéle*, and that Roberts thus has "'a rare chance for investment'" (22). But when the merchant meets the transfer-agent, the man seems unwilling to do business with him:

> "In my official capacity I have not been authenticated to you. This transfer-book, now . . . how do you know that it may not be a bogus one? And I, being personally a stranger to you, how can you have confidence in me?"
>
> "Because," knowingly smiled the good merchant, "if you were other than I have confidence that you are, hardly would you challenge distrust that way."
>
> "But you have not examined my book."
>
> "What need to, if already I believe that it is what it is lettered to be?"
>
> "But you had better. It might suggest doubts."
>
> "Doubts, may be, it might suggest, but not knowledge; for how, by examining the book, should I think I knew any more than I now think I do; since, if it be the true book, I think it so already; and since if it be otherwise, then I have never seen the true one, and don't know what that ought to look like." (56)

The transfer-agent immediately links his own identity to that of his book. He asks how the merchant can identify him and the book, but the question is taken to be its own answer: no one, Roberts says, would put his own identity in question if it were truly open to debate. Reading the book, he adds, cannot provide proof of its validity; textual evidence can reveal no more than an internal self-consistency—it cannot guarantee that a text accurately refers to anything outside of it. The "truth" of texts, and of their bearers, may be "believed," but it can never be established through interpretation.

The upshot of these exchanges is a moment of doubt for Roberts:

> "Ah, wine is good, and confidence is good; but can wine or confidence percolate down through all the stony strata of hard considerations, and drop warmly and ruddily into the cold cave of truth? Truth will *not* be comforted. Led by dear charity, lured by sweet hope, fond fancy essays this feat; but in vain; mere dreams and ideals, they explode in your hand, leaving nought but the scorching behind!" (67)

It is only a "fond fancy" that one can reach the truth about the character of others, he concludes. Truth is unattainable through "confidence," its nature diametrically opposed to both charity in interpretation and faith in others.

This bleak conclusion is, however, abandoned almost immediately, as Roberts, "with altered mien, stammeringly confessed, that he was almost as much surprised as his companion, at what had escaped him. He did not understand it; was quite at a loss to account for such a rhapsody popping out of him unbidden" (68). The merchant hopes that his "confidence" has returned, but he remains "mortified" at having accidentally made such "mad disclosures—to himself as to another—of the queer, unaccountable caprices of his natural heart" (68). Roberts' "true" nature, if it exists at all, can only be unaccountable, capricious, and self-contradictory.

This returns us to Chapter 14, where the narrator takes the merchant's "inconsistency" as his subject. "[I]n real life," he argues, "a consistent character is a *rara avis*" (69). Readers object to inconsistent characters, he says, not because of an allegiance to facts, but because of their own "perplexity as to understanding them. But if the acutest sage be often at his wits' ends to understand living character, shall those who are not sages expect to run and read character in those mere phantoms which flit along a page, like shadows along a wall?" (69). If character may prove impossible to interpret in real life, it must be impossible to read in the "shadows" of a textual representation, the pattern of black and white traces that "flit along a page."

It is at this point that the narrator invokes the image of the caterpillar/butterfly to describe the inconsistency of human character. The same image appears a few chapters later, in the dialogue between the Missourian, Pitch, and the man from the Philosophical Intelligence Office. Pitch asserts that "'boyhood is a natural state of rascality'" (117) and unhesitatingly rejects the PIO man's suggestion that boys may "outgrow" their foibles: "'"the child is father of the man;" hence, as all boys are rascals, so are all men'" (119). He assumes a continuity of character over time, a process of development in which identity remains essentially fixed.

The PIO man responds with a series of "'analogies,'" beginning with a textual one: a child, he says, is but a "'loose sort of sketchy thing; a little preliminary rag-paper study, or careless cartoon, so to speak, of a man'" (121). He then shifts to human physiology—the boy will, as an adult, possess a beard, "'an appendix, not less imposing than patriarchal; and for this goodly beard, should we not by generous anticipation give the man-child, even in his cradle, credit?'" (122). This argument would seem to support Pitch's view of a continuously developing character, but the PIO man changes his analogy as he proceeds. "'[C]orrupt qualities,'" he says, like baby teeth, will be replaced by "'sound, even, beautiful and permanent'" ones; these second teeth, he insists, "'follow, but do not come from, the first; successors, not sons'" (123). The child is *not* the father of the man; growth is discontinuous, involving a change in character in which different, unrelated qualities *replace* one another. The child is "the caterpillar," he claims, and the man "the butterfly" (124). Pitch replies that "'the butterfly is the caterpillar in a gaudy cloak; stripped of which, there lies the impostor's long spindle of a body, pretty much worm-shaped as before'" (124). He still maintains the distinction between a true and unchanging inner self and the alterations in its physical appearance, but when the PIO man at last supplies him with the right analogy, comparing a boy's growth to that of an ear of Indian corn, the Missourian softens.

Pitch soon comes to think, however, "that he, the philosopher, had unwittingly been betrayed into being an unphilosophical dupe" (129). But his only explanation for the lapse in logic is one that echoes the PIO man's arguments for the changeableness or inconsistency of the self: "one may wake up wise, and slow of assent," but nevertheless "before night . . . be left in the lurch a ninny. Health and wisdom equally precious, and equally little as unfluctuating possessions to be relied on," he concludes (129–30).

Here and elsewhere in the novel, there is an obvious and unresolved tension between the desire for an absolute and essential identity and the inability to find or create such a consistency in human actions. One may believe in an integral and unchangeable selfhood, but that belief can never be grounded in an examination of actual character, for the self as it can be known or represented is always inconsistent or self-contradictory. It is Pitch's rebuff of the Cosmopolitan a paragraph later that leads to the novel's chief argument for the existence of an absolute moral character, Charlie Noble's story of Colonel Moredock the Indian-hater.[9]

Aside from the question of the context in which Moredock's story is told, to which I will return, the title of Chapter 26, "Containing the *metaphysics* of Indian-hating . . . ," should lead us to examine the argumentative structure of this section (144, my emphasis). The case for a consistent, morally identifiable self is, in fact, riddled by contradictions and inconsistencies. The backwoodsman, we are told, "less hearkens to what others may say about things, than looks for himself, to see what are things themselves" (144). He relies on "his own judgment, though it stand alone" (145). "[D]welling exclusively among the works of God," he presumably has immediate access to "things themselves," a relation he jealously preserves by continually moving away from civilization, "to one more remove from man, one step deeper into nature" (145).

No sooner has the backwoodsman's claim to absolute and direct knowledge been introduced, however, than it is supplanted by a different source for his hatred. "[I]f in youth the backwoodsman incline to knowledge," he turns not to nature and experience but to "his schoolmasters, the old chroniclers of the forest," from whom he hears "histories of Indian lying, Indian theft, Indian double-dealing . . . In these Indian narratives and traditions the lad is thoroughly grounded" (146). The backwoodsman's hatred is "grounded" in stories, not in personal knowledge after all. Individual experience is, in fact, explicitly rejected as evidence: "scarce one among us so self-important, or so selfish-minded, as to hold his personal exemption from Indian outrage such a set-off against the contrary experience of so many others" (148–49).

The belief in a single, unchanging "Indian nature" (148) thus cannot be established experientially. Nor can it be proved logically; for, while such a belief does not create its own evidence, it does exclude all contrary evidence. Indians, for example, cannot "be permitted to testify for themselves" (147). But "when an Indian becomes a genuine proselyte to Christianity," the argument runs, "he will not . . . conceal his enlightened conviction, that his race's portion *by nature* is total depravity" (147, my emphasis). If the Indian's nature is fixed and absolute, however, "a genuine proselyte to Christianity" would seem an impossibility. And even if such a conversion could take place, a crucial question remains: which "race" is depraved—the Indian race or the human race? The Calvinist terminology of the passage suggests the latter; it undermines rather than supports the backwoodsman's racism. He would allow the Indian to speak only in an act of self-incrimination—an Indian who "advances the notion of the benignity of the red race" can be doing so only as "part and parcel" of a "subtle strategy" of evil (147).

The radical evil of the "Indian nature" can only be *posited*—as one pole of an absolute opposition whose other term is the Indian-hater. The second term may have the power to define the first, but it nevertheless depends on the first for its own existence: Indian-hating "will continue to exist, *so long as Indians do*" (142, my emphasis). It is an endlessly self-sustaining opposition, an unbreakable vicious circle—unbreakable because neither term, neither Indian nor Indian-hater, can exist in the absolute form the opposition requires. "[T]here can be no biography of an Indian-hater *par excellence*, any more than . . . one of a dead man" (150), for Indian-hating requires the extinction of the self. After a farewell as final as a "death-bed adieu," the true Indian-hater "is good as gone to his long home" (149, 150).

Since the Indian-hater *par excellence* exists only as an "ideal type," his nature can only be "surmise[d]" or projected from the character of the "diluted Indian-hater" (151, 150). The "diluted" Indian-hater permits himself "vacations" from his self-destructive mission, even though these "impair the keeping of the character" (150). The inferential process crumbles, however, the moment it is described: just as the absolute evil of the Indian cannot be converted into Christian virtue, the equally absolute nature of the Indian-hater cannot become a "character" to be "kept" or discarded at will. The difference between the "diluted" Indian-hater and the Indian-hater *par excellence* is a difference in kind, not in degree. Melville's Cosmopolitan is right to say that Moredock must be "either misanthrope or nothing" (157)—Indian-hating is an all-or-nothing proposition that may be imagined but never lived.

Moredock's biography reveals more than a simple slip "out of character," however: the opposition between Indian and Indian-hater, like all absolute oppositions, threatens to collapse into an identity. The only way in which Moredock can pursue his foes is to imitate them—repeating their procedure of hunt, ambush, and slaughter. His complexion darkens into "a sultry and tragical brown" (154), closer to red than white. He is a "moccasined gentleman," we are told, even though the combination of Indian moccasins and a gentlemanly character must be a contradiction in terms (154).

The opposition between Indian and Indian-hater is thus both arbitrary and insubstantial, built on skewed logic, suppressed evidence, and faulty inferences. These flaws are far from accidental; they represent Melville's deliberate changes in his source, James Hall's *Sketches of History, Life, and Manners in the West*.[10] Hall makes no special claims for the backwoodsman's direct experience of nature; he emphasizes both the inherited and traditional nature of Indian-hating and its one-sidedness and exaggeration (505–06). The absolute opposition between the Indian's "natural depravity" and the Indian-hater's near-religious devotion is Melville's creation— an addition specifically designed to undermine the argument that contains it.

In this case, the existence and identifiability of moral character is just another story. It is a tale told by one man, Charlie Noble, in the ostensible words of another, Judge Hall, its arguments encased in a double layer of quotation marks.[11] Charlie heard the story as a boy, from "'my father's friend,'" the judge (142)—it has been handed down from one generation to the next in the same way as the Indian-hater's "histories." Charlie's rhetorical aims are also far from clear, aside from a desire to simply make conversation with a potential victim—for Charlie is one of the novel's "confidence men." The whole discussion of Indian-hating thus comes, second-hand, from a clearly unreliable source, one given no special authority in the text itself.[12]

Once again, we are left not with a stable and comfortable identity, but with a dubious narrative. Moral certainties can only be posited *against* the evidence, for the desire for certainty is a longing to escape the demand for rational proof, the necessity of interpretation. It is no coincidence that the Indian-hater echoes that other absolutist, Ahab,[13] who

> came to identify with [Moby Dick], not only all his bodily woes, but all his intellectual and spiritual exasperations. The White Whale swam before him as the monomaniac incarnation of all those malicious agencies which some deep men feel eating in them, till they are left living on with half a heart and half a lung. . . . He piled upon the whale's white hump the sum of all the general rage and hate felt by his whole race from Adam down; and then, as if his chest had been a mortar, he burst his hot heart's shell upon it. (*Moby-Dick*, 160)

The evil of the Indian, like that of the whale, is projected onto him in a self-destructive and irrational act of will. It is the incompletion or instability of

Ahab's own sense of self that generates such projections, his desire for a master term that will put an end to interpretation and uncertainty. The belief in absolute evil is just like the merchant's faith in the transfer-agent's book—each responds to the loss of a unified or stable identity by simply positing the existence of such a stable unity outside the self.

3.

The traditional source of external authority is, of course, the sacred text of the Bible, which is assumed to lie beyond the instability of ordinary language and the vagaries of human interpretation. The Bible, Shakespeare, and other paternal texts are the subjects of numerous allusions throughout the novel. But the very frequency and ease of reference to such texts serves to bring them into the field of interpretation—to equate them with, rather than differentiate them from, ordinary texts.

If Melville simply absorbed Shakespearean diction and dramatic techniques into the fabric of *Moby-Dick*, his use of *Romeo and Juliet* in *Pierre* places it outside the narrative, in an ironic relation to events. Shakespearean texts lack even this stable position in *The Confidence-Man*, however; they are invoked and discussed, but they prove no more authoritative than the labels on the herb-doctor's remedies.

The doctor quotes from *The Merchant of Venice* (5.1.13–14) to support his claims for the power of his herbs:

> "Is it not writ, that on a moonlight night,
>   'Medea gathered the enchanted herbs
>   That did renew old Æson?'
> Ah, would you but have confidence, you should be the new Æson,
>   and I your Medea." (79)

These lines are spoken by Jessica to her lover Lorenzo in the garden at Belmont, but they are part of a patterned exchange, and the herb-doctor omits Lorenzo's reply:

>   In such a night
> Did Jessica steal from the wealthy Jew,
> And with an unthrift love did run from Venice,
> As far as Belmont. (5.1.14–17)[14]

Lorenzo's answer undercuts the Ovidian myth with a reminder of the facts of Jessica's elopement and theft, and this suppressed context undermines the herb-doctor's allusion in a similar fashion, opening up the possibility that he, too, may be a thief. The Shakespearean text, even though it is safely detached from the herb-doctor's argument in an indented quotation, nevertheless erodes his claims about his medicine and himself.

A sick man later responds to the doctor's talk of "countersigns" with his own reference to the play: "'you preach to me distrust,'" he says, "'Ah, truth will out!'" (83). His allusion is to Launcelot Gobbo's playful conversation with his blind father: "it is a wise father that knows his own child," the clown says, but "truth will come to light; murder cannot be hid long; a man's son may, but in the end truth will out" (2.2.76–80). The "truth" that comes to light in the play is Launcelot's own identity, which he has been withholding from his father. But the truth of a father/son relation, whose restoration acknowledges the father's authority, should be the basis of faith and confidence, not distrust. Is the truth of the father/son relation— including that between *literary* father and son—one of distrust, after all? Or is it merely that paternal texts are defenseless against manipulation and reinterpretation by readers/sons?

Such ancestral texts must necessarily remain equivocal—they can be neither absolutely trusted nor distrusted, for their very nature and intent depends on interpretation. This, at least, is the lesson of Charlie Noble's conversation with the Cosmopolitan, Frank Goodman. Charlie takes issue with the "'selfishness'" of Polonius' advice to Laertes in *Hamlet*, calling it "'false, fatal, and calumnious'" (169, 170), speaking with

> a degree of ardor befitting one resenting a stigma upon the family escutcheon, "and for a father to give his son—monstrous. . . . The son is going abroad, and for the first. What does the father? Invoke God's blessing upon him? Put the blessed Bible in his trunk? No. Crams him with maxims smacking of my Lord Chesterfield, with maxims of France, with maxims of Italy." (170)

Paternal authority is here embodied in the father's *choice of texts*, and Charlie attacks Polonius for not invoking the ultimate authority of the Bible. The father's duty, according to Charlie, is to support and continue the line of faith that derives from Scripture—Polonius is thus for him only "'an irreligious warner'" (171).

Frank, however, offers a more "charitable" reading of Polonius' speech, quoting a passage in favor of firm friendship—but Charlie sees this too as only another example of self-interest. The possibility of two diametrically opposed readings of a single couplet distresses Frank: "'your suggestions have,'" he says, "'put things in such a strange light to me as in fact a little to disturb my previous notions of Polonius and what he says. . . . you have, I know not how, unsettled me; so that now I don't exactly see how Shakespeare meant the words he puts in Polonius' mouth'" (171). Given their opposite interpretations of the speech, Frank turns to the question of authorial intention in hopes of resolving the difficulty. But no clear intention can be found on which to ground a reading: "'At times seeming irresponsible, [Shakespeare] does not always seem reliable. There appears to be a certain—what shall I call it?—hidden sun, say, about him, at once enlightening and mystifying'" (171–72). Frank declines to say whether this "hidden sun" is "the true light," however, describing Shakespeare as "'a kind of deity. Prudent minds, having certain latent thoughts concerning him, will reserve them in a condition of lasting probation'" (172). The ambiguities of the Shakespearean text must remain, for the author is finally as inconsistent and inscrutable in his writing as all men are in their actions. There can be no reliance on literary authority, for the paternal figure of the author cannot be known, or even approached, through the ambiguities of his texts.

If this is true for Shakespeare as "a kind of deity," it also applies to God, "the author of authors," and his Biblical text. It is 1 and 2 Corinthians that provide the ground for the book's key term, "confidence." The first words quoted in the novel, those on the deaf-mute's slate, are Biblical quotations—from 1 Corinthians 13. The deaf-mute's inscriptions all begin with Paul's (and Augustine's) key term, "charity": "Charity thinketh no evil"; "Charity suffereth long, and is kind"; "Charity endureth all things"; "Charity believeth all things"; "Charity never faileth" (4–5). "The word charity, as originally traced, remained throughout uneffaced, not unlike the left-hand numeral of a printed date, otherwise left for convenience in blank" (5). "Charity" is fixed and absolute, but in the narrator's description its constancy is a matter of mere "convenience." Even the Bible can be dated; its timelessness is only relative.

The man in the gray coat and white tie also invokes St. Paul after receiving a contribution: "'Yea, you can say to me as the apostle said to the Corinthians, "I rejoice that I have confidence in you in all things"'" (45). His reference to 2 Corinthians 7:16 links the terms "confidence," "faith," and "charity," as does a miser's plea to the transfer-agent in its echo of Mark 9:24, "'I confide, I confide; help, friend, my distrust!'" (76).

But the same text that supports unquestioning confidence and faith also counsels men to question and disbelieve. In describing the signs and countersigns that distinguish his "'genuine medicine'" from its imitators, the herb-doctor asks this sick man to "'Prove all the vials; trust those which are true,'" echoing I Thessalonians 5:21 (83). His patient, however, sees the difficulty implict in both the herb-doctor's words and his Pauline text: "'to doubt, to suspect, to prove—to have all this wearing work to be doing continually—how opposed to confidence. It is evil!'" (83). Faith, elsewhere defined as antithetical to the "wearing work" of interpretation, is now to be based on it, and the source of this injunction is the Bible itself.

Once such a principle of skepticism and rational analysis has been located within the Scriptures themselves, biblical self-consistency comes to depend even more on the reader's own interpretive efforts. The barber refers to "'what the son of Sirach says in the True Book'" in support of his distrust, quoting from Ecclesiasticus 12:16 and 13:11 (236). The Cosmopolitan seizes on the expression "the True Book," but this emphasis only brings an echo of the merchant's words to the transfer-agent and his acknowledgment that although a book's "truth" can be believed, it cannot be proved through interpretation (56).

Leaving the barbershop, the Cosmopolitan enters the gentlemen's cabin, where an old man sits reading the Bible. As the Cosmopolitan sits, with "a kind of waiting expression," the old man looks up, and comments that his companion looks as eager as if "'I had a newspaper here with great news'":

> "And so you *have* good news there, sir—the very best of good news."
>
> "Too good to be true," here came from one of the curtained berths. . . .
>
> "Why speak you, sir, of news, and all that, when you must see this is a book I have here—the Bible, not a newspaper?" (241)

The old man distinguishes between the timelessness of a book, and of the Bible in particular, and the ephemeral nature of a newspaper. The Cosmopolitan has, however, spoken of the newspaperman's printing press as "'the iron Paul,'" advancing both knowledge and "'righteousness'" (166).

As we have seen in the case of the deaf-mute, the distinction between the timeless and the temporal may not be entirely clear-cut.

After borrowing the volume and reading for a time, the Cosmopolitan asks the man if he can "'resolve me a doubt—a disturbing doubt'" (242). "'There are doubts, sir,'" the old man replies, "'which, if man have them, it is not man that can solve them'" (242). He insists on the absolute difference between faith and doubt and places it beyond the reach of argument or explanation. The Cosmopolitan proceeds, however, to describe his distress at finding the passage cited by the barber to indeed be in the Bible, along with others equally opposed to "confidence":

> "Ah!" cried the old man, brightening up, "now I know. Look," turning the leaves forward and back, till all the Old Testament lay flat on one side, and all the New Testament flat on the other, while in his fingers he supported vertically the portion between, "look, sir, all this to the right is certain truth, and all this to the left is certain truth, but all I hold in my hand here is apocrypha." (243)

The word "apocryphal," he explains, "'implies something of uncertain credit'" (243). The ideas of "certainty" and "creditworthiness" have been major issues in the Cosmopolitan's encounter with the barber (237), but he gives the old man his thanks nevertheless. "'Fact is,'" he says,

> "when all is bound up together, it's sometimes confusing. The un-canonical part should be bound distinct. And, now that I think of it, how well did those learned doctors who rejected for us this whole book of Sirach. . . . how can that be trustworthy that teaches distrust?" (243)

The books of the Apocrypha stand at the hidden center of the Biblical text, the source of both moral and interpretive distrust. They are to be distinguished from the Old and New Testaments through scholarly interpretation, through the use of external or internal "evidence." Absolute truths are thus confirmed by the contingencies of history and textuality; the "chronometrical" is defined by the "horological," to use the terms of Plinlimmon's pamphlet in *Pierre*.

The Cosmopolitan goes on, however, to quote from Proverbs 3:26: "Jehovah shall be thy confidence" (250). The Lord shall give man his faith, the proverb says, but the preceding discussion has implied the opposite—it is man's need for faith that constitutes God's Word as its own ground. The will to believe cannot be based on the authority of paternal texts, for it has given them their authority in the first place. Charity and confidence, even though perhaps morally necessary, cannot finally be grounded in either knowledge or an authoritative Text. God and man remain inscrutable, only inconsistently and partially revealed, in the Bible or in life.

4.

If there is no consistency in human character and no form—bodily, genealogical, or textual—through which it can be known or represented, how is *The Confidence-Man* itself to be understood? It is an intensely self-conscious and insistently self-referential work, continually suggesting possibilities for interpretation and then undermining and disowning them. One clearly cannot ascribe unity and consistency to a work that denies these qualities both to texts in general and to itself in particular. One cannot take an individual episode as an interpretive key, for each chapter is undercut by either its own language or its context.[15] And if the novel offers no synecdochic passages, neither does it authorize an allegorical reading:[16] an interpretive order can be imposed on Melville's novel, but it cannot be derived from the form or content of the book itself.

The narrator describes the *Fidéle* as a microcosm, but it is a microcosm without internal structure, constantly changing in its composition: "though always full of strangers, she continually, in some degree, adds to, or replaces them with strangers still more strange" (8). The ship is not a closed system like the *Neversink*, and it tends toward entropic disintegration, as its passengers embark and disembark without establishing any relation to each other, remaining strangers or becoming "still more" estranged, "involuntarily submitting to that natural law which ordains dissolution equally to the mass as in time to the member" (9).

Even if no whole remains stable over time, the very conception of a whole prevents an accurate perception of its parts. The narrator compiles a paragraph-long list of characters and types aboard the boat, concluding with a description of them as "a piebald parliament, an Anacharsis Cloots congress of all kinds of that multiform pilgrim species, man" (9). But once these individuals are conceived of as members of a species, their individual character is lost: "so these varieties of mortals blended their visage and garb" (9). The chapter closes with the image, not of the *Fidéle* as a closed unit, but with the "Mississippi itself, which, uniting the streams of the most distant and opposite zones, pours them along, helter-skelter, in one cosmopolitan and confident tide" (9). The dominant force in the novel, the narrator suggests, is not the static symbolic structure of a microcosm, but the ceaseless flow or progression of characters and events, in a continual circulation of signs and meanings that tends toward chaos rather than coherence.

Neither can the novel be unified through its central narrative consciousness. Its narrator is even more mysterious and unreliable than *Pierre*'s, seeming to claim omniscience at some points (129–30, for example) and to disclaim it at others (17, 106, 237). Many episodes begin *in medias res*, with fragments of dialogue between unnamed speakers—the narrator's refusal to provide links between events or to embed them in a narrative progression is emphasized again and again (7, 93, and 106, for example).

The links between various characters are generally established, not by the narrator, but by other characters. Black Guinea, of course, provides a list of people who will vouch for him, but only a few of them appear, and some of his descriptions may apply to several characters. It is left for the passengers to identify others as the men referred to by the cripple—the merchant "recognizes" the man with the weed, for instance, and the man in a gray coat and white tie is found by a clergyman (18, 29). The identifications may be correct, but they take place within the action of the novel, without narrative confirmation or support.

If the narrator does not consistently structure his story, neither does he withdraw. He is, at times, unaccountably intrusive, insisting on his mediating presence between reader and character. Chapters 10, 17, and 23, for example, open in the present tense, as the narrator sets the scene for the ensuing dialogue with a conspicuous air of stage management. At other points, he appropriates and retells his characters' stories, admitting that he alters them in the process. In the case of the man with the wooden leg, the narrator does so to avoid "sarcastic details, unpleasant to repeat," with the result being a more "good-natured version" (30). Both the man with the wooden leg and his tale are, however, decidedly ill-natured, so the narrator's "good-natured version" cannot be faithful to the original.

Another example of such narrative revision is the story of the man with the weed. It is at first withheld from the reader, as the narrator describes only the merchant's reaction as he hears the tale (21). But when the merchant goes on to retell it, the narrator steps in: the merchant, he says, "could, perhaps, do better justice to the man than the story, [so] we shall venture to tell it in other words than his, though not to any other effect" (59). Is the problem that the merchant is a poor storyteller, or that the story itself does not "do justice to" the man with the weed?

Such ambiguities are, in fact, the narrator's stock in trade; his language is constantly turning on itself and subverting its own representational power. His equivocations reinforce the story's ambiguities instead of clarifying them, making it impossible to describe either the man with the weed or his wife as good or evil, sane or insane. No tale, this implies, can ever "do justice to" or adequately represent the self.

The narrator continually insists that his own text is equivocal and self-contradictory, dependent on the reader's interpretive activity for its meaning and coherence. Just as the title of Chapter 12 calls upon the reader to judge the true character of the man with the weed, so other chapter titles leave their ambiguities deliberately unresolved: Chapter 14 is "Worth the consideration of those to whom it may prove worth considering" (69), and Chapter 33 "may pass for whatever it may prove to be worth" (182). Both of these chapters are self-referential, moments at which the narrator describes his own text—*The Confidence-Man* as a whole is thus made dependent on the reader's interpretive assumptions and propensities.

In Chapter 14, as we have seen, the narrator defends the inconsistency of his characters as truer to reality than an artificial coherence. In Chapter 33, however, he takes an apparently opposite position, becoming himself another example of inconsistency. "A work of amusement," he says, should not be expected to be as dull as "real life," for the reader turns to fiction for diversion, out of weariness with reality (182). But, he continues,

> [since] in real life, the proprieties will not allow people to act out themselves with that unreserve permitted to the stage; so, in books of fiction, they look not only for more entertainment, but, at bottom, even for more reality, than real life itself can show. Thus, though they want novelty, they want nature, too; but nature unfettered, exhilarated, in effect transformed. (182–83)

True character does not simply manifest itself; it must be "acted out," self-consciously represented. And this process of acting out belongs to the world of fiction and the stage, not to "real life." The heightened and "transformed" representation possible in fiction is, according to the narrator, the true reality of human character, freed from the "proprieties" of real life. Fiction thus cannot take "reality" as a ground for its representation of character, for reality is as fictional as fiction is real. The man with the wooden leg says that "'To do, is to act; so all doers are actors'" (31); the narrator here implies that to *be* is to act. Self-representation and impersonation amount to the same thing, for there is no essential self "behind" or "beneath" them, no distinct and separate ground for the play of action and language.

In Chapter 44, "which will be sure of receiving more or less attention from those readers who do not skip it," the narrator discusses the nature of the truly "original character" (238). He distinguishes "original" from merely "singular" characters: "while characters, merely singular, imply but singular forms, so to speak, original ones, truly so, imply original instincts" (239). Originality lies not in the form in which a character is represented, but in the "instinct" behind that representation, in an activity that generates, but lies beyond, all representation. It is not

> something personal—confined to itself . . . the original character, essentially such, is like a revolving Drummond light, raying away from itself all round it—everything is lit by it, everything starts up to it (mark how it is with Hamlet), so that, in certain minds, there follows upon the adequate conception of such a character, an effect, in its way, akin to that which in Genesis attends upon the beginning of things. (239)

In this notion of an "original character," Melville's narrator comes close to describing a pure creative force. Like the white light of Ahab's soul, it is only visible as pure light, "a blankness in itself" (*Moby-Dick*, 175). Its nature can only be surmised from its effects, from the objects it illuminates. Here, almost at the end of the novel, Melville moves to reestablish a principle of representational authority, associating the "original character" with Shakespeare and with God Himself.

The narrator retreats almost immediately, however. The "original character," he says, "cannot be born in the author's imagination—it being as true in literature as in zoology, that all life is from the egg" (239). The creative ground for a work of fiction must lie *outside* the text, in a movement or impulse that cannot be comprehended or represented through the language of the text itself. The next chapter, however, opens with an image strikingly similar to that of the "Drummond light": a "solar lamp" in the gentlemen's cabin, whose shade of ground glass [is] all round fancifully variegated, in transparency, with the image of a horned altar, from which flames rose, alternate with the figure of a robed man, his head encircled by a halo. The light of this lamp, after dazzlingly striking on marble, snow-white and round—the slab of a centre-table beneath—on all sides went rippling off with ever-diminishing distinctness, till, like circles from a stone dropped in water, the rays died dimly away in the furthest nook of the place. (240)

The description of this "solar lamp" brings into play a number of images of creative power and authority: the "Drummond light," the "hidden sun" of the literary father, and the sun as an image of God. The way the light "ripples off" in a series of expanding circles suggests that the movement of representation is *away* from its unknowable source or center; it is, like Ishmael's weaving, antithetical to Ahab's drive to reach that center, to make the ground of belief into the object of knowledge. Melville acknowledges the necessity of belief but again and again declares it to be incommensurate with knowledge, beyond the representational limits of his text. His lamp grows dimmer and dimmer in the course of the chapter, finally "expiring" (251) and leaving the Cosmopolitan and the old man, the narrator and the reader, and Melville himself, in darkness.

This is the point at which Melville ends his public career as a novelist. If one of its primary themes has been the search for a stable, unassailable selfhood, *The Confidence-Man* is a novel of philosophical and literary exhaustion. It is an embittered critique of Melville's own artistic goals and techniques, a vicious skewering of his own earlier illusions.

5.

The action of *Billy Budd* ends not in darkness but at dawn. Nevertheless, despite its tautness and economy of construction, it too resists any clear and fully determinate reading. *Billy Budd* may draw upon an historical event— the *Somers* mutiny of 1842—but it would be misleading to describe the text as "grounded" in history. For Melville textualizes that history, reworking it into a proliferation of contradictory stories:[17] an "inside narrative," an "official" story, and an apocryphal popular ballad. The first and longest of these versions may be presented as authoritative, but when one turns from the story *in* the text to the story *of* the text's composition, that authority looks more problematic. For Melville actually wrote the last and briefest version—the ballad—first. It is not just the "official" version that is a revision or reinterpretation; so is the "inside" story. There is no historical truth to be found in *Billy Budd*, only, perhaps, a prior interpretation.

Billy Budd is dedicated to Jack Chase, the real "handsome sailor" Melville had described in *White-Jacket*.[18] In many ways, however, it is a bitterly ironic revision of that novel.[19] It is in *White-Jacket* that Melville comes closest to describing an ideal of democratic brotherhood, in the comradeship of the main-top (396–97). There is, of course, a first among these equals, one upon whom this entire order depends—Chase, handsome and eloquent, the man whose language and presence alone can obtain "liberty" for the men of the *Neversink* (213–15). But if language is a means of liberation for Chase and his companions, it is only another form of entrapment for Billy Budd.

Billy does not, obviously, have Chase's verbal fluency, his ability to represent himself and others. Billy's stutter is a physical impediment that disrupts and frustrates speech; the blow that kills Claggart is Budd's attempt to force his body into expression. All he does, of course, is deepen and reify the blockage. In this case, self and body are fatally at odds; in asserting his innocence, Billy establishes his guilt.

In the last analysis, however, the difference between Chase and Budd lies not in the anomaly of Billy's stutter, but in Melville's altered view of representation itself. For such self-contradiction and ambiguity are continuous with and characteristic of all discourse in *Billy Budd*. If pure and unmediated representation were possible, then the world of the novel would be one in which "handsome is as handsome does (and says)." But Billy's handsome physique *cannot* communicate his moral innocence, and when Claggart remarks that "'handsome is as handsome did it,'" he is rejecting such direct or immediate self-representation with sarcastic contempt (72).

The irony is not just Claggart's, however; it is Melville's as well. It is not just the master-at-arms who is "equivocal" (64); the narrator himself works "by indirection" (74), speculating and insinuating when it serves his purpose. Like the slippery narrator of *The Confidence-Man*, he has his own "sinister dexterity" with words (49). There is a subversive, ironic potential in all statement, regardless of its source or intention.

And if all language is susceptible to ironic interpretation, so too is Billy's. He enters and leaves the novel in two highly dramatic farewell scenes, each of which pivots on a single sentence: in the first case, "'good-bye to you too, old *Rights-of-Man*'" (49), and in the second, "'God bless Captain Vere'" (123). It is in response to the first that the narrator describes Billy as incapable of irony: "To deal in double meanings and insinuations of any sort," he insists, "was quite foreign to his nature" (49). But this is, and *must be*, an assertion without evidence. For goodness cannot manifest itself directly, not without recourse to a mode of representation that will vitiate it. The narrator's conclusion is a statement of belief in a goodness that his language cannot hope to represent. It is *essentially* unrepresentable, *necessarily* unseen.

The conflict between such belief and the defining force of language and the law is played out in Captain Vere. The fatherless Billy may find a paternal figure in his captain, but this father/son relation can never be reconstituted. For the law that gives Vere his patriarchal character also subverts and denies the bond between the father who passes sentence and the son who cannot speak. The law, as Vere rightly notes, concerns itself only with facts, with Billy's deed (110). And if that deed—that insurrectionary, implicitly parricidal political act—cannot touch on or represent the individual's true nature, then the law cannot do so either—except, that is, with the killing touch of the letter. So it is that "'the angel must hang'" (101).

Billy Budd is, finally, an "inside narrative" that denies both the privileged status of the "inside" and the very possibility of access to the interior of the self. For all the densely religious imagery used to describe his execution, Billy's benediction and his "ascension" may be either symbolic or ironic. The duplicity and slipperiness of Melville's words makes it impossible to decide. Choosing one or the other is neither more nor less than an act of interpretive faith, a bestowal of critical confidence.

Melville thus leaves his readers with the same interpretive dilemma as in *The Confidence-Man*. Belief and knowledge may be incommensurable, but "confidence"—faith in oneself, in others, and in God—remains an unquestionable virtue, a moral necessity. Such confidence is also, however, the naive gullibility of a "confidence-man's" victim. The tension between these two meanings illustrates the doubleness and unreliability of all language, the instability that makes it impossible to base belief on or represent it in language. A "confidence-man" is in one sense a believer, and in another a deceiver—or, of course, he may simply be one who raises the issue of confidence, in a novel like *The Confidence-Man*.

The only conclusion Melville offers is a set of paradoxes: the fictionality of the real self and the reality of the fictional self, the impossibility of knowing or representing a real self and the necessity of believing in its existence. Captain Vere speaks of the "mystery of iniquity" (*Billy Budd*, 108), but goodness must remain equally mysterious. If the self is the point from which we start, the ground on which we engage the world, then it is the first and last of mysteries—in this sense, there are indeed no mysteries out of ourselves.

Notes

UNLESS OTHERWISE NOTED, references to Melville's works will be to the Northwestern-Newberry edition now in progress:

The Writings of Herman Melville, ed. Harrison Hayford, Hershel Parker, and G. Thomas Tanselle (Evanston and Chicago: Northwestern UP and the Newberry Library).

Vol. 1, *Typee* (1968)
Vol. 2, *Omoo* (1968)
Vol. 3, *Mardi* (1970)
Vol. 4, *Redburn* (1969)
Vol. 5, *White-Jacket* (1970)
Vol. 7, *Pierre* (1971)
Vol. 10, *The Confidence-Man* (1984)

The primary exceptions are references to *Moby-Dick*, *Billy Budd*, and the *Letters*, which will be to the following editions:

Moby-Dick, ed. Harrison Hayford and Hershel Parker (New York: Norton, 1967).

Billy Budd, Sailor (An Inside Narrative), ed. Harrison Hayford and Merton M. Sealts, Jr. (Chicago: U of Chicago P, 1962).

The Letters of Herman Melville, ed. Merrell R. Davis and William H. Gilman (New Haven, CT: Yale UP, 1960).

I: Introduction

1. Melville, *Moby-Dick*, ed. Hayford and Parker (New York: Norton, 1967), 238. All further references will be to this edition.

2. Quoted in Leon Howard, Historical Note, *Typee*, *Writings* 1: 279. All further references to the novel will be to this edition.

3. *The Letters of Herman Melville*, ed. Davis and Gilman (New Haven, CT: Yale UP, 1960), 130. All further references to Melville's letters will be to this edition.

4. Descartes' rejection of bodily identity comes in the second of his *Meditations on First Philosophy*, his reassertion of the body's existence in Meditation VI (*The Philosophical Works of Descartes*, tr. Elizabeth S. Haldane and G.R.T. Ross [Cambridge: Cambridge UP, 1931], 1: 149–57, 185–99).

5. *Moby-Dick*, 55. A paragraph earlier, Ishmael has said that sensations or "qualities" can be known only "by contrast." Closing one's eyes eliminates the visual contrast between the body and the world, so embodiment cannot be a "quality" of this kind.

Warwick Wadlington invokes Gerard Manley Hopkins' notion of "selftaste" to describe the "reflexive sense" of personal identity that eludes "cognitive processes" (*The Confidence Game in American Literature* [Princeton, NJ: Princeton UP, 1975], 75).

6. The term was originated by Sir Charles Sherrington in his 1906 *The Integrative Action of the Nervous System* (rpt. New Haven, CT: Yale UP, 1947); see 132–33.

For a further discussion of the concept, see Oliver Sacks, *The Man Who Mistook His Wife for a Hat and Other Clinical Tales* (New York: Summit, 1985), 42–43. Sacks describes proprioception as providing "the fundamental, organic mooring of identity—at least that of corporeal identity, or 'body-ego'" (50).

For Wittgenstein, as Sacks notes, one's sense of one's own body seems to be a limit case, a kind of awareness so fundamental that it almost cannot be called "knowledge" and so cannot be subject to doubt (*On Certainty*, ed. G.E.M. Anscombe and G.H. von Wright, tr. Denis Paul and G.E.M. Anscombe [New York: Harper, 1969], 25, sec. 178).

7. In *The Passions of the Soul*, Descartes does distinguish among "perceptions which we relate to objects which are without us," "perceptions which we relate to our body," and "perceptions which we relate to our soul" (*Philosophical Works*, 1: 342–43). Even though the body is perceived differently than are other objects, Descartes nevertheless holds, in *The Principles of Philosophy*, that we in turn "know our mind better than our body" (*Philosophical Works*, 1: 223).

Francis Barker places Descartes at the center of a seventeenth-century shift away from the spectacular, corporeal self of the Jacobean theater toward a bourgeois self that is both alienated from the body and divided against itself (*The Tremulous Private Body: Essays on Subjection* [New York: Methuen, 1984], esp. 52–67). Barker's Foucauldian historical scheme can only be applied to Melville with some difficulty, for he combines (or seeks to combine) elements of both the "old" and "new" orders. See also my discussion of Foucault in connection with *White-Jacket* below.

8. For a discussion of the problem of "knowing" another's pain or bodily sensations, see Stanley Cavell, "Knowing and Acknowledging," in *Must We Mean What We Say?* (Cambridge: Cambridge UP, 1976), 238–66.

9. Jacques Lacan, "The mirror stage as formative of the I as revealed in psychoanalytic experience," *Écrits*, tr. Alan Sheridan (New York: Norton, 1977), 1–7.

10. I put these expressions in quotation marks because they both imply a distinction between body and self—the very distinction I see Melville as trying to escape.

11. Melville, *Typee*, 220.

12. Melville, *White-Jacket*, *Writings* 5: 142. Babbalanja takes the same position in *Mardi*: " 'at the last day,' " he says, " 'every man shall rise in the flesh' " (Melville, *Writings* 3: 505). All further references will be to these editions.

13. This is the position taken by Sharon Cameron in *The Corporeal Self: Allegories of the Body in Melville and Hawthorne* (Baltimore: Johns Hopkins UP, 1981), 15–75. For further discussion of Cameron's reading, see Chapter II.

14. To make a further distinction, my concern is with the body as a physical space or object, not as an erotic or sexual one. For a reading of Melville that emphasizies male sexuality, see Robert K. Martin, *Hero, Captain, and Stranger* (Chapel Hill: U of North Carolina P, 1986).

15. *An Essay Concerning Human Understanding* (2nd. ed. 1694); rpt. in *Personal Identity*, ed. John Perry (Berkeley: U of California P, 1975), 39.

16. Locke, *Essay Concerning Human Understanding*, 39–40.

17. *A Treatise of Human Nature*, ed. L.A. Selby-Bigge (Oxford: Clarendon, 1888), 252. All further references will be to this edition.

18. Nietzsche takes a similar position in *The Will to Power*: " 'The subject' is the fiction that many similar states in us are the effect of one substratum: but it is we who first created the 'similarity' of these states; our adjusting them and making them similar is the fact, not their similarity (—which ought rather to be denied—)" (tr. Walter Kauffmann and R. J. Hollingdale, ed. Walter Kauffmann [New York: Vintage, 1968], 269).

Nietzsche's critique of Descartes (268) leads him to take "[t]he body and physiology" as "the starting point": "Belief in the body is more fundamental than belief in the soul," he argues (271).

19. *Essays on the Intellectual Powers of Man* (1785); rpt. in *Personal Identity*, ed. Perry, 116.

20. Melville, *Redburn*, *Writings* 4: 312; my emphasis. All further references will be to this edition.

21. "Conditions and Limits of Autobiography," tr. James Olney, in *Autobiography: Essays Theoretical and Critical*, ed. Olney (Princeton, NJ: Princeton UP, 1980), 35.

22. "The Style of Autobiography," tr. Seymour Chatman, in *Autobiography*, ed. Olney, 74. For Gusdorf, this division is a gain: "autobiography is a second reading of experience, and it is truer than the first because it adds to experience itself consciousness of it" (38).

23. "The Veto of the Imagination: A Theory of Autobiography," in *Autobiography*, ed. Olney, 278–79. All further references will be to this edition.

24. "To Write: An Intransitive Verb?" in *The Structuralist Controversy: The Languages of Criticism and the Sciences of Man*, ed. Richard Macksey and Eugenio Donato (Baltimore: Johns Hopkins UP, 1972), 140.

25. "Autobiography as De-facement," *MLN* 94 (1979): 922. All further references will be to this edition. For a commentary on the essay, see Jacques Derrida's "Mnemosyne," tr. Cecile Lindsay, *Mémoires for Paul de Man* (New York: Columbia UP, 1986), 22–29.

26. "Some Versions of Memory/Some Versions of *Bios*: The Ontology of

Autobiography," in *Autobiography*, ed. Olney, 239. Janet Varner Gunn employs a variant of this spatial model: she describes time as "experienced more like the thickness of a palimpsest. . . . The past provides fullness to the present as both a push and pull behind its surface" (*Autobiography: Toward a Poetics of Experience* [Philadelphia: U of Pennsylvania P, 1982], 14).

27. Melville, *The Confidence-Man, Writings* 10: 193. All further references will be to this edition.

28. See Thompson, *Melville's Quarrel with God* (Princeton, NJ: Princeton UP, 1952); Herbert, *Moby-Dick and Calvinism* (New Brunswick, NJ: Rutgers UP, 1977); Karcher, *Shadow Over the Promised Land* (Baton Rouge: Louisiana State UP, 1980); and Martin, *Hero, Captain, and Stranger*.

My selections, in this and the following note, are, of course, neither complete nor perhaps even representative. I wish only to emphasize the general separation in the criticism between thematic and formal approaches.

29. See Matthiessen, *American Renaissance* (New York: Oxford UP, 1941); Bezanson, "*Moby-Dick*: Work of Art," in *Moby-Dick: Centennial Essays*, ed. Tyrus Hillway and Luther S. Mansfield (Dallas, TX: Southern Methodist UP, 1953), 31–58; and Berthoff, *The Example of Melville* (Princeton, NJ: Princeton UP, 1962).

30. Throughout the text, I speak most often of Melville's works as "narratives" rather than "novels." The key point, for my purposes, is that he attempts to work out his responses to philosophical and psychological questions within the limits of *narrative*. Those narratives are indeed fictional, but my emphasis, by and large, is on their internal features rather than the accuracy of their references to an external "truth." For a discussion of Melville's discomfort with fictional texts, see Nina Baym, "Melville's Quarrel with Fiction," *PMLA* 94 (1979): 909–23.

31. See Feidelson, *Symbolism and American Literature* (Chicago: U of Chicago P, 1953), 154–55; and Brodhead, *Hawthorne, Melville, and the Novel* (Chicago: U of Chicago P, 1976), 124–26.

32. *Melville's Thematics of Form: The Great Art of Telling the Truth* (Baltimore: Johns Hopkins UP, 1968), 35, 36–37.

33. *Subversive Genealogy: The Politics and Art of Herman Melville* (New York: Knopf, 1983), ix.

34. Many readers would, of course, take literature as "representing" or "reflecting" society and politics; something of this approach to literature as illuminating historical "fact" lies behind the New Historicism. The extreme form of this subordination, of course, would be the notion of a cultural "superstructure," now consigned to the category of "vulgar Marxism."

35. "The Poetics of Union in Whitman and Lincoln: An Inquiry toward the Relationship of Art and Policy," in *The American Renaissance Reconsidered, Selected Papers from the English Institute, 1982–83*, ed. Walter Benn Michaels and Donald Pease (Baltimore: Johns Hopkins UP, 1985), 184.

36. *Visionary Compacts: American Renaissance Writings in Cultural Context* (Madison: U of Wisconsin P, 1987), ix.

37. I have discussed this subject at greater length in "Melville's *Israel Potter*: Autobiography as History as Fiction," forthcoming in *American Literary History*.

38. See *Visionary Compacts*, 10, 25. The thrust of my study, as should be clear by now, runs directly counter to Pease's "anti-modernist," anti-deconstructive reading.

39. "The Subject and Power," *Critical Inquiry* 8 (1982): 778, 777. All further references will be to this edition of the essay.

40. Foucault also resembles Melville in his view of history: he seeks, he says, "to understand how we have been *trapped in* our own history" (790, my emphasis).

41. Poirier, "Writing off the Self," *Raritan* 1 (Summer 1981): 108, 122–24. For Bloom's description of this tradition, see "Agon: Revisionism and Critical Personality" in the same issue, 20–21.

II: Bodily Identity

1. According to Frederick O'Brien, Vaekehu, the Marquesan queen who actually visited the *United States* while Melville was aboard, had only one leg tattooed; she was converted to Christianity before the other leg could be done (cited in James Baird, *Ishmael* [Baltimore: Johns Hopkins UP, 1956], 114–15).

2. Leon Howard, Historical Note, *Typee*, 283.

3. Chase, for example, offers psychological interpretations of both leg and jacket (*Herman Melville: A Critical Study* [New York: William Sloane, 1949], 12, 25). More recently, so have Rogin (*Subversive Genealogy: The Politics and Art of Herman Melville* [New York: Knopf, 1983], 44) and Tolchin (*Mourning, Gender, and Creativity in the Art of Herman Melville* [New Haven, CT: Yale UP, 1988], 40). For Arvin's reading of Ahab's leg, see below.

4. *The Corporeal Self: Allegories of the Body in Melville and Hawthorne* (Baltimore: Johns Hopkins UP, 1981), 15–75).

5. I also differ from Cameron regarding her insistence that in *Moby-Dick* hermeneutic or interpretive issues are a "surface," beneath which lie "more primitive questions about identity" (*The Corporeal Self*, 19). One of my primary themes is the way in which "primitive questions" resolve or dissolve into problems of interpretation in Melville's work. (And one of my secondary points is that the distinction between surface and depth is a good deal more complex and unstable than Cameron suggests.)

6. Ishmael considers the differences between burial on land and at sea in Chapter 7 of *Moby-Dick*, "The Chapel." The loss of bodies at sea, he suggests, denies "resurrections to the beings who have placelessly perished without a grave" (41); the body's preservation in the afterlife depends upon its symbolic preservation in a specific burial place on earth: as Ahab puts it, the coffin is "'an immortality-preserver'" (433). See my discussion of this chapter and the issues it raises—especially the substitution of text for body in a memorial "tablet"—in Chapter IV below.

7. Ishmael suggests that cannibalism adulterates rather than strengthens the native's identity: Queequeg's "royal" blood has been "sadly vitiated" by the cannibalism of his youth (*Moby-Dick*, 56). The body cannot "absorb" part of another body and still remain itself; to put it mildly, the cannibal's body is no longer "pure."

8. In *The Body in Pain: The Making and Unmaking of the World* (New York: Oxford UP, 1985), Elaine Scarry describes how "the person in great pain experiences his own body as the agent of his agony" (47).

9. Charles Anderson suggests that Melville misidentified the "leech": "Melville's description identifies him beyond question as an inspirational priest," who attempts to heal Tommo's leg through exorcism (*Melville in the South Seas* [New York: Columbia UP, 1939], 169). If this is indeed an exorcism, the priest's infliction of pain makes sense as an attempt to drive an evil spirit out of the body; in this case, the cause of Tommo's illness would be perceived as internal after all.

10. Even though it may be greatly diminished, Tommo's fear of cannibalism never entirely disappears. When he is shown a pile of empty calabashes and coconut shells, for instance, he describes it as "not unlike a cenotaph of skulls" (160).

11. In *White-Jacket*, Catholic sailors have crosses tattooed on their arms as symbols of their faith—to ensure "a decent burial in consecrated ground" (170). Paradoxically, violation of the body's surface thus ensures the preservation of both body and soul.

12. The artist's tools are not tools but weapons from Tommo's perspective. (For a discussion of the transformation of ordinary objects into weapons, see Scarry, *The Body in Pain*, 40–45, 173.) In *Moby-Dick*, Ishmael first takes Queequeg's tattoos to be wounds covered with sticking plasters (28).

13. "The whole system of tattooing," Tommo believes, is connected with the Typees' religion: "they were resolved to make a convert of me" (220). Edgar Dryden emphasizes the "conversion" implied by the tattoo as "both a rejection of [Tommo's] old self and an acceptance of the new. For this reason the tattooing is a threat to his identity which results in the revival of his sense of temporal duration," driving him "to define his identity by the life he lived before and after the present moment" (*Melville's Thematics of Form: The Great Art of Telling the Truth* [Baltimore: Johns Hopkins UP, 1968], 43).

In *Omoo*, Melville's narrator mentions the case of Lem Hardy, an Englishman living among the Tahitians: Hardy's tattoo horrifies the narrator, who describes it as "an impress . . . [f]ar worse than Cain's" (Melville, *Writings* 2: 27; all further references will be to this edition). It is not, however, simply a sign of human mortality, for it marks Hardy as a "renegado from Christendom *and humanity*" (my emphasis). For a discussion of this passage in terms of the dangers of acquiescing in Tahitian indolence, see William B. Dillingham, *An Artist in the Rigging: The Early Work of Herman Melville* (Athens: U of Georgia P, 1972), 91–92.

14. Richard Chase argues that Tommo fears "cannibalism in general, but specifically . . . castration" (*Herman Melville*, 12).

15. In one respect the *Neversink* resembles the nineteenth-century prison and factory as characterized by Michel Foucault in *Discipline and Punish*, tr. Alan Sheridan (New York: Vintage, 1979). The boat is compared to a "State Prison" on a number of occasions, and linked to the prison as factory in that the sailor's uniform is "aptly manufactured for him in a State Prison ashore" (378). The frigate's disciplinary order is itself a machine, "a system of cruel cogs and wheels, systematically grinding up in one common hopper all that might minister to the moral well-being of the crew" (374–75).

But *White-Jacket*, appearing at a transitional moment just before the abolition of flogging, also records the persistence of this "older" form of penality. On the *Neversink*, the spectacle of bodily punishment coexists with, without contradicting, a more "modern" regime of discipline and surveillance. This is possible at least in part because the sailors have already been deprived of liberty; within a system of ostensibly non-punitive confinement, in which there is no "judicial process" to speak of, the retention of a public and theatrical penality is less surprising.

16. The model for such an analogy between the captain's body and the "social body" of the ship is of course the concept of "the king's two bodies," in which the personal and social are metaphorically fused. Melville's Captain Claret is indeed a despot: "a ship is a bit of terra firma cut off from the main; it is a state in itself; and the captain is its king" (23). Melville's attack on "the captain's two bodies" is part and parcel of his critique of arbitrary naval authority exercised in the name of the democratic "main" for which it is ostensibly a synecdoche: naval law "should conform to the spirit of the political institutions of the country that ordains it" (23). (The extreme form of such a fusion is, of course, that enforced by Ahab: " 'Ye are not other men, but my arms and my legs; and so obey me' " [*Moby-Dick*, 465].)

17. The regulation of space aboard the *Neversink* is complemented by an equally rigorous temporal order. Meals are served to the crew at 8:00 a.m., noon, and 4:00 p.m., a "barbarous" schedule that leaves them hungry for sixteen hours overnight (29). And the sequence of watches often leaves one group with three hours sleep or less—this, White-Jacket claims, is "One Reason why Men-of-war's-men are, generally, Short-lived" (82).

18. During a race, in fact, the Captain uses his men as "make-weights," positioning them in the forward part of the ship in order to generate more speed (272). Similarly, in *Moby-Dick* Ahab regards his men as "tools" (183).

19. Ishmael will speak of a "democratic dignity . . . which has no robed investiture," an "immaculate manliness we feel within ourselves, so far within us, that it remains intact though all the outer character seem gone" (*Moby-Dick*, 104). In *Moby-Dick*, the split between inner and outer selves has become the norm.

20. The welts left by the cat are "bars" (137, 224) just like those Karky would draw across Tommo's face. Whether the seaman be flogged or placed in the brig, he is thus placed behind bars, his body reduced to a sign of confinement rather than freedom.

21. In *Moby-Dick*, Steelkilt manifests a resolve much like White-Jacket's: " 'if you flog me,' " he whispers to the *Town-Ho*'s captain, " 'I murder you!' " (219).

This kind of confrontation is reenacted on a seriocomic level in the "Massacre of the Beards" (355). The captain orders the men to have their beards trimmed to regulation length, but they object to this "last insult" and "unkindest cut of all," for "the beard is the token of manhood" (357, 368). All but one accede to this symbolic castration, however, although they choose to remain cleanshaven thereafter. "[T]he ancient Captain of the Forecastle," Ushant, refuses, asserting that " 'My beard is my own, sir!' " (363, 365), and he submits to flogging and imprisonment rather than sacrifice a part of his body.

22. Willard Thorp notes that the surgeon of the *United States*—Melville's model for the *Neversink*—was "emphatically not the original of" Cuticle (Historical

Note, *White-Jacket*, 414). Since most of Melville's characters do correspond to members of the *United States'* crew, this grisly fictional insertion must be read as both an intensification of his critique of naval order and an attack on contemporary medical practice. (See Howard P. Vincent, *The Tailoring of Melville's* White-Jacket [Evanston, IL: Northwestern UP, 1970], 135–47.) Scarry's discussion of the link between medicine and torture (*The Body in Pain*, 42) is also relevant here.

23. Richard Manley Blau describes the jacket as "a surrogate self," "a kind of fictive body," and associates its whiteness with Tommo's untattooed skin (*The Body Impolitic*, *Costerus* 22 [Amsterdam: Rodopi, 1979], 32, 38). Chase argues that the jacket's whiteness symbolizes "the mystery of the young man's paternity . . . the moral immaculateness of the dead father" (*Herman Melville*, 25).

24. I shall discuss the question of writing in *White-Jacket* in Chapter IV, in connection with White-Jacket's position as narrator.

25. The same thing happens to Tommo and his provisions early in *Typee* (42–43).

26. Dillingham contrasts Cuticle's operation and the "Massacre of the Beards" with White-Jacket's cutting himself free of his jacket, describing them as two different and opposed types of "amputation": the former are "destructive and degrading," the latter "necessary and ennobling" (*An Artist in the Rigging*, 78). For him, the jacket represents White-Jacket's youthful illusions, which must be abandoned if he is to reach "manhood." Such a view both assigns a symbolic meaning to the jacket—a different approach from my emphasis on it as a physical object—and endorses White-Jacket's view of his garment as a part of the body itself.

27. Later in the novel, Melville considers the case of an invisible division *within* the body—the breaking of the spinal cord. The resulting paralysis only objectifies the philosopher Grando's sense of alienation from his body; the psychological and philosophical split generates the literal one, and leads to the philosopher's death (505–06).

28. Gibbon labels the story of Belisarius' blindness a "fiction of latter times," but if Melville learned of the general through Gibbon, as was probably the case, he would also have encountered the "fiction" (*The Decline and Fall of the Roman Empire* [New York: Modern Library, 1932], chap. xliii, 2:660).

29. In a letter to Hawthorne (1 June 1851), Melville responds to a "saying" of Goethe's, "*Live in the all*": "your separate identity is but a wretched one,—good; but get out of yourself, spread and expand yourself . . . What nonsense!" (*Letters*, 130–31). He does acknowledge the existence of "the *all* feeling," but insists that it is only "temporary," not to be universally applied (131).

30. In bed at the Spouter Inn, Queequeg's "bridegroom clasp" is as tight "as though naught but death should part us twain" (33). He later tells Ishmael "that henceforth we were married; meaning . . . he would gladly die for me, if need should be" (53). The distinction between a symbolic link that does eventually save Ishmael's life and the literal one that merely endangers it is what I wish to emphasize here. The *Pequod's* cruise is, in fact, characterized by destructive linkages, to which Ishmael's relationship with Queequeg stands as an alternative: the "monkey-rope," true to its name, makes Queequeg seem like "a dancing-ape" held on a leash by an "organ-

boy" (270); and on a deeper level, Starbuck feels that an "ineffable thing has tied me to [Ahab]; tows me with a cable I have no knife to cut" (148). For more on the image of the line in *Moby-Dick*, see Chapter IV.

31. This illusion of transcendence has another price as well: the whale that is being processed has been "dearly purchased" (348), for it is in this lowering that Pip leaps from Stubb's boat and goes insane. For more on Pip, see below.

32. The break is typographical as well as thematic: the two sections of the chapter are separated by a row of asterisks.

33. Daniel Hoffman argues that in "A Squeeze of the Hand" Ishmael discovers "the organic unity of man with fellow-man," and that this chapter represents a "counter-ritual" to Ahab's (*Form and Fable in American Fiction* [New York: Norton, 1973], 235; see also 267–68). Such a view, the standard one, does not take into account the second half of the chapter, but instead jumps forward to the turning point of "The Try-works" two chapters later.

Cameron describes such a fusion of identities as the "fantasy" of *Moby-Dick*, and suggests that Melville invokes both the desire for selves to be able to "go outside of their delimited boundaries" and "the idea that such projection is impossible except as projection" (*The Corporeal Self*, 2, 21).

34. "[T]wo different things were warring" within Ahab, Ishmael says, and the contrast between them is illustrated by that between the captain's "live leg" and his "dead limb"—"On life and death this old man walked" (200).

35. Newton Arvin sees Ahab's leg as "an equivocal symbol both of his own impotence and of the independent male principle directed cripplingly against him" (*Herman Melville* [New York: William Sloane, 1950], 172). What I would emphasize here is the progression from Tommo's merely *symbolic* castration in *Typee* to a *literal* emasculation here.

36. Descartes takes dreams as an example of how the senses may be deceived; he uses them to place the existence of the body in doubt in Meditation I (*Philosophical Works*, tr. Elizabeth S. Haldane and G.R.T. Ross [Cambridge: Cambridge UP, 1931], 1: 145–46). Here Melville uses Ahab's dreams to reveal the fragmentation not only of the body but of the mind as well.

37. David Simpson describes Ahab's pursuit as "a quest for completion, for the capture of what is lacking," undertaken because the captain has been "robbed of his leg, and probably of something else besides, by the white whale" (*Fetishism and Imagination: Dickens, Melville, Conrad* [Baltimore: Johns Hopkins UP, 1982], 76). "Whales," he says, are "analogues of human self-completion" (77), and Moby Dick in particular is the image of the lost phallus (80).

38. Cameron argues that Ahab's desire must be to consume the body of the whale and make it one with his own; the self, she says, acknowledges "the world that lies outside of it . . . only in the process of trying to appropriate it" (*The Corporeal Self*, 4–5). For her, *Moby-Dick* consistently replaces the desire for knowledge with one for a merging of self and reality: "Not being separate would replace knowledge" (25).

Leo Bersani, on the other hand, argues that the desire for plenitude is "intrinsically violent" because it assumes the "annihilation of everything alien to it"; its fantasies include "a spontaneous fury at those invincible forces (both in the world and in ourselves) which have condemned us to the loss of ecstasy" (*A Future for Astyanax: Character and Desire in Literature* [Boston: Little, Brown, 1970], 13).

39. In this respect Ahab resembles the "cannibal" sharks feeding alongside the *Pequod*, who, when attacked with whaling-spades, "viciously snapped, not only at each other's disembowelments, but . . . bent round, and bit their own" (257). The harpoon he forges for Moby Dick will indeed be his own " 'branding-iron' " (404).

40. Ishmael has described Ahab's soul as "shut up in the caved trunk of his body" like a hibernating bear in a tree (134).

41. Ishmael describes the front of the sperm whale's head as "a dead, blind wall," a featureless "mass" of bonelike toughness without sensation (284–85). The echo of Ahab's image is unmistakeable—for Ishmael too, the whale's head represents sheer physical otherness, but he sees it as "impregnable" and "uninjurable" (285).

42. Freud speaks of a "spot in every dream at which it is unplumbable—a navel, as it were, that is its point of contact with the unknown. . . . at that point there is a tangle of dream thoughts which cannot be unravelled" (*The Interpretation of Dreams, Standard Edition of the Complete Psychological Works of Sigmund Freud*, tr. and ed. James Strachey [London: Hogarth Press, 1953], 4: 111, 5: 525).

43. A fusion of sorts does take place between Ahab and Fedallah; it is not a fusion of bodies, but rather a fusion of bodies and shadows: "Ahab chanced so to stand, that the Parsee occupied his shadow; while, if the Parsee's shadow was there at all it seemed only to blend with, and lengthen Ahab's" (278). Fedallah is here a projection or representation of Ahab, not a part of him. Unlike Ishmael, Ahab dreams of impermeability rather than fusion: his "desirable pattern" for a man calls for a blind and heartless monster (390).

44. Sacks describes a "phantom limb" like Ahab's as "essential if an artificial limb is to be used"; the phantom in fact allows the prosthesis to be integrated into the patient's "body-image" (*The Man Who Mistook His Wife for a Hat and Other Clinical Tales* [New York: Summit, 1985], 64). Ahab obviously refuses to attempt such an integration, and the result is a rupture of his body-image, which, according to Sacks, leads to a loss of the sense of self (51).

45. " 'Oh God! that man should be a thing for immortal souls to sieve through!' " Ahab laments (427). " 'I'm all aleak myself,' " he says to Starbuck, when the mate tells him that a cask is leaking in the hold (393).

46. Ahab also invokes this harvest imagery in "The Symphony," the last chapter before the three days of the chase: " 'they have been making hay somewhere under the slopes of the Andes . . . toil how we may, we all sleep at last on the field' " (445).

III: Genealogical Identity

1. R.W.B. Lewis speaks of Melville's relation to European literature as "queer and vigilant . . . at once hospitable and hostile, at once unlimited and uneasy" (*The American Adam* [Chicago: U of Chicago P, 1955], 145). My emphasis here is on the

freedom with which Melville would draw upon and "transfigure" (the term is Lewis's) the work of his literary forefathers. His "anxiety" about literary influence seems to have been focused more on the work of contemporaries such as the Transcendentalists, whose views he combated directly and repeatedly. It is not until *The Confidence-Man* that Melville begins to treat his literary antecedents (Shakespeare and the Bible in particular) as distant and unknowable, discrete texts whose ambiguities are to be defended against rather than simply absorbed into his own writing.

2. Richard Chase sees a mythic structure in Melville's work, in which "a fatherless boy and young man painfully resurrect[s] his past" as he matures and discovers his true relation to his dead father (*Herman Melville: A Critical Study* [New York: William Sloane, 1949], 2). The hero, he says, moves between two sets of symbolic polarities, chief among which are "the mythical abode of the gods and the fathers from which the young man has fallen [which] has the symbolic qualities of the father, and the earthbound world of the fallen hero [which] has the symbolic qualities of the son . . . The son [here] is the father bereft of his positive qualities" (35). Chase's reading yields a number of insights, but its linear, biographical emphasis minimizes both the progression of Melville's thought and the differences between his novels.

3. Arvin says that Moby Dick "embodies neither the father merely nor the mother but, by a process of condensation, the *parental* principle inclusively" (*Herman Melville* [New York: William Sloane, 1950], 172). Sundquist calls Ahab's hunt parricidal, but then stops and associates the whale with "both father and mother, womb and phallus" (*Home as Found: Authority and Genealogy in Nineteenth-Century American Literature* [Baltimore: Johns Hopkins UP, 1979], 148).

4. Tolchin also does some projecting of paternal attributes, comparing Ahab to both Allan and Maria Melvill (*Mourning, Gender, and Creativity in the Art of Herman Melville* [New Haven, CT: Yale UP, 1988], 118, 133); Durand, " 'The Captive King': The Absent Father in Melville's Fiction," in *The Fictional Father: Lacanian Readings of the Text*, ed. Robert Con Davis (Amherst: U of Massachusetts P, 1981), 50.

5. See Larzer Ziff, *Literary Democracy* (New York: Penguin, 1982), 10, for a further discussion of the Typees' sense of time.

6. In *Omoo*, Melville's narrator comments on a cultivated "grove of cocoa-nut and bread-fruit trees" as an exception to the general rule, "as if, for once the improvident Polynesian had thought of his posterity" (261). This is "the only instance" of such planning "which ever came under my observation," he says (261). The natives' lack of agricultural management is, for him, evidence of their inability to see themselves as linked to future generations.

According to Charles Anderson, Melville is simply wrong about this: "The Marquesans were thrifty enough to take precautions against a future shortage by planting breadfruit and cocoanut trees with great care, especially upon the birth of a child" (*Melville in the South Seas* [New York: Columbia UP, 1939], 144). Melville's observation thus says a great deal more about his sense of the difference between Western and native cultures than it does about the Polynesians themselves.

7. Missionaries on Imeeo educate their children separately from the natives,

"the avowed reason being, to preserve the young whites from moral contamination. The better to insure this end, every effort is made to prevent them from acquiring the native language," comments the narrator of *Omoo* (188).

8. For a description of *Redburn*'s initiatory structure and the criticism that describes it, see James Shroeter, "*Redburn* and the Failure of Mythic Criticism," *AL* 39 (1967): 179–97; and Michael D. Bell, "Melville's *Redburn*: Initiation and Authority," *NEQ* 46 (1973): 558–72. Christopher W. Sten offers a reading of the novel in terms of "identity formation" in "Melville's 'Gentleman Forger': The Struggle for Identity in *Redburn*" *TSLL* 21 (1979): 347–67.

For a discussion of the figure of the father in terms of a search for an American identity, see Sacvan Bercovitch, "Melville's Search for National Identity: Son and Father in *Redburn*, *Pierre*, and *Billy Budd*," *CLAJ* 10 (1967): 217–28.

9. Redburn goes to sea at age 14; Melville embarked on his "first voyage," also to Liverpool, when he was 18. But Melville turned 14 in 1833—the year after the deaths of both his father and paternal grandfather and a fire that destroyed the Gansevoort mansion in Albany (Rogin, *Subversive Genealogy: The Politics and Art of Herman Melville* [New York: Knopf, 1983], 30).

10. Allan Melvill's 1818 journey to Liverpool was a similar combination of continuity and rupture: Melville's father travelled to Scotland to establish a connection between the American branch of the family and their Scots ancestors; but he went on to Paris, to establish connections for the importing business he was going to open in New York—after moving his family away from his father in Boston (see Rogin, *Subversive Genealogy*, 23–24).

11. Durand suggests that "the traditional pattern of initiatory symbolism is reversed" here: "the guidebook leads to no new knowledge or discovery, but simply to a return of the dead father" ("'The Captive King': The Absent Father in Melville's Text," 54). Redburn's voyage to Liverpool is indeed an attempt to recapture the dead father's presence, but this moment does not seem to me the "intrusion of *Unheimlichkeit*" that Durand describes. It is, after all, the *impossibility* of the dead father's return that the episode demonstrates.

Lewis also emphasizes this incident, but describes it as "the moment when Melville's hero realizes that he is an orphan," "betrayed" by his dead father (*The American Adam*, 137, 138).

12. Chase describes Ishmael as "no longer held prisoner by the lost father," but "free to search for (among other things) the meaning and value of paternity" (28). He seeks, according to Chase, "to become the complete Promethean-Oedipean man, in whom father and son are reconciled" (*Herman Melville*, 34–35).

13. Ann Douglas cites this passage in connection with Melville's assertion of "masculine" values and images, and links it to his critique of nineteenth-century liberal Protestantism (*The Feminization of American Culture* [New York: Knopf, 1977], 305–06).

14. Leslie Fiedler describes the relationship between Ishmael and Queequeg as representing "the redemptive love of man and man," but acknowledges that such love remains "suspect" (*Love and Death in the American Novel* [New York: Stein and Day, 1966], 370).

15. Redburn's memory of a June day in his childhood is a memory of his father—Ishmael's memory, on the other hand, is built around the father's absence.

16. In *White-Jacket*, the narrator describes the *Neversink*'s main-top-men as "brothers," a "fraternity of fine fellows" who "loaned ourselves to each other with all the freedom in the world" (15). This state of interchangeable brotherhood is, however, vulnerable both to the genealogically based Articles of War on which the ship's hierarchy depends and to the passage of time itself—the crew, including the main-top-men, will scatter when the ship reaches port. White-Jacket's only narrative recourse is to suspend temporality, to "leave the ship on the sea" and the main-top-men in an artificial timelessness, "a brother-band . . . all spliced together" forever (396).

Douglas sees the issue underlying the novel's flogging scenes as "paternalism versus fraternity." She describes "the fundamental struggle in American culture" as "the Oedipal one of son against father" but treats such genealogical conflict as an expression of an "essentially political and class-oriented" struggle (*The Feminization of American Culture*, 297–98).

17. Henry A. Murray suggests that the white whale "has received the projection of Captain Ahab's Presbyterian conscience" and that it thus represents "the Freudian Superego": "most specifically, he symbolizes the zealous parents," both father and mother ("In Nomine Diaboli," in *Moby Dick Centennial Essays*, ed. Tyrus Hillway and Luther S. Mansfield [Dallas, TX: Southern Methodist UP, 1953], 12).

I would agree that Ahab's rebellion against genealogy does color and animate his pursuit of Moby Dick, but I would resist the temptation to reduce the whale to a mere symbol of the Parent. For Ahab, Moby Dick represents an inscrutable otherness that is physical and epistemological as well as genealogical.

18. Chase at one point describes Ahab as "both the father and the son," but later says that because Ahab and his purpose are "unfathered," he cannot be the cultural force Melville symbolizes as the father (*Herman Melville*, 49, 63).

19. This speech has, until recently, been assigned to Ishmael, but the editors of the Northwestern-Newberry edition have judged the context to require its ascription to Ahab. I have, in this instance, turned to the Northwestern-Newberry text as published in the Library of America volume containing *Redburn*, *White-Jacket*, and *Moby-Dick* (New York: Library of America, 1983). See 1318 and the editor's note on 1436.

The change has little impact on my argument, but it is a crucial one for readings that cite the passage as an example of Ishmael's circular or relativistic perspective. See, for example, Wadlington, *The Confidence Game in American Literature* (Princeton, NJ: Princeton UP, 1975), 73–103.

20. Melville, *Writings* 7: 3, 11. All further references will be to this edition.

21. Edgar Dryden notes that Pierre's relationship to his mother and his longing for a sister "subtly entangle the genealogical line by disrupting its temporal development" ("'The Entangled Text': Melville's *Pierre* and the Problem of Reading," *Boundary 2* 7.3 [1979]: 149, 150). Dryden, however, overlooks the fact that Pierre's mother is the primary source of this generational confusion.

22. Douglas argues that Pierre's "essential conflict is with his mother," and that he takes his father as a model of masculine "virility" opposed to her feminized and domesticated image of her son (*The Feminization of American Culture*, 309, 310). But given his father's absence, Douglas says, "Pierre can find no focus, no real significance for his rebellion" (311).

23. This substitutive repetition is incomplete in another way, for it excludes Pierre's mother; he cannot act as both his father's son and his mother's—he can no longer be "himself." Michael Ragussis suggests that Pierre's failure to acknowledge Isabel as "sister" "repeats his father's crime; he refuses Isabel her natural familial title" (*Acts of Naming: The Family Plot in Fiction* [New York: Oxford UP, 1986], 56).

24. Sundquist points out that "the paradox of Pierre's resolve to save Isabel and protect his father's sacred memory lies in the fact that his very desire to keep the father's name untarnished insures that it will die out with Pierre" (*Home as Found*, 154).

25. Brodhead describes Pierre's vision of Encedalus as a "moment of self-comprehension" for both him and the novel, "showing how his relation to his mother breeds in him a mixture of sexual desire and reverential love" (*Hawthorne, Melville, and the Novel* [Chicago: U of Chicago P, 1976], 188). Here, according to Brodhead, "the book's conflicts of sexuality and idealism within the self and its conflicts between spiritual self and worldly society become figures for each other" (188).

Brook Thomas characterizes Pierre's attempt to "write disembodied transcendental truths" as "incestuous," a "bachelor quest" that ends by "denying difference and embracing purely an image of the self" ("The Writer's Procreative Urge in *Pierre*: Fictional Father or Convoluted Incest?" *SNNTS* 9 [1979]: 422).

IV: Textual Identity

1. Melville resembles his contemporary Kierkegaard in this respect. One wrote under various pseudonyms (Kierkegaard) and the other through pseudonymous narrators (Melville); just as Kierkegaard at once acknowledged his authorship in his *Concluding Unscientific Postscript* (1846) and also insisted on his complete separation from his personae, so Melville says that he is and is not the writer of *Typee*.

2. William B. Dillingham discusses this problem in connection with *Typee*, emphasizing the discrepancy between Tommo's experience in the valley and his romanticized memories of it. "An experience such as Tommo's," he argues, "is complex and organic and does not end abruptly but undergoes transformation as it continues to be a part of his mind. The pure past, then, is irrecoverable" (*An Artist in the Rigging: The Early Work of Herman Melville* [Athens: U of Georgia P, 1972], 24). But, he adds, Tommo "never seems to grasp the nature of the past or to realize that he cannot go back" (24).

3. Book length examples of this approach would include Paul Brodtkorb's *Ishmael's White World: A Phenomenological Reading of "Moby-Dick"* (New Haven, CT: Yale UP, 1965) and Bainard Cowan's *Exiled Waters: Moby-Dick and the Crisis of Allegory* (Baton Rouge, LA: Louisiana State UP, 1982), among others. I could also cite many chapters of books; Sharon Cameron's chapter in *The Corporeal Self:*

Allegories of the Body in Melville and Hawthorne (Baltimore: Johns Hopkins UP, 1981) and Ramón Saldívar's in *Figural Language in the Novel* (Princeton, NJ: Princeton UP, 1984) are only two recent examples.

4. "The Flawed Grandeur of Melville's *Pierre*," in *New Perspectives on Melville*, ed. Faith Pullin (Kent, OH: Kent State UP, 1978), 162–96. Another study that emphasizes Melville's changing attitudes toward his audience and its expectations is Ann Douglas' *The Feminization of American Culture* (New York: Knopf, 1977).

5. William H. Gilman describes this "disrupting shift in the angle of vision" as a "ruinous defect" (*Melville's Early Life and "Redburn"* [New York: New York UP, 1951], 208–09). Most subsequent critics have agreed, though some—F.O. Matthiessen, for example—locate this shift at an earlier point in the novel (*American Renaissance* [New York: Oxford UP, 1941], 391).

Merlin Bowen, on the other hand, argues that the adult commentary is the narrator's, not Melville's, and that the novel's major problem lies in the flawed structure of its second half rather than in its use of perspective ("*Redburn* and the Angle of Vision," *MP* 52 [1954]: 100–09).

6. Dillingham emphasizes this foreshadowing, pointing out that Redburn's copy of Adam Smith had been given to him by his brother's friend Mr. Jones, who had been given the book by his father. Jones himself has either discarded or never read this paternal text, judging from the amount of dust on the volume (*An Artist in the Rigging*, 51).

7. For Edgar Dryden, the narrator's imaginary recreation of his friend is a successful "artistic resurrection" (*Melville's Thematics of Form: The Great Art of Telling the Truth* [Baltimore: Johns Hopkins UP, 1968], 67). From his perspective, Melville's narrators self-consciously and contentedly fictionalize their experience to produce meaning and order.

8. Reprinted in *White-Jacket*, 487.

9. White-Jacket describes the doors that close off areas of the ship as "like the gloomy entrances to family vaults of buried dead" (127). Régis Durand sees White-Jacket's exploration of the closed space of the frigate as associated with the return of primitive elements, involving a primal scene in which the subject penetrates to recover a father figure ("'The Captive King': The Absent Father in Melville's Text," in *The Fictional Father: Lacanian Readings of the Text*, ed. Robert Con Davis [Amherst: U of Massachusetts P, 1981], 56–57).

10. The sailor-poet Lemsford, for example, finds writing almost impossible aboard ship: "In a frigate, you can not sit down and meander off your sonnets, when the full heart prompts; but only, when more important duties permit" (40). He also has White-Jacket's problem of a lack of space; he, too, must have his verses "accessible at all times," but cannot find a hiding place for his "casket" of poems (41).

11. My contention here is that the entire text of *Moby-Dick* is contained within and shaped by Ishmael's narration, just as in *Redburn* and *White-Jacket*. Melville does, of course, break the frame of first-person narration in both the dramatic chapters and at those points at which Ishmael seems to claim a limited omniscience, but the book retains the psychological dynamic and autobiographical trajectory of its predecessors. Melville's presence is thus continuous, but always indirect and implicit, even if more visible.

Glauco Cambon argues that the novel's shifts in form are deliberate experiments by Melville, not lapses in artistic control. He describes the dramatic chapters as reflecting "the natural movement of memory striving to recapture lost actuality" ("Ishmael and the Problem of Formal Discontinuities in *Moby-Dick*," *MLN* 16 [1961]: 522).

Alfred Kazin and W.B. Dillingham, among others, argue for Ishmael's complete control over the text: see Kazin, "An Introduction to *Moby-Dick*," rpt. in *Discussions of Moby-Dick*, ed. Milton R. Stern (Boston: Heath, 1960), 52–59; and Dillingham, "The Narrator of *Moby-Dick*," *English Studies* 49 (1968): 20–29. Charles Feidelson, on the other hand, sees author and narrator as interchangeable (*Symbolism and American Literature* [Chicago: U of Chicago P, 1953], 31, 184); Richard Chase sees Ishmael as disappearing into the voice of the omniscient author (*The American Novel and Its Tradition* [New York: Anchor, 1959], 94).

12. The epilogue was omitted from the first English edition of *Moby-Dick*, entitled *The Whale*. Several reviewers took Melville to task for his supposed error in narrative mechanics, asking, in the words of the London *New Quarterly Review*, "As there was no survivor of the catastrophe, how became the author or Mr. Bentley possessed of all these minute and painful details?" (quoted in *Moby-Dick as Doubloon*, ed. Hershel Parker and Harrison Hayford [New York: Norton, 1970], 79. See also reviews from the London *Literary Gazette* and the *Dublin University Magazine* (*Moby-Dick as Doubloon*, 61, 88).

13. Carl F. Strauch also begins his consideration of *Moby-Dick* with the epilogue. He notes the figure of the vortex here and elsewhere and attributes a "painfully injurious" psychological effect to Ishmael's experience within it ("Ishmael: Time and Personality in *Moby-Dick*," *SNNTS* 1 [1969]: 469).

14. Walter E. Bezanson makes this distinction between Ishmael as character and as narrator. He takes Ishmael to be "the real center of meaning and the defining force of the novel" ("Moby-Dick: Work of Art," in *Moby-Dick Centennial Essays*, ed. Tyrus Hillway and Luther S. Mansfield [Dallas, TX: Southern Methodist UP, 1953], 53). "[T]he Ishmael voice," he says, "is there every moment," from the first word of the novel to the last (41). The book's different structural levels, he argues, reflect Ishmael's attempts to find a form adequate to his purpose. Bezanson does, however, assume that the "young" and "old" Ishmael are continuous: "Narrator Ishmael is merely young Ishmael grown older" (37); "young Ishmael" will simply "become the narrator in due time" (38).

Merlin Bowen also sees Ishmael the narrator as only more experienced and mature than Ishmael the character. But he does admit that the actual moment of the "transformation" is never shown (*The Long Encounter: Self and Experience in the Writings of Herman Melville* [Chicago: U of Chicago P, 1960], 241).

Paul Brodtkorb argues that Ishmael's consciousness pervades and constitutes the world and text of the novel. He acknowledges that Ishmael appears as both character and narrator, but Brodtkorb's phenomenological approach requires him to conflate the two, usually treating them as a single consciousness. He describes Ishmael the narrator as taking an ironic view of himself as character, but this ironic distance is not a problem or discontinuity within the "Ishmaelian consciousness" (*Ishmael's White World*, 3).

Grant McMillan notes the limits of Brodtkorb's view and describes the shifts and oscillations in the text as evidence of a tension within Ishmael as narrator. Ishmael, in McMillan's reading, is both attracted to and terrified by Ahab's projection of spiritual significance onto material objects; his narrative reversals and ambiguities show Ishmael to be repeatedly drawn toward Ahab's project, only to withdraw from and attempt to repress that desire ("Ishmael's Dilemma: The Significance of the Fiery Hunt," *Centennial Review* 15 [1971]: 204–17).

Bainard Cowan makes this temporal division a central feature of the allegorical structure he finds in the novel. *Moby-Dick*, he says, is an "allegory of allegory" (*Exiled Waters*, 58). The gap between Ishmael the survivor and Ishmael the seafarer is, he says, "absolute," but the distance enables the former to find an allegorical meaning in the latter's experience (60). Cowan's notion of allegory, derived from Benjamin, is of a redemptive "turn" away from reality that "empties [living things] of all life" but "fills them with significance" (161). "Allegory" here shapes and gives meaning to experience in the way that "fiction" does in Dryden's reading. Cowan assumes, of course, that Melville sees allegory in these terms and can accept the loss inherent in such allegorical structures—a loss of meaning as anything more than a potential but unrealizable presence and as loss of the self as more than an entity constituted by a difference or "turn" within itself. I differ with Cowan not over his analysis of the "crisis" Melville describes in *Moby-Dick*, but on the question of whether allegory is regarded as an adequate response to it.

15. Dryden invokes a distinction between Ishmael as "teller" and as "actor," but argues that he constructs a purely verbal identity for himself as narrator, and ensures his survival by turning away from the real world to create "an imaginative reality," a self-reflexive fiction (*Melville's Thematics of Form*, 84). Dryden's interpretation assumes that Ishmael is content with such a verbal, fictional identity, a new self "who will inhabit a world of words rather than objects" (110), and that the events of his narrative no longer represent a threat or problem for him once they have been textualized.

Dillingham's reading is closer to my own. He compares Ishmael to Coleridge's Ancient Mariner, describing Melville's narrator as compelled to tell and retell his story. It is the experience of "almost unendurable loneliness" in his abandonment at sea that leaves him with this burden of narration, Dillingham claims ("The Narrator of *Moby-Dick*," 25–29). In this connection, see also Barry A. Marks's "Retrospective Narration in Nineteenth-Century Literature," (*CE* 31 [1970]: 366–75), which describes *Moby-Dick* as Ishmael's "quest for a conception of himself as a narrator" (372).

16. Warner Berthoff describes the relationship between Melville's first-person narrators and their readers as a recuperative, comic bond that operates to contain the destabilizing and subversive effects of tragic experience. Melville's narrators, for Berthoff, are observers and commentators unconstrained by their experience; their detachment and distance are unqualified freedoms (*The Example of Melville* [Princeton, NJ: Princeton UP, 1962], 115–32). I take Ishmael's relation to both his readers and his own experience to be more complex and troubled; he is neither free from his memories nor secure against them in a contract with the reader.

A. Robert Lee also reads "Loomings" as enticing or cajoling the reader into complicity with the text. But in deemphasizing Ishmael's narrative presence, Lee overlooks the ways in which Ishmael distances himself from his reader ("Moby-Dick: The Tale and the Telling," in *New Perspectives on Melville*, 86–127).

Brodtkorb's reading of the chapter (*Ishmael's White World*, 51, 104–05, 123–24) is closer to mine, although he emphasizes Ishmael's boredom on land. Robert Zoellner also cautions against taking Ishmael's jovial tone at face value, describing him as a "suicidal neurotic" (*The Salt-Sea Mastodon* [Berkeley: U of California P, 1973], 120). But he sees Ishmael as redeemed in the course of the novel.

Warwick Wadlington notices the shifts in tone and distance in Chapter 1, but sees Ishmael's rhetoric as designed to engender "selftaste" in the reader "by manipulating the reader's distance from him and the world of his fiction" (*The Confidence Game in American Literature* [Princeton: Princeton UP, 1975], 92). This educative process, according to Wadlington, reproduces the sequence of "allurement and distancing, attraction and disengagement" that characterizes Ishmael's experience (92).

17. Ishmael also describes going to sea as an alternative to suicide when characterizing the *Pequod*'s blacksmith (402).

18. See John T. Irwin, *American Hieroglyphics* (New Haven, CT: Yale UP, 1980), 288–89, for a similar reading of this passage. Zoellner takes the Narcissus image as the site at which the "constitutive metaphors" of the novel converge (*The Salt-Sea Mastodon*, 52).

19. John Seelye associates Ahab's quest with the line of the story and Ishmael's expository passages with a circular relativism (*Melville: The Ironic Diagram* [Evanston, IL: Northwestern UP, 1970], 6–7). He describes the cetological chapters as Ishmael's attempts to "block and impede the forward movement of the narrative" (63). But Seelye's view of Ishmael as relativist is more sanguine than his description of Melville's own ironic questioning. I regard Ishmael as more desperate for certainties—about himself, especially—and thus not simply opposed to Ahab. Ishmael's text attempts to master and transform the linearity of Ahab's quest, not simply to escape or oppose it.

20. The walls of the entryway to the Spouter Inn, for example, suggest two different ways of encountering the whale. The painting on one wall offers a surface image that eludes interpretation; "reading" cannot discover the "object" represented. The picture's meaning must, finally, be projected onto it by the viewer. The other wall bears a collection of weapons, lances, and harpoons, one of which is "like a corkscrew now"; these suggest a direct and dangerous penetration of the whale's body (21).

21. Brodtkorb cites this passage as an example of Ishmael's circular reasoning, which begins and ends with emotional responses to death. But he takes the change in tone as Ishmael grows merry again to mark an "inexplicable" change in mood for Ishmael *as character* (*Ishmael's White World*, 17). Brodtkorb sees Ishmael the narrator as only passively reproducing his earlier thoughts, albeit from an ironic distance. The shift can, however, be explained in terms of Ishmael's active manipulation of tense and person, a process similar to the narrator's use of both "White-Jacket" and the first person in *White-Jacket*.

22. W.H. Auden sees the sermon as setting forth the moral norm of the novel

(*The Enchaféd Flood* [New York: Vintage, 1950], 116–19), as does Luther S. Mansfield ("Symbolism and Biblical Allusion in *Moby-Dick*," *ESQ* 28 [1962]: 20–23). Robert F. Bergstrom takes Mapple to be a false prophet, part of Melville's critique of orthodox Christianity ("The Topmost Grief: Rejection of Ahab's Faith," *Essays in Literature* 2 [1975]: 171–80). Nathalia Wright sees Mapple as modelled on Old Testament prophets; she reads his sermon as a blend of the stories of Jonah and Jeremiah that foretells the end of the narrative (*Melville's Use of the Bible* [Durham, NC: Duke UP, 1949], 82–93).

23. Zoellner notes Ishmael's lack of response to the sermon but takes it as a sign of his rejection of orthodox Christianity. For Zoellner's reading of the sermon as a call for self-alienation, see *The Salt-Sea Mastodon*, 59–64.

24. Harrison Hayford notes this shift between Chapters 23 and 24, but attributes it to Melville's return to an earlier draft in Chapter 24. For Hayford, such modulations in tone take place within Melville's writing alone, not Ishmael's ("Unnecessary Duplicates: A Key to the Writing of *Moby-Dick*," in *New Perspectives on Melville*, 148–49).

25. These alternatives are analogous to those described by Auden: "the poetic shell," which promises an escape from self-consciousness through an immersion in nature; and "the Euclidean stone," whose truth also involves a loss of self, in a transformation into "a purely self-conscious ego" (*The Enchaféd Flood*, 81–87).

26. Zoellner describes Ahab as event-oriented in his attempt to dive through the interface of phenomenal experience to the truth of things in themselves. Where Ahab distinguishes between perceiver and perceived, Ishmael, in Zoellner's reading, comes to see them as parts of a seamless whole (*The Salt-Sea Mastodon*, 27–28). Zoellner emphasizes the instability of Ishmael's position as narrator, taking character and narrator to be a stable unity in epistemological opposition to Ahab.

27. Carolyn Porter sees Ahab's authority as ultimately dependent on a "discourse of dramatic, ritual action," such as that created here, rather than on the verbal discourse of dialogue ("Call me Ishmael, or How to Make Double-Talk Speak," in *New Essays on Moby-Dick*, ed. Richard Brodhead [Cambridge: Cambridge UP, 1986], 103).

28. Here and elsewhere, Ishmael's text goes well beyond the limits of his direct experience. Given his willingness to manipulate and delay his narrative, it would not be inconsistent for him to extrapolate from his own experience and construct soliloquies for Ahab and others. Just as his expository chapters offer sometimes unreliable commentaries on and extensions of events, so his dramatic chapters extend and "deepen" his characterizations.

Ishmael himself addresses this issue at the end of Chapter 33, discussing his presentation of Ahab:

> I must not conceal that I have only to do with a poor old whale-hunter like him; and, therefore, all outward majestical trappings and housings are denied me. Oh, Ahab! what shall be grand in thee, it must needs be plucked at from the skies, and dived for in the deep, and featured in the unbodied air. (130)

Soliloquies, like the dramatic mode in general, are dives into a postulated "depth" of character that can only be "featured in the unbodied air" of Ishmael's imagination.

Dillingham describes Ishmael as *"recreating* the story, both from what he actually witnessed and heard, and from what he pieces together in his imagination" ("The Narrator of *Moby-Dick*," 23). He sees Ishmael as "profoundly disturbed" by his experience, "half-crazy" at times (23). For a similar view, see Zoellner, *The Salt-Sea Mastodon*, xi.

Richard B. Sewall, on the other hand, sees Melville taking control of the novel as tragic dramatist, abandoning Ishmael's consciousness (*The Vision of Tragedy* [New Haven, CT: Yale UP, 1957], 92–105). R.P. Blackmur argues that Melville shifts from consciousness to consciousness "at will without sense of consistency" and that this shows the weakness of his novelistic technique ("The Craft of Herman Melville," *VQR* 14 [1938]: 269). Herbert S. Donow mounts a Jamesian attack on Melville's "misuse" of point of view and overt manipulation of characters and diction ("Herman Melville and the Craft of Fiction," *MLQ* 25 [1964]: 181–86).

One may attribute these sections to Ishmael's imagination or to Melville's impatience with narrative, but in either case, first-person narrative becomes a limiting condition, a form that must be escaped or transcended to represent the "truth" of events.

29. Thomas Woodson takes this passage as linking Ishmael's "dive" into Ahab's character with the captain's pursuit of the whale ("Ahab's Greatness: Prometheus as Narcissus," *ELH* 33 [1966]: 351–69). In this connection see also Brodtkorb, *Ishmael's White World*, 61–62.

30. Brodtkorb also describes a downward movement into the vortex as an escape from the circularity of time and notes its association with a loss of identity in death or madness (*Ishmael's White World*, 37–39). But he does not distinguish Ahab's representation of truth as depth from Ishmael's experimentation with the image in constructing the formal features of his text.

Brodtkorb here follows Georges Poulet, who calls such a dive out of time an escape into the freedom of a fabulous or mythic time without determination or succession. But the diver can never succeed, Poulet says; he will be forced to return to the circularity and determinism of human time (*Studies in Human Time*, tr. Elliott Coleman [New York: Harper, 1959], 337–41). Auden offers a slightly different contrast, between the "one-direction historical time" and necessity of a voyage and "cyclical natural time" (*The Enchafèd Flood*, 68–70).

31. Cambon compares these two acts of naming, arguing that Chapter 41 is an attempt by Ishmael to understand the preceding events and himself ("Ishmael and the Problem of Formal Discontinuities in *Moby-Dick*," 518–19).

32. Cambon notes the structural similarity between the "Candles" and "Quarter-deck" sequences and takes the later group as the point at which Ishmael's presence as character and narrator begins to recede ("Ishmael and the Problem of Formal Discontinuities in *Moby-Dick*," 521). He sees this withdrawal as a positive step, however, as "the liberation of imaginative objectivity" rather than a tacit admission of narrative failure (523).

33. James Guetti takes the open-endedness of Ishmael's consideration of whiteness and of the whale itself to indicate the limits of linguistic possibility. Ishmael's refusal to commit himself to a single rhetorical technique, according to Guetti, shows his awareness that "language can only illuminate itself; it . . . continually and

inevitably recreates itself in a permanent circularity, never reaching away from itself toward the reality" (*The Limits of Metaphor* [Ithaca, NY: Cornell UP, 1967], 28). Guetti's argument is convincing but limited, for it assumes a narrative detachment, a calculated playfulness, that Ishmael does not seem to me to possess. Even if he pulls back from Ahab's drive to achieve a fixed inner meaning, Ishmael is still tormented by the ineffability of the world, the whale, and the self.

34. Rodolphe Gasché takes Ishmael's subject in "Cetology" to be the scene of writing itself. I take from Gasché the notion of Ishmael's classification as the projection of "a spatial object upon a plane surface" ("The Scene of Writing: A Deferred Outset," *Glyph* 1 [Baltimore: Johns Hopkins UP, 1977], 152). He goes on to argue, however, that the whale itself "rolls" in a movement of pure displacement and deviation, unfolding and projecting itself, breaking and disrupting the textual surface (152).

35. For other interpretations of this weaving imagery, see Matthiessen, *American Renaissance*, 129–30; Dryden, *Melville's Thematics of Form*, 106–09; and Daniel G. Hoffman, "*Moby-Dick*: Jonah's Whale or Job's?" *Sewanee Review* 69 (1969): 205–24. Cowan sees Ishmael's examination of the whale's body as a playful "carnivalization," a turn away from rather than an extension of his attempt to weave a spatial matrix or grid (*Exiled Waters*, 114–19).

36. My primary interest here is in Ishmael's narrative management of "The Town-Ho's Story," not in the tale's thematic relationship to the rest of the novel. The latter subject has been discussed by a number of critics; see, among others: Sherman Paul, "Melville's 'The Town-Ho's Story,'" *AL* 21 (1949): 212–21; Don Geiger, "Melville's Black God: Contrary Evidence in 'The Town-Ho's Story,'" *AL* 25 (1954): 464–71; William K. Spofford, "Melville's Ambiguities: A Re-evaluation of 'The Town-Ho's Story,'" *AL* 41 (1969): 264–70.

37. Berthoff discusses "The Town-Ho's Story" as an effort by Ishmael to "exert and renew his story-teller's authority over experience" (*The Example of Melville*, 137). The dramatized scene in Lima calls attention to Ishmael's act of recollection and narration, making it as important as the story itself. Berthoff goes on to defend Melville's emphasis on the "told story," with its "doubled focus—on the event, and on the recapturing of it" at some length (145, 139–49). For him, this doubled focus is an extension of the possibilities of the novel—an advantage rather than a narrative problem.

38. Noah Webster, *An American Dictionary of the English Language* (Springfield, MA: Merriman, 1851), 701. W.H. Matthews rejects this etymological link (*Mazes and Labyrinths: Their History and Development* [1922; rpt. New York: Dover, 1970], 180). True or false, this information would have been available to Melville.

39. In "Circles and Orphans," Darrell E. Griffiths focuses on the circle imagery here and in "The Castaway" and the three chapters of "The Chase," noting that penetrating to the vision within the circle (into the womb) results in its destruction and the orphaning of the self (*Books at Brown* 24 [1971]: 68–81).

Leslie Fiedler, on the other hand, cites this chapter in his argument that penetration to a watery depth is redemptive, "a life-giving immersion in nature or the id" (*Love and Death in the American Novel* [New York: Stein and Day, 1966], 381). He describes Ishmael's recovery by the *Rachel* as a return to the Mother and Ahab's death as the result of his conflict with the Father—a reading that cannot encompass Ishmael's struggles, as narrator, to gain and preserve authority over the text.

Marius Bewley compares Ishmael's vision with Dante's *Paradiso*, Canto XXVIII. He uses this chapter to further his argument for Leviathan as a symbol of godlike goodness (*The Eccentric Design* [New York: Columbia UP, 1963], 201–05). Ishmael, in Bewley's view, is "resurrected" because of his resistance to Ahab and his ability to see the whale as a symbol of creation itself (206–11).

Zoellner takes this chapter to be a redemption of the image of the vortex by the whale (*The Salt-Sea Mastodon*, 204–05). Ishmael finds life rather than death in the heart of this vortex, as he will in the Epilogue, according to Zoellner. He sees this as an affirmation of Ishmael's "redemptive cyclism" and a rejection of Ahab's "entropism."

40. Ishmael has invoked this image earlier, in Chapter 58, "Brit": "as this appalling ocean surrounds the verdant land, so in the soul of man there lies one insular Tahiti, full of peace and joy, but encompassed by all the horrors of the half known life. . . . Push not off from that isle, thou canst never return" (236). This distinction between the insular self and the "horrors" outside it is reminiscent of Starbuck's claim in Chapter 38 that "that horror's out of me!" (148). But Ishmael speaks as one who *has* pushed off from this island within himself—for such an integrity can only be known as *already lost*, sacrificed in the very moment of its self-conscious recognition. Bowen describes this island self as lost, but nevertheless claims that its stillness can be recovered through self-discipline (*The Long Encounter*, 39–44).

41. Cowan takes Chapters 87, 93, 94, and 96 as versions of a "leap into being," which show how such a leap "either cannot be made, results in death, or cannot be maintained long enough to be grasped in language" (*Exiled Waters*, 158).

42. Various critics have regarded the "The Try-Works" as the point at which Ishmael finally rejects Ahab and his quest. These readers also tend to minimize Ishmael's narrative role, treating him only as character. See Sewall, *The Vision of Tragedy*, 99–100; Strauch, "Ishmael: Time and Personality in *Moby-Dick*," 473–74; and Milton R. Stern, *The Fine Hammered Steel of Herman Melville* (Urbana, IL: U of Illinois P, 1957), 242–44.

43. Brodhead offers a similar reading of this image; he does, however, see in *Moby-Dick*, and in Ishmael, a "peculiar willingness . . . to be in uncertainty," and proposes a rather sanguine reading of "The Gilder" to support his case (*Hawthorne, Melville, and the Novel* [Chicago: U of Chicago P, 1976], 151). R.W.B. Lewis reads the movement of this passage as reflecting Melville's spiritual growth and the eagle image as representing his intellectual and artistic vision in writing *Moby-Dick* (*The American Adam* [Chicago: U of Chicago P, 1955], 131–34).

44. Zoellner contrasts Ahab's view of reality as mirror with Ishmael's discovery of an "intuitional transparency" in the "oceanic interface" (*The Salt-Sea Mastodon*, 44, 46). Simpson describes the coin as Ahab's image, "the thing that purports to be outside him, but that is in fact within in its essential purposes" (*Fetishism and Imagination: Dickens, Melville, Conrad* [Baltimore: Johns Hopkins UP, 1982], 81).

45. Feidelson argues that a "dive" in pursuit of "the totality of symbolic

meaning" leads to the destruction of individuality (*Symbolism and American Literature*, 33). Symbolic vision, he says, at once "implies a complex of logical oppositions," multiple meanings, and "tends to obscure these real and important differences" (33).

46. According to Zoellner, the "ideational" aspect of *Moby-Dick* ends with "The Symphony," as Ishmael attains a "true apprehension of the nature of things," a final harmony with his world (*The Salt-Sea Mastodon*, 238). The three days' chase, in his reading, belongs to the "dramatic" part of the novel.

Marks also sees Ishmael's disappearance at the end of the novel as a victory, as he overcomes his obsessive need for explanations. Ishmael takes up "the stance of omniscient, third-person narrator" in the last three chapters, achieving an "unselfconsciousness" ("Retrospective Narration in Nineteenth-Century Literature," 373). For Marks, the epilogue, with its explanation of Ishmael's survival, allows him to escape death only by returning to "incapacitating self-consciousness" (364).

David H. Hirsch takes Ishmael's absence from "The Chase" as a sign of his suppression of his own ego, as he melts into the crew in an affirmation of fraternal love ("The Dilemma of the Liberal Intellectual: Melville's Ishmael," *TSLL* 5 [1963]: 169–88).

47. Thomas notes that "Pierre's father did not write the sacred text himself," and suggests that Pierre's aunt may have done the embroidering. He goes on to compare this paternal text to Plinlimmon's works, which are actually composed by his disciples ("The Writer's Procreative Urge in *Pierre*: Fictional Father or Convoluted Incest?" *SNNTS* 9 [1979]: 419, 420). Dryden also emphasizes that the handkerchief is "an object totally separated from its originating source" ("'The Entangled Text': Melville's *Pierre* and the Problem of Reading," *Boundary 2* 7.2 [1979]: 169).

48. Sundquist associates this imagery of an Arctic, feminine Truth with Isabel's guitar and its music, describing them as empty and silent maternal spaces, where "signification has been mutilated or erased" (*Home as Found: Authority and Genealogy in Nineteenth-Century American Literature* [Baltimore: Johns Hopkins UP, 1979], 169, 172). He does not, however, consider Isabel's reliance on paternal signs rather than her music in presenting and identifying herself to Pierre.

49. Brodhead says that *Pierre*'s "quality of language in excess of its occasion . . . makes the novel's world seem perpetually out of focus," and that the book is "marked by a persistent quality of distortion" (*Hawthorne, Melville, and the Novel*, 163, 164).

50. Douglas claims that in *Pierre* "Melville makes the sentimental romance into a cage in which he deliberately confines his main character—and himself—both to define the limits of the form and to test the possibility of breaking out and destroying it" (*The Feminization of American Culture*, 312). See also Brodhead (*Hawthorne, Melville, and the Novel*, 164, 171) for a discussion of Melville's attitude toward the convention within which he works.

51. Brodhead sees Melville as challenging not only the adequacy of novelistic conventions, but "the credentials of any representational art" (*Hawthorne, Melville, and the Novel*, 129).

V: In Confidence

1. Melville's manuscripts are reproduced in the Editorial Appendix to the Northwestern-Newberry edition of *The Confidence-Man*. I quote here from the editors' final reading of fragment #10, which they label Version III, second fair copy (441). Melville had earlier written "contradictory to" instead of "much at variance with," and he eventually deleted the phrase "it is with man as with his maker."

2. This quotation is taken from the editors' final reading of fragments #10 and #11 (441, 443). Melville cut the second sentence from the published version.

3. Parker's characterization is offered in his Norton edition of the novel [(New York, 1971), x].

4. Key contributions to this interpretation are Foster's Introduction and Notes (New York: Hendricks House) and John W. Shroeder's "Sources and Symbols for Melville's *Confidence-Man*," *PMLA* 66 (1951): 363–80; rpt. in *The Confidence-Man*, ed. Parker, 291–316.

For attacks on the orthodox view, see Philip Drew, "Appearance and Reality in Melville's *The Confidence-Man*," *ELH* 31 (1964): 418–42; and Paul Brodtkorb, Jr., "*The Confidence-Man*: The Con-Man as Hero," *Studies in the Novel* 1 (1969): 421–35.

5. For characterizations of this unifying figure as gamesman or archetypal trickster, see Warwick Wadlington, *The Confidence Game in American Literature* (Princeton, NJ: Princeton UP, 1975), 137–70; and Gary Lindberg, *The Confidence Man in American Literature* (New York: Oxford UP, 1982), 5–47.

6. See E.L. Grant Watson, "Melville's Testament of Acceptance," *NEQ* 6 (1933): 319–27; Phil Withim, "*Billy Budd*: Testament of Resistance," *MLQ* 20 (1959): 115–27; E.M. Cifelli, "*Billy Budd*: Boggy Ground to Build On," *Studies in Short Fiction* 8 (1976): 463–69.

7. See Rogin, *Subversive Genealogy: The Politics and Art of Herman Melville* (New York: Knopf, 1983), 296–315 for a political reading; Chase, *Herman Melville: A Critical Study* (New York: William Sloane, 1949), 269–77 for a psychological one; and Thompson, *Melville's Quarrel with God* (Princeton, NJ: Princeton UP, 1952), 355–414 for a religious one.

8. "Melville's Fist: The Execution of *Billy Budd*," *SiR* 18 (1979): 567–99.

9. This section is "the crux of the book" in Parker's "standard line," which takes its absolute terms as those according to which the novel is to be read (the first phrase comes from Parker's "The Metaphysics of Indian-Hating," *NCF* 18 (1963), rpt. in *The Confidence-Man*, ed. Parker, 330n.

10. (Philadelphia: Harrison Hall, 1835). The relevant passages (2:74–82) are reprinted in the Northwestern-Newberry edition, to which I will refer below.

11. I have omitted these multiple quotation marks—*triple* quotation marks in this context—solely to avoid confusion.

12. As Michael Davitt Bell puts it, "Like everything else in *The Confidence-Man*, including *The Confidence-Man* itself, the Story of Colonel John Moredock is only a story" (*The Development of American Romance: The Sacrifice of Relation* [Chicago: U of Chicago P, 1980], 237). Bell seems to agree that the Indian-hating chapters are central to the book, but notes that the "ambiguous" narration acts to "subvert" the "moral distinction" it would establish (236).

13. Moredock resembles Ahab in a number of ways: the Colonel's hate is a "vortex from whose suction scarce the remotest chip of the guilty race may reasonably feel secure" (149), for example. Both hunters come to resemble their enemies—just as Moredock takes on Indian traits, both Ahab and the whale are compared to pyramids (*Moby-Dick*, 115, 292), and both Indian-hater and whale-hunter either long for or become partly mechanized beings (*The Confidence-Man*, 132–33; *Moby-Dick*, 390).

14. Quotations from Shakespeare are taken from *The Riverside Shakespeare*, ed. G. Blakemore Evans (Boston: Houghton Mifflin, 1974).

15. H. Bruce Franklin, among others, takes Black Guinea's list to be a central clue or subtext, and he spends a good deal of effort in tracking down the characters that correspond to the cripple's descriptions (*The Confidence-Man: His Masquerade*, ed. Franklin [Indianapolis, IN: Bobbs-Merrill, 1967], xx–xxiv). He ignores the distrust of physical appearances to which Guinea's list is a response, and finds, of course, that some of the descriptions may apply to several characters or to none at all. R.W.B. Lewis responds to this difficulty by calling these figures red herrings, further evidence of "Guinea's guile" (Afterword, *The Confidence-Man: His Masquerade* [New York: NAL, 1964], 267).

16. It is widely assumed that many figures in the novel are "avatars" or disguises of a single "Confidence-Man." The point I wish to make is that this is an interpretive assumption—it is based on "evidence" supplied by characters and narrator, but it is a conclusion that the narrator himself never even suggests.

For Franklin, in fact, the novel presents an interpretive ultimatum: he takes Melville's remark that there can only be one "original character" in a work (239) to mean that "If the Cosmopolitan cannot be seen as the embodiment of all, the resulting conflict is chaos; order is possible only if the reader can resolve the apparently opposing principles into a transcendent unity" (331n).

17. This is also his technique in "Benito Cereno" and *Israel Potter*, in which history itself becomes a textual or interpretive construction.

18. *Billy Budd, Sailor*, ed. Hayford and Sealts (Chicago: U of Chicago P, 1962), 42. All further quotations will be from this edition.

19. In *White-Jacket*, Melville speaks directly of the *Somers* affair as fact (303), while in *Billy Budd* he submerges historical "fact" beneath layers of interpretive and narrative problems. For a fine comparison between *Billy Budd* and both *White-Jacket* and the *Somers* affair, see Rogin, *Subversive Genealogy*, 294–316.

Index

ACC0947   10/15/90

PS
2388
I35
B4
1990

0 00 02 0498019 7
MIDDLEBURY COLLEGE